The ROOSEVELT ERA

Edited by

Milton Crane

With a Foreword by
Jonathan Daniels

✳

Boni and Gaer New York

COPYRIGHT 1947 BY MILTON CRANE

PUBLISHED BY BONI & GAER, INC.
133 WEST 44 STREET
NEW YORK 18, N. Y.

for Sibylle

PRINTED IN THE UNITED STATES OF AMERICA
BY J. J. LITTLE & IVES COMPANY, NEW YORK

CONTENTS

I

II

Foreword

Foreword

I t seems a long time ago. Franklin Roosevelt has been dead less than three years but already his time seems as sharply defined as the block of stone above his grave at Hyde Park. Sometimes there seems to have been almost a conspiracy, engaged in by both his friends and his enemies, to push the period of his impact upon America as quickly and as far into history as possible. No people have been quite as insistent that the New Deal is over and done as some of these who under Roosevelt were parts of it. Their personal dismay and political despair is only matched by those who are enlisted in the improbable task of recreating America exactly as it was before Roosevelt arrived in the Presidency. Sometimes, indeed, only Westbrook Pegler in his energetic defilement of a dead enemy seems unwilling to relinquish the period of Roosevelt to the past. It is behind us and what is behind us, of course, is history. The amazing, the heartening and also the disturbing thing is, as Milton Crane shows us in this book, that that time was not only America then but also America now—lacking only the leadership of the man who gave his name to the period.

I had not read—or re-read—the splendid collection of vivid writing about the period which he has brought together here when I first talked to Milton Crane about this book. I am afraid I expected just another anthology. I was aware then across a luncheon

table in a club only that I was in the presence of a diffident young
professor eager to share his feeling for the period as life and not
merely facts and words. He was not merely engaged in collecting
"the literature" of the time between the Saturday when Roosevelt
arrived in the White House and the Thursday afternoon twelve
years later on which he died. Mr. Crane was certainly not concerned as Harvard Ph.D. with the reduction of the crowded years
between to the phrases and formulae of formal social history. The
pieces he has put together here, he collected in the exciting understanding that he was letting the period speak for itself in self-pity
and self-analysis, in anger and fear, and in comedy as well as
courage. The writers of that time and in this company recorded
not only the events and the conflicts, they wrote of broken hearts
and stuffed shirts as well. What Crane has shaped from their work
into the revealing and moving pattern of this book is not history
for Americans but the inescapable years behind us all as living
Americans who continue as people beyond a period.

Milton Crane was 15 years old when the Roosevelt occupancy of
the White House began; he was a 28-year-old professor when Roosevelt died at Warm Springs. The Roosevelt years were the American
years so far as he was concerned. Indeed, no American under forty
today ever had a chance to vote in a Presidential election in which
Roosevelt was not elected. In a real sense, therefore, this book is
not only our history but the only history we have ever known—
certainly for most of us the only personalized period in which the
great majority of Americans were so long so confident that they
were headed in the right direction under the right man. Many, of
course, were always equally confident that Roosevelt was not so
much leading us away from the horse and buggy days as he was
heading us for hell in a hack. He may have been just lucky to have
arrived at the hour of American despair and to have departed at
the height of American prosperity and power. Hardly anybody,
however, will deny that it was a dramatic procession. He made
"good copy." There was a fresh seeing—sometimes angry, occasionally satirical, sentimental and comic—of the American scene against

which he stood. And in this book in the work of contemporary journalists, poets, dramatists, politicians and novelists, Milton Crane has put together both the biography and the picture of the time.

He has done something more important than that, I think. In the works of diverse writers he has given us a full sense of the variety, the vitality, the courage and the fear of our own times, too. Roosevelt is history. But even in these fattest and sometimes most fatuous seeming American years, the sharp American contrasts remain, rich and poor, green and gully red, the chromium and the confusion. The men with big bank accounts whom John Dos Passos saw in the transcontinental airliner high above the hitch hikers in the early thirties are flying high again. There are not so many bums below them but there is an unmentioned suggestion in the cumulative effect of the pieces collected here that in the continuing American drama they may be waiting in the wings for cues as loud as thunder. Even beyond victory, the war dead are as restless as they were when Irwin Shaw spoke the fears of World War II long before it began. I have a feeling that Milton Crane has given us not merely a book but a bridge, not the dead past but a vivid prelude. Indeed, if this book is social history, it is as restlessly alive as Roosevelt's ghost in a world whistling uneasily by his gravestone.

JONATHAN DANIELS

Editor's Note

This is not a book about President Roosevelt. It is an effort to communicate, through the words of many writers, something of the ideas, the problems, and the actions of men and women in Franklin Roosevelt's America between 1932 and 1945. The degree to which that age, or any age, expresses itself in its literature must remain ultimately unknown and unknowable. The editor who wrenches out of context those writings and portions of writings that seem to him capable of evoking significant moments or experiences is both privileged and handicapped by the unearned gift of historical hindsight. He can decide—although not without trepidations—that a given short story or poem captures the flavor of a moment in time. He is aware of the irony with which time can invest the most casual sketch or can nullify the most portentous prophecy or analysis. But, in his eagerness to find epitomes, he may give undeserved importance to an apparently symbolic work that actually sprang from purely local and personal motives; thus, Mr. James Thurber has been so kind as to explain that one of his admirable stories "was by no means the result of the period in America in any economic or political sense, but was written simply because a certain young woman had been for several months driving me nuts."

The editor may also become aware (as this one has) that some notable literary figures are missing from his compilation. But the purpose of this book has not been to excerpt the finest literary works published while Mr. Roosevelt was president, but rather to assemble a coherent and connected group of materials for a social history of the age. The work of Thomas Wolfe, for example, cannot be ignored by any literary historian of the Thirties; but it has little to contribute to such a book as this, partly because Wolfe's concerns were so predominantly personal, and also because his work must be read extensively to produce its characteristic effect.

At the same time, there are many cross-currents of political history that are unquestionably important but have failed to leave their mark in literature. The editor knows, for example, that the huge body of writing spawned by the forces opposing Mr. Roosevelt remains unrepresented except in the distorting mirrors of E. B. White and Frank Sullivan. The opposition to Mr. Roosevelt was one of the most notorious phenomena of his terms in office. Yet how is one to find among the official or semi-official statements of the opposition anything that stands the test of time well enough to deserve perpetuation in print? Not even Mrs. Luce's speeches can qualify. So the humorous sketches of Mr. White and Mr. Sullivan must stand for numberless articles, books, speeches, snarls, and all that bitter talk whose origins must be sought in abnormal psychology. And, in spite of the general veneration with which the late President has come to be regarded, the statements of some public figures indicate only too clearly that death is no warrant against slander.

The literature from which the contents of this book have been drawn marked a sharp break with the literature of the Nineteen-Twenties. The years following the First World War had seen in this country a small-scale renaissance in letters, a flowering of imaginative literature in which the United States itself figured largely either as a subject for satirical description or as a fearsome Babbitt-warren of Puritanism and Philistinism (few people paused long enough in their reading of *The American Mercury* to distinguish between the terms, far less to define them). The writers of the Twenties retreated from America to Europe or into the well-furnished havens of their own minds. But such agreeable despair is an expensive luxury; a Poictesme must be paid for by a Big Bull Market.

The writers of the Thirties and Forties had no such avenues of escape open to them. Theirs was no longer a world in which well-to-do ironists could write satirical fables proving that Middle-Westerners had no taste in art and no discrimination in wine. The misery which many people were slowly beginning to accept as the irremediable condition of normal existence forced its way into their works and made them treat, as best they could, the economic and political problems that surrounded them. Some were led to more or less satisfying forms of political activity; others were content to transmute imaginatively their reactions to their new awareness of the world. The realization that American life was lived not alone by artists and intellectuals was not, of course, peculiar to the literature of the Thirties, but it can be considered a leading characteristic.

The determination to see, to know, and to tell with courage and honesty the facts of American life shines through writing in the three large divisions of the Roosevelt years that have been adopted for the purposes of this book, and that correspond roughly to the three administrations. The period of what Basil Rauch has called "the first New Deal" were the years of uncertainty and hope, in which almost anything could be faced except the continuation of the intolerable present. Joseph Mitchell's cave dwellers escaped from their Central Park refuge to fantastic comfort; Martha Gellhorn's Mrs. Maddison undertook her hopeless effort to feed her miserable family by returning to the land; and the groping, questioning men and women of Carl Sandburg's poems sought a half-forgotten peace and security lest they be overtaken by a Buzz Windrip and the terrors of an American Fascism.

After Mr. Roosevelt's crushing defeat of Governor Landon in 1936, it became effectively clear that the President could look to the mass of the people for support, although the "national unity" of those first epoch-making months of the New Deal had long ago disappeared. The middle Thirties were the great days of "New Deal art": of the admirable state and city guides of the Federal Writers Project, that fed a new popular interest about the land and the people; and of the youthful and exciting Federal Theatre. But a growing threat of war, combined with the damaging economic recession of 1937, sowed fear and bewilderment. One month after the débâcle of Munich, Orson Welles's broadcast of H. G. Wells's fantasy, *The War of the Worlds,* was capable of throwing huge numbers of listeners into a state of hysterical panic. Dr. George Gallup (contemporary America has not produced a phenomenon more characteristic of itself) compiled the data from which Professor Hadley Cantril was able to show that the panic had been touched off largely by economic insecurity and the fear of war.

The last period of Mr. Roosevelt's tenure of office comprises the war years, in which his many extraordinary gifts combined to make an overwhelming contribution to the winning of the military victory he did not live to see. These were years of self-examination, in which we asked ourselves, with Archibald MacLeish, whether we had not contrived our own destruction, and persuaded ourselves, with Reinhold Niebuhr and Margaret Mead, that we had to forego our flattering illusions if we were to survive—or wondered, with Mrs. Lindbergh, whether we could or even should resist "the wave of the future." The defeat of Germany and Japan has resolved only the most immediate of our problems.

Mr. Roosevelt is the hero, rather than the subject, of this book, for its components are the thoughts, writings, and actions which his personality helped to shape, and the smoke of his cigarette pervades its atmosphere. *The Roosevelt Era* is a memorial to the influence of one of America's great men on the country he led for so many years. Whether it is also an epitaph to the period we have named for him is what that country must now decide.

My greatest debt is to the writers whose names appear in the table of contents. It is a special pleasure to record also the names of five men who have generously given their suggestions and criticism: Charles Boni, who suggested this book; Jonathan Daniels, Dwight C. Miner, Arthur M. Schlesinger, Jr., and Mark Van Doren.

New York   M. C.
August, 1947

I

First of all, let me assert my firm belief that the only thing we have to fear is fear itself—nameless, unreasoning, unjustified terror which paralyzes needed efforts to convert retreat into advance. In every dark hour of our national life a leadership of frankness and vigor has met with that understanding and support of the people themselves which is essential to victory.

(First Inaugural Address, March 4, 1933)

The Roosevelt Era

The Roosevelt era began in an economic depression and ended in a war. It seems fitting, therefore, to begin with a glance backwards to the chaos and misery which marked the end of Mr. Hoover's administration; John Dos Passos's "Vag," the wanderer on the roads, who tightens his belt as he watches the transcontinental airplane pass overhead, can stand as a symbol of the problems with which the new president had to deal. Morris Markey's detached account of the 1933 inauguration recalls the skepticism and the hope which preceded the startling events of Mr. Roosevelt's first months in office. And the oddly contrasting views of Walter Lippmann and Frederick Lewis Allen on the first year of the New Deal effectively recreate the period and suggest that both the enthusiasm of the first and the considered judgment of the second continue to be subject to revision.

JOHN DOS PASSOS

Vag

❦

THE YOUNG MAN waits at the edge of the concrete, with one hand he grips a rubbed suitcase of phony leather, the other hand almost making a fist, thumb up

that moves in ever so slight an arc when a car slithers past, a truck roars clatter; the wind of cars passing ruffles his hair, slaps grit in his face.

Head swims, hunger has twisted the belly tight,

he has skinned a heel through the torn sock, feet ache in the broken shoes, under the threadbare suit carefully brushed off with the hand, the torn drawers have a crummy feel, the feel of having slept in your clothes; in the nostrils lingers the staleness of discouraged carcasses crowded into a transient camp, the carbolic stench of the jail, on the taut cheeks the shamed flush from the boring eyes of cops and deputies, railroadbulls (they eat three squares a day, they are buttoned into wellmade clothes, they have wives to sleep with, kids to play with after supper, they work for the big men who buy their way, they stick their chests out with the sureness of power behind their backs). Git the hell out, scram. Know what's good for you, you'll make yourself scarce. Gittin' tough, eh? Think you kin take it, eh?

The punch in the jaw, the slam on the head with the nightstick, the wrist grabbed and twisted behind the back, the big knee brought up short into the crotch,

the walk out of town with sore feet to stand and wait at the edge of the hissing speeding string of cars where the reek of ether and lead and gas melts into the silent grassy smell of the earth.

Eyes black with want seek out the eyes of the drivers, a hitch, a hundred miles down the road.

Overhead in the blue a plane drones. Eyes follow the silver Douglas that flashes once in the sun and bores its smooth way out of sight into the blue.

(The transcontinental passengers sit pretty, big men with bankaccounts, highlypaid jobs, who are saluted by doormen; telephonegirls say good-morning to them. Last night after a fine dinner, drinks with friends, they left Newark. Roar of climbing motors slanting up into the inky haze. Lights drop away. An hour staring along a silvery wing at a big lonesome moon hurrying west through curdling scum. Beacons flash in a line across Ohio.

At Cleveland the plane drops banking in a smooth spiral, the string of lights along the lake swings in a circle. Climbing roar of the motors again; slumped in the soft seat drowsing through the flat moonlight night.

Chi. A glimpse of the dipper. Another spiral swoop from cool into hot air thick with dust and the reek of burnt prairies.

Beyond the Mississippi dawn creeps up behind through the murk over the great plains. Puddles of mist go white in the Iowa hills, farms, fences, silos, steel glint from a river. The blinking eyes of the beacons reddening into day. Watercourses vein the eroded hills.

Omaha. Great cumulus clouds, from coppery churning to creamy to silvery white, trail brown skirts of rain over the hot plains. Red and yellow badlands, tiny horned shapes of cattle.

Cheyenne. The cool high air smells of sweetgrass.

The tight-baled clouds to westward burst and scatter in tatters over the strawcolored hills. Indigo mountains jut rimrock. The plane breasts a huge crumbling cloudbank and toboggans over bumpy air across green and crimson slopes into the sunny dazzle of Salt Lake.

The transcontinental passenger thinks contracts, profits, vacationtrips, mighty continent, between Atlantic and Pacific, power, wires humming dollars, cities jammed, hills empty, the indiantrail leading into the wagon-road, the macadamed pike, the concrete skyway; trains, planes; history the billiondollar speedup,

and in the bumpy air over the desert ranges towards Las Vegas

sickens and vomits into the carton container the steak and mushrooms he ate in New York. No matter, silver in the pocket, greenbacks in the wallet, drafts, certified checks, plenty restaurants in L. A.)

The young man waits on the side of the road; the plane has gone; thumb moves in a small arc when a car tears hissing past. Eyes seek the driver's eyes. A hundred miles down the road. Head swims, belly tightens, wants crawl over his skin like ants:

went to school. books said opportunity, ads promised speed, own your home, shine bigger than your neighbor, the radiocrooner whispered girls, ghosts of platinum girls coaxed from the screen, millions in winnings were chalked up on the boards in the offices, paychecks were for hands willing to work, the cleared desk of an executive with three telephones on it;

waits with swimming head, needs knot the belly, idle hands numb, beside the speeding traffic.

A hundred miles down the road.

MORRIS MARKEY

Washington Weekend

THE PARADE went marching up Pennsylvania Avenue, flags in the wind, and drums, and the General on a fine white horse. The most expensive seats in the wooden reviewing stands cost seven dollars each, and all those seats were filled. Bands went by, and citizen soldiers wearing glorious uniforms with white plumes, red plumes; and the Ladies' Auxiliary of the colored Elks looking mighty smart with their gold-and-purple capes, their yellow canes flashing as they walked along.

Then the parade was over, and Mr. Hoover was weeping as his train drew out of the station toward obscurity. And up at the White House

Permission the author. Originally published in *The New Yorker*. Copyright 1933. The F-R. Publishing Corporation.

crowds hung like birds along the iron fences, trying to catch a glimpse of
the statesmen who were hurrying there to struggle with catastrophe. There
were many lights in the White House, and sometimes a vague, enviable
shadow crossed a window. Motorcars swept into the long, curving drive-
way and paused a moment before the white pillars of the doorway and
swept out again. Down at the entrance to the Executive Offices in the west
wing of the White House a hundred newspapermen, all very tired, stood
waiting for news as horses wait for oats.

We knew about the New York banks, of course. It had happened that
morning. About the Illinois banks and about Michigan, where they already
had had three weeks' experience of this business. The more dramatic-
minded of the newspapermen were full of glee.

"Gentlemen, it's revolution. I'm telling you. Finee for the grand and
glorious old American institutions. I can see 'em now, howling up Fifth
Avenue with blood in their eye, howling up Market Street and Beacon
Street and Michigan Avenue."

"Who?"

"Why, the birds that get hungry, that's who. And I've already picked my
side. I'm going to join me a good Communist club."

"Ain't we got fun!"

The lights burned in the White House, and the newspaper reporters
were almost unanimous in their happy predictions of calamity, and downtown Amos 'n' Andy (in person) put out the S.R.O. sign. The other moving picture houses, having no such compelling attraction, did a boom business, nevertheless. The hotels posted notices that "owing to the confused
banking situation" they would be unable to cash checks or money orders.
In the lobbies of those hotels there were many senators and representatives. About each there congregated a little crowd of listeners, and voices
boomed along:

"In my sober opinion, there is not the least cause for worry. Mr. Roosevelt's speech this morning indicated clearly enough that he has the courage
and the ability to command the situation. We face a test of the American
people, their resourcefulness and wisdom—and who of us can doubt for
a moment . . ."

Ten thousand people paid five dollars each to stand in a solid crowd
at the Inaugural Ball. Nobody could possibly dance. The President was
not there. Yet the ball was very gay. The guests accepted its colossal dis-
comforts, its confusion and violent noise, precisely as they accepted the
impending crisis in affairs. They laughed. They talked a little feverishly.
They had, at the last, no earthly idea of their reason for being there or

their reason for not leaving, but they lingered—talking, talking, talking, and applauding loudly the distinguished figure of Mr. Vice-President Garner when he bowed to them from a box.

Quiet did not settle upon the city until long after dawn. Even then, with the sun coming up, you could hear the tramp of feet on the pavements and the quavering harmonies of "Sweet Adeline" drifting against the gray columns of the Treasury Building. In the White House, the lights were never extinguished.

Sunday wore through. The city came awake slowly and then waited, for there was no word at all from the White House. All day long a press of cars moved past the mansion and their occupants stared at the lovely, uncommunicative façade. Occasionally, across the lawn beyond the great elms, there was the flash of a silk hat in the sunlight, the flutter of a gaily colored dress. In the hotel lobbies, a sharp, nervous voice would exclaim now and then, "But listen! I've got to get home, I tell you! You'll just have to cash this check, I tell you! It's a matter of absolute necessity." And, in reply, "I will let you speak to the manager, but I don't think we can do anything."

Almost imperceptibly a certain tension began to appear. In the more popular hotels, where the good, honest sightseers were gathered, the tension manifested itself in a new readiness to giggle, in wheezes like "Well, brother, I've got nine U. S. Cigar Store certificates. Ought to get a ham sandwich for 'em, eh?" In the suave teaparties that they gave in homes out Georgetown way, and in Wardman Park, the change was naturally more subtle.

It was visible first in the women. You could see the curious brightness in their eyes, the half-hidden pleasure at trouble in a man's world—the same mystic delight that women find in days when war is coming on. They might even (you could feel them nurturing this), they might even have the chance to endure, to suffer, to display all the finer nobilities, if the men would only let things get into a slightly worse mess. They urged their servants to hasten the trays of cocktails. They almost lost their ability to conceal their amusement as the men leaned over them with grave, polite assurances that matters would adjust themselves, that the greatest and richest nation on earth certainly could not and would not . . .

In the evening there were magnificent receptions. The foreign diplomats wore their handsome uniforms and their medals, and managed to hide behind a schooled politeness their inescapable glow of satisfaction.

Champagne and caviar, and music from a group of opera singers gathered in the city for a concert.

A girl's voice: "Lordy, I feel like a kid when the schoolhouse has burned down."

A man's voice: "It will turn out to be a fine thing for the country. May I have your glass filled?"

Another girl's voice: "I'm so lucky! Ever since I was a little girl, my father has given me the gold pieces he gets for attending directors' meetings. My deposit box is almost full of them."

The butler spoke to a senator, who bent politely over a girl celebrated for her horses, and the senator left quickly, saying, "They have sent for me and I must get to the White House. Please explain to our hostess."

Toward midnight, I telephoned to a newspaperman, the Washington correspondent for a New York paper. I asked, "What is the news?"

"You'd better come on down and see it happen."

In his office a few people were sitting—men and women in evening clothes. They were all silent, listening to the newspaperman's voice as he spoke to New York over the telephone.

". . . nothing at all from the White House except the proclamation itself. No other statement. . . . Oh, certainly. They are still there. Still with the President. Suppose they will be, all night."

He hung up. Other telephones were ringing, and every minute or two a reporter would come in with word from somebody, news from somebody.

"Here's a statement from Huey Long."

"Well, what's the Kingfish got to say?"

"Same thing he said last week."

"Throw it away."

The reporters were disheveled and tired, but full of automatic energy. We felt a little silly, leaning back in our chairs and watching them work at the business of closing all the banks in America; for the reporters were really closing the banks—they were telling the banks not to open their doors in the morning.

That brilliant reception out in Wardman Park, the diplomats and the ravishing girls and the opera singers and the champagne, seemed far away and long ago.

We sat in the newspaperman's office until about four o'clock. The telegraph instruments clucked away, spelling "All banks will be closed tomorrow" with the same idiotic chatter they would use to spell "The first lady wore black and carried a black fan."

It was very dark and very cold when we started home. We went through the empty streets. We went past the White House. The windows in the Executive Offices were all bright, and upstairs in the White House the lights were burning in four or five rooms. The radiance they cast fell across the lawn, through the bare trees, and struck wanly against the great wooden stands built for the parade. The stands cost forty thousand dollars, and nobody had had the time, yet, to wreck them.

Monday was not a gloomy day. Was not the Congress called for Thursday? The air was charged with the excitement of action. Things were being done. What things? Nobody bothered much about that, for it would be the wildest guesswork anyway. Just as long as something was being done, anything, that would suffice to keep spirits up. But they had stopped giggling. Even the senators and the representatives were stilled—hoping to be called into conference at the White House; for once unready with glib solutions.

The lucky few who were called to the conferences came out with an air of mystery. They confined themselves to a single set speech: "Everything will be all right."

They were shocked into a strange reticence at the novel experience of being taken seriously by the country.

They were, perhaps, more deeply shocked at their own competence when, the Congress having met at last, they passed bills, accomplished the President's will, with so little of their accustomed absurdity.

So the dark Inaugural. So the queer, impersonal confusion of men against events—like the queer, impersonal confusion of troops wandering over a battlefield, fighting when they can find somebody to fight against, shunting human lives about in whatever way seems possible amidst so many bleak impossibilities.

WALTER LIPPMANN
The First Roosevelt Year

THE ACHIEVEMENTS of the past year can be measured statistically. But there is perhaps a better measure. A year ago men were living from hour to hour, in the midst of a crisis of enormous proportions, and all they could think about was how they could survive it. Today they are debating the problems of long term reconstruction.

It is a decisive change. When Mr. Roosevelt was inaugurated, the question in all men's minds was whether the country could "recover." The machinery of government was impotent. The banking system was paralyzed. Panic, misery, rebellion, and despair were convulsing the people and destroying confidence not merely in business enterprise but in the promise of American life. No man can say into what we should have drifted had we drifted another twelve months. But no man can doubt, if he knows the conditions—which responsible observers hardly dared to describe at the time for fear of aggravating the panic—that the dangers were greater than they have been at any time in the experience of this generation of Americans. Today there are still grave problems. But there is no overwhelmingly dangerous crisis. The mass of the people have recovered their courage and their hope. They are no longer hysterically anxious about the immediate present. They have recovered not only some small part of their standard of life but also their self-possession. The very fact that they can take a lively interest in the air mail contracts and the bill to regulate the stock exchange and the permanence of N.R.A. is the best kind of evidence that the crisis has been surmounted. Last winter nobody would have given two thoughts to the air mail contracts. The question then was how to stay out of the bread line, and whether there would be money to supply a bread line, and how to avoid foreclosure or eviction or bankruptcy.

The questions about the future which agitate Mr. Mark Sullivan and Mr. David Lawrence and other critics of the Administration are very important. They should be discussed thoroughly. But we should not be in a position to discuss them thoroughly if the President had not pulled the country out of the pit and brought about a recovery.

By permission of The Macmillan Co., Publishers. From *Interpretations* 1933-1935, by Walter Lippmann. Copyright 1936 by Walter Lippmann.

That he is entitled to full credit for inducing recovery seems to me to be demonstrably certain. It is often said that world recovery began in the summer of 1932, and that, therefore, we should have had recovery without intervention from Washington. Let us see. Let us suppose for the sake of the argument that only those things done in Washington have contributed to recovery which have been done also in other advanced industrial and agricultural countries. That is a reasonable test. If we find that some one of the Roosevelt measures, let us say N.R.A. for example, has been adopted only in the United States, then by this test we may say that whatever the virtues of N.R.A. it has not been of direct importance in promoting recovery.

Using this criterion, we may recall the most important moves made by the Administration. The first one was the decision to end the political deadlock by bringing about a concentration of authority. This has been done in every country which was severely affected. Where it has been long delayed, as in France, the consequences have been serious. The President achieved this at once and demonstrated it by three actions which only a powerful government could have taken. He closed the banks. He reopened them almost immediately. He demonstrated his control over the budget by the Economy Act. The net result of all this was to establish a center of order and power in the midst of panic and confusion.

*   *   *

This took about four weeks. When it was done, the Administration was in a position to adopt measures for recovery which would otherwise have caused more panic and more confusion. The first of them was to go off the gold standard, and thus break the deflationary forces set in motion by the collapse of gold prices. Attempts have been made to argue that the American departure from gold differed from that of England and other countries. The circumstances may have been different. The broad consequences and the general significance were the same, and the best proof is to be found in the fact that only those countries can be said to be having recovery which have reduced the gold value of their currencies.

The next important move, it seems to me, was the decision to use the monetary freedom arising from the gold embargo to put purchasing power in the hands of the people. Money has been pumped out through a number of conduits, to the farmers through the agricultural contracts, through refinancing of mortgages, to the unemployed through direct relief, through the Civilian Conservation Corps, through civil works and public works, through wage increases. These inflationary measures, combined with the rise of commodity and security prices brought on in part by the actual revaluation of the dollar and in part by speculation, have greatly increased the money incomes of large sections of the people. They have in some degree brought purchasing power above the dead weight of fixed charges, and thus have enabled a considerable part of agriculture and of industry to earn small profits.

This inflationary expenditure has no counterpart in other countries. It is, therefore, debatable as to whether it has been the best method to use. That it involves risks cannot be denied, and the risks ought certainly not to be forgotten. Direct inflationary government expenditure is easier to start than to curtail and stop. The justification for it lies in the fact that our situation differed substantially in several respects from that of England. We were more severely deflated. We had a higher level and a larger volume of debts. And we had a paralyzed banking system which is only now beginning to show signs of being able to function. The British have inflated—the last figures I have seen put their inflation at about eighteen per cent since 1932—but they have been able to manage their inflation in a more conventional way because their banking system was in working order.

*   *   *

My view is that the three decisive chapters in the Roosevelt program for recovery have been: first, the organization of political leadership; second, the departure from gold and the revaluation of the dollar; third, the pumping out of funds to consumers of goods.

What, then, about all the other things: the A.A.A. and its schemes for the control of agriculture, the N.R.A. and its codes, the Securities Act and the banking legislation and the stock exchange regulation? They, I think, belong to a wholly different order of things. They have to do with the deeper problems of American life, with the future of agriculture, with the relations of capital and labor, with the regulation of industry, with the conservation of natural resources, with the setting up of new financial standards, with the control of speculation, with the distribution of national income. They are concerned with the possibility of a better life, of greater equality and more justice, with the protection of the social order, the stabilization of our economy, with efforts to control the next boom and mitigate the next depression. They are designed to apply the lessons of the disaster we have been through. They are intended to avert another, and at least to reduce the evil practices which not only cause so much actual evil but engender popular resentments that might become too violent for the safety of the republic.

It would be absurd to pretend that these long term measures of re-construction are more than hastily contrived schemes. It would be unreasonable to regard them as perfected revelation of the New Deal when every man who knows anything knows they were put together in a hurry by harassed men and are being administered by men who are too busy to think about them. It is fair to ask that critics of these measures should be, if not disinterested, then at least candid about their interest in wishing to change them. But these reforms are not sacrosanct. They are experiments and only experiments in the long and difficult task of making the modern economic system work with enough efficiency to give security and with sufficient justice to command the loyalty of the people.

FREDERICK LEWIS ALLEN

New Deal Honeymoon

§ 1

SATURDAY, March 4, 1933.

Turn on the radio. It's time for the inauguration.

There is a tension in the air today—a sense of momentousness and of expectation. When you went downtown this morning you found the banks shut; if you lived in New York State or in Illinois this may have been your first inkling of the general bank closing, since the closing orders in those states had come too late for the early editions of the morning papers of March 4. On the door of each bank was pasted a little type-written notice that it had been closed at the Governor's order; people by twos and threes went up and read the sign and walked away. Your first thought, perhaps, was that you had only a little money in the house—five dollars, was it? ten dollars?—and you wondered how you would manage when this was used up, and what would happen next. Then you began to realize the significance of this financial stoppage.

Well, it's come at last, you thought. Here is that day of doom that people have been dreading. Just now it isn't so bad; there is a tingle of excitement, the sort of thrill you get from a three-alarm fire. But what next?

From *Since Yesterday*, by Frederick Lewis Allen. Copyright 1939, 1940 by Harper & Brothers.

This may be only the beginning of the crack-up. The one thing you want to hear, that everybody wants to hear, is the inaugural address. All over the country people are huddled round their radios, wondering what Roosevelt's answer to disaster will be.

Here's the voice of a radio reporter describing the preparations for the inauguration ceremony at the east front of the Capitol in Washington—the notables coming to their places on the platform, the dense crowds flooding the Capitol square below under a chill, cloudy sky. The reporter is talking with all the synthetic good cheer of his kind—bearing down hard on the note of optimism, in fact, for he knows that worried and frightened people are listening to him. He describes Hoover coming alone, gravely, to his place on the platform; then Roosevelt coming up a ramp on the arm of his son James. The ceremony begins. You hear Chief Justice Hughes administer the oath of office; you hear Roosevelt's reply, phrase by phrase, uttered clearly and firmly. Then comes the inaugural.

The new President's voice is resolute. It comes into your living room sharply.

"President Hoover, Mr. Chief Justice, my friends," the voice begins. "This is a day of national consecration, and I am certain that my fellow Americans expect that on my induction into the Presidency I will address them with a candor and a decision which the present situation of the nation impels. This is pre-eminently the time to speak the truth, frankly and boldly. Nor need we shrink from honestly facing conditions in our country today. This great nation will endure as it has endured, will revive and will prosper. So, first of all, let me assert my firm belief that the only thing we have to fear is fear itself—nameless, unreasoning, unjustified terror which paralyzes needed efforts to convert retreat into advance."

This doesn't sound like "prosperity is just around the corner" talk. It sounds like real confidence.

The voice goes on to blame "the rulers of the exchange of mankind's goods" for the troubles of the country. "True, they have tried, but their efforts have been cast in the pattern of an outworn tradition. . . . The money changers have fled from their high seats in the temple of our civilization." Through the radio comes a burst of applause: after the bank smash-ups and scandals, this condemnation of the big financiers expresses the mood of millions of Americans.

The voice speaks of the primary need of putting people to work; of the need for "making income balance outgo"; of the need for an "adequate but sound currency" (sharp applause for that!); promises a "good neighbor" policy in foreign affairs, but says domestic affairs must come first. Most striking of all, however, is the constant emphasis upon the need for action. Again and again comes the word "action." And after the new President has said he believes that the sort of action which is needed may be taken under the Constitution, the loudest applause of all comes for his declaration that if the occasion warrants he will not hesitate to ask for "broad executive power to wage a war against the emergency, as great as the power that would be given to me if we were in fact invaded by a foreign foe."

A ten-strike, this declaration. For the people have been sick of watching an Executive devote his strongest energies to opposing action, however questionable: they want a positive policy.

"We do not distrust the future of essential democracy," the President continues. "The people of the United States have not failed. In their need they have registered a mandate that they want direct, vigorous action. They have asked for discipline and direction under leadership. They have made me the present instrument of their wishes. In the spirit of the gift I take it."

You can turn off the radio now. You have heard what you wanted to hear. This man sounds no longer cautious, evasive. For he has seen that a tortured and bewildered people want to throw overboard the old and welcome something new; that they are sick of waiting, they want somebody who will *fight* this Depression for them and with them; they want leadership, the thrill of bold decision. And not only in his words but in the challenge of the very accents of his voice he has promised them what they want.

If only the performance measures up to the promise!

§ 2

Action there was, in abundance; and it came fast.

On Sunday, March 5, the day after the inauguration, the new President not only called Congress to meet in special session on Thursday, but also issued a proclamation putting the bank holiday on a national basis and prohibiting the export of gold and all dealings in foreign exchange. (Thus the country went at least part way off the gold standard—on a temporary basis.)

On Thursday Congress met and passed with a whoop a law validating everything that the executive had done to date and tightening still further its control over banking operations, gold, silver, currency, and foreign exchange.

On Friday the President asked Congress for immediate action to cut Federal expenses to the bone—and Congress rushed at the task, despite the political distastefulness of slashing the veterans' allowances.

On Saturday—after a week of furious activity at the Treasury, during which regulations were devised and altered, plans for the issue of clearing-house certificates were made and abandoned, plans for the issue of new currency were promulgated, and a rough classification of banks into more and less sound was made with the aid of advice from Federal Reserve Banks and chief national bank examiners—the President announced that most of the banks of the country would open the following Monday, Tuesday, and Wednesday.

On Sunday night the President, in his first "fireside chat," explained to the people of the country with admirable simplicity, clarity, and persuasiveness just how the re-opening of the banks would be managed and how his hearers could help to make the process orderly.

On Monday, the 13th of March, the banks began to open. And on the same day the President asked Congress to legalize beer—thus closing his tremendous first ten days of office on a note of festivity.

Such were the bare facts of those ten days. But the mere catalogue of them gives little idea of their overtones of significance, or of what those ten days were like to the American people.

The predicament of the incoming Administration was staggering. A new President and new Cabinet, unaccustomed even to the ordinary routine of their positions, largely unacquainted with their staffs, and forced to rely heavily upon the services of Hoover officials who stayed on to help them, had to deal with an unprecedented emergency which confronted them with unforeseen problems. Everything had to be done at top speed. Nobody could tell what might be the future cost of mistakes made under such pressure. Nobody could be sure, for that matter, that this was not just the first of a progressive series of emergencies which would bring conditions infinitely worse. Never did a green Administration seem to be walking into such a potential hornet's nest of difficulties.

But other circumstances aided them. In the first place, the accident of fate which had been so cruel to Hoover gave the country an Administration which could start from scratch in its race against panic, unhandicapped by memories of previous failures. It is traditional for the American people to feel kindly toward a new administration and support its first moves; in this case the friendly feeling was not only ready-made but intense. An enormous majority of the population desperately wanted the New Deal to succeed. Even the Wall Street bankers were ready to give Roosevelt full powers and wish him well, wince though they might at being called money changers who had "fled from their high seats in the temple." They were badly frightened, their institutions were demoralized, their collective reputation was besmirched anyhow, their only hope lay in Roosevelt's success. The newspapers, too, were loud now with enthusiasm. For weeks they had been burying bank-panic news in the back pages; now they could let go—and out gushed, on the news pages and in the editorials, all that zest for whooping it up, for boosting, for delivering optimistic fight talks, that was innate and habitual in the American temperament. Congress, usually divided in opinion and intractable, became almost as unanimous and enthusiastic as a cheering section—because public opinion told them to. The Congressmen's mail was heavy, and the burden of it was "Support the President." It was as if a people rent by discords suddenly found themselves marching in step.

There was another favorable circumstance. In *The Folklore of Capitalism,* Thurman W. Arnold tells of a conversation he had, before the bank panic, with a group of bankers, lawyers, and economists. They were one and all aghast at the possibility of a general bank closing. "My mind," said one of them, "fails to function when I think of the extent of the catastrophe that will follow when the Chase National Bank closes its doors." Mr. Arnold told his friend Professor Edward S. Robinson about this conversation, and found him unaccountably cheerful. "Do you think," asked Professor Robinson, "that when the banks all close people will climb trees and throw coconuts at each other?" Mr. Arnold replied that this seemed to him a little unlikely but that a bank crash of such magnitude suggested to him rioting and perhaps revolution. Whereupon Professor Robinson said, "I will venture a prediction. . . . When the banks close, everyone will feel relieved. It will be a sort of national holiday. There will be general excitement and a feeling of great interest. Travel will not stop; hotels will not close; everyone will have a lot of fun, though they will not admit that it's fun at the time."

Despite the fact that indirectly the bank holiday brought new distress, through new curtailments of business and new layoffs, and intensified the suffering of many people who were already hard hit, Professor Robinson was essentially right. The majority of Americans felt a sense of relief at having the lid of secrecy blown off. Now everything was out in the open. They felt that this trouble was temporary. They felt no shame now in being short of money—everybody seemed to be. They were all in the same boat. And they responded to one another's difficulties good-naturedly.

The grocer lent credit (what else could he do?), most hotels were glad to honor checks, shops were cordial about charge accounts. The diminished advertising columns of the newspapers contained such cheerful announcements as "IN PAYMENT FOR PASSAGE WE WILL ACCEPT CHECKS OR PROPERLY AUTHORIZED SCRIP" (this was in the early days of the bank holiday, when the issue of clearing-house scrip appeared likely); "RADIO CITY HAS

CONFIDENCE IN AMERICA AND ITS PEOPLE—until scrip becomes available our box offices will accept checks"; "WE WILL TAKE YOUR CHECK DATED THREE MONTHS AHEAD for a three months' supply of Pepsodent for yourself and your family."

True, the shopping districts were half deserted; on the upper floors of department stores, clerks were standing about with no customers at all; there was a Saturday air about the business offices, trains were sparsely filled, stock exchanges and commodity exchanges were closed. But in the talk that buzzed everywhere there was less of foreboding than of eager and friendly excitement. "Are they going to put out scrip?—and how do we use it?" "What's a 'conservator'—is that a new word?" "You say you had thirty dollars on you when the banks closed? Well, you're in luck. I had only three-fifty—I'd planned to go to the bank that morning." "They say the Smiths stocked their cellar with canned goods last week—three months' supply; they thought there was going to be a revolution!" "Did you see those pictures of the gold hoarders bringing bags full of gold back to the Federal Reserve Bank? Those birds are getting off easy, if you ask me." "Mrs. Dodge beat the bank holiday all right—overdrew her account last Friday. No, not intentionally. Just a mistake, she says. Shot with luck, I call it." "Stop me if you've heard this banker story: it seems that a banker died and when he got to the gates, St. Peter said. . . ."

To this public mood President Roosevelt's first fireside chat was perfectly attuned. Quiet, uncondescending, clear, and confident, it was an incredibly skillful performance. (According to Raymond Moley's *After Seven Years,* the first draft of this chat was written by Charles Michelson of the Democratic publicity staff; Arthur Ballantine, Under Secretary of the Treasury for Hoover, completely rewrote it; Roosevelt revised it.) The banks opened without any such renewed panic as had been feared. They might not have done so had people realized that it was impossible, in a few days, to separate the sound banks from the unsound with any certainty, and that errors were bound to be made. The story goes that one bank had been in such bad shape that its directors decided not even to put in an application to reopen; through a clerical slip this bank was put on the wrong list, received a clean bill of health, and opened with flying colors! In some places, to be sure, there were bank runs even after the opening—runs which had to be met unquestioningly with Federal funds, lest the whole trouble begin over again. And so many banks had to be kept shut anyhow that ten per cent or more of the deposits of the country were still tied up after March 15, and the national economic machinery thus remained partially crippled. On the whole, however, the opening was an immense success. Confidence had come back with a rush; for the people had been captivated and persuaded by a President who seemed to believe in them and was giving them action, action, action.

The New Deal had made a brilliant beginning.

§3

The next few months in Washington provided a spectacle unprecedented in American history. The pace at which the New Deal had started its career slackened hardly at all. The administrative hopper produced bill after bill, the President passed the bills on to Congress with terse recommendations for passage, and Congress—almost as if mesmerized—passed them, often with scant debate, sometimes without an opportunity for all the members to read them, much less comprehend their full significance. Never before except in wartime had the Executive been so dominant over Congress. Never before, even in wartime, had a legislative program been pushed through with such terrific speed and daring.

The very air of Washington crackled. Suddenly this city had become unquestionably the economic as well as the political capital of the country, the focus of public attention. The press associations had to double their staffs to fill the demand for explanatory dispatches about the New Deal bills. And into Washington descended a multitude of men and women from all over the country.

First there were bankers by the thousands, thronging the corridors of the Treasury, buttonholing their Senators to explain just why their banks should be permitted to re-open, and converging upon an emergency office set up in the Washington Building by the Acting Comptroller of the Currency—an office in which four men found themselves the bottleneck of communication between the banking system and the government. Amid the hammering of workmen putting up partitions, these men were trying simultaneously to hire stenographers and clerks, to draft regulations and letters, to interview importunate bankers, and to deal with incoming telephone calls which were backed up two and three days by the congestion of appeals from all over the country. Every banker had his own story to tell—his own account of how his mortgages had been undervalued by the bank examiners, or an entire community was dependent upon his institution. Some of them brought their directors along. Who could deal with these men? So terrific was the strain of those first days that on at least two nights the Acting Comptroller of the Currency went home only to take a shower, change his clothes, and go back to work; when he did snatch a few hours' sleep, his wife had to sit by a constantly ringing telephone and explain that he might not be disturbed. Another high official would lie down on a couch in the office of the Secretary of the Treasury, go to sleep, be awakened by a question, answer it, and drop off to sleep again.

In that GHQ at the Treasury during the bank holiday there was an almost continuous executive conference, day and night. Woodin and Moley, Democrats; Mills, Ballantine, and Awalt, Republicans, were the nucleus of a group which labored without thought of party. Even in their brief intervals of rest the problems remained with them; at breakfast on the Tuesday morning after the Inauguration little Woodin reported to Moley how he had solved the knotty question of whether and how to issue scrip: "I played my guitar a little while and then read a while and then slept a little while and then awakened and then thought about this scrip thing and then played some more and read some more and slept some more and thought some more. And, by gum, if I didn't hit on the answer that way! . . . We don't have to issue scrip!" The ordeal of twenty-hour days was too much for Secretary Woodin; his health had not been good, and there are those who think that it was the labor and responsibility of those weeks in March which killed him; he died the following year.

Droves of Democratic office-seekers, too, were descending upon Washington: so many of them that Postmaster-General Farley, whom they knew to be the chief patronage dispenser of the Administration, found them haunting the corridors of his hotel; he "virtually had to slip back and forth to his office like a man dodging a sheriff's writ," and he found that the only way to get rid of the hordes that packed his reception room at the Old Post Office Building was to make the rounds of the room five or six times a day with his secretary, taking down the name of each individual and a brief description of the sort of job he sought.

Experts and specialists of all sorts were coming into town to help in the framing of new laws and regulations and in the setting up of new government agencies. Financiers and their lawyers and brief-case-toting assistants were coming to take the witness stand in Ferdinand Pecora's intermittently sensational investigation of the scandals of the banking world. Special emissaries from Great Britain, Canada, France, Italy, Argentina, Germany, Mexico, China, Brazil, Japan, and Chile arrived in quick succession, each with his entourage, to consult with the President and his advisers on economic and diplomatic problems; from Great Britain came Ramsay MacDonald, the Prime Minister; from France came Edouard Herriot, the Premier; there were receptions, conferences, dinners, long discussions between groups of experts, in endless and fatiguing succession.

To Washington as by a magnet were drawn, too, innumerable idealists, enthusiasts, radical national-planners, world-savers of all degrees of hard- and soft-headedness, each with his infallible prescription for ending the Depression.

Meanwhile into the White House poured thousands of plans for re-covery, for the great American public wanted to help. They ranged, these plans, from semi-literate scrawls on ruled paper to 175-page mimeo-graphed booklets with graphs and statistical tables, and they displayed a touching confidence that the President himself would carefully consider their suggestions. (All these plans were read, considered, and politely acknowledged—but not by him.) "In the present national emergency," began a characteristic letter, "surely I will be pardoned if it is presump-tuous to bring views to your attention. If the ideas are in the least beneficial then the end will justify the beginning." And another: "Being one of those Americans who love their country and having a sort of an idea which may have some merit, I am taking the presumptuous liberty of passing it along to you in this letter." Business men, bankers, students, house-wives, unemployed laborers, they had ideas and threw them into the hopper.

Furious work was being done in Washington in that spring of 1933. The lights burned late in government offices as the architects of the New Deal, official and unofficial, drafted bills and regulations and memoranda, tore their drafts to pieces and began all over again, and then rushed off to consult other groups and revise and revise again. In the vast new office buildings along the Mall there was sublime confusion as new jobholders arrived and began searching for their offices, for desks, for people who could tell them what they were supposed to do. Government departments were overflowing into office buildings everywhere; and the streets were full of apartment-hunters, while the real-estate men of Washington rubbed their hands at the sudden boom in the housing market.

§ 4

Out of all this pandemonium emerged in short order an extraordinary array of new legislative measures. To summarize the chief ones very briefly:—

1. Devaluation.

After the banks opened there was a prompt improvement in business, but during the first few weeks it was only moderate. The President be-came impatient; and Congress, likewise impatient, became so enamoured of the idea of inflating the currency that a bill sponsored by Senator Wheeler of Montana, providing for the free coinage of silver on the old

Bryan basis of 16 to 1, almost passed the Senate despite Roosevelt's opposition. Under these circumstances Roosevelt took the plunge off the gold standard. Half convinced that some sort of inflation was necessary anyhow as a shot in the arm for the American economy; unwilling to let Congress take the initiative away from him and force the country into some ill-devised inflation scheme; and convinced that if it were done when 'tis done, then 'twere well it were done quickly, Roosevelt on April 19th placed an embargo on gold—thus serving notice that the gold standard had been definitely abandoned. Then he laid before Congress a bill—which was passed—giving him permissive authority to inflate in any one of five ways if he saw the need to do so.

Shortly afterward there followed a law which forbade the issue of bonds, governmental or corporate, payable in gold, and which abrogated all existing contractual obligations to pay bonds in gold. Still later, when the World Economic Conference, assembling in London, turned to the international stabilization of currencies as its first important task, Roosevelt heaved a bombshell into it—with distressing damage to the prestige of his own delegation—by refusing to let the United States be a party to even a vague and general stabilization agreement at that juncture. And from time to time, while these moves were going on, he declared his intention to raise American prices "to such an extent that those who have borrowed money will, on the average, be able to repay that money in the same kind of dollar which they borrowed." (It was not until later in 1933 that he devalued the American dollar progressively to 59.06 cents, in terms of its former gold value, through the amazing—and none too successful—scheme of progressively raising the price which the United States would bid for gold.)

The result of these various orders, laws, and statements in the spring of 1933 was to bring about a quick jump in prices, a burst of upward activity on the stock exchanges and commodity exchanges, a hurried buying of supplies by business men for their inventories in expectation of further rises in prices, and a much sharper recovery of business than had previously seemed likely. It is difficult to disentangle causes and effects when a government is doing everything at once, but the evidence would seem to show that the shot in the arm administered in the spring of 1933 had a definitely stimulating effect. (In fact, there would seem to be room for the somewhat cynical comment that of all the economic medicines applied to the United States as a whole during the nineteen-thirties, only two have been of proved general effectiveness, and both of these have a habit-forming tendency and may be lethal if too often repeated: these two medicines are devaluation and spending.)

2. Crop Control.

The New Deal came to the rescue of the farm population with a bill which aimed to raise the prices of the major American farm crops by offering payments to farmers to leave part of their acreage unplanted. The money for the payments was to be raised by a processing tax, which in effect was a light sales tax on the consumption of these crops—penalizing everybody a little in order to help the hard-hit farm population. (With cotton the method was different: the crop having already been planted, rewards were offered for plowing up part of it.) The complicated business of administering this Act was entrusted to an Agricultural Adjustment Administration—AAA for short.

The promise of the AAA program, along with the promise of inflation, lifted farm prices sharply in the spring of 1933, and thus brought early and substantial relief to the farmers; the effect of the AAA after it went into full operation in 1934 was more debatable, and was obscured anyhow by subsequent droughts.

3. Stimulating Employment.

Roosevelt's pet scheme for putting a quarter of a million young men into the woods for conservation work was quickly approved by Congress, and presently the young men of the CCC were off to army camps and then to the forests. There was also passed a bill providing $3,300,000,000 for public works—a staggering sum by Hoover standards. (Roosevelt's heart was not in the public-works program, it was difficult to spend any large amount of money quickly and yet wisely on dams, bridges, and other major works, and therefore slow progress was made; a good deal of the $3,300,000,000 was diverted into relief and national defense.)

4. Federal Relief.

To aid the unemployed—whose condition was desperate—the Federal government went for the first time on a large scale into the distribution of relief funds. These, in the early months of the New Deal, were mostly dispensed through state and local machinery; but the new assumption of responsibility was nevertheless significant.

5. The Tennessee Valley Experiment.

Not only did a bill passed in May, 1933, provide for the Federal operation of that subject of long previous argument, the dam at Muscle Shoals; it provided also for an ambitious development of the whole Tennessee Valley through the building of other Federal dams, through the sale of power from them at low prices, and through Federal subsidizing of conservation measures in the Valley. This bill—which went considerably beyond Roosevelt's campaign proposals—was perhaps the most revolutionary measure of the early New Deal in its long-term significance, for it put the government directly into industry and into a dominating position in developing a whole section of the country.

6. *Lightening the Debt Burden.*

Federal agencies were set up to refinance farm and home mortgages, lowering the interest rate on them and putting a Federal guarantee behind them, thus easing the back-breaking pressure of debt on farmers and other householders—and, incidentally, further freezing the debt-structure of the country.

7. *Financial Reforms.*

A Securities Act was passed which provided that those who issued securities must provide the government with full—in fact voluminous—information about the enterprises to be financed. And a banking act was passed which, though it did not grapple with the knotty problem of unifying the banking system of the country, struck at certain conspicuous abuses: it provided that no banking house might both accept deposits and issue securities, and it forbade commercial banks to have securities affiliates. (These reforms were the forerunners of others to come.)

Last in our list, but far from least, there was set up

8. *The NRA.*

The genesis and motivation of the NRA provide a beautiful example of the wild confusion of those honeymoon days of the New Deal, and deserve special mention. The NRA's paternity was multiple, to say the least.

Soon after the bank holiday Senator Hugo Black (of subsequent Supreme Court fame) pushed through the Senate a bill decreeing a thirty-hour week in all businesses engaged in interstate commerce; and although the measure was held up by a motion to reconsider, the size of the Senate vote and the fact that the House was giving a favorable reception to a similar measure (the Connery Bill), showed that Congress meant business. (Here was NRA idea No. 1: spread employment by shortening hours of labor.) Thereupon Secretary of Labor Frances Perkins insisted any such bill must contain a minimum-wage provision. (Here was idea No. 2: "put a floor under wages.") By this time the President and various members of his Administration had become worried over the possibility that wholesale and inflexible legislation on hours and wages might prove a Pandora's box of troubles, and had begun to wrestle with ideas for a more flexible and comprehensive Administration measure, which could be substituted somewhat as the discretionary inflation bill had been substituted for the Wheeler Bill.

.A number of business men also swung into action. For a long time the Chamber of Commerce of the United States had been opposing what it called "cut-throat competition" and had wanted the Sherman Anti-Trust Act modified so that trade associations might set wages and adopt "codes of practice" with governmental permission. Hoover had flatly opposed any such scheme as monopolistic—as allowing established companies to combine to prevent, not only "cut-throat competition," but all real competition of any sort. Roosevelt seemed to have no such fears—and the business men saw their opportunity. (Thus arose idea No. 3: "self-government for business," with the trade associations doing the governing under government auspices.)

Meanwhile there was also much enthusiasm among the young liberals in Washington for the idea of "national planning" for industry. Impressed by the Russian Five-Year Plan, they wanted the government to regulate the functioning of the helter-skelter American business system. (Here was idea No. 4.) There was a widespread hope, too, chiefly among these same liberals, that purchasing power might be expanded by a concerted raising of wages—on the theory that if the raising were general no business would suffer and all would benefit. (Idea No. 5.)

Each of these ideas was represented in the framing of the National Industrial Recovery Act.

After numerous conferences of various groups of men of diverse economic philosophies, there emerged as the principal artificer of the project a man whose own central interest was in the Chamber of Commerce idea: a former Army officer, former plow manufacturer, and protégé of Bernard Baruch named General Hugh S. Johnson, who had worked in the Brain Trust group during the campaign and now had a desk in the office of Raymond Moley, the new Assistant Secretary of State. And there emerged a bill which provided that each industry, through its trade association, would write for itself a "code" prescribing maximum hours and minimum wages and rules of fair competition for that industry, subject to the approval of the government. What was thus prescribed and approved might be done regardless of the Sherman Act, and in fact might not be transgressed under penalty of the law. Since the men who were thus to be allowed to organize and write their own codes were the employers, the Department of Labor insisted that their employees should also be permitted to organize; and so was written into the National Industrial Recovery Act the famous Section 7a, which stated that "employees shall have the right to organize and bargain collectively through representatives of their own choosing, and shall be free from the interference, coercion, or restraint of employers of labor or their agents." For further protection for labor and for consumers there were elaborate pro-

visions for setting up Labor Advisory Boards and Consumers' Advisory
Boards, to make sure that every interest was consulted.

On June 16, 1933, the National Industrial Recovery Act was signed
amid much fanfare. Said President Roosevelt, "History probably will
record the National Industrial Recovery Act as the most important and far-
reaching legislation ever enacted by the American Congress." On that
same day General Johnson was named Administrator of the NRA. And it
became obvious that this unprecedented organization was to be the focal
point of the whole New Deal program of 1933.

Having produced the NRA, Congress adjourned, bringing to an end
what was indeed an extraordinary session.

§5

The contrasts between this 1933 New Deal program and the Hoover
program were sharp. It was not a program of defense but of multiple and
headlong attack. In most of the laws and certainly in the intent behind
them there was a new emphasis on the welfare of the common man; a
new attempt, as was often said, to build prosperity from the bottom up
rather than from the top down. There was a new willingness to expand
the scope of government operations; for a long time past these had been
expanding out of sheer political and economic necessity, as the inevitable
long-term tendency toward centralization took effect upon government
as well as upon business, but now the brakes were removed and the
expansion was abrupt. Also in contrast was the visible distrust by Roosevelt of the bankers and corporate insiders of Wall Street; Hoover had
leaned upon them for advice and assistance (which was not always forthcoming), Roosevelt disregarded them. He preferred the assistance of supposedly impartial (if impractical) professors to that of supposedly practical (if partial) business men. There was a new encouragement of labor
unions, a new hospitality to liberal and radical ideas which would reduce
the power of the owning class. The governmental center of gravity had
moved to the left.

At the same time the program represented a strange jumble of theories.
For example, the Economy Act—and to a certain extent the financial
reform measures—had a deflationary effect; whereas devaluation—and to
a certain extent the public-works plan and the Federal relief plan—had an
inflationary effect. The AAA bill tried to bring recovery by inducing
scarcity—as did much of the NRA as it later developed; whereas the
public-works and TVA plans operated on the abundance theory. The
conferences with foreign emissaries and the plans for international economic co-operation ran head on into the devaluation policy—with a re-

sounding explosion in London. The financial reform measures sought to discourage concentrations of economic power; the NRA—in practice—tended to encourage them.

In addition to these conflicts of theory, there were numerous collisions between governmental organizations trying to do the same thing, between organizations trying to do opposite things, between old policies being pursued as a matter of habit and new ones being introduced.

Some of these conflicts were due, of course, to the sheer impossibility of achieving legislative and administrative perfection at a hand gallop. Some were due to the fact that Washington was full of able and eager men with contrasting ideas: in a multitude of counselors there is confusion. Some were due to the political necessity of devising measures which could win the support of diverse interests. And some were due to the fact that the New Deal program of those first few months was like a geological formation built up in several layers. At the bottom were the old-fashioned liberal measures, the economy and reform measures, of the 1932 platform. On top of these were the more ambitious programs adumbrated by the Brain Trust during the campaign and after, and other measures hustled into action when the bank panic produced a much graver crisis than had been foreseen in early 1932. Then there were the measures which grew, perforce, out of the bank panic itself—including, if you wish, devaluation. On top were the bright ideas that bloomed in the fertile spring of 1933; chief among these was the NRA, which was a whole plum pudding of contrasting elements in itself. Yet even if one took account of all these reasons for inconsistency, there remained something in Roosevelt's try-everything attitude which reminded one of the man who, feeling unwell, took in quick succession all the tonics on the shelf.

But if the President preferred bold action to careful deliberation, so too did the country. The sickness of the economic system was infinitely complicated and little understood. Now a physician had come along who had a lot of medicines in his bag, who had an air of authority and an agreeable bedside manner; and the American people hailed him with delight. His medicines were better than most which were currently suggested, and certainly the patient's morale was improved by having a friendly physician who was willing to do something and not just wait for nature to effect a cure. In the spring and summer of 1933 the American economic system took its new medicines cheerfully, sat up in bed, and said, "I feel better already."

§ 6

What a flood tide of returning hope was running in those first six months of the New Deal!

That was the season when the Chicago Fair opened—that Fair whose intention to chronicle "A Century of Progress" had seemed only a few months before so unmitigatedly ironical. What did Chicagoans care if Sally Rand stole the show with her fan dance? She too had been a victim of the Depression, earning a precarious living dancing in small-time cabarets in Western cities, and her fortunes had sunk low in 1932; in her own reported words, she had "never made any money until she took off her pants"; but now the crowds surged to see her come down the velvet-covered steps with her waving fans (and apparently nothing else) before her, and Chicago profited. General Balbo's armada of Italian airplanes flew to the fair; and in that same summer of 1933 Charles and Anne Lindbergh, leaving behind them for a time the scenes of their tragedy, flew to Greenland, to proceed thence to Europe and Africa and—*Listen! The Wind*—to South America.

That was the season when the Senate Banking Committee drew from the Morgan partners the story of the "preferred lists" of subscribers to the stock of their corporations; and when the orderly processes of financial exemplification were interrupted, to everybody's dismay, by a circus promoter who placed a midget in J. P. Morgan's lap. It was the season when the country first became wonderingly aware of the extent to which the amiable First Lady of the land embodied the law of perpetual motion; and when her husband, after putting his name to the National Industrial Recovery Act, climbed aboard the little *Amberjack II,* put on his oil-skins, and went sailing up the New England coast to Campobello.

That was the season when Max Baer knocked out Schmeling in the tenth, and the massive Primo Carnera knocked out champion Jack Sharkey in the sixth, and an unidentified man almost knocked out Huey Long in the Sands Point washroom, and Glenn Cunningham began breaking the running records for the mile, and *Anthony Adverse* began breaking records for fiction sales as it enthralled lovers of vicarious adventure on thousands of summer porches.

Once more the business men of the country began to know hope. The Federal Reserve Board's adjusted index figure for Industrial Production in the bank-holiday month of March, 1933, had been 59 (as against 58 for the preceding July, the month of the Bonus March). In April it jumped from 59 to 66; in May it jumped to 78; in June, to 91; in July, to 100 (as against a 1929 high of 125). There was no such proportionate gain in employment, to be sure; for as the pace of business increased, there was much slack to be taken up simply by working factories full time that had been working part time, by working office clerks overtime, by keeping shopgirls on the run. Still there remained millions of unemployed men, whose poverty was as yet unrelieved by any Federal expenditures for their aid. So greatly had the Depression stimulated working efficiency and the installation of labor-saving devices that a far sharper increase in production than this would be needed to give jobs to those men. Nor were the men who went back to work any too tractable. They had suffered, they had become embittered, and as hope returned, anger rose with it: strikes began to increase in number. The mood of the farm population was still rebellious, for until their crops were harvested the rise in farm prices would do them little good; the speculators would get the money. There were still riots and disorders in the farm belt. But the prospects were promising. "Give us just a few months more of this improvement . . ." men said to themselves.

The speculators leaped into action. As the stock market spurted, out of the highways and byways came the little stock gamblers. For three and a half years they had been telling themselves—if they had any money left—that speculation was no more for them. During the past few months they had been in the grip, most of them, of a mounting distrust of Wall Street bankers in particular and all bankers in general, and had been telling and re-telling derisive anecdotes in which bankers figured. But when they began to see the plus signs among the stock quotations, back to the brokers' offices they thronged, ready to stake their last savings on Commercial Solvents and Standard Brands and the alcohol stocks; and meanwhile as cold-blooded a lot of pool operators as had ever been seen in the unregenerate days of 1929 manipulated and unloaded, manipulated and unloaded. The Securities Act had been signed, reform was the order of the New Deal day, one might have expected these gentry to be newly cautious; but all such considerations apparently meant nothing to them. So violently did the stock market boil, so frequently were there five- and six-million-share days, that the total volume of trading in the month of June, 1933, and again in the month of July, 1933, was greater than it had been in any single month in the Big Bull Market of 1929—with the sole exception of the Panic month of October. Meanwhile the grain market and the other commodity markets boiled too. Who could lose? argued the little speculators. "If we don't have prosperity we'll at least have inflation." (In 1932 the thought of inflation had prompted selling, now it prompted buying: the mood had changed.)

Late in July the stock and commodity markets broke badly, and day after day the speculators' favorites tumbled; one of these favorites, American Commercial Alcohol, actually collapsed from $89\frac{7}{8}$ to $29\frac{1}{8}$ in four days. But at that very moment the President was having distributed to business men all over the country the blanket NRA code that would "start the wheels turning." It was difficult to find a daily paper which did not contain somebody's glowing tribute to the NRA. It had "abolished child labor," it was introducing "a new era of co-operation between industry and government," it was "an attempt to substitute constructive co-operation for destructive competition," it would cause "management and labor to join hands," it would "end the flat-wallet era," and it held out "the promise of a new day." The break in the markets checked confidence a bit; but was it not predicted that millions of men would go back to work "before the snow flies"?

In Washington the excitement was still feverish. Congress had adjourned, but now the business men were there by the bewildered thousands to draw up NRA codes. Up and down the interminable corridors of the Commerce Building they tramped, buttonholing any hatless man to ask their way, under the impression that he must be a high official. They wanted their own codes, industry by industry, and each of them had his own idea of what ought to go into his code to stop the particular kind of "cut-throat competition" that his company hated. But first these men had to find out what industry they belonged to. Was candlewick-bedspread-making a part of the cotton-textile industry, or should it have a code of its own? Shouldn't the dog-food industry insist on special treatment? And where should the academic costume men go to solve their code problems? And the fly-swatter manufacturers? Where was General Johnson's office? And who was this "Robbie" whose ear it was considered so valuable to get? And might it not be better to go back to the Mayflower and confer there, even though the hotel telephone service was so jammed that you couldn't get a connection?

In the center of this wild confusion—as Jonathan Mitchell wrote—General Johnson "sat at ease, coat off, blue shirt open at the neck, redfaced, and looking uncannily like Captain Stagg in Stallings and Anderson's 'What Price Glory.' Like captured peasants, squads of sweating business men . . . were led in before him." Part cavalry officer, part veteran business man, part economic seer, part government administrator (he could assume any of these roles at will, said Mitchell) the General coaxed or prophesied or wisecracked or thundered as the occasion seemed to warrant, and the business men would go forth obediently—or so they felt at the moment—to do his bidding. So completely did the General captivate the Washington newspaper men that they began to regard the

NRA as the center of the government exhibit and the White House as a side show. His vehement oratory, his references to "cracking down on the chiselers" and to the "dead cats" of criticism, his torrential enthusiasm, held the country spellbound. General Johnson had become the personification of Recovery.

When you went to the movies to see "Cavalcade" (that life-preserver with TITANIC on it!), or "Mädchen in Uniform," or "Reunion in Vienna," you would see also a short picture, accompanied by a voice thrilling with patriotism, telling how America was marching on to prosperity under the slogan "We do our part." The Blue Eagle appeared in shop windows, in advertisements. There were splendid NRA parades, with thousands marching and airplanes droning overhead. Grover Whalen organized a New York compliance campaign enlivened by the appearance of Miss Nira (short for National Industrial Recovery Act) and Miss Liberty; 150 women from the Bronx marched to NRA headquarters bearing 250,000 pledges and accompanied by a brass band; it was estimated that a quarter of a million people marched in New York and a million and a half looked on, and it cost $4,980.70 to clean up the streets afterwards.

Yes, America was on its way. Though the stock market looked ragged as the summer came to an end, and the business indices had slipped back from the pinnacle of July, and doubts and disagreements were beginning to cloud the brightness of the economic and political skies, still the prevailing mood of the general public was aptly reflected in the song of the three little pigs in Disney's new picture, then going the rounds of the movie houses: America had learned to sing "Who's Afraid of the Big Bad Wolf?"

The homeless people who made a home in Central Park found their way into Joseph Mitchell's story and into Robert Nathan's gentle fairy-tale, One More Spring. *But the wry humor of the former and the inverted optimism of the latter can hardly conceal the cold terror that inspired both writers. The rural equivalent is Martha Gellhorn's reworking of the case histories she collected as a relief field worker. Tess Slesinger captured the hopelessness of men and women for whom a job was merely an incredible and brief interruption of the normal state of unemployment. And the four stories from that admirable experiment,* 365 Days, *are semi-journalistic, semi-fictional responses to economic stresses.*

JOSEPH MITCHELL

The Cave Dwellers

THE WINTER OF 1933 was a painful one. It seems like a hundred and thirty-three years ago, but I remember it distinctly. That winter, I was a reporter on a newspaper whose editors believed that nothing brightened up a front page so much as a story about human suffering. "The man on the street is so gloomy nowadays," one of the editors used to say, "that a story about somebody else's bad luck cheers him up." In the three weeks preceding Christmas there was, of course, an abundance of such stories, and for one reason or another I was picked to handle most of them. One morning I spent a harried half-hour in the anteroom of a magistrate's court talking with a stony-faced woman who had stabbed her husband to death because he took a dollar and eighty cents she had saved for Christmas presents for their children and spent it in one of the new repeal gin mills. "I sure fixed his wagon," she said. Then she began to moan. That afternoon I was sent up to the big "Hoover Village" on the Hudson at Seventy-fourth Street to ask about the plans the people there were making for Christmas. The gaunt squatters stood and looked at me with a look I probably never will get over; if they had turned on me and pitched me into the river I wouldn't have blamed them. Next day I was sent out to stand on a busy corner with a Salvation Army woman whose job was to ring a bell and attract attention to a kettle in the hope that passers-by would drop money into it for the Army's Christmas Fund. "Just stand there three or four hours," I was told, "and see what happens; there ought to be a story in it." The bellringer was elderly and hollow-eyed and she had a head cold, which I caught.

Day in and day out, I was sent to breadlines, to relief bureaus, to evictions; each morning I called on cringing, abject humans who sat and stared as I goaded them with questions. My editors sincerely believed that such interviews would provoke people to contribute to the various Christmas funds, and they undoubtedly did, but that did not help me conquer the feeling that I had no right to knock on tenement doors and catechize

Originally published in *The New Yorker*. Reprinted from *McSorley's Wonderful Saloon* by Joseph Mitchell by permission of the publishers Duell, Sloan & Pearce, Inc. Copyright 1938 by Joseph Mitchell.

men and women who were interesting only because they were miserable in some unusual way. Also, the attitude of the people I talked with was disheartening. They were without indignation. They were utterly spiritless. I am sure that few of them wanted their stories printed, but they answered my questions, questions I absolutely had to ask, because they were afraid something might happen to their relief if they didn't; all of them thought I was connected in some way with the relief administration. I began to feel that I was preying on the unfortunate. My faith in human dignity was almost gone when something happened that did a lot to restore it.

Early one bitter cold morning, only a few days before Christmas, a man telephoned the newspaper and said that the evening before, while walking his dog in Central Park, he had come upon a man and woman who said they had lived for almost a year in a cave in the park. This was one of the caves uncovered when the old lower reservoir was emptied and abandoned, an area since filled in for playgrounds. He said he had discovered the man and woman squatting in the cave beside a little fire, and had been afraid they would freeze to death during the night, so he had persuaded them to leave the Park and had put them up in a furnished room.

"I wish your newspaper would run a story about them," said the man on the telephone. "It might help them get jobs."

I went up to see the man and woman. They were living in one of a cluster of brownstone rooming houses on West Sixtieth Street, off Columbus Avenue, two blocks from the Park. They were on the fourth floor. An inch and a half of snow had fallen during the night and there was a ridge of it on the window sill of their furnished room. The man said his name was James Hollinan and that he was an unemployed carpenter. He was small, wiry, and white-haired. He wore corduroy trousers and a greasy leather windbreaker. The woman was his wife. Her name was Elizabeth and she was an unemployed hotel maid. When I arrived, Mr. Hollinan was preparing to go out. He had his hat on and was getting into a tattered overcoat. I told him who I was.

"I'd like to ask a few questions," I said.

"Talk to my wife," he said. "She does all the talking."

He turned to his wife. "I'll go get some breakfast," he said.

"Get egg sandwiches and some coffee," she said, taking a few coins out of her purse and placing them, one by one, in his hand, "and we'll have seven cents left."

"O.K.," he said, and left.

I asked Mrs. Hollinan to tell me about their life in the cave. While she answered my questions she made the bed, and she appeared to get a lot of pleasure out of the task. I could understand it; it was the first bed she had made in a long time.

"Well, I tell you," she said, smacking a pillow against the iron bed-stead, "we got dispossessed from a flat up in Washington Heights the middle of last December, a year ago. When we went to the relief bureau they tried to separate us. They wanted to send my husband one place and me another. So I said, 'We'll starve together.' That night we ended up in Central Park. We found the cave and hid in it. Late at night we built a fire. We been doing that almost every night for a year."

She smoothed out the counterpane until there wasn't a wrinkle in it and then rather reluctantly sat down on the bed. There was only one chair in the room.

"Of course," she continued, "some nights it got too cold and rainy. Then we'd go to a church uptown that's left open at night. We'd sleep in a pew, sitting up. Most mornings we'd part and look for work. He hardly ever found anything to do. It was worse for him. He's older than me. Couple of times a week I'd pick up a cleaning job and that would mean a few dollars, and we'd eat on that. We'd carry water to the cave and make stews."

"How did you sleep in the cave?" I asked.

"We'd take turns snoozing on a bed we made of a pile of cardboard boxes," she said. "We kept a fire going. A little fire, so the cops wouldn't run us off. The Park cops knew we were there, but so long as we didn't build up a big fire and attract attention, they'd let us alone. Last summer the cave was better than a house. But lately, when it rained, we'd get rheumatism, and it was awful."

Mrs. Hollinan's dress was nearly worn out, but it was clean and neat. I wondered how she had kept so clean, living in a cave. I think she guessed what was on my mind, because she said, "We'd go to a public bath about twice a week, and I used to put my dresses and his shirts in an old lard stand in the cave and boil them." We talked for about fifteen minutes and then her husband returned. He had a cardboard container of coffee and two sandwiches in a paper bag. I knew they didn't want me around while they ate breakfast, so I said goodbye.

"I hope we get some relief this time," said Mrs. Hollinan as I went out of the door, and I realized she thought I was a relief investigator. I didn't have the nerve to tell her she was mistaken.

I wasn't especially interested in Mr. and Mrs. Hollinan; compared with some of the people I had seen that winter, they were living off the fat of the land. In the story I wrote about them I mentioned the incident in which Mrs. Hollinan told her husband that when breakfast was paid for they would have seven cents left, and I gave the address of the rooming house in case someone wanted to offer Mr. Hollinan a job. The story was in the late editions.

Next day was my day off, but that afternoon I dropped by the office to get my mail. My box was stuffed with letters from people who had read the story about Mr. and Mrs. Hollinan, and attached to many of the letters were bills or checks to be turned over to them. The biggest check, one for twenty-five dollars, was from Robert Nathan. His novel, "One More Spring," which concerned some derelicts who lived a winter in a drafty Central Park toolhouse, had been published earlier that year. In all, there was eighty-five dollars, and there were two telegrams, offering jobs.

I had a date to meet a girl and help her with Christmas shopping, and I telephoned her that I couldn't keep it, that I had to go give eighty-five dollars to a man and woman who had spent a year in a cave. She wanted to go with me. I met her at Columbus Circle and we walked over to the rooming house. The streets were crowded with Christmas shoppers and store windows were full of holly and tinsel and red Christmas bells. The cheerful shoppers depressed me. "How can men and women be so happy," I thought, "when all over the city people are starving?".

The landlady of the rooming house met us at the door. She appeared to be in an angry mood. I told her I was the reporter who had come to see Mr. and Mrs. Hollinan the day before. She said people had been calling on them since early morning, bringing them money and food.

"They read that story you had in the paper last night," the landlady said. "They keep coming, but I haven't let anybody upstairs this afternoon. That was a lot of baloney you had in the paper. Why, those cave people are upstairs celebrating."

"I don't blame them," said my girl.

"Well, I do," said the landlady.

She wouldn't let my girl go upstairs with me.

"You'll have to wait here, young lady," she said severely.

I went on upstairs carrying the fistful of letters. I knocked on their door and someone shouted, "Come on in!" I opened the door. The room was in magnificent disorder. On the table were two big steamer baskets, cellophane-wrapped, with red ribbons tied to their handles. The steamer baskets looked odd in the shabby room. Also on the table were bottles of beer and gin and ginger ale and some half-eaten sandwiches. The floor was strewn with wrapping paper and boxes and cigar butts. Mrs. Hollinan was sitting on the bed with a tumbler in her hand. A cigar was sticking out of a corner of Mr. Hollinan's mouth and he was pouring himself a drink of gin. They were quite drunk, without a doubt. Mr. Hollinan looked at me, but he didn't seem to recognize me.

"Sit down and make yourself at home," he said, waving me to the bed. "Have a drink? Have a cigar?"

"It's that sneak from the newspaper," said Mrs. Hollinan. "Give him hell, Jim."

Mr. Hollinan stood up. He wasn't very steady on his feet.

"What did you mean," he said, "putting that writeup in the paper?"

"What was wrong with it?" I asked.

"You said in that writeup we only had seven cents left, you liar."

"Well, that's what your wife told me."

"I did not," said Mrs. Hollinan, indignantly. She got up and waved her tumbler, spilling gin and ginger ale all over the bed. "I told you we had *seventy* cents left," she said.

"That's right," said Mr. Hollinan. "What do you mean, putting lies about us in the paper?"

Mr. Hollinan took a square bottle of gin off the table. He got a good grip on it and started toward me, waving the bottle in the air.

"Wait a minute," I said, edging toward the door. "I brought you some money."

"I don't want your money," he said. "I got money."

"Well," I said, holding out the telegrams, "I think I have a job for you."

"I don't want your help," he said. "You put a lie about us in the paper."

"That's right, Jim," said Mrs. Hollinan, giggling. "Give him hell!"

I closed the door and hurried to the stairs. Mr. Hollinan stumbled out of the room and stood at the head of the stairs, clutching for the railing with one hand. Just as I reached the landing on the second floor he threw the bottle of gin. It hit the wall above my head and broke into pieces. I was sprayed with gin and bits of wet glass. I ran on down the stairs, getting out of Mr. Hollinan's range. All the way down the stairs I could hear Mrs. Hollinan up in the room, yelling, "Give him hell, Jim!"

"Mother of God," said the landlady when I got downstairs, "what happened? What was that crash?"

"You smell like a distillery," said my girl.

I was laughing. "Mr. Hollinan threw a bottle of gin at me," I said.

"That's nothing to laugh about," said the landlady sharply. "Why don't you call an officer?"

"Let's get out of here," I said to my girl.

We went to a liquor store over on Columbus Circle. I bought a bottle of Holland gin and had it wrapped in Christmas-gift paper, and I gave the liquor-store man Mr. Hollinan's address and told him to deliver the order. My girl thought I was crazy, but I didn't mind. It was the first time I had laughed in weeks.

Early the following morning I went back to the rooming house. I had decided it was my duty to make another attempt to give the money to Mr. and Mrs. Hollinan.

"Those cave people are gone," the landlady told me. "A gentleman came here last night in a limousine, with a chauffeur. He took them away. I had a talk with him before he went upstairs, and I told him how they'd been cutting up, but he didn't care. He gave me a five-dollar bill. 'Here,' he said, 'take this for your trouble. If any mail comes for these good people, send it along to me, and I'll see they get it.' He put them in the back seat with him. He told me he was going to give Mr. Hollinan a job on his farm."

The landlady was quite angry. "They were still drunk," she said, "but that man in the limousine didn't seem to care. He was drunk, too. Drunker than they were, if you ask me. He kept slapping them on the back, first one and then the other. And when they got in the limousine they were laughing and falling all over theirselves, and that Mrs. Hollinan, that lowdown woman, she rolled down the window and thumbed her nose at me."

She had the benefactor's name and address written down and I made a note of them. It was a New Jersey address. I went back to the office and wrote letters to all the people who had sent money to Mr. and Mrs. Hollinan, returning it. I told them Mr. Hollinan had found a job and had declined their contributions.

Until perhaps a week before Christmas of the following year, I forgot about Mr. and Mrs. Hollinan. Then I recalled the experience and began to wonder about them. I wondered if the man in the limousine did give Mr. Hollinan a job and if he was getting along all right. I kept thinking about them all that week and on Christmas Eve I decided to try and get in touch with them and wish them a merry Christmas and a happy New Year. I searched through a stack of old notebooks in the bottom drawer of my desk and finally found their benefactor's name and address. I asked Information to get me his telephone number in New Jersey and I put in a call for him. He answered the telephone himself. I told him I was the reporter who wrote the story about the man and woman he had befriended last Christmas, the cave dwellers. I started to ask him if he would let Mr. Hollinan come to the telephone, but he interrupted me.

"Have you seen them lately?" he asked, irrelevantly. His voice was blurry.

"Why, no," I said. "Aren't they out there with you any longer?"

"I certainly would like to see them," he answered. "To tell you the God's truth, I was just thinking about them. I was sitting here by the fire having a few drinks and I was thinking how much I'd like to see them. I used to have a few drinks at night with old man Hollinan. He was good company, and so was the old lady. He was a funny old crock." He paused.

"What happened?" I asked.

"Well," he said, "I have a little farm here and he took care of it for me when I was in the city. He was the caretaker, sort of. They stayed until about the end of March, and then one day the old boy and his wife just wandered off and I never saw them again. Just wandered off, free people. Free people, yes sir, free as birds."

"I wonder why they left."

"I don't know for sure," he said, "but you know what I think? I think living in that cave ruined them. It ruined them for living in a house. I think they left me because they just got tired of living in a house."

"Well," I said, "merry Christmas."

"Same to you," he said, and hung up.

MARTHA GELLHORN

Mrs. Maddison Returns to the Land

IN THE RELIEF OFFICE they had read the bulletins coming from Washington via State headquarters, and they had received a good many visitors called field supervisors and field representatives. Under pressure and feeling theirs-not-to-reason-why, they had shipped unemployed families back to the land. It was a Project, which made it vast and important, possible of endless interpretation and confusion, and above all it had to be done quickly. Some of the Relief workers, who had lived long in these parts and knew conditions and what you had to have to farm, and what kind of land they were putting people on, and what the houses meant in ill-health, shook their heads grimly but in wise silence. Rural rehabilitation: in itself a magnificent idea. A chance for men to be again self-supporting;

their own masters; captains of their destinies, souls, pocket-books. "It's a fine idea," Mrs. Cahill said, "only nobody seems to have thought much about those Negro shanties we're putting our folks in." Mrs. Lewis, who worked out towards the sawmill district, said it certainly was a fine idea, but she thought there'd be some trouble about medical aid: she also shook her head. "The malaria," Mrs. Lewis said. Miss Ogilvie, who had a sharper tongue than the others, and used to lie awake at night furtively being ashamed of herself for having such a nice bed, said: "It sez, in the bulletins, $105.80 a year is the average cost to the govment for rural rehab families; for everything personal. Lissen to me," she said, with the sun shining on her eyeglasses. "That just isn't human. And to think those northerners made all that fuss about slaves. I don't think they got their heads screwed on right up there."

Mrs. Cahill brooded over the present and future of Mrs. Maddison and her children. She realised that Mrs. Maddison was starving herself, doing some very fine and tricky work with her Relief money in order to coddle Tiny. She liked Mrs. Maddison and thought Tennessee was stupid, sexually awake only, selfish, and that Tiny had so few chances of being a decent or healthy citizen that Mrs. Maddison's sacrifice probably came under the heading of heroic if senseless gestures.

She wanted very much to get Mrs. Maddison away from Tennessee's disaffection, and she also liked Alec, and thought he could do with something to eat for a change. But rural rehabilitation. . . . Something about the name upset Mrs. Cahill, who was fairly simple and usually said what she meant. It was such a vast sound, such a stupendous and splendid idea, and when you got right down to it, it was a chance to live in an abandoned Negro shanty or a badly made, too small, new house; without adequate water, heat or light, with inadequate provision for staple groceries or clothes or medical care: and work until your back broke to raise a crop for which there might or might not be buyers. Obviously it was easier to be in debt to the Government than to private landowners. The Government, being so much bigger, sometimes got a little entangled and forgot to collect on time or just lent you more money to pay back with. But the idea distressed her, still. She talked this problem over with the local administrator and finally she approached Alec, calling on him one day when he was sitting on the river-bank fishing quite hopelessly, but fooling himself into feeling busy.

"Alec," Mrs. Cahill said, "have you ever thought about farming?"

"No'm."

"Would you like to go on a farm?"

Alec thought. He thought about farms as he remembered them and they seemed not unpleasant. Anyhow, a lot better than this overcrowded hut he was living in. And vaguely he had an idea that his mother had baked pies. There would, of course, be a catch in it somewhere.

"I'm not gonna take no Relief," he said rather sulkily.

"It isn't Relief, Alec, it's a loan the Government makes you and you've got some years to pay it back. They give you a certain amount of stuff, farm animals, and tools, and feed, and fertiliser, and seed, and groceries and such; and you make a crop and you pay some money back to the Government."

"Like on shares," Alec said.

"Well." Mrs. Cahill was a little embarrassed. She knew that most enlightened people did not feel the share cropper system was all that might be hoped. However. "Well. Sort of."

"Who'll go, just me and Sabine or all of us?"

"Well, I thought if we could arrange it, you and your mother and your wife would go—the houses aren't very big and Tiny's so small, it might be better for her to stay here with Tennessee."

"Where'll they live then? Tennessee can't live way off down here with that drunk husband of hers around."

"No, I thought Tennessee could take Mrs. Maddison's house while you're on the farm. That way it'd be all right."

"I'll think about it." Alec was careful not to show pleasure or surprise; he mistrusted the Government and all employers, deeply. It always sounded better than what you got in the end. No sense acting happy; then they'd cut you down even more. But a series of new ideas started in his head: satisfactory images and plans. The first picture he evoked was one of a table groaning with food, home-made preserves and things from the garden and fried chicken from their own backyard and pitchers of milk and corn bread and good pale butter. He tightened his jeans around him and wandered back to find Sabine and tell her warily about the future.

Sabine was sick of their cabin and especially now that Tennessee and the baby were there, and it was so crowded she couldn't properly wash things out, or cook, or ever be quiet. Without saying anything to Alec or comparing notes she too had a vision of wonderful food. And maybe a good dress for coming in to town after the first crop; and some new silk stockings and even a permanent. She said casually that it looked all right to her and better ask Mrs. Maddison.

Mrs. Maddison's reasons were very simple: Tennessee and the baby would have a nice house if she left and then she wouldn't have to go around acting to the neighbours as if she and Tennessee saw each other and behaved as daughter and mother should. When, in fact, Tennessee didn't speak and Mrs. Maddison felt more and more lonely and unwanted every day. And she was getting headaches from the sewing-room; her ten cent store glasses didn't seem to be so good after all. And then again, food. And maybe a garden. She saw the house in her mind: a neat little white house with roses all over it and several large magnolia trees and things on shelves in jars, very good to eat, which she had made herself, and curtains at the windows. The Maddisons agreed. Mrs. Cahill wangled. Many papers were made out and signed. Mrs. Maddison had a grand time rushing up to the Relief office, panting and flushed and clamouring for her rights and being stern and saying, I know Mr. Roosevelt wouldn't mean for us not to have oil lamps.

Finally after a month of negotiations they were put into an intimidated Ford truck with whatever baggage they thought necessary or pleasant, and driven to their new start in life. They returned to the land.

* * *

"Oh," Mrs. Maddison said. She stood with a rolled patchwork quilt under one arm, and in her other hand, a market basket full of oddments, notably an alarm clock, a potato masher, two bars of laundry soap and some rope for hanging up the wash.

Sabine stared too but she could find nothing to say; and behind her, alarmed but not realising the extent of the disaster, stood Alec with his mouth open.

"Gimme a hand bud," the truck-driver said. "I'll help you get the big pieces in but I gotta hurry along; I got some other famblies moving out to-day."

Alec helped lift down the rusted stove they had brought from his shack; bed-posts; a table; a chest. He went in the house finally, with a chair resting over his head, and stopped in the middle of the floor, looking about him. He didn't know what to do. His instinct and his first desire were to cry out to this man, who was going to leave, "Don't go, don't leave us here." And then quickly, he thought: if only we could go back with him ... They were so far away; they were so alone and so helpless. What would they do here; how could they live in this place. Suddenly he realised that farming was not a job like salvaging iron: you had to know what to do, and when. And also you had to know what to expect.

Sabine was crying softly behind him. "They shoulda told us," she kept saying. "It ain't right."

Mrs. Maddison was still outside; she had not moved. She didn't notice that the handle of the market basket was eating into her hand and that her arm and shoulder were getting stiff, holding the quilt. These things took time: when you had made a picture, clear and neat in your mind, it took time to erase it. She saw plainly the house she had imagined: white, with roses growing untidily all over it. There should perhaps have been a grey cat asleep on the doorstep in the sun. The curtains would already be up ... Mrs. Cahill had been very uncertain about moving white families into abandoned Negro shanties: these houses weren't even desirable for Negroes she had felt, and that—by local tradition—was saying a good deal. It's got a tired look, Mrs. Maddison thought, tired and worn-out and dirty. The kind of place you thought you'd die in, on the days when you were blue. Mrs. Maddison felt that it was too late to start again; what kind of God was it, who was after her. Driving her from one filthy rattletrap shack to another, driving and driving. She had a right to be tired; she had a right not to try any more.

"Where's Ma?" Alec said.

"Outside."

"C'mon in, Ma," Alec shouted, and there was irritation and despair in his voice; "c'mon in and see the fine house your Relief got us."

She waited a moment longer. It would take a little more courage to go inside, though she could imagine how it was. And she thought: they're young and they're not used to things. I'm the one's got to say something cheerful.

She climbed up the rickety steps. There were two front rooms, both having doors on to the porch. Behind one of them there was a lean-to addition, for a kitchen. It was the simplest form of house. She looked at both rooms and bent a little getting through the low door into the kitchen.

"Well," she said.

They waited. Somehow they felt this was her fault. She was older. She should have known the kind of place they were coming to. They looked at her without kindness.

"Well," Mrs. Maddison said, "I reckon Sabine and me can fix it up so's it'll be all right. It'll be all right in a coupla years."

Alec laughed: "We'll be dead first. We'll freeze in this place in winter. Look," he said. Angrily he ripped more of the torn paper from the walls; light showed through the gaps. "Rain," he said, "we'll be washed outa bed, that's what. And how're we gonna git warm in a place like this." Sabine, catching his anger, kicked her heel hard against the floor and the planking splintered and went through.

"Don't do that," Mrs. Maddison said. "You don't have to show me. But we gotta live here. We don't have no other place to live. So we better get busy about it."

"Your Relief," Alec said in fury. "It's your Relief's doing."

Mrs. Maddison put down her bundles on the floor. She stood up before him, a thin old woman with her hair tightly wobbed on top of her head, sharp-faced and tired, her cheeks fallen in where teeth were missing.

"Lissen to me, Alec Maddison. Don't you talk like that to me. And don't go on saying foolishness. I'd of been dead if it warn't for that Relief. And Miss Lucy's a good woman. And Mr. Roosevelt's a fine man. He's got a good kind face and he's doing what he can for us. Only it takes time. They gotta make mistakes like everybody. But don't you go blaming everything on them. And you jest get busy and set up that bed there, and put the stove where it belongs, and get the pipe fixed up on it, and Sabine, you get busy with a broom and clean out this place and don't look like somebody's stole your last penny. If we gotta live here, we gotta live here. No sense talking."

Resentfully they obeyed her. Mrs. Maddison unpacked what china and pots and pans they had: put clothes and odd bits of linen into the chest. She sang thinly as she worked. She made a lot of noise, too, trying to keep a silence from settling on the house. It's up to me, she thought, they're too young yet. They get discouraged. It's up to me. Suddenly she felt a great pride that their three lives and their happiness and success depended on her: that she was the one who would keep things going, and somehow make a triumph out of this gloomy and decrepit house. It had to be done; it was another job. One more thing to get through before she died. She'd manage it too. The worst thing, Mrs. Maddison decided, would be ever to admit that you didn't have any hope left at all, and that living was too much for you.

*　　*　　*

Alec was a bad farmer, and Sabine an unwilling housewife. Mrs. Maddison, with love, sought to make excuses for them. It was true that they had little to work with. The mule named Thomas was old, embittered and weary. It was no joke ploughing up the field, holding the plough down with blistered hands, behind that languid and uncertain animal. Thomas had a tendency to wander off, suddenly bored by the straight line. It was also true that Alec had to haul water on a crude handmade sled, from a well about fifteen minutes walking down the road. There was no well on the place: they rationed water as if they were on a raft, with the salt ocean swelling ominously about them. And she and Sabine had to take their clothes to a pond over the hill, a greenish pond, where mosquitoes sang their welcome, to wash them. And there were no screens, and no mosquito-nets for the beds, so that sleeping was uneasy, a drugged, resentful fight against the whining pests. And the house; oh yes, Mrs. Maddison told herself, it's bad. But still. She could not keep herself from singing, a thin monotonous song, as she worked. In the evenings she sat on the porch alone, beside her pot of evil-burning rags, and looked over the land. With contentment, and a kind of proud peacefulness that Alec and Sabine found maddening.

Alec was planting cotton: it was the only pay crop (if there were buyers) and the Government demanded this. The farm was twenty acres in all; and he intended to put in eight acres of cotton. By turns, and depending on his anger or where he'd been ploughing, he said: the land's clay . . . it's nothing but sand, no cotton nor nothing else'll grow . . . rocks, rocks, God I oughta be ploughing with dynamite. . . . The vegetable garden became Mrs. Maddison's affair: turnips and squash, peas, beans, beets, carrots, lettuce, potatoes, corn and suddenly, from nowhere, mysteriously, she produced flower seeds: larkspur and asters and a few brown, frail-looking rose plants, carefully embedded by the porch pillars. Mrs. Maddison saw everything green and rich already. Later, she thought, when we've made the crop, we'll buy chickens and a cow. The fullness of life. There might be money for paint too, and new planks to nail over the rotting floor boards, and windows later, and yards of bright print for curtains. It would be a home. She'd live long enough to make it into a home.

Sabine would get up in the morning, with a fretful look on her mouth, and say "'Tain't no use doing anything with this house." In silence Alec hitched the plough behind Thomas and set out for the fields. Sabine and Alec worked against their disgust, wearily, and came back at nights to hate this place where they had to live. Mrs. Maddison could find no words to encourage them. Now, before the garden came up, they had to live sparingly on corn bread and sorghum and turnip greens which she bought at the cross roads store five miles away: and the coffee was thin, trying to use as little of it as possible, only coloured water: and the milk was oily and yellowish from the can. . . . But in June the garden would be coming on, and there'd be flowers on the cotton. And all summer afterwards they could eat their own things, the fresh green things from their own land; and by September—only five months, only five months—they'd be picking cotton. And then. Maybe Miss Lucy could get them a cow before then. She dreamed as she worked.

There wasn't much to do about the house. The grey, unpainted walls, darkened in places from smoke, always seemed dirty. But, being spring, the broken windows didn't matter so much. She thought about them a good deal and finally wrote a letter with difficulty, to Mrs. Cahill, saying that there were five windows in the house and all broken: now if she could get some cheese-cloth to tack over them, that would anyhow keep out the flies, and maybe when next Alec went to town he could pick up a few boards for shutters in case it rained. And so maybe it would be best if she just knocked out the windows altogether, since they were jagged-like and ugly; and could Mrs. Cahill maybe get her some cheese-cloth. The cheese-cloth arrived, together with a box of tacks, and Mrs. Maddison was as excited as if she'd suddenly been given velvet curtains to hang sumptuously over French windows. . . .

She dug up the garden and planted the seeds. Alec and Sabine together planted the cotton seed in the brown narrow furrows of earth in the fields. Mrs. Maddison was alone in the house all day. There wasn't much cooking to do because, finally it always seemed to be pan bread or corn bread and sorghum and whatever else she could find or invent or afford to eke this out. She wanted the garden to be big and the Government had been generous with seeds. She wrote a few letters, almost drawing the words as if each one were a picture, asking for magazines—she would again paper the walls gaily and cleanly. Mrs. Cahill, who could not forget the old woman in that evil, decaying shack, sent her several yards of cheap print in startling colours. Mrs. Maddison made curtains and bed spreads, and hung a length of it over the low door to the kitchen, which at least shut off the sight of that place, if not the smell.

It grew hot. Alec was working without a hat in the fields and he would come back at noon ominously white with the heat. Sabine made a bonnet for herself from newspapers; she worked in bent, broken, high-heeled slippers, the heels catching in the earth, suddenly jerking her ankle sideways. Before they drank the last of the water that they'd hauled in a keg, it was warmish and had a grey flat taste. Mrs. Maddison tended the garden with passion and delicacy, almost luring the seeds to take root and grow. She lay awake at nights thinking of the feathery short green things that would be coming out of the earth. She particularly thought of the flowers. Alec's and Sabine's room had the walls papered now with advertisements: there weren't enough magazines despite Mrs. Cahill's efforts, to do both rooms. In the winter, Mrs. Maddison thought, when there isn't so much work outside, Sabine and I can make rag rugs so it'll be warmer underfoot. In two years, in three years, this place would be a good place: safe and quiet, with things in jars for the winter and every summer plenty in the garden, and a little money coming from the cotton for extras. Safe and quiet: Tennessee and the baby could come too. They'd save money for timber and put up another room. She'd have her family around her. If only they could live it out until the first crop got sold. There were days when her head ached and the garden went black before her eyes: I'm getting old she thought. And then too she was so sick of the food they ate that it was hard to swallow; it rested uneasily on her stomach. She was thinner.

Alec and Sabine were hoeing now, cutting out the plants that grew too close together, weeding, keeping the grass off, breaking the light dry crust of earth that formed over the plants after rain. They never talked: all three of them lived in an agony of fatigue, hurrying, trying each day to keep ahead of the land which didn't want to be worked over and driven; caring for the seeds which seemed animate, each one with its own fragile and demanding life. At night after supper, Alec and Sabine went to bed. And Mrs. Maddison too weary for sleep, sat on the porch, leaning against one of the thin posts that held it up, trying to ease the aches in her body before she lay down. For a while she would sit quietly thinking of nothing but only identifying the places in her body that meant pain: the shoulders, the centre of her back, her knees, her wrists. She waited for the aches to stop being sharp and separate, knowing that they'd merge into a general weariness that was not hard to bear. And then she could look out over the fields, and her garden beside the house. And look at the sky. Things seemed sure to her now: her life and her children's lives were no longer dependent on other people, on the strange fancies of employers, and the rules and regulations of the Government. Yes, they were in debt: but the Government was going to give them time to pay. It wasn't like being on shares or a tenant, when you never knew where you stood. As long as we grow things, Mrs. Maddison thought. She liked the emptiness of the land before her. It's good land, Mrs. Maddison said to herself, and we're making something to last. Something for the children. There's nothing wrong with being poor, Mrs. Maddison decided proudly, if you've got your own place, and no one coming to holler about the rent and throw you out; and if you know there's food in your garden, and you don't need to go begging around at every store. It's the begging and not knowing where you're going to be next. "And work," she said suddenly aloud, "Land's sake, no one's ever gonna call my chilrun nocount loafers."

*   *   *

A man came and talked with Alec about the cotton; he said he was the farm supervisor for the rural rehabilitation families around here. A woman came and talked to Mrs. Maddison about groceries and what they needed in the house: she was the home visitor out this way. The callers made Alec mutely angry. He didn't want anybody butting in his business. Even if they acted nice about it. He could get along. Next time they came Mrs. Maddison could just tell them to get the hell out; he'd manage his own farm. Mrs. Maddison, who had an entirely personal conception of Government, was encouraged by these visits. For her, simply, it meant that Mr. Roosevelt and Mrs. Cahill were not forgetting her. If they couldn't come themselves they'd send their people. She was glad of this: she knew Miss Lucy wasn't forgetting her because there was the cheese-cloth and the print. But those things were gifts and had nothing to do with the Government. The Government was supposed to be interested and come around every once in a while and ask how you were getting on and ask if they could help. Government was like that. She had been rather boastful with Miss Blythe, who was Mr. Roosevelt's representative out that way. She'd shown off her not yet producing garden and her house, and extended her arm largely to exhibit their land, the acres which were theirs, which made them respectable steady rooted people with a future. Miss Blythe had been flattering about the house and said she'd try to get their grocery order raised. "Of course," Miss Blythe said, "if you can manage with it being so small—well that's just that much less money to pay back later." Mrs. Maddison liked that too; she was borrowing money, she wasn't begging.

Mrs. Maddison told Alec that Mr. Roosevelt had some right nice people working for him out this way; but Alec was neither interested nor pleased.

Sabine and Alec were more than silent; they were sullen now. They hated everything about the farm, and they had no faith in it. Alec used to say bitterly he knew his cotton would be bad, or it'd rain too much later, or there'd be boll weevil; or no buyers. He didn't believe anything could come of this; he saw the future as a long half-starved drudgery, slaving for nothing. And the silent days and the silent nights. Sabine saw herself growing ugly, her hair straight and unkempt, her hands coarse; no clothes, no finery, no fun. No girls to gossip with and no dances or any of the things she wanted. At least, in town, they could get together with their friends and have a little drink and somebody could always play a fiddle and they could go up-town and look at the stores anyhow. But this: working yourself to death and nothing to show for it. Those hateful ugly selfish little cotton plants.

Mrs. Maddison was going calling. She was in such a good humour that she had to share it. She walked over the dusty reddish roads, with her hat sitting up on top of her head, where it would shade her, but not press down and give her headache. Her gingham dress was darned till it seemed to be covered with white sores. None of this worried her; she was going graciously to pay a call on Mrs. Lowry and pass the time of day, and talk brightly of the future.

Mrs. Lowry was sitting on her porch fanning herself. She was about Mrs. Maddison's age. Mrs. Maddison said, "Howdy, Mrs. Lowry, fine weather we're having," and they sat down to talk. Mrs. Lowry said it was a treat, she never saw anybody for a month of Sundays and she'd have come to see Mrs. Maddison but they were that busy. "Farming," Mrs. Lowry said; "you just gotta keep at it every second till you die." But she seemed proud of it on the whole. Mrs. Maddison liked her. She thought it would be nice in the winter, when they had more time, and she and Mrs. Lowry could swap recipes and patterns for crocheting. Later, when the vegetables had been canned and the cotton sold.

Mrs. Lowry had been in her house a year. "Lawd knows it's nothin' to look at," she said. "But you ought of seen it when we come. Dirty, I never seen such a place. Now we got our own vegetables put up, and such-like; we're gettin' on all right. It's worst the first year."

Mrs. Maddison agreed.

"The bad thing is the young folks," Mrs. Lowry said. "There's no fun for them. And they don't have no patience, poor things."

"Later," Mrs. Maddison said to Mrs. Lowry, her eyes shining with the thought of it, "when we're all fixed up and everybody's not working so hard, we'll get together and have a barn dance. I see you gotta barn here, and we could sweep it out and fix it up pretty, and everybody bring a little something themselves, and have a real party."

She had said this breathlessly, hurrying before the vision failed her. In her mind, the barn was filled with young men and girls, dressed as she had been dressed when she was young and went to a party. They'd be doing square dances, and the fiddlers thumping with their feet on the floor to keep time. And apple-bobbing. And blind man's buff. All the neighbours there together, being gay and serene, and every man sure of his home, sure of to-morrow, and easy with to-day.

Mrs. Lowry understood her excitement. "If only the young folks'll wait," she said. "We'll have a good time yet before we die."

*   *   *

Alec lay in his darkened room and Sabine talked to Mrs. Maddison in savage whispers.

"We're going," she said. "Soon's he can move we're going. We're not gonna stay out here to get ourselves killed. Sunstroke," she said, and her whisper was shrill. "He'll be laying in the fields dead next. And me with the malaria. What kinda life is that? They can't make us stay. We hate this place n'we're going quick; n'we're never coming back. So."

Mrs. Maddison twisted her hands in her lap. There were roses now, climbing up the door posts, and even if the posts were unpainted and the house grey and streaked behind them, these were real roses. Next year there would be more and maybe paint, too. The garden was green and just looking at it made you feel rich and safe. She'd been serving her own vegetables now for weeks. Next year, if they had a cow, there'd be butter to put on the new tender carrots and the beets, and the fresh green peas. The cotton was coming out thinly in the fields, but it was only the beginning. She'd gone down and picked a boll, and held the soft white fluff in her hands gently. This was money; of course there'd be a buyer and fine prices. This was more lumber for another room, and shoes, and a buggy, maybe. The worst was over. Things were growing. Larkspur and roses and squash and potatoes and cotton. This was what life meant if life was good. She'd even gotten her room papered in advertisements now. With money, they could buy boards, make furniture, a solid roof, a whole floor, and paint to make it clean and gay. They had only now to live a little carefully and everything would come to them. They were safe now and what lay ahead was more safety and even ease. In the winter, when they couldn't work after dark and there was nothing much to do anyhow, there were the neighbours. All the things she'd planned and dreamed.

"Sabine," she said softly, "he'll get over it in a day or so. N'you'll get over the malaria. Miss Blythe said she'd send some quinine. We done the work, Sabine. You can't go now. The worst is all over."

"We're going. And don't you try to stop us, neither. You're old and you don't expect to get any fun outa life. But we're young. And we're not gonna stay around here and kill ourselves."

"You won't have any fun back in that old shack of yours. You won't even have stuff to eat. What kinda life is that, then? Sabine, we worked so hard," Mrs. Maddison said. There were tears in her eyes, but she was not looking at the younger woman. She was looking out the door, at the roses. For the last month it had seemed to her that not only Mr. Roosevelt and Mrs. Cahill were remembering her, but God also. The things she wanted: a home, and roses, and food, and quiet when the work was over, and a place to live and be. Tennessee could come in the fall; when they had a little money, too. She was an old woman and she was a lucky one: she had everything she could want.

She cried out against this dreadful and wanton thing they meant to do: leave the land when things were growing; leave the cotton unpicked and the garden going to weeds and waste. And the house they'd made into something like a home; let it rot back again into a worn-out Negro shanty. But she knew they wouldn't listen to her. Miss Blythe came and argued and so did the farm foreman: he even threatened Alec, saying "You'll never get a loan again" and "You're a low quitter, that's what you are." Alec was ill, and hysterically obstinate; something had happened to him. He hated the land beyond any explanation. He would rather starve than stay there; it was a slavery to him and a bleak, empty, exhausting life, with none of the things that made for pleasure. Sabine chattered with chills and burned with fever, and cursed the home visitor and the farm foreman and Mrs. Maddison, and said she'd crawl to town on her hands and knees if she had to, but she wasn't going to stay out here in this hole and kill herself, and get ugly, and go crazy with the work, and no fun ever, ever, ever.

The entire neighbourhood got drawn into this, and Mrs. Lowry stood on the porch with Mrs. Maddison, one day at sunset, looking out over the white beginnings of the cotton, and the greenness of the garden and said: "It's a sin and a shame, Flora. They'll be sorry, too."

Mrs. Cahill drove out in her uncertain Ford and tried to talk to Alec, who wouldn't listen. Mrs. Maddison could not stay on alone; the work was too much for her. She couldn't keep the cotton cultivated and do the garden too. "You'd be having sunstroke next," Mrs. Cahill said and smiled.

"He did have a sunstroke," Mrs. Maddison said abruptly. "It was a real bad sunstroke and he was sick's a baby."

"I know." Mrs. Cahill put her hand on Mrs. Maddison's shoulder. The old woman would defend those no-count children if they did murder.

"Would you like to take home some roses, Miss Lucy, or some larkspur? It's all gonna be wasted now."

She stood beside her flowers weeping quietly and helplessly. "All wasted," she said. "It all come to nothing."

"Alec deserves a beating," Mrs. Cahill said furiously. "He's selfish, and he's being stupid, too. Sabine's a fool and you couldn't expect anything else of her. But Alec. I'd like to get some big strong man to give him the beating of his life."

"It's only that he's not hisself. He's still weakish from that there sunstroke. But it's gonna be too late when he sees what he done. We'll of lost the place then."

Mrs. Cahill put her arm around Mrs. Maddison's shoulder. "You've done your best, darling. Nobody'll ever blame you. You made a fine place here and somebody'll be lucky to get it, and they'll know what a good worker you are. We'll see you get taken care of all right in town. I'm sorry. I'm sorrier than I can tell you."

"We were all fixed," Mrs. Maddison said. "We could of lived like real people again. Well," she said, "how's things in the sewing-room, Miss Lucy?"

Finally Mrs. Cahill drove Alec and Sabine back with her. She thought it would be easier for Mrs. Maddison to have them out of the way. The driver would come with the truck to-morrow or the next day and move Mrs. Maddison and their possessions back into town. The land couldn't be wasted; someone would have to work it and try to profit by it and pay back the debt. Mrs. Cahill drove in angry silence. Once Sabine started to talk to her and she turned and said: "You're a no-count girl, Sabine, and you've got a no-count husband, and I don't want any truck with you. You've broken that poor old woman's heart and you deserve anything that comes to you. I'll drive you to town but I won't act friendly with you."

Mrs. Maddison had something to do. Before it grew dark, before she slept. Now that her son had really done this thing; gone away, not caring for the land or the money he owed. She got out a block of ruled paper and a stubby pencil and began: Dear Mr. Roosevelt. . . .

It was a long letter. She explained Alec's sunstroke and Sabine's malaria, and how hard it had been for over four months, working with so little and the house cheerless and such poor food. She told about everything which excused Alec in his desertion; but loyally, she said too, that the garden was fine now, and the cotton coming up. She hoped he wouldn't be too disappointed in Alec, but Alec was young, and when you were young you were foolish, and did bad things without knowing. She hoped he would excuse Alec. She was grateful for the things Mr. Roosevelt had done, and she would work to pay back the money they owed but she was afraid it would take a long time. Work was so hard to get and money so scarce. She enclosed a short spray of larkspur because she wanted him to know that it was a fine place she was leaving. . . .

She sat alone on the front porch and watched the stars come out. It had all come to nothing. The safety and the ease that was ahead, and the good times, and having a place and being someone. Nothing. The land was fine and beautiful, she thought, and she could smell the roses in the dark.

TESS SLESINGER

Jobs in the Sky

❧

IT MEANT that you wanted to hold your job like nobody's business if you managed to get in ahead of Mr Keasbey whose name had been first in Mrs Summers' section-book and the section-books of her predecessors for a noble fifteen years. Mr Keasbey signed in daily at eight-forty (ten minutes before the deadline), and on the dot of eight-fifteen on pep-speech days (a good ten minutes before Mrs Summers reluctantly counted you late)—and daily, after removing the cover from his table of Important New Fiction and flicking his books with his private duster, stood with his fine white head bowed, waiting reproachfully like the best boy in the class. But on the day before Christmas, the Monday which was the last day of the Christmas rush, 1934, and the morning for which Mr Marvell's Christmas speech had been announced (Mr Marvell being the 'M' in 'M & J'), Joey Andrews, No. 191-23, 167B, who had been till three weeks before without a number in the army of the unemployed, wrote his name and number on the top line of Mrs Summers' fresh page at exactly eight-eleven. Mrs Summers asked Mr Andrews if he had fallen out of bed; she said it was nice to see some face beside Mr Keasbey's so early in the morning; and she said she had sat up in the bathroom all night (not to wake *Mister* S) going over her records and trying to make them tally. . . And Mrs Summers, who limped before nine and immediately after five-thirty because there was not, she said, very much sitting on her job, limped off with the salesbooks for the hat-girls who were also part of her section.

Once more as Joey Andrews looked down from the mezzanine onto the great sleeping main floor below he felt in his stomach the dull ball of fear which a lover experiences when he recalls how nearly he missed going out on that particular Tuesday on which he met his love. But propping the biography of Dostoievsky against the Memoirs of a Grand Duchess on his own table of History and Biography, Joey Andrews felt that any recollection of his eight-months' nightmare among the unhired was unworthy of No. 191-23, 167B of a great department store. And won-

Reprinted from *Time: The Present,* by permission of Simon and Schuster, Inc. Copyright 1935 by Tess Slesinger.

dering to what table Jane Eyre belonged (for surely it was not a biography?), "I must forget about the Washington Square gang," he scolded himself, "I don't belong with them any more;" and went to lay Jane Eyre tentatively on Miss Bodkin's table of Classics.

Downstairs the perfume girls were drifting in; the floor-walkers adjusting their button-holes and their smiles, moved here and there with dignity. Having arranged his own table, Joey Andrews looked about his beloved book department for some way to be helpful, some way to live up to the Christmas spirit of M & J. He didn't quite dare to fix Miss Bodkin's table; and he was just pulling the long white nightgown off Mr Keasbey's New Fiction when Mr Keasbey himself walked in—it was the dot of eight-fifteen—and, forewarned by the section-book violated, bearing another's name before his own, gave Joey a haughty, suspicious look and began flying around his table making kissing sounds until his fingers came safely to rest on the handle of his very own duster.

Now the cosmetic girls were mounting stacks of cold cream on their counters while near the doors the cheap stockings stretched coyly over amputated limbs. On the mezzanine behind the book department the hat girls in their drab black dresses and exquisitely sheer-hosed legs began clapping the hats on stalks like flowers. Mrs White who kept the lending library at the back came next; the Hierarchy permitted Mrs White and Mr Keasbey to bow with formal recognition of mutual virtue—Mrs White had been with M & J a noble twelve years to Mr Keasbey's noble fifteen—before Mr Keasbey hurried to return Rebecca of Sunnybrook Farm, which he borrowed every night that it had not been taken by a customer, for his mother who was eighty and had stopped sleeping. Mrs White began driving the hair-pins into the pretzel high on her head; and when Mr. Keasbey laid Rebecca on the table before her, pointed her mouth like a pencil and made a check-mark with her head: down—one, two; hold; up—one, two—and Mrs White and Mr Keasbey part for the day.

Miss Paley of the Modern Library and movie-editions, to whom the Hierarchy does not permit Mr Keasbey to bow, mounts the mezzanine stairs with a look of resigned bewilderment on her melancholy face. Two decades of teaching school have left her permanently surprised at finding herself daily entering the Commercial World (and how had she ever, in the teeth of Mr Neely the Principal's disapproval, made the Change!)— and also there have been rumors breathed by Miss Bodkin that Miss Paley's life in the Commercial World is to be very brief indeed, and it may be that some of these rumors have even reached Miss Paley. Yet here she is, daily from nine to five-thirty, not selling children's books, as surely, she complains to Joey Andrews who rushes forth to help her with her jungle of cheap editions, as surely she had, after two decades of teaching little children, every reason to expect? had she not, as Mr Neely (who put things so well!) had put it, a gift for understanding children? But Mr Neely warned me, she whispers through her closed white mask, that the Commercial World was something else again . . . and drawing out the handkerchief (given her by the best-speller's mother) from her place in the Modern Library copy of the Old Wives' Tale which she reads at idle moments in the day, Miss Paley dismisses Joey with a kindly, authoritative nod as though he were the first-grade pupil who had just collected the rulers. And Joey, rather glad to get away, for ever since Miss Bodkin breathed the rumor, Miss Paley has been touched for him with some infectious germ, takes up his stand by his table of History and Biography.

Miss Willows the buyer trips over to her desk and lays her hat in the bottom drawer. But as yet no Miss Bodkin. Miss Willows bites at her pearls as she makes a hasty survey of the book department, arranges Christmas calendars with her head on one side like a bird. Still no Miss Bodkin (Joey Andrews hates to think of no Miss Bodkin.) "Heavens knows," murmurs Miss Paley to Mrs Summers on the subject of varicose veins in which they both specialize; and Miss Bodkin's chum Miss Rees slips in on the stroke of eight-twenty, the deadline, and carelessly pulls the cover off The Young Girls Series for which Miss Paley would cheerfully trade her miniature set of Proust; and "*I* know as well as Heaven," returns Mrs Summers humorously, and she has forty minutes more of the luxury of limping. Beautiful Miss Fern Stacy who is so dumb (according to Miss Bodkin) that she can hardly make change, takes her place behind the stationery counter—Mr Keasbey had fought bitterly against its ignoble presence in the book department, even for the Christmas rush week. Mr Keasbey stands with his arms folded, his head lifted; a fit citizen in the world of M & J, fit door-man to the gate of Heaven: perhaps one day Mr Marvell will pause and glance at his noble mien, his professorial posture, and will think to himself, What a man! what a faithful employee. . . And there suddenly is Miss Bodkin, having signed in fraudulently in the space left blank by her good friend Miss Rees, a Miss Bodkin defying a gullible world to imagine that she was not present at least as early as Mr Keasbey, and that she does not every Saturday of her life make off with a first edition hidden away under one of Mrs White's lending library covers . . . Joey Andrews feels waves of purple sliding shamefully down his spine at the sight of Miss Bodkin's gooseberry breasts squeezed tight under her black satin dress; he remembers that it has been a long time since he has dared to ask a girl for a date, and that tonight is Christmas Eve.

Eight-thirty; and Mr Keasbey, for the fifteenth annual successive time, leads his class as though he were the monitor, down the mezzanine stairs for Mr Marvell's Christmas speech.

"and Mr Marvell who needs no introduction has come all the way from White Plains at this early hour to give us one and all his Christmas message." (Mr Sawyer of the Personnel speaking—O thank you, thank you for nothing, murmured Miss Bodkin, her small face expressing sarcastic devotion; Mr Keasbey delivered a withering glance; and Joey Andrews, though sick with admiration for her gooseberry breasts, moved away from her contaminating influence, for Joey, having had a Job for only three weeks was still more in love with the job than he was with Miss Bodkin.)

Beyond where the shoe-clerks were gathered a white-haired man rose and bowed. "What a fine face," whispered Miss Paley; "he has Mr Neely's eyebrows exactly." Faint applause, led by smart clapping of department heads, while the great man smiled dreamily.

"My friends. (Mister God in person, murmured Miss Bodkin mouthlessly; and Joey Andrews stared for comfort at the graveyard of boils on the back of Mr Keasbey's neck.) I only wish it were possible to know each and every to shake each and every to wish each and every but—the . femilay . of . M & J . is . too . large. (Laughter, the lingerie girls throwing themselves in fake passion against their shrouded counters; under cover of the polite sounds Miss Willows the buyer leaned across Joey Andrews and hissed Miss Bodkin kindly stop that talking. The white hairs in Mr Keasbey's ears bristled sexagenarian triumph.) My friends, a spaycial responsibility toward your countray, your fellow-men the femilay of M & J have you ever stopped to think how the department stores contribute to the good cheer of this heppy holiday come rich and poor alike gifts for his loved ones differences forgotten all men are equal at Christmas and who has the honor the privilege the blessing (Bring on the castor oil, groaned Miss Bodkin.)

"Who . but . you . my friends. And this year in especial when so many renegades and complainers of course a bad year but take the good with the bad life wouldn't be moch fon if we didn't have our ups and downs like our good friends the ladies of the elevators here—and our slogan is down with the complainers friends, we don't want 'em here why up at Princeton we used to wash out their mouths with soap maybe we ought to enlist the parfume gehls to do the same thing here. (Haw haw roared the shoe-clerks remembering public school but the book department merely smiled condescendingly, such humor was beneath them and they knew was meant to be.) Bear in mind my good friends a job for every good man or woman in this countray if you don't like this countray you can go to another if you don't like your job here you can leave it always plenty only glad step in shoes.

"One word in closing to the new friends taken on to help us in this merry busy season. We wish we could permanently retain each and every make a permanent member of the femilay of M & J each and every but let me say to each and every WE will do OUR BAIST if YOU will do YOUR baist . . . and this is YOUR big chance to prove yourselves invaluable to US, on this last day of the Christmas rush when SOME of our friends unfortunately MUST BE DROPPED (the book department glances briefly and guiltily at Miss Paley, who continues to stand with her hands clasped as though Mr Marvell were the Principal leading assembly.) And I say this not merely to our new but it applies also to our old this is the day for EACH and EVERY.

"In conclusion it is good-will that counts good cheer is the baist policy the spirit of Christmas all year round is our slogan we are one big femilay and we spread our good cheer our customers expect it demand it PAY for it and now my friends I wish each and every a merry and profitable Christmas KEEP ON YOUR TOES ALL DAY OUR PROFIT IS YOUR PROFIT IT MAY BE THAT YOU CAN WIN YOURSELF A PERMANENT POSITION my friends I thank you each and every one."

Smatter of applause, Mr Keasbey clapping on and on like an old Italian listening to the opera, while the section managers turned back toward their sections; but a thin man in a striped tie (Gadowsky who edited the monthly M & J Banner) leaped to a counter and cried: "Just one moment, friends. Let's give Mr Marvell a hearty send-off to show our appreciation—altogether now, M and J 'Tis of Thee ..." The song straggled out across the floor; heads craned for a last glimpse of Mr Marvell, but Mr Marvell was on his way back to White Plains; the song died.

O God, if the gang could see me now, thought Joey, taking his place for this day of days before his careful table of History and Biography. (Y'oughta forget that bunch, y'don't belong with them any more. And look around, look around, Jesus it's like heaven to be working.) Now there steals over the book department, the hat department, the entire floor below, a period of hurried hush, of calm excitement; a poised expectancy, denoting the birth of the Store for this great day. Now the aisles lie flat and virgin, waiting, breathless and coy, for merry and profitable defilement. (Remember Pete . . . passed his examinations for the bar . . . in between starving he handed out grocers' handbills . . . and Dopy Simpson, turned down a job for $11 . . . said he wouldn't stay straight under $25 per.) Now you can hear Miss Bodkin whispering with Miss Rees about the rumored romances of Miss Fern Stacy the stationery girl: "when she said *three* I knew she was lying, there aren't three men in the city fool enough to propose to a girl a depression year like this." (Remember Rounds . . . been a scholarship boy at a swell prep-school until the Depression cut down the scholarship fund . . . went around saying over Latin verbs to himself . . . Dad said I'd meet swell fellows in New York, but he didn't think I'd find 'em on a park bench.) Now the large clock over the entrance doors jumps to eight-fifty-three; Miss Paley stands sweet and serious like a school-teacher—and God, it's as safe as being in school again, thinks Joey, coming here every day, nice and warm, watching the clock jump like that on its way to nine . . . Mrs Summers, her eyebrows dancing like harassed ghosts, limps like a nervous shepherd among her flock; only seven minutes more of that limping, Mrs Summers! M & J expects courtesy health good cheer of its employees, the customers expect it demand it *pay* for it . . .

Now Miss Paley closes the Old Wives' Tale with the best-speller's handkerchief in her place, and stands lifting her melancholy mask like a lamp waiting to be lighted. Behind her you can see tucked over a row of books her pocketbook, another of her many crumpled handkerchiefs, a pocket-comb; for Miss Paley has moved in (despite the rumors), Miss Paley has settled in (she has not heard the rumors), among the cheap books, as she had for two decades in her class-room, this is YOUR day, Miss Paley, to prove yourself invaluable, and YOURS too, Joey Andrews, and YOURS and YOURS and YOURS, each and every . . . (Remember Jonesy, a real bum, Jonesy . . . turned Christian and left the gang, went and hung about with the Christers on the Y breadlines . . . pan-handling and spending his pennies on Sterno, which he converted into alcohol by filtering it through his handkerchief at the horse-trough at the end of the Bowery . . . in his Sterno he thought or pretended he thought he was Jesus. But Rounds who had been a scholarship boy said he'd go Red before he'd stand on a breadline or sing Onward Christian Soldiers like Jonesy.) Now you can hear Miss Bodkin: "I hate this Goddamn place, they fix the quotas high so nobody can possibly make a commission except the week before Christmas." Foolish Miss Bodkin! a daughter of the femilay of M & J: doesn't she know when she's well off? take care, Miss Bodkin, this is YOUR day too. (Remember fumbling in the ash-can for a paper before

turning in—those nights you hadn't the wherewithal for a flop—turning
in on the grassy center of Washington Square, surrounded by those
beautiful houses . . . dreaming and planning with Rounds the One
Perfect Hold-up—can Mrs Summers read the mind? . . . remembering,
because you couldn't sleep, how long it had been since you had had a
girl . . . remembering, because you couldn't sleep for the drunks singing
at the other end of the park, *If you've said your prayers Joey my son no
harm can come to you.*) Now Mr Keasbey stands at the top of the mezzanine stairs with a dignity like the dignity of a Painless Dentist, his
arms folded, threatening and somber, as he turns and prepares for his
victims. Miss Willows herself descends from her desk and takes a position
in the middle of the floor sucking her beads, a débutante hostess waiting,
leaning forward from the hips, to greet the crowds that must be stamping outside in the Christmas cold. Now the outside entrance doors are
thrown open and you can see the waiting customers pour into the
vestibule sliding and coming to a stop like beads in a box. Now the big
clock jumps to eight-fifty-eight; Mrs Summers can limp for two minutes
more, and she limps from clerk to clerk, her eyebrows dancing, begging
everybody to remember the Christmas spirit, and that extra pencils will
be under each cash register.

(*You can get anywhere in this country with an education my son* said
his father . . . oh gee pop, you were right, if you could only see me now!
I want you to have a high-school diploma son.) Now the aisles below lie
flat and smooth like roads, and the customers stamping in the lobby are
a frenzied herd of cattle. "Watch the customers sharply," said Miss Willows; "and remember there are plenty of store detectives in disguise all
over the store *watching every move you make.*" Remember there are plenty
of detectives, remember this is YOUR day, remember the Christmas spirit
. . . remember they stood on a corner of fourteenth street where a young
man promised them a bad Winter and Rounds said "I'd sooner go Red
than stand on a breadline," and Joey Andrews shook in his thin-soled
shoes for he knew he'd starve sooner than stand on a breadline and he
felt he'd stand on a breadline sooner than go Red . . . remember KEEP
ON YOUR TOES ALL DAY THERE WILL BE DETECTIVES
WATCHING EVERY MOVE YOU MAKE THIS IS YOUR BIG
DAY TO PROVE . . . remember Washington Square Park . . .
Where a bench was turned permanently outward, making a cosy little
entrance to the grass hotel, a gateway to the open-air sleeping quarters
for which no rent was charged, to which one came democratically without
luggage, without even a full stomach. Remember you stood at the gateway, fumbling in a refuse barrel with your head well in, select a *Times*—

the Tabloids are better reading but too narrow for practical use—for your blanket, mattress, pillow, bedlamp, water-carafe and chamber-pot. On the grass you chose a spot among the reclining forms and lit your goodnight butt. "Lousy flop-house joints," your neighbor murmured; "a plate of soup, a free wash—who in hell wants a wash?" Bug-Eye the one-leggeder from the World War had to show off by springing over the fence instead of coming in nicely through the revolving doors. "They say he can still feel that leg . . . do you believe that?" "Shut up and give me a Chesterfield—oh well, a Lucky will do." "Amo, amare . . . amas, amat," murmured Rounds regretfully, as he picked himself up to go again to the toilet at the side of the park; he was having serious trouble with his stomach, no green vegetables. . . . "there'll be pie in the sky by and by," sang Dopey Simpson. "Shut up, there, lights out, no more talking."

Stars in the sky overhead, pie in the sky, moon in the sky, dreams, girls, pie, jobs in the sky too.

"Move over." It is Jonesy the Christer, lit on Sterno. "If you believe, believe, believe on the Lord. . ." "Smart Aleck, dirty sucker, hanging around the Y . . . mamma's boy. . ." *Papa can anybody in the country be the president?*

Three drunks sitting on the bench too happy to go to bed (sitting in the lobby of their swell hotel, drinking, guzzling, gossiping.) "Yesh shir, the mosht turrible thing in thish country is the bootlegger liquor . . . all the lovely young college boys going to their raksh and ruinsh. . ." "If you believe, believe, believe. . ." *Yes my son and remember Abraham Lincoln was born in a log cabin and Our Lord was born in a Manger.* "In the war we had such nice warm mud. . ." "Shut up, Bug-Eye, what'd it get you?" "In the war we had such nice warm blood. . ." "If I wash preshident of the United Statesh, firsht thing I'd do I'd forbid the lovely young college boys. . ." *Just close your eyes Joey if you've said your prayers nothing can happen to you.* "Such nice warm mud. . ." "Sometimes I think Bug-Eye's just plain nuts." "I lost my leg in Avalon. . ." "Onward Christian so-o-oldiers" . . . "When we ask them for something to e-a-t . . ." Rounds came back from the toilet: "I can't remember a deponent verb, I hate to forget all that." "If you believe, believe, believe. . ." *Do I have to eat spinach mamma? Yes Joey think of the little Belgian boys who haven't any—and it will make you big and strong.* "Work and pray, live on hay, there'll be jobs in the sky by and by." Rounds said all the comfort stations in the world wouldn't bring him comfort any more . . . he needed steamed vegetables . . . he said he'd go Red before he'd stand on a breadline. "Work and pray, live on hay, there'll be jobs in the sky. . ." "Onward Chrisssstian Soldiers. . ." One of the drunks on the bench was putting into action an experiment he had heard of: thoughtfully tapping one knee with the side of his hand to see if he was still alive. He was not. He toppled over onto his cold bed beneath the stars and if those gay boys sitting up and singing in their open-air dormitory thought they weren't spending that night with a corpse they were making just one hell of a mistake. . . Remember how that morning, remember how all that day, remember . . . REMEMBER THIS IS YOUR DAY, JOEY ANDREWS. . .

The bell rings, it is nine o'clock. Miss Willows wets her lips against the first polite speech of the day. Mr. Keasbey goes rigid with desire. Mrs. Summers stands erect at last on her varicose legs.

The heavy doors swing open. The mob in the vestibule surges and squirms, animals stampeding in panic inside a burning barn; then breaks suddenly, spilling like thick syrup down the aisles.

The machinery starts with a roar; unorganized come into conflict with organized; the clerks are over-powered, the floor-walkers swept along with the stream of customers; the aisles are drowned; arms reach like fishing-rods into the piled bargains on every counter. But gradually the frantic haphazard customers are subdued and controlled by the competent motions of well-trained officers, who reason, who separate, who mollify and implore. Still mad, but under direction at last, the crowd settles around counters screaming to be fed.

The mezzanine grows tense with desire for invasion.

The first customer toys with one foot on the stairs; pinches her pocketbook and climbs laboriously upward. Miss Bodkin's short, smart legs run to capture; but over Miss Bodkin's black banged head Mr Keasbey has already made a dignified assignation; like one hypnotized the customer makes her way surely and pointedly toward those grave commanding eyes. Miss Bodkin turns back in anger; meets Joey Andrews' admiring eye, and irresponsibly sticks out her tongue. Joey Andrews feels his confidence in No. 191-23, 167B slip a little as he sees with a pang Miss Bodkin guessing he is absolutely no good with girls.

"Mrs Summerssss sssign please!" Miss Bodkin bags the day's next sale.

Surely these determined ladies and gentlemen (or are all the gentlemen detectives?) are not the same race as those tentative unhurried customers who loitered and weighed two weeks ago. Now they hurried fiercely, became insane people at indecision, rapidly bought two if they could not decide upon one. After favoring her customer with a cheap Lorna Doone from her classics table, Miss Bodkin with malice and caution sells her the latest detective story right off Mr Keasbey's beautifully stacked table, right under Mr Keasbey's bristling but dignified nose. Mr Keasbey bending his stately professorial back takes out his feather-duster and gives his books where Miss Bodkin has ravaged them a quick indignant flick. Miss Bodkin retires with the slyness of a nun to her own table.

A lady grazing close to Joey Andrews is captured by Mr Keasbey two strides ahead of Miss Bodkin who retires viciously blowing her bang off her eyes, and in passing murmurs, "If I printed what I thought about the sixty-year-old teacher's pet, it would make a book too awful even for my own Classics table." But all the lady wanted, and she said so too frankly, was a ninety-five cent copy of Robinson Crusoe for the kids and when Mr Keasbey lost out trying to explain the value of the three-fifty illustrated issue on his own table, he turned her over in haste to Miss Paley; because Christmas is here, and Miss Paley's cheap editions are petty game at this season to an old hunter like Mr Keasbey. . . But Miss Paley receives the gift gratefully and looking at Mr Keasbey's dignified face, who knows but she forgets for a minute Mr Neely. Now Joey Andrews has his day's first customer, and he will never forget her kind eyes and brown fur coat as she stands eagerly waiting for him to wrap her package with the Christmas twine. Miss Paley on her knees hunting and hunting for Robinson Crusoe which is hard to find because it is exactly the color and size of the Romance of Leonardo da Vinci, lifts a face modestly benign with the joy of laboring to catch her breath, for Miss Paley knows from her last decade's experience that if she rises too quickly she is likely to get the least little bit of swimming in the head.

The invisible electric wire carried rumors from clerk to clerk. Free lunch would be served in the basement; twenty minutes to eat. A hat-girl had been arrested for stealing change. A shop-lifter had been caught downstairs. The man in the gray felt hat was a Store detective. The Store had already done one-eighth more business than it had done by eleven-thirty of last year's Christmas Eve. Miss Bodkin's sales were higher than Mr Keasbey's. Miss Stacy had run out of Christmas stickers three times. Mrs White had sent down a twenty-dollar bill to be changed (no clerk was permitted to make change of anything higher than a ten out of his cash register) and the bill had not come back, after thirty minutes.

The first batch went to the free lunch at eleven-forty-five. They came back. They talked. They conquered. There was no second batch, except Miss Paley who went for a cup of tea. Miss Bodkin said the lunch was made of pieces of wrapping paper from returned purchases of 1929.

Mrs Summers asked Joey Andrews if he thought he could make out without any lunch. Joey Andrews said sure and dashed off to his next customer.

Joey Andrews was drunk. If for a moment he found himself without a customer he ran up to one lady after another like a lost child seeking its mother.

Miss Willows forgot that for the last two years she had been buyer for the book department; the fire of selling caught in her veins again; she sold passionately. Let Miss Bodkin take the credit down in her salesbook, let Mr Keasbey receive the commission—but let Miss Willows sell again! Her pearls caught on the edge of a table; scattered underfoot—Miss Willows laughed; turned to a customer and kicked the pearls recklessly out of her way. Miss Willows too was drunk.

Miss Bodkin whispered that her sales had reached $150.

Miss Willows greeting customers at the top of the stairs had lost her débutante coolness and become a barker for a three-ring circus.

Mr Keasbey broke down a reserve of years and squeezed Joey's arm as he pushed him out of his way.

Miss Paley, weak from no lunch, brushed her hand across her eyes and smiled until her whole head ached.

So it went on, and Mrs Summers passed among them, conspicuous for her white head, for her customer-like lined face, and in the back of her distracted eyes lurked worry like guilt.

Who shall say that even Mr Keasbey was actively, consciously motivated by the few cents' commission he was piling up? Each one was simply part of a great selling team, schooled and trained to perfection, each part functioned perfectly. All the time the crowd was changing, but imperceptibly; the stream which fed it must be flowing as fast as the stream which ebbed away. Now one was handing fifty-seven cents change to a gentleman with a green tie, now one was looking through the crowd for the lady with the feather.

In all his life Joey Andrews had never been so happy. His day was measured by customers, not by sales. He was mad with the delight of being necessary to so many people at once, with being efficient for his great team, with knowing exactly what part he had to play.

Miss Willows' voice grew hoarse, strangely naked she looked without her beads too—this way for calendars, this way for the latest fiction—Miss Willows was selling herself and was lost in passion.

But worry was growing out of Mrs Summers' eyes. She hovered for a brief second about Miss Paley as she stung open the drawer of her cash register. The invisible wires hummed again: Has Miss Paley, maybe Miss Paley, it looks as if Miss Paley. . . But Miss Paley, blind and dazed and cheerful, still flies among her cheap editions, still makes her way mildly in the Commercial World.

Still the crowd filled the aisles, covered the floor. Only now the incoming stream was heavier than the out-going, complemented by clerks and secretaries from Brooklyn to the Bronx. There was no slack, no shading. Even as there was no telling how the crowd melted and swelled again, there was no telling whether one's feet hurt or did not hurt; not only did no one attend to bodily functions, it was as if they had ceased to exist.

To get to your cash register now meant a hand-to-hand battle. The little bells rang as clerks shot out their drawers, counted rapidly, slammed them shut again. Joey Andrews clicked his open; good God, the bills under the weight were rising mountainously. He wasted a second of M & J's time: he felt with his finger the soft resistant pad of bills.

Mrs. Summers with her kind and tortured smile, her worried eyes, her dancing brows, hovered briefly about Joey Andrews' cash register. Mr Andrews . . . Mr Andrews . . . Joey Andrews gave her a bright child's look with eyes which looked swiftly away, beyond her, in liaison with his next customer.

Feet were like rubber tires now. Bodies were conveyors of books. Minds were adding machines. Fleeting glimpses of strained and happy faces—it might be Christmas, it might be the warm contact of body with body, of air made of the mingling of human breaths, it might be the happy exchange of one human tribe with another, the excitement, the warmth, the continuous roar of sound. . .

There was a slight lull, as there is sometimes a lull in a storm. Joey Andrews, running like a mountain goat, caught Miss Bodkin's round black eyes, caught Mrs Summers' level worried look . . . and then he found the eye of a lady with a scar on her throat, who was holding out a book to him, begging, begging for the kindness of his service. . . And then there was a flurry of ladies with anxious faces and Boy Scout nephews in small towns; Miss Rees had a sudden success with her Green Mountain Boys and Joey Andrews deserted History and Biography to take on her overflow. And the human storm was loose again, wrapping them all together in an efficient human mass. . . Mrs Summers stands like a bird of ill omen hovering over Miss Paley's cash register.

The invisible electric wires are humming again. Six hat-girls are going to be dropped, three of them old employees, three of them just taken on for the Christmas rush. They don't tell them, says Miss Bodkin viciously, until the last minute—so they'll keep on selling to the end. Miss Bodkin knows everything before anyone else. Paley's going to get hers, too, I know it, says Miss Bodkin—and Joey Andrews wonders what Miss Bodkin is doing tonight, on Christmas Eve, he wonders if he might have the nerve. . .

Five-twenty-five. Joey Andrews flew to his cash register, back to the cus-

tomer with the scar on her throat, back to his beloved cash register. "Well,"
says Miss Paley to Mrs Summers, "it can't be helped and it can't be
helped." It has happened. Miss Paley's got the sack. They've told Miss
Paley they're letting her go. This is Miss Paley's last day. What do you
think, Paley's just been fired. Jesus, poor old Paley . . . Joey Andrews has
a customer who wants something in green to match her library curtains.
"Heavens knows," Miss Paley said, "I cannot understand, cannot comprehend. . ." and everybody knows that Miss Paley is using big words to
keep from crying, and to show that she was a teacher for twenty years.
Joey Andrews' customer would prefer something a shade darker; maybe
that Oscar Wilde. Mrs Summers with her eyebrows going like an orchestra leader's baton: "I just feel terrible about this, Miss Paley, just terrible, I knew it last night and I couldn't sleep, they don't let us tell you
till the last minute." Joey Andrews' customer doesn't see why they don't
put out a Shakespeare in green suède—or even a dictionary.

Someone wants to buy Miss Paley's copy of the Old Wives' Tale. Such
a nice lady, Miss Paley would like to tell her how much she loves that
book. "Next to my Jane Austen," she almost says, holding her side as she
graciously hands over the book. "The Commercial World," says Miss
Paley, reaching over for the wrapping paper. "My principal told me,"
Miss Paley said. "A natural teacher. Born, not made. He told me in so
many words. . ."

The clock jumps to five-twenty-seven. Three minutes more in the Commercial World, Miss Paley. Three minutes more of non-limping, Mrs
Summers. Three minutes more of being a human being, Miss Willows!

Mr Keasbey is smiling like a boy. Christmas Eve—he hasn't missed one
in sixty years with his mother; bought her a shawl, he had, on the third
floor, got the employees' discount; had it for her in his locker. Good cook,
the old lady, probably'd spend the whole day getting up his Christmas dinner. "My principal told me," Miss Paley said; "he is a man who never
minces words. Myra Paley, he told me. . ." Joey Andrews flies back to his
cash register, he does not like to look at Miss Paley any more, Mrs Summers is standing tentatively: "Mr Andrews, oh Mr Andrews." Joey Andrews eyes her with with his bright-eyed look, punching at the buttons
which make the drawer slide out and tap him gently in the stomach:
"Mr Andrews—I see you are too busy now." "My job at the school," Miss
Paley says, "is gone; it's gone, my principal told me." Mrs Summers is off
again, non-limping her last two minutes, like an unwilling bird of ill-
omen off with her little messages—the hat-girls now.

And at last the closing bell rang and customers clung where they had
been indifferent before and sales-clerks turned cold who had been them-

selves leeches ten seconds earlier, and customers would not, could not, tear themselves away until Stars Fell on Alabama was sent to Arkansas and the Motion Picture Girls to Far Rockaway and until they had made ab-so-lutely sure that the price was erased from the Grosset and Dunlap edition of The Bridge of San Luis Rey—and Joey Andrews, making out a final sales-check, catches Miss Bodkin's eye on him at last, kindly at last, friendly at last, as if at last she were perceiving him, and Joey Andrews' heart leaps with the thought of Christmas Eve and the chance, the bare chance, that Miss Bodkin, with her gay little bobbing breasts. . .

"My principal told me," says Miss Paley, not sitting as she had last night, on a counter and girlishly swinging her legs as she added up her sales—but standing off a little, apart from them, as the great store empties, as the people whom the employees of M & J have served all day go home and leave the Store to the clerks, to whom it properly belongs, Miss Paley stands all by herself, while Mrs Summers (avoiding her now, for Miss Paley is dead) moves like a plague from hat-girl to hat-girl, infecting them, six of them, with the poison from headquarters that has killed Miss Paley. Miss Bodkin, although she has higher sales than anyone else with the possible exception of Mr Keasbey (who bends his hand over his sales-book as though he fears someone might copy his sums) subdues her joy in her sales as a man uncovers his head for a passing funeral—and there is no doubt about it now at all, Miss Bodkin is definitely smiling at Joey Andrews as if she liked him.

They handed Miss Paley her handkerchiefs and pencils in silence. For all they were kind to her, and patted her shoulders, they were really hurrying her a little, too, hurrying her out of their lives—Miss Paley was bad luck. "Maybe your next job will be a sitting-down one, honey," said Mrs Summers, limping at last. They all wished Miss Paley would hurry. It is not nice to see someone dead. "Goodbye, all," Miss Paley said, and with a last bewildered look set her feet on the stairs to make her exit from the Commercial World. And they watched Miss Paley float out with her handkerchiefs, her pencils, and her varicose legs, and all of them knew they would never see her again—and Joey Andrews, turning back with relief to his salesbook, gathered courage to return Miss Bodkin's smile.

Mrs Summers is bearing down upon Joey, smiling too, suddenly everyone is smiling at Joey, Joey Andrews is a good boy and everyone is smiling very kindly at him and Joey happily smiles back. "Different with you, you are young," Mrs Summers is saying. Young, yes, Joey Andrews is young as hell, and Miss Bodkin evidently thinks she has smiled at him too boldly, for now she lowers her eyes to her salesbook again. "You are young and life holds many opportunities," Mrs Summers says, smiling and smiling. "They don't let us tell them till the last minute, I tried to tell you but you were so busy, you were so happy, but it's different with you, you're so young," says Mrs Summers, smiling pleading for forgiveness. Of course I am young, thinks Joey Andrews, impatient with the old, with the white-haired Mrs Summers—and he tries to catch Miss Bodkin's eye again and signal her, We're both young, tonight's Christmas Eve—but the old will never have done talking to the young, and Mrs Summers goes on: "and so if you will leave your things tonight on my desk, and come for your pay-check next Thursday. . ." Nobody is smiling at Joey Andrews now, everybody is looking down very conscientiously at his own salesbook, he feels without knowing quite why that they are anxious to have him go, he hurries through counting the sales he scored for M & J, he stands apart a little as Miss Paley had, and when Miss Bodkin, not smiling any more now, comes and asks him in a low voice if he would like to come to her party tonight, just a few friends, just Miss Rees and herself and a few of the fellows, Joey Andrews says stiffly, "Thanks very much, I have a date," for Joey Andrews knows now why Miss Bodkin took to smiling at him so suddenly, Miss Bodkin knows everything ahead of everyone else—and Joey Andrews is not going to hang around people and be bad luck.

1934

WILLIAM MARCH, HILAIRE HILER, PAUL ENGLE, KAY BOYLE

Four Stories

"UNEMPLOYED CROWD BENCHES OF NEW YORK PARKS AS NEW YEAR BEGINS"

WILLIAM MARCH

CHARLIE HUDDLED in the doorway, protected somewhat from the tugging wind; but when he saw the old lady approaching with her dog, he squared his shoulders and walked towards her with something of his old carelessness. He whispered: 'It'll be easier, the first time, to ask an old dame. It won't be so shameful.' The old woman stopped and peered over her nose glasses at Charlie, surveying his wrecked shoes, his dirty reddened hands, his unshaven face. The terrier bitch stepped forward, dancing in the cold, and sniffed his trousers, making a whining sound.

All at once Charlie's jauntiness vanished. The set speech which he had rehearsed in the doorway went out of his mind. He spoke rapidly in his terror: This was the first time he had ever begged. She must believe that, for God's sake. He wasn't a bum. He'd had a good job until just a few months ago. This was the first time, and he hadn't eaten for almost two days. He was a man with self-respect and she must believe that. It was important. She must believe that, for God's sake.

The old woman opened her bag. She dropped a dime into his palm.

Charlie sat on a bench in Washington Square, clutching the coin tightly, crushing with his heels clods of soiled and brittle snow. In a little while he would get up and buy something hot for his gnawing belly; but first he must sit here a little longer and adjust himself to shame. He rested his face against the iciness of the iron bench, hoping that nobody could guess his degradation by looking at him. He thought: 'I sold out pretty cheap, didn't I?'

Depression takes Toll of Human Life in Hollywood

HILAIRE HILER

IF YOU WALK around behind the 'Brown Derby' (which is made just like a brown derby, and a darn cute idea, I think), and past the 'drive-in-and-eat-from-your-own-car' place where they have the grillburgers, you find the 'Desert Song' just back of Sonia Witowski's 'Ye Olde Beautie Shoppe.' Mrs. Fawcett has fixed it pretty natty without spending too much money. She's a right tasty woman, and between buying things at Woolworth's and making little handmade knicknacks, she has her place fixed up real cute and cosylike. 'The Hydrangeas' next door is run by Mrs. Spellacy and she don't seem to care quite so much about making her roomers happy and comfortable, although to tell you the honest truth they aren't too happy in either place. They're about the cheapest places around here and most of the people who get real disappointed about the movies go to one or the other, kind of as a last resort. This morning I heard Mrs. Spellacy talking to Mrs. Fawcett, and they were talking about Depression and Roosevelt and all that, and they got around to the point where they were talking about suicide being so common now. 'You know,' one of them

Permission the author. Reprinted from *365 Days*.

says to the other, 'if there's anything I hate it's these people cutting their throats. They make so much noise and everything before they pass out, and it's awfully messy. It's unbelievable how much blood there can be in a single person!' 'Personally, I prefer to have them do it outside the place,' said the other one. 'Taking poison's not so bad, at least it doesn't soil things much as a rule unless they get to vomiting.' 'We're at a disadvantage compared to New York' said Mrs. Fawcett, 'with these California-style bungalows. Anyone threw themselves out of the highest window I got wouldn't hardly shake themselves up.' 'As a matter of fact,' said Mrs. Spellacy, 'I don't give a D. what they do, but there's one thing I'm getting sick and tired of, and I know none of these good-looking extra girls would ever do if they knew how it makes them look, and that's having them use up my good gas. It runs up the bill something terrible, Mrs. Fawcett,' she said.

AMERICAN PASTORAL

PAUL ENGLE

AFTER DRINKING the cup of cool well water for which I had stopped, I looked around and saw that the larger pig pen was closed up and unused. 'Cholera?' I asked.

'No. The government. They paid me to slaughter the brood sows and the young pigs. Lovely Poland Chinas. Clean-skinned. Always farrowed big litters, maybe three a year.'

At the building the heavy July sun had broken the door down and nailed the shadows to the wall. The spiders, nervous and methodical, had propped up the ceiling with their thin beams. The tangy dark smell that a pig-sty, though abandoned, never loses, moved through the air.

'I buried them in the cornfield,' he went on. 'It's the damnedest kind of farming I've ever seen. A man works his tail off all his life, doubles the yield of his land, puts up new buildings, gets better bulls and boars, and then some bastard off in Washington that doesn't know a milch cow from a steer or his ass from a hole in the ground writes a business called a code, and you have to plough up your wheat and kill half your stock. It's not farming. It's just a kind of damn fool game, and the farmers and the people that's hungry get it in the neck.'

The wood of the slop trough was hard and whole even yet. There were dried corn cobs lying like black bones on the floor.

'By Christ,' he continued, 'they can't say there's over-production when there's millions right today hungry for a loaf of good honest-to-God bread

Permission the author. Reprinted from *365 Days*.

and a side of bacon, and waiting for a chance to let a notch out of their belts instead of putting another one in.'

We went on to the government-sealed corn cribs.

Marathon Dance Contest

KAY BOYLE

'THE WALK-A-SHOW MARATHON opened at eight o'clock on the fifth with Jack White, a Cleveland boy whom you all know, and his partner, lovely Edna Winters, representing Western Oil Incorporated. They will have to outdance Fred Plummer and his partner Alice Wilson, representing Lynex Hosiery, Elmer Barnes and Mildred Penn, representing Harris's Bread, and a dozen other well-known long distance dancing couples. The battle of champions has been keeping this city and the state at large right up on its toes, and we know you'll be sorry to hear that Les Ayres was disqualified this afternoon for leaning for half a minute against the band stand although he kept his feet going and that his partner, May Lou Boyd, representing Pinny Chain Drug Stores, is going right on dancing like there was nothing wrong at all. Her feet are so swollen that they had to cut her shoes off this morning but a little thing like that don't phase pretty May Lou. Now I'm going to let the Reverend Wilbur Hotchkiss talk to you for a few minutes, folks, and if you're a little surprised at hearing a minister talk to you on our programme that's nothing compared to the surprise you're going to get when you hear what he has to say. Now we're taking you right over to the studio and giving the Reverend the microphone.'

'Ladies and gentlemen,' said the voice of the Reverend Hotchkiss gently to the air, 'you have all, I am sure, been watching with the keenest interest this dance contest which has stirred us all, and I think I may truthfully say that the courage and perseverance of Jack White and Edna Winters has appealed to the sense of fair play and sportsmanship in each and everyone of us. I am sure you have come to regard them almost like personal friends, having lived with them, through the medium of our announcer, day by day and night by night in the intense moments of this grilling ordeal.

'Now the directors of Western Oil Incorporated have just confided a previous secret to me and I have been requested to let you in on it too. Those two brave young people, Jack White and Edna Winters, still going strong in the Marathon at this instant, have learned to love each other, really to love each other, and I am proud indeed to invite you all to tune in on the wedding service tomorrow evening when I shall perform the marriage ceremony right on the dance floor without any interruption in the movement of the dancers. Tune in on Station WFBE at eight-thirty and take part in a ceremony more sacred than many held in churches, and hear little Edna promise to love, honour, and . . .'

Here is a small mixed garland of reactions to a rising political radicalism that fed on the misery chronicled above. Clifford Odets's powerful denunciation of class injustice in Waiting For Lefty *was before long to be reduced to left-wing dramatic and lyric clichés, as S. J. Perelman's travesty suggests. Heywood Broun tells with patient humor of his encounter with the egregious Mrs. Elizabeth Dilling (later to figure as a defendant in the botched sedition trials); Broun's spiritual hegira, ending in the bosom of Rome, was to prove one of the familiar patterns of salvation for intellectuals in his time. E. B. White's dialogue between Diego Rivera and Nelson Rockefeller and Archibald MacLeish's impressive* Frescoes *comment quite adequately on each other and on Radio City.*

S. J. PERELMAN

Waiting For Santy

A Christmas Playlet

(WITH A BOW TO MR. CLIFFORD ODETS)

Scene: The sweatshop of S. Claus, a manufacturer of children's toys, on North Pole Street. Time: The night before Christmas.

At rise, seven gnomes, Rankin, Panken, Rivkin, Riskin, Ruskin, Briskin, and Praskin, are discovered working furiously to fill orders piling up at stage right. The whir of lathes, the hum of motors, and the hiss of drying lacquer are so deafening that at times the dialogue cannot be heard, which is very vexing if you vex easily. (Note: The parts of Rankin, Pan-

ken, Rivkin, Riskin, Ruskin, Briskin, and Praskin are interchangeable, and may be secured directly from your dealer or the factory.)

RISKIN *(filing a Meccano girder, bitterly)*—A parasite, a leech, a blood-sucker—altogether a five-star no goodnick! Starvation wages we get so he can ride around in a red team with reindeers!

RUSKIN *(jeering)*—Hey, Karl Marx, whyn'tcha hire a hall?

RISKIN *(sneering)*—Scab! Stool pigeon! Company spy! *(They tangle and rain blows on each other. While waiting for these to dry, each returns to his respective task.)*

BRISKIN *(sadly, to Pankin)*—All day long I'm painting "Snow Queen" on these Flexible Flyers and my little Irving lays in a cold tenement with the gout.

PANKEN—You said before it was the mumps.

BRISKIN *(with a fatalistic shrug)*—The mumps—the gout—go argue with City Hall.

PANKEN *(kindly, passing him a bowl)*—Here, take a piece fruit.

BRISKIN *(chewing)*—It ain't bad, for wax fruit.

PANKEN *(with pride)*—I painted it myself.

BRISKIN *(rejecting the fruit)*—Ptoo! Slave psychology!

RIVKIN *(suddenly, half to himself, half to the Party)*—I got a belly full of stars, baby. You make me feel like I swallowed a Roman candle.

PRASKIN *(curiously)*—What's wrong with the kid?

RISKIN—What's wrong with all of us? The system! Two years he and Claus's daughter's been making goo-goo eyes behind the old man's back.

PRASKIN—So what?

RISKIN *(scornfully)*—So what? Economic determinism! What do you think the kid's name is—J. Pierpont Rivkin? He ain't even got for a bottle Dr. Brown's Celery Tonic. I tell you, it's like gall in my mouth two young people shouldn't have a room where they could make great music.

RANKIN *(warningly)*—Shhh! Here she comes now! *(Stella Claus enters, carrying a portable gramophone. She and Rivkin embrace, place a record on the turntable, and begin a very slow waltz, unmindful that the gramophone is playing "Cohen on the Telephone.")*

STELLA *(dreamily)*—Love me, sugar?

RIVKIN—I can't sleep, I can't eat, that's how I love you. You're a double malted with two scoops of whipped cream; you're the moon rising over Mosholu Parkway; you're a two weeks' vacation at Camp Nitgedaiget! I'd pull down the Chrysler Building to make a bobbie pin for your hair!

STELLA—I've got a stomach full of anguish. Oh, Rivvy, what'll we do?

PANKEN (*sympathetically*)—Here, try a piece fruit.

RIVKIN (*fiercely*)—Wax fruit—that's been my whole life! Imitations! Substitutes! Well, I'm through! Stella, tonight I'm telling your old man. He can't play mumblety-peg with two human beings! (*The tinkle of sleigh bells is heard offstage, followed by a voice shouting, "Whoa, Dasher! Whoa, Dancer!" A moment later S. Claus enters in a gust of mock snow. He is a pompous bourgeois of sixty-five who affects a white beard and a false air of benevolence. But tonight the ruddy color is missing from his cheeks, his step falters, and he moves heavily. The gnomes hastily replace the marzipan they have been filching.*)

STELLA (*anxiously*)—Papa! What did the specialist say?

CLAUS (*brokenly*)—The biggest professor in the country . . . the best cardiac man that money could buy. . . . I tell you I was like a wild man.

STELLA—Pull yourself together, Sam!

CLAUS—It's no use. Adhesions, diabetes, sleeping sickness, decalcomania—oh, my God! I got to cut out climbing in chimneys, he says—me, Sanford Claus, the biggest toy concern in the world!

STELLA (*soothingly*)—After all, it's only one man's opinion.

CLAUS—No, no, he cooked my goose. I'm like a broken uke after a Yosian picnic. Rivkin!

RIVKIN—Yes, Sam.

CLAUS—My boy, I had my eye on you for a long time. You and Stella thought you were too foxy for an old man, didn't you? Well, let bygones be bygones. Stella, do you love this gnome?

STELLA (*simply*)—He's the whole stage show at the Music Hall, Papa; he's Toscanini conducting Beethoven's Fifth; he's—

CLAUS (*curtly*)—Enough already. Take him. From now on he's a partner in the firm. (*As all exclaim, Claus holds up his hand for silence.*) And tonight he can take my route and make the deliveries. It's the least I could do for my own flesh and blood. (*As the happy couple kiss, Claus wipes away a suspicious moisture and turns to the other gnomes.*) Boys, do you know what day tomorrow is?

GNOMES (*crowding around expectantly*)—Christmas!

CLAUS—Correct. When you look in your envelopes tonight, you'll find a little present from me—a forty-per cent pay cut. And the first one who opens his trap—gets this. (*As he holds up a tear-gas bomb and beams at them, the gnomes utter cries of joy, join hands, and dance around him shouting exultantly. All except Riskin and Briskin, that is, who exchange a quick glance and go underground.*)

HEYWOOD BROUN

Redder than the Roosevelts

A KIND CLIENT has sent to me my dossier from Mrs. Albert Dilling's *The Red Network*, which unfortunately I had not read at all. This single all-too-slender biography has sold the book to still another customer. I am fascinated not only by the subject matter but caught up with the manner of the telling. The style is terse and also free. Mrs. Dilling is, I suspect, own cousin to the Garble sisters, whose dialogues are featured by Hi Phillips in his Sun Dial column.

But let me quote and try to show how completely an endearing revolutionary can be limned within the span of a couple of sticks. Had they been chafed together, think of the fire which might have been engendered. That is not the Dilling method. Dispassionately the author states her case and lets the reader soak it in. Here goes:

Broun, Heywood: New York *World-Telegram* newspaperman; resigned from Socialist Party recently, saying, it was reported, that it was not radical enough for him; Rand School; wife, Ruth Hale of Lucy Stone Lg . . . went to Boston to help stage last-minute Sacco-V. protest meeting (N. Y. *Post,* Aug. 10, 1927); ousted as columnist for N. Y. *World* because of friction over his abuse of the authorities in the Sacco-V. matter; at once engaged by radical *Nation;* principal speaker at Level Club, N. Y. C., blacklist party of speakers barred by D. A. R. as subversives, May 9, 1928. James Weldon Johnson, colored radical, was master of ceremonies and mock trial for revocation of D. A. R. charter was held, Norman Thomas being the judge and Arthur Garfield Hays one of the attorneys; nat. com. W. I. R., 1929: nat. com. W. R. Lg., 1930-31; L. I. D. (bd. dir., April, 1931); Recep. Com. Soviet Fliers; Fed. Unemp. Wkrs. Lgs. N. Y., 1933; contrib. *New Masses,* 1933; Nat. Scottsboro Com. of Action, 1933; Emer. Com. Strike Rel., 1933; Il Nuovo Mondo Nat. Com.; supporter Rand Sch., 1933; nat. coun. Berger Nat. Found.: Nat. Com. to Aid Vic. G. Fascism; pres. and org. Am. Newspaper Guild, 1933; Conf. Prog. Pol. Act., 1933-4; Roosevelt appointee, Theatrical Code Authority, 1933.

It is true that I am the pres. but I am not the org. of the Am. News-paper Guild and most bitterly do I wish to enter a denial of the last ac-cusation hurled by Mrs. Dilling. President Roosevelt did not appoint me to the Theatrical Code Authority. In all fairness to Mrs. Dilling it must be admitted that she did not weave this serious charge out of whole cloth. I must admit that I sat at one hearing before the theatrical code adminis-trator and that Mrs. Rumsey had informed me that I was there to rep-resent the consuming public. But I was not alone in this reckless deed. Side by side with me sat Joseph Wood Krutch, who, as I later learned, is bd. of eds. and drm. ctc. and lit. ctc. of the *Nat.* At the end of the session, in which William A. Brady, thr. pd., made a long and eloquent speech, a Mr. Rosenblatt asked me if I wanted to say anything. I told him no. He then asked Joseph Wood Krutch, ed. radical *Nat.*, who was almost as eloquent. I was informed that I could get my expenses by turning in an account at the proper office but it happened to be at the far end of the Commerce Building on one of the uncharted corridors and so I said, "Oh, what the hl. I'll stake my country to the $6.15." And that, as Jvh. (Bibl. dty.) is my witness, is the only warrant for the charge that I was appointed to the Thl. Cd. Athy.

That was all the consuming or the theatrical public ever heard from me. And in justice to Mr. Rosenblatt it should be added that undoubtedly when he asked me if I had anything to say he was not cognizant of the fact that I was nat. com. W. I. R. In bringing this matter to light I'll freely confess that Mrs. Dilling has me worried. Indeed, this one revelation in *The Red Network* keeps me tossing and turning at night. Like the young lady in the song, I couldn't say yes and I couldn't say no. Nor is it sufficient to ask indulgence on account of the fact that this was way back in 1929 when I was a young man only nineteen years out of college. How on earth can I explain or justify my being nat. com. W. I. R. when I have not the slightest recollection of what the W. I. R. may be?

Of course, it could be World Institute Reds or Wabbling Into Repub-licanism. Or for that matter the When in Rome Society. The best I can do is to say that, whether I was a W. I. R. or not in the past, its purposes and its practices elude me now. I can truthfully say that I haven't been to any W. I. R. dance, banquet, or business meeting in the last five years. It must be that I was trying to forget and in this I have succeeded ad-mirably. But there is just one tragic possibility. Perhaps Mrs. Dilling has also forgotten. Come on, Mrs. D., be a good scout and tell me what the W. I. R. is or was so that I can make amends and once more sleep peace-fully at night.

Mrs. Dilling has fallen into an inaccuracy in stating that Broun, Heywood (with a little better detective work she might have dug out the "Campbell" for the middle) was "ousted as columnist for N. Y. *World* because of friction over his abuse of authorities in the Sacco-V. matter." My abuse of the authorities did lead to a situation during which I absented myself from the columns of the *World* for several months. That was of my own volition. I got fired by Ralph Pulitzer, almost a year later, after I had returned to the job. The offense was an article in the "radical *Nation*" attacking the editorial policy of the N. Y. *World* as administered largely by Walter Lippmann, p.s.b. Lest there be confusion I may state that p.s.b. is in no sense a radical organization. Some of the most respectable people in the American community belong to it. I appointed them myself. Nicholas Murray Butler is a member and William Randolph Hearst might very appropriately be the org. of this large and inclusive fraternal organization. Madison Square Garden being solidly booked for the season, the members of the p.s.b. have no clubhouse at the moment, although I believe guest privileges have been offered them by the S.N.S.S.—Society of Native Stuffed Shirts.

But to get back to Mrs. Dilling and her all-too-brief biography of Broun, Heywood. Much as I regret to say it, I feel that we have both failed. She has not made out her case and I do not deserve the accolade she has offered. As I read the account of the activities of this "*World-Telegram* newspaperman" I find, not the solid outlines of a red, but merely the portrait of a joiner. Better luck next time, Mrs. D.

E. B. WHITE

I Paint What I See

A BALLAD of Artistic Integrity, on the Occasion of the Removal of Some Rather Expensive Murals from the RCA Building.

"What do you paint, when you paint on a wall?"
 Said John D.'s grandson Nelson.
"Do you paint just anything there at all?

Permission the author. Originally published in *The New Yorker*. From *The Fox Of Peapack* by E. B. White. Copyright 1933 by E. B. White. Harper & Brothers.

"Will there be any doves, or a tree in fall?
"Or a hunting scene, like an English hall?"

"I paint what I see," said Rivera.

"What are the colors you use when you paint?"
Said John D.'s grandson Nelson.
"Do you use any red in the beard of a saint?
"If you do, is it terribly red, or faint?
"Do you use any blue? Is it Prussian?"

"I paint what I paint," said Rivera.

"Whose is that head that I see on my wall?"
Said John D.'s grandson Nelson.
"Is it anyone's head whom we know, at all?
"A Rensselaer, or a Saltonstall?
"Is it Franklin D? Is it Mordaunt Hall?
"Or is it the head of a Russian?"

"I paint what I think," said Rivera.

"I paint what I paint. I paint what I see.
"I paint what I think," said Rivera.
"And the thing that is dearest in life to me
"In a bourgeois hall is Integrity:
"However. . . ."
"I'll take out a couple of people drinkin'
"And put in a picture of Abraham Lincoln;
"I could even give you McCormick's reaper
"And still not make my art much cheaper.
"But the head of Lenin has got to stay
"Or my friends will give me the bird today,
"The bird, the bird, forever."

"It's not good taste in a man like me."
Said John D.'s grandson Nelson.
"To question an artist's integrity
"Or mention a practical thing like a fee.
"But I know what I like, to a large degree,
"Though art I hate to hamper.
"For twenty-one thousand conservative bucks
"You painted a radical. I say shucks,
"I never could rent the offices—
"The capitalistic offices.

"For this, as you know, is a public hall
"And people want doves, or a tree in fall.
"And though your art I dislike to hamper,
"I owe a *little* to God and Gramper.
  "And after all.
  "It's *my* wall . . ."

  "We'll see if it is," said Rivera.

ARCHIBALD MacLEISH

Frescoes for Mr. Rockefeller's City . . .

I

LANDSCAPE AS A NUDE

SHE LIES on her left side her flank golden:
Her hair is burned black with the strong sun:
The scent of her hair is of rain in the dust on her shoulders:
She has brown breasts and the mouth of no other country:

Ah she is beautiful here in the sun where she lies:
She is not like the soft girls naked in vineyards
Nor the soft naked girls of the English islands
Where the rain comes in with the surf on an east wind:

Hers is the west wind and the sunlight: the west
Wind is the long clean wind of the continents—
The wind turning with earth: the wind descending
Steadily out of the evening and following on:

The wind here where she lies is west: the trees
Oak ironwood cottonwood hickory: standing in
Great groves the roll on the wind as the sea would:
The grasses of Iowa Illinois Indiana

Run with the plunge of the wind as a wave tumbling:

Under her knees there is no green lawn of the Florentines:
Under her dusty knees is the corn stubble:
Her belly is flecked with the flickering light of the corn:

She lies on her left side her flank golden:
Her hair is burned black with the strong sun:
The scent of her hair is of dust and of smoke on her shoulders:
She has brown breasts and the mouth of no other country:

2

WILDWEST

There were none of my blood in this battle:
There were Minneconjous: Sans Arcs: Brules:
Many nations of Sioux: they were few men galloping:

This would have been in the long days in June:
They were galloping well deployed under the plum-trees:
They were driving riderless horses: themselves they were few:

Crazy Horse had done it with few numbers:
Crazy Horse was small for a Lakota:
He was riding always alone thinking of something:

He was standing alone by the picket lines by the ropes:
He was young then: he was thirty when he died:
Unless there were children to talk he took no notice:

When the soldiers came for him there on the other side
On the Greasy Grass in the villages we were shouting
'Hoka Hey! Crazy Horse will be riding!'

They fought in the water: horses and men were drowning:
They rode on the butte: dust settled in sunlight:
Hoka Hey! they lay on the bloody ground:

No one could tell of the dead which man was Custer . . .
That was the end of his luck: by that river:
The soldiers beat him at Slim Buttes once:

They beat him at Willow Creek when the snow lifted:
The last time they beat him was the Tongue:
He had only the meat he had made and of that little:

Do you ask why he should fight? It was his country:
My God should he not fight? It was his:
But after the Tongue there were no herds to be hunting:

He cut the knots of the tails and he led them in:
He cried out 'I am Crazy Horse! Do not touch me!'
There were many soldiers between and the gun glinting ...

And a Mister Josiah Perham of Maine had much of the
land Mister Perham was building the Northern Pacific
railroad that is Mister Perham was saying at lunch that

forty say fifty millions of acres in gift and
government grant outright ought to be worth a
wide price on the Board at two-fifty and

later a Mister Cooke had relieved Mister Perham and
later a Mister Morgan relieved Mister Cooke:
Mister Morgan converted at prices current:

It was all prices to them: they never looked at it:
why should they look at the land: they were Empire Builders:
it was all in the bid and the asked and the ink on their books ...

When Crazy Horse was there by the Black Hills
His heart would be big with the love he had for that country
And all the game he had seen and the mares he had ridden

And how it went out from you wide and clean in the sunlight

Footnote: Black Elk's memories of Crazy Horse recorded by Neihardt.

3

BURYING GROUND BY THE TIES

Ayee! Ai! This is heavy earth on our shoulders:
There were none of us born to be buried in this earth:
Niggers we were Portuguese Magyars Polacks:

We were born to another look of the sky certainly:
Now we lie here in the river pastures:
We lie in the mowings under the thick turf:

We hear the earth and the all-day rasp of the grasshoppers:
It was we laid the steel on this land from ocean to ocean:
It was we (if you know) put the U. P. through the passes

Bringing her down into Laramie full load
Eighteen mile on the granite anticlinal
Forty-three foot to the mile and the grade holding:

It was we did it: hunkies of our kind:
It was we dug the caved-in holes for the cold water:
It was we built the gully spurs and the freight sidings:

Who would do it but we and the Irishmen bossing us?
It was all foreign-born men there were in this country:
It was Scotsmen Englishmen Chinese Squareheads Austrians . . .

Ayee! but there's weight to the earth under it:
Not for this did we come out—to be lying here
Nameless under the ties in the clay cuts:

There's nothing good in the world but the rich will buy it:
Everything sticks to the grease of a gold note—
Even a continent—even a new sky!

Do not pity us much for the strange grass over us:
We laid the steel to the stone stock of these mountains:
The place of our graves is marked by the telegraph poles!

It was not to lie in the bottoms we came out
And the trains going over us here in the dry hollows . . .

4

OIL PAINTING OF THE ARTIST AS
THE ARTIST

The plump Mr. Pl'f is washing his hands of America:
The plump Mr. Pl'f is in ochre with such hair:

America is in blue-black-grey-green-sandcolor:
America is a continent—many lands:

The plump Mr. Pl'f is washing his hands of America:
He is pictured at Pau on the *place* and his eyes glaring:

He thinks of himself as an exile from all this:
As an émigré from his own time into history—

(History being an empty house without owners
A practical man may get in by the privy stones—

The dead are excellent hosts: they have no objections—
And once in he can nail the knob on the next one

Living the life of a classic in bad air with
Himself for the Past and his face in the glass for Posterity)

The Cinquecento is nothing at all like Nome
Or Natchez or Wounded Knee or the Shenandoah:

Your vulgarity Tennessee: your violence Texas:
The rocks under your fields Ohio Connecticut:

Your clay Missouri your clay: you have driven him out:
You have shadowed his life Appalachians purple mountains:

There is much too much of your flowing Mississippi:
He prefers a tidier stream with a terrace for trippers and

Cypresses mentioned in Horace or Henry James:
He prefers a country where everything carries the name of a

Countess or real king or an actual palace or
Something in Prose and the stock prices all in Italian:

There is more shade for an artist under a fig
Than under the whole damn range (he finds) of the Big Horns

5

EMPIRE BUILDERS

The Museum Attendant:
This is *The Making of America in Five Panels:*

This is Mister Harriman making America:
Mister-Harriman-is-buying-the-Union-Pacific-at-Seventy:
The Santa Fe is shining on his hair:

This is Commodore Vanderbilt making America:
Mister-Vanderbilt-is-eliminating-the-short-interest-in-Hudson:
Observe the carving on the rocking chair:

This is J. P. Morgan making America:
(The Tennessee Coal is behind to the left of the Steel Company:)
Those in mauve are braces he is wearing:

This is Mister Mellon making America:
Mister-Mellon-is-represented-as-a-symbolical-figure-in-aluminum-
Strewing-bank-stocks-on-a-burnished-stair:

This is the Bruce is the Barton making America:
Mister-Barton-is-selling-us-Doctor's-Deliciousest-Dentifrice:
This is he in beige with the canary:

You have just beheld the Makers making America:
This is *The Making of America in Five Panels:*
America lies to the west-southwest of the Switch-Tower:
There is nothing to see of America but land:

The Original Document
under the Panel Paint:
'To Thos. Jefferson Esq. his obd't serv't
Mr. Lewis: captain: detached:
                                        Sir:

Having in mind your repeated commands in this matter;
And the worst half of it done and streams mapped:

And we here on the back of this beach beholding the
Other ocean—two years gone and the cold

Breaking with rain for the third spring since St. Louis:
The crows at the fishbones on the frozen dunes:

The first cranes going over from south north:
And the river down by a mark of the pole since the morning:

And time near to return, and a ship (Spanish)
Lying in for the salmon: and fearing chance or the

Drought or the Sioux should deprive you of these discoveries—
Therefore we send by sea in this writing:

                                        Above the
Platte there were long plains and clay country:
Rim of the sky far off: grass under it:

Dung for the cook fires by the sulphur licks:
After that there were low hills and the sycamores:

And we poled up by the Great Bend in the skiffs:
The honey bees left us after the Osage River:

The wind was west in the evenings and no dew and the
Morning Star larger and whiter than usual—

The winter rattling in the brittle haws:
The second year there was sage and the quail calling:

All that valley is good land by the river:
Three thousand miles and the clay cliffs and

Rue and beargrass by the water banks
And many birds and the brant going over and tracks of

Bear elk wolves marten: the buffalo
Numberless so that the cloud of their dust covers them:

The antelope fording the fall creeks: and the mountains and
Grazing lands and the meadow lands and the ground

Sweet and open and well-drained:
                       We advise you to
Settle troops at the forks and to issue licenses:

Many men will have living on these lands:
There is wealth in the earth for them all and the wood standing

And wild birds on the water where they sleep:
There is stone in the hills for the towns of a great people ...'

You have just beheld the Makers making America:

They screwed her scrawny and gaunt with their seven-year panics:
They bought her back on their mortgages old-whore-cheap:
They fattened their bonds at her breasts till the thin blood ran
    from them:

Men have forgotten how full clear and deep
The Yellowstone moved on the gravel and grass grew
When the land lay waiting for her westward people!

6

BACKGROUND WITH REVOLUTIONARIES

And the corn singing Millennium!
Lenin! Millennium! Lennium!

When they're shunting the cars on the Katy a mile off
When they're shunting the cars when they're shunting the cars on
   the Katy
You can hear the clank of the couplings riding away

Also Comrade Devine who writes of America
Most instructively having in 'Seventy-four
Crossed to the Hoboken side on the Barclay Street Ferry

She sits on a settle in the State of North Dakota
O she sits on a settle in the State of North Dakota
She can hear the engines whistle over Iowa and Idaho

Also Comrade Edward Remington Ridge
Who has prayed God since the April of 'Seventeen
To replace in his life his lost (M.E.) religion

And The New York Daily Worker *goes a'blowing over Arkansas*
The New York Daily Worker *goes a'blowing over Arkansas*
The grasses let it go along the Ozarks over Arkansas

Even Comrade Grenadine Grilt who has tried since
August tenth for something to feel about strongly in
Verses—his personal passions having tired

I can tell my land by the jays in the apple-trees
Tell my land by the jays in the apple-trees
I can tell my people by the blue-jays in the apple-trees

Aindt you read in d' books you are all brudders?
D' glassic historic objective broves you are brudders!
You and d' Wops and d' Chinks you are all brudders!
Havend't you got it d' same ideology? Havend't you?

When it's yesterday in Oregon it's one A M in Maine
And she slides: and the day slides: and it runs: runs over us:
And the bells strike twelve strike twelve strike twelve
In Marblehead in Buffalo in Cheyenne in Cherokee
Yesterday runs on the states like a crow's shadow

For Marx has said to us Workers what do you need?
And Stalin has said to us Starvers what do you need?
You need the Dialectical Materialism!

She's a tough land under the corn mister:
She has changed the bone in the cheeks of many races:
She has winced the eyes of the soft Slavs with her sun on them:
She has tried the fat from the round rumps of Italians:
Even the voice of the English has gone dry
And hard on the tongue and alive in the throat speaking:

She's a tough land under the oak-trees mister:
It may be she can change the word in the book
As she changes the bone of a man's head in his children:
It may be that the earth and the men remain . . .

There is too much sun on the lids of my eyes to be listening

While the bold experiment of TVA, under the gifted and thoughtful leadership of David Lilienthal, was giving Americans a new conception of what public ownership of public utilities could mean, the growing dangers at home and abroad were becoming sinister and unmistakable. Irwin Shaw's Bury the Dead *expressed the diehard pacifism of a new generation that could find no justification for any war, but was before long to find itself justifying its participation in the greatest of all wars. In* It Can't Happen Here *Sinclair Lewis showed American Fascism in action, with all his unequalled talent for making fiction sound like the morning newspaper. And Carl Sandburg, in those rugged accents which are so peculiarly his own, reaffirmed his faith in the people, warning that the people would little longer tolerate the groping uncertainty that harassed them.*

DAVID LILIENTHAL

The People's Dividend

THE STORY thus far as I have recounted it has been chiefly one of physical changes in the Tennessee Valley. But what has been the yield to the people—to those who live in the region, and to the people of the country as a whole who advanced most of the funds?

First of all, the level of income of the region's people is definitely rising. By 1940, and before the effect of war expansion, the per capita income had increased in the seven valley states 73 per cent over the level of 1933; while for the same period the increase in the country as a whole was

Permission the author. From *TVA: Democracy on the March.* Harper & Brothers. Copyright 1944, by David E. Lilienthal.

only 56 per cent. The same trend is reflected in income payment statistics. Between 1933 and 1943 the seven valley states show an increase in per capita income payments which substantially exceeds the index for the country as a whole. The rate of increase in each of the seven valley states is above the index for the country. The same is true of total income payments: the rate of increase for all the valley states, and for each of the states, exceeds the national index of rate of increase. Bank deposits increased 76 per cent between 1933 and 1939 compared to 49 per cent in the country, and retail sales increased 81 per cent compared to 71 per cent for the country.

All the available figures—and the evidence of one's eyes—show that our income level is rising. But the Tennessee Valley is still a region of low income, about half the United States average.

INDUSTRIAL EXPANSION

What has happened to the businesses of the people? Farming is the most important private enterprise in this region; that business, as I have indicated, is moving upward as the fruitfulness and stability of the land increase. What of business in the industrial sense? That too is developing, and at a rapid rate. Even before the war the valley saw the addition or expansion of several large industries devoted to the basic materials of modern industry, such as aluminum, ferro-silicon, heavy chemicals; these included two of the largest phosphatic chemical works in the country.

The war has added mightily to the list. For reasons of security little of this expansion can now be told. But when the full story of a once industrially laggard valley's part in production for war can be revealed, it will rank as one of the miracles of American enterprise, the kind of miracle that is marvelled at when it occurs across the seas, rarely comprehended close at home.

At least as important as these heavy industries is the rise of new light industries and the expansion of plants that existed before 1933. The industries added since 1933 range from those for the processing of frozen foods and the production of cheese to the manufacture of aircraft and mattresses, bottle washers, stoves, flour, inlaid wood, barrel heads and staves, electric water heaters, furniture, hats and shoes, pencils, carbon electrodes, boats, horse collars, ground mica, oxygen and acetylene, metal dies, ax handles, and barites. Many new small industries are the immediate result of opportunities for profit provided by the chain of lakes that make the Tennessee River a new arc of beauty through the countryside.

We have a long way yet to go in the valley. There are many factories yet to be built, in an area with such great potential wealth and with less than its economic share of the nation's industry and manufacturing. There are many new jobs to be created by the laboratories and businessmen out of the region's dormant resources. There are millions of acres yet to be restored to full productiveness. When TVA began its work in 1933, of the total of eight and a half million acres of cultivated land in the valley, erosion in varying degrees had damaged seven million acres. On more than a million acres the top soil had entirely disappeared. There are more trees to plant, houses, schools, roads, and hospitals to build. Many new skills have been learned—among farmers, industrial workers in the new factories, the tens of thousands of men and women who have added to their skills in the course of their work for the TVA —but lack of training is still a heavy handicap to be overcome. The task is barely begun—but the Tennessee Valley is on its way.

THE HUMAN RESOURCES

Democracy is on the march in this valley. Not only because of the physical changes or the figures of increased income and economic activity. My faith in this as a region with a great future is built most of all upon what I have come to know of the great capacities and the spirit of the people. The notion that has been expressed that the region's problem, as one commentator has put it, is one of "human salvage" completely misses the mark. The human resources of this valley are its greatest asset and advantage. The people have seized upon these modern tools of opportunity and have raised up their own leadership. They have shown an ability to hold themselves to tough assignments with a singleness of purpose and a resourcefulness in doing much with little that will be difficult to match anywhere in the country.

This advent of opportunity has brought with it the rise of a confident, sure, chesty feeling. The evidence is everywhere. It is epitomized in an editorial in the Decatur, Alabama, *Daily* for May 18, 1943. The editor, a community leader, candidly relates the doleful past and contrasts it with the optimistic and fruitful present. Seven years ago Decatur was in great trouble; today it is one of the most enterprising and promising small cities in the interior United States. "What has happened in these seven years?" he asks, and then he answers:

We can write of great dams . . . of the building of home-grown industry and of electricity at last coming to the farms of thousands of farm people in the valley. *Yet the significant advance has been made in the thinking of a people.* They are no longer afraid. *They have caught the vision of their own powers.* They can stand now and talk out in meeting and say that if industry doesn't come into the Valley from other sections, then we'll build our own industry. This they are doing today.

These changes of a decade were not, of course, wrought by TVA alone: in point of fact, the very essence of TVA's method in the undertaking, as I shall later indicate in detail, was at every hand to minimize what it was to do directly and to encourage and stimulate the broadest possible *coalition* of all forces. Private funds and private efforts, on farms and in factories; state funds and state activities; local communities, clubs, schools, associations, co-operatives—all have had major roles. Moreover, scores of federal agencies co-operated—the Civilian Conservation Corps; the Department of Agriculture through such agencies as the Farm Security Administration, the Rural Electrification Administration, the scientific research bureaus, the Agricultural Adjustment Administration, the Commodity Credit Corporation, the co-operative loan banks and the Forest Service; the Public Health Service; the Army Corps of Engineers which prior to 1933 had prepared a preliminary survey of the Tennessee River widely known as "House Document 328"; the Coast Guard; the Public Works Administration; several of the bureaus of the Interior Department, the Bureau of Reclamation which prepared designs for early Norris and Wheeler dams, the Geological Survey, the Bureau of Mines, the Bureau of Fish and Wildlife Service, the National Park Service; the Geodetic Survey and the Weather Bureau—and so on; the list, if complete, would include most national agencies.

THE PEOPLE'S MONEY

How much of the public's money has the TVA spent in these ten years? Has it been worth that cost as measured in dividends to the people?

It is as important that a public enterprise should produce benefits and values as great as or greater than their cost as it is when the undertaking is a private one. And, to those who are studying the feasibility of developments of a comparable character, the question of cost and the balancing of investment of materials and manpower against the yield the investment produces are considerations of the first consequence.

I shall not, of course, go into all the possible technical refinements of TVA's financial affairs, since they are of little interest to the general reader. The facts are all readily available in TVA's financial statements, in its annual reports to Congress, in thousands of pages of testimony before Congressional committees, and in technical books and writings on the subject. I shall here only summarize the basic facts and the considerations that may be useful in judging the significance of those facts.

Capital Investment

The funds used by the TVA have all been advanced from funds appropriated by Congress with two major exceptions: 65 millions of TVA bonds and about 50 millions supplied by electric rate-payers and reinvested in dams and equipment. To avoid unduly complicating the statement, however, I shall treat the funds expended as if they *all* had been advanced directly from the federal treasury; the exceptions do not affect the principles. The American people who advanced these funds are entitled to a return from them.

The Varied Benefits

In judging whether they have received such a return and whether the product of TVA's investment of the people's money has been worth the outlay, it must be remembered that much of the return, to the Tennessee Valley and the nation, is in benefits which cannot be exactly measured. It is only the investment in power facilities that yields the federal taxpayers a return in dollars in addition to other benefits. For power is the only major product of the TVA investment that is sold for dollars. For the other expenditures little if any of the return is in dollars, but instead is realized in benefits to citizens and their communities and business enterprises.

The benefits of a navigable channel, for example, go to shippers, to industries using the channel, to consumers of grain, oil, gasoline, and so on. This is true, of course, not only on the Tennessee but also on the Ohio, the Illinois, the Missouri, all of the many rivers where millions of federal funds have been expended for a century and more. So it is not possible to record the same precise dollar measure of navigation benefits as it is with power. But simply because they do not appear on TVA's books as income does not mean, of course, that there are no benefits.

Likewise, the benefits of flood control produced by these dams extend all the way down the Mississippi River to the mouth of the Red. But since TVA is not paid for those benefits in dollars, the taxpayers' return cannot be measured in that way. And so it is with TVA's expenditures to produce phosphate plant food, and to demonstrate its use to control soil erosion not only in the Tennessee Valley but in Minnesota, Wisconsin, New York, Iowa, and seventeen other states outside this region. So with forestry, industrial research, mapping.

The *cost* of such development work appears on *TVA's books as a net expense; but the benefits appear on the balance sheet of the region and of the nation.* And, as with public improvement expenditures generally the country over, it was anticipated that such expenditures would be repaid to the taxpayers not directly in dollars, but indirectly in benefits.

TVA EXPENDITURES

Turning now to TVA's expenditures, and first the cost of developing the river: TVA's financial balance sheet shows that to provide a 650-mile navigable channel, flood protection, and power supply, the TVA has an investment in completed plant as of June 30, 1943, totaling about $475,-000,000. By the end of 1944, with several additional dams completed, the figure was in excess of $700,000,000. Of this amount approximately 65 per cent, or $450,000,000, will represent the power investment. The river control works will then be substantially completed.

THE PEOPLE'S DIVIDENDS

What dividends for the people does this investment yield? Do the expenditures yield a product that justifies this cost?

As to power the answer is a relatively easy one, since the power is sold and the revenues provide a dollar measurement, and one that is reassuring. In the fiscal year ended June 30, 1943, the sale of power yielded revenues to TVA in excess of $31,500,000. Operating expenses to produce that power, including about $2,000,000 of tax payments and about $6,000,-000 (or almost 20 per cent of each dollar of revenue) in depreciation charges, left a surplus of revenue over cost of more than $13,000,000.

Actual earnings in the first months of the current fiscal year indicate that the total net income from power since the beginning of the TVA in 1933 to June 30, 1944, has been well over $40,000,000. This substantial surplus will have been accumulated in only five or six years, for between 1933 and 1937 the TVA was not a going power concern; the system was incomplete and operations were beset by a multiplicity of lawsuits and injunctions which prevented the normal sale of the power produced by the river. The size of this net income indicates pretty clearly that the power asset of the Tennessee River certainly is worth its cost.

These calculations take into account only dollar returns to TVA, and none of the indirect benefits. But such benefits are many. Among them are the $10,000,000 annual savings to consumers as a result of greatly reduced rates, the effects on the region's business enterprises of large amounts of low-cost power, the benefits that have resulted to business in other regions of the country, as well as the fact that 80 per cent of the equipment and materials purchased by TVA were produced in factories located in regions outside the Tennessee Valley. Nor do they seek to measure the value to the country of the fact that it was largely because of power from this river that in 1943 America was able to build huge fleets of bombers to send over Europe and the South Pacific.

What of the Future?

Will the current revenues and surpluses continue in the future? The end of the war will mean that large amounts of power will no longer be used for direct war production. The future of electricity, however, as an industrial necessity in the production of light metals and chemical products seems assured. The conversion of most of TVA's present industrial consumers of power to civilian production in these electro-chemical and metallurgic fields appears a reasonable prospect. There is every reason to expect a large increase in the valley's domestic and farm use of electricity, carrying forward the trend interrupted by the war. Short of a prolonged major depression after the war, power revenue will continue to cover all costs, including straight-line depreciation, and in addition will provide a large net income probably between $10,000,000 and $15,000,000 annually.

Revenues from power and surpluses show a favorable relation to the capital invested to produce that income. On the basis of actual experience to date, power surplus could repay the American people their total power investment in TVA without interest within the next thirty years. Since much of the investment is in land or in property of almost indefinite life—a concrete dam is almost as indestructible as the rock on which it rests—this is a brief period indeed for the repayment of this investment.

At the end of that thirty-year period of repayment the situation would be this: (1) Payments from users of TVA power would have repaid to the people of the nation their total investment which has been used to transform the energy of the river into usable electricity and to construct a transmission network to reach the communities throughout the valley. (2) This $450,000,000 property, entirely repaid by the valley consumers of TVA electricity, will be in first-class operating condition and reserves will be available to keep it intact by reason of a conservative straight-line depreciation accumulation, charged currently against the rate-payers. (3) Large surplus income from a "paid-out" investment will continue to flow into the federal treasury.

There is another way by which the soundness of the nation's power investment in the Tennessee Valley can be tested. Only a small portion of the investment, $65,000,000, is represented by bonds issued by TVA. With this exception, Congress preferred the policy of appropriating funds directly. But Congress might have followed another method. Since the federal taxpayer seems to me clearly entitled to a money return on his investment in a direct revenue-producing operation (as distinguished from an activity such as navigation or soil erosion control that does not yield revenue in dollars), Congress might have authorized TVA to issue bonds for the total power investment, with an obligation to pay interest to the private purchasers of those bonds. In this way the federal government would have shifted the burden of capital advance from general taxpayers to individual investors. The interest payments would go to those individual private investors.

If such bonds had been issued, bearing a 2 per cent interest rate, TVA surplus revenues could meet the interest payments, the physical property could be kept intact through maintenance and replacement, the investment in the property could be kept intact through straight-line depreciation charges, and sixty years from now the bonds would be completely liquidated out of earnings. If the interest rate were 2½ per cent the same result could be reached; the retirement of the bonds would extend over a longer period, about eighty years.

These figures should be read in the light of the fact that rarely, if ever, do public utilities and railroads provide in this way for the retirement of their entire capitalization. And it is important also to bear in mind that few utilities, in whose bonds private individuals invest, follow as conservative a practice of charging depreciation as do the TVA and its associated local distributing agencies.

To sum up, in the case of the TVA (1) this method of financing would liquidate the original capital debt, (2) it would pay interest, and (3) the nation's taxpayers would still own and possess through the federal government a going concern with property intact and productive of further net income.

Inasmuch as the nation's taxpayers, though the capital they advanced will have been repaid, will still own the properties, repayment with interest in so short a period compared with the life of the properties may not be fair to this region. It may prove to be wiser to spread repayment over a longer period, and to use that added margin for reductions in TVA wholesale power rates at some future time.

By either of these measures—repayment in thirty years, or repayment in sixty or eighty years plus interest—the power investment stands as a sound proposition.

NAVIGATION AND FLOOD CONTROL

But there is an additional value that attaches to the power facilities of the river not to be overlooked in resource development. For the total investment of $700,000,000 in river development produces not only power, but also the benefits of navigation and flood control. *By combining these three functions in single structures* that serve all three purposes, so that costs common to all three may be shared, great economies were produced. Navigation and flood control benefits have thereby been secured at a lower cost. Similarly, because navigation and flood control are combined in the same structure with power, power is produced more cheaply than if the sole purpose of the structure were power.

Congress directed that TVA set down on its books what appeared to the Board to be the proper portions of the total investment attributable severally to power, to navigation, and to flood control. Of the total river development investment, approximately 65 per cent will be allocated to power, 15 per cent to navigation, and 20 per cent to flood control. (These figures are tentative because not all the projects are completed as of the date of this writing.) These allocations have been made on the basis of elaborate technical studies.

Even if the total investment for power, navigation, and flood control—the entire $700,000,000—were *all* charged against power, revenues from electricity would repay that entire amount, in less than sixty years. This would be grossly unfair to electric consumers in this valley, for Congress has never applied such a policy in the development of other rivers; nor is it a policy that should be followed. I cite the fact merely to show that, regardless of how the capital cost may be allocated, this is a good investment.

The expense of providing navigation and flood control in the fiscal year 1943 was $2,035,000. This figure includes not only the costs of operation but also substantial charges for depreciation. From the beginning of the enterprise to the end of fiscal year 1943 the total net cost of supplying navigation and flood control has been about $10,000,000.

What this expenditure has yielded I have summarized in a preceding chapter. The benefits produced by these expenditures cannot be measured exactly in terms of dollars, of course. A saving of about three and a half million dollars a year already accrues to shippers using the channel; after a reasonable period of development this is expected to reach a total of more than eight million dollars annually. Savings in flood damage in a single year exceed a million dollars. The direct stimulus that this channel and flood protection have provided to the growth of private business has already been shown to be great. While it cannot be proved statistically, there is every reason to believe that the value of the benefits justifies the investment allocable to navigation and flood control, which will be about $250,000,000 and an annual operating cost, including depreciation, of about $3,000,000.

LAND RESTORATION

Leaving the river and turning to the cost of land restoration, TVA's balance sheet shows that in the fiscal year ended June 30, 1943, this program resulted in a net cost of $3,344,000. This includes not only the production of fertilizer but the administration of the demonstration farm activity in the Tennessee Valley and in twenty-one other states of the Union. The expense of mapping, forestry, industrial, and all other kinds of research—in short, the entire development program that I have heretofore summarized—totaled $2,595,000 for the year. These, too, are expenditures that do not yield a return in dollars, but they do yield a return in the building of a region and a nation. During the ten-year period the net expense of TVA's land restoration and all other development work has been $39,800,000; in addition $8,383,000 has been spent on fertilizer plants and equipment, including the phosphate plant at Muscle Shoals and the phosphate ore reserves, which are, of course, capital investments. The total TVA capital expenditure for every purpose whatever to June 30, 1944, was in the neighborhood of $750,000,000.

Are the expenditures for this development worth their cost to the country? There is, of course, no way of settling the question by statistical proof. You must look at the valley, appraise what the expenditure of these funds has done in increasing the productivity of the region and of the nation. You must look at the effect of the growing strength and new vitality of the valley on the total strength of the whole country in war and peace. One has to consider what it is worth to the country to provide opportunity to thousands of men and women in this valley—farmers, businessmen engaged in new enterprises, workers in new factories.

This is not a question that accountants or financial experts can answer for us. Whether the over-all results in this region are worth what they have cost is something the citizen must answer for himself as a matter not of arithmetic but of the highest public policy.

*   *   *

Decentralization

ANTIDOTE FOR REMOTE CONTROL

But it is not wise to direct everything from Washington.
> —PRESIDENT ROOSEVELT, Message to the Congress
> respecting Regional Authorities, June 3, 1937

WHAT I HAVE BEEN DESCRIBING is the way by which in this region we are working toward a decentralized administration of the functions of the central government.

The chief purpose of such methods of decentralization is to provide greater opportunity for a richer, more interesting, and more responsible life for the individual, and to increase his genuine freedom, his sense of his own importance. Centralization in administration promotes remote and absentee control, and thereby increasingly denies to the individual the opportunity to make decisions and to carry those responsibilities by which human personality is nourished and developed.

I find it impossible to comprehend how democracy can be a living reality if people are remote from their government and in their daily lives are not made a part of it, or if the control and direction of making a living—industry, farming, the distribution of goods—is far removed from the stream of life and from the local community.

"Centralization" is no mere technical matter of "management," of "bigness versus smallness." We are dealing here with those deep urgencies of the human spirit which are embodied in the faith we call "democracy." It is precisely here that modern life puts America to one of its most severe tests; it is here that the experience in this valley laboratory in democratic methods takes on unusual meaning.

Congress established the TVA as a national agency, but one confined to a particular region. This provided an opportunity for decentralization. A limited region, its outlines drawn by its natural resources and the cohesion of its human interests, was the unit of federal activity rather than the whole nation.

To the degree that the experiment as administered helps to solve some of the problems raised by the flight of power to the center and the isolation of the citizen from his government, history may mark that down as TVA's most substantial contribution to national well-being and the strengthening of democracy.

TVA's methods are, of course, not the only ones that must be tried. There will be different types and other methods of administration suitable to other problems and different areas. Diversity will always be the mark of decentralized administration, just as surely as uniformity (often for its own sake) is the mark of central and remote control.

Decentralization in action has been anything but an easy task. Its course will never be a smooth one, without setbacks and disappointments. Everywhere, nevertheless, the problem must be faced if we are to conserve and develop the energies and zeal of our citizens, to keep open the channels through which our democracy is constantly invigorated.

THE GROWTH OF CENTRALIZATION

Overcentralization is, of course, no unique characteristic of our own national government. It is the tendency all over the world, in business as well as government. Centralization of power at our national capital is largely the result of efforts to protect citizens from the evils of overcentralization in the industrial and commercial life of the country, a tendency that has been going on for generations. Chain stores have supplanted the corner grocery and the village drug store. In banks and theaters, hotels, and systems of power supply—in every activity of business—local controls have almost disappeared. To be sure, business centralization has brought advantages in lower unit costs and improved services. Except by the village dressmaker, or the owner of the country store or hotel, the advantages of centralization, at the beginning, at least, were gratefully received. People seemed to like a kind of sense of security that came with uniformity.

The paying of the price came later when towns and villages began to take stock. The profits of local commerce had been siphoned off, local enterprise was stifled, and moribund communities awoke to some of the ultimate penalties of remote control. When a major depression struck in 1929, business centralization made us more vulnerable than ever before to the disruption that ensued. Power had gone to the center, decisions were made far from the people whose lives would be affected. Cities and states were powerless to meet the evils that were bred; the federal government had to act. The tendency to centralization in government was quickened.

It was ironic that centralized businesses should become, as they did, eloquent advocates of the merits of decentralization in government. From their central headquarters they began to issue statements and brochures. And a wondrous state of confusion arose in the minds of men: they ate food bought at a store that had its replica in almost every town from coast to coast; they took their ease in standard chairs; they wore suits of identical weave and pattern and shoes identical with those worn all over the country. In the midst of this uniformity they all listened on the radio to the same program at the same time, a program that bewailed the evils of "regimentation," or they read an indignant editorial in their local evening papers (identical with an editorial that same day in a dozen other newspapers of the same chain) urging them to vote for a candidate who said he would bring an end to centralization in government.

THE DUTY OF GOVERNMENT

I am not one who is attracted by that appealing combination of big business and little government. I believe that the federal government must have large grants of power progressively to deal with problems that are national in their consequences and remedy, problems too broad to be handled by local political units. I am convinced, as surely most realistic men must be, that in the future further responsibilities will have to be assumed by the central government to deal with national issues which centralized business inevitably creates. The war has advanced this trend.

The people have a right to demand that their federal government provide them an opportunity to share in the benefits of advances in science and research, the right to demand protection from economic abuses beyond the power of their local political units to control. But they have the further right to insist that the methods of administration used to carry out the very laws enacted for their individual welfare will not atrophy the human resources of their democracy.

It is folly to forget that the same dangers and the same temptations exist whether the centralization is in government or in mammoth business enterprises. In both cases the problem is to capture the advantages that come with such centralized authority as we find we must have, and at the same time to avoid the hazards of overcentralized *administration* of those central powers.

It can be done. It can be done in many business operations as well as in government activities. I have described the way in which the operations of the Tennessee Valley's power system have been brought close to the people of this valley. Certainly that makes clear that no blind fear of bigness underlies my conviction of the necessity for decentralized administration. Here we have centralized only the activities in connection with electric supply which are common to a large integrated area and can best be carried on by a single agency, that is, producing the power and then transmitting it from the dams and stream-electric plants to the gates of communities. But, as I have pointed out, in the Tennessee Valley system the ownership and management of the distribution systems are decentralized. Here, I believe, is one example, among many, of an effective combination of the advantages of the *decentralized administration of centralized authority*.

ADMINISTRATION IN THE FIELD

The distinction between authority and its administration is a vital one. For a long time all of us—administrators, citizens, and politicians—have been confused on this point. We have acted on the assumption that because there was an increasing need for centralized authority, the centralized execution of that authority was likewise inevitable. We have assumed that, as new powers were granted to the government with its seat at Washington, these powers therefore must also be administered from Washington. Out of lethargy and confusion we have taken it for granted that the price of federal action was a top-heavy, cumbersome administration. Clearly this is nonsense. *The problem is to divorce the two ideas of authority and administration of authority.*

Our task is to invent devices of management through which many of the powers of the central government will be administered not by remote control from Washington but in the field.

A national capital almost anywhere is bound to suffer from lack of knowledge of local conditions, of parochial customs. And in a country as vast as the United States, in which local and regional differences are so vital and so precious, many citizens and administrators are coming to see more and more that powers centrally administered from Washington cannot take into account the physical and economic variations within our boundaries. The national strength and culture that flows from that very diversity cannot be nourished by centralized administration.

It has become common observation that in Washington it is too easy to forget, let us say, the centuries of tradition that lie behind the customs of the Spanish-American citizens in New Mexico and how different their problems are from those of the men and women whose lives have been spent in the mountains of the South. It is hard, from a distance, with only memoranda before him, for an administrator to be alive to the fact that the ways of suburban New Jersey are alien to the customs of the coast of eastern Maine. And yet the fact that the ancestors of these people brought dissimilar customs from their homelands, that they have earned their living in different manners, that the climates in which they live are not the same—this is all deeply important when a national program is brought to the men and women in cities and villages and farms for application, when their daily lives are visibly affected. When those differences in customs are not comprehended, statutes seem irrelevant or harsh. They destroy confidence, and disturb rather than promote people's welfare.

Centralization at the national capital or within a business undertaking always glorifies the importance of pieces of paper. This dims the sense of reality. As men and organizations acquire a preoccupation with papers they become less understanding, less perceptive of the reality of those matters with which they should be dealing: particular human problems, particular human beings, actual things in a real America—highways, wheat, barges, drought, floods, backyards, blast furnaces. The reason why there is and always has been so much bureaucratic spirit, such organizational intrigue, so much pathologic personal ambition, so many burning jealousies and vendettas in a capital city (any capital city, not only Washington), is no mystery. The facts with which a highly centralized institution deals tend to be the men and women of that institution itself, and their ideas and ambitions. To maintain perspective and human understanding in the atmosphere of centralization is a task that many able and conscientious people have found well-nigh impossible.

THE HUMAN ELEMENT

Making decisions from papers has a dehumanizing effect. Much of man's inhumanity to man is explained by it. Almost all great observers of mankind have noted it. In *War and Peace* Tolstoy makes it particularly clear. Pierre Bezukhov is standing a captive before one of Napoleon's generals, Marshal Davout.

At the first glance, when Davout had only raised his head from *the papers where human affairs and lives were indicated by numbers,* Pierre was merely a circumstance, and Davout could have shot him without burdening his conscience with an evil deed, but now he saw in him a human being . . .

To see each citizen thus as a "human being" is easy at the grass roots. That is where more of the functions of our federal government should be exercised.

The permanence of democracy indeed demands this. For the cumulative effect of overcentralization of administration in a national capital is greatly to reduce the effectiveness of government. It is serious enough in itself when, because of remoteness and ignorance of local conditions or the slowness of their operation, laws and programs fail of their purposes. We are threatened, however, with an even more disastrous sequence, the loss of the people's confidence, the very foundation of democratic government. Confidence does not flourish in a "government continually at a distance and out of sight," to use the language of Alexander Hamilton, himself a constant advocate of strong central authority. On the other hand, said Hamilton,

the more the operations of the national authority are intermingled in the ordinary exercise of government, the more the citizens are accustomed to meet with it in the common occurrences of their political life, the more it is familiarized to their sight and to their feelings, the further it enters into those objects which touch the most sensible chords and put into motion the most active springs of the human heart, the greater will be the probability that it will conciliate the respect and attachment of the community.

When "the respect and attachment of the community" give place to uneasiness, fears develop that the granting of further powers may be abused. Ridicule of the capriciousness of some government officials takes the place of pride. Democracy cannot thrive long in an atmosphere of scorn or fear. One of two things ultimately happens: either distrustful citizens, their fears often capitalized upon by selfish men, refuse to yield to the national government the powers which it should have in the common interest; or an arrogant central government imposes its will by force. In either case the substance of democracy has perished.

We face a dilemma; there is no reason to conceal its proportions. I do not minimize the complexities and difficulties it presents. We need a strong central government. This is plain to everyone who sees the changed nature of our modern world. But I have deep apprehension for the future unless we learn how many of those central powers can be decentralized in their administration.

The Core of Democracy

Every important administrative decision need not be made in Washington. We must rid ourselves of the notion that a new staff, with every member paid out of the federal treasury, has to administer every detail of each new federal law or regulation. We who believe devoutly in the democratic process should be the first to urge the use of methods that will keep the administration of national functions from becoming so concentrated at the national capital, so distant from the everyday life of ordinary people, as to wither and deaden the average citizen's sense of participation and partnership in government affairs. *For in this citizen participation lies the vitality of a democracy.*

Federal functions can be decentralized in their administration. But it requires a completely changed point of view on the part of citizens and their representatives. For this business of centralization is not wholly the fault of government administrators. Statutes are rarely designed to provide an opportunity for ingenuity in the development of new techniques in administration. Only infrequently do you find a new law which in its terms recognizes the hazards of overcentralization.

Our recent history shows that many public men and editorial writers prefer the privilege of berating administrators as "bureaucrats" to suggesting and supporting ways through which the vices of bureaucracy would have less opportunity to develop. Congress has usually taken the easy course, when new laws are passed, of piling upon the shoulders of an already weary (but rarely unwilling) official the responsibility for supervising a whole new field of federal activity. He has been given a fresh corps of assistants perhaps, but upon his judgment decisions of great detail ultimately rest.

This country is too big for such a pyramiding of responsibilities. In the general atmosphere of bigness, men continue to come about the same size. There is a limit to the energy and wisdom of the best; the ancient lust for power for its own sake burns in the worst.

In the case of TVA, Congress did enact a statute which permitted a decentralized administration. Had not Congress created that opportunity, the TVA could not have developed its administration at the grass roots. An area of manageable proportions—the watershed of a river as its base— was the unit of administration. Decisions could be made and responsibility taken at a point that was close to the problems themselves. That is the test of decentralization.

It is not decentralization to open regional offices or branches in each state, if decisions have to be made in Washington and the officers in the field prove to be merely errand boys. Genuine decentralization means an entirely different point of view in the selecting and training of personnel. It means an emigration of talent to the grass roots. But if the important tasks, the real responsibilities, are kept at the center, men of stature will not go to the "field."

Touchstones of Decentralization

Neither is it decentralization when bureaus or departments are moved out of crowded Washington. It may be necessary and entirely wise—but it is not decentralization. You do not get decentralization as we know it in the TVA unless you meet two tests:

First, do the men in the field have the power of decision?

Second, are the people, their private and their local public institutions, actively participating in the enterprise?

There is generous lip service to decentralization on every hand. But little will be done about it unless there is real understanding of what it means, and an urgent and never ceasing demand from citizens.

When methods such as those the TVA has used are proposed, the chief objection usually made is that local communities, state agencies, or the field officers of federal agencies cannot be trusted to carry out national policies. Usually the reason is dressed up in more tactful language, but, however disguised, it is the doctrine of the élite nevertheless. The burden of proving that the men who at the time are federal officials in Washington are the only ones competent to administer the laws enacted by Congress certainly lies upon those who advance that reason. Actually such statements often prove the desperate hazards of centralization to the health of a democracy, for they exhibit, in the minds of those who put them forward, a low esteem or affectionate contempt for the abilities of anyone outside the capital city, or else a slavish concern for the existing rituals of bureaucracy.

There are of course many instances where the facts appear to support the claim that good administration of national concerns cannot be obtained through the co-operation of local agencies. Local politics, ineptitude, lack of interest and experience in public matters and in administration, brazen partisanship, even corruption—all these stand in the way. I am sure these hazards exist. I am sure, for we have encountered most of them in this valley. But what are the alternatives? Fewer citizens participating in governmental administration. Less and less local community responsibility. More federal employees in the field armed with papers to be filled out and sent to Washington for "processing," because only there is "good administration" possible. The progressive atrophy of citizen interest. An ever wider gulf between local communities and national government, between citizens and their vital public concerns. Such are the alternatives.

The often flabby muscles of community and individual responsibility will never be invigorated unless the muscles are given work to do. They grow strong by use; there is no other way. Although it is true that decentralization at times is ineffective because of the quality of local officials or field officers, the virtues, by comparison, of what can be done in central headquarters are somewhat illusory. For, without the co-operation of citizens (an admittedly difficult goal) and of institutions familiar to them, no detailed and far-reaching economic or social policy and no democratic planning can be made effective. Surely there can be little doubt about the truth of this statement, as I write these words, with our country at war. The daily experience of the average citizen confirms it unanswerably.

THE EVILS OF CENTRALIZATION

The shortcomings of highly centralized administration of national policies are not due simply to the stupidity or wrongheadedness of particular individuals. Naming a scapegoat whenever a mess is uncovered, a favorite editorial and lay custom, is of little help; it usually misses the mark. We need perspective about such things, lest we foolishly take out our anger and frustration for ineptitudes upon this man and that, this party or that, instead of turning our attention where it usually belongs, *viz.,* upon the limitations and dangers of centralization.

These evils are inherent in the overcentralized administration of huge enterprise, because it ignores the nature of man. There is light on this matter in the words of de Tocqueville, writing a century ago of the relatively simple society of the United States.

However enlightened and however skillful a central power may be (he wrote in his *Democracy in America*) it cannot of itself embrace all the details of the existence of a great nation. . . . And when it attempts to create and set in motion so many complicated springs, it must submit to a very imperfect result, or consume itself in bootless efforts. Centralization succeeds more easily, indeed, in subjecting the external actions of men to a certain uniformity . . . and perpetuates a drowsy precision in the conduct of affairs, which is hailed by the heads of the administration as a sign of perfect order . . . in short, it excels more in prevention than in action. Its force deserts it when society is to be disturbed or accelerated in its course; and if once the co-operation of private citizens is necessary to the furtherance of its measures, the secret of its impotence is disclosed. Even while it invokes their assistance, it is on the condition that they shall act exactly as much as the government chooses, and exactly in the manner it appoints. . . . These, however, are not conditions on which the alliance of the human will is to be obtained; its carriage must be free, and its actions responsible, or such is the constitution of man the citizen had rather remain a passive spectator than a dependent actor in schemes with which he is unacquainted.

Out of my experience in this valley I am as acutely aware as anyone could be of the difficulties of securing the active participation of citizens at the grass roots. I know "what a task" (again using the words of de Tocqueville) it is "to persuade men to busy themselves about their own affairs." But our experience here has in it more of encouragement than of despair. For in this valley, in almost every village and town and city, in every rural community, there has proved to be a rich reservoir of citizen talent for public service. The notion that brains, resourcefulness, and capacity for management are a limited commodity in America—and this it is that is behind most of the skepticism about decentralization—is a myth that is disproved in almost every chapter and page of the story of the development of this valley.

Need for Confidence and Co-operation

The fact that TVA was not remote but close at hand has been the most effective way to dissipate the considerable initial suspicion of this enterprise and secure from citizens of every point of view the existing wide measure of warm co-operation. In the case of the power program of the TVA, for example, if TVA were not in the region and of it, if it could not make decisions until Washington, hundreds of miles away, had "processed" the papers and reached a conclusion, only a few of these valley communities, in my opinion, would have signed a contract with the TVA for power supply. Remote control from Washington would not have seemed greatly to be preferred to remote control from a holding company office in New York. And if TVA had not in turn decentralized its own operations the plan would work badly. TVA's division and area managers and other field officials are not merely office boys with imposing titles but no standing or authority. They are selected, trained, given broad responsibility and discretion, and compensated accordingly.

The decentralized administration of federal functions is no infallible panacea. Of course mistakes are made at the grass roots too. But even the mistakes are useful, for they are close at hand where the reasons behind them can be seen and understood. The wise decisions, the successes (and there are many such), are a source of pride and satisfaction to the whole community. If, as I strongly believe, power must be diffused, if it is vital that citizens participate in the programs of their government, if it is important that confidence in our federal government be maintained, then decentralization is essential.

I speak of decentralization as a problem for the United States of America. But the poison of overcentralization is not a threat to us here alone. Decentralized administration is one form of antidote that is effective the world over, for it rests upon human impulses that are universal. Centralization is a threat to the human spirit everywhere, and its control is a concern of all men who love freedom.

IRWIN SHAW

Bury the Dead

*". . . what is this world that
you cling to it?"*

To My Mother

CAST OF CHARACTERS

PRIVATE DRISCOLL
PRIVATE MORGAN
PRIVATE LEVY
PRIVATE WEBSTER
PRIVATE SCHELLING
PRIVATE DEAN
JOAN BURKE
BESS SCHELLING
MARTHA WEBSTER

JULIA BLAKE
KATHERINE DRISCOLL
ELIZABETH DEAN
Generals One, Two and Three.
A Captain, a Sergeant, and four infantrymen,
   employed as a burial detail.
A Priest, a Rabbi, a Doctor.
A Reporter and an Editor.
Two Whores.

TIME

The second year of the war that is to begin tomorrow night.

SCENE

*The stage is in two planes—in the foreground, the bare stage, in the rear,
not too far back, going the entire length of the stage, a platform about seven
feet above the level of the stage proper. No properties are used to adorn the
stage save for some sandbags, whole and split, lying along the edge of the
raised platform and some loose dirt also on the platform. The entire platform is painted dull black. It is lighted by a strong spotlight thrown along
it at hip-height from the right wing. It is the only light on the stage. The
platform is to represent a torn-over battlefield, now quiet, some miles behind the present lines, where a burial detail, standing in a shallow trench
dug in the platform, so that the audience sees them only from the hip up,
are digging a common grave to accommodate six bodies, piled on the right*

Permission of the author.

of the platform, wrapped in canvas. A sergeant stands on the right, on the edge of the grave, smoking. . . . The soldier nearest him, in the shallow trench, stops his digging . . . .

FIRST SOLDIER. Say, Sergeant, they stink . . . . (*Waving his shovel at the corpses*) Let's bury them in a hurry. . . .

SERGEANT. What the hell do you think you'd smell like, after you'd been lyin' out for two days—a goddamn lily of the valley? They'll be buried soon enough. Keep digging.

SECOND SOLDIER. (*Scratching himself.*) Dig and scratch! Dig and scratch! What a war! When you're not diggin' trenches you're diggin' graves. . . .

THIRD SOLDIER. Who's got a cigarette? I'll take opium if nobody's got a cigarette.

SECOND SOLDIER. When you're not diggin' graves you're scratchin' at fleas. By God, there're more fleas in this army than . . .

FIRST SOLDIER. That's what the war's made for—the fleas. Somebody's got to feed 'em. . . .

FOURTH SOLDIER. I used to take a shower every day. Can you imagine?

SERGEANT. All right, Mr. Lifebuoy, we'll put your picture in the *Saturday Evening Post*—in color!

SECOND SOLDIER. When you're not scratching at fleas, you're bein' killed. That's a helluva life for a grown man.

THIRD SOLDIER. Who's got a cigarette? I'll trade my rifle—if I can find it—for a cigarette. For Christ's sake, don't they make cigarettes no more? (*Leaning, melancholy, on his shovel*) This country's goin' to the dogs for real now. . . .

SERGEANT. Lift dirt, soldier. Come on! This ain't no vacation.

THIRD SOLDIER. (*Disregarding him.*) I heard of guys packin' weeds and cow-flop into cigarettes in this man's army. They say it has a tang. (*Reflectively*) Got to try it some day. . . .

SERGEANT. *Hurry up!* (*Blowing on his hands*) I'm freezin' here. I don't want to hang around all night. I can't feel my feet no more. . . .

FOURTH SOLDIER. I ain't felt my feet for two weeks. I ain't had my shoes off in two weeks. (*Leaning on his shovel*) I wonder if the toes're still connected. I wear a 8A shoe. Aristocratic foot, the salesman always said. Funny—going around not even knowin' whether you still got toes or not. . . . It's not hygienic really. . . .

SERGEANT. All right, friend, we'll make sure the next war you're in is run hygienic.

FOURTH SOLDIER. In the Spanish-American War more men died of fever than . . .

FIRST SOLDIER. *(Beating viciously at something in the grave)* Get him! Get him! Kill the bastard!

FOURTH SOLDIER. *(Savagely)* He's coming this way! We've got him cornered!

FIRST SOLDIER. Bash his brains out!

SECOND SOLDIER. You got him with that one! *(All the soldiers in the grave beat at it, yelling demoniacally, triumphantly.)*

SERGEANT. *(Remonstrating)* Come on now, you're wasting time. . . .

FIRST SOLDIER. *(Swinging savagely)* There. That fixed him. The goddamn . . .

FOURTH SOLDIER. *(Sadly)* You'd think the rats'd at least wait until the stiffs were underground.

FIRST SOLDIER. Did you ever see such a fat rat in your whole life? I bet he ate like a horse—this one.

SERGEANT. All right, all right. You're not fightin' the war against rats. Get back to your business.

FIRST SOLDIER. I get a lot more pleasure killin' rats than killin' them. *(Gesture toward the front lines.)*

SERGEANT. Rats got to live, too. They don't know no better.

FIRST SOLDIER. *(Suddenly scooping up rat on his shovel and presenting it to* SERGEANT*)* Here you are, Sergeant. A little token of our regard from Company A.

SERGEANT. Stop the smart stuff! I don't like it.

FIRST SOLDIER. *(Still with rat upheld on shovel)* Ah, Sergeant, I'm disappointed. This rat's a fine pedigreed animal—fed only on the choicest young men the United States's turned out in the last twenty years.

SERGEANT. Come on, wise guy. (FIRST SOLDIER *goes right on.*)

FIRST SOLDIER. Notice the heavy, powerful shoulders to this rat, notice the well-covered flanks, notice the round belly—bank clerks, mechanics, society-leaders, farmers—good feeding—*(Suddenly he throws the rat away)* Ah—I'm gettin' awful tired of this. I didn't enlist in this bloody war to be no bloody grave-digger!

SERGEANT. Tell that to the President. Keep diggin'.

SECOND SOLDIER. Say, this is deep enough. What're we supposed to do—dig right down to hell and deliver them over firsthand?

SERGEANT. A man's entitled to six feet a' dirt over his face. We gotta show respect to the dead. Keep diggin'. . . .

FOURTH SOLDIER. I hope they don't put me too far under when my turn comes. I want to be able to come up and get a smell of air every once in so often.

SERGEANT. Stow the gab, you guys! Keep diggin'. . . .

FIRST SOLDIER. They stink! Bury them!

SERGEANT. All right, Fanny. From now on we'll perfume 'em before we ask you to put them away. Will that please you?

FIRST SOLDIER. I don't like the way they smell, that's all. I don't have to like the way they smell, do I? That ain't in the regulations, is it? A man's got a right to use his nose, ain't he, even though he's in this god-damn army. . . .

SERGEANT. Talk respectful when you talk about the army, you!

FIRST SOLDIER. Oh, the lovely army . . . *(He heaves up clod of dirt.)*

SECOND SOLDIER. Oh, the sweet army . . . *(He heaves up clod of dirt.)*

FIRST SOLDIER. Oh, the scummy, stinking, god-damn army . . . *(He heaves up three shovelfuls in rapid succession.)*

SERGEANT. That's a fine way to talk in the presence of death. . . .

FIRST SOLDIER. We'd talk in blank verse for you, Sergeant, only we ran out of it our third day in the front line. What do you expect, Sergeant, we're just common soldiers . . .

SECOND SOLDIER. Come on. Let's put 'em away. I'm getting blisters big enough to use for balloons here. What's the difference? They'll just be turned up anyway, the next time the artillery wakes up. . . .

SERGEANT. All right! All right! If you're in such a hurry—put 'em in. . . . *(The soldiers nearest the right-hand edge of the grave jump out and start carrying the bodies over, one at each corner of the canvas. The other soldiers, still in the trench, take the bodies from them and carry them over to the other side of the trench, where they lay them down, out of sight of the audience.)*

SERGEANT. Put 'em in neat, there. . . .

FIRST SOLDIER. File 'em away alphabetically, boys. We may want to refer to them, later. The General might want to look up some past cases.

FOURTH SOLDIER. This one's just a kid. I knew him a little. Nice kid. He used to write dirty poems. Funny as hell. He don't even look dead. . . .

FIRST SOLDIER. Bury him! He stinks!

SERGEANT. If you think *you* smell so sweet, yourself, Baby, you oughta wake up. You ain't exactly a perfume-ad, soldier. *(Laughter.)*

THIRD SOLDIER. Chalk one up for the Sergeant.

FIRST SOLDIER. You ain't a combination of roses and wistaria, either, Sergeant, but I can stand you, especially when you don't talk. At least you're alive. There's something about the smell of dead ones that gives me the willies. . . . Come on, let's pile the dirt in on them. . . . *(The* SOLDIERS *scramble out of the grave.)*

SERGEANT. Hold it.

THIRD SOLDIER. What's the matter now? Do we have to do a dance around them?

SERGEANT. We have to wait for chaplains. . . . They gotta say some prayers over them.

FIRST SOLDIER. Oh, for Christ's sake ain't I ever going to get any sleep tonight?

SERGEANT. Don't begrudge a man his prayers, soldier. You'd want 'em, wouldn't you?

FIRST SOLDIER. God, no. I want to sleep peaceful when I go. . . . Well, where are they? Why don't they come? Do we have to stand here all night waiting for those guys to come and talk to God about these fellers?

THIRD SOLDIER. Who's got a cigarette? *(Plaintively.)*

SERGEANT. Attention! Here they are! *(A Roman Catholic priest and a rabbi come in.)*

PRIEST. Is everything ready?

SERGEANT. Yes, Father . . .

FIRST SOLDIER. Make it snappy! I'm awful tired.

PRIEST. God must be served slowly, my son. . . .

FIRST SOLDIER. He's gettin' plenty of service these days—and not so slow, either. He can stand a little rushin'. . . .

SERGEANT. Shut up, soldier.

RABBI. Do you want to hold your services first, Father?

SERGEANT. There ain't no Jewish boys in there. *(Gesture to grave)* Reverend, I don't think we'll need you.

RABBI. I understand one of them is named Levy.

SERGEANT. Yes. But he's no Jew.

RABBI. With that name we won't take any chances. Father, will you be first?

PRIEST. Perhaps we had better wait. There is an Episcopal bishop in this sector. He expressed the desire to conduct a burial service here. He's doing that in all sectors he is visiting. I think we had better wait for him. Episcopal bishops are rather sensitive about order. . . .

RABBI. He's not coming. He's having his supper.

FIRST SOLDIER. What does God do while the bishop has his supper?

SERGEANT. If you don't keep quiet, I'll bring you up on charges.

FIRST SOLDIER. I want to get it over with! Bury them! They stink!

PRIEST. Young man, that is not the way to talk about one of God's creatures. . . .

FIRST SOLDIER. If that's *(Gesture to grave)* one of God's creatures, all I can say is, He's slippin' . . .

PRIEST. Ah, my son, you seem so bitter. . . .

FIRST SOLDIER. For God's sake, stop talking and get this over with. I want to throw dirt over them! I can't stand the smell of them! Sergeant, get 'em to do it fast. They ain't got no right to keep us up all night. We got work to do tomorrow.... Let 'em say their prayers together! God'll be able to understand....

PRIEST. Yes. There is really no need to prolong it. We must think of the living as well as the dead. As he says, Reverend, God will be able to understand.... (*He stands at the head of the grave, chants the Latin prayer for the dead. The* RABBI *goes around to the other end and recites the Hebrew prayer. In the middle of it, a groan is heard, low, but clear. The chants keep on. Another groan is heard.*)

FIRST SOLDIER. (*While the Hebrew and Latin go on*) I heard a groan. (*The* RABBI *and* PRIEST *continue*) I heard a groan!

SERGEANT. Shut up, soldier! (*The Latin and Hebrew go on.*)

FIRST SOLDIER. (*Gets down on one knee by side of grave and listens. Another groan*) Stop it! I heard a groan ...

SERGEANT. What about it? Can you have war without groans? Keep quiet! (*The prayers go on undisturbed. Another groan. The* FIRST SOLDIER, *jumps into the grave.*)

FIRST SOLDIER. It's from here! Hold it! (*Screaming*) Hold it! Stop those god-damned parrots! (*Throws a clod of dirt at end of trench*) Hold it! Somebody down here groaned.... (*A head appears slowly above the trench rim at the left end, a man stands up, slowly facing the rear. All the men sigh—the service goes on.*)

SERGEANT. Oh, my God ...

FIRST SOLDIER. He's alive....

SERGEANT. Why the hell don't they get these things straight? Pull him out!

FIRST SOLDIER. Stop them! (*As the services go on*) Get them out of here! Live men don't need them....

SERGEANT. Please, Father, this has nothing to do with you.... There's been some mistake....

PRIEST. I see. All right, Sergeant. (*He and* RABBI *join, hand in hand, and leave. Nobody notices them. All the men are hypnotically watching the man in the trench, arisen from the dead. The* CORPSE *passes his hand over his eyes. The men sigh—horrible, dry sighs.... Another groan is heard from the left side of trench.*)

FIRST SOLDIER. (*In trench*) There! (*Pointing*) It came from there! I heard it! (*A head, then shoulders appear over the rim of trench at left side. The* SECOND CORPSE *stands up, passes his hands over eyes in same gesture which drew sighs from the men before. There is absolute silence as the men watch the arisen corpses. Then, silently, a corpse rises in the middle of the trench, next to the* FIRST SOLDIER. *The* FIRST SOLDIER *screams, scram-*

*bles out of the trench in rear, and stands, bent over, watching the trench,
middle-rear. There is no sound save the very light rumble of the guns.
One by one the* CORPSES *arise and stand silently in their places, facing the
rear, their backs to the audience. The* SOLDIERS *don't move, scarcely
breathe, as, one by one, the* CORPSES *appear. They stand there, a frozen
tableau. Suddenly, the* SERGEANT *talks.)*

SERGEANT. What do you want?

FIRST CORPSE. Don't bury us.

THIRD SOLDIER. Let's get the hell out of here!

SERGEANT. *(Drawing pistol)* Stay where you are! I'll shoot the first man
that moves.

FIRST CORPSE. Don't bury us. We don't want to be buried.

SERGEANT. Christ! *(To men)* Carry on! *(The men stand still)* Christ! *(The*
SERGEANT *rushes off, calling)* Captain! Captain! Where the hell is the
Captain? *(His voice fades, terror-stricken. The* SOLDIERS *watch the
corpses, then slowly, all together, start to back off.)*

SIXTH CORPSE. Don't go away.

SECOND CORPSE. Stay with us.

THIRD CORPSE. We want to hear the sound of men talking.

SIXTH CORPSE. Don't be afraid of us.

FIRST CORPSE. We're not really different from you. We're dead.

SECOND CORPSE. That's all. . . ?

FOURTH. All—all . . .

FIRST SOLDIER. That's all . . . ?

THIRD CORPSE. Are you afraid of six dead men? You, who've lived with the
dead, the so-many dead, and eaten your bread by their side when there
was no time to bury them and you were hungry?

SECOND CORPSE. Are we different from you? An ounce or so of lead in our
hearts, and none in yours. A small difference between us.

THIRD CORPSE. Tomorrow or the next day, the lead will be yours, too. Talk
as our equals.

FOURTH SOLDIER. It's the kid—the one who wrote the dirty poems.

FIRST CORPSE. Say something to us. Forget the grave, as we would forget
it. . . .

THIRD SOLDIER. Do you—do you want a cigarette? (SERGEANT *re-enters with*
CAPTAIN.)

SERGEANT. I'm not drunk! I'm not crazy, either! They just—got up, all together—and looked at us. . . . Look—look for yourself, Captain! *(The*
CAPTAIN *stands off to one side, looking. The men stand at attention.)*

SERGEANT. See?

CAPTAIN. I see. *(He laughs sadly)* I was expecting it to happen—some day.

So many men each day. It's too bad it had to happen in my company. Gentlemen! At ease! (*The men stand at ease. The* CAPTAIN *leaves. The guns roar suddenly. Fadeout.*)

The spotlight is turned on to the lower stage, right, below the platform on which the action, until now, has taken place. Discovered in its glare are three GENERALS, *around a table. The* CAPTAIN *is standing before them, talking.*

CAPTAIN. I'm only telling the Generals what I saw.

FIRST GENERAL. You're not making this up, Captain?

CAPTAIN. No, General.

SECOND GENERAL. Have you any proof, Captain?

CAPTAIN. The four men in the burial detail and the Sergeant, Sir.

THIRD GENERAL. In time of war, Captain, men see strange things.

CAPTAIN. Yes, General.

SECOND GENERAL. You've been drinking, Captain.

CAPTAIN. Yes, General.

SECOND GENERAL. When a man has been drinking, he is not responsible for what he sees.

CAPTAIN. Yes, General. I am not responsible for what I saw. I am glad of that. I would not like to carry that burden, along with all the others. . . .

FIRST GENERAL. Come, come, Captain, confess now. You were drinking and you walked out into the cold air over a field just lately won and what with the liquor and the air and the flush of victory . . .

CAPTAIN. I told the General what I saw.

SECOND GENERAL. Yes, we heard. We forgive you for it. We don't think any the worse of you for taking a nip. It's only natural. We understand. So take another drink with us now and forget your ghosts. . . .

CAPTAIN. They weren't ghosts. They were men—killed two days, standing in their graves and looking at me.

FIRST GENERAL. Captain, you're becoming trying. . . .

CAPTAIN. I'm sorry, Sir. It was a trying sight. I saw them and what are the Generals going to do about it?

SECOND GENERAL. Forget it! A man is taken for dead and put in a grave. He wakes from his coma and stands up. It happens every day—you've got to expect such things in a war. Take him out and send him to a hospital!

CAPTAIN. Hospitals aren't for dead men. What are the Generals going to do about them?

THIRD GENERAL. Don't stand there croaking, "What are the Generals going to do about them?" Have em examined by a doctor. If they're alive send them to a hospital. If they're dead, bury them! It's very simple.

CAPTAIN. But ...

THIRD GENERAL. No buts, Sir!

CAPTAIN. Yes, Sir.

THIRD GENERAL. Take a doctor down with you, Sir, and a stenographer. Have the doctor dictate official reports. Have them witnessed. And let's hear no more of it.

CAPTAIN. Yes, Sir. Very good, Sir. *(Wheels to go out.)*

SECOND GENERAL. Oh, and Captain ...

CAPTAIN. *(Stopping)* Yes, Sir.

SECOND GENERAL. Stay away from the bottle.

CAPTAIN. Yes, Sir. Is that all, Sir?

SECOND GENERAL. That's all.

CAPTAIN. Yes, Sir. *(The light fades from the* GENERALS. *It follows the* CAPTAIN *as he walks across the stage. The* CAPTAIN *stops, takes out a bottle. Takes two long swigs. Blackout.)*

The guns rumble, growing louder. They have been almost mute during GENERALS' *scene. The light is thrown on the burial scene again, where the* DOCTOR *is seen examining the* CORPSES *in their graves. The* DOCTOR *is armed with a stethoscope and is followed by a soldier stenographer, two of the* SOLDIERS, *impressed as witnesses, and the* CAPTAIN. *The* DOCTOR *is talking, as he passes from the first man.*

DOCTOR. Number one. Evisceration of the lower intestine. Dead forty-eight hours.

STENOGRAPHER. *(Repeating)* Number one. Evisceration of the lower intestine. Dead forty-eight hours. *(To witnesses)* Sign here. *(They sign.)*

DOCTOR. *(On the next man)* Number two. Bullet penetrated the left ventricle. Dead forty-eight hours.

STENOGRAPHER. Number two. Bullet penetrated the left ventricle. Dead forty-eight hours. *(To witnesses)* Sign here. *(They sign.)*

DOCTOR. *(On the next* CORPSE*)* Number three. Bullets penetrated both lungs. Severe hemorrhages. Dead forty-eight hours.

STENOGRAPHER. *(Chanting)* Number three. Bullets penetrated both lungs. Severe hemorrhages. Dead forty-eight hours. Sign here. *(The witnesses sign.)*

DOCTOR. *(On next* CORPSE*)* Number four. Fracture of the skull and avulsion of the cerebellum. Dead forty-eight hours.

STENOGRAPHER. Number four. Fracture of the skull and avulsion of the cerebellum. Dead forty-eight hours. Sign here. *(The witnesses sign.)*

DOCTOR. *(Moving on to next* CORPSE*)* Number five. Destruction of the genito-urinary system by shell-splinters. Death from hemorrhages. Dead forty-eight hours. Ummn. (*Looks curiously at* CORPSE's *face*) Hum . . . (*Moves on.*)

STENOGRAPHER. Number five. Destruction of the genito-urinary system by shell-splinters. Death from hemorrhages. Dead forty-eight hours. Sign here. (*The witnesses sign.*)

DOCTOR. (*On the next* CORPSE) Number six. Destruction of right side of head from supra-orbital ridges through jaw-bone. Hum. You'd be a pretty sight for your mother, you would. Dead forty-eight hours . . .

STENOGRAPHER. Number six. Destruction of right side of head from supra-orbital ridges through jaw-bone. You'd be a pretty sight for your mother you would. Dead forty-eight hours. Sign here.

DOCTOR. What are you doing there?

STENOGRAPHER. That's what you said, Sir. . . .

DOCTOR. I know. Leave out—"You'd be a pretty sight for your mother you would . . ." The Generals wouldn't be interested in that.

STENOGRAPHER. Yes, Sir. Sign here. (*The witnesses sign.*)

DOCTOR. Six, is that all?

CAPTAIN. Yes, Doctor. They're all dead? (*The* FOURTH CORPSE *offers the* THIRD SOLDIER *a cigarette. The* THIRD SOLDIER *hesitates a second before taking it, then accepts it with a half-grin.*)

THIRD SOLDIER. Thanks, Buddy. I—I'm awful sorry—I—Thanks . . . (*He saves cigarette.*)

DOCTOR. (*Eyes on* FOURTH CORPSE *and* THIRD SOLDIER) All dead.

CAPTAIN. A drink, Doctor?

DOCTOR. Yes, thank you. (*He takes the proffered bottle. Drinks long from it. Holds it, puts stethoscope in pocket with other hand. Stands looking at the* CORPSES, *lined up, facing the rear, nods, then takes another long drink. Silently hands bottle to* CAPTAIN, *who looks around him from one* CORPSE *to another, then takes a long drink. Blackout.*)

Spotlight on the GENERALS, *facing the* CAPTAIN *and the* DOCTOR. *The* FIRST GENERAL *has the* DOCTOR's *reports in his hands.*

FIRST GENERAL. Doctor!

DOCTOR. Yes, Sir.

FIRST GENERAL. In your reports here you say that each of these six men is dead.

DOCTOR. Yes, Sir.

FIRST GENERAL. Then I don't see what all the fuss is about, Captain. They're dead—bury them. . . .

CAPTAIN. I am afraid, Sir, that that can't be done. . . . They are standing in their graves. They refuse to be buried.

THIRD GENERAL. Do we have to go into that again? We have the doctor's report. They're dead. Aren't they, Doctor?

DOCTOR. Yes, Sir.

THIRD GENERAL. Then they aren't standing in their graves, refusing to be buried, are they?

DOCTOR. Yes, Sir.

SECOND GENERAL. Doctor, would you know a dead man if you saw one?

DOCTOR. The symptoms are easily recognized.

FIRST GENERAL. You've been drinking, too. . . .

DOCTOR. Yes, Sir.

FIRST GENERAL. The whole damned army is drunk! I want a regulation announced tomorrow morning in all regiments. No more liquor is to be allowed within twenty miles of the front line upon pain of death. Got it?

SECOND GENERAL. Yes, General. But then how'll we get the men to fight?

FIRST GENERAL. Damn the fighting! We can't have stories like this springing up. It's bad for the morale! Did you hear me, Doctor, it's bad for the morale and you ought to be ashamed of yourself!

DOCTOR. Yes, Sir.

THIRD GENERAL. This has gone far enough. If it goes any farther, the men will get wind of it. We have witnessed certificates from a registered surgeon that these men are dead. Bury them! Waste no more time on it. Do you hear me, Captain?

CAPTAIN. Yes, Sir. I'm afraid, Sir, that I must refuse to bury these men.

THIRD GENERAL. That's insubordination, Sir. . . .

CAPTAIN. I'm sorry, Sir. It is not within the line of my military duties to bury men against their will. If the General will only think for a moment he will see that this is impossible. . . .

FIRST GENERAL. The Captain's right. It might get back to Congress. God only knows what *they'd* make of it!

THIRD GENERAL. What are we going to do then?

FIRST GENERAL. Captain, what do you suggest?

CAPTAIN. Stop the war.

CHORUS OF GENERALS. Captain!

FIRST GENERAL. *(With great dignity)* Captain, we beg of you to remember the gravity of the situation. It admits of no levity. Is that the best suggestion you can make, Captain?

CAPTAIN. Yes. But I have another— If the Generals would come down to the grave themselves and attempt to influence these—ah—corpses—to lie down, perhaps that would prove effective. We're seven miles behind the line now and we could screen the roads to protect your arrival. . . .

FIRST GENERAL. *(Coughing)* Umm—uh—usually, of course, that would be—

uh ... We'll see. In the meantime it must be kept quiet! Remember that! Not a word! Nobody must know! God only knows what would happen if people began to suspect we couldn't even get our dead to lie down and be buried! This is the god-damnedest war! They never said anything about this sort of thing at West Point. Remember, not a word, nobody must know, quiet as the grave, *mum! ssssh! (All the* GENERALS *repeat the ssssh after him.)*

The light fades—but the hiss of the GENERALS *hushing each other is still heard as the light falls on another part of the stage proper, where two soldiers are on post in the front lines, behind a barricade of sandbags. The sound of guns is very strong. There are flashes of gun-fire.*

BEVINS. *(A soldier past forty, fat, with a pot-belly and graying hair showing under his helmet)* Did you hear about those guys that won't let themselves be buried, Charley?

CHARLEY. I heard. You never know what's gonna happen next in this lousy war.

BEVINS. What do you think about it, Charley?

CHARLEY. What're they gettin' out of it, that's what I'd like to know. They're just making things harder. I heard all about 'em. They stink! Bury 'em. That's what I say.

BEVINS. I don't know, Charley. I kinda can see what they're aimin' at. Christ, I wouldn't like to be put six foot under now, I wouldn't. What the hell for?

CHARLEY. What's the difference?

BEVINS. There's a difference, all right. It's kinda good, bein' alive. It's kinda nice, bein' on top of the earth and seein' things and hearin' things and smellin' things. . . .

CHARLEY. Yeah, smellin' stiffs that ain't had time to be buried. That sure is sweet.

BEVINS. Yeah, but it's better than havin' the dirt packed onto your face. I guess those guys felt sorta gypped when they started throwin' the dirt in on 'em and just couldn't stand it, dead or no dead.

CHARLEY. They're dead, ain't they? Nobody's puttin' them under while they're alive.

BEVINS. It amounts to the same thing, Charley. They should be alive now. What are they—a parcel of kids? Kids shouldn't be dead, Charley. That's what they musta figured when the dirt started fallin' in on 'em. What the hell are they doin' dead? Did they get anything out of it? Did anybody ask them? Did they want to be standin' there when the lead poured in? They're just kids, or guys with wives and young kids of their own. They wanted to be home readin' a book or teachin' their kid c-a-t spells cat or takin' a woman out into the country in a open car with the wind blowin'. . . . That's the way it musta come to them, when the dirt smacked on their faces, dead or no dead. . . .

CHARLEY. Bury them. That's what I say. . . . *(There is the chatter of a machine gun off in the night.* BEVINS *is hit. He staggers.)*

BEVINS. *(Clutching his throat)* Charley—Charley . . . *(His fingers bring down the top sandbag as he falls. The machine gun chatters again and* CHARLEY *is hit. He staggers.)*

CHARLEY. Oh, my God . . . *(The machine gun chatters again. He falls over* BEVINS. *There is quiet for a moment. Then the eternal artillery again. Blackout.)*

A baby spotlight, white, picks out the FIRST GENERAL, *standing over the prone forms of the two soldiers. He has his fingers to his lips.*

FIRST GENERAL. *(In a hoarse whisper)* Sssh! Keep it quiet! Nobody must know! Not a word! Sssh! *(Blackout.)*

A spotlight picks out another part of the stage—a newspaper office. EDITOR *at his desk,* REPORTER *before him, hat on head.*

REPORTER. That's the story! It's as straight as a rifle-barrel, so help me God.

EDITOR. *(Looking down at manuscript in hand)* This is a freak, all right. I never came across anything like it in all the years I've been putting out a newspaper.

REPORTER. There never was anything like it before. It's somethin' new. Somethin's happening. Somebody's waking up. . . .

EDITOR. It didn't happen.

REPORTER. So help me God, I got it straight. Those guys just stood up in the grave and said, "The hell with it, you can't bury us!" God's honest truth.

EDITOR. *(Picks up telephone)* Get me Macready at the War Department. . . . It's an awfully funny story. . . .

REPORTER. What about it? It's the story of the year—the story of the century—the biggest story of all time—men gettin' up with bullets in their hearts and refusin' to be buried. . . .

EDITOR. Who do they think they are—Jesus Christ?

REPORTER. What's the difference? That's the story! You can't miss it! You goin' to put it in? Lissen—are you goin' to put it in?

EDITOR. Hold it! *(Into telephone)* Macready!

REPORTER. What's he got to do with it?

EDITOR. I'll find out. What are *you* so hot about? . . . Hello? Macready?

Hansen from the New York ... Yeah. ... Listen, Macready, I got this story about the six guys who refuse to be ... Yeah. ...

REPORTER. What does he say?

EDITOR. Okay, Macready. Yeah, if that's the way the Government feels about it. ... Yeah. ...

REPORTER. Well?

EDITOR. (Putting down telephone) No.

REPORTER. Holy god-damn, you got to. People got a right to know.

EDITOR. In time of war, people have a right to know nothing. If we put it in, it'd be censored anyway.

REPORTER. Ah, this is a lousy business. ...

EDITOR. Write another human interest story about the boys at the front. That'll keep you busy. You know ... that one about how the boys in the front-line sing "I Can't Give You Anything but Love," before they go over the top. ...

REPORTER. But I wrote that last week.

EDITOR. It made a great hit. Write it again.

REPORTER. But these guys in the grave, Boss. Lloyds are giving three to one they won't go down. That's a story!

EDITOR. Save it. You can write a book of memoirs twenty years from now. Make that "I Can't Give You Anything but Love" story a thousand words, and make it snappy. The casualty lists run into two pages today and we got to balance them with something. ... (Blackout)

Rumble of guns. The spotlight illuminates the grave on the platform, where the CORPSES *are still standing, hip-deep, facing the rear. The burial squad is there, and the* CAPTAIN, *and the* GENERALS.

CAPTAIN. There they are. What are the Generals going to do about them?

FIRST GENERAL. (Pettishly) I see them. Stop saying "What are the Generals going to do about them?"

SECOND GENERAL. Who do they think they are?

THIRD GENERAL. It's against all regulations.

FIRST GENERAL. Quiet, please, quiet. Let's not have any scenes. ... This must be handled with authority—but tactfully. I'll talk to them! (He goes over to brink of grave) Men! Listen to me! This is a strange situation in which we find ourselves. I have no doubt but that it is giving you as much embarrassment as it is us. ...

SECOND GENERAL. (Confidentially to THIRD GENERAL) The wrong note. He's good on artillery, but when it comes to using his head, he's lost. ... He's been that way ever since I knew him.

FIRST GENERAL. We're all anxious to get this thing over with just as quickly and quietly as possible. I know that you men are with me on this. There's no reason why we can't get together and settle this in jig time. I grant, my friends, that it's unfortunate that you're dead. I'm sure that you'll all listen to reason. Listen, too, to the voice of duty, the voice that sent you here to die bravely for your country. Gentlemen, your country demands of you that you lie down and allow yourselves to be buried. Must our flag fly at half-mast and droop in the wind while you so far forget your duty to the lovely land that bore and nurtured you? I love America, gentlemen, its hills and valleys. If you loved America as I do, you would not . . . *(He breaks down, overcome)* I find it difficult to go on. *(He pauses)* I have studied this matter and come to the conclusion that the best thing for all concerned would be for you men to lie down peaceably in your graves and allow yourselves to be buried. *(He waits. The* CORPSES *do not move.)*

THIRD GENERAL. It didn't work. He's not firm enough. You've got to be firm from the beginning or you're lost.

FIRST GENERAL. Men, perhaps you don't understand. *(To* CORPSES*)* I advise you to allow yourselves to be buried. *(They stand, motionless)* You're dead, men, don't you realize that? You can't be dead and stand there like that. Here . . . here . . . I'll prove it to you! *(He gets out* DOCTOR'S *reports)* Look! A doctor's reports. Witnessed! Witnessed by Privates McGurk and Butler. *(He reads the names)* This ought to show you! *(He waves the reports. He stands on the brink of the grave, middle-rear, glaring at the* CORPSES. *He shouts at them)* You're dead, officially, all of you! I won't mince words! You heard! We're a civilized race, we bury our dead. Lie down! *(The* CORPSES *stand)* Private Driscoll! Private Schelling! Private Morgan! Private Levy! Private Webster! Private Dean! Lie down! As Commander-in-Chief of the Army as appointed by the President of the United States in accordance with the Constitution of the United States, and as your superior officer, I command you to lie down and allow yourselves to be buried. *(They stand, silent and motionless)* Tell me—What is it going to get you, staying above the earth? *(Not a sound from the* CORPSES*)* I asked you a question, men. Answer me! What is it going to get you? If I were dead I wouldn't hesitate to be buried. Answer me . . . what do you want? What is it going to get you . . . *(As they remain silent)* Tell me! Answer me! Why don't you talk? Explain it to me, make me understand . . .

SECOND GENERAL. *(In whisper to* THIRD GENERAL, *as* FIRST GENERAL *glares hopelessly at the* CORPSES.*)* He's licked. It was a mistake—moving him off the artillery.

THIRD GENERAL. They ought to let me handle them. I'd show 'em. You've got to use force.

FIRST GENERAL. *(Bursting out—after walking along entire row of* CORPSES *and back)* Lie down! *(The* CORPSES *stand, immobile. The* GENERAL *rushes out, moaning)* Oh, God, oh, my God . . . *(Blackout.)*

Spotlight, red, picks out two WHORES, *dressed in the uniform of their trade, on a street corner.*

FIRST WHORE. I'd lay 'em, all right. They oughta call me in. I'd lay 'em. There wouldn't be any doubt in anybody's mind after I got through with 'em. Why don't they call me in instead of those Generals? What do Generals know about such things? *(Both* WHORES *go off into fits of wild laughter)* Call the War Department, Mabel, tell 'em we'll come to their rescue at the prevailing rates. *(Laughs wildly again)* We're willing to do our part, like the papers say—share the burden! Oh, my Gawd, I ain't laughed so much . . . *(Laugh again. A* MAN *crosses their path. Still laughing, but professional)* Say, Johnny, Johnny, what'cha doin' tonight? How'd ya like . . . ? *(The* MAN *passes on. The women laugh)* Share the burden—Oh, my Gawd . . . *(They laugh and laugh and laugh, clinging to each other. . . . Blackout. But the laughter goes on.)*

*The spotlight illuminates the grave—*SOLDIERS *of burial detail are sitting around a covered fire.* SECOND SOLDIER *is singing "Swing Low, Sweet Chariot."*

THIRD SOLDIER. This is a funny war. It's rollin' downhill. Everybody's waitin'. Personally, I think it's those guys there that . . . *(He gestures to grave.)*

SERGEANT. Nobody asked you. You're not supposed to talk about it.

FIRST SOLDIER. Regulation 2035a . . .

SERGEANT. Well, I just told ya. *(SECOND SOLDIER starts to sing again.* SERGEANT *breaks in on him)* Say, lissen, think about those guys there. How do you think they feel with you howlin' like this? They got more important things to think about.

SECOND SOLDIER. I won't distract 'em. I got an easy-flowin' voice.

SERGEANT. They don't like it. I can tell.

FIRST SOLDIER. Well, I like to hear him sing. And I'll bet they do, too. I'm gonna ask 'em . . . *(He jumps up.)*

SERGEANT. Now, lissen! *(FIRST SOLDIER slowly approaches the grave. He is embarrassed, a little frightened.)*

FIRST SOLDIER. Say, men, I . . . *(CAPTAIN comes on. FIRST SOLDIER stands at attention.)*

CAPTAIN. Sergeant . . .

SERGEANT. Yes, Sir!

CAPTAIN. You know that none of the men is to talk to *them*. . . .

SERGEANT. Yes, Sir. Only, Sir . . .

CAPTAIN. All right. *(To* FIRST SOLDIER*)* Get back there, please.

FIRST SOLDIER. Yes, Sir! *(He salutes and goes back.)*

SERGEANT. *(Under his breath to* FIRST SOLDIER*)* I warned ya.

FIRST SOLDIER. Shut up! I wanna listen to what's goin' on there! (CAPTAIN *has meanwhile seated himself on the edge of the grave and has brought out a pair of eyeglasses with which he plays as he talks.)*

CAPTAIN. Gentlemen, I have been asked by the Generals to talk to you. My work is not this . . . *(He indicates his uniform)* I am a philosopher, a scientist, my uniform is a pair of eye-glasses, my usual weapons test-tubes and books. At a time like this perhaps we need philosophy, need science. First I must say that your General has ordered you to lie down.

FIRST CORPSE. We used to have a General.

THIRD CORPSE. No more.

FOURTH CORPSE. They sold us.

CAPTAIN. What do you mean—sold you!

FIFTH CORPSE. Sold us for twenty-five yards of bloody mud.

SIXTH CORPSE. A life for four yards of bloody mud.

CAPTAIN. We had to take that hill. General's orders. You're soldiers. You understand.

FIRST CORPSE. We understand now. The real estate operations of Generals are always carried on at boom prices.

SIXTH CORPSE. A life for your yards of bloody mud. Gold is cheaper, and rare jewels, pearls and rubies. . . .

THIRD CORPSE. I fell in the first yard. . . .

SECOND CORPSE. I caught on the wire and hung there while the machine gun stitched me through the middle to it. . . .

FOURTH CORPSE. I was there at the end and thought I had life in my hands for another day, but a shell came and my life dripped into the mud.

SIXTH CORPSE. Ask the General how he'd like to be dead at twenty. *(Calling, as though to the* GENERAL*)* Twenty, General, twenty . . .

CAPTAIN. Other men are dead.

FIRST CORPSE. Too many.

CAPTAIN. Men must die for their country's sake—if not you, then others. This has always been. Men died for Pharaoh and Cæsar and Rome two thousand years ago and more, and went into the earth with their wounds. Why not you . . . ?

FIRST CORPSE. Men, even the men who die for Pharaoh and Cæsar and

Rome, must, in the end, before all hope is gone, discover that a man can die happy and be contentedly buried only when he dies for himself or for a cause that is his own and not Pharaoh's or Cæsar's or Rome's. . . .

CAPTAIN. Still—what is this world, that you cling to it? A speck of dust, a flaw in the skies, a thumb-print on the margin of a page printed in an incomprehensible language. . . .

SECOND CORPSE. It is our home.

THIRD CORPSE. We have been dispossessed by force, but we are reclaiming our home. It is time that mankind claimed its home—this earth—its home. . . .

CAPTAIN. We have no home. We are strangers in the universe and cling, desperate and grimy, to the crust of our world, and if there is a God and this His earth, we must be a terrible sight in His eyes.

FOURTH CORPSE. We are not disturbed by the notion of our appearance in the eyes of God. . . .

CAPTAIN. The earth is an unpleasant place and when you are rid of it you are well rid of it. Man cheats man here and the only sure things are death and despair. Of what use, then, to remain on it once you have the permission to leave?

FIFTH CORPSE. It is the one thing we know.

SIXTH CORPSE. We did not ask permission to leave. Nobody asked us whether we wanted it or not. The Generals pushed us out and closed the door on us. Who are the Generals that they are to close the door on us?

CAPTAIN. The earth, I assure you, is a mean place, insignificantly miserable. . . .

FIRST CORPSE. We must find out for ourselves. That is our right.

CAPTAIN. Man has no rights. . . .

FIRST CORPSE. Man can make rights for himself. It requires only determination and the good-will of ordinary men. We have made ourselves the right to walk this earth, seeing it and judging it for ourselves.

CAPTAIN. There is peace in the grave. . . .

THIRD CORPSE. Peace and the worms and the roots of grass. There is a deeper peace than that which comes with feeding the roots of the grass.

CAPTAIN. (Looks slowly at them, in turn) Yes, gentlemen . . . (Turns away and walks off. FIRST SOLDIER moves slowly up to the grave.)

FIRST SOLDIER. (To the CORPSES) I . . . I'm glad you . . . you didn't . . . I'm glad. Say, is there anything we can do for you?

SERGEANT. Lissen, soldier!

FIRST SOLDIER. (Passionately, harshly) Shut up, Sergeant! (Then very softly and warmly to FIRST CORPSE) Is there anything we can do for you, Friend?

FIRST CORPSE. Yeah. You can sing . . . (There is a pause in which the FIRST

SOLDIER *turns around and looks at the* SECOND SOLDIER, *then back to the* FIRST CORPSE.

Then the silence is broken by the SECOND SOLDIER'S *voice, raised in song. It goes on for a few moments, then fades as the light dims.)*

Colored spotlights pick out three BUSINESS MEN *on different parts of the stage.*

FIRST BUSINESS MAN. Ssh! Keep it quiet!

THIRD BUSINESS MAN. Sink 'em with lead. . . .

SECOND BUSINESS MAN. Bury them! Bury them six feet under!

FIRST BUSINESS MAN. What are we going to do?

SECOND BUSINESS MAN. We must keep up the morale.

THIRD BUSINESS MAN. Lead! Lead! A lot of lead!

SECOND BUSINESS MAN. What do we pay our Generals for?

CHORUS OF BUSINESS MEN. Ssssh! *(Blackout)*

Spotlight on the congregation of a church, kneeling, with a PRIEST *praying over them.*

PRIEST. O Jesus, our God and our Christ, Who has redeemed us with Thy blood on the Cross at Calvary, give us Thy blessing on this holy day, and cause it that our soldiers allow themselves to be buried in peace, and bring victory to our arms, enlisted in Thy Cause and the cause of all righteousness on the field of battle . . . Amen . . . *(Blackout.)*

FIRST GENERAL. *(In purple baby spotlight)* Please, God, keep it quiet . . . *(Spotlight on newspaper office.)*

REPORTER. Well? What are you going to do?

EDITOR. Do I have to do anything?

REPORTER. God damn right you do. . . . They're still standing up. They're going to stand up from now till Doomsday. They're not going to be able to bury soldiers any more. It's in the stars. . . . You got to say something about it. . . .

EDITOR. All right. Put this in. "It is alleged that certain members of an infantry regiment refuse to allow themselves to be buried. . . ."

REPORTER. Well?

EDITOR. That's all.

REPORTER. *(Incredulous)* That's all?

EDITOR. Yes, Christ, isn't that *enough? (Blackout.)*

Spotlight on a radio-loudspeaker. A VOICE, *mellow and beautiful, comes out of it.*

THE VOICE. It has been reported that certain American soldiers, killed on the field of battle, have refused to allow themselves to be buried. Whether this is true or not, the Coast-to-Coast Broadcasting System feels that this must give the American public an idea of the indomitable spirit of the American doughboy in this war. We cannot rest until this war is won —not even our brave dead boys . . . *(Blackout.)*

Guns. Spotlight on FIRST GENERAL *and* CAPTAIN.

FIRST GENERAL. Have you got any suggestions . . . ?

CAPTAIN. I think so. Get their women. . . .

FIRST GENERAL. What good'll their women do?

CAPTAIN. Women are always conservative. It's a conservative notion—this one of lying down and allowing yourself to be buried when you're dead. The women'll fight the General's battle for them—in the best possible way—through their emotions. . . . It's the General's best bet. . . .

FIRST GENERAL. Women— Of course! You've got it there, Captain! Get out their women! Get them in a hurry! We'll have these boys underground in a jiffy. Women! By God, I never thought of it. . . . Send out the call. . . . Women! *(Fadeout.)*

A baby spotlight on the loudspeaker. The VOICE *again, just as mellow, just as persuasive.*

VOICE. We have been asked by the War Department to broadcast an appeal to the women of Privates Driscoll, Schelling, Morgan, Webster, Levy, and Dean, reported dead. The War Department requests that the women of these men present themselves at the War Department Office immediately. It is within their power to do a great service to their country . . . *(Blackout.)*

The spotlight illuminates the FIRST GENERAL, *where he stands, addressing six women.*

FIRST GENERAL. Go to your men . . . talk to them . . . make them see the error of their ways, ladies. You women represent what is dearest in our civilization—the sacred foundations of the home. We are fighting this war to protect the foundations of the homes of America! Those foundations will crumble utterly if these men of yours come back from the dead. I shudder to think of the consequences of such an act. Our entire system will be mortally struck. Our banks will close, our buildings collapse . . . our army will desert the field and leave our fair land open to be overrun by the enemy. Ladies, you are all Gold Star mothers and wives and sweethearts. You want to win this war. I know it. I know the high fire of patriotism that burns in women's breasts. That is why I have called upon you. Ladies, let me make this clear to you. If you do not get your men to lie down and allow themselves to be buried, I fear that our cause is lost. The burden of the war is upon your shoulders now. Wars are not fought with guns and powder alone, ladies. Here is your chance to do your part, a glorious part. . . . You are fighting for your homes, your children, your sisters' lives, your country's honor. You are fighting for religion, for love, for all decent human life. Wars can be fought and won only when the dead are buried and forgotten. How can we forget the dead who refuse to be buried? And we *must* forget them! There is no room in this world for dead men. They will lead only to the bitterest unhappiness—for you, for them, for everybody. Go, ladies, do your duty. Your country waits upon you. . . . *(Blackout.)*

Spotlight immediately illuminates the place where PRIVATE SCHELLING, CORPSE TWO, *is talking to his wife.* MRS. SCHELLING *is a spare, taciturn woman, a farmer's wife, who might be twenty or forty or anything in between.*

BESS SCHELLING. Did it hurt much, John?

SCHELLING. How's the kid, Bess?

BESS. He's fine. He talks now. He weighs twenty-eight pounds. He'll be a big boy. Did it hurt much, John?

SCHELLING. How is the farm? Is it going all right, Bess?

BESS. It's going. The rye was heavy this year. Did it hurt much, John?

SCHELLING. Who did the reapin' for you, Bess?

BESS. Schmidt took care of it—and his boys. Schmidt's too old for the war and his boys are too young. Took 'em nearly two weeks. The wheat's not bad this year. Schmidt's oldest boy expects to be called in a month or two. He practices behind the barn with that old shotgun Schmidt uses for duck.

SCHELLING. The Schmidts were always fools. When the kid grows up, Bess, you make sure you pump some sense into his head. What color's his hair?

BESS. Blond. Like you. . . . What are you going to do, John?

SCHELLING. I would like to see the kid—and the farm—and . . .

BESS. They say you're dead, John. . . .

SCHELLING. I'm dead, all right.

BESS. Then how is it . . . ?

SCHELLING. I don't know. Maybe there's too many of us under the ground now. Maybe the earth can't stand it no more. You got to change crops sometime. What are you doing here, Bess?

BESS. They asked me to get you to let yourself be buried.

SCHELLING. What do you think?

BESS. You're dead, John. . . .

SCHELLING. Well . . . ?

BESS. What's the good . . . ?

SCHELLING. I don't know. Only there's something in me, dead or no dead, that won't let me be buried.

BESS. You were a queer man, John. I never did understand what you were about. But what's the good . . . ?

SCHELLING. Bess, I never talked so that I could get you to understand what I wanted while I—while I—before . . . Maybe now . . . There're a couple of things, Bess, that I ain't had enough of. Easy things, the things you see when you look outa your window at night, after supper, or when you wake up in the mornin'. Things you smell when you step outside the door when summer's on and the sun starts to turn the grass brown. Things you hear when you're busy with the horses or pitchin' the hay and you don't really notice them and yet they come back to you. Things like the fuzz of green over a field in spring where you planted wheat and it's started to come out overnight. Things like lookin' at rows of corn scrapin' in the breeze, tall and green, with the silk flying off the ears in the wind. Things like seeing the sweat come out all over your horse's fat flank and seein' it shine like silk in front of you, smelling horsey and strong. Things like seein' the loam turn back all fat and deep brown on both sides as the plough turns it over so that it gets to be awful hard walkin' behind it. Things like taking a cold drink of water outa the well after you've boiled in the sun all afternoon, and feelin' the water go down and down into you coolin' you off all through from the inside out. . . . Things like seein' a blond kid, all busy and serious, playin' with a dog on the shady side of a house. . . . There ain't nothin' like that down here, Bess. . . .

BESS. Everything has its place, John. Dead men have theirs.

SCHELLING. My place is on the earth, Bess. My business is with the top of the earth, not the under-side. It was a trap that yanked me down. I'm not smart, Bess, and I'm easy trapped—but I can tell now . . . I got some stories to tell the farmers before I'm through—I'm going to tell 'em. . . .

BESS. We could bury you home, John, near the creek—it's cool there and quiet and there's always a breeze in the trees. . . .

SCHELLING. Later, Bess, when I've had my fill of lookin' and smellin' and talkin' . . . . A man should be able to walk into his grave, not be dragged into it. . . .

BESS. How'll I feel—and the kid—with you walkin' around—like—like that . . . ?

SCHELLING. I won't bother you. . . . I won't come near you. . . .

BESS. Even so. Just knowin' . . .

SCHELLING. I can't help it. This is somethin' bigger'n you—bigger'n me
It's somethin' I ain't had nothin' to do with startin'. . . . It's somethin'
that just grew up outa the earth—like—like a weed—a flower. Cut it
down now and it'll jump up in a dozen new places. You can't stop it.
The earth's ready for it. . . .

BESS. You were a good husband, John. For the kid—and me—won't you?

SCHELLING. (*Quietly*) Go home, Bess. *Go home!* (*Blackout.*)

The spotlight picks out CORPSE NUMBER FIVE, PRIVATE LEVY, *where he stands
in the grave, with his back to the audience. His woman, a pert, attractive young lady, is sitting next to him, above him, facing him, talking
to him.*

JOAN. You loved me best, didn't you, Henry—of all of them—all those
women—you loved me the best, didn't you?

LEVY. (FIFTH CORPSE) What's the difference, now?

JOAN. I want to know it.

LEVY. It's not important.

JOAN. It's important to me. I knew about the others, about Doris and that
shifty-eyed Janet. . . . Henry, you're not a live man, are you, Henry?

LEVY. No, I'm all shot away inside.

JOAN. Must wars always be fought in the mud like this? I never expected
it to look like this. It . . . it looks like a dump heap.

LEVY. You've gotten your shoes muddy. They're pretty shoes, Joan.

JOAN. Do you think so, Henry? They're lizard. I like them too. It's so
hard to get a good pair of shoes nowadays.

LEVY. Do you still dance, Joan?

JOAN. Oh, I'm really much better than I used to be. There are so many
dances back home nowadays. Dances for orphan relief and convalescent
hospitals and Victory Loans. I'm busy seven nights a week. I sold
more Victory Loans than any other girl in the League. I got a helmet . . .
one of *their* helmets . . . one with a bullet-hole in it for selling eleven
thousand dollars' worth.

LEVY. Out here we get them for nothing, by the million—bullet-holes and
all.

JOAN. That sounds bitter. You shouldn't sound bitter.

LEVY. I'm sorry.

JOAN. I heard Colonel Elwell the other day. You know Colonel Elwell,
old Anthony Elwell who owns the mill. He made a speech at the
monthly Red Cross banquet and he said that that was the nice thing
about this war, it wasn't being fought bitterly by our boys. He said it was

just patriotism that kept us going. He's a wonderful speaker, Colonel Elwell; I cried and cried. . . .

LEVY. I remember him.

JOAN. Henry, do you think we're going to win the war?

LEVY. What's the difference?

JOAN. Henry! What a way to talk! I don't know what's come over you. Really, I don't. Why, the papers say that if *they* win the war, they'll burn our churches and tear down our museums and . . . and rape our women. (LEVY *laughs*) Why are you laughing, Henry?

LEVY. I'm dead, Joan.

JOAN. Yes. Then why—why don't you let them bury you?

LEVY. There are a lot of reasons. There were a lot of things I loved on this earth. . . .

JOAN. A dead man can't touch a woman.

LEVY. The women, yes—but more than touching them. I got a great joy just from listening to women, hearing them laugh, watching their skirts blow in the wind, noticing the way their breasts bounced up and down inside their dresses when they walked. It had nothing to do with touching them. I liked to hear the sound of their high heels on pavements at night and the tenderness in their voices when they walked past me arm in arm with a young man. You were so lovely, Joan, with your pale hair and long hands.

JOAN. You always liked my hair. (*A pause*) No woman will walk arm in arm with you, Henry Levy, while you cheat the grave.

LEVY. No. But there will be the eyes of women to look at and the bright color of their hair and the soft way they swing their hips when they walk before young men. These are the things that mean life and the earth to me, the joy and the pain. These are the things the earth still owes me, now when I am only thirty. Joy and pain—to each man in his own way, a full seventy years, to be ended by an unhurried fate, not by a colored pin on a General's map. What do I care for the colored pins on a General's map?

JOAN. They are not only pins. They mean more. . . .

LEVY. More? To whom? To the Generals—not to me. To me they are colored pins. It is not a fair bargain—this exchange of my life for a small part of a colored pin. . . .

JOAN. Henry, how can you talk like that? You know why this war is being fought.

LEVY. No. Do you?

JOAN. Of course, everybody knows. We *must* win! We must be prepared to sacrifice our last drop of blood. Anyway, what can you do?

LEVY. Do you remember last summer, Joan? My last leave. We went to Maine. I would like to remember that—the sun and the beach and your soft hands—for a long time.

JOAN. What are you going to do?

LEVY. Walk the world looking at the fine, long-legged girls, seeing in them something deep and true and passionately vital, listening to the sound of their light voices with ears the Generals would have stopped with the grave's solid mud. . . .

JOAN. Henry! Henry! Once you said you loved me. For the love of me, Henry, go into the grave. . . .

LEVY. Poor Joan. (*Stretches out his hand tenderly as if to touch her.*)

JOAN. (*Recoiling*) Don't touch me. (*Pause*) For love of me.

LEVY. Go home, Joan! *Go home!* (*Blackout.*)

The spotlight picks out the THIRD CORPSE, PRIVATE MORGAN, *and* JULIA BLAKE, *he with his back to the audience, standing in the grave, she above and to the right.* JULIA *sobs.*

MORGAN. Stop crying, Julia. What's the sense in crying?

JULIA. No sense. Only I can't stop crying.

MORGAN. You shouldn't have come.

JULIA. They asked me to come. They said you wouldn't let them bury you—dead and all. . . .

MORGAN. Yes.

JULIA. (*Crying*) Why don't they kill me too? I'd let them bury me. I'd be glad to be buried—to get away from all this . . I—I haven't stopped crying for two weeks now. I used to think I was tough. I never cried. Even when I was a kid. It's a wonder where all the tears can come from. Though I guess there's always room for more tears. I thought I was all cried out when I heard about the way they killed Fred. My kid brother. I used to comb his hair in the morning when he went to school . . . I—I . . . Then they killed you. They did, didn't they?

MORGAN. Yes.

JULIA. It's hard to know like this. I—I know, though. It—it makes it harder, this way, with you like this. I could forget easier if you . . . But I wasn't going to say that. I was going to listen to you. Oh, my darling, it's been so rotten. I get drunk. I hate it and I get drunk. I sing out loud and everybody laughs. I was going through your things the other day—I'm crazy . . . I go through all your things three times a week, touching your clothes and reading your books. . . . You have the nicest clothes . . . . There was that quatrain you wrote to me that time you were in

Boston and . . . First I laughed, then I cried, then . . . It's a lovely poem—
you would have been a fine writer. I think you would have been the
greatest writer that ever . . . I . . . Did they shoot your hands away,
darling?

MORGAN. No.

JULIA. That's good. I couldn't bear it if anything happened to your hands.
Was it bad, darling?

MORGAN. Bad enough.

JULIA. But they didn't shoot your hands away. That's something. You
learn how to be grateful for the craziest things nowadays. People have
to be grateful for something and it's so hard, with the war and all. . . .
Oh, darling, I never could think of you dead. Somehow you didn't seem
to be made to be dead. I would feel better if you were buried in a fine
green field and there were funny little flowers jumping up around the
stone that said, "Walter Morgan, Born 1913, Died 1937." I could stop
getting drunk at night and singing out loud so that people laugh at me.
The worst thing is looking at all the books you piled up home that
you didn't read. They wait there, waiting for your hands to come and
open them and . . . Oh, let them bury you, let them bury you . . .
There's nothing left, only crazy people and clothes that'll never be used
hanging in the closets . . . Why not?

MORGAN. There are too many books I haven't read, too many places I
haven't seen, too many memories I haven't kept long enough. . . . I
won't be cheated of them. . . .

JULIA. And me? Darling, me . . . I hate getting drunk. Your name would
look so well on a nice simple chunk of marble in a green field. "Walter
Morgan, Beloved of Julia Blake . . ." With poppies and daisies and
those little purple flowers all around the bottom, and . . . (*She is bent
over, almost wailing. There is the flash of a gun in her hand, and she
totters, falls*) Now they can put my name on the casualty lists, too. . . .
What do they call those purple flowers, darling . . . ? (*Blackout.*)

The spotlight follows KATHERINE DRISCOLL *as she makes her way from*
CORPSE *to* CORPSE *in the grave, looking at their faces. She looks first at*
CORPSE SIX, *shudders, covers her eyes and moves on. She stops
at* CORPSE FIVE.

KATHERINE. I'm Katherine Driscoll. I—I'm looking for my brother. He's
dead. Are you my brother?

FIFTH CORPSE. No. (KATHERINE *goes on to* CORPSE FOUR, *stops, looks, moves
on to* CORPSE THREE.)

KATHERINE. I'm looking for my brother. My name is Katherine Driscoll. His name—

THIRD CORPSE. No. (KATHERINE *goes on, stands irresolutely before* CORPSE TWO.)

KATHERINE. Are you . . . ? (*Realizes it isn't her brother. Goes on to* CORPSE ONE) I'm looking for my brother. My name is Katherine Driscoll. His name—

DRISCOLL. I'm Tom Driscoll.

KATHERINE. Hel—Hello. I don't know you. After fifteen years— And . . .

DRISCOLL. What do you want, Katherine?

KATHERINE. You don't know me either, do you?

DRISCOLL. No.

KATHERINE. It's funny—my coming here to talk to a dead man—to try to get him to do something because once long ago he was my brother. They talked me into it. I don't know how to begin. . . .

DRISCOLL. You'll be wasting your words, Katherine. . . .

KATHERINE. They should have asked someone nearer to you—someone who loved you—only they couldn't find anybody. I was the nearest, they said. . . .

DRISCOLL. That's so. You were the nearest. . . .

KATHERINE. And I fifteen years away. Poor Tom . . . It couldn't have been a sweet life you led these fifteen years.

DRISCOLL. It wasn't.

KATHERINE. You were poor, too?

DRISCOLL. Sometimes I begged for meals. I wasn't lucky. . . .

KATHERINE. And yet you want to go back. Is there no more sense in the dead, Tom, than in the living?

DRISCOLL. Maybe not. Maybe there's no sense in either living or dying, but we can't believe that. I travelled to a lot of places and I saw a lot of things, always from the black side of them, always workin' hard to keep from starvin' and turnin' my collar up to keep the wind out, and they were mean and rotten and sad, but always I saw that they could be better and some day they were going to be better, and that the guys like me who knew that they were rotten and knew that they could be better had to get out and fight to make it that way.

KATHERINE. You're dead. Your fight's over.

DRISCOLL. The fight's never over. I got things to say to people now—to the people who nurse big machines and the people who swing shovels and the people whose babies die with big bellies and rotten bones. I got things to say to the people who leave their lives behind them and pick up guns to fight in somebody else's war. Important things. Big things. Big enough to lift me out of the grave right back onto the earth into the middle of men just because I got the voice to say them. If God could lift Jesus . . .

KATHERINE. Tom! Have you lost religion, too?

DRISCOLL. I got another religion. I got a religion that wants to take heaven out of the clouds and plant it right here on the earth where most of us can get a slice of it. It isn't as pretty a heaven—there aren't any streets of gold and there aren't any angels, and we'd have to worry about sewerage and railroad schedules in it, and we don't guarantee everybody'd love it, but it'd be right here, stuck in the mud of this earth, and there wouldn't be any entrance requirement, like dying to get into it. . . . Dead or alive, I see that, and it won't let me rest. I was the first one to get up in this black grave of ours, because that idea wouldn't let me rest. I pulled the others with me—that's my job, pulling the others . . . They only know what they want—I know how they can get it. . . .

KATHERINE. There's still the edge of arrogance on you.

DRISCOLL. I got heaven in my two hands to give to men. There's reason for arrogance. . . .

KATHERINE. I came to ask you to lie down and let them bury you. It seems foolish now. But . . .

DRISCOLL. It's foolish, Katherine. I didn't get up from the dead to go back to the dead. I'm going to the living now. . . .

KATHERINE. Fifteen years. It's a good thing your mother isn't alive. How can you say good-bye to a dead brother Tom?

DRISCOLL. Wish him an easy grave, Katherine.

KATHERINE. A green and pleasant grave to you, Tom, when finally . . . finally . . . green and pleasant. (*Blackout.*)

The spotlight illuminates PRIVATE DEAN, *the* SIXTH CORPSE, *where he stands with his back to the audience, listening to his mother, a thin, shabby, red-eyed woman of about forty-five, sitting above and to the right, in the full glare of the spotlight.* DEAN *is in shadow.*

MRS. DEAN. Let me see your face, son . . .

DEAN. You don't want to see it, mom . . .

MRS. DEAN. My baby's face. Once, before you . . .

DEAN. You don't want to see it, mom. I know. Didn't they tell you what happened to me?

MRS. DEAN. I asked the doctor. He said a piece of shell hit the side of your head—but even so. . . .

DEAN. Don't ask to see it, mom.

MRS. DEAN. How are you, son? (DEAN *laughs a little—bitterly*) Oh, I forgot.

I asked you that question so many times while you were growing up, Jimmy. Let me see your face, Jimmy—just once. . . .

DEAN. How did Alice take it when she heard . . . ?

MRS. DEAN. She put a gold star in her window. She tells everybody you were going to be married. Is that so?

DEAN. Maybe. I liked Alice.

MRS. DEAN. She came over on your birthday. That was before this—this happened. She brought flowers. Big chrysanthemums. Yellow. A lot of them. We had to put them in two vases. I baked a cake. I don't know why. It's hard to get eggs and fine flour nowadays. My baby, twenty years old . . . Let me see your face, Jimmy, boy. . . .

DEAN. Go home, mom. . . . It's not doing you any good staying here. . . .

MRS. DEAN. I want you to let them bury you, Baby. It's done now and over. It would be better for you that way. . . .

DEAN. There's no better to it, mom—and no worse. It happened that way, that's all.

MRS. DEAN. Let me see your face, Jimmy. You had such a fine face. Like a good baby's. It hurt me when you started to shave. Somehow, I almost forget what you looked like, Baby. I remember what you looked like when you were five, when you were ten—you were chubby and fair and your cheeks felt like little silk cushions when I put my hand on them. But I don't remember how you looked when you went away with that uniform on you and that helmet over your face. . . . Baby, let me see your face, once. . . .

DEAN. Don't ask me . . . You don't want to see. You'll feel worse—forever . . . if you see . . .

MRS. DEAN. I'm not afraid. I can look at my baby's face. Do you think mothers can be frightened by their children's . . .

DEAN. No, mom . . .

MRS. DEAN. Baby, listen to me, I'm your mother. . . . Let them bury you. There's something peaceful and done about a grave. After a while you forget the death and you remember only the life before it. But this way—you never forget. . . . it's a wound walking around forever, without peace. For your sake and mine and your father's . . . Baby . . .

DEAN. I was only twenty, mom. I hadn't done anything. I hadn't seen anything. I never even had a girl. I spent twenty years practising to be a man and then they killed me. Being a kid's no good, mom. You try to get over it as soon as you can. You don't really live while you're a kid. You mark time, waiting. I waited, mom—but then I got cheated. They made a speech and played a trumpet and dressed me in a uniform and then they killed me.

MRS. DEAN. Oh, Baby, Baby, there's no peace this way. Please, let them . . .

DEAN. No, mom . . .

MRS. DEAN. Then once, now, so that I can remember—let me see your face, my baby's face . . .

DEAN. Mom, the shell hit close to me. You don't want to look at a man when a shell hits close to him.

MRS. DEAN. Let me see your face, Jimmy . . .

DEAN. All right, mom . . . Look! (*He turns his face to her. The audience can't see his face, but immediately a spotlight, white and sharp, shoots down from directly above and hits* DEAN's *head.* MRS. DEAN *leans forward, staring. Another spotlight shoots down immediately after from the extreme right, then one from the left, then two more, from above. They hit with the impact of blows and* MRS. DEAN *shudders a little as they come, as though she were watching her son being beaten. There is absolute silence for a moment. Then* MRS. DEAN *starts to moan, low, painfully. The lights remain fixed and* MRS. DEAN's *moans rise to a wail, then to a scream. She leans back, covering her eyes with her hands, screaming. Blackout. The scream persists, fading, like a siren fading in the distance, until it is finally stilled.*)

The spotlight on CORPSE THREE, PRIVATE WEBSTER, *and his wife, a dumpy, sad little woman.*

MARTHA WEBSTER. Say something.

WEBSTER. What do you want me to say?

MARTHA. Something—anything. Only talk. You give me the shivers standing there like that—looking like that. . . .

WEBSTER. Even now—after this—there's nothing that we can talk to each other about.

MARTHA. Don't talk like that. You talked like that enough when you were alive—It's not my fault that you're dead. . . .

WEBSTER. No.

MARTHA. It was bad enough when you were alive—and you didn't talk to me and you looked at me as though I was always in your way.

WEBSTER. Martha, Martha, what's the difference now?

MARTHA. I just wanted to let you know. Now I suppose you're going to come back and sit around and ruin my life altogether?

WEBSTER. No. I'm not going to come back.

MARTHA. Then what . . . ?

WEBSTER. I couldn't explain it to you, Martha. . . .

MARTHA. No! Oh, no—you couldn't explain it to your wife. But you could explain it to that dirty bunch of loafers down at that damned garage of yours and you could explain it to those bums in the saloon on F Street. . . .

WEBSTER. I guess I could. (*Musing*) Things seemed to be clearer when I was talking to the boys while I worked over a job. And I managed to talk so people could get to understand what I meant down at the saloon on F Street. It was nice, standing there of a Saturday night, with a beer in front of you and a man or two that understood your own language next to you, talking—oh, about Babe Ruth or the new oiling system Ford was putting out or the chances of us gettin' into the war. . . .

MARTHA. It's different if you were rich and had a fine beautiful life you wanted to go back to. Then I could understand. But you were poor . . . you always had dirt under your finger nails, you never ate enough, you hated me, your wife, you couldn't stand being in the same room with me. . . . Don't shake your head, I know. Out of your whole life, all you could remember that's good is a beer on Saturday night that you drank in company with a couple of bums. . . .

WEBSTER. That's enough. I didn't think about it then . . . but I guess I was happy those times.

MARTHA. You were happy those times . . . but you weren't happy in your own home! I know, even if you don't say it! Well, I wasn't happy either! Living in three damned rooms that the sun didn't hit five times a year! Watching the roaches make picnics on the walls! Happy!

WEBSTER. I did my best.

MARTHA. Eighteen-fifty a week! Your best! Eighteen-fifty, condensed milk, a two-dollar pair of shoes once a year, five hundred dollars' insurance, chopped meat, God, how I hate chopped meat! Eighteen-fifty, being afraid of everything—of the landlord, the gas company, scared stiff every month that I was goin' to have a baby! Why shouldn't I have a baby? Who says I shouldn't have a baby? Eighteen-fifty, no baby!

WEBSTER. I woulda liked a kid.

MARTHA. Would you? You never said anything.

WEBSTER. It's good to have a kid. A kid's somebody to talk to.

MARTHA. At first . . . In the beginning . . . I thought we'd have a kid some day.

WEBSTER. Yeah, me too. I used to go out on Sundays and watch men wheel their kids through the park.

MARTHA. There were so many things you didn't tell me. Why did you keep quiet?

WEBSTER. I was ashamed to talk to you. I couldn't give you anything.

MARTHA. I'm sorry.

WEBSTER. In the beginning it looked so fine. I used to smile to myself when I walked beside you in the street and other men looked at you.

MARTHA. That was a long time ago.

WEBSTER. A kid would've helped.

MARTHA. No, it wouldn't. Don't fool yourself, Webster. The Clarks downstairs have four and it doesn't help them. Old man Clark comes home drunk every Saturday night and beats 'em with his shaving strap and throws plates at the old lady. Kids don't help the poor. Nothing helps the poor! I'm too smart to have sick, dirty kids on eighteen-fifty. . . .

WEBSTER. That's it. . . .

MARTHA. A house should have a baby. But it should be a clean house with a full icebox. Why shouldn't I have a baby? Other people have babies. Even now, with the war, other people have babies. They don't have to feel their skin curl every time they tear a page off the calendar. They go off to beautiful hospitals in lovely ambulances and have babies between colored sheets! What's there about them that God likes that He makes it so easy for *them* to have babies?

WEBSTER. They're not married to mechanics.

MARTHA. No! It's not eighteen-fifty for them. And now . . . now it's worse. Your twenty dollars a month. You hire yourself out to be killed and I get twenty dollars a month. I wait on line all day to get a loaf of bread. I've forgotten what butter tastes like. I wait on line with the rain soaking through my shoes for a pound of rotten meat once a week. At night I go home. Nobody to talk to, just sitting, watching the bugs, with one little light because the Government's got to save electricity. You had to go off and leave me to that! What's the war to me that I have to sit at night with nobody to talk to? What's the war to you that you had to go off and . . . ?

WEBSTER. That's why I'm standing up now, Martha.

MARTHA. What took you so long, then? Why now? Why not a month ago, a year ago, ten years ago? Why didn't you stand up then? Why wait until you're dead? You live on eighteen-fifty a week, with the roaches, not saying a word, and then when they kill you, you stand up! You fool!

WEBSTER. I didn't see it before.

MARTHA. Just like you! Wait until it's too late! There's plenty for live men to stand up for! All right, stand up! It's about time you talked back. It's about time all you poor miserable eighteen-fifty bastards stood up for themselves and their wives and the children they can't have! Tell 'em *all* to stand up! Tell 'em! *Tell 'em!* (*She shrieks. Blackout.*)

A spotlight picks out the FIRST GENERAL. *He has his hands to his lips.*

FIRST GENERAL. It didn't work. But keep it quiet. For God's sake, keep it quiet.... (*Blackout.*)

A spotlight picks out the newspaper office, the REPORTER *and the* EDITOR.

REPORTER. (*In harsh triumph*) It didn't work! Now, you've got to put it in! I knew it wouldn't work! Smear it over the headlines! It didn't work!

EDITOR. Put it in the headlines.... They won't be buried! (*Blackout—Voices call....*)

VOICE. (NEWSBOY *spotted*) It didn't work! Extra! It didn't work!

VOICE. (*In dark. Hoarse whisper*) It didn't work! They're still standing.... Somebody do something....

VOICE. (*Spotted, a clubwoman type*) Somebody do something....

VOICE. (NEWSBOY *spotted*) Extra! They're still standing....

VOICE. (CLUBWOMAN) Don't let them back into the country....

REPORTER. (*Spotted. Triumphantly.*) They're standing. From now on they'll always stand! You can't bury soldiers any more .... (*Spotted, a group, owners of the next four voices.*)

VOICE. They stink. Bury them!

VOICE. What are we going to do about them?

VOICE. What'll happen to our war? We can't let anything happen to our war....

VOICE. (*A* PRIEST, *facing the three men*) Pray! Pray! God must help us! Down on your knees, all of you and pray with your hearts and your guts and the marrow of your bones....

VOICE. (REPORTER *spotted, facing them all*) It will take more than prayers. What are prayers to a dead man? They're standing! Mankind is standing up and climbing out of its grave.... (*Blackout.*)

VOICE. (*In dark*) Have you heard. ..? It didn't work....

VOICE. (*In dark*) Extra! Extra! It didn't work! They're still standing! (*Spotted,* MRS. DEAN, MRS. SCHELLING, JULIA BLAKE.)

MRS. DEAN. My baby....

MRS. SCHELLING. My husband....

JULIA BLAKE. My lover.... (*Blackout.*)

VOICE. (*In dark*) Bury them! They stink! (*The next set of characters walks through a stationary spotlight.*)

VOICE. (*A* FARMER) Plant a new crop! The old crop has worn out the earth. Plant something besides lives in the old and weary earth....

VOICE. (*A* NEWSBOY, *running*) Extra! It didn't work!

VOICE. (*A* BANKER. *Frantic*) Somebody do something! Dupont's passed a dividend!

VOICE. (*A* PRIEST) The Day of Judgment is at hand. . . .

VOICE. (*The* FIRST WHORE) Where is Christ? (*Blackout.*)

VOICE. (*In dark*) File 'em away in alphabetical order. . . . (*Spotlight on a man in academic robes, reading aloud from behind a table, after he adjusts his glasses.*)

VOICE. We don't believe it. It is against the dictates of science. (*Blackout— Spot on* SECOND GENERAL.)

SECOND GENERAL. Keep it quiet! (MRS. SCHELLING *walks in front of him. The others follow.*)

BESS SCHELLING. My husband. . . . .

JULIA BLAKE. My lover. . . .

MRS. DEAN. My baby. . . . (*Blackout.*)

VOICE. (*A* CHILD) What have they done with my father? (*Spot on* BANKER *at telephone.*)

BANKER. (*Into phone*) Somebody do something. Call up the War Department! Call up Congress! Call up the Roman Catholic Church! Somebody do something!

VOICE. We've got to put them down!

REPORTER. (*Spotted*) Never! Never! Never! You can't put them down. Put one down and ten will spring up like weeds in an old garden. . . . (*Spots at various parts of the stage.*)

VOICE. (*The* THIRD GENERAL) Use lead on them, lead! Lead put 'em down once, lead'll do it again! Lead!

VOICE. Put down the sword and hang the armor on the wall to rust with the years. The killed have arisen.

VOICE. Bury them! Bury the dead!

VOICE. The old demons have come back to possess the earth. We are lost. . . .

VOICE. The dead have arisen, now let the living rise, singing. . . .

VOICE. Do something, for the love of God, do something. . . .

VOICE. Extra! They're still standing.

VOICE. Do something!

VOICE. (*In dark*) We will do something. . . .

VOICE. Who are you?

VOICE. (PRIEST *in spot*) We are the Church and the voice of God. The State has tried its ways, now let the Church use the ways of God. These corpses are possessed by the devil, who plagues the lives of men. The Church will exorcise the devil from these men, according to its ancient rite, and they will lie down in their graves like children to a pleasant sleep, rising no more to trouble the world of living men. The Church which is the Voice of God upon this earth, amen. . . . (*Blackout.*)

CHORUS OF VOICES. Alleluia, alleluia, sing . . . . (*The scream of the bereft mother fades in, reaches its height, then dies off as the holy procession of priests moves solemnly on with bell, book and candle. A* PRIEST *sprinkles the* CORPSES *with holy water, makes the sign of the cross over them and begins in the solemn Latin of the service. At the end he goes into English—his voice rising in ritualistic passion.)*

PRIEST. I exorcise thee, unclean spirit, in the name of Jesus Christ; tremble, O Satan, thou enemy of the faith, thou foe of mankind, who hast brought death into the world, who hast deprived men of life, and hast rebelled against justice, thou seducer of mankind, thou root of evil, thou source of avarice, discord, and envy. (*Silence. Then the* CORPSES *begin to laugh, lightly, horribly. There is a sign from the living men present, and the priestly procession goes off, its bell tinkling. The laughter goes on. Blackout. The* VOICES *again. . . .*)

VOICE. No. . . .

VOICE. NO!

VOICE. It didn't work. . . .

VOICE. We are deserted by God for our evil ways. It is the new flood, without rain. . . .

NEWSBOY. They're licked.

VOICE. This isn't 1918! This is today!

VOICE. See what happens tomorrow!

VOICE. Anything can happen now! Anything!

VOICE. They're coming. We must stop them!

VOICE. We must find ways, find means!

VOICE. (*The* REPORTER, *exulting*) They're coming! There will be no ways, no means!

SEMI-CHORUS. (*Mocking*) What are you going to do?

CHORUS. *What are you going to do?* (*They laugh sardonically.*)

THIRD GENERAL. Let me have a machine gun! Sergeant! A machine gun! (*A bolt of light comes down to a machine gun set to the left of the grave, mid-way between the edge of the grave and the wings. The* GENERALS *are clustered around it.*)

THIRD GENERAL. I'll show them! This is what they've needed!

FIRST GENERAL. All right, all right. Get it over with! Hurry! But keep it quiet!

THIRD GENERAL. I want a crew to man this gun. (*Pointing to* FIRST SOLDIER) You! Come over here! And you! You know what to do. I'll give the command to fire. . . .

FIRST SOLDIER. Not to me, you won't. . . . This is over me. I won't touch that gun. None of us will! We didn't hire out to be no butcher of dead men. Do your own chopping. . . .

THIRD GENERAL. You'll be court-martialed! You'll be dead by tomorrow morning. . . .

FIRST SOLDIER. Be careful, General! I may take a notion to come up like these guys. That's the smartest thing I've seen in this army. I like it. . . . (*To* DRISCOLL) What d'ye say, Buddy?

DRISCOLL. It's about time. . . . (*The* THIRD GENERAL *draws his gun, but the other* GENERALS *hold his arm.*)

FIRST GENERAL. Stop it! It's bad enough as it is! Let him alone! do it yourself! Go ahead, do it!

THIRD GENERAL. (*Whispers*) Oh, my God. . . . (*He looks down at gun, then slowly gets down on one knee behind it. The other* GENERALS *slide out behind him. The* CORPSES *come together in the middle of the grave, all facing the gun.* THIRD GENERAL *fumbles with the gun.* VOICES *call.*)

REPORTER. Never, never, never!

JULIA. Walter Morgan, Beloved of Julia Blake, Born 1913, Died 1937.

MRS. DEAN. Let me see your face, Baby?

MARTHA WEBSTER. All you remember is a glass of beer with a couple of bums on Saturday night.

KATHERINE DRISCOLL. A green and pleasant grave . . .

BESS SCHELLING. Did it hurt much, John? His hair is blond and he weighs twenty-eight pounds.

JOAN. You loved me best, didn't you, Henry? . . . best . . .

VOICE. Four yards of bloody mud . . .

VOICE. I understand how they feel, Charlie. I wouldn't like to be underground . . . now . . .

REPORTER. Never, never!

VOICE. Never!

MARTHA WEBSTER. Tell 'em all to stand up! Tell 'em! *Tell 'em!* (*The* CORPSES *begin to walk toward the left end of the grave, not marching, but walking together, silently. The* THIRD GENERAL *stiffens, then starts to laugh hysterically. As the* CORPSES *reach the edge of the grave and take their first step out, he starts firing, laughing wildly, the gun shaking his shoulders violently. Calmly, in the face of the chattering gun, the* CORPSES *gather on the brink of the grave, then walk soberly, in a little bunch, toward the* THIRD GENERAL. *For a moment they obscure him as they pass him. In that moment the gun stops. There is absolute silence. The* CORPSES *pass on, going off the stage, like men who have leisurely business that must be attended to in the not too pressing future. As they pass the gun, they reveal the* THIRD GENERAL, *slumped forward, still, over the still gun. There is no movement on the stage for a fraction of a second. Then, slowly, the* FOUR SOLDIERS *of the burial detail break ranks. Slowly they walk, exactly as the* CORPSES *have walked, off toward the left, past the* THIRD GENERAL. *The last* SOLDIER, *as he passes the* THIRD GENERAL, *deliberately, but without malice, flicks a cigarette butt at him, then follows the other* SOLDIERS *off the stage. The* THIRD GENERAL *is the last thing we see, huddled over his quiet gun, pointed at the empty grave, as the light dims —in the silence.)*

Curtain

SINCLAIR LEWIS

It Can't Happen Here

Those who have never been on the inside in the Councils of State can never realize that with really high-class Statesmen, their chief quality is not political canniness, but a big, rich overflowing Love for all sorts and conditions of people and for the whole land. That Love and that Patriotism have been my sole guiding principles in Politics. My one ambition is to get all Americans to realize that they are, and must continue to be, the greatest Race on the face of this old Earth, and second, to realize that whatever apparent Differences there may be among us, in wealth, knowledge, skill, ancestry or strength—though, of course, all this does not apply to people who are *racially* different from us—we are all brothers, bound together in the great and wonderful bond of National Unity, for which we should all be very glad. And I think we ought to for this be willing to sacrifice any individual gains at all.

Zero Hour, Berzelius Windrip.

BERZELIUS WINDRIP, of whom in late summer and early autumn of 1936 there were so many published photographs—showing him popping into cars and out of aëroplanes, dedicating bridges, eating corn pone and side-meat with Southerners and clam chowder and bran with Northerners, addressing the American Legion, the Liberty League, the Y.M.H.A., the Young People's Socialist League, the Elks, the Bartenders' and Waiters' Union, the Anti-Saloon League, the Society for the Propagation of the Gospel in Afghanistan—showing him kissing lady centenarians and shaking hands with ladies called Madame, but never the opposite—showing him in Savile Row riding-clothes on Long Island and in overalls and a khaki shirt in the Ozarks—this Buzz Windrip was almost a dwarf, yet with an enormous head, a bloodhound head, of huge ears, pendulous cheeks, mournful eyes. He had a luminous, ungrudging smile which (declared the Washington correspondents)' he turned on and off deliberately, like an electric light, but which could make his ugliness more attractive than the simpers of any pretty man.

His hair was so coarse and black and straight, and worn so long in the back, that it hinted of Indian blood. In the Senate he preferred clothes that suggested the competent insurance salesman, but when farmer constituents were in Washington he appeared in an historic ten-gallon hat with a mussy gray "cutaway" which somehow you erroneously remembered as a black "Prince Albert."

In that costume, he looked like a sawed-off museum model of a medicine-show "doctor," and indeed it was rumored that during one lawschool vacation Buzz Windrip had played the banjo and done card tricks and handed down medicine bottles and managed the shell game for no less scientific an expedition than Old Dr. Alagash's Traveling Laboratory, which specialized in the Choctaw Cancer Cure, the Chinook Consumption Soother, and the Oriental Remedy for Piles and Rheumatism Prepared from a World-old Secret Formula by the Gipsy Princess, Queen Peshawara. The company, ardently assisted by Buzz, killed off quite a number of persons who, but for their confidence in Dr. Alagash's bottles of water, coloring matter, tobacco juice, and raw corn whisky, might have gone early enough to doctors. But since then, Windrip had redeemed himself, no doubt, by ascending from the vulgar fraud of selling bogus medicine, standing in front of a megaphone, to the dignity of selling bogus economics, standing on an indoor platform under mercury-vapor lights in front of a microphone.

He was in stature but a small man, yet remember that so were Napoleon, Lord Beaverbrook, Stephen A. Douglas, Frederick the Great, and the Dr. Goebbels who is privily known throughout Germany as "Wotan's Mickey Mouse."

Doremus Jessup, so inconspicuous an observer, watching Senator Windrip from so humble a Bœotia, could not explain his power of bewitching large audiences. The Senator was vulgar, almost illiterate, a public liar easily detected, and in his "ideas" almost idiotic, while his celebrated piety was that of a traveling salesman for church furniture, and his yet more celebrated humor the sly cynicism of a country store.

Certainly there was nothing exhilarating in the actual words of his speeches, nor anything convincing in his philosophy. His political platforms were only wings of a windmill. Seven years before his present credo

—derived from Lee Sarason, Hitler, Gottfried Feder, Rocco, and probably the revue *Of Thee I Sing*—little Buzz, back home, had advocated nothing more revolutionary than better beef stew in the county poor-farms, and plenty of graft for loyal machine politicians, with jobs for their brothers-in-law, nephews, law partners, and creditors.

Doremus had never heard Windrip during one of his orgasms of oratory, but he had been told by political reporters that under the spell you thought Windrip was Plato, but that on the way home you could not remember anything he had said.

There were two things, they told Doremus, that distinguished this prairie Demosthenes. He was an actor of genius. There was no more overwhelming actor on the stage, in the motion pictures, nor even in the pulpit. He would whirl arms, bang tables, glare from mad eyes, vomit Biblical wrath from a gaping mouth; but he would also coo like a nursing mother, beseech like an aching lover, and in between tricks would coldly and almost contemptuously jab his crowds with figures and facts—figures and facts that were inescapable even when, as often happened, they were entirely incorrect.

But below this surface stagecraft was his uncommon natural ability to be authentically excited by and with his audience, and they by and with him. He could dramatize his assertion that he was neither a Nazi nor a Fascist but a Democrat—a homespun Jeffersonian-Lincolnian-Clevelandian-Wilsonian Democrat—and (sans scenery and costume) make you see him veritably defending the Capitol against barbarian hordes, the while he innocently presented as his own warm-hearted Democratic inventions, every anti-libertarian, anti-Semitic madness of Europe.

Aside from his dramatic glory, Buzz Windrip was a Professional Common Man.

Oh, he was common enough. He had every prejudice and aspiration of every American Common Man. He believed in the desirability and therefore the sanctity of thick buckwheat cakes with adulterated maple syrup, in rubber trays for the ice cubes in his electric refrigerator, in the especial nobility of dogs, all dogs, in the oracles of S. Parkes Cadman, in being chummy with all waitresses at all junction lunch rooms, and in Henry Ford (when he became President, he exulted, maybe he could get Mr. Ford to come to supper at the White House), and the superiority of anyone who possessed a million dollars. He regarded spats, walking sticks, caviar, titles, tea-drinking, poetry not daily syndicated in newspapers and all foreigners, possibly excepting the British, as degenerate.

But he was the Common Man twenty-times-magnified by his oratory, so that while the other Commoners could understand his every purpose, which was exactly the same as their own, they saw him towering among them, and they raised hands to him in worship.

In the greatest of all native American arts (next to the talkies, and those Spirituals in which Negroes express their desire to go to heaven, to St. Louis, or almost any place distant from the romantic old plantations), namely, in the art of Publicity, Lee Sarason was in no way inferior even to such acknowledged masters as Edward Bernays, the late Theodore Roosevelt, Jack Dempsey, and Upton Sinclair.

Sarason had, as it was scientifically called, been "building up" Senator Windrip for seven years before his nomination as President. Where other Senators were encouraged by their secretaries and wives (no potential dictator ought ever to have a visible wife, and none ever has had, except Napoleon) to expand from village back-slapping to noble, rotund, Cice-ronian gestures, Sarason had encouraged Windrip to keep up in the Great World all of the clownishness which (along with considerable legal shrewdness and the endurance to make ten speeches a day) had endeared him to his simple-hearted constituents in his native state.

Windrip danced a hornpipe before an alarmed academic audience when he got his first honorary degree; he kissed Miss Flandreau at the South Dakota beauty contest; he entertained the Senate, or at least the Senate galleries, with detailed accounts of how to catch catfish—from the bait-digging to the ultimate effects of the jug of corn whisky; he challenged the venerable Chief Justice of the Supreme Court to a duel with sling-shots.

Though she was not visible, Windrip did have a wife—Sarason had none, nor was likely to; and Walt Trowbridge was a widower. Buzz's lady stayed back home, raising spinach and chickens and telling the neighbors that she expected to go to Washington *next* year, the while Windrip was informing the press that his "Frau" was so edifyingly de-voted to their two small children and to Bible study that she simply could not be coaxed to come East.

But when it came to assembling a political machine, Windrip had no need of counsel from Lee Sarason.

Where Buzz was, there were the vultures also. His hotel suite, in the cap-ital city of his home state, in Washington, In New York, or in Kansas City, was like—well, Frank Sullivan once suggested that it resembled the office of a tabloid newspaper upon the impossible occasion of Bishop Cannon's setting fire to St. Patrick's Cathedral, kidnaping the Dionne quintuplets, and eloping with Greta Garbo in a stolen tank.

In the "parlor" of any of these suites, Buzz Windrip sat in the middle of the room, a telephone on the floor beside him, and for hours he shrieked at the instrument, "Hello—yuh—speaking," or at the door, "Come in—come in!" and "Sit down 'n' take a load off your feet!" All day, all night till dawn, he would be bellowing, "Tell him he can take his bill and go climb a tree," or "Why certainly, old man—tickled to death to support it—ultility corporations cer'nly been getting a raw deal," and "You tell the Governor I want Kippy elected sheriff and I want the indictment against him quashed and I want it damn quick!" Usually, squatted there cross-legged, he would be wearing a smart belted camel's-hair coat with an atrocious checked cap.

In a fury, as he was at least every quarter hour, he would leap up, peel off the overcoat (showing either a white boiled shirt and clerical black bow, or a canary-yellow silk shirt with a scarlet tie), fling it on the floor, and put in on again with slow dignity, while he bellowed his anger like Jeremiah cursing Jerusalem, or like a sick cow mourning its kidnaped young.

There came to him stockbrokers, labor leaders, distillers, anti-vivisec-tionists, vegetarians, disbarred shyster lawyers, missionaries to China, lob-byists for oil and electricity, advocates of war and of war against war. "Gaw! Every guy in the country with a bad case of the gimmes comes to see me!" he growled to Sarason. He promised to further their causes, to get an appointment to West Point for the nephew who had just lost his job in the creamery. He promised fellow politicians to support their bills if they would support his. He gave interviews upon subsistence farming, backless bathing suits, and the secret strategy of the Ethiopian army. He grinned and knee-patted and back-slapped; and few of his visitors, once they had talked with him, failed to look upon him as their Little Father and to support him forever. . . . The few who did fail, most of them newspapermen, disliked the smell of him more than before they had met him. . . . Even they, by the unusual spiritedness and color of their attacks upon him, kept his name alive in every column. . . . By the time he had been a Senator for one year, his machine was as complete and smooth-running—and as hidden away from ordinary passengers—as the engines of a liner.

On the beds in any of his suites there would, at the same time, repose three top-hats, two clerical hats, a green object with a feather, a brown derby, a taxi-driver's cap, and nine ordinary, Christian brown felts.

Once, within twenty-seven minutes, he talked on the telephone from Chicago to Palo Alto, Washington, Buenos Aires, Wilmette, and Okla-homa City. Once, in half a day, he received sixteen calls from clergymen asking him to condemn the dirty burlesque show, and seven from theat-rical promoters and real-estate owners asking him to praise it. He called the clergymen "Doctor" or "Brother" or both; he called the promoters "Buddy" and "Pal"; he gave equally ringing promises to both; and for both he loyally did nothing whatever.

Normally, he would not have thought of cultivating foreign alliances, though he never doubted that some day, as President, he would be leader of the world orchestra. Lee Sarason insisted that Buzz look into a few international fundamentals, such as the relationship of sterling to the lira, the proper way in which to address a baronet, the chances of the Archduke Otto, the London oyster bars and the brothels near the Boulevard de Sebastopol best to recommend to junketing Representatives.

But the actual cultivation of foreign diplomats resident in Washington he left to Sarason, who entertained them on terrapin and canvasback duck with black-currant jelly, in his apartment that was considerably more tapestried than Buzz's own ostentatiously simple Washington quarters. . . . However, in Sarason's place, a room with a large silk-hung Empire double bed was reserved for Buzz.

It was Sarason who had persuaded Windrip to let him write *Zero Hour*, based on Windrip's own dictated notes, and who had beguiled millions into reading—and even thousands into buying—that Bible of Economic Justice; Sarason who had perceived there was now such a spate of private political weeklies and monthlies that it was a distinction not to publish one; Sarason who had the inspiration for Buzz's emergency radio address at 3 A.M. upon the occasion of the Supreme Court's throttling the N.R.A., in May, 1935. . . . Though not many adherents, including Buzz himself, were quite certain as to whether he was pleased or disappointed; though not many actually heard the broadcast itself, everyone in the country except sheepherders and Professor Albert Einstein heard about it and was impressed.

Yet it was Buzz who all by himself thought of first offending the Duke of York by refusing to appear at the Embassy dinner for him in December, 1935, thus gaining, in all farm kitchens and parsonages and barrooms, a splendid reputation for Homespun Democracy; and of later mollifying His Highness by calling on him with a touching little home bouquet of geraniums (from the hot-house of the Japanese ambassador), which endeared him, if not necessarily to Royalty yet certainly to the D.A.R., the English-Speaking Union, and all motherly hearts who thought the pudgy little bunch of geraniums too sweet for anything.

By the newspapermen Buzz was credited with having insisted on the nomination of Perley Beecroft for vice-president at the Democratic convention, after Doremus Jessup had frenetically ceased listening. Beecroft was a Southern tobacco-planter and storekeeper, an ex-Governor of his state, married to an ex-schoolteacher from Maine who was sufficiently scented with salt spray and potato blossoms to win any Yankee. But it was not his geographical superiority which made Mr. Beecroft the perfect running mate for Buzz Windrip but that he was malaria-yellowed and laxly mustached, where Buzz's horsey face was ruddy and smooth; while Beecroft's oratory had a vacuity, a profundity of slowly enunciated nonsense, which beguiled such solemn deacons as were irritated by Buzz's cataract of slang.

Nor could Sarason ever have convinced the wealthy that the more Buzz denounced them and promised to distribute their millions to the poor, the more they could trust his "common sense" and finance his campaign. But with a hint, a grin, a wink, a handshake, Buzz could convince them, and their contributions came in by the hundred thousand, often disguised as assessments on imaginary business partnerships.

It had been the peculiar genius of Berzelius Windrip not to wait until he should be nominated for this office or that to begin shanghaiing his band of buccaneers. He had been coaxing in supporters ever since the day when, at the age of four, he had captivated a neighborhood comrade by giving him an ammonia pistol which later he thriftily stole back from the comrade's pocket. Buzz might not have learned, perhaps could not have learned, much from sociologists Charles Beard and John Dewey, but they could have learned a great deal from Buzz.

And it was Buzz's, not Sarason's, master stroke that, as warmly as he advocated everyone's getting rich by just voting to be rich, he denounced all "Fascism" and "Naziism," so that most of the Republicans who were afraid of Democratic Fascism, and all the Democrats who were afraid of Republican Fascism, were ready to vote for him.

CARL SANDBURG

The People, Yes

87

THE PEOPLE learn, unlearn, learn,
a builder, a wrecker, a builder again,
a juggler of shifting puppets.
    In so few eyeblinks
    In transition lightning streaks,
the people protect midgets into giants,
the people shrink titans into dwarfs.

    Faiths blow on the winds
    and become shibboleths
    and deep growths
    with men ready to die
for a living word on the tongue,
for a light alive in the bones,
for dreams fluttering in the wrists.

For liberty and authority they die
though one is fire and the other water
and the balances of freedom and discipline
are a moving target with changing decoys.

Revolt and terror pay a price.
Order and law have a cost.
What is this double use of fire and water?
Where are the rulers who know this riddle?
On the fingers of one hand you can number them.
How often has a governor of the people first learned to govern himself?
The free man willing to pay and struggle and die for the freedom for him-
    self and others
Knowing how far to subject himself to discipline and obedience for the

sake of an ordered society free from tyrants, exploiters and legalized frauds—
This free man is a rare bird and when you meet him take a good look at
him and try to figure him out because
Some day when the United States of the Earth gets going and runs smooth
and pretty there will be more of him than we have now.

107

The people will live on.
The learning and blundering people will live on.
They will be tricked and sold and again sold
And go back to the nourishing earth for rootholds,
The people so peculiar in renewal and comeback,
You can't laugh off their capacity to take it.
The mammoth rests between his cyclonic dramas.

The people so often sleepy, weary, enigmatic,
is a vast huddle with many units saying:
"I earn my living.
I make enough to get by
and it takes all my time.
If I had more time
I could do more for myself
and maybe for others.
I could read and study
and talk things over
and find out about things.
It takes time.
I wish I had the time."

The people is a tragic and comic two-face:
hero and hoodlum: phantom and gorilla twisting to moan with a gargoyle mouth: "They
buy me and sell me . . . it's a game . . .
sometime I'll break loose . . ."

Once having marched
Over the margins of animal necessity,
Over the grim line of sheer subsistence
Then man came
To the deeper rituals of his bones,

To the lights lighter than any bones,
To the time for thinking things over,
To the dance, the song, the story,
Or the hours given over to dreaming,
    Once having so marched.

Between the finite limitations of the five senses
and the endless yearnings of man for the beyond
the people hold the humdrum bidding of work and food
while reaching out when it comes their way
for lights beyond the prison of the five senses,
for keepsakes lasting beyond any hunger or death.
    This reaching is alive.
The panderers and liars have violated and smutted it.
    Yet this reaching is alive yet
    for lights and keepsakes.

The people know the salt of the sea
and the strength of the winds
lashing the corners of the earth.
The people take the earth
as a tomb of rest and a cradle of hope.
Who else speaks for the Family of Man?
They are in tune and step
with constellations of universal law.

The people is a polychrome,
a spectrum and a prism
held in a moving monolith,
a console organ of changing themes,
a clavilux of color poems
wherein the sea offers fog
and the fog moves off in rain
and the labrador sunset shortens
to a nocturne of clear stars
serene over the shot spray
of northern lights.

The steel mill sky is alive.
The fire breaks white and zigzag
shot on a gun-metal gloaming.

Man is a long time coming.
Man will yet win.
Brother may yet line up with brother:

This old anvil laughs at many broken hammers.
There are men who can't be bought.
The fireborn are at home in fire.
The stars make no noise.
You can't hinder the wind from blowing.
Time is a great teacher.
Who can live without hope.

In the darkness with a great bundle of grief the people march.
In the night, and overhead a shovel of stars for keeps, the people march:
                              "Where to? what next?"

"I SEE a great nation, upon a great continent, blessed with a great wealth of natural resources. Its hundred and thirty million people are at peace among themselves; they are making their country a good neighbor among the nations. I see a United States which can demonstrate that, under democratic methods of government, national wealth can be translated into a spreading volume of human comforts hitherto unknown, and the lowest standard of living can be raised far above the level of mere subsistence.

But here is the challenge to our democracy: In this nation I see tens of millions of its citizens—a substantial part of its whole population—who at this very moment are denied the greater part of what the very lowest standards of today call the necessities of life.

I see millions of families trying to live on incomes so meager that the pall of family disaster hangs over them day by day.

I see millions whose daily lives in city and on farm continue under conditions labeled indecent by a so-called polite society half a century ago.

I see millions denied education, recreation, and the opportunity to better their lot and the lot of their children.

I see millions lacking the means to buy the products of farm and factory and by their poverty denying work and productiveness to many other millions.

I see one-third of a nation ill-housed, ill-clad, ill-nourished.

(Second Inaugural Address, January 20, 1937)

Mr. Roosevelt's second administration began triumphantly enough, but bad days were ahead. The inexplicable myopia of the democratic powers, who lost their first battle in Spain, made war in Europe virtually a certainty. And few Americans could be so sanguine as to imagine their nation long abstaining from a war between Great Britain and Nazi Germany. Jay Franklin looks back, from that curious island in time which was the United States in 1940, to those crucial years 1937 and 1938. And Thurman Arnold coolly and ironically exposes our folklore in that period as if he were discussing Trobriand Islanders or Kwakiutls. The Thirties had seen the advent of such demagogues as Father Charles E. Coughlin, Gerald L. K. Smith, and the late Huey Long, who made a dubious but vivid impression on American life, arousing the amused interest of even so cynical a connoisseur of rabble-rousers as H. L. Mencken, and moving James Far rell to set down the type in the character of Father Moylan, the inspirer of Tommy Gallagher's crusade. America could produce its own Fascists, it realized a little ruefully; but Richard Boyer learned one night in York-ville that Adolf Hitler was prepared to furnish not only the inspiration and the model, but also the leaders of American Fascism.

JAY FRANKLIN

Democratic Suicide (1937-1938)

✖

MR. ROOSEVELT had his mandate. His effort to give the American people the reforms for which they had voted was blocked by the slow suicide of the Democratic Party during the next two years.

The three things which chiefly thwarted this "Third New Deal" were: the world-wide trend away from government by consent and toward government by force; an economic depression of which the poor suffered the major effects; and the division of the New Deal—which resulted in a loss of headway for the people's program and ended in cruel disillusion at the polls in 1938.

Early in March of 1936, I had left Tugwell's office in order to return to political journalism. After the 1936 election and the tremendous authority it gave to Mr. Roosevelt, I set to work to interpret what was happening, on the basis of my knowledge of the men and measures of the New Deal high command. It was an exciting period for a political reporter.

The events of these two years of increasing New Deal frustration and failure cannot be understood apart from what was happening in the rest of the world. Americans like to imagine that they make their political decisions in a continental vacuum, but this has never been true and, in an age of speedy and even instantaneous communication, it was impossible that the New Deal should escape the political influence of events abroad. The Franco rebellion against the Spanish Republic was swiftly unveiled as an Italo-German filibustering expedition, designed to bring pressure against France and England, with the moral support of large sections of the Catholic hierarchy. In France, the Popular Front government of

From *1940* by Jay Franklin. Copyright, 1940, by John Franklin Carter. By permission of The Viking Press, Inc., New York.

Léon Blum was gradually driven from power by its own inhibitions and by British diplomatic pressure. Spain was overrun and conquered by the rebels, while English policy veered more and more sharply to support of the revisionist claims of Italy and Germany. Japan embarked upon the conquest of the Chinese Republic. Soviet Russia became increasingly isolationist in sentiment and relaxed intervention in Spain and in China. Germany was permitted to annex Austria, under rather abrupt circumstances, and then proceeded to partition, dominate, and finally annex Czecho-Slovakia, with the full consent of Paris and London. By the time our midterm elections rolled around, the democratic nations, which had seemed to be firmly in the saddle in 1936, were everywhere on the defensive, while the United States was forced to consider the first major threat to the Monroe Doctrine since it was announced in 1823. The disillusion was world-wide and it affected Mr. Roosevelt's followers no less than it did Chiang Kai-shek's armies before Hankow or the Spanish Loyalists along the Ebro. In assigning historical causes for the Roosevelt reverses of this period it seems to me impossible to escape the conviction that much of the responsibility lay with the sense of moral let-down, if not of hopelessness, which discouraged the believers in popular sovereignty throughout the world.

For the purposes of an American election, the economic depression of 1937-38 alone had assured Mr. Roosevelt's party of serious losses. As early as December 1936, Leon Henderson of the WPA called to my attention the uneconomic price-raising by leading American manufacturers. This, he told me, would insure a business depression within six or eight months. Henderson kept hammering on this theme all through the winter and by the spring of 1937 he had sufficiently impressed the Administration to induce Mr. Roosevelt to make a statement that certain prices—especially of copper—were too high. This warning was greeted with hoots of derision by the Tories, and the President himself seems promptly to have forgotten it and to have ignored the economics of his spending program.

By August of 1937, the Government was, for the first time since the depression, taking in more money in taxes than it was laying out. Profiteering had become so outrageous and so general that buying-strikes had developed, yet in early September I was told at Hyde Park that what was checking national reform was the general condition of prosperity, a condition which the Administration apparently regarded as both wide and deep, though I argued that it was obviously neither. In spite of storm-signals and slumps in the Stock Market, Henry Morgenthau was allowed to commit the Government to a program of retrenchment and budget-balancing at a moment when the sharpest business recession ever recorded overtook the country. Industrial purchasing was curtailed on a scale which tempted many New Dealers to suspect the existence of an organized sit-down strike by capital. Men were sent onto relief and WPA by millions, catching many political agencies—including the Government—quite unprepared and making a mockery of the proud New Deal claim of prosperity through planning.

By the spring of 1938, Louis Bean, the crack statistician of the Department of Agriculture, worked out, on the basis of the business figures and the voting record in previous periods of depression, an estimated gain of eighty seats by the Republicans in the coming elections. His estimate came far closer to the actual result than did the predictions of the political experts. In addition to the industrial shut-down, the farmers were cursed with abundant harvests. The New Deal's wheat control plan was not yet in effect, owing to deliberate Congressional sabotage; the foreign markets for wheat and other farm products had dwindled; and the industrial payrolls had fallen so as to reduce domestic demand. Low farm prices plus industrial unemployment led to political revolt. When all was said and done, however, the real fault lay with failure of the Government—including Congress and the courts—to adopt a sound economic and social program. Large-scale spending and lending had been useful in 1933 but could not serve indefinitely without a greater degree of control over industrial policies and agricultural production, without a tax program which would prevent uneconomic concentration of idle capital, and without a wider distribution of social income to labor and other disadvantaged groups of producers and consumers. Between reactionary court decisions, Congressional balkiness, and confused Administration policies, little had been accomplished along those lines. The rich continued to get richer and to regard their taxes as the Great Whore of Babylon, while the poor suffered and starved in a land of abundance. The technological chickens were coming home to roost and were making a mess of the New Deal's neatly scheduled plans for progressive and gradual (oh! how gradual!) reform. So, where Mr. Roosevelt was the beneficiary of the discontented vote in 1932, his party suffered from national discontent six years later—and rightly so. For the attempt to substitute watered-down "social justice" for economic reform had not only left empty pockets still empty but had given rise to resentment against unsubstantial social doctrines.

For this condition, Mr. Roosevelt's party was clearly responsible. It had thrice received a popular mandate by grace of the large independent vote which decides American elections. Now the party itself disintegrated. The chief elements in its strength were the Catholics, the labor unions, and the middle economic and professional classes. These, plus the Old Guard machine politicians, made for New Deal victories. Vatican approval and hierarchical backing for the anti-democratic Franco rebellion in Spain divided and confused Catholic sentiment in America. Father Coughlin was openly in opposition, having sponsored an ineffective third-party movement in the '36 campaign. Transmontane influences among the clergy on the Eastern seaboard were encouraging American Catholics to look with suspicion and hostility on Jews and Marxists, and were breaking up the Jewish-Catholic solidarity which had been forged by the 1928 Bigotry Campaign and kept alive by the initial moves of the Hitler Revolution. Arguments over the bombing of Guernica, the burning of churches, "Communism," and dogma were depriving the New Deal of the driving power of the Catholic liberalism of the Great Encyclicals. Of the four American Cardinals, only one—Mundelein of Chicago—remained as a visible symbol of the moral forces on which Mr. Roosevelt had relied to make reform effective. In 1932, I had inquired at the Vatican whether the Church was prepared to sacrifice her American wealth in the interest of social justice. The answer had then been "Yes." By 1938, however, a cleavage had developed between the wealthier Catholics of the East and their poorer coreligionists west of the Alleghenies. Here again—as in 1803 and 1914—the power of European politics to disrupt American democracy was made evident.

No such excuse justified the split in the ranks of labor. Both the American Federation of Labor and the group of industrial unions organized by John L. Lewis into the CIO had supported Mr. Roosevelt in 1936. With the beginning of 1937, the CIO began to make tremendous headway in organizing the automobile and steel workers through the newly devised sit-down strike technique. This technique—being simple and effective—alarmed the farming and the professional classes, which had never felt more than a sentimental identity with the interests of industrial labor. The A. F. of L., led by William Green, John P. Frey, and other conservatives, shifted into angry and even violent opposition to the Lewis movement. From jealousy, from fear, and from an educated sense of bread-and-butter values, the Federation hastened, without shame, to ingratiate itself with the conservative business interests and with the Republican opposition, and took the extreme step in 1937 of delaying Federal legislation for minimum wages and maximum hours in industry, and two years later opposed Federal relief and undertook strikes in the WPA.

All through 1937, the CIO sit-down and other organizing methods registered wide gains, at the cost of reducing much of industrial America to condition approaching civil war. By 1938, the rivalry of the A. F. of L. and CIO had produced a kind of gang-warfare between the two groups, espcially on the West Coast, and led to a complete breach in the political and economic unity of organized labor. This was a double disaster for the New Deal. It not only robbed Mr. Roosevelt's party of its strongest voting battalions (Mr. Green openly gloated over the defeat of CIO-endorsed candidates who were friendly to labor, by avowed reactionaries); it also alienated many sections of America—particularly in the West and South —where labor organization was akin to social revolution and where the nice-minded idealistic middle-class groups were shocked by the spectacle of a real change in social relationships.

These latter groups were actually lost from the moment that Mr. Roosevelt sought to give reality to his 1936 mandate by a program of realistic reforms. These reforms included a proposal to bring the courts, including the Supreme Court, into tune with the twentieth century by enlarging the judicial personnel; a plan to control major farm crops by a system of acreage limitation; a plan to increase social income by a Federal Wages and Hours Law; taxes on the corporate surpluses of large-scale economic enterprises, in order to force a distribution of income and earnings; and a long-overdue set of well-considered proposals to reorganize the executive agencies of the Federal Government.

As early as the Democratic National Convention at Philadelphia in 1936, party leaders had known that the Third New Deal must embody such proposals, and conservative Democrats, inspired by Vice-President Garner, had laid plans to block the program. By the beginning of 1937, it was only a question of whether they or the President would strike first. The issue was touched off by an article in *The Saturday Evening Post* by Dr. Stanley High, entitled "Whose Party Is It?" I had seen Dr. High during the '36 campaign when, as head of the Good Neighbor League, he stood high in the confidence of the White House and had assumed that he would be suitably rewarded. Unfortunately, the President was unwilling to give this idealist what he really wanted and so he shot boldly into opposition. His article was the opening gun of a two-year fight to make an honest woman of the Democratic Party. Early in 1936, the conservative Democrats had forced the President to turn much of the Federal patronage over to them, and in September, when even a babe knew that Landon was licked, they had gone solemnly to Hyde Park and begged Roosevelt to fight, lest all be lost! On the publication of Dr. High's article, they went to the White House and demanded a showdown.

They got it, in the form of proposals to reform the Supreme Court, proposals which served as a touchstone to divide those who really wanted to do something to improve American conditions from the stand-pat politicians who saw no need to hurry or worry. The Court proposals were, paradoxically, the work of a conservative group in the Administration and were correspondingly insincere and slovenly. They were promptly utilized by the conservatives of both parties as a means to filibuster against the entire New Deal reform program. The Crop Control Law was delayed until the beginning of 1938, the Wages and Hours Law was not passed until the spring of 1938, the tax program was emasculated by Senator Pat Harrison of Mississippi. The Reorganization Bill was the center of one of the fiercest parliamentary and propagandist struggles of our history, and was finally betrayed in the House of Representatives by John J. O'Connor, brother of the President's former law partner. The Court battle ended in the death of Joe Robinson, Mr. Roosevelt's sole loyal ally among the leading Senatorial conservatives, and the appointment of the liberal Hugo L. Black of Alabama to the Supreme Court.

Nearly every Presidential promise was manhandled or betrayed by the President's supposed followers. The Southern Democrats—and their conservative Northern allies—were fighting for control of what they foolishly imagined to be an unbeatable party organization. Mr. Roosevelt was forced by the expensive method of trial-and-error to discover whom he could trust among men who had been elected on a platform of loyalty to himself. The sheep were few in number and were themselves exposed to relentless partisan malice. Hugo Black was accused of Klan bigotry by some of the very men who were opposing an anti-lynching bill. Jimmy Roosevelt, the President's son, was libeled in magazine articles. Tom Corcoran and Ben Cohen were spotlighted as "amateur Machiavellis." At one critical moment in the fight for the Reorganization Bill, two relatively unimportant men, neither of whom was connected with the Government at all, found themselves in sole command of the New Deal forces. It was a slaughter.

The battle for public opinion was almost as one-sided. Conservative columnists like Walter Lippmann, Mark Sullivan, David Lawrence, Dorothy Thompson, Hugh Johnson, and Westbrook Pegler blanketed the Tory press. On the liberal side were Heywood Broun, the late Rodney Dutcher, Mrs. Roosevelt, Allen and Pearson, and myself. It was worse on the radio, where national hook-ups were made available to Miss Thompson, General Johnson, Fulton Lewis, Boake Carter, Cameron of Ford Motor Company fame, for regular blasts against reform. It was not until midsummer of 1938 that the National Broadcasting Company put me on the air in a series of talks on "The State of the Nation," while during the real battle the only people who could reach the microphone for the Administration were avowed partisans like Lewis Schwellenbach and Sherman Minton or Cabinet officers. During the '36 campaign, 80 percent of the press had been hostile to Roosevelt; by 1938, the proportion had risen to over 95 percent, while every major national magazine was against the New Deal policies. The wealthy property interests were mobilized against the President, and a public which had responded in 1932 to the rather simple idea that nobody must starve in wealthy America, applauded one candidate who said that what he would do for the unemployed was to put a chicken dinner at the top of a flagpole and then grease the pole!

Finally, President Roosevelt—blocked in Congress by the members of his own party, many of whom owed their elections directly to his popularity—tried to undo in five months what he had done to build up their individual political power over the previous five years. He tried to purge his unbeatable party of the men who had embezzled the election returns. It was too late. By the aid of New Deal patronage, his enemies had cemented their grip on State and local Democratic machinery. The primary campaigns of 1938 were a dismal commentary on the New Deal's lack of foresight. The President's friend, Senator Barkley of Kentucky, was renominated and re-elected, as was Senator Thomas of Oklahoma. Roosevelt endorsed Bulkley in Ohio, who won the primary and lost the election. He endorsed McAdoo in California, who rightly lost the primary. He opposed George in Georgia, Smith in South Carolina, and Tydings in Maryland, all of whom were renominated and therefore re-elected. He opposed John J. O'Connor in New York, who lost the Democratic but won the Republican primary and had to be licked all over again in the general election. Pope in Idaho was defeated, as was McGill in Kansas. Such comfort as the President derived from the defeat of Lonergan in Connecticut and the near-defeats of conservatives like Van Nuys of Indiana and Gillette of Iowa was cold and clammy.

The whole episode registered a tremendous deflation of the optimism of the Democrats in their suicidal struggle for power over an "unbeatable" party. The Democrats who subordinated their duty to give effect to the mandate of 1936 to the question of "Whose Party Is It?" forgot that no American party has ever been unbeatable or proof against internal dissension. Their failure promptly to enact the Third New Deal program plunged the nation deeper into economic depression than was ever necessary, while the fierce feuds over European developments, labor organization, and party control checked the headway which Roosevelt's New Deal had accumulated during four years of hard and patriotic effort.

After the votes of November 8, 1938, had been counted and the size of the Republican gains analyzed, there was no longer much point to that record of achievement. The only question was whether the Roosevelt party could reorganize itself in time and hold its legislative measures steadily enough in force to bring economic recovery by 1940 and thus win the national election of that year, or whether the Republican effort to solve present complexities by a synthetic resurrection of vanished American simplicities would push the nation over the edge of a far-reaching and painful conservative revolution.

THURMAN ARNOLD

The Folklore of 1937

IN which it is explained how the great sciences of law and economics and the little imaginary people who are supposed to be guided by these sciences affect the daily lives of those who make, distribute, and consume our goods.

THE FOLKLORE of 1937 was expressed principally by the literature of law and economics. Here were found elaborately framed the little pictures which men had of society as it ought to be. Of course, this literature was not called folklore. No one thought of sound principles of law or economics as a religion. They were considered as inescapable truths, as natural laws, as principles of justice, and as the only method of an ordered society. This is a characteristic of all vital folklore or religion.[1] The moment that folklore is recognized to be only folklore it ceases to have the effect of folklore. It descends to the place of poetry or fairy tales which affect us only in our romantic moments. For example, years ago Mr. Justice Cardozo pointed out that law was really literature. This is true. Yet if it were generally recognized to be true, the particular kind of literature known as law would not have the kind of influence it has today.

The effect of the peculiar folklore of 1937 was to encourage the type of organization known as industry or business and discourage the type known as government. Under the protection of this folklore the achievements of American business were remarkable. There was no questioning of myth which supported independent empires by those engaged in those enter

---

Permission of the author. From *The Folklore of Capitalism*. Yale University Press.

[1] Polybius, writing about the Roman social order before the birth of Christ, observed:

"But it seems to me the most distinctive superiority of the Roman political and social order is to be found in the nature of their religious convictions; and I mean the very thing which other peoples look upon with reproach, as superstition. But it nevertheless maintains the cohesion of the Roman state." (*Polybius*, VI, 56.)

prises. So-called private institutions like General Motors never lost their direction through philosophical debate. The pioneer efforts at industrial organization in this country had been wasteful beyond belief, but bold and confident.

With respect to political government, however, our superstitions had the opposite effect. They were not a cohesive force, but a destructive and disintegrating one. The pioneer efforts of the Government were timid, indecisive, and ineffective. When it became necessary for the Government to fill gaps in the national structure in which private business enterprise was an obvious failure, the myths and folklore of the time hampered practical organization at every turn. Men became more interested in planning the culture of the future—in saving posterity from the evils of dictatorship or bureaucracy, in preventing the American people from adopting Russian culture on the one hand, or German culture on the other—than in the day-to-day distribution of food, housing, and clothing to those who needed them. Mystical attacks on practical measures achieved an astonishing degree of success. Debaters and orators rose to the top in such an atmosphere and technicians twiddled their thumbs, unable to use their skills.

The operation of this legal and economic folklore which paralyzed organizations with the name "government" attached to them will make a fascinating study for the future historian. He will note a striking resemblance to the medieval myths which impeded medical knowledge for hundreds of years. He will observe men refusing benefits obviously to their practical advantage when tendered by the Government, because they violated current taboos. A few incidents will illustrate how men constantly sacrificed present advantage in order to avoid the future retribution supposed to result from the violation of these taboos.

In the spring of 1936 the writer heard a group of bankers, businessmen, lawyers, and professors, typical of the learned and conservative thinkers of the time, discussing a crisis in the affairs of the bankrupt New York, New Haven, and Hartford Railroad—once the backbone of New England, the support of its institutions and its worthy widows and orphans. They were expressing indignation that a bureaucratic Interstate Commerce Commission, operating from Washington, had decreed that passenger rates be cut almost in half. Every man there would directly benefit from the lower rate. None were stockholders. Yet all were convinced that the reduction in rate should be opposed by all conservative citizens and they were very unhappy about this new outrage committed by a government bent on destroying private business by interfering with the free judgment of its managers.

This sincere indignation and gloom had its roots not in selfishness nor the pursuit of the profit of the moment, but in pure idealism. These men, though they owned no stock, were willing to forego the advantage of lower fares to save the railroad from the consequences of economic sin. They took a long-range view and decided that in the nature of things the benefits of the lower rates would be only temporary, because they had been lowered in violation of the great principle that government should not interfere with business. Some sort of catastrophe was bound to result from such an action. The writer tried to get the picture of the impending catastrophe in clearer detail. Did the gentlemen think that, under the new rates, trains would stop running and maroon them in the City of Elms? It appeared that no one quite believed this. The collapse which they feared was more nebulous. Trains would keep on running, but with a sinister change in the character of the service. Under government influence, it would become as unpleasant as the income taxes were unpleasant. And in the background was an even more nebulous fear. The Government would, under such conditions, have to take over the railroad, thus ushering in bureaucracy and regimentation. Trains would run, but there would be no pleasure in riding on them any more.

There was also the thought that investors would suffer. This was difficult to put into concrete terms because investors already had suffered. The railroad was bankrupt. Most of the gentlemen present had once owned stock, but had sold it before it had reached its present low. Of course, they wanted the stock to go up again, along with everything else, provided, of course, that the Government did not put it up by "artificial" means, which would be inflation.

The point was raised as to whether the Interstate Commerce Commission was right in believing that the road would actually be more prosperous under the lower rates. This possibility was dismissed as absurd. Government commissions were always theoretical. This was a tenet of pure faith about which one did not even argue.

In addition to faith, there were figures. One gentleman present had the statistical data on *why* the railroad would suffer. In order to take care of the increased traffic, new trains would have to be added, new brakemen and conductors hired, more money put into permanent equipment. All such expenditures would, of course, reflect advantageously on the economic life of New Haven, remove persons from relief rolls, stimulate the heavy goods industries, and so on. This, however, was argued to be unsound. Since it was done in violation of sound principle it would damage business confidence, and actually result in less capital goods expenditures, in spite of the fact that it appeared to the superficial observer to be creating more. And besides, where was the money coming from? This worry was also somewhat astonishing, because it appeared that the railroad actually could obtain the necessary funds for the present needed improvements. However, the answer to that was that posterity would have to pay through the nose.

And so the discussion ended on a note of vague worry. No one was happy over the fact that he could travel cheaper. No one was pleased that employment would increase, or that the heavy industries would be stimulated by the reduction of rates. Out of pure mystical idealism, these men were opposing every selfish interest both of themselves and the community, because the scheme went counter to the folklore to which they were accustomed. And since it went counter to that folklore, the same fears resulted from every other current scheme which violated traditional attitudes, whether it was relief, housing, railroad rates, or the Securities Exchange Act. Anything which could be called governmental interference in business necessarily created bureaucracy, regimentation, inflation and put burdens on posterity.

All this discussion was backed by much learning and theory. Yet it was easy to see its emotional source. These men pictured the railroad corporation as a big man who had once been a personal friend of theirs. They were willing to undergo financial sacrifice in order to prevent injustice being done to that big man. The personality of the corporation was so real to them that it was impossible to analyze the concept into terms of selfish interest. Does one think of personal gain when a member of one's family is insulted? With that emotional beginning, the balance of the discussion flowed out of the learned myths of the time, and ended where all the economic arguments of the time ended, in a parade of future horrors. The thinking was as primitive and naïve as all such thinking must be when it is divorced from practical issues and involved in prevailing taboos. As to the merits of the rate reduction from a practical point of view, neither the writer, nor any member of the group, knew anything. Yet such was the faith of these men in the formula they recited, that they felt that knowledge of details was completely unnecessary in having a positive and unchangeable opinion.

The way of thinking illustrated by the above incident is a stereotype. Its pattern is the same to whatever problems it is applied. It starts by reducing a situation, infinitely complicated by human and political factors, to a simple parable which illustrates fundamental and immutable principles. It ends by proving that the sacrifice of present advantage is necessary in order to protect everything we hold most dear. All such discussions end with arguments based on freedom, the home, tyranny, bureaucracy, and so on. All lead into a verbal crusade to protect our system of government. In this way certainty of opinion is possible for people who know nothing whatever about the actual situation. They feel they do not have to know the details. They know the principles.

Take another example. In 1937 a new device known as the "sit-down" strike was most effectively used against the General Motors Corporation. Here was a fascinating struggle to develop labor unity and leadership in this country, headed by a great organizer, John L. Lewis. As in all combat situations, both sides believed intensely in the morality and sacredness of their cause. A realist observing the struggle without the moral preconceptions of either of the opposing organizations might make a guess as to the final outcome of the labor movement. He would realize, however, that it was only a political guess and that a guess based on a search for the proper fundamental principles of how strikes "should" be conducted by right-thinking conservative strikers would have no validity whatever.

But here again editorial table-pounders in our most respectable publications insisted that the real issue was whether, using the analogy of the sit-down strike, irresponsible men would not feel that they had the right to destroy our homes by conducting sit-down strikes in the parlors. Liberty, freedom, the home, were again at stake as they had been in the case of the New Haven rate cut. Nothing could have been more absurd than the suggestion that this great industrial struggle was in reality concerned with the right of individuals to undisturbed possession of their homes. Yet this was the position usually taken by most of the so-called "thinking" people who filed income-tax returns.

The great debate in 1937 over President Roosevelt's proposal to put more liberal judges on the Supreme Court of the United States offers another example of this way of thinking. There was, of course, every reason for those who opposed the extension of national power represented by Roosevelt's program to cling to the Court as a last line of defense against a popular mandate. Here was a way of taking away from a great popular majority the fruits of their recent victory at the polls. Yet much of the opposition to the proposal came not from those who were opposed but from those in favor of the main outlines of the Roosevelt policies. They were actually afraid of the exercise of an admitted constitutional power to reform the attitude of the judiciary. The argument centered on the familiar symbols of regimentation, bureaucracy, freedom, and the home, which actually had as little to do with the issues involved as they had to do with the enforced reduction of rates on the New Haven Railroad.

We use as an illustration of this type of argument the issue of the *American Bar Association Journal* for April, 1937. In this issue eight distinguished and alarmed leaders of the bar and one editor made it abundantly clear that the proposal to increase the membership of that Court was fundamentally immoral. That being so, it followed that the wages of sin is death. Grave peril of a somewhat unspecific character lay in wait for us. The nation was about to lose its immortal soul and become at best a bureaucracy, and at worst a tyranny. The whole issue was keyed to a note of warning of impending doom.

For example, President Stinchfield, who contributed the first article, told us that if we adopted the plan "we shall have government from Washington covering a territory of 130 million people." The superficial observer might have thought that this was one of the objectives for which the Civil War was fought and therefore had its good points. But President Stinchfield went on to say: "We must inevitably become a government by bureaucracy. . . ." Such mysterious matters, of course, could not be proved, but President Stinchfield's faith in the malevolence of Congress was such that he didn't think proof necessary. He said: "I think we are in great danger at the moment."

Mr. Olney, who followed Mr. Stinchfield, was also gloomy and sad about the remote future, through whose mists his prophetic vision penetrated without any difficulty. He was particularly worried because he was afraid that labor unions would disappear if the President's proposal was passed. He said that the measure would put them "at the mercy of a President and Congress who choose to pass a law forbidding the persuasion of men to join a union." This was a very odd thing to worry about just after the triumph of John L. Lewis. However, Mr. Olney explained how foolish it was for labor to be cheerful about the future right to organize. He said: "It is no answer to this to say that such a thing could not happen in this country. It has happened elsewhere in countries no less civilized than ours. It has happened in Germany and Italy."

Elsewhere in the article Mr. Olney pointed out that Germany and Italy were not the only countries we may come to resemble. We might also become like the South American republics, of whose judiciary Mr. Olney seemed to have a low opinion. The trouble with Germany, Italy, and the South American republics was that in their blindness they bowed down to the wrong principles, like the heathen. This, Mr. Olney thought, was hard on Germany, but it was a lucky break for us, because as a result labor and the underprivileged groups in this country could now see the dangers of getting what they want.

Mr. Olney's analysis made the complex conditions in Europe and South America simple and easy to understand and showed just why we are on the verge of becoming like these countries.

The next article was by Louis A. Lecher, a distinguished member of the

Milwaukee Bar. It was evident that he had been thinking along the same lines as Mr. Olney. However, he was more specific. The Potato Act was, he thought, not only an unwise agricultural measure, but also a subtly concealed attack on human liberty.

George Wharton Pepper contributed an article in which he said of the President's proposal: "Here the question is not whether A or B shall be elected to political office but whether A and B shall be deprived of their guaranties of civil and religious liberty."

He saw in the plan danger to labor and the Jews and the Catholics and the schools, and pointed out that professors like the writer were foes of education within its own household, because they did not realize that the defeat of the plan was essential to academic freedom. He observed that "unless labor leaders, Jews, Catholics, educators and editors come to their senses before it is too late they will find themselves in an America which is anything but a land of the free."

Mr. Donovan then spoke. He analyzed the groups that were in imminent danger from the plan. They were religious groups, racial groups, citizens of foreign descent, labor unions, and persons charged with crime. All of these people would, in Mr. Donovan's opinion, be in a bad way if more justices were added to the Court under the plan.

These symbolic arguments were almost identical with the arguments in the preceding presidential campaign, because they were the automatic response to the same kind of irritation. This same pattern of argument always greets the struggle of any new organization to find a logical place among traditional institutions.

Let us go back to the Middle Ages for our final example of this way of thinking. In the seventeenth century the University of Paris, supported by an ancient learned tradition, with faculties of law, medicine, and theology, occupied a position in medicine not unlike the position of the Supreme Court of the United States in government today. It was the duty of these carefully chosen scholars to make a unified whole out of the learning of the time. They spent their lives studying those fundamental principles, the violation of which brings ruin. Their logic was as unassailable as the economic and legal logic of today. They had the same distrust of immediate practical advantage, the same fear of mysterious and impending moral disaster lying in wait to destroy the national character of a people who deserted fundamental principles to gain present ends. The medieval physician could see no profit in saving a man's body if thereby he lost his soul. Nor did he think that any temporary physical relief could ever be worth the violation of the fundamental principles of medicine.

The remedy for fever established by the learning of the time was the art of bleeding to rid the body of those noxious vapors and humors in the blood which were the root of the illness. Of course, patients sickened and died in the process, but they were dying for a medical principle, so it was thoroughly worth-while. To depart from that principle would have the same effect on human health as the failure to shoot strikers occupying the plant of an industrial concern in a sit-down strike, or as the tampering with the Supreme Court of the United States has today on social well-being.

Magic had the same importance in the art of healing physical ills in the Middle Ages that it has today in the determination of governmental policy. Practical remedies, like sanitation, were not sufficiently mysterious to be respected. A people accustomed to living in filth had great faith in the curative properties of filth. There was more magic in disagreeable drugs than in pleasant ones, because disease was personified as an evil element that had to be attacked and driven away through some sort of combat in which pleasant remedies were a sign of weakness in the face of the enemy. The tactics in the war against disease bore a striking resemblance to the tactics in the modern war against social problems, in that the principles of medicine were much more sacred and important than the health of the patient.

Such were the attitudes of those learned in medicine in 1638 when the Jesuits in Peru discovered quinine. The cures which were accomplished by the use of this drug were marvelous, due in part to its own merit and in part to the fact that patients escaped the bleeding process. It was natural that such a radical departure from established precedent should be viewed with alarm. Therefore, it was not surprising that the University of Paris declared the use of quinine unconstitutional and banned the drug as dangerous.

The reasoning of the faculty was clear and persuasive. Since quinine did nothing to relieve the noxious vapors in the blood, immediate benefits must necessarily be an "artificial" cure or "panacea" which left the patient worse off than before in spite of his own temporary delusion that he felt better. The use of quinine was an attack on the whole fundamental theory of medicine, which had been carefully correlated with religion and theology. Certainly the temporary relief of a few sufferers could never be worth the overthrow of medical principles to the confusion of all the learning and experience of the past. They talked about it like this "What is the emergency at present which should force the people to adopt the dictatorial rather than the democratic method for the solution of the very real constitutional problems which undoubtedly exist? There is none." (James Truslow Adams, "The Court Issue and Democracy," *New York Times Magazine,* February 21, 1937.)

However, it was more than a medical problem. It was a moral problem which affected the character, the freedom, and the homes of everyone. Fortunately, the unlearned people of the time, like those of today, were constantly forgetting the great moral issues of the future for the practical comfort of the moment. Hence the use of quinine eventually became common. The significant thing, however, was that it had to be introduced by a quack who concealed it in a curious compound of irrelevant substances.

In such an atmosphere there was at least a chance that a quack would be right; there was a certainty that a physician would be wrong. The Jesuits were considered by their enemies the most dangerous religious bureaucrats of the time, a fanatical group of zealots for whom the end always justified the means. They had made many people uncomfortable with their crusading. One could not adopt their remedies without adopting their principles any more than the United States today can develop national power without becoming like the Germans under Hitler. And so the dreaded specter of Jesuitism hung over the use of quinine, as Communism and Fascism hang over soil conservation and crop insurance today.

This way of thinking is as old as the desire of men to escape from the hard necessity of making practical judgments in the comfort and certainty of an appeal to priests. It controlled the thinking about the human body in the Middle Ages. It controls our thinking about the body politic today. Out of it have been spun our great legal and economic principles which have made our learning about government a search for universal truth rather than a set of observations about the techniques of human organization.

Medieval Attitudes in Law and Economics

The years before and during the great depression in America, which were feudal in their economic organization, present a spectacle of a continuous search for a set of rational formulas designed to enable men to govern with a minimum of exercise of judgment, and with a minimum of personal power. The historian of the future will be amazed at a great people's simple belief that sound legal and economic principles, discovered by close students of these mysteries, were the only means to national salvation. He will be equally amazed at the naïve fears that opportunistic action or judgment based not upon learning but on political expediency, whatever its temporary benefit, would necessarily lead to disaster if it did not fit into some preconceived theory. The history of the time is the story of men who struggled gallantly and unsuccessfully to make government correspond to this theory about it. It is intelligible only if we start out with a bird's-eye view of what men thought were the principles which made the social structure survive.

We have already analyzed the conception of the "thinking man" which was essential to all political debate. Without him, public discussion of rational principles and systems of government would have been impossible. He was the great spirit which hovered over all governmental institutions.

This particular type of folklore had ceased to affect medicine in 1937. Medical principles were not supposed to be a matter which was to be thought out, in the way governmental principles were thought out. The difference between the attitudes of medical science and physical science was very subtle, particularly since the political scientist of 1937 always *claimed* to be doing the same thing as the physical scientist. That difference therefore cannot be defined; it can only be illustrated.

Thirty years ago medical men were still fighting for principle, just as political men are fighting for it today. There were the homeopathic and the allopathic schools of medicine. The thinking man was supposed to choose between these two schools in hiring his physician. There was much public debate on their merits. Disciples of each school were supposed to stand together as a matter of party loyalty. They were the missionaries of a medical creed.

Today the public is no longer asked to choose between conflicting medical principles (at least not to the same extent). Medicine has been taken over by men of skill rather than men of principle. The medical sects, such as chiropractic, which still argues fundamental principle in the way the political scientist argues it, are unimportant. There is little left in medicine for thinking men to debate. Physicians are chosen on a guess as to their expertness. Hospitals no longer take sides. Therefore the concept of the "thinking man" is no longer essential.

In advertising the "thinking man" has gone so completely that a modern advertising agency would be amazed at the suggestion that the best way to sell goods is by making a rational appeal.

In government the concept still reigns supreme. Men are still asked to diagnose the ills of social organization through the darkened lenses of "schools" of legal or economic theory. They still worry about choosing a "system" of government. Fact-minded persons who do not believe in the "thinking man" and who do not expect to gain political objectives by making rational appeals to him are not considered respectable. They are called "politicians" and not "political scientists." The political scientists are the high priests of our governmental mythology. The politician is still in the position of the Jewish money lender of the Middle Ages.

In examining that curious folklore, still a powerful influence in 1937, the future historian will observe that during the first half of the twentieth century the principles of government were divided into two great branches, law and economics. Each had its specialists, who were supposed to work hand in hand in the joint enterprise of discovering the true principles of government. The law, on the one hand, preserved those great moral values of freedom and individualism by pointing out that the opportunistic action, which seemed best for the moment, often concealed dangerous moral traits. It was supposed to guard us against well-meaning individuals who, in their desire to alleviate human suffering and promote efficiency for the present, were leading us into future bureaucracy, regimentation, and dictatorship. Economics, on the other hand, supplied the principles which, if properly studied, would make incoherent legislative bodies act with unity and coherence, and which, if properly propagandized among the solid citizenry, would insure the selection of legislators who could distinguish between sound and unsound principles. Between the two sets of principles it was thought possible to avoid the personal element in government.

The future historian will also mark the paradox that there was little agreement on what were the sound theories in 1937, and at the same time almost unanimous agreement that good government followed only upon the selection of sound theories. No program for the alleviation of any pressing problem could win any sort of acceptance without having behind it some theory logically consistent with the more general superstitions concerning the function of government. Men believed that there were several defined systems of government—Capitalism, Communism, Fascism—which bright men had thought up and lesser men accepted, all of them in operation in various parts of the world. It was the duty of the American people to make a free-will choice between them. The great ideological battle in 1937 was whether Capitalism was worth preserving. Most people thought it should be preserved. There were many intelligent humanitarian people, however, who thought that it should be abandoned and a new system inaugurated, usually called Socialism. This new system on paper seemed preferable to Capitalism. Yet it was constantly pointed out by its opponents that if one tried to obtain Socialism, one got either Fascism or Communism, with their attendant evils of regimentation, bureaucracy, dictatorship, and so on, and that individualism disappeared.

It was a complicated business, this preservation of the capitalistic system in 1937 against the other "isms" and alien ideals. There was first the task of defining what Capitalism really was. This was a constant process. It had to be done every day and each new restatement led only to the necessity of further definition. The preservation of Capitalism also required that practical plans be tested by expert economic theorists who looked at each practical measure through the spectacles of economic abstractions, in order not to be confused by immediate objectives. Thus child labor had to be debated, not on the basis of whether it was desirable for children to work, but in the light of its effect on the American home in ten years, if it were followed to its logical conclusion. Measures for the conservation of oil, or regulation of agriculture, had to be considered without relation to immediate benefits either to oil or agriculture. Tendencies were regarded as far more important than immediate effects, and the danger to posterity actually seemed more real than the danger to existing persons.

The capitalistic system in America had two sets of rules, one economic and the other legal, determining what the limits of governmental control should be. Economic theory had no separate institution to speak ex cathedra, other than the two political parties, each of which hired experts to study it and advise them. Whatever was produced by any political platform had to have its background of scholarly research. It was the duty of each party to consult only sound economists. Legal theory, on the other hand, was manufactured by the Supreme Court of the United States. There were two parties in the Supreme Court of the United States, each with its own legal theory. However, it was generally agreed that what the majority of judges thought was the real essence of the Constitution. It was not left to the people to decide between sound and unsound legal theory, and therefore the opinions of dissenting judges, unlike the opinions of dissenting economists, were not available in political debate, at least prior to Roosevelt's attack on the Court. This was because law concerned the spiritual welfare of the people and preserved their form of government, whereas economics concerned only their material welfare. In spiritual things it is essential that men do right according to some final authority. There was thought to be no such compelling reason to prevent them from ruining themselves economically.

The general idea of the Supreme Court's function is represented by a cartoon, in which the economic and social legislation of the day is thrown out of the august portals of the Supreme Court, stripped of the plausible humanitarian disguises which had deceived both the President and Congress. This gives a very accurate picture of what the great mass of conservative people thought the Court was doing for them. They did not trust themselves to decide whether a humanitarian or practical scheme was really government by edict, or would lead to government by edict. They knew that such things seldom appeared on the surface, and that they required great learning to analyze. However, more intelli-

gent people required a more complicated explanation, because they preferred long words to pictures. Hence the years of the depression produced
thousands of learned dissertations, which came to every possible sort of
conclusion as to the constitutionality of various measures. These articles
did not make the law clear. They did, however, make it clear that there
was such a thing as law, which experts could discover through reason.

It was this faith in a higher law which made the Supreme Court the
greatest unifying symbol in American government. Here was the one
body which could still the constant debate, and represent to the country
the ideal of a government of fundamental principles. On this Court the
whole ideal of a government of laws and not of the competing opinions of
men appeared to depend. Here only was there a breathing spell from the
continual din of arguments about governmental philosophy which were
never settled.

The legislative branches of the Government were under constant suspicion, and their acts were presumed to be malevolent. The incompetency
of Congress was an assumed fact everywhere. The great trouble with the
legislative branches was that they were influenced by an unlearned, un-
theoretical, illogical, and often corrupt force called "politics." Politics was
continually putting unworthy persons in power, as opposed to business,
where, because of economic law, only worthy persons rose to the top. A
body influenced by political considerations could not give any disinterested
judgment as to the soundness of any economic theory. Hence Congress
was constantly picking unsound theories, listening to unsound economists,
and letting the practical convenience of the moment overweigh the needs
of posterity. Politicians were the kind of people who would not care if a
thing called bureaucracy was established as long as it gave them jobs.

The only trustworthy check against unsound economic theory was not
the politician, but that great body of thinking men and women who composed the better class of the public. Yet even such people were easily confused in those days when the noise of competing theories was loudest. The
only way of straightening them out was by constant preaching, which had
the weakness of all preaching throughout the centuries, in that sin and
heresy were always rising against it. Hence the age-old cry of the disappointed preacher to his erring flock was constantly heard in the land. As
typical of this, a distinguished economist from Columbia University spoke
the discouragement of his brethren in 1936 as follows:

NEED REALISTIC WARNINGS.—Professor Ralph West Robey, of Columbia University, appealed to professional economists to make more realistic warnings of
economic disaster if present conditions continued. He had pointed out that,
despite an 86 per cent increase in federal revenue since 1932, the nation was

faced with the largest peace time deficit in its history. He added that the cost of government in the United States is now about one-third of the national income, and that if this deficit were provided for by taxation, the average per capita tax would be some 20 per cent higher than that in England.

But, he added, the public no longer listens to economists who foresee trouble ahead.

PUBLIC DEAF TO WARNINGS.—"The result has been," he said, "that the public has ceased to be frightened when it hears economists prophesying collapse and disaster. It has come to believe, if I may steal the phrase of a friend, that when an economist yells 'Wolf! Wolf!!' it probably means nothing more significant than that the administration has pulled another white rabbit out of the hat.

"Such a situation, it seems to me, is most distressing. I think it is distressing because I have the utmost confidence in economic reasoning and in economic principles." (*New Haven Register,* May 11, 1936.)

Economists generally felt in those dark days as Dr. Robey did. Here was careful scholarly work, leading to a set of theories which, if followed, would cure social disease as well as the imperfect nature of man permitted it to be cured. And here was an ungrateful public which would not listen to Dr. Robey's sound economics. It might seem strange, therefore, to the reader, examining this most interesting folklore from a detached point of view, that the sound economists did not demand a Supreme Court of Economics. Why should they entrust to popular judgment this scholarly task, when they refused to entrust to popular judgment the somewhat easier task of legal reasoning?

The answer to this question takes us into some of the unexamined religious assumptions which the folklore of 1937 had in common with the Christian religion which was its heritage. It went back to the paradox of the relationship of sin and virtue, and the mystical nature of free will. God, according to an earlier theology, had his choice of making men keep to the straight and narrow path by discipline, or by persuasion. Weighing the advantages of these two different methods, he preferred to make him free to sin in order to make a more noble fellow out of him. Neither God nor the economists of 1937 desired a nation of slaves. Therefore the economists would have rejected as unthinkable the organization of a Supreme Court of Economics, on the ground that even a benevolent dictatorship is bad because it abolishes freedom. It had been evident for a long time that the only possible method of making *laissez faire* economics, or indeed any other planned system of economic principles work, would be to force people to accept them. But it was far better to trust to the feeble judgment of the common herd, and to guide them through love of virtue and fear of hell, of Inflation, or Bureaucracy, or Regimentation, or whatever name hell happened to have in the particular field of learning, at the particular time. Of course, the results were discouraging to the economist. They regretted man's tendency to follow false economic reasoning, just as the preachers regretted man's tendency to sin. Nevertheless, they felt that the only refuge was in a deeper search for the Word and in more fervent preaching.

This was the way that most intelligent, socially minded, "thinking men" thought. Of course, those who actually ran the Government were compelled to act on an entirely different set of assumptions. Politicians were interested in getting votes, and such high-sounding theory had nothing whatever to do with the process. Everybody knew this, but it was regarded as a shameful thing that it should be so. Therefore, the efforts of reformers were directed toward abolishing this distressing phenomenon. They argued that if men who did not stoop to use political tricks would only go into politics, and if people only would elect them, then political tricks would disappear from government. The efforts along this line achieved about the same success as the age-old effort to abolish sensuality from love. Everyone realized this, but considered it no excuse for abandoning the effort.

LAW AND OBEDIENCE TO AUTHORITY

There was only one area where the prevailing theory limited the operation of group free will. Men could choose between sound and unsound economic theories, but they must not be permitted to choose between sound and unsound constitutional theories. To prevent them from erring on this point, a scholargarchy was set up, with complete autocratic power. To a superficial observer, this might seem a denial of the beauty of group free will, but closer examination showed that it was not. For the function of the Supreme Court was not to prevent people from choosing what kind of constitution they desired, but to prevent them from changing their form of government *without knowing it*. Congress in its ignorance was constantly passing laws with purely practical objectives, which really changed the constitution without giving the people a chance to exercise their free will on that important subject. Therefore, some autocratic power had to be set up to apply the complicated scholarly techniques to such measures, not to prevent the people from exercising their free will on the Constitution, but to prevent them from doing it inadvertently.

Immersed in such theories, no student of government, economics, or law could look at the conduct of the institutions about which he was thinking without the same sort of nausea that an idealistic lover of bees and butterflies feels when she overturns a stone and sees some big black bugs crawling about in a loathsome manner. A similar attitude produced the same results in the study of government as it would have produced in biology. Facts about social organization of which men did not approve were not treated as facts, but as sins.

From this point of view it became the duty of everyone to denounce organized political factions as low things unworthy of the attention of courageous statesmen. Party platforms were the only reality—not the social and political pressures which force such platforms into a series of inconsistent compromises. The remedy was to ignore the pressures and make the platforms courageous and consistent. We were supposed to elect to office only those persons who did not care whether they were reëlected or not.

Of course, no political party could carry out these principles without political suicide, but this only meant that political parties were shot through with politics. Hence everyone demanded the kind of political party which thought more of posterity than getting votes for its leaders. Everyone realized, of course, that this was impossible, and the conflict created spiritual trouble, indecision, and a greater variety of literary and oratorical nonsense than the world has ever known heretofore.

To find peace, men denounced government by men, and sought relief by reciting principles. The fundamental assumption of the folklore about government during the great depression was that principles could be more trusted than organizations. Organizations were dangerous because of their tendency to err and stray. Principles, provided that they were sound, endured forever, and could alone make up for the constant tendency of social groups to backslide.

The Dawn of a Different Attitude toward Individual Maladjustments

All this folklore persisted in a time when the theory of free will, sin, and repentance was disappearing from the thinking about individuals' troubles. Psychiatrists and psychologists no longer explained individual conduct on the basis of a free-will choice between good and evil. Such a way of thinking had led in the past to curing the insane by preaching away the devil which had entered the patient. By 1937 people had lost interest in theoretical ethical principles for maladjusted individuals. The term "sinner" had gone from all sophisticated psychology. The concept of the devil had disappeared from the anatomy of the individual mind. Indeed, the idea that any man was a single integrated individual had disappeared, and it was recognized that each individual was a whole cast of characters, each appearing on the stage under the influence of different stimuli. In diagnosing an individual's maladies, the psychiatrist found out what his fantasies were and, without bothering whether they were true or false, attempted to cure him by recognizing these fantasies as part of the problem.

The psychiatrists, like physicians, were not concerned with the theoretical definition of the good mind, or the perfect human body. Even where they read of such definitions by their more theoretical brethren, they did not attempt to fit their particular patients into these molds. Ignoring the speculation of what the man would be in twenty years, or the effect of their treatment on posterity, they proceeded to make the insane person as comfortable and as little of a nuisance to himself and his fellow man as possible, from day to day. They did not spend their time deploring insanity, or the existence of psychopathic personalities. Their attitude toward their patients was rather one of intense interest. And in this atmosphere curative techniques developed, and men actually learned.

The Faith in Principles Rather than Organizations

In 1937 there was little of this point of view in legal or economic thinking. The point of view of the psychiatrist had long been part of the stock in trade of that low class called politicians. However, the attitude seldom was in evidence when respectable people talked or thought about government. There were exceptions here and there in colleges, but that influence had failed to reach the minds of respectable editorial writers, forward-looking reformers, or molders of public opinion. The conception of social institutions as having free will, and winning their salvation by a free-will selection of the right principles; the idea that politics, pressure groups, lobbying, powerful political machines existed because people had sinful yearnings in that direction; the economic idea that depressions were the result of tinkering with economic laws and preventing the automatic working of an abstract law which would have functioned properly had it not been for bad men who threw this law out of gear—these were held as articles of faith by conservatives and radicals alike.

This faith, held so implicitly, was sorely tried during the years of the great depression. As in every time of great travail, from the great plagues on to today, prayers went up in all directions. These prayers, from businessmen, labor leaders, and socialists, had one element in common. They all showed distrust of any form of organized control. No one would admit that man should govern man. No one would observe the obvious fact that lay everywhere under their noses, the human organizations' rise to power, not by following announced creeds, but by the development of loyalties and institutional habits. All these devoted people thought that the world could only attain that state of static perfection which alone was worth aiming at, by studying and developing the proper theories, and then following them, not by force, but by their own free will. Thus far the ideals of the Socialist party, the Liberty League, Dr. Townsend, and the budget balancers were all identical. The only difference between them was the proper application of the general principles on which all right-thinking men agreed.

The prayers of the house of bishops of industry were well illustrated by a typical speech of Mr. Sloan, at an annual dinner of the Association of Manufacturers in 1936. The speaker wanted American Industry, which he personified in a very beautiful way, to operate on an unselfish, or non-profit basis, and he wanted businessmen to assume the rôle of statesmen. The way to attain this was by making their minds pure and getting them to think about the right things. Within the General Motors Corporation, of which he was President, Mr. Sloan would never have substituted preaching for control. The lack of central control and the substitution of free will aided by preaching would have demoralized the concern within a year. However, it offered a marvelous intellectual escape for a man who felt the absolute necessity of business control, and at the same time could not fit actual control into his political religion. Portions of his speech which we have just analyzed are set forth, because they are so completely typical of the thinking of the day.

At the annual dinner last night, in accordance with the custom of the National Association of Manufacturers, the guests of honor were introduced separately as "men outstanding in the formulation of national industrial policy." Mr. Sloan, introduced as "one in the forefront of this group," delivered the address of the occasion, entitled "Industry's responsibilities broaden." (*New York Times,* December 5, 1935.)

He said in part:

"Industry must further expand its horizon of thinking and action. *It must assume the rôle of an enlightened industrial statesmanship.*[1] To the extent that it accepts such broadened responsibilities, to that degree does it assure the maintenance of private enterprise, and with it the exercise of *free initiative,* as the sole creator, just as it must always be the most efficient creator of wealth.

"During the past few years it has become the vogue to discredit every instrumentality of accomplishment, be it the individual or the machine. It has been said that American industry is selfish. It would be far more just to say that it has been preoccupied—preoccupied in exploring the secrets of nature and creating a continuous flow of new products.

"But, as we look forward, and as we analyze the evolution that has occurred, I am convinced that industry's responsibilities can no longer be adequately discharged, however efficient and effective it may be, *with the mere physical production of goods and services.*

"First, let us ask whether our wealth-creating agencies, particularly that of

---

[1] Italics on this page, and all succeeding pages, unless otherwise indicated, are the author's.

industry, are to be based upon private enterprise or political management. I cannot see how any intelligent observer can have any possible faith in the capacity of political management to provide either stability or progress, if it should set out to operate the agencies of wealth creation, particularly industry. It is my firm conviction that any form of 'Government Regulation of Industry' is bound to result in an ever-increasing interference with the broad exercise of initiative—the very foundation of the American system. That is the natural evolution of bureaucracy. If that be so, might not the ultimate logical result be the necessity for the socialization of industry through the break down of the *profit system* induced by the accumulative effect of the ever-increasing political management? We do not need to go far afield to see definite evidences of that possibility." (*New York Times,* December 5, 1935.)

The medieval idea, that just because sin had always existed and probably always would exist, we were not justified in regarding it as commonplace or inevitable, was illustrated at the same meeting at which Mr. Sloan talked. In the platform of the organization it was pointed out that

"The American System . . . offers greater assurance than any other of equality of opportunity for all men, with rewards in accordance with the contribution of each." By speakers during the day, the "American System" was contrasted with the New Deal, which was variously denounced as "an alien importation" and as *"an Oriental philosophy."*
Government officials and legislators in general who had departed from the "American System" were denounced in the platform as having done so "in spite of their oath of office." (*New York Times,* December 6, 1935.)

Nevertheless, this American system would only work, in the opinion of the convention, if the invisible government of politics were kept out. The convention noted with horror the existence of men of influence in government who had not been elected, and commented on it by resolution:

A supplementary resolution later added to the denunciation a body otherwise unnamed called "the invisible government." The resolution read in part:
"It is a matter of grave concern that the germs of a dangerous invisible government have appeared in our national government. *It is a matter of common observation that our governmental powers, decisions and policies are being largely dictated by persons who have not been elected to official position and who are not responsible to the people for their acts, decisions and policies.* This is an unhealthy incubus in our national body politic which endangers the very life of our representative government and should be stamped out." (*New York Times,* December 6, 1935.)

In order to stamp out this invisible government by influential men not elected by the people, it was obviously necessary for influential men not elected by the people to enter into the business of influencing government. Thus another resolution was introduced to this effect, the report of which is as follows:

The "direct entrance" of industry into politics on this platform was declared to be a necessity by Charles H. Prentis Jr., president of the Armstrong Cork Company, who introduced it. Further, the declaration of entrance into politics the previous day by Clinton L. Bardo, president of the National Association of Manufacturers, was implemented yesterday by S. Wells Utley, who had been selected to make a broadcast convention address on the political tactics to be followed. (*New York Times,* December 6, 1935.)

There were very many, of course, who considered the Chamber of Commerce and the Manufacturers' Association hidebound groups of selfish people, pursuing their own interests under the guise of unselfishness. This attitude made the members of these organizations so speechless with indignation that they constantly reiterated that they had become too frightened and angry to assume the leadership which the crisis demanded. Criticism of this kind impeded recovery by scaring the natural-born leaders into such a state that they could only hide in cyclone cellars. Unfortunately, however, the critics were also engaged in a search for the holy grail, and therefore their deliberations resulted in the same kind of a hunt for two things: heresy and corruption. As a result of this, Socialists split into two wings, and the believers in true principles ousted the non-believers at a stormy convention in Cleveland. They wanted no patching up of a capitalistic religion. They wanted the true religion, if they had to go through chaos to get it.

We are using these speeches only to illustrate a common belief that social remedies could be found in the formulation of principles rather than in control and organization. In this respect radicals and conservatives were exactly alike.

Dr. Townsend belonged to the same church. He wanted goods distributed to the poor, but was convinced that the very worst way of doing this was to build a practical organization of human beings to do it. He, like his conservative foes, wanted an automatic scheme which would work for all time by encouraging free bargaining. His sole aim was to encourage private initiative by creating a proper credit system. His scheme was no more nor less utopian than the *laissez faire* economics of the conservative wing of the great medieval church to which he belonged. It would have worked if human beings had only been like the little abstract man in the back of his head. So also would *laissez faire,* if only human beings would leave things alone, and all act like good skilful traders who took their medicine when beaten, and did not try to overreach each other by unfair means. Thus we find Dr. Townsend endorsing a conservative general position in 1936 as follows:

Dr. Townsend, on the other hand, in addition to his fundamental plan of paying $200-a-month old age pensions from the proceeds of a transactions tax, remarked that "there are many fortunes which will have to be dissipated by the income tax and the inheritance tax route."

To Fight "Dictatorship."—"We are presenting a common front against the dictatorship in Washington," said Dr. Townsend, showing a glint of gold teeth beneath his tiny mustache.

"Add to that Communism and Farleyism, and you have our platform," added the Louisiana preacher, a red-faced gentleman who talks in a succession of tub-thumping phrases.

Dr. Townsend, who said that he considered the Supreme Court and the Constitution "a great safeguard," said that President Roosevelt "knew beyond doubt beforehand that his measures were unconstitutional," and that he had put them through in order to arouse resentment against the Supreme Court. Some one asked whether he believed the Supreme Court would find his proposals constitutional.

"They will if it is shown that they represent the will of the great majority of the people," replied Dr. Townsend in a grim tone. Later, however, he remarked that if it were possible to "capture the government" a constitutional amendment could easily be put through. (*New York Herald Tribune,* June 2, 1936.)

There is obviously nothing in these general principles to which the Liberty League could not have subscribed, in principle. There is a hint of breaking up large fortunes in both of them, in order to get back to the grand old days of free bargaining before large fortunes existed. In those days of the great depression everyone believed in the same God, and only fought about details of the service.

In such a situation there was only one safe speech which could be made, and that was to invoke all religions at once, and lump them under the phrase, "moral conscience and integrity." Such speeches, seeking the remedy through God, were therefore heard through the length and breadth of the land. Typical of them was the following from Governor Landon.

In the stress and confusion of recent years and in the din of conflicting counsel, we have lost our bearings and we have listened in vain for the commanding voice that might at once dispel our doubts and uncertainties and point us into safe courses.

We have waited and hesitated, the courage and resolution of old has seemed to fail us, and our moral fiber has seemed to weaken.

There is peril in that situation.

Our economic welfare may be threatened for the moment, and our industrial progress may be retarded for a season without final or total disaster.

Far more serious is the possible collapse of character, a possible paralysis of individual initiative, and a deadened sense of personal obligation and responsibility....

What is this intangible, yet very real thing we call the spirit of America? It may be found in the Bible. It is the slow groping of human thought toward the value of human personality and toward the one God in whose sight all men are equal. (*New York Times,* May 24, 1936.)

Of course, the God to lead us out of our economic bewilderment was not always the God of the Church. Lawyers found one in the Constitution. Huge organizations like the Liberty League and the Crusaders sought the truth from this document and the learned decisions elaborating it. They produced briefs, law-review articles, and sermons in publications devoted to the elucidation of the law. Like all great bodies of literature, the Constitution marched in all conceivable directions. An inflation of legal learning took place, the like of which the world has never seen. In the Middle Ages, men sought the "Word" just as diligently, but the available material resources did not permit so many thousands to seek it at the same time, and the printing presses were not so efficient then as now.

The Constitution, however, was only one symbol. Men feverishly attempted to make all written law march toward safety, security, and peace, through logical certainty. Millions were spent on restating all the law at once, and hundreds of learned men were employed by an organization called the "American Law Institute." Prominent lawyers gathered from all parts of the nation to hear the law, as it ought logically to be, read to them for their agreement and approbation.

The purely religious character of these exercises was shown in the complete lack of selfish interest in nearly all of those who participated in them. They sought nothing for themselves in this quest for simplified principle. No discouragement halted that search. Indeed, the obstacles were what made the search entrancing. The American Law Institute was ceremony of the very purest sort, dedicated to the ideal that this was a government of law and not of men. Some of the members of the Liberty League may have had a few selfish interests to further, but it is very doubtful if even these people thought about those interests directly, so absorbed were they in the search for ultimate truth, so preoccupied in contemplation of the future to the exclusion of the present. And in so far as the great membership of this institution was concerned, most of them were acting directly against the common sense interests which they would instantly have recognized if the phobias which motivated them had been brushed aside.

A poll of the Institute of Public Opinion showed that at least 30 per cent of even the unemployed men preferred the conservative to the liberal label. Persons on relief who had seen better days and were imbued with middle-class culture felt it only proper that they should be pauperized before aid was extended them. It was common to find persons who had gone bankrupt devoting the rest of their lives to working for their creditors. Some of these persons demanded new philosophies of government and became Socialists, or Communists, or whatnot. Few of them demanded with any articulate political force actual bread instead of religious principles. Only a few groups like the ex-soldiers, a few of the industrial leaders, and the politicians seemed to catch the beauty of the old proverb that "a bird in the hand is worth two in the bush." They achieved cash bonuses out of the tangled political situation, while most of their fellows were seeking symbols.

The deep hold which this highly religious folklore had upon the small business or professional man, a majority of our industrial leaders, and our press is evidenced by the fact that in 1936 the Constitution became for them a sort of abracadabra which would cure all disease. Copies of the Constitution, bound together with the Declaration of Independence and Lincoln's Gettysburg Address, were distributed in cigar stores; essays on the Constitution were written by high-school students; incomprehensible speeches on the Constitution were made from every public platform to reverent audiences which knew approximately as much about the history and dialectic of that document as the masses in the Middle Ages knew about the Bible—in those days when people were not permitted to read the Bible. The American Liberty League was dedicated to Constitution worship. Like the Bible, the Constitution became the altar whenever our best people met together for tearful solemn purposes, regardless of the kind of organization. Teachers in many states were compelled to swear to support the Constitution. No attempt was made to attach a particular meaning to this phrase, yet people thought that it had deep and mystical significance, and that the saying of the oath constituted a charm against evil spirits. The opponents of such oaths became equally excited, and equally theological about the great harm the ceremony might do. Nor was Constitution worship limited to upper strata. The Ku Klux Klan and similar disorderly organizations took the Constitution as their motto for the persecution of Jews and Catholics. In May, 1936, Michigan discovered a state-wide organization of misguided psychopathic personalities which had conducted a series of floggings simply because it was caught up by the solemnity of a ritual. No one could belong who did not take a solemn oath that he was a supporter of the Constitution. The most interesting fact about this order was that it was recruited largely from the underprivileged and the unemployed.

Only radical parties refused to worship the Constitution, but the spirit of the age was such that they, too, put their faith in the written doctrines which they themselves had framed. Thus, the Socialist party, a group which could have no other conceivable purpose than to organize a protest vote, split wide apart in the crucial year of 1936 on purely theological doctrine.

When in 1937 the President proposed to put more liberal judges on the Court, liberals like Oswald Garrison Villard and John T. Flynn joined with the *New York Herald Tribune* to denounce this sacrilege. A group of men with completely irreconcilable views joined together in reciting the book of common prayer.

The essential characteristics of this type of thinking may be described as follows:

1. Everyone was so completely preoccupied with government as it ought to be that no action which was politically possible could escape condemnation in the terms of that ideal. Expediency was not a good public excuse for necessary imperfections.

2. Everyone was so much more concerned with the future life of social institutions than with the present that it seemed immaterial what happened to the legislation of the day directed only at temporary needs. Nothing could be considered really important unless it fitted into what was conceived to be the moral future of the nation. No one could quite explain what the moral future of the nation was, and therefore on such a question they were always willing to accept the word of any duly constituted authority whose remarks fitted their particular prejudices.

3. Everyone was more interested in the spiritual government than in the temporal. Temporal government consisted of business and politics. The theory was that these things ran themselves, the one being impelled by beneficent economic laws, which operated because of the inherent balance of human nature, and the other being an invention of the devil which ran automatically because of the weakness of human nature.

4. No one ever read the economic theory or the constitutional theory which kept the spiritual government in bounds. Nor was there any faith in any particular type of expert. The faith was in the pontifical nature of the utterances ex cathedra, and the belief in the centuries of learning supposed to lie back of them. Not everyone liked the particular set of such principles which happened to be uppermost. But they were convinced that further study and the elimination of politics from government would give them a set which they would like.

The attitude which we have just been describing colored all thinking and all public utterance wherever the activities of government were concerned. It completely confused the activities of government by subjecting them to unreal standards under which no human organization could operate. The election of 1936 brought out the fact that a very large number of people, roughly representing the more illiterate and inarticulate masses of people, had lost their faith in the more prominent and respected economic preachers and writers of the time, who for the most part were aligned against the New Deal. They repudiated the advice of the newspapers which they bought and read because they were more immediately affected by the economic pressures of the time which were depriving them of security. Nevertheless, after the election, people continued to talk in the old phrases as before. The political leadership which was demanded was also required to be cast in old formulas and these old formulas continued to confuse its direction. Although there were signs of a change in attitude everywhere, organized learning had not yet caught up.

H. L. MENCKEN

Beaters of Breasts

ON SEPTEMBER 1, in the presidential campaign year of 1936, I received an office chit from Paul Patterson, publisher of the Baltimore *Sunpapers,* proposing that I go to Boston to cover the Harvard tercentenary orgies, then just getting under way. On September 3, after a day given over, at least in theory, to prayer and soul-searching, I replied as follows:

The more I think over the Harvard project, the less it lifts me. I'd much prefer to join Alf Landon. I like politicoes much better than I like professors. They sweat more freely and are more amusing.

My prayer and soul-searching, of course, were purely bogus, as such exercises only too often are. I had actually made up my mind in favor of the politicians a great many years before, to wit, in 1900 or thereabout, when I was still an infant at the breast in journalism. They shocked me a little at my first intimate contact with them, for I had never suspected, up to then, that frauds so bold and shameless could flourish in a society presumably Christian, and under the eye of a putatively watchful God. But as I came to know them better and better I began to develop a growing admiration, if not for their virtue, then at least for their professional virtuosity, and at the same time I discovered that many of them, in their private character, were delightful fellows, whatever their infamies *ex officio*. This appreciation of them, in the years following, gradually extended itself into a friendly interest in quacks of all sorts, whether theological, economic, military, philanthropic, judicial, literary, musical or sexual, and including even the professorial, and in the end that interest made me a sort of expert on the science of rooking the confiding, with a large acquaintance among practitioners of every species. But though I thus threw a wide net I never hauled in any fish who seemed to me to be the peers of the quacks political—not, indeed, by many a glittering inch. Even the Freudians when they dawned, and the chiropractors, and the penologists, and the social engineers, and the pedagogical wizards of Teachers College, Columbia, fell a good deal short of many Congressmen and Senators that I knew, not to mention Governors of sovereign American states. The Governors, in fact, were for long my favorites, for they constituted a class of extraordinarily protean rascals, and I remember a year when, of the forty-eight then in office, four were under indictment by grand juries, and one was actually in jail. Of the rest, seven were active Ku Kluxers, three were unreformed labor leaders, two were dipsomaniacs, five were bogus war heroes, and another was an astrologer.

My high opinion of political mountebanks remains unchanged to this day, and I suspect that when the history of our era is written at last it may turn out that they have been one of America's richest gifts to humanity. On only one point do I discover any doubt, and that is on the point whether those who really believe in their hocus-pocus—for example, Woodrow Wilson—are to be put higher or lower, in entertainment value, to those who are too smart—for example, Huey Long. Perhaps the question answers itself, for very few of the second class, in the long run, are able to resist their own buncombe, and I daresay that Huey, if the Japs had not cut him down prematurely, would have ended by believing more or less in his share-the-wealth apocalypse, though not, of course, to the extent of sharing his share. After the death of William Jennings Bryan, in 1926, I printed an estimate of his life and public services which dismissed him as a quack pure and unadulterated, but in the years since I have come to wonder if that was really just. When, under the prodding of Clarence Darrow, he made his immortal declaration that man is not a mammal, it seemed to me to be a mere bravura piece by a quack sure that his customers would take anything. But I am now more than half convinced that Jennings really believed it, just as he believed that Jonah swallowed the whale. The same phenomenon is often visible in other fields of quackery, especially the theological. More than once I have seen a Baptist evangelist scare himself by his own alarming of sinners, and quite as often I have met social workers who actually swallowed at least a third of their sure-cures for all the sorrows of the world. Let us not forget that Lydia Pinkham, on her deathbed, chased out her doctors and sent for a carboy of her Vegetable Compound, and that Karl Marx (though not Engels) converted himself to Socialism in his declining years.

It amazes me that no one has ever undertaken a full-length psychological study of Bryan, in the manner of Gamaliel Bradford and Lytton Strachey, for his life was long and full of wonders. My own contacts with him, unhappily, were rather scanty, though I reported his performances, off and on, from 1904 to 1926, a period of nearly a quarter of a century. The first time I saw him show in the grand manner was at the Democratic national convention of 1904, in St. Louis. He had been the party candidate for the presidency in 1896 and 1900, and was to be the candidate again in 1908, but in 1904 the gold Democrats were on top and he was rejected in favor of Alton B. Parker, a neat and clean but bewildered judge from somewhere up the Hudson, now forgotten by all save political antiquarians. Jennings made a stupendous fight against Parker, and was beaten in the end only by a resort to gouging *a posteriori* and kneeing below the belt. On a hot, humid night, with the hall packed, he elbowed his way to the platform to deliver what he and everyone else thought would be his valedictory. He had prepared for it by announcing that he had come down with laryngitis and could scarcely speak, and as he began his speech it was in a ghostly whisper. That was long before the day of loud-speakers, so the gallery could not hear him, and in a minute it was howling to him to speak louder, and he was going through the motion of trying to do so. In his frayed alpaca coat and baggy pants he was a pathetic figure, and that, precisely, is what he wanted to appear.

But galleries are always brutal, and this one was worse than most. It kept on howling, and in a little while the proceedings had to be suspended while the sergeants-at-arms tried to restore order. How long the hiatus continued I forget, but I well remember how it ended. One of the dignitaries in attendance was the late J. Ham Lewis, then in the full splendor of his famous pink whiskers. He sat at a corner of the platform where everyone in the house could see him, and so sitting, with the fetid miasma from 15,000 Democrats rising about him, he presently became thirsty. Calling a page, he sent out for a couple of bottles of beer, and when they came in, sweating with cold, he removed the caps with a gold opener, parted his vibrissae with a lordly gesture, and proceeded to empty the beer down his esophagus. The galleries, forgetting poor Jennings, rose on their hind legs and gave Ham three loud cheers, and when they were over it was as if an electric spark had been discharged, for suddenly there was quiet, and Jennings could go on.

The uproar had nettled him, for he was a vain fellow, and when he uttered his first words it was plain that either his indignation had cured his laryngitis or he had forgotten it. His magnificent baritone voice rolled out clearly and sonorously, and in two minutes he had stilled the hostility of the crowd and was launched upon a piece of oratory of the very first chop. There were hundreds of politicians present who had heard his Cross of Gold speech in Chicago in 1896, and they were still more or less under its enchantment, but nine-tenths of them were saying the next day that this St. Louis speech was even more eloquent, even more gaudy, even more overpowering. Certainly I listened to it myself with my ears wide open, my eyes apop and my reportorial pencil palsied. It swept up on wave after wave of sound like the *finale* of the first movement of Beethoven's Eroica, and finally burst into such coruscations that the crowd first gasped and then screamed. "You *may* say," roared Jennings, "that I have not fought a good fight. [*A pause.*] You *may* say that I have not run a good race. [*A longer pause, with dead silence in the galleries.*] But *no* man [*crescendo*] shall say [*a catch in the baritone voice*] *that I have not kept the faith!!!!*"

That was long, long ago, in a hot and boozy town, in the decadent days of an American era that is now as far off as the Würm Glaciation, but I remember it as clearly as if it were last night. What a speech, my masters! What a speech! Like all really great art, it was fundamentally simple. The argument in it, so far as I can recall it at all, was feeble, and the paraphrase of II Timothy iv, 7 was obvious. But how apt, how fit and meet, how tremendously effective! If the galleries had been free to vote, Bryan would have been nominated on the spot, and to the tune of ear-splitting hallelujahs. Even as it was, there was an ominous stirring among the delegates, boughten though most of them were, and the leaders, for ten minutes, were in a state of mind not far from the panicky. I well recall how they darted through the hall, slapping down heresy here and encouraging the true faith there. Bryan, always the perfect stage manager, did not wait for this painful afterglow. He knew that he was done for, and he was too smart to be on hand for the formal immolation. Instead, he climbed down from the platform and made his slow way out of the hall, his huge catfish mouth set in a hard line, his great eyes glittering, his black hair clumped in sweaty locks over his epicycloid dome. He looked poor and shabby and battered, but he was pathetic no more. The Money Power had downed him, but his soul was marching on. Some one in the galleries started to sing "John Brown's Body" in a voice of brass, but the band leader shut it off hastily by breaking into "The Washington *Post* March." Under cover of the banal strains the leaders managed to restore law and order in the ranks. The next morning Parker

was nominated, and on the Tuesday following the first Monday of the
ensuing November he was laid away forever by Roosevelt I.

I missed Bryan's come-back in 1908, but I saw him often after that,
and was present, as I have recorded, at his Gethsemane among the Bible
searchers at Dayton, Tenn., though I had left town before he actually
ascended into Heaven. He was largely responsible for the nomination of
Woodrow Wilson at Baltimore in 1912, and was rewarded for his services
by being made Secretary of State. In New York, in 1924, after howling
against Wall Street for nearly three weeks, he accepted the nomination
of its agent and attorney, John W. Davis, of Piping Rock, W. Va., and
took in payment the nomination of his low comedy brother, Charlie,
to second place on the ticket. During the great war upon the Rum Demon
he hung back until the triumph of Prohibition began to seem inevitable,
and then leaped aboard the band-wagon with loud, exultant gloats. In brief,
a fraud. But I find myself convinced, nevertheless, that his support of the
Good Book against Darwin and company was quite sincere—that is, as
sincerity runs among politicoes. When age began to fetch him the fear
of Hell burgeoned out of his unconscious, and he died a true Christian
of the Hookworm Belt, full of a malignant rage against the infidel.

Bryan was essentially and incurably a yap, and never had much of a
following in the big cities. At the New York convention of 1924 the
Tammany galleries razzed him from end to end of his battle against
the Interests, and then razzed him again, and even more cruelly, when
he sold out for the honor of the family. He made speeches nearly every
day, but they were heard only in part, for the moment he appeared
on the platform the Al Smith firemen in the galleries began setting off
their sirens and the cops on the floor began shouting orders and pushing
people about. Thus the setting was not favorable for his oratory, and
he made a sorry showing. But when he had a friendly audience he was
magnificent. I heard all the famous rhetoricians of his generation, from
Chauncey M. Depew to W. Bourke Cockran, and it is my sober judgment, standing on the brink of eternity, that he was the greatest of them
all. His voice had something of the caressing richness of Julia Mar-
lowe's, and he could think upon his feet much better than at a desk.
The average impromptu speech, taken down by a stenographer, is found
to be a bedlam of puerile clichés, thumping non sequiturs and limping,
unfinished sentences. But Jennings emitted English that was clear, flowing
and sometimes not a little elegant, in the best sense of the word. Every
sentence had a beginning, a middle and an end. The argument, three
times out of four, was idiotic, but it at least hung together.

I never traveled with him on his tours of the cow country, but it was my good fortune to accompany various other would-be heirs to Washington and Lincoln on theirs, and I always enjoyed the experience, though it meant heavy work for a reporter, and a certain amount of hardship. No politician can ever resist a chance to make a speech, and sometimes, in the regions where oratory is still esteemed, that chance offers twenty or thirty times a day. What he has to say is seldom worth hearing, but he roars it as if it were gospel, and in the process of wearing out his vocal chords he also wears out the reporters. More than once, accompanying such a geyser, I have been hard at it for eighteen hours out of the twenty-four, and have got nothing properly describable as a meal until 11.30 p.m. Meanwhile, unless there is an occasional lay-over in some hotel, it is hard to keep clean, and in consequence after a couple of weeks of campaigning the entourage of a candidate for the highest secular office under God begins to smell like a strike meeting of longshoremen.

Of all the hopefuls I have thus accompanied on their missionary journeys—it is perhaps only a coincidence that each and every one of them was licked—the most amusing was Al Smith. By the time he made his campaign in 1928 he was very well known to the country, and so he attracted large crowds everywhere. Sometimes, of course, those crowds were a good deal more curious than cordial, for Al passed, in the pellagra and chigger latitudes, as no more than a secret agent of the Pope, and it was generally believed that he had machine-guns aboard his campaign train, and was ready to turn them loose at a word from Rome. But the only time he met with actual hostility was not in the tall grass but in the metropolis of Louisville, and the persons who tried to fetch him there were not credulous yokels but city slickers. His meeting was held in a large hall, and every inch of it was jammed. When Al and his party got to the place they found it uncomfortably warm, but that was hardly surprising, for big crowds always engender calories. But by the time the candidate rose to speak the heat was really extraordinary, and before he was half way through his speech he was sweating so copiously that he seemed half drowned. The dignitaries on the platform sweated too, and so did the vulgar on the floor and in the galleries. Minute by minute the temperature seemed to increase, until finally it became almost unbearable. When Al shut down at last, with his collar a rag and his shirt and pants sticking to his hide, the thermometer must have stood at 100 degrees at least, and there were plenty who guessed that it stood at 110. Not until the campaign party got back to its train did the truth reach it. There then appeared an apologetic committee with the news that the city administration of Louisville, which was currently Republican, had had its goons fire up the boilers under the hall, deliberately and with malice prepense.

The plan had been to wreck the meeting by frying it, but the plotters had underestimated the endurance of a politico with an audience in front of him, and also the endurance of an American crowd feasting its eyes upon a celebrated character. It took Al twenty-four hours to cool off, but I had noted no falling off in his oratorical amperage. He had, in fact, hollered even louder than usual, and his steaming customers had howled with delight. What his speech was about I can't tell you, and neither, I daresay, could anyone else who was present.

The truth is that some of his most effective harangues in that campaign were probably more or less unintelligible to himself. The common report was that he knew nothing about national issues, and that he had never, in fact, been across the North river before he was nominated, or even so much as looked across, so he carried a Brain Trust with him to help him prove that this report was all a lie, and its members prepared the first draft of every one of his set speeches. Its chief wizard was the famous Mrs. Belle Israels Moskowitz, but she did not travel with the candidate; instead, she remained at his G.H.Q. in New York, bossing a huge staff of experts in all the known departments of human knowledge, and leaving the field work to two trusties—the Hon. Joseph M. Proskauer, a justice of the Supreme Court of New York, and the Hon. Bernard L. Shientag, then a justice of the New York City court. The two learned judges and their secretaries sweated almost as hard every day as Al sweated in that hall in Louisville. They had a car to themselves, and it was filled with files, card indexes and miscellaneous memoranda supplied from time to time by Mrs. Moskowitz. Every morning they would turn out bright and early to concoct Al's evening speech—usually on some such unhappy and unfathomable subject (at least to the candidate himself) as the tariff, the League of Nations, Farm Relief, the Alaskan fisheries, or the crimes of the Chicago Board of Trade. They would work away at this discourse until noon, then stop for lunch, and then proceed to finish it. By three or four o'clock it was ready, and after a fair copy had been sent to Al it would be mimeographed for the use of the press.

Al's struggles with it were carried on *in camera,* so I can't report upon them in any detail, but there is reason to believe that he often made heavy weather of mastering his evening's argument. By the time he appeared on the platform he had reduced it to a series of notes on cards, and from these he spoke—often thunderously and always to the great delight of the assembled Democrats. But not infrequently his actual speech resembled the draft of the two judges only to the extent that the ritual of the Benevolent and Protective Order of Elks resembles the Book of

Mormon and the poetry of John Donne. The general drift was there, but that was about all—and sometimes even the drift took a new course. The rest was a gallimaufry of Al's recollections of the issues and arguments in a dozen New York campaigns, with improvisations suggested by the time, the place and the crowd. It was commonly swell stuff, but I'd certainly be exaggerating if I said it showed any profound grasp of national issues. Al, always shrewd, knew that a Chicago crowd, or a rural Missouri crowd, or a crowd in Tennessee, Michigan or Pennsylvania did not differ by more than four per cent. from a New York crowd, so he gave them all the old stuff that he had tried with such success in his state campaigns, and it went down again with a roar. Never in my life had I heard louder yells than those that greeted him at Sedalia, Mo., in the very heart of the no-more-scrub-bulls country. His meeting was held in the vast cattle-shed of a county fair, and among the 20,000 persons present there were some who had come in by flivver from places as far away as Nebraska, Oklahoma, and even New Mexico. The subject of his remarks that night, as set by the two judges, was the tariff, but he had forgotten it in five minutes, and so had his audience. There were stenographers present to take down what he said, and transcripts of it were supplied to the press-stand sheet by sheet, but only a few correspondents actually sent it out. The rest coasted on the judges' draft, disseminated by the press associations during the late afternoon and released at 8 p.m., as he arose to speak. Thus all the Americans who still depended on the newspapers for their news—and there were plenty of them left in 1928— were duped into accepting what the two laborious juris-consults had written for what Al had actually said. I do not know, but the thought has often crossed my mind, that Hoover's overwhelming victory in November may have been due, at least in part, to that fact.

Al bore up pretty well under the rigors of the campaign, but now and then he needed a rest, and it was provided by parking his train on a side-track for a quiet night, usually in some sparsely settled region where crowds could not congregate. After his harrying of Tennessee, and just before he bore down upon Louisville to be fried, there was such a hiatus in rural Kentucky. When I turned out in the morning I found that the train was laid up in a lovely little valley of the Blue Grass country, with nothing in sight save a few farmhouses and a water-tank, the latter about a mile down the track. My colleague, Henry M. Hyde, suggested that we go ashore to stretch our legs, and in a little while we were hanging over a fence some distance to the rear of the train, admiring a white-painted house set in a grove of trees. Presently two handsome young girls issued from the house, and asked us prettily to have breakfast with their mother, who was a widow, and themselves. We accepted at once, and were very charmingly entertained. In the course of the conversation it appeared that another daughter, not present, aspired to be the postmistress of the village behind the tank down the track, and Hyde, always gallant, promised at once that he would see Al, and get her a promise of the appointment come March 4, 1929.

When we got back to the train Hyde duly saw Al, and the promise was made instantly. Unhappily, Hoover won in November, and it seemed hopeless to ask his Postmaster-General to make good on Al's pledge. Four years of horror came and went, but the daughter down in the Blue Grass kept on hugging her ambition. When Roosevelt II was elected in 1932 her mother got into communication with Hyde, suggesting that the new administration should be proud and eager to make good on the promise of the Democratic standard-bearer four years before, even though that standard-bearer had since taken his famous walk. Hyde put the question up to Jim Farley, and Farley, a man very sensitive to points of honor, decided that Roosevelt was bound to carry out the official promises of his predecessor, however revolting they might be. An order was thereupon issued that the daughter be made postmistress at the water-tank at once, and Hyde went to bed that night feeling that few other Boy Scouts had done better during the day. But alas and alas, it turned out that the tank was a fourth-class post office, that appointments to such offices were under the Civil Service, and that candidates had to be examined. Farley so advised the widow's daughter and she took the examination, but some other candidate got a higher mark, and the scrupulous Jim decided that he could not appoint her. Hyde and I often recall the lamentable episode, and especially the agreeable first canto of it. Never in all my wanderings have I seen a more idyllic spot than that secluded little valley in the Blue Grass, or had the pleasure of being entertained by pleasanter people than the widow and her daughters. The place was really Arcadian, and Hyde and I wallowed in its bucolic enchantments while Al caught up with lost sleep on his funeral train.

He was, in his day, the most attractive of all American politicoes, but it would be going too far to say that he was any great shakes as an orator. Compared to Bryan he was as a BB shot to a twelve-inch shell, and as he was passing out of public life there was arising a rhetorician who was even greater than Bryan, to wit, Gerald L. K. Smith. As I have said, I have heard all the really first-chop American breast-beaters since 1900, and included among them have been not only the statesmen but also the divines, for example, Sam Jones, Gipsy Smith, Father Coughlin and Billy Sunday, but among them all I have encountered none worthy of being put in the same species, or even in the same genus, as Gerald. His own early training was gained at the sacred desk but in maturity he switched to the hustings, so that he now has a double grip upon the diaphragms and short hairs of the *Anthropoidea*. Add to these advantages of nurture the natural gifts of an imposing person, a flashing eye, a hairy chest, a rubescent complexion, large fists, a voice both loud and mellow, terrifying and reassuring, *sforzando* and *pizzicato,* and finally, an unearthly capacity for distending the superficial blood-vessels of his temples and neck, as if they were biceps—and you have the makings of a boob-bumper worth going miles to see and hear, and then worth writing home about. When I first heard Gerald, at the convention of the Townsend old-age pension fans at Cleveland in 1936, I duly wrote home about him to the *Sunpaper,* and in the following fervent terms:

His speech was a magnificent amalgam of each and every American species of rabble-rousing, with embellishments borrowed from the Algonquin Indians and the Cossacks of the Don. It ran the keyboard from the softest sobs and gurgles to the most ear-splitting whoops and howls, and when it was over the 9000 delegates simply lay back in their pews and yelled.

Never in my life, in truth, have I ever heard a more effective speech. In logical content, to be sure, it was somewhat vague and even murky, but Dr. Townsend's old folks were not looking for logical content: what they had come to Cleveland for was cheer, consolation, the sweet music of harps and psalteries. Gerald had the harps and psalteries, and also a battery of trumpets, trombones and bass-drums. When he limned the delights of a civilization offering old-age pensions to all, with $200 cash a month for every gaffer and another $200 for the old woman, he lifted them up to the highest heaven, and when he excoriated the Wall Street bankers, millionaire steel magnates, Chicago wheat speculators and New Deal social engineers who sneered at the vision, he showed them the depths of the lowest hell. Nor was it only the believing and in fact already half dotty old folks who panted under his eloquence: he also fetched the minority of sophisticates in the hall, some of them porch-climbers in Dr. Townsend's entourage and the rest reporters in the press-stand. It is an ancient convention of American journalism, not yet quite outlawed by the Newspaper Guild, that the press-stand has no opinion—that its members, consecrated to fair reports, must keep their private feelings to themselves, and neither cheer nor hiss. But that convention went out of the window before Gerald had been hollering five minutes. One and all, the boys and gals of the press abandoned their jobs, leaped upon their rickety desks, and gave themselves up to the voluptuous enjoyment of his whooping. When the old folks yelled, so did the reporters yell, and just as loudly. And when Gerald, sweating like Al at Louisville, sat down at last, and the press resumed its business of reporting his remarks, no one could remember what he had said.

A few weeks later I saw him give an even more impressive exhibition of his powers. At the Townsend convention just described one of the guest speakers had been the Rev. Charles E. Coughlin, the radio priest, who, in return for Dr. Townsend's politeness in inviting him, invited the doctor and Gerald to speak at his own convention, scheduled to be held in Cleveland a few weeks later. But Gerald's immense success apparently sicklied him o'er with a green cast of envy, and when the time came he showed a considerable reluctance to make good. Finally, he hit upon the device of putting Gerald and the doctor off until the very end of his convention, by which time his assembled customers would be so worn out by his own rabble-rousing that nothing short of an earthquake could move them. On the last day, in fact, they were so worn out, for Coughlin kept banging away at them from 10 a.m. to 8 p.m., with no breaks for meals. The device was thus a smart one, but his reverence, for all his smartness, was not smart enough to realize that Gerald was actually an earthquake. First, old Townsend was put up, and the general somnolence was only increased, for he is one of the dullest speakers on earth. But then, with the poor morons hardly able to keep their eyes open, Gerald followed— and within five minutes the Coughlin faithful had forgotten all about their fatigues, and also all about Coughlin, and were leaping and howling like the Townsend old folks. It was a shorter speech than the other, for Coughlin, frowning, showed his itch to cut it off as soon as possible and Gerald was more or less uneasy, but it was even more remarkable. Once more the boys and gals in the press-stand forgot their Hippocratic oath and yielded themselves to pure enjoyment, and once more no one could recall, when it was over, what its drift had been, but that it was a masterpiece was agreed by all. When Gerald came to Cleveland it was in the humble rôle of a follower of the late Huey Long, jobless since Huey's murder on September 10, 1935. But when he cleared out after his two speeches it was in the lofty character of the greatest rabble-rouser since Peter the Hermit.

Coughlin, it seems to me, is a much inferior performer. He has a velvet voice, and is thus very effective on the radio, but like his great rival on the air, Roosevelt II, he is much less effective face to face. For one thing, he is almost totally lacking in dramatic gesture, for his long training at the mike taught him to stick firmly to one spot, lest the fans lose him in the midst of his howling. It is, of course, impossible for an orator with passion in him to remain really immovable, so Coughlin has developed a habit of enforcing his points by revolving his backside. This saves him from going off the air, but it is somewhat disconcerting, not to say indecent, in the presence of an audience. After the convention of his half-wits in Cleveland in 1936 a report was circulated that he was experimenting with a mike fixed to his shoulders by a stout framework, so that he could gesture normally without any risk of roaring futilely into space, but if he actually ever used it I was not present, and so cannot tell you about it.

JAMES T. FARRELL

Tommy Gallagher's Crusade

I

"READ *Christian Justice!* Father Moylan's *Christian Justice,* ten cents a copy! See page three of this issue and learn what Father Moylan says of the Red menace. Get your *Christian Justice,* ten cents a copy!"

Tommy Gallagher stood on the curb in front of his parish church in Brooklyn, selling his magazines as the last Sunday mass let out. Tommy was a lad of twenty-five, husky, broad-shouldered, with a large round face with sensuous lips and dark brows which contributed to the ferocity of his expression when he frowned. The parishioners poured out of the church. Small knots of people gathered on the sidewalk to talk for a moment or two, while many others moved away.

Young fellows whom Tommy knew, some of them grammar school classmates of his, grinned at him. Now and then older people nodded, parishioners he had known for many years, friends of his mother and father. Most of the people were not interested in his magazine and passed him by. Several men faced him with unmistakable hostility but said nothing. A man of middle age in shabby clothes came up to him and bought a copy. The man said that Father Moylan was the real one for the common fellow. Tommy said sure he was. The man said that he had been out of work for two years, had been on relief, W.P.A., had looked for odd jobs, and he was fed up and felt that the only one who had

From *To Whom It May Concern.* Reprinted by permission of Vanguard Press Inc. Copyright, 1939, by James T. Farrell.

spoken out for the poor devils like himself was Father Moylan. Tommy agreed. The man folded his copy of *Christian Justice* under his arm and walked on, a seedy, broken-looking figure.

"Read Father Moylan's *Christian Justice!* Ten cents a copy! Read *Christian Justice* and kick the Reds out of America!"

The crowd was almost gone now. Tommy stood there, hoping to make a last sale. He held up a copy of the magazine. It was printed in bold type, looked something like a newspaper, had large headlines and a picture on the front page. But he guessed that he'd have to call it quits. Jimmy Powers, a thin, overdressed lad of Tommy's age, came over to him, smiling as he approached.

"What the hell, Tommy, when did you become a Red?" Jimmy asked.

"What's that?" Tommy retorted, taken by surprise.

"Ain't you a Red, selling magazines on the street?"

"Father Moylan's magazine! Read it and see what the Reds and the eagle-beaks are doin'," Tommy replied, holding up a copy.

"Oh! I thought it was only Reds and newsboys who sold magazines and papers an the streets."

"Here, Jimmy, buy one, it's only a dime."

"What'll I do with it?" Jimmy asked.

"Read it!"

"Sounds too much like work."

"Jimmy, it'll open your eyes. Come on, buy one," Tommy said, trying to thrust a copy into Jimmy's hand.

"Hell, Gallagher, *The Brooklyn Eagle* gives me enough readin' matter."

They were alone now in front of the church. Jimmy lit a cigarette. He offered Tommy one and held up a lighted match while Tommy lit his.

"Jimmy, you're a Christian and an American, ain't you?" Tommy asked.

"I guess so. And I'm a Dodger fan, too."

"Well, you ought to buy this magazine."

"Workin', Tommy?"

"I'm sellin'. Sellin' this," Tommy answered, and again he held up a copy.

"Hell, that ain't work," Jimmy said.

"I ain't ashamed of selling *Christian Justice*. You don't understand, Jimmy. Let me explain it to you."

"Explain what?"

"Oh, about Father Moylan and what he's doin'."

"I got to trot along. I got to get out to Ebbets Field early today if I want a seat. They're gonna pitch Van Lingle Mungo and I want to see the big boy come back. Tell me another time. Good luck, and hope you make a few pennies with your work there," Jimmy said, and he walked off.

Tommy looked after him, dour. He guessed he never liked that guy. He stuck his hands in his pockets and fingered his change. He'd only sold ten copies this morning. Hadn't made much dough. Well, he had about five bucks of his own. Maybe he'd have better luck next week. Carrying his bundle of magazines, he started toward home.

2

The Gallagher family sat down to their Sunday dinner. The father was a lean man in his fifties with graying hair; for years he had worked for the telephone company as a repairman. A mild-mannered and genial man, he had never manifested much interest in politics. He had always voted the Democratic ticket and let it go at that. Mrs. Gallagher was a plump woman with lovely black hair that was beginning to streak with white. The oldest boy, Joe, was tall and lean like his father. He had a pretty good job working in the pay roll department of the telephone company. Bill was twenty-one, heavier and more burly than Tommy, with a jolly face and light hair. He was a clerk in an office in Manhattan and earned thirty dollars a week. All during the depression, Bill, Joe, and the father had been fortunate in retaining their jobs, and the family was comfortably enough situated to satisfy their normal wants.

The father and Joe had been talking about the telephone company and the dinner was progressing when Mrs. Gallagher suddenly looked at Tommy and said:

"I saw Mrs. Malone at early mass today. She was nice as pie, and told me that her son had a good job, and then she says she sees you in front of church every Sunday selling newspapers."

"He works for kikes. Catch me workin' for one of them eagle-beaks," Tommy blurted out.

"Why don't you say catch you working, and stop there?" Bill said, looking across the table at Tommy.

"Say, you punk, when you was still in school I had a job," Tommy countered.

"And you sure overworked yourself getting out of jobs and losing 'em ever since."

"Why don't you cut it out?" Mr. Gallagher asked.

"It seems to me that you ought to show a little consideration for the rest of us. You ought to be able to get something better to do with that outfit you run around with besides selling newspapers," Joe said.

"I don't sell newspapers. I sell a magazine and I do it because it's my duty," Tommy answered.

Bill burst into hearty laughter.

"You talking about duty. You're gettin' so funny they ought to put you on the radio," Bill said.

Tommy glared at Bill. There was a dense expression on his face. He was trying to think of a quick comeback.

"That's what you say," Tommy finally said.

"Tommy, I don't know what's happening to you. You're gettin' touchy and always go around with a chip on your shoulder," Mr. Gallagher observed.

"I got my eyes opened," Tommy answered.

"And I'm gettin' mine open, too. Here Joe and I are saving our dough to get married, and he won't even look for a job," Bill said.

"How you gonna get a job when the Jewrocracy runs the country? Maybe if I had a name like Rosenstein, I'd have a good job."

"Well, why don't you change your name to Rosenstein then and get a job?"

No one spoke for a few moments, and they went on eating. Tommy was smouldering. He hadn't been able to think up anything to say to Bill's last crack.

. "Tommy, the last time I went to a Holy Name Communion breakfast, I was talking to a young priest, Father Smith. He's a damned bright priest and well educated. I asked him about Father Moylan, and he said he couldn't go along with Father Moylan on this Jewish business, and it was going to give the Church a bad name. A priest shouldn't be mixing in politics like he does. If he does, what are the fellows on the other side of the fence gonna think?" Mr. Gallagher said.

"You don't understand," Tommy answered.

"Well, I'm tryin' to find out. Now, I used to think Father Moylan was all right, but when he turned against Roosevelt in the last election, that wasn't right. President Roosevelt is doin' the best he can, and if we pull along with him, he's goin' to get us out of all this mess."

"Rosenfeld," Tommy sneered.

"What's that?" Joe asked.

"I told you, Rosenfeld. And Mrs. Rosenfeld is a Red."

"Why, Mrs. Roosevelt is a lovely woman. I read her column every da' in the newspaper, and it's wonderful," Mrs. Gallagher said.

"Tommy, that's no way to talk about the President of the United State and his wife," Mr. Gallagher reproached him.

"Hitler kicks the Jews out, and we make them governors of our states and let 'em walk all over us," Tommy said.

"Joe, what do you think he'll do when he takes over Roosevelt's job?" Bill asked sarcastically, nodding his head toward Tommy.

"Listen, you, I'm fed up with your insults!"

"Well, what you gonna do about it?" Bill asked, looking straight at Tommy.

"No fighting! Not in this family. This is a home not a street corner," the father interposed.

"That'll be news to him. He doesn't act like it was," Bill said.

"I told you, you punk!"

Bill jumped to his feet in anger and challenged:

"Try tellin' me with something besides that tongue of yours!"

Joe and the father were on their feet. Joe grabbed Bill and told him not to be doing anything rash. The father gazed from one to the other, disturbed.

Mrs. Gallagher banged on the table. They sat down and were quiet. Tommy ate hastily now. He pouted.

"There's going to be no more fighting at this table. Not while I'm alive," Mrs. Gallagher declared with determination.

"I didn't start it. Don't look at me," Tommy said.

Bill looked enigmatically at Tommy, smiled sardonically, said nothing.

"I don't know, but it seems to me we all ought to live and let live. That's my philosophy, and it's always been that. It's the same for the Jews as for everybody else. There's good and bad in all kinds. We have too much fighting and hating in the world as it is, and the world is never going to get any better until it stops all this hating and fighting. We all got to make up our minds that we're gonna live and let live," Mr. Gallagher said.

Tommy looked arrogantly at his father. He was silent.

3

Tommy Gallagher marched in the picket line carrying a sign which read:

FREE CHRISTIAN AMERICA FROM JEWRY

The line was moving back and forth in front of the entrance to a large building in the Fifties in which were located the offices of a radio station that had refused to sell Father Moylan time because of the priest's provocative address and because he had been widely charged with having made false statements.

There were about three hundred people in the picket line. It had been organized by the Association for Christian Freedom to which Tommy belonged. He and many others in the line wore buttons on their coat lapels testifying to their membership in this organization. The main body of the demonstration consisted of young men, many of them unemployed. A number of them were dressed poorly; frayed collars and cuffs and an occasional shiny seat to a pair of trousers could be noticed in the moving line. The remainder of the crowd was mixed, including older men, girls, and corpulent women. Back and forth the line moved, going on the outside of the sidewalk by the curb, turning some distance down from the entrance to come back on the inside. In the crowd one could see fanatical faces, harried expressions, surly and sneering stares, sudden smiles. But the dominant mood of the demonstration was one of pugnacity. The crowd was spoiling for a fight. Policemen were lining the curb and were grouped at either end of the sidewalk area which the pickets covered. Passers-by and bystanders were hurried along, crowds and groups were not allowed to congregate. No magazine venders were permitted except those selling magazines to which the demonstrators were not hostile. Every now and then a few persons would join the demonstration and a loud cheer of approval would sweep down the marching line. In single file, they paraded back and forth in front of the building entrance.

Tommy was thrilling with pride as he marched. In front of him there was a little fellow with one elbow almost out of his coat. He carried a sign which read:

FOR A CHRISTIAN AMERICA

What this little fellow lacked in size he made up in voice, and at times even drowned out Tommy's yells. The lad behind him was shorter than Tommy. He was snappily dressed in a stylish suit with pleated trousers. He had a pin-point mustache, and as he marched, he constantly fingered it and smoothed down his greasy black hair. He wore a button, and carried a sign bearing the slogan:

BREAK THE RULE OF THE ATHEISTIC JEWS

Tommy kept looking at those passing in line on the opposite side of the sidewalk. He nodded frequently as he recognized faces of people he had met at meetings of the Association. Spotting Al O'Reilley, he smiled and read the sign Al was carrying.

SMASH COMMUNISM

He walked in line, feeling a sense of unity with all these people. He felt that he was one with them, and that they were one with him, all ready to fight together. He thought what a fine sight it was to see this picket line of Christian Americans who had all come out like this in defense of Father Moylan.

A trim little girl of about eighteen, with blonde hair, passed on the opposite side and let out a screeching yell.

Twenty million Christians murdered in Russia!

Exercising all of his strong lung power, Tommy repeated her shout and was pleased when he got a smile from her. The yell spread up and down the line of marchers and it reverberated with increasing volume and swelling hatred. Again and again it was taken up and shrieked out.

Twenty million Christians murdered in Russia!

The slogan was dropped as suddenly as it had been picked up. A sudden roar demanding free speech for Father Moylan arose and died down. Tommy saw a man with a red nose and gray hair swagger by, carrying a picket sign which demanded:

KEEP AMERICA OUT OF WAR

He started thinking that if there were any attempt to break this line, he would haul off and go swinging into the center of the melee and more than one dirty Red disrupter and hook-nose would know he'd been hit.

The marchers began singsonging another slogan:

Free speech for Father Moylan!

Tommy reiterated the slogan without thinking of what he was saying. Flashes of himself in the role of a heroic street warrior, slugging the Reds and Jews, kept coming and going in his mind. His arms tired because of the sign he carried and he wished that he were not lugging it in the demonstration. Al O'Reilley went by again, and he noticed that Al had gotten rid of his sign.

Tommy trudged along, and he thought how this demonstration was bringing people together. This sense of unity thrilled him. And at the same time he wanted to stand out from these people and be noticed. He joined in a new cry, seeking to send his voice soaring above all the others.

Defend Catholic Mexico!

He walked self-consciously erect and flung back his head as he again exploded the new slogan. He ought to stand out from the shrimps ahead of and behind him. He threw back his shoulders and put on his fiercest frown. He walked now with his shoulders held back so tensely that the muscles of his back hurt, and his arm was tired from the weight of the sign. He watched out of the corner of his eye to see whether or not those passing him would look. He read a sign carried by a red-haired woman:

NO MORE CHRISTIAN MARTYRS TO RED ATHEISM

He frowned, grimaced, made faces. He had to relax his posture a little because he was fagging himself out by holding himself too firmly. No use wearing himself out this way because he'd need what it took if there was a fight. He marched on.

A swarthy girl in summery clothes that brought out her figure passed, and her sign read:

FREE SPEECH FOR FATHER MOYLAN AND ALL CHRISTIAN AMERICANS

He'd like to know her.

Suddenly he noticed that there were newspaper photographers around taking pictures. Nearing two photographers, he contorted his features and let out a roaring demand for free speech for Father Moylan. He had hoped that they would snap him in action, and that then his picture would be in the newspapers tomorrow. But no pictures were taken when he passed the cameramen. He shuffled along, scraping his feet on the sidewalk. He looked at those opposite him, dragging along as if they were starting to get pooped out. It seemed as if many were now becoming weary of shouting. They walked more slowly, they yelled more sporadically, and they just drooped on. He hoped that the photographers would not go away before he passed them again.

"Snap it up. This ain't no way to walk," he said to the fellow in front of him.

"You tell 'em that. I can't go any faster than the one ahead of me."

He tramped along. A yell arose and spread up and down the line.

We demand free speech for Father Moylan!

But it soon faded out. The demonstration was losing its unity and its energy now. The slogans were being shouted out with only a momentary display of spirit.

Tommy again walked toward the photographers. He threw his shoulders back and held himself erect. But suppose that he were snapped and his picture did appear in the papers tomorrow morning, and the Reds saw it and recognized him, and then one day, he might be alone some place, walking along, minding his business, and they would remember him from the picture and pile on him? But no, that wasn't likely to happen. And he could take care of himself. He could handle plenty of 'em. Everybody knew they were worms.

We demand free speech for Father Moylan!

The cry died out spiritlessly.

Like a speaker had said at one of the Association meetings, the Reds were all yellow. And yet it made him kind of afraid. Suppose five or ten of them jumped him? Just as he was thinking of this, he came in camera range, and the photographers were taking pictures. He averted his gaze without even exercising any volition; it was like a reflex action. He walked on, dragging his feet, and he began thinking how he hated the Jews and the Communists.

Buy Christian!

It was a girl who started this cry, and they took it up like a college crowd shouting a cheer.

Buy Christian! Buy Christian! Buy Christian!

The spirit of the marchers suddenly lifted as they chanted the slogan. They marched now, and many tried to keep step. And they kept up their chant.

Buy Christian! Buy Christian! Buy Christian!

But again they dropped their cry and straggled. Tommy was now passing the cameras. He conquered his inclination to look away and looked bravely into the lenses, clenching his lips and holding the muscles of his face taut to seem tough. He walked on.

We demand free speech for Father Moylan!

The demonstration began to break up. Many were leaving it. There were gaps in the lines. Tommy remained in line until the crowd dispersed.

4

After the demonstration had broken up, Al O'Reilley asked Tommy to come along with a couple of the fellows and have a drink. Tommy was introduced to them. Pete Sullivan was a burly young man wearing a shiny blue suit. Then he met Eddie Slavin, a skinny lad of about twenty-one with a pimply face, small and suspicious black eyes, and buck teeth. Tommy noticed that he had on a neat suit. He was glad that his own gray suit was still in good condition.

A fellow belonging to the Association was going to a parish house where they often met, and took the signs in his automobile, and that relieved them. They went over to a bar on Ninth Avenue, and sat together at a table having beer and sandwiches while a radio was blaring swing music, and several fellows lined up at the bar were talking knowingly about prize fighters. They were enthusiastic and excited because of the demonstration and talked about it for a while, and then they got to talking about jobs.

"I'm in slavery," Eddie Slavin exclaimed.

"You're lucky," Pete Sullivan said.

"You wouldn't think so if you had my job. I'm a doorman in an apartment hotel down near Washington Square. The bastards make me work ten hours a day, and with the little dough I get, one of the guys there is trying to steam me up to join a goddamn union and pay 'em dues," Eddie said.

"Is the guy a Red?"

"I guess so. I see him comin' to work and goin' home with books under his arm, and he acts like a screwball," Eddie said.

"If you need any help, just say the word, boy," Al remarked.

"Boy, am I fed up! Some of the people livin' in the place are fine people, but then, others aren't. Christ, there's one damned bitch who's always belly-aching about me. And most of the people who come to see her got noses that make me suspicious. And goddamn it, I don't see why I, a freeborn white American, have to be a flunky for Jews, open doors and elevators for 'em, say yes sir and yes ma'm to 'em, run their goddamn errands, take crap from sheenies. I tell you, I'm fed up," Eddie Slavin went on. With a resolute gesture he lifted his glass of beer and took a drink.

"You're a lucky bastard, Al, with your old man doing good," Pete said.

"Me and Father Moylan are O.K. with my old man. He likes what I do and says it's for the good of the country," Al explained.

"You know, my old man just can't get anything into his head. He thinks I'm a screwball," Tommy complained.

"Well, I'm fed up, boys, and so is the old man. He had a hat store out in Flushing and he was doin' good, and then with bad times it went ker-flooie, and he's on his ear now. He works for the W.P.A. and he's always down in the mouth," Pete said.

"You want to explain to him what's wrong, tell him it's the Jews," Al told Pete.

"I got it figured out that if there weren't so many dames working, why, guys like us would be better off," Eddie Slavin said.

"That's why Hitler told the dames to stay home where they belong and have babies, and let the men work," Al declared.

"Say, Slavin, any chance of my gettin' a job where you are?" Pete asked.

"Gee, I don't know. They're full up, but guys are always comin' and goin'. If there's any chance, I'll tip you off."

"Do, will yuh," Pete urged.

"Sure I will. Only it's one goddamn lousy job, if you want to know."

"I don't care. I'm fed up," Pete said.

Tommy thought to himself that they could just catch him being a door-man and wearing a flunky's uniform. Catch him!

They had another round of beers.

Pete told a story he'd heard about the Reds and their girl friends, and they discussed girls. When they finished their beer, they paid their checks.

Pete Sullivan said he was lucky he could pay his share. He'd had a pretty good week selling *Christian Justice*. They left and walked four abreast over to Eighth Avenue.

Tommy wanted something exciting to happen. He felt a kind of let-down after the afternoon's activity. He wanted girls, drinking, fun, action. He remembered how often he had felt just like this, having nothing to do, and wanting a little fun and excitement, and how he'd cruised around with guys he knew, looking for something to happen, and nothing had, and he'd gone home feeling that another night had gone down the sewer. He was kind of afraid that tonight might be the same. All his life, he'd had a feeling that something big was going to happen to him, and it never had. Since he'd gotten interested in Father Moylan and joined the Association for Christian Freedom, this feeling had gotten stronger in him. And damn it, life had gotten more exciting. He had things to do that gave him a feeling of his own place in the world that he'd never had before. Yes, he had the feeling now more than ever that something big was going to come to him that he'd never had before and that he'd always wanted and waited for.

They turned onto Eighth Avenue and heard the rumbling of the subway underneath the sidewalk. A few feet ahead, Tommy saw a couple strolling toward him, and both were clearly Semitic. The fellow was smaller than Tommy, and the girl was good-looking and had a nice figure outlined by her dress.

"Close ranks, boys!" Tommy said quickly and under his breath.

They linked arms. The couple came face to face with them, surprised to find their path blocked by four sneering, tough-looking young men. The Jewish fellow was taken aback. The girl clung to his arm and her lips trembled.

"Lots of sidewalk out there," Tommy said curtly, pointing beyond the curb.

The fellow and girl tried to go around Tommy on the right, and a few pedestrians paused to watch what was happening. Tommy and his companions moved over.

"Get out on the street and make it fast!" Eddie Slavin yelled.

The Jewish lad blanched. He moved over to the curb, stepped off, walked with the girl on the street for a few feet, and then regained the sidewalk. The four boys laughed heartily, and spectators didn't know what was happening. The Jewish lad and his girl were lost in the crowd. Tommy and the boys walked on, laughing.

"Before we finish, boys, there won't be a Jew in New York," Tommy boasted.

They walked on. Pete Sullivan remarked that the two Hebes were lucky they didn't get worse. Tommy looked dour. He wanted excitement. Maybe a fight! With the others along, it wouldn't be too dangerous. No, he wanted it to be dangerous. And he knew himself that he didn't want this. And knowing it himself, it filled him with hate and envy.

"How about another beer, boys?" Al suggested.

5

Feeling low, Tommy woke up and saw that it was already eleven o'clock. He got out of bed but felt dizzy. He went back to bed and turned his eyes away from the light. Lying down, he felt all right. He tried to remember last night. They'd gone to several bars, and he recalled how he'd almost gotten into a fight in one of them. But he couldn't remember clearly just what had happened.

He was going over to New York to sell the magazine on the street, but he could stay in bed a little while longer and go down in the afternoon. He had to sell, too, because he was broke. He'd spent all his dough last night. He dozed off to sleep and awakened a half hour later. He lay in bed, attracted by his own imaginings of his fighting ability, and he began knocking Jews and Reds all over in his mind. He dozed off to sleep in the midst of his fantasy and got up at twelve-thirty, feeling a little better for the extra sleep.

He got dressed and went out into the kitchen for breakfast. His mother didn't say a word to him. He was hoping she wouldn't be sore because he didn't want to be quarreling with her.

"Hello, Mom," he said with forced cordiality.

"Up late, Tommy," she answered.

"I know, Mom. I didn't get in early last night."

"Neither did your brother Bill, but he was up bright and early this morning and over to work at his office."

"He's lucky. He's got a decent job."

"You'll never find a decent job if you go out looking for it at this time of day."

"I've been looking for jobs so long, I'm fed up."

"Whenever you had jobs, you lost them."

"It wasn't my fault. I ain't responsible for conditions. And then, at most of my jobs they never liked me. The last place, the boss was against me. How can you have a job when the boss is against you for no good reason?"

"Sit down and have your breakfast," she said.

He dropped into a chair at the kitchen table. He remembered that he didn't have a red cent. He'd have to ask her for money again. He'd been a damned fool for not getting up early, because then it'd have been easier to get something off her. But he couldn't have done it, feeling like he did. He was still low and nervous and breaking out with sudden fits of sweating. But he'd get over it. A bigger problem was how he was going to ask her for money.

"Gee, Mom, you don't have to act so sore at me," he complained in a whining, injured voice when his mother set coffee and toast before him.

"I'm not angry with you," she replied curtly.

"Well, gee, what's the matter then?"

"Eat your breakfast. I've got lots to do. We can't afford servants in this house," she said, leaving the kitchen.

He sat munching toast and drinking coffee. He lit a cigarette. He only had a few left, and didn't even have the price of another pack. He felt sorry for himself. He was getting a raw deal. He had never had a decent job in his life. Most of the jobs he'd had were lousy and he'd had to go to work and ride in the subways in dirty old work clothes while others went to work and came home dressed up. They were all against him. Mom was treating him like a stepson. They were all against him, and they didn't understand.

Sulking, he finished his cup of coffee, went to the stove and poured another, and came back to the table and sat down with it. He still sulked.

He broke out in another sweat. He felt weak. Gee, how was he going to get through the day? And how was he going to get any money from Mom when she seemed so sore at him?

His coffee was lukewarm. He dumped the cup in the sink.

6

It was a sunny afternoon in the middle of the week. Tommy stood on the corner opposite the New York Public Library at Forty-second Street and Fifth Avenue selling *Christian Justice*. He had a good position, but near-by were three girls selling a magazine hostile to Father Moylan. Four cops stood around to prevent trouble. There had been a small riot on the same corner only two days before, but Tommy hadn't been there that day. Today it was quiet. The presence of the cops made Tommy feel more at ease. Several of the boys were supposed to have come around to protect him in case there was any trouble. But they hadn't shown up, and he'd given up hope now that they would come. But anyway, they wouldn't be needed when there were only girls around selling that magazine.

"Anti-Semitism is un-American!" the girl selling the magazine cried to the passers-by, while her two companions stood at her side.

Tommy called out his magazine, holding up a copy. He tried to watch the girls out of the corner of his eye, but people kept getting in his way. He wanted to see if they were selling more than he was. The girls didn't look Jewish, and the one with the magazines in her hand was pretty, with dark hair, a slim figure, and nice legs. She looked as if she might even be Irish. He couldn't seem to keep his eyes off her. She was more than good-looking enough to date up.

"Read Father Moylan's *Christian Justice!* Read it and see who are un-American and un-Christian! Read *Christian Justice!* Father Moylan's *Christian Justice,* ten cents a copy. Get *Christian Justice* and kick the Reds out of America!" he cried out.

"Yes, and kick Father Moylan out with them," a middle-aged woman screamed at him as she walked by. A cop frowned but said nothing.

Tommy scowled after the woman.

There was a steady flow of people along the sidewalk. A number hastened or drifted by without paying attention to any of the venders. Others strolling along paused to look at the girls and at Tommy, stood gaping for a few moments, and then passed on. Whenever too many people collected and remained too long to watch, the cops told them curtly to break it up and move on. Now and then pedestrians stopped to talk to the cops, to ask questions, and to protest about one or another of the magazine sellers.

"Go on back to Russia," a well-dressed man with a sleek shiny face said to Tommy.

"Read Father Moylan and toss the Reds out of America," Tommy yelled quickly.

A man halted and stood gazing at Tommy. He was powerfully built and looked as if he were a Swede. He said nothing. He placed his hands on his hips and stared. Tommy was so disconcerted that he could not meet this stranger's cold blue eyes.

"*Christian Justice,* ten cents a copy," Tommy cried out rather weakly, so disturbed by the man that he toned down his sales cry.

Tommy tried to appear busy and unaware of him. Suddenly he was drawn to look directly at him. The man sneered. He spat on the sidewalk. He walked on. Tommy looked after him.

"Another Red sonofabitch!" he muttered to himself.

He scowled ferociously.

"Hitler kicks 'em out. Read what we do for 'em in *Christian Justice!*" he bawled out, holding a copy aloft.

A passing girl gave him a smile. He smiled after her and wished she'd said something, or he'd had something on the tip of his tongue to say to attract her. Maybe standing here, a swell-looking girl would pick him up. He wandered off in his thoughts and forgot to call out his magazine. Suddenly he looked down and saw the black-haired girl selling a copy.

"Twenty million Christians murdered in Spain, Russia, and Mexico. Read *Christian Justice!*" he barked.

A little fellow came up to him.

"Why do you do this?" the little fellow asked in a sad voice.

"Huh?"

"Why do you spread the fires of race hatred like this, young fellow?" the man asked.

"Scram!" Tommy said.

The man walked off, shaking his head. Tommy stood there, scowling, grimacing, barking out his cries, feeling to himself that if he looked tough as hell, it would make them afraid, and that was half the battle won. But he wasn't making many sales. He'd only sold about nine copies. He glanced down at the girls. They seemed to be selling some, but he didn't know how many.

And the endless crowd filed past Forty-second Street and Fifth Avenue, and the steady stream of traffic poured by. He was getting fed up. His arm was beginning to tire from holding up the magazine. He shifted his bundle to his right arm and held a copy before his chest with his left hand. It seemed as if at least a half hour went by without a sale. One person after another passed, either not seeing him or else looking at him with a hasty, apathetic glance. Out of the corner of his eye he saw the girl sell another copy. He clenched his teeth. Someone ought to tear the damned rag out of her hand and slap her face.

"Why don't you get a job, you bum?" a passing woman yelled at him.

"I will when you Jews are thrown out of America," he yelled after her.

"I'm a better American than you are," she retorted.

"Read *Christian Justice* and save America," he barked.

"Bum!" the woman said before passing on.

A well-dressed man gave Tommy a dime. Tommy handed him the magazine and said thanks. The man casually moved off, tearing the magazine up and tossing the scraps in a large wire basket used as a public trash receptacle. Tommy cursed and grimaced.

And the crowd flowed by. No more sales.

"Here you are, Father Moylan's *Christian Justice,* only magazine in America telling the truth about international bankers. Read *Christian Justice* and smash the Reds! Ten cents a copy!"

And suddenly he was finding out that he could not check himself from looking down at the black-haired girl.

"Read it! Read it! Here you are, read it, a defense of American morality, *Christian Justice!"*

She was taking all his business away, and for what? To sell a filthy Communist rag!

The crowd passed on. Few people now showed any interest in either magazine vender. Neither Tommy nor the girl was making many sales. And the crowd passed them in an endless stream.

"Read *Christian Justice!"*

"Anti-Semitism is un-American!"

7

"Joe, here's the newsboy," Bill remarked when Tommy got home.

Tommy didn't answer. He went to his room and left his magazines in the closet, and then came to the living room.

"Extry paper! Read it and save the world! Read it and weep!"

"Sell any papers today, Tom?" Bill asked.

"What's it to you?"

"From newsboy to dictator," Joe said.

"You guys mind your own business," Tommy said curtly. He walked across the room and stood looking out of the window, his eyes fastened vacantly on the red brick two-story building across the street. Once a sweet girl named Mary Cecilia Connor had lived there, and he had used to sit here and watch for her to come out and had thought of her a lot and of how he would like to take her out and be in love with her, and he had never gotten beyond a nodding acquaintance with her. Her family had moved out to Jackson Heights, and he'd never heard anything about her again. She had been a nice girl, and he was suddenly nostalgic, nostalgic for the days when he would sometimes see her come out of that building, and sometimes pass her on the street and say hello. He finally turned from the window and glared at his brothers.

"Aw, let him alone," Bill said, winking at Joe.

"You guys mind your own goddamn business," Tommy snapped.

"Didn't I tell you to let him alone?" Bill said.

"And you too, shut your mouth!"

Scowling, he stamped out of the room. Both brothers laughed.

8

"They didn't build America! The Christian built America!" the lean baldish speaker said in his deep bass voice, drawing a roar of applause from the one hundred and fifty-odd persons attending the meeting in the little hall on Third Avenue in the Sixties.

He paused and looked dramatically at his audience, which consisted mainly of young fellows like Tommy and middle-aged women. Just as the shouts died down, an elevated train rumbled by outside, drowning out the voices within. Behind the speaker there was a banner of the Christian American Party, a small political organization under whose auspices the meeting was being held. It was part of the Association for Christian Freedom. Around the hall there were signs and banners calling for the destruction of the Red Menace and for the freedom and prosperity of Christian America. The speaker was the last one on the evening's program, a man from out of town. The previous speakers had worked up the audience for him, so that when he had begun, he had them in a frenzied mood, ready to yell and applaud almost his every sentence. And he had played upon them and was now going along full steam, with the audience having become almost a unit in its cheering, roaring, hissing, catcalling, and yelling as the appropriate stimuli were issued.

Tommy sat near the exit in a row of camp chairs, and beside him were young men, all wearing the Association button. Tommy was slouched a bit in his chair, and there was a faraway look on his face.

"*They* didn't do the pick and shovel work to make America what it is today. Oh, no, not *they!*" the speaker said, emphasizing his words with a heavy and obviously sarcastic tone of voice.

Again he paused while he heard sarcastic laughter. Tommy's face seemed to light up with sudden interest, and he sat erect and attentive.

"It was the Christians who did the pick and shovel work to build America!" the speaker yelled, accompanying his words with flourishing gestures.

The audience roared agreement. Tommy thought that this was true, and told himself that since it was, why should Christians, Christians like himself, have to do the pick and shovel work today? Why should he have to take a laborer's job and ride in the subway in dirty clothes and let everybody see he couldn't be any better than a common workman? Let *them* do that!

As the applause died down, a stout woman with a pudgy face yelled in a loud voice:

"Name them!"

"My fellow Christians, I don't have to name *them*," the speaker replied, smiling unctuously.

A lean woman, whose face was beginning to crack with wrinkles, jumped to her feet.

"I'll name them!" she cried in a shrill, high-pitched voice. "I'll name them! The dirty *Jews!*"

"Hear! Hear!" a red-faced little Irishman shouted.

There were many boos and catcalls.

"Down with the Jews!" Tommy boomed.

"Up the Gentile!" the red-faced little Irishman shouted.

"Down with the kikes!" Tommy boomed, but an elevated train drowned out his cry.

The speaker stood poised, and when he could proceed he smiled knowingly.

"Far be it from me, my fellow Christians, to be an anti-Semite," he said suavely, and many of the audience laughed good-naturedly. He continued. "Anti-Semite is now the gutter phrase which the Reds use to cast scorn on those who would do their Christian and patriotic duty."

More boos and catcalls.

"I am not afraid of the word when aliens, Reds, hook-nosed parasites hurl it at me," he cried out in a rising voice. "No, when I am called that by such ilk, it is a badge of honor. When they call me that, they prove that I am not veering from the right course."

He paused to receive an outburst of cheers.

"Down with the Reds!" Tommy shouted with all his lung power, and his cry was taken up.

"I am not here to talk against this race or that," the speaker continued. "I am here to talk about American conditions, about the problems which are facing Christian America in its gravest and darkest hour of peril."

More cheers.

"My fellow Christians, what has America come to when a man of God, a clergyman, a great American, a great Christian, a champion of the common people, is barred from speaking over the radio in the name of justice because he tells the truth?" He waited for the catcalls, hisses, and boos. "Why is he barred from the radio?"

"Ask the Jews!" a woman screamed.

"Why is he barred? Because he tells the truth."

The audience cheered hysterically, rising to its feet, climbing on the chairs, drowning out the rumble of another passing elevated train. Tommy was on his chair, yelling until he was hoarse and out of breath.

"He tells the truth, and certain gentlemen, so-called, do not like to hear the truth. And, my Christian friends, I might add that these gentlemen are not named Murphy, or Gallagher, or O'Reilley. No, they aren't named Smith or Jones, either."

He paused for another reverberating catcall.

"But what of it? Do these gentlemen, so-called, care for the truth? Ask me another. Do the rulers of Red Russia care for the truth?"

"Save America from the Jews!" a red-haired woman screamed, and many took up her cry, shouting it in unison.

"Save America! Yes, my Christian compatriots, save America! Save America from all the enemies within her gates!" he shouted with the practiced inflection of one who knew how to mold his audience. And then he waited for the proper response of assent. Another elevated train interfered with this assent, and then he was able to continue.

"But America will be saved!"

Roars.

"And America will be Christian!"

Hysterical roars.

"Last week," the speaker continued in a lower key, "I spoke in Philadelphia, and six hundred people joined our party, six hundred Christian Americans."

The audience once more was on its feet, exploding all its lung power in enthusiastic greeting of this announcement. Tommy, once more on his chair, was shouting and thinking of how things were moving, and he was thrilling with the sense of belonging to something that was growing in power and numbers.

"Two weeks ago, I spoke in Chicago. Two thousand joined us." The speaker produced another wave of cheers. "Two thousand Christian Americans who see eye to eye with us."

From without came the sirens of fire engines, and the hall seemed like a bedlam.

"Tremble, Judea!" a tall, emaciated woman cried, standing on a chair and waving bony arms.

She was cheered. The fire engine sirens were heard again. The tall woman was waving her arms and lost her balance, but as she fell from the chair, two men caught her. Tommy and some of the other young men laughed.

"My friends, our movement is greater than the Crusades. It is the New Crusade."

More noise.

Poised and waiting, his face beaming with smiles, the speaker watched the audience seethe. He casually poured water from the pitcher on the table beside him, took up a glass, drank.

"And that reminds me," he went on, smiling disingenuously, his voice in a low key. "That reminds me." They knew something was coming, and waited. "Where did the Crusaders go in the Crusades of the Middle Ages?"

"Jewrusalem," a woman yelled, and many parroted her, and there was much laughter.

"And the new crusaders are coming to Jew York," the red-haired woman yelled.

"Down with the Jews of Jew York!" Tommy boomed.

"That reminds me of something funny that happened to me when I came to this town to make my speech here. You know, when I came in, the custom inspector stopped me, and I had trouble smuggling in my Bible with the New Testament. And I had forgotten my passport. You know, coming here, I forgot that I was coming into a foreign country."

There was more laughter; then hisses, boos, and more catcalls.

He went on. Tommy felt that he wanted to be in with everybody here, to yell with them, boo with them, shout out cries which would make them laugh and yell, and make them turn and look at him, see that he'd made them laugh and yell, feel that they liked it and respected him and thought he was all right and regular. The speaker continued. Tommy suddenly wasn't listening. He remembered how when he'd been a kid in school, he would always find himself not able to listen to what was said, and sometimes now he found he still couldn't listen for a long time. He leaned forward in his chair and told himself that he would listen. He kept thinking and telling himself now what could his family say if they knew all this, heard and saw this here tonight, came here? And how could the Reds answer this man? What would people say who insulted him, gave him dirty looks, made dirty cracks at him when he stood on the street selling the magazine? What would they say if they were here tonight?

"It *they* did not control the press, the radio, Hollywood, even some of the highest offices in the land, then, then the Christians of this country would know of the danger facing them. But *they* do control so much that they pull the wool over the eyes of the decent Christians of America. And it is the old, old story. *They* have climbed on the backs of others, and it is to *their* interest that the truth be strangled and treated with contempt, that the truth be denied to the Christians of this country."

Tommy was still leaning forward, attentive, straining and forcing himself to listen to every word. And he reminded himself that he would have to remember some of the things this man said and use them when he was out selling *Christian Justice*.

The speaker went on, describing plots and revolutionary schemes to drench America in blood and turn it into a Soviet state. These plots were being hatched in Mexico, and a Red Army was being organized to march into America and to turn it into another Spain, another Russia, another

Mexico. He said that, in fact, these other countries had only provided the dress rehearsals for the terror now being planned for America.

"If *they* have *their* way, *they* will get more than Shylock's pound of flesh!" he shouted.

"Kill *them*. Kill the Jews! Kill the Reds!" a hysterical woman shouted, and her cry was taken up fanatically.

By the time the speaker had finished, there was a unified mood of hostility and fanaticism pervading those present. Tommy was stirred. He wanted to strike a blow immediately for the cause the speaker had glorified. He was afraid, too. At times during the evening he and many others had trembled when the speaker had described what the Reds would do if their revolution succeeded. He had even imagined himself being tortured, torn limb from limb by Reds. He wanted to see them stopped before they got too powerful, and perhaps it was too late already.

With the meeting over, women were crowded around the speaker. A neat well-dressed man with a mustache was signing up seven recruits to the party, and literature was being sold at a table by the exit door. Tommy stood indecisive. He wanted to go up and tell the speaker he was with him, give him his name, bring himself to the attention of the speaker. Just as he started up, Al O'Reilley came up to him.

"Doin' anything, Gallagher?"

"Why?"

"Give him some of the stickers, Frank," Al said.

A dark-browed fellow handed Tommy stickers on which was printed the slogan BUY CHRISTIAN. Tommy took them.

"We're goin' out to paste these around," Al said.

"Can you wait a minute?" Tommy asked.

"Why? What for?"

"I wanted to go up and say a word to the speaker," Tommy answered.

"Come on, do it another time. We got to get busy. It's gettin' late," Al snapped at him.

Disappointed that he was missing the chance to make himself known to the speaker, Tommy left with Al and six others.

They went along Third Avenue, pasting their signs on darkened store windows and elevated posts. They bumped into a lone fellow with a large nose and Semitic features. Tommy and Al clouted him in the face, and the fellow was knocked groggy and unable to defend himself. They surrounded him, jeered him as a Jew, and punched him some more. Al laughed while Tommy pasted a sticker on his coat. Then Al gave him a kick and told him to beat it. The man staggered away. One of the fellows found an old tomato, and whizzed it after him, but missed. They hooted until the Jew was out of sight, and went on pasting up their stickers.

When they reached Fourteenth Street, they had used up all they had. They walked over to Union Square, making dirty cracks as they walked. At Union Square there was a small group on a street corner discussing politics. The boys busted into the group and began arguing. The group was dispersed by cops. One of the fellows, with a Yiddish accent, demanded that the cops arrest Tommy and his pals, and the cop told him that he had better blow, and blow quickly. The cop then told Tommy and the boys to watch their step in this neighborhood with all the Reds around. Al said that he knew of a school run by the Socialist Party, more Reds, near by, that they ought to do a job on. They made their way to an old loft building on a dark street off Union Square.

9

Tommy, Al O'Reilley, and a number of the boys had been going around, starting street fights with persons whose features were clearly Semitic, and breaking up street meetings. They had usually been successful in these tactics. They had had fun, and had escaped serious injuries. Al and Pete Sullivan had been arrested, and in court. The judge had warned them to stop and count fifty before they got into any more fights, and then let them go. This had made them heroes, and Tommy had envied them their honors. When they broke up street meetings, they used a regular technique. They would saunter up to a meeting in twos and threes and place themselves strategically in the crowd, with a number of them up in front to be in a good position to rush the speaker and beat him up. Before they would get down to the serious business of bruising and punching, they would first try to disrupt the meeting, frighten the speaker and listeners, and make their work easier by a preliminary process of demoralization. They would mill about, push and shove, step on toes, heckle, interrupt, and boo.

On a pleasant Saturday evening, a number of them took a subway up to the Bronx, planning to break up a street meeting. They had broken one up at the same corner two weeks previously, manhandling a number of the listeners and slugging the speaker. Tommy had carried off honors in this fray. He had moved about during the fracas doling out rabbit punches in the back of the neck that had had telling effects. They had learned that despite their work, meetings were still being held in the same place, and they decided to drive them off that corner for good.

It was a corner by a vacant lot in a workers' district, and there were small brick buildings along both sides of the street. The speaker stood on a stand from which an American flag drooped. This evening the speaker was a gray-haired man with a rich, full voice. The crowd was larger than it had been on the night the boys had broken up the meeting. A number of the crowd appeared to be workingmen, but a still larger proportion were youths, radical lads and girls, many of whom were students. There was also a good sprinkling of the inquisitive, those people who look at building construction going on, watch fires, listen to harangues from soap boxes just in order to pass the time. Some of the youths looked pretty burly and they were to be found in the crowd in groups, one group of ten or twelve standing directly before the speaker's stand. Only ten fellows had come along to break up the meeting: Al O'Reilley, Tommy, Pete Sullivan, Eddie Slavin, a little fellow named Johnny Brown, and five bruisers whom Tommy didn't know. Coming up on the subway, they had had a lot of fun kidding with Pete and Al about counting fifty before they hauled off on a Red or crashed their fists into an eagle-beak. They sauntered up to the meeting in the usual fashion, but since there were fewer of them than they had expected and the crowd was a little large, they stuck close together on the right wing of the crowd. Before they had come, there had been some bitter heckling of the meeting, coming from a group of Communists. The speaker had countered the hecklers, and finally they had marched off in dudgeon after calling on all workers assembled to shun this Trotskyite meeting like a plague. After they left, the meeting proceeded in an orderly fashion. Gradually, people out strolling had stopped to listen. When Tommy arrived, he gazed about with an apprehensive look, because there was a bigger crowd than he had counted on. The first words that he heard were:

"When the Fascists rear their heads here, only the revolutionary working class can smash them and liberate all mankind from fascism and capitalism. Comrades, fellow workers, friends, this is the lesson of revolutionary defeats suffered in Europe, and this is the lesson we must learn in America before it is too late."

Tommy grinned. The usual boushwah of the Reds, he reflected. He thought how he might be arrested, and get out scot free, and that would be something to raise his stock. He smiled to himself, wondering what the family would think if he got pinched.

"That is why we have issued calls for a Workers Defense Guard to be prepared to smash the Fascist gangs when they raise their heads in America as they have begun to do," the speaker went on.

Tommy frowned. What did this bastard mean? Well, in a couple of minutes he'd eat his words, and maybe he'd eat them along with a couple of his own teeth that would be knocked down his throat. He looked around. The crowd was growing, and some of those around liked what this Red louse was saying. He noticed, too, that a number of Jews were listening. And some of the Jews, he reflected, said that the Jews weren't Red. Well, they were. And still, there were some big guys around here. Well, maybe it was just as he heard speakers say at meetings, the Reds had no guts. And again he glanced around. Some of the guys here were pretty husky.

"Let's get going," Al whispered to Tommy.

"They ain't worth smacking down, these bums," Tommy said quietly to Al.

"What's the matter, gettin' yellow?" Al answered in a low voice, and all the while the speaker was continuing his harangue, launching into an attack on Father Moylan.

"Who's yellow?"

"Well, why did you make that crack?" Al said.

"They're punks," Tommy said.

"Punks or not, we're gonna get 'em! Now, let's start grinding the organ. Start yelling out at 'em," Al said.

Neither of them observed that they were being closely watched, and that a group of youths and men edged through the crowd and stood near them.

"Comrades, you know the Moylanites broke up our last meeting. Comrades . . ."

"Litvinov's name is Bronstein and Trotsky's is Finklestein," Tommy yelled.

He had blurted it out before he knew exactly what he was saying. He trembled now, and he was nervous. But this would show that he wasn't yellow.

"Get down off there, Finklestein!" a husky yelled.

"Quit hidin' behind the flag, Finklestein!" Al O'Reilley yelled.

There was movement in the crowd. Some started edging away. Others, mainly youths, began going over toward the hecklers.

"Do not let yourself be provoked, comrades! Defend yourselves and your meeting if attacked," the speaker yelled.

People around Al, Tommy and the others were telling them to shut up. Near Tommy, an argument about Americanism broke out. A tall Slav with a foreign accent told the Moylanite boys to shut up and leave the meeting.

"This is a free country, and we're Americans," Eddie Slavin replied to him.

There was a tension pervading the meeting now, but suddenly the audience was quiet, and the speaker was going on.

"Who is this sanctimonious hypocrite who bellows Fascism over the radio?" the speaker said, raising his voice.

"Don't say that again, you!" Tommy bellowed.

"Quit hidin' behind the flag!" Al yelled.

The tall Slav told them that they should shut up or leave the meeting. Arguments were breaking out in the crowd, and the speaker couldn't be heard.

"Quit hidin' behind the flag!" Al O'Reilley yelled again.

All his companions started shouting this cry in unison. Somebody was pushed. Someone had his toe stepped on. A girl yelled. There were scuffles. Pete Sullivan suddenly rushed a youth and they traded blows. Tommy saw Al O'Reilley slip on brass knuckles and cut the jaw of a fellow in a blue shirt. Tommy caught the fellow off balance and clipped him on the other jaw. The fellow's knees sagged. The fighting was general. The crowd opened up, and there was slugging on all sides, curses, screams, yells. Many who had stopped to listen hurried away, while others stepped aside and watched. The youths near the stand closed in on Tommy and his companions.

Tommy moved to polish off a little Jew in front of him. Just as he took a step forward with fists cocked, he was smashed in the left eye. He seemed to see streaks of irregular light. He felt a sharp pain in his eye. He had a sick thudding headache. His whole body seemed to grow weak and powerless. He bent forward, holding his eye. He was pounded on the face until he dropped. He moaned.

Everything now was like a nightmare to him. Curses, cries, angry taunts, screams, groans, swinging fists, clashing bodies were all about him. His head cleared a little. He noticed there was blood on his hands. He tried to rise and he was knocked down. Groggy, he staggered off to one side.

Al O'Reilley was backing away with a welt on his cheek. Pressing him was a broad-shouldered worker whose face was streaming blood, but who came at him pumping his hands like dynamos. Al swung out but not so swiftly as his opponent, and the broad-shouldered laborer sent him spinning backward. Eddie Slavin, his shirt ripped half off, suddenly bolted out of the crowd and ran lickety-split down the street.

Women were screaming, and spectators were yelling for the police to come. People came running down the street from the near-by houses.

"Kill the Fascists!" many began to cry.

"Inhuman, barbarous," a man watching was saying.

"Is this democracy, heh?" a Jewish man with gray hair said on the side-lines.

All those who had come with Al and Tommy to disrupt the meeting were backing off. Tommy's head had cleared a little. He was like a sick animal. He could feel his eye swelling. He saw the brawling and slugging with his good eye. It looked bad for the boys. He slunk away from the fighting.

Al and the other boys continued to retreat, taking severe punishment. They were now outnumbered, and the defenders of the meeting fought with fury. A young Jewish boy yelled, "Down with Fascism," and rushed headlong at Pete Sullivan. Pete caught him coming in, square on the jaw with an uppercut. The boy half turned from the force of the blow, and his knees gave way. He dropped on the street, unconscious. Pete was smashed in the nose. He turned and ran off. Police sirens were heard. Al and all the others beat it down the street, followed by taunts, angry cries, and a few flying bricks.

10

"Boy, your face looks like a slow-motion sunset," Bill said.

Tommy frowned. He looked grotesque. There was a yellowish, purplish-black spot around his left eye, covering the swollen lid and circling down under the eye. The eye was bloodshot and watered constantly so that while he ate, he had to keep dabbing at it with a handkerchief. He found also that he could not chew on the left side without his jaw hurting.

"Let him alone," Mr. Gallagher said.

"He's got it coming to him. He goes around telling us we don't understand, as if he knew something. He had it coming to him, the hoodlum," Joe spoke up.

"It wasn't a hoodlum fight," Tommy said.

Mr. Gallagher looked pained.

"All I want to say is I'm fed up with him. Why doesn't he get a job and not expect others to feed him?" Bill said.

"Tommy, I hope you learned your lesson. You might get killed going out this way," Mr. Gallagher added.

"I swear I don't know what the world's coming to, with this fighting. And when I saw him Sunday morning, I thought I was seeing a ghost," Mrs. Gallagher exclaimed.

"Or a cartoon for Ripley's," Bill said.

Tommy glared at Bill. His eye watered. He dabbed it with his handkerchief. He felt humiliated.

"Well, he wasn't only afraid to be the newsboy yesterday morning in front of church. He was afraid to go to mass for fear somebody would see that interior decorating on his face," Bill said.

"I can take it, don't worry about me. And let me tell you, the kikes will pay for this."

"Tommy, why don't you cut this stuff out and try and get a job? You know there's no good in all this fighting, no good is ever going to come of it. I don't care what you say you're fighting for, it's no good. You got to learn to live and let live, and if you do, the other fellow'd be the same to you," Mr. Gallagher said.

"Maybe you want to have 'em walk all over you. Well, I don't," Tommy answered.

Joe and Bill burst into laughter.

"You sure look like you got stepped on and tramped over," Bill said.

Tommy jumped from his chair and stalked out of the room. His mother followed him, while Joe and Bill told each other that nobody should give him sympathy now, because he'd gotten what was coming to him. Mrs. Gallagher found him sitting on his bed with his chin sunk in his cupped hands.

"Thomas, you come and eat your supper," she said.

"I don't want any," he answered.

"Please, for my sake."

"Can't you let me alone? You're all against me," he whined.

"I'm your mother!"

"Please, leave me alone. You don't understand."

"Now, Thomas . . ." she began.

He walked past her and went into the bathroom. He locked the door. He looked at his eye in the mirror. It was watering, and he touched his handkerchief to it. Pains, coming and going in that region, stabbed him repeatedly. He had never had a shiner like this in all his life. He kept examining it carefully, thinking that the bastards had made his face look like a rainbow. He went back to his room, closed the door, and lay on his bed with a handkerchief over his eyes. Immediately he began to think how it might have been different. They'd been outnumbered. Some of the guys who said they were coming hadn't shown up. Suddenly he was arguing with himself against his brothers. They could let him alone, couldn't they? It wasn't their business.

Maybe he shouldn't have gone Saturday night. He wished he hadn't. He tried to console himself by thinking that he was a martyr, but he couldn't find any consolation in this thought, not with a badge of shame stamped on his face. He was afraid even to go out of the house and let people see it.

He felt a new pain in the eye. He was afraid that he might be permanently disabled.

After his brothers left, he went out to the kitchen and finished his supper. His father came out and sat with him.

"Tommy, tell me what this business is all about. It looks bad to me," Mr. Gallagher said.

"You don't understand."

"Tom, I saw Joe Cannon today. His brother owns a three-story building, and Joe thinks his brother needs a superintendent, and I spoke to him about you getting the job. It's not so much of a job, but after all it's work, and will you take it as soon as you're . . . feeling better?"

Tommy didn't answer. He was fed up with everything here at home. He ate with a brooding look on his face, carefully chewing because of his jaw.

"Will you take it?"

Tommy nodded. He and his father sat in the kitchen, saying nothing.

When the swelling had almost gone, Tommy went to work as the superintendent of the building owned by Joe Cannon's brother. He hated the work, and told himself over and over again that superintendent was a high-toned word for janitor. He had to empty garbage wearing dirty clothes, and this he hated more than any other thing he had to do. And two of the tenants were Jewish. He could scarcely be civil to them. And he kept thinking how in the winter it would be damned cold in the mornings and he'd have to be up early, before dawn, to tend to the furnace. After a week he gave up the work. He decided to go back selling the magazine. After all, it was a cause and it would pay him in the end. Why should he be a dope?

The family was angry and disappointed when they learned that he had given up his new job. He resumed selling *Christian Justice*. He came home one Sunday morning after selling in front of the parish church, feeling glum because he'd had few sales. During the first part of the meal no one talked to him. But Bill and Joe kept glancing at him accusingly. He got sore.

"Cut it out!" he snapped.

"Nobody's saying anything to you," Bill replied.

"I ain't doin' nothin' to you," Tommy said.

"Goddamn you! I'm fed up!" Bill yelled, and he jumped to his feet and rushed around the table.

Tommy started to get out of his chair, but as he was doing so, Bill caught him on the jaw and tumbled him over the chair. Tommy gazed up at Bill, bewildered, holding his jaw. Mrs. Gallagher was on her feet and in tears. Joe and Mr. Gallagher got between Tommy and Bill.

"Fine guy you are, hitting me before I had a chance," Tommy said.

"Shut up, you bum! I'll give you worse than you got!" Bill cried.

Again Joe and the father tried to pacify Bill. They led him back to his chair, and he sat down. Mrs. Gallagher sobbed.

"You wouldn't do that to me outside," Tommy said.

Bill had calmed down. He looked at Tommy scornfully.

"Tommy, your brother lost his temper, but he's right. You got to turn over a new leaf. You made me look like a monkey running out on the job I got you," Mr. Gallagher said.

"I didn't ask you to do it," Tommy answered.

"Who the hell's going to feed you?" Mr. Gallagher asked, suddenly losing his temper.

"Jesus Christ, but ain't you a nervy sonofabitch," Joe said.

Bill was pushing his chair back. Mrs. Gallagher screamed and yelled out that she would not stand for this. Her tears stopped Bill. While she shook with sobs, Tommy got to his feet.

"All right, if that's the way you feel about it," he said, leaving the room.

Her head bent, Mrs. Gallagher wiped her eyes. The front door was heard to slam.

"He'll come back. That guy likes a meal ticket," Bill said.

"Come now, Mother," the father said as he put his hand tenderly on her shoulder.

"I'm damned glad I socked him," Bill remarked.

II

Tommy was bitter. He walked alone in the milling Sunday night crowd on Broadway, past the lighted theaters where crowds waited in line to be admitted. The brightness of the street, the many people, the atmosphere of pleasure-seeking, all emphasized to him his aloneness. He looked at fellows with girls. He saw a number of foreign or Semitic faces, and every time he saw one, hatred flared in his soul. They were the kind who were to blame for his plight. He smoked his last cigarette and walked with hands stuck in his pockets. Then he wanted another smoke. He thought of bumming the price of a pack off someone, and he didn't have the nerve to. He told himself again and again that he couldn't go home, he wouldn't. They didn't understand him. He was never going home. They all thought they had him down, did they! Well, they had another guess coming.

Aimless, he wandered along, going over to Fifth Avenue. Many people strolled by, walking slowly, looking in windows, drifting on. A bus stopped beside him, and from the top came the laughter and joshing of two young couples. He looked at them with envy. He strolled along, titillated by shapes of the women who passed. He turned at Forty-second Street and wandered back over to Broadway. He paused in front of a motion picture theater that presented Russian movies, and he cursed Russia and the Reds. He told himself that somebody ought to throw a stink bomb in the place. He wandered on. He picked a cigarette butt off the curb and smoked it. He wandered back to mill along with the slow-moving crowds on Broadway, and to watch the people.

He wandered about Broadway, Seventh Avenue and Fifth Avenue until around midnight. Dismally, he spent his last nickel on subway fare and slumped in a seat in a partially filled subway car. Across from him were several couples on a date, now homeward bound. Seeing fellows with girls like this made him feel more alone. Directly across from him was a tired couple, and the girl rested her blonde head on the fellow's shoulder, while he had his arm around her. A little way down was a good-looking, red-haired girl with a greasy-looking fellow who had a small mustache. They held hands, rubbed knees, and talked low and intently, acting like a couple in love. And he had no girl. And he wanted one. Hell, even if he did have one, he wouldn't have any dough to spend on her. He'd always been a football to be kicked around. He was fed up. His goddamn brother, too, the punk, cracking him when he was sitting down and didn't have a chance to defend himself.

He looked around the car at the couples. His mood changed. He was filled with contempt for those he saw. He wanted to stand up in the car and curse them all with the most obscene words he knew. He dozed off, fell asleep. But luckily he awakened at his station.

He sneaked quietly into the apartment. Bill, who was in the living room reading the baseball scores in the Monday morning edition of the *News,* heard him come in. Tommy went quietly to his room, quickly took off his clothes, and got into bed. When Bill came into the room to go to bed, Tommy lay with his face to the wall, feigning sleep. Bill looked at him with contempt.

"You haven't even got the guts to sleep in the park," Bill said, beginning to undress.

Tommy pretended not to hear. Making a little noise, Bill finally got undressed, turned the light off, and went to bed. Tommy lay there unable to sleep. He lay awake, pitying himself, telling himself that he was brave, thinking of his hatreds, vowing over and over again that his day was coming, and assuring himself that when it did come, it would be a day of bitter vengeance. Look at Hitler in Germany! Hitler had known days like this, too!

RICHARD O. BOYER

Nazi Meeting

A FEW NIGHTS ago I attended a regular weekly meeting of the Amerikadeutscher Volksbund, Yorkville branch. I was a little uneasy. After all, I did not belong to it, and if its members were plotting to overthrow the government and establish a Fascist dictatorship, as Congressman Dickstein and others declare, they might not like to have a reporter present.

The meetings are held at the New York Turnverein, on Lexington Avenue at Eighty-fifth Street. It was reassuring to find a German restaurant with red-checked tablecloths at the front of the building, and as I passed I could see a little orchestra and waiters rushing around with steins of beer. The entrance to the hall where the meeting was to be held was on Eighty-fifth Street, around the corner from the restaurant. Just inside six men were standing in a line. They wore Sam Browne belts over gray shirts trimmed with black, black forage caps resembling the Legion's, and black trousers. I joined the line of pleasant, middle-aged Germans who were shuffling by them in single file toward the door, where a uniformed man sat at a card table. In exchange for fifteen cents he gave each one a little green ticket like those at the movies.

He took my fifteen cents as readily as if I were a Nazi. Yet he must have known that I was not a member, for without change of expression he handed me a paper marked "Application for Membership." It stated that the initiation fee was a dollar, that monthly dues were seventy-five cents, and its first sentence read, "I am of Aryan origin, free from Jewish or colored blood."

Inside the door, I looked around. The hall was rectangular. At the back was a line of uniformed men who stood with their hands behind them and stared rigidly forward at half-empty rows of seats which extended to a platform at the front. Some of the men wore spectacles. Many were not young and their coatless uniforms and snug-fitting trousers revealed the saggingly bulging contours of middle age. On the platform was a narrow rostrum, a brown swastika painted on its front. On the wall behind it was the shield of the United States to the right and a swastika to the left.

Permission of the author. Originally published in *The New Yorker*. Copyright, 1937, The F-R. Publishing Corporation.

Nearby was a door, its glass top suggesting that it led to an office. The lower half of the walls were panelled in green-stained wood; the upper half, on each of the two sides, held an identical mural. In each a hound was about to bring down a fleeing stag and a red-coated hunter in the distance was bounding over a hill on his steed. Near the rostrum was an electric phonograph—a small, boxlike model, attached by an electric-light cord to a socket in the wall.

The lighting was rather dim but the atmosphere was cheerful, perhaps because one could hear the clink of glasses, the lulling murmur of voices, and the strains of the violin in the restaurant. I did not realize in what easy communication we were with the restaurant until a man with a handlebar mustache waddled to a little panel in the rear wall and tapped on it. A waiter opened it and presently handed the man a stein of beer.

I was about to follow the same procedure when a young man in civilian clothes handed me his card, clicked his heels, and bowed. "You are not a member?" he asked. I explained that I was a reporter, and read the name on his card. It was "James Wheeler-Hill." I asked why he had so British a name and so German an accent, and he replied with pleasant finality, "It is just a habben so."

The meeting, he said, would not start for a half-hour or more, and added politely that the name for the organization in English was the German-American Bund. I asked him about the membership. He said there were 17,000 members in New York City and between 95,000 and 120,000 in the entire country. There were seventy-nine units, he said, in seventy-nine cities, but this was merely a meeting of a neighborhood "branch," the smallest organizational division of the Bund. He said the object of the Bund was to fight for Nazi principles under the American Constitution and to train its members to combat a Communist uprising. I asked him who was the head of the Bund and he pointed at the door at the front of the hall.

"He's in the office there," he said. "Fritz Kuhn."

"Can I see him? Will he attend the meeting?"

"He is too busy. Maybe you can see him during the intermission. The first half is in German, the second in English. There is an intermission between."

We watched people enter the hall. There seemed to be a timidity about many. They entered separately and sat alone when there was room to do so, as if ill-at-ease. I wondered if these people came because they were lonely in a strange country. Most of them, I found, had not come to the United States until after the World War. Often, as they passed through the door, they gave a jerky little salute, swinging up the right forearm, the elbow held stiffly pressed against the side. Mr. Wheeler-Hill said that this was the colloquial, informal Nazi salute. It was "Hello" in Nazi sign language, he said, as contrasted with the more formal outstretched arm which meant "Hail!"

A stout woman with a large bag of black gumdrops settled herself in a chair. A man with a Hitler mustache bowed stiffly and moved the chair next to her a little away before he sat down. I felt that if I had not seen the uniforms and known the nature of the meeting, I might not have guessed that the audience was German. It resembled any crowd on a subway platform. Fully half of those present were women, and Mr. Wheeler-Hill said they were members of the women's auxiliary of the Bund, the Frauenschaft. Some of their husbands, he said, were in uniform at the back of the hall. He said these men in uniform were members of the Ordnungsdienst, which meant order keepers. I glanced at the line which had stood there so rigidly for so long a time and asked what its members were in civil life.

"Oh, clerks, bakers, butchers," Mr. Wheeler-Hill said carelessly, and walked away.

In the centre of the line stood the tallest trooper, those on either side of him progressively shorter until the two smallest were at either end. He didn't look very military. He had a plain, scholarly face and rimless spectacles gripped his nose. He seemed embarrassed when I asked him why he had joined the Bund and continued to gaze straight ahead as if he wished I'd go away and let him hold his military posture unmolested.

"Why, I don't know," he said. "I—I—" he stammered, and his accent was so Teutonic that I didn't know whether he was having trouble with his English or with expressing his thoughts. "In Germany everything is so nice, so—" He tried for words and then said, *"Gemütlich."*

"In Germany everybody is so—" he sneaked a glance at me and said, "When your wife is sick and you go down the street everybody says, 'How is the wife today?'" He gave up, but it seemed clear that he had joined the Bund because of homesickness. When I asked him if he had been a Nazi in Germany, he seemed even more embarrassed. Finally he said, "I was a Communist there." He explained that he quit before coming to this country in 1924 when they told him one night to go home and get a gun and meet the comrades in a field at dawn.

"Not for me," he said, and gave me a quick grin and then snapped his head back and froze his face into a becoming dignity.

We both could feel the disapproval of the others in the line. I walked away, and a uniformed officer came up and looked me all over. He asked no question. He simply examined me in a very cool way. I might have

felt uneasy had not a strapping young fellow, as blond as Mr. Hitler could
wish, and with his chest straining against his Sam Browne belt, come
up to me and said, "You are a stranger, yes?" He seemed crammed with
an elephantine eagerness to serve. He saw a pencil in my coat pocket
and took it out and said, "You would like it sharpened, yes?" He was
disappointed when I said that I wouldn't. He was taking me around
the hall, showing me the coats of arms of German states and cities painted
on the shades of electric lights that hung from the ceiling, when there was
a whirring, mechanical noise and at the same time everyone stood up.
There were about three hundred in the hall.

The noise came from the phonograph. It was playing "The Star-
Spangled Banner." The troopers in the back stood at military salute, the
crowd at attention. Only one person in the audience sang—a slim little
woman who had not the slightest trace of an accent. She was very serious
and exalted about it.

I was disappointed during the first half of the meeting, the part in German. Mr. Wheeler-Hill took the platform and said that the Bund employment service could offer a woman light housework for room and
board. Then he introduced a little man whose brown face barely peeked
above the rostrum. This was Herr Nicholai—I think that was his name—
the Bund's Eastern organizer. He talked on and on for more than
an hour trying to prove that President Roosevelt was plotting to lead us
into a war against Germany. Almost everyone listened with great attention, even when he repeated himself.

I, however, was scarcely listening when he suddenly switched over into
English. "I should have talked in English then," he said, "and I will do
so now. It was in Philadelphia at the German Day. I was making the
principal speech in German and some hoodlums started to boo. I would
have gladly talked in English then and given them a piece of my German mind, but I did not think. One of them passed an unusually insulting remark when we sang our Horst Wessel song and I am glad to
report that he got what was coming to him!"

There was polite applause, and thus encouraged, Herr Nicholai continued for twenty minutes more. Finally his speech was over and there
was an intermission. A line of people formed at the little panel in the rear
of the hall and a waiter passed beer through to them. I was watching
this proceeding when Mr. Wheeler-Hill tapped me on the shoulder and
said, "Der Führer has consented to see you." I followed him the length
of the hall to the door that led to the office.

He preceded me into it, halted respectfully before a large man behind a
large desk, and declaimed, "*Fritz Kuhn, Führer des Amerikadeutschen*

Volksbundes." Der Führer acknowledged neither me nor the introduction. His head drooped over the keyboard of a portable typewriter on his desk, and two thick index fingers hovered uncertainly above the typewriter, which he seemed to be trying to operate by sheer force of will. He wore a black suit with a Norfolk jacket, and his white expanse of face seemed as expressionless as a cliff.

There were two books on his desk. One was a copy of Hitler's "Mein Kampf," the other a blue-bound volume of the *Social Register*. I was looking at a picture on the wall of the American Führer presenting a book to the German Führer when the former glanced up and said, "Yes, take a good look at everything. Don't miss anything."

His accent was thick and held a curiously angry note.

"Look at the luxurious Oriental rug on the floor!" There was a thin strip of dirty carpet. "Don't miss the perfume! You smell the perfume?"

I sniffed uncertainly, smelled no perfume, and said, "Why?"

"All the writers smell the perfume. Always in their stories about me, lies, lies, lies. I don't give a damn. Don't miss anything. See the swastika? The picture of Hitler? Of Roosevelt?"

I was almost surprised to see these on the wall.

"I just wanted to tell you I was enjoying the meeting."

He did not answer. He still seemed angry.

"You believe in freedom?" he asked, and the question was like a sneer. "A man with a half a million holding a chob he is not suited for, while good men go hungry. Is that freedom?"

He did not give me a chance to answer, but went on in a guttural stream that seemed to hint of interior pressures seeking relief. "Freedom of the press! I send an article to the paper and they do not print it. Nothing but lies about Germany! Is that freedom?"

He was walking up and down the room now, and his body was so thick and angular that he seemed short despite his height. He turned accusingly and said, "Freedom to work under the bayonets of the C.I.O!" I said nothing and he asked angrily, "Is that freedom? Freedom to have your bank fail and lose your money. Is that freedom? Ach," he said with scornful finality, "freedom to get a cup of coffee, that's the only freedom here." Then he accompanied me to the door and added, "They got that freedom in every country if you got the money."

I stepped out into the friendliness of the hall. Some of the audience were still drinking beer and there was still the faint, far-away sound of the violin in the restaurant. As I walked back to my seat, the intermission was coming to an end. The hinged panel in the rear wall through which the beer had been passed was closed and those in uniform were standing at frozen-faced attention in a line at the rear of the hall. Herr Nicholai took the platform again and said he wanted to introduce "Bob Wood, who talked to us four years ago and still has the same enthusiasm." As Herr Nicholai talked, a slim young man with large ears walked down the aisle, smiling and shooting up his right arm in jerky Nazi salutes. He was twenty-one and a junior, I found later, at Columbia College. As he mounted the platform, Herr Nicholai draped a paternal arm around his shoulders and said, "Give him a kindly ear, for while he is young in fighting years, he's got the spirit we need."

Bob Wood stood silent and smiling a moment, enjoying the audience and letting the audience enjoy him. He was a ramroddish little fellow with the authentic preacher's manner and almost professionally youthful. Ladies ducked their heads together and made appreciative cluckings. He was so winning and boyish and clean and his face shone so that one knew he had ideals. Suddenly he clicked his heels, raised his hand, and shouted *"Heil!"* and he did it just as authentically as if he were really a German instead of a student at Columbia.

"Herr Nicholai is wrong," he began, "very wrong." An old man next to me, with a round face and a grizzled, shaved head that sloped into a creased neck, nudged me and said approvingly, "He's a fine one, that boy! He don't care what he says!" Wood smiled to show that he didn't really mean it and continued, "He said I had the same enthusiasm. My dear friends of the Bund, I come back from Germany with ten times the enthusiasm I had before!"

As young Mr. Wood continued, it developed that he didn't like the newspapers. They had refused to publish all but one of the stories he had sent from Germany. He didn't mind for himself, he said. He could stand it. But he did resent it in the larger sense, in the sense that it was an injustice to a great nation. He would read these rejected stories, he said, and the audience could judge for itself the reason for the rejections. While describing things he'd seen in Germany, he frequently asked, "And how much of that did you read in the papers, I wonder."

He read his first article with much expression. " 'Munich,' " he began, holding his dispatch in his hand. " 'When I saw legion after legion of German youth marching forward and onward today, heads high, eyes bright, marching for ten hours, I thought—' " He paused and looked upward and said slowly, " 'And I thought a lot.' "

He was very solemn now before continuing. The hall was still. In the pause I found myself thinking and thinking a lot. The audience gazed as intently at the speaker as if he were a young prophet.

" 'I thought,' " he repeated, " 'and I thought a lot!' " He was not reading his dispatch now. He was declaiming it, as if he knew it by heart.

" 'I thought that Germany today is being led by an ideal. What is this ideal? I doubt if anyone could answer. But this ideal is proving itself in the fact that German youth is marching toward a clean and honorable goal.

" 'I love my city. I love my college life. But no one could fail to be impressed by the German student. He is fearless in fighting for the truth. He keeps himself clean and neat. He holds himself proudly erect. He will not indulge in filth or profanity or excess. But he will fight for his ideals.' "

There was no applause, for such was the speaker's solemnity it would have been like applauding a prayer. Wood just stood there a moment, looking down at his impressed elders. "I want to read you excerpts from another article," he said, and slowly added, as his voice slid into a more sombre register, "one—that—was—not—accepted."

There was a polite deprecatory murmur from the audience. Wood began to read, and he couldn't have done it better had he been an elocution teacher. Yet despite his exquisite enunciation, his winsome, cultured modulation, I couldn't quite understand what he was driving at. The speech seemed to reveal Wood, the mystic, and my sympathies were with the editor who rejected it.

It was from Munich too. They were evidently honoring sixteen men who had been killed in street fights, and there was a procession. " 'As I watched them pass,' " Wood read from the rejected manuscript, " 'I thought and I thought deeply. The procession made me think of my likes and my dislikes, of my admirations and my prejudices. Soldiers in black, soldiers in brown shirts without arms—' " Somehow I lost the thread. Perhaps the picture of Wood thinking and thinking deeply obscured the music of his words.

" 'And I thought,' " Wood concluded, " 'that the reverence, honesty, truth, and loyalty displayed on this day were sincere, a God-given gift to a people.' " Again he looked down upon the expatriates. "That article," he said slowly, "was not accepted."

Wood moved on to his ordeal in France. "The people actually did not seem to care if they were clean," he said, "and didn't care much if the streets were clean." He made the statement as if it were an unbelievable revelation. There were little cries of horror from three or four women in the audience. "I was simply infuriated by the waiters and everyone in Paris, simply by their manner. Since the People's Front came to power there it is taboo to say 'merci.' You see what a government can do for its people. If the Soviets come to power in France, you will push your own mother out of the way to get a seat in a bus."

By way of contrast he described his farewell at Munich, where he took the train for Paris. A German student, he said, came down to see him off. In describing the student, Wood stood straighter, held his head higher, and looked a bit more noble, so that we could get some idea of the student.

" '*Auf Wiedersehen!*' " Wood quoted his friend. " '*Heil Hitler! Heil Deutschland!*' " Wood's arm pumped up and down with each "*Heil!*" as he reconstructed the scene.

He couldn't stand France and went on to England, "the home of my blood, where I had the greatest awakening of my life." Wood's awakener was a beggar who stood singing outside a restaurant in which the young man was eating with an English companion. When Wood suggested that they give the beggar some money, the Englishman refused. This awakened Wood, he said, to the decadence of the British Empire, and later investigation proved to him that it was typical.

"Before I left," he said, "I stood before the monument to Nelson at Trafalgar Square. 'Oh, England,' I thought, 'you are the land of my blood and I love you very, very much, but I am praying for something to come and do away with all this rot!' But they are working there with the Communists, and we all know where that leads. How sorry I am that England hasn't Edward! It's not the fault of the people.

"Coming back, I was forced to share my cabin with a Jewish lad." He said it softly, evenly, making light of his hardship. One woman cried, "How horrid!" and Wood went on, "One day he took up my sweater and looked at the trademark and said, 'But you bought this in Germany!' and I said 'Yes' and he said, 'Why did you buy it there?' and I said, 'Because I wanted to.'

"I talked to the lad at greater length later. He said that seven generations of his folk had been born in Germany, but that they did not live there now. We happened to be near a piano and I began to play some of the divine old German airs. 'Why do you play that rot?' he asked. 'It's too sentimental.' "

The speaker was silent, permitting the audience to savor the sacrilege. I fancied I could see him tightening for his final effort. I was right. His voice sang out in his closing message, and it was really thrilling, because he was so young and sincere.

" 'That's just it!' I told the lad. 'There is a fundamental difference between us! I am not German-born, but I can feel! But you, no matter how long you live in Germany, you cannot feel!' "

"I had felt the same thing before. An American professor was visiting me in Germany and threw paper on my floor. I picked it up and he said, 'I think it's nice to throw paper on the floor and let it stay there.'

" 'That's just it!' I cried. 'There is a fundamental difference between us! We want order! We want discipline! And we can't have it based on disorder!' " That was the message of the evening, and Wood stood motionless for a moment. Suddenly he jerked himself into a rigid line, shot his right arm stiffly forward, shouted *"Heil!"* and skipped boyishly from the platform.

He got a big hand. The audience made so much noise that uniformed members of the Ordnungsdienst ran in from the corridor, where some had been smoking cigarettes. They crowded swiftly into line at the back of the hall until some fifty of them were standing at an extravagant attention. The crowd was standing up too, and James Wheeler-Hill had come to the platform.

Wheeler-Hill shot out his arm and snapped, *"Sieg!"* The word means victory.

"Heil!" roared the crowd.

"Sieg!" said Wheeler-Hill.

"Heil!" roared the crowd.

"Sieg!" snapped Wheeler-Hill.

"Heil!" the audience bellowed in one sharp shout.

With arms still outstretched, they were singing the Horst Wessel song, the favorite Nazi anthem. The men's voices were deep, militant, the women's shrill with intensity. It sounded like a hymn.

> *Kamaraden alle: ihr braune Schar,*
> *die Fahne pflanzt auf der Türme Knauf!*
> *Das Wort macht wahr:*
> *Horst Wessel fiel, und Deutschland steht auf!*

The hands dropped as the song ended and the stiff, rigid saluters became people once more. There was laughter and talk of more beer as the crowd moved out of the hall. Many of the troopers had shabby overcoats over their uniforms, and the clash of civilian and military haberdashery gave their appearance a pleasant incongruity. I walked out with Bob Wood, and he said, "I was late. Did they begin by singing the national anthem?"

"No, they sang 'The Star-Spangled Banner.' "

"That's what I meant," he said. "After all, I'm still an American."

The delicate art of Roosevelt-hating took every form, as Frederick Lewis Allen has well reminded us, from the quasi-humorous Pullman anecdote to the well organized whispering campaign. Frank Sullivan's cliché expert and E. B. White's drunken liberal were, sad to say, painted from life. I well remember a scurrilous and relatively literate document circulated in Washington during the 1944 campaign; it purported to be an authoritative memoir of the President by "an old friend of the family." The virulence of the hatred that touched off such attacks may be measured by the fact that the campaign of vilification has persisted so long since the President's death.

E. B. WHITE

Liberal in a Lounge Car

THIS TRAIN (he said to the man next to him) exactly suits my purposes. It's the only efficient way to go to Boston. I can wade through a pile of work in the morning, clear my desk by 10:30, give dictation, then put a battery of girls to work getting up the letters. Just before the train pulls out, my secretary, Birdsall, brings the whole wad of stuff aboard for signature, revision, and so forth. That was Birdsall you probably saw. I put through those that are O.K., and take the others along with me; then at Boston I have a public stenographer meet me and handle the load at the other end. I can integrate this train perfectly with my work schedule, and the food is good, too, if you treat the dining-car captain generously. Would you mind just pushing that button behind you, I'd like another highball. Thanks. Will you have a cigar? Here you are, boy. *Encore le* Scotch-and-Soda. Don't you know what *encore* means? Guess you didn't go to the right school. Well, just bring me another drink like a good fellow. And an afternoon paper, please.

I follow the Sino-Japanese crisis very closely. It's the crux of the present recession—even more than this man down in Washington. The absorption of China is inevitable, of course; but the amusing thing is the effect abroad, particularly in England. I've watched England losing ground for years now, and the implications, both in the Orient and in Spain, are highly significant as bearing on the gradual dissipation of England's imperial structure. Funny how few people realize the way England's going. It's really the most amusing development of the past two years. Naturally she bears the brunt of the Italian threat because of India. England knows perfectly well she'd never hold India in the event of serious trouble. I'd like more fizz, please, my boy. The next two years will see the lid blow off without question. I've been in England a good deal, and I think I can say honestly I understand the English temperament. It's appalling, what the last two years have seen.

Will you have a drink with me? I don't go for the hard stuff, ordinarily, but I'm beginning to feel this morning's extra pressure. Business is a tough egg these days, with empires falling and rising. You have to play ball, if you want the figures to come out right. Of course, the social experiment in this country is really an amazing thing. And a good thing. Most people don't grasp it, but I welcome it. The world is on the march, and if you don't believe me all you have to do is glance over these headlines. Spain. Italy. Russia. Japan. All turbulent. With England on the wane, and America holding the bag. All you hear in the business world is belly-aching; but I prefer to play ball. I have the best lawyers in the country helping me watch the curves as they come over the plate, and that's something. But even more than that is my mental attitude. You've got to be philosophical and you've got to have a liberal point of view in tune with the times. Hell, I welcome a recession such as this. It helps me understand myself better. And I play along with the boys in Washington. I've never been able to understand these liverish fellows who jump out of the window just because their arithmetic doesn't check. Why, a good friend of ours jumped in the crash of '29—a man worth three quarters of a million even after he'd been cleaned. A man who had everything to live for— lovely wife (a really swell person, I knew her extremely well) and two fine children. That's all that matters in life, anyway. I'm beginning to see things so much clearer. Why should we pile up dough indefinitely? Look here, I happen to have more than I want—literally. That's not a boast, I'm just talking straight to you. But listen. I've got five kids, and that's my asset side of the ledger right there. Those kids. I planned to have four, but my wife went off the deep end and threw twins the last time, and I tell you I wouldn't trade one for the whole of Russia. Literally wouldn't. But the thing about kids is to give them an intelligent break— know what makes them tick. And I'm letting *my* children understand what goes on in their country—not bringing them up in some crazy dream world. They face hard facts.

Of course, you've got to have an understanding of child psychology. And you can't be ambitious. I want my children to be normal kids, in every way. Come the revolution, I want them to go out and take their place shoulder to shoulder with the masses of people. I'm watching it already, keeping my finger right on it. In the first place, I don't let my kids see too much of me. Why? Simply because I don't want them to become precocious. In school, I never urge them to go after perfect marks. Never! I want 80's. No 90's, no 100's, in my family. They learn to be democratic, too, by God. In my house there's no darn little aristocrats running around, I'll tell the world. My wife and I not only let the children play with their inferiors, but we encourage it. Why, only last week I saw one of my youngsters playing around with the laundress's kid. Why shouldn't he, for heaven's sake? I suppose the neighbors think we're crazy, but what do we care?

And money! That's where so many people go wrong in relation to children. Take Christmas. Fortunately situated though I am, I insisted on a completely frugal Christmas last December. I mapped out the entire occasion, and put it through. Each of the children received exactly three presents—one gift that they wanted, one gift that they would learn something from, and one gift that they didn't know existed. All other presents, from outside sources, my wife and I confiscated in advance and distributed to the poor. Furthermore, my kids did their own shopping—actually bought the things they were to give us out of their own allowance. Of course, Mamselle went with them to the shops, but they did the selecting. In that way they got the true meaning of Christmas. They presented me with the god-damnedest ash trays you ever saw, but listen: I have those ash trays sitting right on my desk at the office, and I'll be looking at them the rest of my life, and loving it. Oh, I don't fool myself about children. Nobody knows better than I do that you can't plan their lives for them. If one of my boys wants to become a railway conductor, I'll be the first to say Go to it. Matter of fact, I imagine my oldest lad is heading for journalism. Guess he comes by it honestly, as far as that goes. I've always been able to pick up a paper and get the meat out of it. Just a glance at this edition is enough. Just a question of stripping a thing down to its essentials. Foreign news—all disguised these days. Have to read between th' lines. These Fascist powers. Inter'sting. Inter'sting to an executive, p'ticularly. Triumph of efficient organization. Man like Mussolini: threat to our traditional notions, perhaps; not above criticism, perhaps; but magnificent in victory. Nothing clumsy about that kind of government. He doesn't ask 'em, he tells 'em. That's thing England can't understand. This man Van Zeeland. Includes England as one of the great powers in his plan for economic c'llaboration. Big mistake to include England. England hardly need be considered any more, strength so far diss'pated. I would like another drink—would you mind pushing that button just behind your head? Thank you very much.

FRANK SULLIVAN

The Cliché Expert Testifies as a Roosevelt Hater

MR. ARBUTHNOT: No sir! Nobody is going to tell *me* how to run my business.

Q: Mr. Arbuthnot, you sound like a Roosevelt hater.

A: I certainly am.

Q: In that case, perhaps you could give us an idea of some of the clichés your set is in the habit of using in speaking of Mr. Roosevelt.

A: S-s-s-s-s-s-s!

Q: I beg your pardon?

A: I was hissing. Our set always hisses whenever Roosevelt's name is mentioned or his picture shown.

Q: Oh, to be sure. I forgot. Well now, to return to Mr. Roosevelt—

A: S-s-s-s-s-s!

Q: Mr. Arbuthnot, it might simplify matters if we took the hissing for granted from now on. I mean to say, whenever I mention Mr. Roosevelt's name we'll just assume that you have countered with a hiss. Is that agreeable to you?

A: Certainly, if you insist.

Q: I think it would expedite matters, if you don't mind. Now then, what I want to know first is what you Roosevelt haters call the President.

A: Why, the—!

Q: Oh, I don't mean that kind, Mr. Arbuthnot.

A: Well, we call him That Madman in the White House, or That Fellow Down in Washington. Sometimes we call him *Mister* Roosevelt, or Your *Friend,* Franklin D.—just like that.

Q: Sort of sarcastic, eh?

A: And how!

Q: I see. Please proceed and give me your frank opinion of the President.

A: Well, I voted for him in 1932. I think he did a good job when the banks were closed, but . . .

Q: Yes. Go on.

A: Now don't misunderstand me. I'm a liberal. I'm in favor of a lot of these reforms Roosevelt has been trying to put over, but I don't like the way he's going about it.

Q: Why?

A: Because he's trying to destroy the American way of life.

Q: For instance?

A: Well, you take the Supreme Court. Where Roosevelt made his big mistake was in attacking the Court.

Q: I see.

A: And where Roosevelt made his big mistake was in arousing all this class hatred. You know, all this forgotten-man stuff.

Q: Yes.

A: And where Roosevelt made his big mistake was in starting all this pump priming. You can't spend your way out of a depression.

Q: Really?

A: Certainly not. Where's the money coming from to pay for all this— this—

Q: Do you mean "orgy of spending"?

A: That's just the phrase I was searching for. You know how it's all going to wind up?

Q: How?

A: Inflation. We're going to have the worst inflation in this country you ever saw. These taxes. Twenty-five cents out of every dollar goes for taxes. Why, our children and our children's children will be paying for all this long after you and I are dead and gone. Now, you take relief. I certainly think it's all right to help people who deserve help, but I don't believe in all this coddling, as Governor La Follette says. The trouble with half the people on relief is they don't *want* to work. You can't tell me that most of these people can't find work. If a man wants a job bad enough he'll find one all right. Half these people on relief are foreigners, anyhow.

Q: And what is it these foreigners do, Mr. Arbuthnot?

A: They come over here and take the bread out of our own people's mouths. Let 'em go on back home where they came from. We haven't got enough jobs to go around as it is. And you take the C.I.O.

Q: Yes?

A: A bunch of Communists. In my opinion, no man should be forced to join a labor union against his will. I think Henry Ford has got the right idea. And I certainly object to a radical like that John L. Lewis run-ning this country.

Q: Does John L. Lewis run this country?

A: Why certainly he runs it. He's got Roosevelt so scared he don't dare say his soul's his own. They say Lewis has a key to a back door of the White House.

Q: What about the WPA, Mr. Arbuthnot?

A: Oh, the shovel brigade. I'm against the WPA and the PWA and all this alphabet-soup stuff. Say, speaking of the WPA, did you hear the one about the WPA worker and King Solomon? Why is a WPA worker like King Solomon?

Q: I heard it. Now then—

A: Because he takes his pick and goes to bed.

Q: Is that the funniest New Deal joke you know, Mr. Arbuthnot?

A: Oh, no. Here's the funniest. Have you heard there's only Six Dwarfs now?

Q: Only six?

A: Yeah. Dopey's in the White House.

Q: Mr. Arbuthnot, you slay me. Well, go on. Tell us more. Why don't you like Mr. Roosevelt? What's the matter with him?

A: Well, the trouble with Roosevelt is he's an idealist.

Q: Yes?

A: And the trouble with Roosevelt is he's destroyed individual initiative.

Q: Do tell.

A: And the trouble with Roosevelt is he's a Communist.

Q: I see. Go on.

A: The trouble with Roosevelt is he's a Fascist.

Q: A Fascist, too?

A: Certainly. He wants to be dictator. Don't tell *me* he hasn't got his eye on a third term.

Q: Sakes alive! Has he?

A: And the trouble with Roosevelt is his vanity. That's what makes him so stubborn. He just won't listen to reason. And the trouble with Roosevelt is he's got no right to spend the taxpayers' money to build up his own personal political machine. Even at that, the trouble with Roosevelt isn't so much Roosevelt himself, it's that bunch he's got himself surrounded with down there in Washington.

Q: What bunch?

A: Oh, this fellow Corcoran. This fellow Cohen. This fellow Frank-furter. This fellow Arnold. This fellow Tugwell.

Q: But this fellow Tugwell isn't there any more.

A: Well, you know who I mean. This bunch of college professors he's got down there. Brain Trusters. I'd rather have Farley, at that. Poor Farley.

Q: Why "poor Farley"?

A: Poor Farley, he takes the rap for all Roosevelt's mistakes. He's the goat. By the way, they're all washed up, you know.

Q: Who's all washed up?

A: Roosevelt and Farley. I have it on good authority that they aren't friends any more. Roosevelt fights with all his old friends sooner or later, just like Wilson did. But can you imagine—a lot of crackpot college professors telling businessmen how to run their business. This country would be all right if Roosevelt would let it alone.

Q: You mean the country is—

A: Basically sound. Right. The trouble with this country is too much government interference in business. A businessman never can tell what That Fellow in the White House is going to do next. All your profits go for taxes, anyhow.

Q: And I suppose you discount the statistics showing a rise in national income because . . .

A: Because those figures are based on the fifty-cent Roosevelt dollar.

Q: What is it business needs, Mr. Arbuthnot?

A: Business needs a breathing spell.

Q: Thus far Mr. Arbuthnot, your comments have been confined to Mr. Roosevelt's policies. Have you, as an expert in the jargon of the Roosevelt haters, anything to say about his private, personal life?

A: Have I? Oh boy! Why, he's a rich man's son. He never did a tap of work in his life. Where does *he* get off, posing as a champion of the people?

Q: A traitor to his class, eh?

A: Oh, we don't use that chestnut any more. It's out of date. What Roosevelt wants to do is set up a dynasty. He's got most of his family on the public payroll down there in Washington now. Don't worry, they're feathering the old nest.

Q: I believe you boys refer to James Roosevelt as the Crown Prince, do you not?

A: Well, yes, only we add a little twist to that and call him the Clown Prince.

Q: Mr. Arbuthnot, I know that you Roosevelt haters have quite a collection of spicy stories about the Roosevelt family. Could you summarize all these in one cliché?

A: Certainly. How can you expect Roosevelt to run the country when he can't even control his own family?

Q: What about Mrs. Roosevelt?

A: She ought to stay home and tend to her own business instead of gallivanting around the country making a holy show of herself. I should think the First Lady would have a little dignity.

Q: What about the President's fishing trips?

A: Fishing trips! Look at the country, the shape it's in, and he goes fishing. On a battleship, too. You know who pays for those junkets, don't you?

Q: Who?

A: The taxpayers, that's who. Oh well, it won't be long now.

Q: What do you mean?

A: I mean Franklin D. is on his way out. He's finally overreached himself. You know what the voters are going to deliver Franklin Delano Roosevelt this fall?

Q: What?

A: A stinging rebuke, that's what. He's lost his hold on the people. He's been sitting down there in his ivory tower too long, listening to these college professors and forgetting his campaign promises. He's lost touch. He don't know what's going on throughout the country.

Q: You think so?

A: Sure do. The old Roosevelt charm won't work this time. The old Roosevelt smile and that "my friends" baloney won't get him anywhere this fall. The people are onto him at last.

Q: You're quite sure of this?

A: Well, in a way I am and in a way I ain't. Look at how he's spending the taxpayer's money to further his own personal ambition. After all, you can't beat Santa Claus.

The portrait of Henry Luce by Wolcott Gibbs, a masterpiece of what Russell Maloney has called the knee-in-the-groin school of biography, throws light on a number of journalistic and political developments of the Thirties. Mary McCarthy's Portrait of the Intellectual as a Yale Man (*easily the best title of the era*) *explores some aspects of life on the liberal weeklies before transporting its hero to more fortunate climes. Miss McCarthy's Yale man is a unique figure—two or three, by some accounts—but his history includes fragments of many personal histories of those years. James*

Thurber's inquiry into the quaint ways of Leftist literary criticism is both a splendid potting of jargon on the wing and a salutary reminder that all who speak in the name of the working class do not necessarily remember— if they ever knew—that workers are first of all men, and not the noble savages who stride mightily through the proletarian novels. At the opposite pole from the abstractions of Mr. Thurber's literary critics is Joseph Curran of the National Maritime Union, who emerged as a significant figure during the Roosevelt era and who could probably have appeared at no earlier time.

WOLCOTT GIBBS

Time . . . Life . . . Fortune . . . Luce

SAD-EYED in October, 1936, was nimble, middle-sized *Life*-President Clair Maxwell as he told newshawks of the sale of the fifty-three-year-old gag-mag to *Time*. For celebrated name alone, price: $85,000.

Said he: "*Life* . . . introduced to the world the drawings . . . of such men as Charles Dana Gibson, the verses of . . . James Whitcomb Riley and Oliver Herford, such writers as John Kendrick Bangs. . . . Beginning next month the magazine *Life* will embark on a new venture entirely unrelated to the old."

How unrelated to the world of the Gibson Girl was this new venture might have been gathered at the time from a prospectus issued by enormous, Apollo-faced C. D. Jackson, of Time, Inc.

"*Life*," wrote he, "will show us the Man-of-the-Week . . . his body clothed and, if possible, nude." It will expose "the loves, scandals, and personal affairs of the plain and fancy citizen . . . and write around them a light, good-tempered 'colyumnist' review of these once-private lives."

29,000 die-hard subscribers to *Life*,[1] long accustomed to he-she jokes, many ignorant of Duke of Windsor's once-private life (*Time,* July 25,

Originally published in *The New Yorker*. Reprinted by permission of Dodd, Mead & Company, Inc. From *A Bed of Neuroses* by Wolcott Gibbs. Copyright, 1936, by Wolcott Gibbs.
[1] Peak of *Life* circulation (1921): 250,000.

1936, *et seq.*), will be comforted for the balance of their subscription periods by familiar, innocent jocosities of *Judge*. First issue of new publication went out to 250,000 readers, carried advertisements suggesting an annual revenue of $1,500,000, pictured Russian peasants in the nude, the love life of the Black Widow spider, referred inevitably to Mrs. Ernest Simpson. By March, 1937, circulation had touched a million; form and content remained essentially the same.

Behind this latest, most incomprehensible Timenterprise loomed, as usual, ambitious, gimlet-eyed, Baby Tycoon Henry Robinson Luce, co-founder of *Time,* promulgator of *Fortune,* potent in associated radio & cinema ventures.

"High-Buttoned . . . Brilliant"

Headman Luce was born in Tengchowfu, China, on April 3, 1898, the son of Henry Winters & Elizabeth Middleton Luce, Presbyterian missionaries. Very unlike the novels of Pearl Buck were his early days. Under brows too beetling for a baby, young Luce grew up inside the compound, played with his two sisters, lisped first Chinese, dreamed much of the Occident. At 14, weary of poverty, already respecting wealth & power, he sailed alone for England, entered school at St. Albans. Restless again, he came to the United States, enrolled at Hotchkiss, met up & coming young Brooklynite Briton Hadden. Both even then were troubled with an itch to harass the public. Intoned Luce years later: "We reached the conclusion that most people were not well informed & that something should be done. . . ."

First publication to inform fellowman was *Hotchkiss Weekly Record;* next *Yale Daily News,* which they turned into a tabloid; fought to double hours of military training, fought alumni who wished to change tune of Yale song from *Die Wacht am Rhein.* Traditionally unshaven, wearing high-buttoned Brooks jackets, soft white collars, cordovan shoes, no garters, Luce & Hadden were Big Men on a campus then depleted of other, older Big Men by the war. Luce, pale, intense, nervous, was Skull & Bones, Alpha Delta Phi, Phi Beta Kappa, member of the Student Council, editor of the *News;* wrote sad poems, read the *New Republic,* studied political philosophy. As successful, less earnest, more convivial, Hadden collected china dogs, made jokes.[1] In 1920 the senior class voted Hadden Most Likely to Succeed, Luce Most Brilliant. Most Brilliant he, Luce sloped off to Christ Church, Oxford, there to study European conditions, take field trips into the churning Balkans.

---

[1] Once, watching Luce going past, laden with cares & responsibilities, Hadden chuckled, upspoke: "Look out, Harry. You'll drop the college."

Best Advice: Don't

Twenty months after commencement, in the city room of Paperkiller Frank Munsey's *Baltimore News,* met again Luce, Hadden. Newshawks by day, at night they wrangled over policies of the magazine they had been planning since Hotchkiss. Boasted the final prospectus: *"Time* will be free from cheap sensationalism . . . windy bias."

In May, 1922, began the long struggle to raise money to start *Time.* Skeptical at the outset proved Newton D. Baker, Nicholas Murray Butler, Herbert Bayard Swope, William Lyon Phelps. Pooh-poohed *Review of Reviews* Owner Charles Lanier: "My best advice . . . don't do it." From studious, pint-sized Henry Seidel Canby, later editor of Lamont-backed *Saturday Review of Literature,* came only encouraging voice in this threnody.

Undismayed Luce & Hadden took the first of many offices in an old brownstone house at 9 East 17th Street, furnished it with a filing cabinet, four second-hand desks, a big brass bowl for cigarette stubs, sought backers.[1]

JPMorganapoleon H. P. Davison, Yale classmate of Luce, Hadden, great & good friend of both, in June contributed $4,000. Next to succumb: Mrs. David S. Ingalls, sister of Classmate William Hale Harkness; amount, $10,000. From Brother Bill, $5,000. Biggest early angel, Mrs. William Hale Harkness, mother of Brother Bill & Mrs. Ingalls, invested $20,000. Other original stockholders: Robert A. Chambers, Ward Cheney,

---

[1] In return for $50 cash, original investors were given two shares 6% Preferred Stock with a par value of $25, one share Class A Common Stock without par value. 3,440 Preferred, 1,720 Class A Common were so sold.

170 shares of Class A Common, 8,000 shares of Class B Common, also without par value, not entitled to dividends until Preferred Shares had been retired, were issued to Briton Hadden, Henry R. Luce, who gave one-third to associates, divided remainder equally.

In 1925, authorized capital of Time, Inc., was increased to 19,000 shares; of which 8,000 were Preferred, 3,000 Class A; as before, 8,000 Class B.

In June, 1930 (if you are still following this), the Preferred Stock was retired in full & dividends were initiated for both Common Stocks. Corporation at this time had 2,400 shares Class A, 7,900 Class B outstanding.

By the spring of 1931 *Time* had begun to march, shares were nominally quoted at $1,000. Best financial minds advised splitting stock on basis of twenty shares for one. Outstanding after clever maneuver: 206,400 shares Common.

In 1933, outlook still gorgeous, each share of stock was reclassified into 1/10th share of $6.50 Dividend Cumulative Convertible Preferred Stock ($6.50 div. cum. con. pfd. stk.) and one share of New Common Stock. New div. cum. con. pfd. stk. was convertible into a share and a half of New Common Stock, then selling around $40 a share, now quoted at over $200.

Present number of shares outstanding, 238,000; paper value of shares, $47,000,000; conservative estimate of Luce holding, 102,300 shares; paper value, $20,460,000; conservative estimate of Luce income from *Time* stock, $818,400; reported Luce income from other investments, $100,000; reported Luce bagatelle as editor of Time, Inc., $45,000; reported total Lucemolument, $963,400.

Boy!

F. Trubee Davison, E. Roland Harriman, Dwight W. Morrow, Harvey S. Firestone, Jr., Seymour H. Knox, William V. Griffin. By November Luce & Hadden had raised $86,000, decided to go to work on fellowman.

"Snaggle-Toothed ... Pig-Faced"

Puny in spite of these preparations, prosy in spite of the contributions of Yale poets Archibald MacLeish & John Farrar, was the first issue of *Time* on March 3, 1923. Magazine went to 9,000 subscribers; readers learned that Uncle Joe Cannon had retired at 86, that there was a famine in Russia, that Thornton Wilder friend Tunney had defeated Greb.

Yet to suggest itself as a rational method of communication, of infuriating readers into buying the magazine, was strange inverted Timestyle. It was months before Hadden's impish contempt for his readers,[1] his impatience with the English language, crystallized into gibberish. By the end of the first year, however, Timeditors were calling people able, potent, nimble; "Tycoon," most successful Timepithet, had been coined by Editor Laird Shields Goldsborough; so fascinated Hadden with "beady-eyed" that for months nobody was anything else. Timeworthy were deemed such designations as "Tom-tom" Heflin, "Body-lover" MacFadden.

"Great word! Great word!" would crow Hadden, coming upon "snaggle-toothed," "pig-faced." Appearing already were such maddening coagulations as "cinemaddict," "radiorator." Appearing also were first gratuitous invasions of privacy. Always mentioned as William Randolph Hearst's "great & good friend" was Cinemactress Marion Davies, stressed was the bastardy of Ramsay MacDonald, the "cozy hospitality" of Mae West. Backward ran sentences until reeled the mind.

By March, 1924, the circulation had doubled, has risen since then 40,000 a year, reaches now the gratifying peak of 640,000, is still growing. From four meagre pages in first issue, *Time* advertising has now come to eclipse that in *Satevepost*. Published *Time* in first six months of 1936, 1,590 pages; *Satevepost*, 1,480.

No Slugabed, He ...

Strongly contrasted from the outset of their venture were Hadden, Luce. Hadden, handsome, black-haired, eccentric, irritated his partner by playing baseball with the office boys, by making jokes, by lack of respect for autocratic business. Conformist Luce disapproved of heavy drinking, played hard, sensible game of tennis, said once: "I have no use for a man who

---

[1] Still framed at *Time* is Hadden's scrawled dictum: "Let Subscriber Goodkind mend his ways!"

lies in bed after nine o'clock in the morning," walked to work every morning, reproved a writer who asked for a desk for lack of "log-cabin spirit."

In 1925, when *Time* moved its offices to Cleveland, bored, rebellious was Editor Hadden; Luce, busy & social, lunched with local bigwigs, addressed Chamber of Commerce, subscribed to Symphony Orchestra, had neat house in the suburbs. Dismayed was Luce when Hadden met him on return from Europe with premature plans to move the magazine back to New York. In 1929, dying of a streptococcus infection, Hadden still opposed certain details of success-formula of *Fortune,* new, beloved Lucenterprise.

Oats, Hogs, Cheese . . .

In January, 1930, first issue of *Fortune* was mailed to 30,000 subscribers, cost as now $1 a copy, contained articles on branch banking, hogs, glassblowing, how to live in Chicago on $25,000 a year. Recent issue went to 130,000 subscribers, contained articles on bacon, tires, the New Deal, weighed as much as a good-sized flounder.[1]

Although in 1935 *Fortune* made a net profit of $500,000, vaguely dissatisfied was Editor Luce. Anxious to find & express "the technological significance of industry," he has been handicapped by the fact that his writers are often hostile to Big Business, prone to insert sneers, slithering insults. In an article on Bernard Baruch, the banker was described as calling President Hoover "old cheese-face." Protested Tycoon Baruch that he had said no such thing. Shotup of this was that Luce, embarrassed, printed a retraction; now often removes too-vivid phrasing from writers' copy.

Typical perhaps of Luce methods is *Fortune* system of getting material. Writers in first draft put down wild gossip, any figures that occur to them. This is sent to victim, who indignantly corrects the errors, inadvertently supplies facts he might otherwise have withheld.

March of Time in approximately its present form was first broadcast on March 6, 1931, paid the Columbia System for privilege, dropped from the air in February, 1932, with Luce attacking radio's "blatant claim to be a medium of education." Said he: "Should *Time* or any other business feel obliged to be the philanthropist of the air; to continue to pay for radio advertising it doesn't want in order to provide radio with something worthwhile?" So popular, so valuable to the studio was *March of Time* that it was restored in September of the same year, with Columbia donating its time & facilities. Since then *March of Time* has been sponsored by Remington-Rand typewriter company, by Wrigley's gum, by its own

---

[1] Two pounds, nine ounces.

cinema *March of Time,* has made 400 broadcasts.[1] Apparently reconciled to philanthropy is Luce, because time for latest version is being bought & paid for by his organization.

No active connection now has Luce with the moving-picture edition of *March of Time,* which was first shown on February 1, 1935, appears thirteen times a year in over 6,000 theatres, has so far failed to make money, to repay $900,000 investment. Even less connection has he with *Time's* only other unprofitable venture. Fifty-year-old *Architectural Forum,* acquired in 1932, loses still between $30,000 and $50,000 a year, circulates to 31,000.

Letters, five-cent fortnightly collection of *Time's* correspondence with its indefatigable readers, was started in 1931, goes to 30,000, makes a little money.

For a time, Luce was on Board of Directors of Paramount Pictures. Hoped to learn something of cinema, heard nothing discussed but banking, resigned sadly.

Fascinating Facts . . . Dreamy Figures . . .

Net profits of Time, Inc., for nine years:

1927	3,860
1928	125,787
1929	325,412
1930	818,936
1931	847,447
1932	613,727[2]
1933	1,009,628
1934	1,773,094
1935	$2,249,823[3]

In 1935 gross revenue of *Time-Fortune* was $8,621,170, of which the newsmagazine brought in approximately $6,000,000. Outside investments netted $562,295. For rent, salaries, production & distribution, other expenses went $6,594,076. Other deductions: $41,397. Allowance for federal income tax: $298,169.

Time's books, according to Chicago Statisticians Gerwig & Gerwig, show total assets of $6,755,451. Liabilities, $3,101,584. These figures, conventionally allowing $1 for name, prestige of *Time,* come far from reflecting actual prosperity of Luce, his enterprises. Sitting pretty are the boys.

---

[1] By some devious necromancy, statisticians have calculated that *March of Time* ranks just behind *Amos & Andy* as most popular of all radio programs; reaches between 8,000,000 and 9,000,000 newshungry addicts.

[2] Hmm.

[3] Exceeded only by Curtis Publishing Co. (*Satevepost*): $5,329,900; Crowell Publishing Co. (*Collier's*): $2,399,600.

Luce . . . Marches On!

Transmogrified by this success are the offices, personnel of *Time-Fortune*. Last reliable report: *Time,* 308 employees; *Fortune,* 103; Cinemarch, 58; Radiomarch, 10; *Architectural Forum,* 40; *Life,* 47. In New York; total, 566. In Chicago, mailing, editorial, mechanical employees, 216. Grand total Time-employees on God's earth, 782. Average weekly recompense for informing fellowman, $45.67802.

From first single office, Timen have come to bulge to bursting six floors of spiked, shiny Chrysler Building, occupy 150 rooms, eat daily, many at famed Cloud Club, over 1,000 eggs, 500 cups of coffee, much bicarbonate of soda. Other offices: Cinemarch, 10th Avenue at 54th Street; Radiomarch, Columbia Broadcasting Building.

Ornamented with Yale, Harvard, Princeton diplomas, stuffed fish, terrestrial globes are offices of Luce & other headmen; bleak, uncarpeted the writer's dingy lair.

Heir apparent to mantle of Luce is dapper, tennis-playing $35,000-a-year Roy Larsen, nimble in Radio & Cinemarch, vice-president & second largest stockholder in Time, Inc. Stock income: $120,000.

Looming behind him is burly, able, tumbledown Yaleman Ralph McAllister Ingersoll, former Fortuneditor, now general manager of all Timenterprises, descendant of 400-famed Ward McAllister. Littered his desk with pills, unguents, Kleenex, Socialite Ingersoll is *Time's* No. 1 hypochondriac, introduced ant palaces for study & emulation of employees, writes copious memoranda about filing systems, other trivia, seldom misses a Yale football game. His salary: $30,000; income from stock: $40,000.

Early in life Timeditor John Stuart Martin lost his left arm in an accident. Unhandicapped he, resentful of sympathy, Martin played par golf at Princeton, is a crack shot with a rifle or shotgun, holds a telephone with no hands, using shoulder & chin, chews paperclips. First cousin of Cofounder Hadden, joined in second marriage to daughter of Cunard Tycoon Sir Ashley Sparks, Timartin is managing editor of newsmagazine, has been nimble in Cinemarch, other Timenterprises, makes $25,000 a year salary, gets from stock $60,000.

$20,000 salary, $20,000 from stock gets shyest, least-known of all Timeditors, Harvardman John S. Billings, Jr., now under Luce in charge of revamped *Life,* once Washington correspondent for the Brooklyn *Eagle,* once National Affairs Editor for *Time.* Yclept "most important man in shop" by Colleague Martin, Billings, brother of famed muralist Henry Billings, is naïve, solemn, absent-minded, once printed same story twice, wanted to print, as news, story of van Gogh's self-mutilation, drives to office in car with liveried chauffeur, likes Jones Beach.

Fortuneditor Eric Hodgins is thin-haired, orbicular, no Big Three graduate. Formerly on *Redbook,* boy & girl informing *Youth's Companion,* Hodgins inherited Pill-Swallower Ingersoll's editorial job two years ago when latter was called to greater glory, higher usefulness, still writes much of content of magazine, is paid $15,000; from stock only $8,000.

Doomed to strict anonymity are *Time-Fortune* staff writers, but generally known in spite of this are former *Times* bookritic John Chamberlain, Meistersinger Archibald MacLeish. Both out of sympathy with domineering business, both irked by stylistic restrictions, thorns to Luce as well as jewels they. Reward for lack of fame: Chamberlain, $10,000; MacLeish, $15,000; each, two months' vacation.

Brisk beyond belief are carryings-on these days in Luce's chromium tower. *Time,* marching on more militantly than ever, is a shambles on Sundays & Mondays, when week's news is teletyped to Chicago printing plant; *Fortune,* energetic, dignified, its offices smelling comfortably of cookies, is ever astir with such stupefying projects as sending the entire staff to Japan; new whoopsheet *Life* so deep in organization that staff breakfasts are held to choose from 6,000 submitted photographs the Nude of the Week; so harried perpetually all editors that even interoffice memoranda are couched in familiar Timestyle,[1] that an appointment to lunch with Editor Luce must be made three weeks in advance.

Caught up also in the whirlwind of progress are *Time, Fortune's* 19 maiden checkers. Bryn Mawr, Wellesley, Vassar graduates they, each is assigned to a staff writer, checks every word he writes, works hard & late, is barred by magazine's anti-feminine policy from editorial advancement.

Cold, Baggy, Temperate . . .

At work today, Luce is efficient, humorless, revered by colleagues; arrives always at 9:15, leaves at 6, carrying armfuls of work, talks jerkily, carefully, avoiding visitor's eye; stutters in conversation, never in speechmaking. In early days kept standing at Luce desk like butlers were writers while he praised or blamed; now most business is done by time-saving memoranda called "Luce's bulls." Prone he to wave aside pleasantries, social preliminaries, to get at once to the matter in hand. Once to interviewer who said, "I hope I'm not disturbing you," snapped Luce, "Well, you are." To ladies full of gentle misinformation he is brusque, contradictory, hostile: says that his only hobby is "conversing with somebody

---

[1] Sample Luce memorandum: "Let *Time's* editors next week put thought on the Japanese beetle. H. R. L."

who knows something," argues still that "names make news," that he would not hesitate to print a scandal involving his best friend.

Because of his Chinese birth, constantly besieged is Luce by visiting Orientals; he is polite, forbearing, seethes secretly. Lunch, usually in a private room at the Cloud Club, is eaten quickly, little attention paid to the food, much to business. He drinks not at all at midday, sparingly at all times, takes sometimes champagne at dinner, an occasional cocktail at parties. Embarrassed perhaps by reputation for unusual abstemiousness, he confesses proudly that he smokes too much.

Serious, ambitious Yale standards are still reflected in much of his conduct; in indiscriminate admiration for bustling success, in strong regard for conventional morality, in honest passion for accuracy; physically, in conservative, baggy clothes, white shirts with buttoned-down collars, solid-color ties. A budding joiner, in New York, Luce belongs to the Yale, Coffee House, Racquet & Tennis, Union, & Cloud Clubs; owns a box at the Metropolitan; is listed in *Who's Who* & *Social Register*.

Colder, more certain, more dignified than in the early days of the magazine, his prose style has grown less ebullient, resembles pontifical *Fortune* rather than chattering *Time*. Before some important body he makes now at least one speech a year, partly as a form of self-discipline, partly because he feels that his position as head of a national institution demands it. His interests wider, he likes to travel, meet & observe the Great. Five or six times in Europe, he has observed many Great & Near Great. Of a twenty-minute conversation with Duke of Windsor, then Prince of Wales, says only "Very interesting." Returning from such trips, he always provides staff members with 10 & 12-page memoranda carefully explaining conditions.

Orated recently of conditions in this country: "Without the aristocratic principle no society can endure. . . . What slowly deadened our aristocratic sense was the expanding frontier, but more the expanding machine. . . . But the aristocratic principle persisted in the United States in our fetish of comparative success. . . . We got a plutocracy without any common sense of dignity and obligation. Money became more and more the only mark of success, but still we insisted that the rich man was no better than the poor man—and the rich man accepted the verdict. And so let me make it plain, the triumph of the mass mind is nowhere more apparent than in the frustration of the upper classes." Also remarked in conversation: "Trouble is—great anti-social development—is the automobile trailer. Greatest failure of this country is that it hasn't provided good homes for its people. Trailer shows that."

Milestones

Good-naturedly amused by Luce tycoon ambitions was Lila Hotz, of Chicago, whom he married there on Dec. 22, 1923. In 1935, the father of two boys, Luce was divorced by her in Reno on Oct. 5. Married in Old Greenwich, Conn., without attendants, on Nov. 23, 1935, were Luce, Novelist-Playwright Clare Boothe Brokaw, described once by Anglo-aesthete Cecil Beaton as "most drenchingly beautiful," former wife of elderly Pantycoon George Tuttle Brokaw.

Two days before ceremony, "Abide with Me," by new, beautiful Mrs. Luce, was produced at the Ritz Theatre. Play dealt with young woman married to sadistic drunkard, was unfavorably reviewed by all newspaper critics.[1]

In a quandary was Bridegroom Luce when *Time's* own critic submitted a review suggesting play had some merit. Said he: "Show isn't that good. . . . Go back. . . . Write what you thought." Seven times, however, struggled the writer before achieving an acceptable compromise between criticism, tact.

A Million Rooms, a Thousand Baths . . .

Long accustomed to being entertained, entertaining, is Mrs. Luce, intimate of Mr. & Mrs. A. Coster Schermerhorn, Mr. and Mrs. Bernard M. Baruch, Jock Whitney, glistening stage & literary stars. Many were invited last summer to 30-acre estate in Stamford to play tennis, croquet, swim; many, too, will come to 7,000-acre, $100,000 Luce plantation, near Charleston, S. C.; will sleep there in four stream-lined, prefabricated guest cottages. Given to first Mrs. Luce in divorce settlement, along with $500,-000 in cash & securities, was French Manoir at Gladstone, N. J., where Luce once planned to raise Black Angus cows, to become gentleman farmer.

Described too modestly by him as "smallest apartment in River House,"[2] duplex at 435 East 52nd Street occupied last winter by Luce contained 15 rooms, 5 baths, a lavatory; was leased furnished from Mrs. Bodrero Macy for $7,300 annually, contained many valuable French, English, Italian antiques, looked north and east on the river. In décor, Mrs. Luce prefers the modern; evasive is Luce. Says he: "Just like things con-

---

[1] Of it said Richard Watts, blue-shirted, moon-faced *Tribune* dramappraiser:
"One almost forgave 'Abide with Me' its faults when its lovely playwright, who must have been crouched in the wings for a sprinter's start as the final curtain mercifully descended, heard a cry of 'author,' which was not audible in my vicinity, and arrived onstage to accept the audience's applause just as the actors, who had a head-start on her, were properly lined up and smoothed out to receive their customary adulation."

[2] Smallest apartment in River House has six rooms, one bath.

venient & sensible." Says also: "Whatever furniture or houses we buy in
the future will be my wife's buying, not mine.":

Whither, Whither?

Accused by many of Fascist leanings, of soaring journalistic ambition,
much & conflicting is the evidence on Luce political faith, future plans. By
tradition a Tory, in 1928 he voted for Alfred E. Smith, in 1932 for Herbert
Hoover, last year for Alfred M. Landon. Long at outs with William Randolph Hearst, it was rumored that a recent visit to California included a
truce with ruthless, shifting publisher. Close friend for years of Thomas
Lamont, Henry P. Davison, the late Dwight Morrow, it has been hinted
that an official connection with the House of Morgan in the future is not
impossible. Vehemently denies this Luce, denies any personal political ambition, admits only that he would like eventually to own a daily newspaper in New York.

Most persistent, most fantastic rumor, however, declares that Yaleman
Luce already has a wistful eye on the White House. Reported this Chicago's *Ringmaster,* added: "A legally-minded friend . . . told him that
his Chinese birth made him ineligible. Luce dashed to another lawyer to
check. Relief! He was born of American parents and properly registered
at the Consulate."

Whatever the facts in that matter, indicative of Luce consciousness of
budding greatness, of responsibility to whole nation, was his report to
Time's Board of Directors on March 19, 1936. Declaimed he: "The expansion of your company has brought it to a point beyond which it will
cease to be even a big Small Business and become a small Big Business.
. . . The problem of public relations also arises. *Time,* the Weekly Newsmagazine, has been, and still is, its own adequate apologist. Ditto, *Fortune.*
But with a motion-picture journal, a nightly radio broadcast, and with
four magazines, the public interpretation of your company's alleged viewpoint or viewpoints must be taken with great seriousness." Certainly to
be taken with seriousness is Luce at thirty-nine, his fellowmen already informed up to their ears, the shadow of his enterprises long across the land,
his future plans impossible to imagine, staggering to contemplate. Where
it all will end, knows God!

MARY McCARTHY

Portrait of the Intellectual as a Yale Man

TO LOOK at him, you would never have believed he was an intellectual. That was the nice thing about Jim Barnett. With his pink cheeks and sparkling brown eyes and reddish brown hair that needed brushing and well-cut brown suit that needed pressing, he might have been any kind of regular young guy, anywhere in America. He made you think of Boy Scouts and starting a fire without matches and Wesley Barry and skinning the cat and Our Gang comedies and Huckleberry Finn. If he had ever been hard up, he could have been a photographic model, and one would have seen his pleasant, vaguely troubled face more often in *The Saturday Evening Post* than in *Esquire*. He might have done very well as the young man who is worried about his life insurance, the young man who is worried about dandruff, the young man whose shirts won't fit him, the young man who looks up happily from his plate of Crunchies, saying, "Gee, honey, I didn't know breakfast food could taste so good!"

In real life, his concerns were of a different order. The year he came down from Yale (where he could have been Bones but wouldn't), he was worried about Foster and Ford and the Bonus Marchers and the Scottsboro Boys. He had also just taken a big gulp of *Das Kapital* and was going around telling people about how he felt afterwards. He would buttonhole a classmate after a few sets of tennis down at the old Fourteenth Street Armory. "You know, Al," he would say, twisting his head upwards and to one side in the characteristic American gesture of a man who is giving a problem serious thought (the old salt or the grizzled Yankee farmer scanning the sky for weather indications), "you know, Al, I never thought so at college, but the Communists *have* something. Their methods over here are a little operatic, but you can't get around their analysis of capitalism. I think the system is finished, and it's up to us to be ready for the new thing when it comes." And Al, or whoever it was, would be doubtful but impressed. He might even go home with a copy of the *Communist Manifesto* in his pocket—in that period, the little social-

ist classic enjoyed something of the popularity of the *Reader's Digest:* it put
the whole thing in a nutshell, let a fellow like Al know just what he was up
against. Later that evening Al might remark to his wife that maybe it
would be a good idea (didn't she think?) to lay in a stock of durable
consumers' goods—in case, oh, in case of inflation, or revolution, or anything like that. His wife would interpret this in terms of cans and leave a
big order for Heinz's baked beans, Campbell's tomato soup, and somebody
else's chicken à la king with the grocer the next day. This was the phenomenon known as the dissemination of ideas.

In much the same tone (that of a man in an advertisement letting
another man in on a new high-test gasoline) Jim began to write about his
convictions in articles and book reviews for the liberal magazines. Capitalism was on the skids, and everybody ought to know about it. He
could never have written, "Capitalism is doomed," any more than he
could have talked about "the toiling masses." At Yale, elevation in speech
had been held to be quite as barbarous as eccentricity in dress or the wrong
sort of seriousness in study; and if Jim had committed an unpardonable
breach of manners in interesting himself in Marxism, his rough-and-tum-
ble vocabulary was a sort of apology for this, a placatory offering to the
gods of decorum, who must have appeared to him in the guise of football
players. Certainly, his vocabulary had something to do with the enthusiasm
his work excited. The ideas he put forward, familiar enough when clothed
in their usual phraseology, emerged in his writing in a state of undress that
made them look exciting and almost new, just as a woman whom one has
known for years is always something of a surprise without her clothes on.
And, in the end, it was not the ideas that counted so much, as the fact that
Jim Barnett held them.

This was the thing that nobody, including Jim himself, could ever quite
get over. Now and then someone would be frank enough to ask him how it
had happened, and he would laugh and say that it had been an accident:
he had had a roommate at college who was literary, and once you got
started reading one thing led to another. But modest men, like boasters, are
never believed, even when they speak the exact truth; and in 1932 everyone
on the left was convinced that this "accident" was really a miracle, a sign
from heaven or history that the millennium was at hand. Most men had
come to socialism by some all-too-human compulsion: they were out of
work or lonely or sexually unsatisfied or foreign-born or queer in one of
a hundred bitter, irremediable ways. They resembled the original twelve
apostles in the New Testament; there was no real merit in their adherence,
and no hope either. But Jim was like the Roman centurion or Saint Paul;
he came to socialism freely, from the happy center of things, by a pure act

of perception which could only have been brought about by grace; and his conversion might be interpreted as a prelude to the conversion of the world.

And, like all miracles, this particular one served to quicken the faith of the stragglers, the tired workers, and the worldlings. Silly people who had gone a little to the left and then begun to wonder whether they had not, after all, made a mistake, had only to look at Jim Barnett to feel reassured. Nobody could possibly object to socialism if it were going to be run by earnest, undogmatic Yale men—some of them out of Shef, to take care of the technical side. On the other hand, serious middle-aged men who had been plugging Marxism for years in little magazines that owed the printer money and never came out on time would have a conversation with Jim and feel heartened, even inspired. If a nice, average boy like that could tumble into the movement, surely the old ideas must be bankrupt at last. When capitalism, intellectually speaking, could no longer feed her favorite children, the end could not but be very, very near.

By simply being the way he was, Jim Barnett made a great many people on the left feel happy, almost sentimental. He was a mascot, a good-luck piece; and there was perhaps some superstition behind the fact that very little was demanded of him—you must not ask too much of a talisman or the power will go out of it, and it is better not to look a gift horse in the mouth. At any rate, unlike most converts of that period, he was not expected to follow the Party line, even on a long leash. From the very first, Jim was an independent in politics, siding now with the Communists, now with the Lovestoneites, now with the Trotskyists, now with the group of middle-class liberals he had known at college who were trying to build a Farmer-Labor party of their own. In anybody else, such behavior would have been politically suspect: the man would have been damned as a careerist, on the one hand, or a dilettante on the other. Yet neither of these allegations was ever made against Jim. His heterodoxy was received by all factions with paternal indulgence. "Let the boy have his head," was the feeling. "A wild oat or two won't hurt him."

With Jim himself it was a point of honor that he should never agree completely with anyone or anything. He had never swallowed Marxism whole, he used to say in a slightly boastful tone, as if he had achieved a considerable feat of acrobatics. It was true; he never swallowed any doctrine whole. Like a finicky eater, he took pride in the fact that he always left something on the plate. There was something peculiarly American and puritanical about this abstemiousness of his; in other countries children are taught that it is bad manners not to finish everything that is set before them. But at Yale a certain intellectual prodigality had been cultivated in the students; it was bad taste to admire anything too wholeheartedly. They thought "bad taste" but they meant "dangerous," for the prodigality was merely an end product of asceticism: you must not give in to your appetites, physical or spiritual; if you did, God knows where it would land you, in paganism, Romanism, idolatry, or the gutter. Like all good Yale men, Jim feared systems as his great-grandfather had feared the devil, the saloon, and the pope.

Naturally, for boys brought up under these influences, systems of thought had a certain wanton, outlawed attractiveness; and Marxism was to become for Jim's generation what an actress had been for the youths of the Gilded Age. During the first years of the New Deal, there were many flirtations, many platonic friendships with the scarlet woman of the steppes. Jim, being courageous, went farther than most. And, at first glance, that balkiness of his, that hesitation, that unwillingness to take the final step, might have appeared to be merely a concession to tradition, another bone thrown to the Eli bulldog, who was always extraordinarily hungry.

Actually, it was deeper and more personal than that. If other people on the left stood in superstitious awe of Jim, Jim also stood in awe of himself. It was not that he considered that he was especially brilliant or talented; his estimation of his qualities was both just and modest. What he reverenced in himself was his intelligent mediocrity. He knew that he was the Average Thinking Man to whom in the end all appeals are addressed. He was the man that Uncle Sam points his finger at in the recruiting posters, that political orators beseech and ad-writers try to frighten; he was the stooge from the audience that the magician calls up on the stage, the foreman on the Grand Jury, the YOU in "This means YOU." He was a walking Gallup Poll, and he had only to leaf over his feelings to discover what America was thinking. There was something sublime about this, but there were responsibilities, too. The danger was that you would lose your amateur standing. It was essential to remain—not aloof, exactly, for that implied some aristocratic hauteur—but accessible, undecided. It was so easy, so fatally easy, to become a professional innocent; one day you were a bona fide tourist, and the next you were a shill in a Chinatown bus. If you were not remarkably alert, you might never know it had happened.

Jim Barnett, however, *was* alert, and he took every possible precaution. His mind and character appeared to him as a kind of sacred trust that he must preserve inviolate. It was as if he were the standard gold dollar against which the currency is measured. It would be wrong to debase it with lead, but it would be equally wrong to put more than the specified amount of gold into it. The dollar was supposed to be impure in certain unalterable proportions: you could not change that without upsetting the whole monetary system. Jim's function, as he saw it, was to ring the new ideas against himself, and let the world hear how they sounded. It was his duty, therefore, to "be himself," and his virtues and his weaknesses were alike untouchable. On the one hand, he could not drop into the life of a Communist front man, because this would have involved a suspension of individual judgment, a surgical sterilization of the moral faculty that was odious to him; on the other hand, he could not lift himself into the world of Marxist scholarship, because, to put it frankly, this might have over-taxed his powers, might (who knows) have crippled him for good.

It did not occur to him, or, indeed, to anyone else, that he was taking the line of least resistance. This state of being unresolved, on call, as it were, was painful to him, and he used to envy his friends who, as he said, were "sure." The inconsistencies he found whenever he examined his own thoughts troubled him a good deal. He found, for example, that he liked to drink and dance and go to medium-smart night clubs with medium-pretty girls. Yet he believed with Veblen that there was no greater folly than conspicuous consumption, and his eyes and ears told him that people were hungry while he had money in his pocket. This was a problem all well-to-do radicals had to face, and there were any number of ways of dealing with it. You could stop being a radical, or you could give your money away. Or you could give a little of it away and say, "I owe some-thing to myself," or give none of it away, and say, "I'm not a saint, and be-sides I have something more important than money to contribute." The Communist Party in those years did its best to settle this delicate question gracefully for prosperous fellow-travelers. It was reported that Browder had declared that there was nothing worse for the movement than what he called "a tired radical," and that men and women would be better workers for the cause if they let themselves go and enjoyed life once in a while. This pronouncement was widely quoted—over cocktails in the Rainbow Room, and sometimes (even) over a bottle of champagne in more intimate boîtes; it was believed that this showed "the human side" of the Party leader, and gave the lie to those perpetual carpers (tired radicals, un-doubtedly) who kept talking about Communist inflexibility. The example of Marx and Engels was also cited: they had had great Christmas parties and had called the young Kautsky a mollycoddle because he would not drink beer. (And how right their judgment had been! Forty years later Kautsky had betrayed the revolution by voting war credits in the German Reichstag, and Lenin had called him, among other things, an old woman.) Jim Barnett tried all these formulas on his conscience, but stretch them as he would, he could not make them cover the abyss between the theory and the practice. He decided, at last, to let the abyss yawn, and in the course of time he fell into it.

The second year Jim was in New York, he went to work as assistant editor on one of the liberal weeklies. The whole staff was instantly delighted with him, from the septuagenarian editor and publisher down to the red-haired telephone girl. He brought a breath of fresh air into the office, the women told each other, while the old man muttered happily about "young ideas," and the men of forty-odd, Harvard graduates who remembered Jack Reed and who were rather dried and historical themselves, they, too, welcomed Jim Barnett in their own way, shaking their heads over him and prophesying with a certain relish that he would soon lose his illusions and resign himself, as they had done, to the world. The gratitude and joy everyone felt translated itself at once into action. The magazine began—with an alacrity that was almost fatuous—to smarten itself up. The advertising manager had herself an expensive permanent, Labor and Industry took to using mascara, the library got a set of modernistic chairs, some of the new lamps with indirect lighting, and a thick-piled gray rug from a neo-cubist furniture store on Eighth Street. Tea was served in the afternoons; a new format was planned for the magazine; the switchboard girl began to listen in to phone calls; and the managing editor asked a well-known Marxist hothead to do a series of articles on the New Deal.

All this attention embarrassed Jim a little. It did not go to his head. He even opposed some of the changes, in the manner of a small boy who says, "Aw, Ma, you're taking too much trouble." There was talk of moving the paper uptown, but Jim squelched this by insisting that the old-fashioned offices had a quaint integrity of their own, that the very editorial policy might be imperiled by a move to more glittering quarters. He perceived that the editors were ready to do anything he wanted—and he did not like it at all. It was true, he was anxious to put over his ideas, but he saw himself accomplishing this by argument, not by ingratiation. In his eyes, there was something ugly about the fact that these seasoned liberals should go to such lengths to please him. It was like having a girl give in too quickly; you felt that she did not take you, as an individual, seriously— she only wanted a man. At the back of his mind he was aware of a contempt for the *Liberal's* editorial board, like the contempt he had felt for the easy makes, the town girls in New Haven; and it was a contempt that was restless and full of fear, since the idea that kept pushing itself in was, "They would have done it for any young guy. They have no political respect for me as a person." This was one of the penalties of being the Average Man, that you were never sure whether people were not mixing you up with someone else. Sometimes you did not feel average so much as anonymous. Jim could never understand quite why it was, but whenever anyone talked about losing yourself in a cause, or in the Common Will, a thrill of horror would go through him, and he would recall the lost feeling, the tangled-up feeling, he got in a certain recurrent dream he had, where he could not find out who he was.

In the editorial staff of the *Liberal,* Jim sensed a great aching unspecific need for somebody, anybody, to think by and live by, as a mother lives by her son. Only the old man, with his long black coat and pompous manners and his eyeglasses on a black ribbon, seemed to be exempt from this necessity, and it was only with him in his private office that Jim felt truly comfortable. The others wanted to be bullied or taken by storm; the old man merely wanted to talk. He was interested in what Jim had to say, while the others, Jim felt, did not so much listen to his remarks as eavesdrop on them, waiting for him to express a preference they could gratify, or a decision they could concur with. It was like walking down Fifth Avenue with your mother or your girl during the Christmas shopping season: you did not dare pause for an instant before a tennis racket, an English sweater, or a toilet case in a store window; if you showed the faintest flicker of interest she would buy the thing for you, whether you wanted it or not. With the old man, however, Jim felt safe. He could say whatever came into his head and know that it would not appear, in a slightly garbled form, in one of the lead paragraphs on the following Wednesday. The two of them would sit in the old man's room, facing each other on a pair of squeaky swivel chairs, and discuss the AAA, the court-packing plan, the Kirov assassination and the execution of the hundred White Guards.

On all of these subjects the old man held opinions that were in the eyes of most of his staff and many of his readers an indication of failing powers. Mr. Wendell was uncompromisingly against what he called, in a public-auditorium voice, this new spirit of bureaucracy, this specter that was haunting the world under the name of progressivism or communism. He believed in socialism, but he held out for an economy of abundance, for a free judiciary, and trial by jury. He stood for inviolable human rights rather than plans or programs; and no plan, he declared, was worth a nickel that would sacrifice these rights at the first hint of trouble. Years later, Jim decided that time had, in each of these instances, proved the old man right. At the moment, he was not so sure. He did not quite agree with his friends who considered Mr. Wendell a tiresome old fuddyduddy. Still, he thought that you could probably trust Mr. Roosevelt and Comrade Stalin to abrogate liberty only just so much as was absolutely necessary—

and always in the right direction, that is, to abrogate your opponent's liberty rather than your own. When he told the old man that he was making a fetish of civil liberties, that the liberties were for the people and not the people for the liberties, Mr. Wendell replied that Jim was making a fetish out of socialism. Jim had to smile a little ruefully, conceding the point.

One day a new argument occurred to him, one he had heard the Communists advance. After all, he said, there has to be a limit to everything. Nobody can be allowed to practice freedom at the expense of everybody else. The government, for instance, has to protect itself against sedition and against the betrayal of state secrets in wartime. He looked up at the old man expectantly, wondering what he could answer. "Doesn't it?" he asked earnestly, when Mr. Wendell remained silent. "I don't believe in war," the old man answered calmly, and Jim blushed. He did not believe in war, either; at least he said he didn't, not in imperialist war anyway; but the words he had just spoken seemed to show that he did, that he believed in it more than anything else, more than free speech, more than the right to agitate against the government. He was so deeply chagrined by this discovery that the thread of the debate slipped from his hands, and it did not occur to him until he lay in bed that night that the old man had not answered the question but only parried it, and in such a way as to assert his moral superiority, to remind Jim of his long and heroic career as a fighter for peace. Jim laughed to himself, and turned over, contentedly. Of course there had to be certain restrictions on liberty; anybody but an anarchist would admit that. Of course there would have to be policemen, even in a classless society. "I'm too much of a realist," Jim said to himself proudly, "to imagine that anywhere, at any time, a state could be run on the honor system." Yet there *was* a problem. People said that you must never forget that the Soviet Union was moving toward greater democracy all the time; you had to look at a thing like this Kirov business *historically*: if you remembered the Czarist repression and the hated Okhrana, you would see that the execution of a few White Guards was a step forward—there were merely a hundred or so of them after all. But that, Jim thought, was like patting a mass killer on the head because this time he had only committed one little murder. "No!" he heard himself say, loudly and defiantly into the darkness. It was wrong to condone an affair like these executions. So far the old man was right. But there must be some middle ground. You ought to hate the sin and love the sinner. That was very difficult in practice, but everything was difficult. At least, he congratulated himself, he had faced the problem, even if he had not solved it. He settled himself comfortably on the horns of the dilemma and fell asleep.

When he married Nancy Hodges, he invited everybody on the *Liberal* to the wedding. Some of the older women looked a little dowdy and were inclined to be skittish about the champagne, but Mr. Wendell made a distinguished appearance, and, in any case, Nancy's parents, good, well-to-do Connecticut people, were not precisely streamlined themselves. The women, on their side, were faintly disappointed in Nancy. She was pretty, everyone conceded that; she had a straight, short nose and blond hair and sweet, direct, blue eyes. Yet somehow, they thought, she was not very *exciting*. She looked too much like her mother, which was a very bad thing in a girl. If Jim had to marry, they felt, it should have been somebody like an actress or a fast society girl or a painter or a burning-eyed revolutionary, somebody out of the ordinary. For Jim to have chosen such a humdrum little person as Nancy was, it seemed to them, a reflection on themselves. Around the office he had been so very careful: a cheerful word and a joke for everybody, but never a lunch or a dinner alone with a female member of the staff. They had not permitted themselves to feel resentment because they knew from the phone operator that there was a girl in the picture; and they had, one and all, persuaded themselves that she must be infinitely more beautiful and glamorous than they were. In this way, their own charms were not called into question. If a man prefers, say, Greta Garbo to you, it does not mean that you are not perfectly all right in your own style, not perfectly adequate to any of the usual requirements. The sight of Nancy in her wedding dress dispelled these comforting illusions. Every moderately young woman on the *Liberal* looked at Nancy and was affronted. "Why not me?" they all thought, as they clasped her small, plump hand, and murmured an appropriate formula.

"I'm afraid it's going to be one of those Dos Passos situations," the literary editor said to the managing editor on the way back on the train. "You know. She won't let him see his friends or do or think anything that her father wouldn't aprpove of. She'll make him buy a house in the country, and they'll live exactly like all the neighbors. She looks sweet, but like all those women she probably has a will of her own."

Jim, however, had been alert enough to consider these possibilities for himself. Nancy was conventional in many ways, but she was not ambitious or priggish or socially insecure. Nancy believed that you ought to have children and that they ought to have good doctors and good schools and plenty of fresh air and wholesome food. She believed that it was nice to go dancing on Saturday nights, and that it was nice to take a vacation trip once a year. She wanted to have big comfortable chairs in their apartment, and a big comfortable colored maid who came in by the day, and the first thing she bought was the very best Beautyrest mattresses for them to sleep on, and the very best box springs for their twin beds. Later, they got a good radio and phonograph combination, and they collected the choicest classical records they could find. Nancy was, from the beginning, careful with Jim's money and she put most of it into things that did not show, like the box springs, or a good plain rug, or life insurance. She subscribed to Consumer's Union, and to the hospitalization plan. She bought her clothes at Best's or Lord and Taylor's, and if she had fifteen dollars to spare from her household budget, she would put it into a new electric mixer for her maid rather than into an after-dinner coffee service for herself.

On the other hand, Nancy gave money to beggars in the street. She was tender-hearted, and she had majored in sociology in college. She knew that conditions under capitalism were horrifying, and she would always sign a check for a worthy cause. Her father showed a tendency to snort over Jim's activities; but Nancy handled this difficult situation perfectly: she took Jim's side but she did not argue; she merely patted her father on the cheek and told him he was an old fogy. "Do you mean to tell me you believe in this communistic talk of his?" the old man would ask. "I don't believe in *all* of it," she would answer with dignity, "but I believe in Jim." The phrasing was a little trite, but the sentiment was unimpeachable, for Nancy's father, like everyone else, believed in Jim, too. He could not help it.

Nancy was limited, but she was good. And she expected things of Jim. This was what drew him. Unlike the people in the *Liberal* office, unlike the radicals of all groups that he had been hobnobbing with, Nancy did not want Jim on any old terms. Nancy was not exacting, and yet there was an unwritten, unspoken contract between them. If she, on her side, had renounced all dreams of fortune and large success, he, on his side, was renouncing the right to poverty, loneliness, and despair. She was not to goad him up the social ladder, but he must never, never let her down. It was understood that he should not be pressed to go against his convictions; it was also understood that she must not go hungry. When he thought about them in the abstract, it seemed to him, now and then, that these guarantees were mutually incompatible, that Clause Z was in eternal obstinate contradiction to Clause A. In practice, however, you could, if you were sufficiently agile, manage to fulfill them both at once. The job on the *Liberal* kept his conscience clean and brought the bottle of Grade A to the door every morning. Many a discord, he thought, which cannot be resolved in theoretical terms, in real life can be turned into perfect harmony; and his own marriage demonstrated to him once again the superiority of pragmatism to all foreign brands of philosophy.

Still, he had misgivings. Sometimes it appeared as if his relation with Nancy were not testing his convictions so much as his powers of compromise. Their wedding had been a case in point. Nancy's parents had wanted a church wedding, and Jim had wanted City Hall. What they had had was a summer wedding on the lawn with a radical clergyman from New York officiating. It was the same way with their choice of friends. Park Avenue and Fourteenth Street were both ruled out. The result was that the people who came to their cocktail parties, at which Nancy served good hors d'oeuvres and rather poor cocktails, were presentable radicals and unpresentable conservatives—men in radio, men in advertising, lawyers with liberal ideas, publishers, magazine editors, writers of a certain status who lived in the country. Every social assertion Nancy and Jim made carried its own negation with it, like the Hegelian thesis. Thus it was always being said by Nancy that someone was a Communist but a terribly nice man, while Jim was remarking that somebody else worked for Young and Rubicam but was astonishingly liberal. Every guest was a sort of qualified statement, and the Barnetts' parties, in consequence, were a little dowdy, a little timid, in a queer way (for they were held in Greenwich Village) a little suburban. For some reason, nobody ever came to the Barnetts' house without his wife, unless she were in the hospital having a baby. They came systematically in pairs, and, once in the apartment, they would separate, as though by decree, and the men would talk, standing up, against the mantelpiece, while the women chattered on the sofa. The same people behaved quite differently at other parties; but here it was if they were under a compulsion to act out, in a kind of ritualistic dance, the dualism of the Barnetts' household, the dualism of their own natures.

Jim recognized that his social life was dull, but he did not object to this. He worked hard during the day; he was alert and gregarious; he had a great many appointments and a great many duties. There were people who believed that he used Nancy as a sedative, to taper off his day, as some men take a boring book to bed with them, in order to put themselves to sleep. Yet this theory, which was popular in the *Liberal* office, was not at all true. Jim loved Nancy with an almost mystical devotion, for Nancy was the Average Intelligent Woman, the Mate. If there was narcissism in this love, there were gratitude and dependence, too, for Jim had a vague notion that Nancy had saved him from something, saved him from losing that precious gift of his, the common touch, kept him close to what he called the facts. Some businessmen say humorously of their wives, "She keeps my nose to the grindstone." Of Nancy, Jim was fond of saying, "She keeps my feet on the ground." The very fact that his domestic life was wholesome and characterless, like a child's junket, was a source of satisfaction to him. He had a profound conviction that this was the way things ought to be, that this was life. In the socialist millennium, of course, everything would be different: love would be free and light as air. Actually, this aspect of the socialist millennium filled Jim with alarm; he hoped that in America they would not have to go so far as to break up the family; it would be enough if every man could have the rock-bottom, durable, practical things, the things Nancy cared about so very, very much.

Moreover, the insipidity of his domestic life was, in a sense, its moral justification. Jim could think of the poor and the homeless now, and conscience no longer stabbed him, for he had purchased his immunity in the true American Way. Unable to renounce money, he had renounced the enjoyment of it. He had sold his birthright to gaiety for the mess of pottage on the dinner table and the right to hold his head up when he walked through the poorer districts in his good brown suit. Christ could forgive himself for being God only by becoming Man, just as a millionaire can excuse his riches by saying, "I was a poor boy once myself." Jim, in a dim, half-holy way, felt that with his marriage he had taken up the cross of Everyman. He, too, was undergoing an ordeal, and the worried look he had always worn deepened and left its mark around his eyes, as if anxiety, hovering over him like a bird, had at last found its natural perch, its time-ordained foothold in bills and babies and dietary disturbances.

Jim was quite sure that his marriage was "real." It pinched him now and then, and that, to his mind, was the test. What disturbed him at times was the fact that it had been so extraordinarily easy to reconcile his political beliefs with his bread and butter. There ought to have been a great tug of war with Nancy at one end and Karl Marx at the other, but the job on the *Liberal* constituted a bridge between the opposing forces, a bridge which he strode across placidly every day, but which he nevertheless suspected of insubstantiality. There was something unnatural about a job that rewarded you quite handsomely for expressing your honest opinions; it was as if you were being paid to keep your virtue when you ought to be paid to lose it. More and more often it seemed to Jim that, if he was "facing facts" at home, in the office he was living in a queer fairy-tale country where everything was comfortable and nothing true. He might, however, have smothered this disquieting notion if he had not heard somebody else put it into words.

It happened at tea in the library one afternoon, when Jim had been married only a short time. Jim did not ordinarily come in for tea, but there was a new girl in the office, an assistant to the literary editor, and at four o'clock, the managing editor had poked her head in at Jim's door and said in a sprightly voice, "You must come and meet our gay divorcee." Jim had no interest in divorcees, and it seemed to him that the managing editor was being a little corny, as he put it, about the facts of life; nevertheless, he obeyed. When he shambled into the library, the girl was sitting across the room in a wing chair, with a cup of tea in her lap. She was telling anecdotes about Reno in a rather breathless voice, as if she were afraid of being interrupted, though everyone in the room was listening to her in fascinated silence. There was something about the scene that Jim did not like, and he went over to the shelves and took down a book.

He had seen the girl before—he knew this at once—somewhere, in a bright-red evening dress that looked too old for her. It must have been at a prom or a football dance at Yale. Suddenly he remembered the whole thing—he had noticed her and thought that she was good-looking and a little bit fast (she had worn long gold earrings), and he had cut in on her without being introduced, just to see what she would say. To his astonishment, she had talked to him about poetry; the mask of the enchantress had dropped from her face and she had seemed excited and happy. In the middle of it, the man she had come with had tapped him on the shoulder with a grumpy air, and danced off with her. Jim had watched her from the sidelines for a little while, admitting to himself that she was having too good a time, or rather, that she was having the wrong kind of good time: she was not floating from man to man as a proper belle should, but talking, laughing, posing, making part of the effort herself. He ought not to have cut in on her without asking her man or some other person to introduce him; yet she had created the sort of lawless atmosphere that provoked such behavior. He did not cut in on her again, and he had never been able to make up his mind whether he liked her or not.

Here she was again, looking rather prettier and younger, almost virginal, he thought, in a black dress with a white organdy ruffle at the neck; and yet again she was somehow out of bounds, and here in the library as on the dance floor she was having too much of a success.

"This is Miss Sargent," the managing editor said, taking his arm and leading him up to the girl's chair.

Jim smiled vaguely.

"I liked your last article," she said, "the one about the smooth-paper magazines."

"Speaking of that," said Labor and Industry, "do you know that Trotsky has been writing for *Liberty?*"

"Writing against Russia," put in the foreign-news man, who was sympathetic with the Communist party.

The managing editor bit her lips. "Oh, dear," she exclaimed plaintively, like a mother who has lost control of her children, "I wish he wouldn't do that! It's such a shame to divide our forces now, when we need unity so badly."

The cup rattled on the new girl's saucer. When Jim looked down he could see that she had spilled her tea. There was a brown pool in the saucer, and her cup dripped as she picked it up again.

"It was just an historical piece," she said stiffly.

Several of the women exchanged smiles. "She's supposed to be a Trotskyist," the advertising manager, who was good-looking, whispered to Jim.

"Is that all?" said the foreign-news man. "It's simply a funny coincidence, I suppose, that it appeared in the place where it could furnish the most ammunition to the enemies of the Soviet Union?"

"You would have been delighted to run it in the *Liberal,* of course," said the girl with an ironical smile.

The managing editor cut in. "Well, no, we wouldn't. We *have* published things by Trotsky, but I think he goes too far. Solidarity on the left is so important at this moment. We can't afford self-criticism now."

"What do you think, Jim?" said Labor and Industry.

Jim cocked his head and considered the question. "I don't agree with Helen," he said finally, nodding toward the managing editor. "Any movement that doesn't dare hear the truth about itself hasn't got much on the ball, in my opinion. But I *would* say that you have to be careful where you print that truth. You want it to be read by your friends, not by your enemies. I think we should have published Trotsky's piece in the *Liberal.* On the other hand, I think Trotsky made a mistake in giving it to *Liberty.* He might just as well have given it to Hearst."

The girl drew a deep breath. She looked stubborn and angry. All at once, Jim was sure that he liked her, for she was going to fight back, he saw, and it took courage to do that on your first day in a new job. He wondered, inspecting her clothes and trying to price them, whether she needed the money.

"It's a delicate problem," she began, speaking slowly, as if she were trying to control her feelings and, at the same time in that stilted way that the Trotskyïsts had, as if they all, like the Old Man, spoke English with an accent, "and it's a problem that none of you, or I, have had to face, because none of us are serious about revolution. You talk," she turned to Jim, "as if it were a matter between you and God, or you and your individual, puritan conscience. You people worry all the time about your integrity, like a débutante worrying about her virginity. Just how far can she go and still be a good girl? Trotsky doesn't look at it that way. For Trotsky it's a relation between himself and the masses. How can he get the truth to the masses, and how can he keep himself alive in order to do that? You say that it would have been all right if he had brought the piece out in the *Liberal*. It would have been all among friends, like a family scandal. But who are these friends? Do you imagine that the *Liberal* is read by the masses? On the contrary, *Liberty* is read by the masses, and the *Liberal* is read by a lot of self-appointed delegates for the masses whose principal contact with the working class is a colored maid."

"The trade-union people read the *Liberal*," said the managing editor, her square, plump face flushing indignantly.

"Who? Dubinsky? Sidney Hillman?" She pronounced the names contemptuously. "I don't doubt it. The point is, though, that you—" she turned again to Jim—"you admit that Trotsky is telling the truth, but you think that nobody is good enough to hear it except a select little circle of intellectuals and *Liberal* readers. What snobbism! Naturally," she went on, "you have to be careful about how you write the article. You have to write it so that anybody who reads it with the minimum of attention will see that what you are saying to them about the Soviet Union is quite a different thing from what the editors of *Liberty* have been saying to them. You know, you might not think so, but it's quite as possible for a revolutionist to make use of Hearst as it is for Hearst to make use of a revolutionist. Lenin went through Germany in a sealed train: the Germans thought they were using him, but he *knew* he was using the Germans. This *Liberty* business is the same thing on a smaller scale. The reactionaries have furnished Trotsky with a vehicle by which he can reach the masses. What would you have him do? Hold up his hands like a girl, and say, 'Oh no! Think of my reputation! I can't accept presents from strange gentlemen!'" Jim laughed out loud, and one or two of the older men snickered. "Besides," she continued, dropping her voice a little, "there's the problem of survival. The liberal magazines haven't shown any desire to stake Trotsky to an orgy of free speech; his organization is poor; would you like it better if he starved?"

She had finished, and she let her breath out in a tired exhalation, as if she had reached the top of a long flight of stairs. Nobody answered her, and after a moment she picked up her tea cup and began to drink with an air of intense concentration. This ostrich maneuver was classically unsuccessful, for everyone in the room continued to watch her, knowing, just as Jim did, that the tea must be stone-cold. At last, one of the older men spoke.

"Well," he said, with a sort of emaciated heartiness, "Trotsky must be a better man than I gave him credit for, to have such a pretty advocate." The remark dropped like a stone into the pool of silence, setting up echoes of itself, little ripples of sound that spread and spread and finally died away.

Jim stopped her on her way out of the office.

"Ride down in the elevator with me," he said.

"I've been thinking," he began as they stood waiting for the car, "you were absolutely right this afternoon. But you won't last long here."

"I know it," she said wryly, getting into the elevator. She shrugged her shoulders.

"Is it true," he asked, "that you're a Trotskyite?"

The girl shook her head.

"I'm not even political," she said.

"But why—?"

"Oh, I don't know. I do admire Trotsky. He's the most romantic man in modern times. And you all sounded so smug." She paused to think. They were standing on the street in the autumn twilight now. "Working on a magazine like the *Liberal* does make you smug. You keep patting yourself on the back because you're not working for Hearst. It's like a lot of kept women feeling virtuous because they're not streetwalkers. Oh yes, you're being true to your ideals; and the kept women are being true to Daddy. But what if Daddy went broke, or the ideals ceased to pay a hundred and a quarter a week? What then? You don't know and you'd rather not think about it. So when something like Trotsky's writing for *Liberty* comes up, it makes you nervous, because it reminds you of the whole problem, and you are all awfully quick to say that *never,* under *any* circumstances, would you do that."

"Yes," Jim said, "I see what you mean. But aren't you being a little romantic? Aren't you trying to say that we all ought to starve for our convictions?"

Miss Sargent smiled.

"I won't say that, because if I said it, then I ought to go and do it, and I don't want to. But I do think, somehow, that it ought to be a litle bit harder than it is for you *Liberal* editors. It generally is, for people who are really independent. Society makes them scramble in one way or another. The thing is, Mr. Wendell did scramble, not financially, because he inherited money, but morally and probably socially, a long time ago. And you people are living off the moral income of that fight, just as you are living off his money income."

"What about you?" said Jim.

"Oh, me, too," said the girl. "But as you say, I won't last long. Neither will you, I hope. The *Liberal* is all right as a stopgap, or as a job to support you while you're writing a book; but the *Liberal* is not a way of life. If you begin to think that, you're finished."

"What about Mr. Wendell?" said Jim. "It's a way of life for him."

"Oh, Mr. Wendell! Mr. Wendell is a crusader. Of course, it's a way of life for him. An honorable one. But the *Liberal* puts him in the red every year, while it puts you and me in the black. That's one reason he's managed to be serious for seventy years—every word costs him something. The good things in life are not free."

"Public opinion is against you there," said Jim.

"Maybe. Well, I must go." She hesitated a moment. "How does the old man feel about the paper?"

"Worried."

"Yes," she said. "Like a self-made man who's tried to give his children all the advantages he didn't have. And then they turn out badly, and he can't understand it. You prove my point for me. Well, good-bye."

He walked to the subway with her, and all the way home he thought about the conversation. He was very much excited and disturbed. At home he told Nancy what had happened.

"She is going to stir up a lot of trouble," said Nancy calmly.

"Yes," Jim answered, smiling, "that's the kind of girl she is. A trouble-maker."

"There must be something wrong with her."

"Yes," said Jim. "I suppose there is."

It was queer, he thought, lying in bed that night (for he still did his thinking, like a boy, with the lights out), it was queer that Nancy had hit on it instantly. *There must be something wrong with her.* On the surface, it might appear that she had everything—looks and brains and health and youth and taste—and yet in a strange way she went against the grain. She was too tense, for one thing. It was as if she lived on excitement, situations, crises, trouble, as Nancy said. And she was not one of those happy trouble-makers who toss the apple of discord around as though it were a child's ball. On the contrary, this afternoon in the library, she had been scared stiff. In one way, he was sure, she had not wanted to speak up for Trotsky at all; she had had to force herself to it, and the effort had left her white. You had to admire her courage for undertaking something that cost her so much; but then, he thought, why do it, why drive yourself if it doesn't come easy? Nothing had been gained; Trotsky was no better off for her having spoken; and she herself, if she went on that way, would lose her job. For the spectator there had been something horrible about the scene; it was like watching a nervous trapeze artist performing on the high bars without a net: if the performer did not have iron nerves, he ought to get out of the business. "The coward dies a thousand deaths," he murmured. "The brave but one."

"What did you say, dear?" asked Nancy from the other bed.

"I didn't know you were awake."

"I've got those cramps in my legs again."

She was seven months pregnant.

"I'm sorry," he said. "I was just thinking out loud."

"About that girl, I bet," she said cheerfully.

"Yes."

"Watch out!" said Nancy in a bantering voice.

"Hell," Jim answered, and his reply had more distaste in it than he had intended to put there. "I wouldn't have her for anybody's money. Besides," he went on, "she's supposed to be engaged. She divorced her husband to marry some other guy. Though when I left her this evening, she looked to me like a girl who didn't have a date. She lingered, you know . . ."

"Yes," said Nancy. "Well, I guess you're safe."

Two months later, en route between a cocktail party and a political dinner, he kissed Miss Sargent in a taxi. Nancy was in the hospital with a new baby girl, and as he leaned down toward his companion, it seemed to him that this fact justified the kiss, lent it indeed the stamp of orthodoxy—young husbands were supposed to go slightly on the loose when their wives were in the hospital having babies; it was the Yale thing, the manly thing, to do. Yet he had hardly framed the excuse to himself when he heard his own voice speaking, a little thick with Martinis and emotion.

"I love you," he said, and listened to the words with surprise, for this was not on the cards at all, and he did not even know if it were true.

"I know," she whispered, and as soon as he heard her say this he was convinced that it *was* true, and he began to feel joyfully unhappy.

"Ever since that Shef dance," he continued. "You wore a red dress." Now he believed (for he was a little tight and every love must have its legend) that he had been fatefully in love with her for years, but that there had been some barrier between them; yet at the same time, kept, as it were, in the cold-storage compartment of his heart, was the certainty that the only barrier that had ever existed was the faint distaste he felt for what was extreme and headstrong and somehow unladylike in her nature.

"I didn't think you remembered," she said. "Why didn't you cut in on me again?"

"You terrified me," he said, knowing, all at once, that this too was true. The taxi had drawn up to the door of a third-rate hotel that was frequently used for left-wing, money-raising evenings.

"Do you want to go in?" he said.

"Of course," she answered, and raised her head for him to kiss her.

He was disappointed. He had half-expected her to say something foolish and passionate like, "Let's keep on driving around all night," or something sultry like, "Come home with me." Her equanimity angered him, for what good was a girl like this unless she *was* foolish and passionate and sultry? He did not kiss her again, but gave her shoulder a slight, friendly push toward the doorman who was waiting to open the cab door. She evaded the doorman's hand and jumped out. By the time Jim had finished paying the cab, she had disappeared into the hotel.

Jim was at the speakers' table, though he was not scheduled to give a formal talk. From where he sat he could see the girl, eating with some people he did not know. He counted them carefully; the number was uneven; unquestionably, she was the extra girl. The discovery gave him a strange kind of satisfaction: she was free, and the evening was not over; anything could still happen; on the other hand, the fact that she was so patently free, dangling there at her table under his eyes, made it easy for him to relinquish her in his mind. He had already decided to go home early and call Nancy the first thing in the morning to tell her how much he loved her, when he looked down at the girl's table and found that she was gone. Her friends were still there; there was only a single empty chair pushed back from the table, as if it had been abandoned in a hurry. He was filled with despair. His prudent, saving self told him that at least he could still call Nancy with a clear conscience—that much had been salvaged from the evening—but the notion no longer pleased him; there is something savorless about a profit that has not been made at somebody else's expense. He began to move about restlessly on his chair, and at the first break between the speeches, he went out to the bar.

She was there, standing beside a fat, middle-aged radical who had his arm around her waist. She was drinking a Scotch and soda and laughing at what the man was saying. The man reached out and tapped Jim on the shoulder as he passed by.

"Hello," he said, with a slight German accent. "The speeches are terrible."

The girl turned and saw Jim.

"Now I know," she said, "why you wanted to pass this up. Can you imagine," she added to the man, "I thought it was my personal charm."

Jim smiled uncomfortably. This Dorothy Parker act rubbed him the wrong way. Especially after what had happened.

"Would you like to go somewhere and dance?" he said.

The girl looked inquiringly at her companion.

"What about it?" she asked.

"I didn't invite Leo," Jim said, trying to make his voice sound light, knowing that he was behaving foolishly, that Leo was a gossip, and that Nancy would probably hear of this.

"Oh, but *I* invite him," said the girl.

"I don't dance," Leo said. "You young bourgeois go along."

In the end, Leo went with them. The two men bought the girl gardenias on a street corner, and there was a great deal of joking competition as to whose gardenia was the biggest and most perfect. They went to a French place on the West Side that had a small orchestra and was not too capitalistic. Jim and the girl danced, and Leo sat at the table like a German papa and made Marxist witticisms about them. The girl did not dance so well as Nancy, but she carried herself as if she were the belle of the evening. When it was time to go home, there was more joking about who should be dropped first, but it was finally agreed that Leo's place was obviously the first stop. As soon as the cab door closed on Leo's stout figure, Jim kissed the girl again.

"I love you," he said.

"It was better to bring Leo along," she murmured as if in answer. "I'm an expert conspirator. I know."

Jim felt a slight chill run through him.

"I don't like conspiracies," he said.

"Oh, neither do I," she said quickly. "But sometimes they're necessary."

Her tone, he thought, was precisely that of an army officer who professes to hate war.

"This time," he said, "they *won't* be necessary, Margaret."

She looked up at him. As they passed a street light, he thought he could see her lips quiver slightly.

"It's funny," she said, "whenever a man starts to tell you he's going to break with you, he uses your first name, even if he's never used it before."

"I wasn't . . ." said Jim.

"Oh yes," she said. "Yes, you were. Well, I'm going to be nice. I'm going to help you out. I'm going to say all the proper things." She took a breath and began to recite. "There is no future in this, it can't lead any-where, it would only hurt us both, it wouldn't be any good unless it were serious and under the circumstances it can't be serious; if we once loved each other, we might not be able to stop, so we had better stop now. Or I could say," her voice dropped, "if we once loved each other, we *would* be able to stop, so let's stop before we find that out."

The taxi drew up in front of her apartment, which was on a street with a quaint name, in the Village.

"Good night," she said. "Please don't see me to the door." She jumped out of the taxi with a kind of exaggerated lightness, just as she had done at the hotel. She ran up the steps and opened the outer door.

"Where to?" said the driver.

Jim could still see her in the entryway, searching in her purse for the key.

"Go on across Seventh Avenue," he said.

The next afternoon he took her home from work on the subway. They went up to her apartment, where they made love. After dinner, he had to leave her to go to see Nancy in the hospital. He stopped and bought some flowers on the way.

It was fortunate, all things considered, that he was called to Washington the following morning. When he got back, Nancy was ready to come home with the baby. Naturally, under the circumstances, there could be no thought of continuing the affair. Miss Sargent, he told himself, was an intelligent girl; she would surely understand . . . the impossibility, et cetera, better to kill the thing quickly . . . more painless in the long run . . . no need to talk about it . . . why stir up the embers? These serviceable phrases rose readily to his mind; it was as if he had memorized them long ago for just such an occasion. The only difficulty was that he could not imagine looking Miss Sargent in the eye and uttering a single one of them.

From her demeanor he could not make out whether she was suffering. It seemed to him sometimes that she was waiting, waiting with a kind of maddening self-control for the word of explanation, the final phrase with which to write off the affair. But it was quite possible that this notion was purely subjective with him, that it arose from his own sense of owing her an explanation and had no basis in fact. It was possible that she had already written off the affair, that she had never expected anything of him, that he was just a guy she had gone to bed with one afternoon, when she had no other engagement. After all, she had never said she loved him. It was he, he thought with a groan, who had said all those things;

she had merely said "I know" in a sweet, wise voice. Recalling his declarations in the taxi that night, he ground his teeth in shame and anger.

"Why the hell did I do it?" he muttered to himself. He considered what alternatives there had been. If he had not let her run away that night? If he had followed her and taken the key from her hand and opened her door? He could imagine himself climbing the stairs behind her. He could see them coming into her small room and turning to face each other, bulky and absurd in their winter coats. Her face would have had that strange, white look, as if she were going to faint. They would have clung to each other just as they were, and he would have pushed her gently down on the couch. He could not see clearly what would have happened afterwards, when they would have begun to talk again; but it would have been something desperately serious. He would have promised to leave Nancy. Suddenly he felt utterly sure that that was what he would have done; and even now, in his office, his mind turned a somersault of terror at the very idea. It was a premonition of this that had made him, in the taxi, acquiesce in her dismissal of him, accept her formulation of why it could not be. He had ridden home in a mood of mournful exaltation, in which a sense of heroic resignation had mingled with relief and joy, as if he had come out of some terrible catastrophe alive.

But when he woke up the next morning, this peculiar happiness, half-elegiac, half-prudent, had vanished, and he was on fire with lust. He knew that he had had a narrow escape, but he knew also that he could not leave the thing as it was. He had an implacable conviction that the affair must be finished off somehow, and he had not been at the office half an hour before he had decided that it was absolutely essential to his peace of mind for him to sleep with the girl. He could not read a manuscript or write a letter; he could not listen when anyone spoke to him; later, when he went out to lunch, he could eat nothing but the quartered pickle that lay beside the sandwich he had ordered. There was no longer any question of love or high tragedy; he had given the girl up the night before; and he saw no reason now to change his mind. He was going to give her up, of course, but he must have her first, and indeed it seemed to him that if he did not have her he could not give her up. All his feelings about her had hardened into a physical need which he endured like a pain, believing from moment to moment that he could not stand it any longer. He said to himself that if he could only bear it for a day or two, it would diminish and finally be dissipated altogether; but, though he knew from observation and experience that this was true, he did not believe it, or rather it seemed irrelevant to him, for, like all sufferers, he had lost the sense of time.

Shortly after lunch, he knew that he had passed the threshold of tolerance, and just as a desperate patient will reach up and deflect the surgeon's arm, no longer caring what the surgeon or the nurse or the attendants think of him, he leapt up from his desk and strode into the literary editor's office. "I'll take you home at five," he said in a grim voice. Both of the women stared at him. "You sound as if you were going to murder her," exclaimed the literary editor, but Jim had already turned and was on his way out.

Immediately, he felt better. His excitement was succeeded by a frozen calm. He was able to go on with his work, able to think about the girl with detachment, able even to feel a premature remorse, as if he had already committed the adultery, and were now doing penance for it. The girl no longer appeared to him so desirable; he could toy with the notion of *not* sleeping with her; in fact, he nearly pesuaded himself that he was going to sleep with her somehow against his inclination and only because he had told her he would take her home. It was as if he had made a contract with her which he would be glad to wriggle out of, but which seemed, alas, binding.

Riding uptown on the subway beside her, he began to dislike her. If only she would flirt or be demure or pretend that she did not know what was going to happen! Then he could feel free to choose her all over again. But she did not speak, and when he looked into her face, he saw there an expression that was like a tracing made with fine tissue paper of his own feelings, an expression of suffering, of resignation, of stoical endurance. It was as if she were his sister, his twin, his tormented Electra; it was as if they were cursed, both together, with a wretched, unquenchable, sterile lust that "ran in the family." Once she turned her head and smiled at him disconsolately, but though he felt a touch of pity, he could not smile back; he had lost the ability to make any human gesture toward her.

In the apartment, he took her twice with a zeal that was somehow both business-like and insane, and then rolled over on his back and sighed deeply, like a man who has completed some disagreeable but salu-ary task. He no longer wanted her; he knew he would never want her again. As if she, too, knew that it was finished, she got up at once, with an air of apology for being naked in unsuitable circumstances. She picked her clothes off the floor where he had tossed them, and went into the bathroom. When she came out, she was dressed. Without a word, he took his own clothes off the chair and went on into the bathroom.

Why the hell, he said to himself now, had he not at least taken her to a decent restaurant for dinner and bought her cocktails and a bottle

of wine? "I could have taken her to Charles," he murmured once. "I
was right around the corner." He banged his fist on the desk until i
hurt him. Instead, they had gone to a Japanese tearoom, where the
had eaten the seventy-five-cent dinner and talked lamely of office politic.
He had called for the check before she had quite finished her chocolat
sundae.

Much later, when his career had been achieved, that afternoon a;
sumed for Jim an allegorical significance. Here, surely, had been th
turning-point; here the hero had been chastened and nearly laid low
here had been the pit, the mouth of hell, the threat of oblivion, th
gleam of redemption. Or, to put it more vaguely, as he did himsel
this unfortunate love affair had somehow been "necessary": he ha
had to go through it in order to pass on to the next stage of his develop
ment. It was like one of those critical episodes in the autobiographi
of great businessmen, as ghostwritten for *The Saturday Evening Post*
the moment of destiny when the future E. W. Sears or Frank Woolwort
is fired by his employer for daydreaming or incompetence, and th
awakened to the necessity of carving his own niche, a moment th
elderly tycoon reverts to in print with tireless gratitude: "If he had n
fired me, I would be a clerk today." In later years, Jim came to hav
this same kind of feeling about Miss Sargent, and, once, when he w;
tight at a party, he tried to tell her about it. "Oh, thank you," she ha
exclaimed, widening her eyes. "I'll have a brass plaque made to har
around my neck, saying, 'Jim Barnett slept here.'" And he had bur
out laughing at once, saying, "Ouch" loudly, because there was no re
vanity in him.

It was a long time, however, before he took this view of the affa
a long time, indeed, before he could think of it without the m(
excruciating remorse. The odd thing was that this remorse seemed
have no connection with Nancy. He did not feel that he had betray
Nancy with the girl in the office; he saw it, in fact, the other w
around. He could almost believe that with Nancy and the new baby
was enjoying an idyllic and respectable liaison, while Miss Sarge
was the neglected wife. He found that he was avoiding her around t
office, fearing a showdown in an empty corridor, fearing equally a k
or a snub. He came in softly, at odd hours, like a married man in a con
strip creeping up the dark stairs with his shoes in his hand. At the sar
time, he found that he was trying to appease her politically. At editor
conferences, he began to reveal certain ultra-leftist tendencies; he wou
make long, earnest speeches, stuttering slightly in the Yale style, a
then raise his eyes furtively for her approval. But still she gave

sign, and as time passed and she continued to behave with impenetrable self-possession, as they never met in the elevator or the library, he began to desire the showdown as greatly as he had feared it. Now he arranged occasions to be alone with her; and he was startled to discover, after several failures, that *she* was avoiding *him*. She came to the office late and left early; the telephone operator reported that she was engaged to a new man. Late that summer she went away, out West somewhere, where she came from; it was understood in the office that she was to get up some articles for the paper and at the same time secure her father's blessing for her second marriage.

As soon as she was gone, Jim felt light and happy again, and the other women in the office told him that he was "more like himself." He threw himself into the job of getting out a special election supplement. This was the sort of work he was well suited to, for he took the election with intense seriousness, regarding his vote as a sum of money which was not to be invested lightly. Unlike the other members of the staff, who were hysterically predisposed in Roosevelt's favor, Jim could look at the array of candidates with the impartial sobriety of the ideal consumer attempting to choose between different brands of soap. He was not deceived by labels, and he saw at once that Landon was not a tory, Lemke was not a fascist, Browder was not a communist, and Roosevelt was not a socialist. He was sent to interview each of the candidates, and he wrote a series of informal character sketches that astonished everyone with their perspicacity and good humor. In the end, he decided to vote for Roosevelt, though he had an uneasy feeling about Norman Thomas, whom Mr. Wendell, alone on the paper, was supporting. The war in Spain, however, seemed to clinch the matter; in times like these, a protest vote was a luxury, and that was enough to outlaw it in Jim's eyes.

He was never sure, afterwards, whether or not it was Miss Sargent's letter that changed his mind. This was a reply to an election questionnaire the paper had sent out to its contributors; Jim came upon it one afternoon in August. She would vote, she wrote, for the Socialist-Labor candidate, whose name she could not remember—would someone in the office please find out for her? Jim stared at the familiar angular handwriting, and felt himself flush with anger. It must be a joke, he said to himself; it was something she had thought up to annoy the managing editor; in fact she could not even have thought it up for herself; her friend Leo must have egged her on to it. "What a damn silly thing to do!" he exclaimed out loud, and he was tempted to destroy the letter to save the girl's face. Then suddenly a large sense of chivalry displaced his annoyance: he was determined to protect her from the consequences of her frivolity. He could announce that he was supporting the Socialist-Labor candidate himself, write an article on that tiny, fierce, incorruptible sect. Something might be done about De Leon and the American socialist movement. But almost immediately he realized that the idea was too outlandish; he could not bring himself to cut so fantastic a figure. Why, for God's sake, couldn't she vote for Thomas, he muttered, and then it came to him as a happy thought that *he* could vote for Thomas: in some indefinable way this would cover her, make a bridge between her and the rest of the staff.

A fine exhilaration quickly took possession of him, and he perceived that he had wanted to vote for Thomas all along. The Roosevelt bandwagon had been far too comfortable—that fact alone should have been a warning to him. He could predict for himself a long talk with Nancy and a short wrangle with the managing editor, but already he could see the article that would appear in next week's issue, "Why I Think I'll Vote for Thomas," by James Barnett. It would be an honest, dogged, tentative, puzzled article that would invite the reader into the author's mind, apologize for the furniture, and beg him to make himself quite at home. In the end, the reader might not be persuaded, but he would be able to leave with the assurance that, however he voted, there would be no hard feelings. With each of Jim Barnett's articles, that, somehow, became the main object. He was like a happy-go-lucky, well-mannered salesman who seems to the prospect delightfully different from other salesmen—as, indeed, he is, since in his eagerness to please he loses sight of his purpose and sells nothing but himself. The born political pamphleteer, like the born salesman, is usually a slightly obnoxious person. Inescapably, Jim had noticed that the two qualities often went together, but it did not appear to him in the light of a general law, but rather as an unhappy accident, a temporary disagreeable state of things which could, with patience, be remedied. And, for a long time, he considered himself the exception which disproved the rule. When it came to him at last that he was not exceptional but irrelevant, when he was, so to speak, *ruled out* as immaterial, having no bearing, incompetent in the legal sense, the shock was terrific.

It was the Moscow trials that made him know, for the first time, that he did not really "belong." Miss Sargent came into his office one day in the fall with a paper for him to sign. (She was back from the Coast and—mysteriously—no longer engaged to be married.) Clearly, the document in her hand was of deep significance for her, and as Jim read it over, his heart swelled with magnanimity, for he saw that he was going to be able to grant her the first request she had ever made of him, and grant it easily, largely, without a second thought, like a millionaire signing a check for a sister of Charity. The statement demanded a hearing for Leon Trotsky, who had been accused in the trials in Moscow of numberless crimes against the Soviet state. It demanded, also, what it called (rather pompously, he thought) the right of asylum for him. Jim had never believed for a moment that Trotsky was guilty of the charges, and this disbelief remained to the bitter end profound and unshakable. Other people wavered, were frightened or coaxed or bribed to resign from the Trotsky Committee; Trotskyites of long standing would wake sweating in the night to ask, "What if Stalin were right?" but Jim was serene and jocular through it all, and the strength of his skepticism came, not from a knowledge of the evidence, nor a sense of Trotsky's integrity, nor an historical view of the Soviet Union, but simply from a deficiency of imagination. Jim did not believe that Trotsky could have plotted to murder Stalin, or to give the Ukraine to Hitler, because he could not imagine himself or anybody he knew behaving in such a melodramatic and improbable manner. People did not act like that; it was all like a bad spy picture that you hissed and booed and applauded (ironically) from the gallery of the Hype in New Haven. And indeed the whole Russian scene appeared to Jim at bottom to be the invention of a movie writer; his skepticism included not only the confessions of the defendants but the *fact* of the defendants' existence. How could there be such people as Romm and Piatakov and the GPU agent, Holtzman? How indeed could there be such a dark and terrible organization as the GPU? It was all so very unlikely. And, in some strange way, Europe itself was unlikely. Jim always had the greatest difficulty in making himself see that Hitler was real, and one reason he had never subscribed to the Popular Front was that whenever he tried to conjure up the menace of fascism, somewhere deep down inside him a Yale undergraduate snickered.

So that it was no problem at all for him to put his signature below Miss Sargent's. Aside from everything else, there was a purely sporting question involved: you don't accuse a man without giving him a chance to answer for himself. Of course Trotsky should be heard. He said as much to Miss Sargent and she smiled at him, and their Anglo-Saxon sense of fair play was warm for a moment between them—he could feel it in his stomach like a shot of whisky. All the shame of that other afternoon was gone suddenly, and he thought what a hell of a nice, straight, clear-eyed girl she was, after all.

This sense of recognition, this spiritual handclasp, lasted only an instant, however, for as soon as she began to speak, her words tripped over each other, and he saw, with disappointment, that she was being intense about the matter. She said something about his "courage," and he reddened and blinked his eyes and twisted his head from side to side, disavowing the virtue. Why, he thought impatiently, was it necessary for Marxists to talk in this high-flown way? There was no question of courage here; it was just a matter of common sense. And he anticipated no trouble. There was never any trouble if you handled these controversies in the right way, kept your head, took it easy, did not let the personal note intrude. It was unfortunate, he had been saying for years, that the radical movement had inherited Karl Marx's cantankerous disposition together with his world-view. The "polemical" side of Marxism was its most serious handicap; here in America, especially, it went against the grain. He was not so simple as to subscribe to the mythology of the conference table (the class struggle was basic, inadjudicable), but surely on the left itself, there could be a little more friendliness, a little more co-operativeness, a little more give-and-take, live-and-let-live and let-sleeping-dogs-lie. And it was really so easy. Take his own case: he had friends of every shade of opinion, argued with them freely, pulled no punches, but never had a quarrel. There had been the time when he had been obliged to throw a classmate out of his apartment for telling an anti-Semitic story, but the guy had come back the next day, sober, and apologized, and they had shaken hands on it, and the incident was forgotten. It only went to show. Unfortunately, however, the bad side of Marxism was precisely what attracted warped personalities of the type of Miss Sargent, who had long lists of people she did not speak to, and who delighted in grievance committees, boycotts, and letters to the editor. So that the evil multiplied a thousandfold. It was like an hereditary insanity that is perpetuated not only through the genes but by a process of selection in which emotional instability tends to marry emotional instability and you end up with the Jukes family. Or you begin with Marx's carbuncles and you end with the Moscow trials.

"Take it easy," he said to the girl, patting her shoulder in token of dismissal.

"I'll try," she answered, lightly enough, but as she turned to go, she flung at him that same sad, desperate smile that she had given him on the subway just before—He closed the door hastily behind her. For an instant it was as if he, too, had heard the chord that announces the return of a major theme, a sound heavy with dread and expectation. *It was all going to begin again,* the same thing, disguised, augmented, in a different key, but irrefragably the same thing. His stomach executed a peculiar drop, and this sensation, also, he remembered. It was the feeling you have on a roller-coaster at Coney Island, when the car has just started

nd you are sitting in the front seat, and you know for sure (you have
een wondering up to this moment) that you do not want to ride on it.
After the first dip, you lose this certainty (you would unquestionably
lie if you kept it), you may even enjoy the ride or suggest a second
rip, become an *aficionado* of roller-coasters, discriminate nicely between
he Cyclone at Palisades Park and the Thunderbolt at Revere Beach.
You are, after all, a human being, with a hundred tricks up your sleeve.
But at the very beginning you *knew*.

However, there seemed at first no cause for alarm. The whole *affaire
Trotsky,* as somebody called it, was going off according to schedule. Miss
Sargent would come to the office every morning in a fever of indignation:
mysterious strangers telephoned her at midnight, she received anonymous
letters and marked copies of the *Daily Worker,* a publisher went back on
a verbal agreement he had made with her, people cut her on the street,
an invitation to a summer writers' conference had been withdrawn. Jim
listened to these stories with a tolerant smile: this was the usual sectarian
hysteria. No doubt some of these things had actually happened to her
(he would not go so far as to say she had made them up), but certainly
she exaggerated, colored, dramatized, interpreted, with very little regard
or probability. Nothing of the sort was happening to him. He was on the
best of terms with his Stalinist friends, who even kidded him a little about
his association with Trotsky; several publishers were after him to do
a book; and he got an offer to join the staff of a well-known news magazine. If anything, his open break with the Party had enhanced his value.
Moreover, he was enjoying himself enormously. He had the true
American taste for argument, argument as distinguished from conversation on the one hand and from oratory on the other. The long-drawn-out,
meandering debate was, perhaps, the only art form he understood or
relished, and this was natural, since the argument is in a sense our only
indigenous folk-art, and it is not the poet but the silver-tongued lawyer
who is our real national bard. The Moscow trials seemed admirably
suited to the medium, and at any cocktail party that season, Jim could
be found in a corner, wrangling pleasantly over Piatakov and Romm, the
Hotel Bristol in Copenhagen and the landing field at Oslo.
However, here, as in the other arts, there were certain conventions to
be observed: statistics were virtually *de rigueur,* but rhetoric was unseemly;
heat was allowed, but not rancor. Jim himself obeyed all the rules with a
natural, unconscious decorum, and in his own circle he felt perfectly
secure in advocating Trotsky's cause. It was at the Trotsky committee meetings that he had misgivings. An ill-assorted group of nervous people would

sit in a bare classroom in the New School or lounge on studio couches in somebody's apartment, listening to Schachtman, a little dark lawyer, demolish the evidence against the Old Man in Mexico. Schachtman's reasoning Jim took no exception to (though it was, perhaps, almost *too* close); what bothered him was the tone of these gatherings. It seemed to him that every committee member wore an expression of injury, of self-justification, a funny, feminine, "put-upon" look, just as if they were all, individually, on trial. They nodded with emphasis at every telling point, with an air of being able to corroborate it from their own experience; ironical smiles of vindication kept flitting from face to face. And not only, Jim thought, did they behave like accused persons; they also behaved like guilty persons; the very anxiety of their demeanor would have convicted them before any jury. Watching them all, Jim would wish that he was the only guy in the world who took Trotsky's side, and he would feel a strong sympathy with Leibowitz, who at Decatur during the Scottsboro case, was supposed to have told the Communists to get the hell out of town. Sometimes, even, listening to Novack read aloud a fiery letter from the Old Man, he would wish that Trotsky himself could be eliminated, or at least held incommunicado, till the investigation was over. The Old Man did not understand Americans.

And after the meeting had broken up, over coffee or highballs, the committee members would exchange anecdotes of persecution, of broken contracts, broken love affairs, isolation, slander, and betrayal. Jim listened with an astonished, impatient incredulity, and he and Nancy used to laugh late at night in their living room over the tales he brought home of Trotskyist suggestibility. They laughed kindly and softly—so as not to wake the baby—over their Ritz crackers and snappy cheese, and Nancy, full-bosomed, a little matronly already in her flowered house coat, seemed to Jim, by contrast with the people he had just left, a kind of American Athena, a true presiding deity of common sense.

Yet occasionally, when he was alone, when an engagement had fallen through and he was left unoccupied, when Nancy was late getting home in the afternoon, he wondered. What if all these stories were true? What if even some of them were true? How did it happen that he was exempt from this campaign of terror? He had not compromised; he had spoken his mind. Did the others, the Stalinists, hope that he would "come around"? Or did they believe that terroristic methods would not work with him? This thought was pleasing and he would hold it at arm's length for a moment, contemplating it, in a kind of Boy Scout daydream of torture and manly defiance, of Indians and the Inquisition, and the boy with his finger in the dike. But humor inevitably challenged this view; the dream dissolved; he was left puzzled. Sometimes, a sort of mild panic would follow. He would be overwhelmed by a sense of trespassing on the Trotsky case. It was as if he had come to dinner at the wrong address and the people were very polite and behaved as if he were expected; out of good breeding they would not allow him to explain his mistake, nor would they set him on his way to the right house. Or it was as if he were an extra who had got onto the stage in the wrong scene: the actors went on acting as if he were not there, and nobody furnished him with a pretext for an exit.

Before long, he began to notice in himself a desire to compete, to have some hair-raising experience of his own and vie in martyrdom with the other members. He was ashamed of his wish; at the same time, it confirmed his skepticism. Here, he felt, was the key to the whole business; nobody wanted to be left out of a thing like this; it was the phenomenon that had been noted again and again at spiritualistic séances: people unconsciously began to co-operate with the medium and with each other, so that no one should seem to be deficient in psychic powers.

This shrewd explanation might have satisfied him—if it had not been for John Dewey. . . . The adherence of the dean of American philosophy, which ought to have reassured Jim, worried him profoundly. It never failed to violate Jim's sense of fitness to see this old man, the very apotheosis of the cracker-barrel spirit, deep in conversation with Schachtman or Stolberg, nodding his white head from time to time in acquiescence to some extravagant statement, smiling, agreeing, accepting, supporting. It was like finding your father in bed with a woman. And the most painful thing about it was that the old man should be so *at home* here, so much more at home than Jim could ever be. *He takes to it like a duck to water,* committee members would say, proudly and affectionately to each other, and Jim could not deny that this was so. Dewey truly appeared to have no reservations; you could not call that mild irony a reservation, for it was a mere habit, like his Yankee drawl, that was so ingrained, so natural, that it seemed to have no specific relation to the outside world, but only to his own, interior life. Whenever Jim heard that dry voice swell out at a mass meeting in anger and eloquence, he squirmed in his seat, not knowing whether to feel embarrassed for Dewey or for himself. The very kinship he felt with the old man served to deepen and define his own sense of alienation, as in a family the very resemblance that exists between the members serves to make more salient the individual differences. It was impossible, moreover, to doubt Dewey's judgment, and when Jim saw that Dewey believed

the stories of persecution (he had indeed been a little bit persecuted-
"annoyed," Dewey put it, himself), Jim, unwillingly, began to believe to

Now the ground was cut from under him. This was perhaps th
first time in his life that he was subscribing to something which he cou
not check against his own experience or psychology, which his own e
perience and psychology seemed, in fact, to contradict. There was
subjective correlative; he was no longer his own man. Yet once he ha
conceded the point, the evidence began rushing in at him. A hundre
incidents that he had forgotten or ignored or discounted marshaled ther
selves before his eyes. He remembered the prominent names that ha
dropped off the committee's letterhead, the queer, defamatory stories
had encountered everywhere about members of the committee, the boo
unaccountably rejected by publishers. What was more devastating,
saw now (a thing he had denied a month before) that the Stalinist ca
paign of intimidation had already had its effect on the *Liberal's* policy.

He read down the contributors' column one day and found it a rost
of new names—youngsters just out of college, professors from obscu
universities, elderly, non-political writers who had been boasting for yea
that they did not "take sides" and who were now receiving their rewa
It was hard to know exactly when they had come in, but suddenly th
were all there. The whole complexion of the magazine had unobtrusiv
changed. It was not, precisely, that it had become Stalinist; rather, li
some timid and adaptive bird, it was endeavoring to make itself as neutr
colored as possible and fade discreetly into the surrounding landsca
The whole process, he saw, had been a negative one. A few months earli
Mr. Wendell had resigned—on account of his age, it was said official
The paper had been made two pages shorter, there were more cartoo
more straight reportage. Shorter articles in larger type, not so mu
political and aesthetic theory. Articles had been limited to two thousa
words apiece; the book-review section had been cut in half and a hum
ous column had been added. Nothing you could put your finger on,
by these innocent measures the paper had effectively purged itself
Trotskyism, for the fact was that the Trotskyists, anarchists, and oth
dissidents *did* run to political and aesthetic theory, to articles more th
two thousand words long, to book reviews of unpopular novelists a
poets.

That same afternoon, he observed for the first time the machinery
exclusion. He came into the literary editor's office; it was her day
seeing book reviewers. A young anti-Stalinist reviewer was standi
despondently in front of the shelves, which usually overflowed w
books (for the literary editor was rather inefficient about getting thi

:viewed on time), but which were now unwontedly, desolately empty. .ight or nine popular novels with garish jackets leaned against each other 1 one corner. The young man had been asking for a new book—Jim id not catch the name. The literary editor shook her head; unfortunately 1e book had just gone out to a professor at Northwestern. He mentioned nother title; that, too, had been assigned—to an instructor at Berkeley. He 1umbled something about an article on Silone; the literary editor was not ncouraging; she wondered whether you *could* do justice to Silone in fteen hundred words; the paper was not printing many general articles; 1e could not promise anything.

She got up from her desk and wandered toward the shelves, gesturing aguely at the popular novels. "Do us a note of a hundred words on one f these—if you feel like it," she said negligently. The young man 1ook his head and shambled out of the office; it was perfectly clear that e would not return. The literary editor murmured something pettish 2out the insularity of New York intellectuals, and Miss Sargent, who ad been sitting all the while with averted head, looked up.

"On Broadway they call that the brush-off," she said.

The literary editor affected not to hear.

Miss Sargent continued, looking straight at Jim, speaking in a louder oice.

"Have you heard? I'm being transferred to Labor and Industry. On ac- 2unt of the curtailment of the book-review section—which we all deplore -my duties are being assumed by a stenographer."

"Oh, Margaret," said the literary editor, "you're becoming perfectly im- 2ssible. I should think you'd be glad to be out of this. I know I would."

The girl did not answer, but kept on looking at Jim. It was impos- ble to misread her gaze, which held in it something challenging and t the same time something feminine and suppliant. He met her eyes 2r an instant, then shook his head hopelessly.

"You girls," he began, intending to say something humorous and pacific, ut he could not finish his sentence. He shook his head again, and re- eated from the office. As soon as he got into the corridor, however, the uncated conversation continued in his mind. That book reviewer, said firm light soprano, that unfortunate boy, with his bad complexion, is blue mesh shirt open at the throat, was Stalin's victim just as surely s the silicosis sufferers who had recently been displayed at a Congres- onal investigation were the victims of industrial capitalism. What the ell, his own voice answered, the young man was probably no great 1akes as a writer (he looked like a punk); it was not a question of life nd death; the kid was on the WPA and the *Liberal's* check could do

no more than buy him a few beers at the Jumble Shop. Ah yes, the firs
voice resumed, martyrs are usually unappetizing personally; that is wh
people treat them so badly; for every noble public man, like Trotsky
you must expect a thousand miserable little followers, but there is reall
more honor in defending them than in defending the great man, who ca
speak for himself. His own voice did not reply, and a visual illusio
succeeded the auditory one. He saw the figure of the book reviewe
splashed on a poster, like the undernourished child in the old Belgia
relief stickers; underneath a caption thundered: WHAT ARE YOU
GOING TO DO ABOUT IT?

That was the first time. Soon it became a regular thing with Jin
to talk to Miss Sargent in his mind. The moment the lights were ou
at night, the cool, light voice would begin its indictment, and his ow
voice, grumbling, expostulating, denying, would take up the defense. An
in the daytime, Jim would find himself thinking up arguments, savin,
them, telling himself, "I must be sure to mention this," just as if it were
real conversation he was going home to. He remembered enough of hi
psychology courses to know that he was not having hallucination
Though the voice sounded perfectly natural, he did not hear it with hi
physical ear, but only with his mind. Moreover, the conversations wer
in some sense, voluntary; that is, he did not like them, he did not wan
to have them, yet they did not precisely impose themselves on him, for i
was he, unwillingly, of his own free will, who was making them up.

Nevertheless, he was alarmed. It was screwy, he told himself, t
spend your time talking to someone who was not there. At the very leas
it showed that the person had a hold on you—a disagreeable, unnervin,
idea. In Jim's world, nobody had a "hold" on anybody else. Yet the fac
was (and he had to face it) he was not in the driver's seat any more. Fo
almost as long as he could remember there had been two selves, a critica
principled self, and an easy-going, follow-the-crowd, self-indulgent, adap
able self. These two characters had debated comfortably in bed, ha
"taken stock," defined their differences, maintained an equilibrium. But i
was as if, during the Moscow trials, the critical principled self had throw,
up the sponge; it had abdicated, and a girl's voice had intruded to tak
over its function. At some point in those recent months, Jim had cease
to be his own severest critic, but criticism, far from being stilled, ha
grown more obdurate. When we pass from "I ought to do this" to "Yo
think I ought to do this," it seems to us at first that we have weakene
the imperative; actually, by externalizing it, we have made it unanswe
able, for it is only ourselves that we can come to terms with. And wher
Jim had once had to meet specific objections from his better nature, h

was now confronted with what he imagined to be a general, undiscriminating hostility, a spirit of criticism embodied in the girl that was capricious, feminine, and absolutely inscrutable, so that he went about feeling continually guilty without knowing just what it was he had done. It haunted him that if he could anticipate every objection, he would be safe, but there was no telling *what* this strange girl might find fault with, and the very limitation of his knowledge of her made the number of possible objections limitless.

He longed to act, he told himself, yet the vague enormity of his situation furnished an apparently permanent excuse for inaction. He believed that he was waiting for an issue big enough to take a stand on, but now all issues seemed flimsy, incapable of supporting his increasing weight. In a curious way, his ego had become both shrunken and enlarged; his sense of inadequacy had made him self-important. He began to talk a good deal about "petty" squabbles, tempests in teapots, molehills and mountains. If he were to resign from the *Liberal,* he said to himself, he would have to do so in his own way, for his own reasons. To resign on behalf of some Eighth Street intellectual would be to accept that intellectual as his ally, to step off the high ground of the *Liberal* into the noisome marsh of sectarian politics. And, above all, Jim feared that terrible quicksand, which would surely, he thought, swallow him up alive, if he so much as set a foot over the edge. Here was the paradox: though his immunity from the Stalinist attacks was the immediate cause of his sense of shame (to be spared, ostentatiously, in a general massacre is a distinction reserved for spies, old men, children, and imbeciles), Jim nevertheless found it temperamentally impossible to venture directly into the melee. What he sought was some formula by which he could demonstrate his political seriousness without embroiling himself in any way—a formula which would, in fact, perpetuate his anomalous situation. It was an irony that Jim did not perceive. He only knew that he must postpone action (for the moment, at least), while he yearned at the same time to be acted *upon.*

If the managing editor would only fire him, for example, he would be free, and nothing he did afterwards could be held against him. He might get a job in an advertising agency, or on one of the news magazines; he would be quit at last of leftist politics, and no one could blame him. "Jim Barnett lost his job over that Trotsky business," they would say. "The poor guy is working for *Newsreel* now." The picture of himself as a victim of circumstances, an object of public sympathy, did not displease him; in fact what his heart cried for was some such outcome for his dilemma, an outcome in which his own helplessness should be underlined.

The managing editor, however, seemed not at all disposed to give him this friendly push, and his self-regard would not permit him simply to disengage himself from the struggle as he might have done from a street brawl. In some way, he felt, he was condemned to "stick it out," perhaps indefinitely, and to pay for his non-intervention by sleeplessness, indigestion, and outbursts of irritability with Nancy.

Nevertheless, when the moment came, Jim found it perfectly simple to quit. The managing editor came into his office one afternoon and told him that in accordance with the magazine's new budget, Miss Sargent would have to go. It was purely a matter of seniority; she was the newest employee; it was only fair that she should be the first, et cetera.

"I wish it hadn't worked out that way," she continued, biting her lips and speaking in a confidential tone. "You know how excitable she is, Jim. She'll be sure to think that it has something to do with politics. That letter, you know . . ."

Jim smiled grimly. The *Liberal,* after months of silence, had endorsed the Moscow trials, and "that letter" was a denunciation of the magazine. It had been signed by Miss Sargent, by a number of ex-contributors to the *Liberal,* and by Jim himself.

"But, of course," the managing editor went on, "I forgot! You signed it too. So that shows . . ." She spread out her hands, leaving the sentence unfinished. "You know I would never deny anybody the right of criticism. I'm glad you spoke out if you felt that way. And Miss Sargent of course, too. And the fact that *you're* continuing on the paper speaks for itself. Still . . ." She paused, "It's the effect on her I'm worried about. She's too bitter already. There's too *much* bitterness in the radical movement. I think we agree about that."

She was silent for a moment. Jim waited.

"Oh, Jim," she burst out at length. "I wish *you* would break it to her. Explain it to her. She'd take it all right coming from you, since you agree with each other politically. You could make her understand . . ."

"You go to hell, Helen," Jim said. The words came as naturally as reflex and even in his first joy, Jim found time to tell himself that it had been morbid to worry about the matter beforehand. You waited until the right time came and then you acted, without thought, without plan, and your character—your character that you had suspected so unjustly—did not betray you.

The managing editor gasped. Jim took his brown coat and hat from he stand and walked deliberately out of the office. He went down the street to a bar he knew and ordered a Scotch and soda. When he was halfway through the drink, he stepped into the phone booth and called up Miss Sargent at the office.

"Come on down here," he said, "and help me write a letter of resignation."

He went back to wait for her at his table, and suddenly he found himself thinking of a book he would like to write. It would deal with the transportation industries and their relation to the Marxist idea of the class struggle. He thought of the filling stations strung out over America, like beads on the arterial highways, and of the station attendants he had seen in the Southwest, each man lonely as a lighthouse keeper in his Socony or his Shell castle: how were you going to organize them as you could organize workers in a factory? He thought also of the chain-store employees as the frontiersmen of a new kind of empire: The Great Atlantic and Pacific Tea Company—the name had the ring of the age of exploration; it brought to mind the Great South Sea Bubble. Monopoly capitalism was deploying its forces, or, rather, it was obliging its historic enemy, the workers, to deploy theirs. As financial and political power became more concentrated, industry was imperceptibly being decentralized. The CIO might find the answer; on the other hand, perhaps the principle of industrial unionism was already superannuated. There was a great book here somewhere, an important contribution, and now he would have the time to write it. It would have been out of the question of course, had he stayed on the *Liberal*. . . .

"Oh boy!" he said to himself, revolving the book in his mind, marveling at it, accepting it as a sort of heavenly tip for services rendered. He clacked his tongue appreciatively against the roof of his mouth. The bartender looked over at him in surprise, and Jim chuckled to himself. He was tremendously elated. He could hardly wait to get home to tell Nancy, and at the same time, he felt a large tenderness toward the girl who was even now making her way toward him through the snowy streets. He owed it all to her, *of course*. Hadn't she told him from the very beginning that the *Liberal* was a dead end, that if he wanted to make anything of himself, he would have to get off it? And it was on account of her, in the end, that he had been able to do it. If they had not decided to fire her, he might never have . . . He stopped short in his reverie, momentarily sobered. In his excitement he had almost forgotten that she had lost her job. Here he was, ready to begin his real work, but for her the prospect was not bright. No doubt she would be glad to hear that she had made such a nuisance of herself that the managing editor could brook

it no longer; there would be the surge of leftist piety, the joy of self
immolation. But, practically speaking, it was going to be hard on her. He
himself had money saved, and, with Nancy's income, he could get along
well enough. The girl was not so fortunately equipped: he could guess
without asking that she had not saved a cent (she was probably in debt)
and it would not be easy for her to find another job. *She is going to have a
tough time,* he said to himself. And she was not going to like it. She would
dramatize her position for a week or so, but when it came down to it
she was not going to enjoy being poor, for Trotsky or anybody else.
The thought of the discomfort she would have to endure bit into his
happiness; it annoyed him that she should behave with such irresponsibility. She had no right, he told himself, to play for high stakes when she
could not afford to lose; it was not ethical; it made the other player
at the table uncomfortable. Already, *in absentia,* she had robbed him of a
little of his joy.

With a slight effort he brought himself back to the projected book.
The excitement revived as he imagined the gray winter afternoons in the
public library, the notes on white cards in the varnished yellow box,
the olive-green filing cabinet he would install in the spare room. "A
second *Das Kapital,*" a voice within him murmured, but though he stilled
it peremptorily, he could not help but grin in an awkward, lopsided way,
as though someone had paid him an absurd, delicious compliment. The
strange thing was, it was the girl's voice that had spoken; perhaps, he
thought, in years to come, she would read the book and *would* say that
to him. By the time the door swung open and she stepped quickly into the
bar, he felt very much pleased with her.

He rose to meet her; she extended her hands. He seized them both; they
were very cold.

"I lost my gloves," she said.

How feminine of her, he thought, how ungrammatical, how charming.
In the last few weeks he had been very unfair to her. This was no Zetkin,
no Luxemburg. If the truth were known, she was probably as much out of
her depth in sectarian politics as he was. He squeezed her hands.

She sat down.

"Well," he said. "You've lost your job."

"Oh," she murmured, looking grave for an instant. Then she shrugged
her shoulders. "I suppose it was about time. But you—" He watched her get
the idea. "Did you——?"

"I walked out," he said.

He stared into his glass and hoped that she was not going to be effusive.

When he finally looked up at her, however, he saw that she was blushing slightly.

"Thank you very much," she said. "I suppose I ought to tell you that you shouldn't have done it."

"Never mind," he said. "It was a good thing to do, anyway. I feel wonderful. I'm going to write a book. It all just came to me while I've been sitting here, though I guess the idea must have been in the back of my mind for quite a while."

He told her about the book.

"It's a very good idea," she said at last.

"You ought to write a book yourself."

She shook her head.

"A fortune teller told me I was born to fritter away my talents. I wouldn't want to go against my destiny."

He grinned at her. It was a silly remark, and characteristic, too, but it was no longer within her power to make him angry. He could barely recall a time when he had wrestled with her all night in a terrible ideological embrace, though it was not yet twenty-four hours since Nancy had spoken from the next bed and begged him to go into the living room if he could not stop tossing.

She went on talking excitedly and he ordered two more drinks. He had forgotten about the letter of resignation, and he did not want her to go. He had gradually become aware that he would like to sleep with her, but he did not know how to broach the suggestion. The fact that it would not be the first time made it more difficult. All those months in which he had not wanted to sleep with her would have to be wiped out with some brief, tactful sentence, but no satisfactory one occurred to him, partly because he was puzzled as to why, on the one hand, he should want to sleep with her now, and why, on the other, he should not have been sleeping with her all along, since she was undoubtedly an attractive girl.

"I was not free . . ." he muttered, experimentally, to himself. But it would not do. She might want to know in what sense he was free now, and had not been before. In relation to Nancy, he was still tied. Did he mean that his time was now his own, than an afternoon of love could—without too much difficulty—be occasionally slipped into his new schedule? No, he thought decidedly, he did not mean that. The idea of a systematic infidelity was offensive to him; the very notion of assignations, trysts, affected him in much the same way that the notion of crop rotation affects the American farmer. It would not be right, he told himself. You oughtn't to plan a thing like that. Besides, he would be too busy. The new book would need all his energies. It was just this once that he wanted her.

"I was not free," he repeated, troubled by these words that had risen to his mind, feeling that they were true in some way that he had not put his finger on. It was as if he had paid off a nagging creditor, a creditor whom for months he had not dared to face, but to whom he could now open the door with the utmost geniality, knowing that there was nothing the man could do to him, knowing that his former fears had been groundless, that the creditor was just a human being like himself.

"You really are a sweet girl," he said, "even if you do act like a Trotskyite dragon."

After the third drink he took her home in a taxi. He decided not to say anything but merely followed her up the stairs and kissed her as she stood in the doorway. She put her hands on his shoulders and pushed him back with a look of astonishment; for a moment, he thought she was going to bar the way to him. She dropped her hands, however, and went on into the apartment. She sank into a chair. He shut the door behind him and waited.

"I'm sorry, Jim," she said. "I'd like to celebrate your resigning and the book and everything, but I just can't."

"It's not a question of a celebration," he said stiffly.

"Well . . ." she conceded, as if not disposed to argue. Her whole aspect was vague and weary. There was a look of strained kindness about her, as she sat in the chair, her coat falling loosely about her; she might have been a schoolteacher kept after hours.

"Margaret," he said, "I can't explain, but the set-up wasn't right before. Working in the same office . . ."

"Yes," she agreed. "It would have been a terrible mess." She smiled.

"It hasn't been any picnic for me, Margaret," he said in an aggrieved tone. "I still feel the same way about you."

"That's wonderful," she said with her first touch of sharpness. "I would like to feel the same way about you (I really would), but I can't. I don't seem to be able to bank my fires. That's a man's job, I suppose."

He frowned. There was some ugly implication in that metaphor of hers, something he did not want to examine at the moment.

With a dim idea of being masterful, he strode across the room and half-lifted her to her feet. He attempted a long close kiss, pressing her body firmly against his. In a moment, however, he let her go, for, though she kissed him back, he could feel no response at all. It was not that she was deliberately stifling her feelings (if he could have believed that, he would have been encouraged to go on); rather, she seemed preoccupied, bored, polite. It was like kissing Nancy when she had toast in the toaster.

She walked to the door with him.

"Good-bye," she said. "Good luck with your book. And don't think I don't appreciate . . ."

"Forget it," he said.

He closed the door behind him, feeling slightly annoyed. In some way, he thought, he had been given the run-around. When you came right down to it, he had quit his job for her sake. What more did she want? "The hell with her," he said, dismissing her from his mind. "After all, she knew I was married." The thought of Nancy brought him up short. Under a street lamp he drew out his watch. If he took a taxi, he would still be in time for dinner. And after dinner, he promised himself, he would make love to Nancy. He would have her put on her blue transparent nightgown, the one he had given her for Christmas and she had only worn once. Making love to her would be more fun than usual because he was still steamed up about that girl. He sensed at once, as he raised his hand for a taxi, that this sexual project of his was distinctly off-color; yet his resolution hardly wavered. In the first place, Nancy would never know; in the second place, he was entitled to some recompense for the moral ordeal he had been through that day. Later on, in bed, his scruples served him well; where a thicker-skinned man would have known that he was simply sleeping with his wife, Jim's active conscience permitted him to see the conjugal act as a perverse and glamorous adultery, an adultery which, moreover, would never land him in a divorce court or an abortionist's waiting room.

No one could ever understand, afterwards, what happened about that book. When his resignation from the *Liberal* was made public, all sorts of people congratulated Jim. Literary columns in the newspapers reported that he was at work on a study of the transportation industries which promised to revise some of the classical conceptions of Marxism. Several publishers wrote him letters, hoping that he would allow them to be the first to see . . . It was felt in general that he was coming into his manhood, that his undeniable talents were at last to be employed in a work of real scope. Jim himself began the task with enthusiasm. He did six months of research in the public library, and amassed a quantity of notes. Then he wrote two chapters. He worked over them diligently, but somehow from the very first sentence, everything was wrong. The stuff lacked punch. Jim saw it at once, and the publishers he sent the chapters to saw it also. It did not sound, they wrote him reluctantly, like the real Barnett. On the other hand, it did not sound (as he had hoped it would) like a major work. It was solemn enough but it was not momentous. What was missing was the thing Jim had found in Marx and Veblen and Adam Smith and Darwin, the dignified sound of a great calm bell tolling the morning of a new age. Jim reread these masters and tried to reproduce the tone by ear, but he could not do it. He became frightened and went back to the public library; perhaps, as someone had suggested, the material was under-researched. He could not bring himself to go on with the writing, for that would be sending good money after bad. When he got an offer from the illustrated magazine *Destiny,* the businessman's *Vogue,* as some-one called it, to do an article on rural electrification, he accepted at once. Traveling with a photographer all over America, he would have the chance, he thought, to see his own subject at first hand. He could do the piece for *Destiny,* and then return to his own work, refreshed from his contact with living reality. However, when the article was done he took a job with *Destiny,* promising himself that he would work on his book over the week ends. He started at ten thousand a year.

The job took more of his time than he had expected, and his friends eventually stopped asking him about his book. Once in a while someone would question Nancy, and she would contract her brows in a little worried frown. He was working much too hard, she would say. He had counted on a vacation to get back to the book, but when the time came, he was on the verge of nervous exhaustion and she had had to take him to Havana for a rest. "You have no idea," she was fond of exclaiming, "what a terrific toll *Destiny* takes of its writers. It burns them right out. If Jim didn't keep up his tennis, and get away to the country every pos-sible week end, he'd be in the hospital right now."

Everyone sympathized with Nancy on this point. The research girls in the *Destiny* office worried a good deal about Jim, and they, too, thought it was a great pity that he did not have time to do his own writing. Jim himself took a certain pride in being overworked, especially since he was not underpaid—the original ten thousand had been raised several times and he got a handsome bonus at Christmas every year. The truth was that he enjoyed working on *Destiny.* Outsiders imagined that his radicalism kept him in hot water there, but this was not true. He wrote about American youth, farm security, South America, musical comedy, and nylon. He said what he pleased, and if the article seemed too "strong," it was given to someone else to modify. He was not obliged to eat his own words. Now he was not so much a writer as a worker on an assembly line. He did his own task conscientiously, and since the finished product was always several removes away from him, it was, in a certain sense, not his concern. He would send an article down from his desk with a droll, schizophrenic, pessimistic air, as if to say, "You're on your own now, God help you." And as his own productions passed more and more beyond his control, he relished more and more the control of data, which was the singular achievement of the *Destiny* machine. Jim liked the facts that were served up to him daily by the girl research workers, liked the feeling that there was nothing, absolutely nothing in the world, that he could not find out by pressing a bell, sending a telegram, or taking a plane. He liked the fact-finding trips that he took with a photographer; he had only to mention the name of the magazine and he would be whisked into a farmer's homestead, an actress' dressing room, a Fifth Avenue mansion, a cold-water flat in an old-law tenement, a girl's college, an army camp, a club, a great hotel. And he saw everything *from the inside;* he was free to examine the laundry lists, the budgets, the toilet facilities, the sleeping arrangements, of any American family he chose to visit; he could ransack a desk or peer into an icebox; nobody but a tax assessor had ever had such freedom, and where the tax assessor was detested, Jim's subjects welcomed him into their homes, their hobbies, their businesses. It pleased them that someone should know *all about them* and write it down and publish it with pictures. It pleased Jim too; it gave him a great feeling of responsibility, as if he were a priest or God.

He believed—most of the time—that he was doing an important work. He still considered himself a Marxist, but he saw that the Marxists were never going to get anywhere until they took a real look at the American scene and stopped deluding themselves with theory. Occasionally, after an argument at some literary cocktail party, he felt that he would like to pick up the whole radical movement by the scruff of its neck and rub its nose hard into the good American dirt. He himself, whatever his failings, was at least setting the facts on record; in a time of confusion like the present this was a valuable thing to do. Moreover, he was playing a part, a rather significant one, in the molding of public opinion. It was true that the publisher of *Destiny* was a reactionary in many ways—potentially, he might even be a fascist—but on certain points he was progressive. He believed that the old-style capitalism would have to go, and now and then he would allow Jim to say so in a signed editorial that was termed by everyone in the office "astonishingly outspoken." Jim had come, he told himself frequently, a long way from the *Liberal,* and he was proud of the fact. He looked back on the years he had spent there with a kind of amazed disgust. How could he have wasted his time so? The *Liberal* was no more revolutionary than *Destiny;* it published nothing but muddle-headed opinion; it paid poorly, and it had no influence. No matter what his mood, Jim never doubted for a moment that his resignation had been the most sensible act of his life.

It was not the memory of the *Liberal* that caused Jim, whenever he got drunk, to abuse the publisher of *Destiny,* to contrast his lot unfavorably with that of his radical friends, to protest with tears in his eyes that he was doing it for the wife and kiddies. This lachrymose, self-accusatory stage was usually followed by an aggressive stage in which he told anyone who was still a socialist how he had waked up to himself in 1937 and what a fine thing it had been for him. These contradictory demonstrations puzzled his interlocutors, who did not see that in the first stage he was comparing his actual work to some imaginary lost vocation, a life of dedication and scholarship which he had in reality never been attracted to, and in the second stage he was comparing his present career on *Destiny* to his former job on the *Liberal.* The majority of Jim's friends paid no attention to the second stage of his drunkenness, ascribing anything he might say to the effects of alcohol ("liquor hits some people that way"); it was the first stage that impressed them. Here, they thought, he spoke from the heart; here the honest, decent man revealed himself to be incorruptible; though obliged to make his living by working on *Destiny,* he did not deceive himself as to its true character; he rebelled, if only on Saturday nights. Actually, however, the utterances of the second stage were "real," and the lamentations were largely histrionic.

The truth was that Jim had changed, though the outward signs of it were still so faint as to pass undetected by his intimates. He got drunk oftener, there was no denying it, but, as Nancy said, the strain of being a writer for *Destiny* had made alcohol "an absolute necessity" for him. His boyish features were now slightly blurred; his awkward, loose-jointed figure was fatter than it had been, and his habitual sprawl was not so becoming to it. Imperceptibly, he had passed from looking pleasantly unkempt to looking seedy. The puzzled frown had become chronic with him; he was, in fact, professionally bewildered. And yet there was something dimly spurious about all this: his gait, his posture, his easy way of talking, half-belied the wrinkles on his forehead. In his young days he had been as lively and nervous as a squirrel; women had been fond of comparing him to some woodland creature. Today that alertness, that wariness, was gone. The sentry slept, relaxed, at his post, knowing that an armistice had been arranged with the enemy. In some subtle way, Jim had turned into a comfortable man, a man incapable of surprising or being surprised. The hairshirt he wore fitted him snugly now; old and well used, it no longer prickled him; it was only from the outside that it appeared to be formidable.

Jim knew that in middle-class intellectual circles his career was regarded as a tragedy of waste. Half-unconsciously, he fostered this illusion, for it permitted him to enjoy what was really a success story, secure from the envy of the less privileged. It was commonly believed that Nancy was the villain, Nancy who had gone and had two more children, Nancy who needed a house in the country, Nancy who kept his nose to *Destiny's* grindstone. And whenever they had friends in, Jim would grumble good-naturedly about expenses, the children's new shoes, the tricycles, the nursery school. Occasionally, during one of these mock tirades someone would look over at Nancy with a touch of concern or curiosity—perhaps these complaints were a little hard on her? But Nancy would always be smiling with genuine sweetness, for Nancy knew the duties of a wife, and knew too that Jim loved the children, the garden, the new radio, just as much if not more than she did.

Undoubtedly, Jim was still a good guy. On the magazine, he was always on the side of the underdog. He treated his subordinates with consideration, and he helped organize the Newspaper Guild chapter. He voted for Roosevelt, though *Destiny* was pro-Willkie, and when the Trotskyites were indicted for sedition in Minneapolis he sent them a check through the Civil Liberties Union. If he showed a certain ruthlessness—socially—to people who did not count, he had the excuse of being extremely busy, preoccupied with the great issues of the day. And he was always interested in the common man. He could spend hours talking to taxi drivers, grocers, swing musicians, real-estate agents, small lawyers or doctors who had married old school friends of Nancy's. These people and their opinions "counted" for Jim; it was only the intellectuals, the unsuccessful, opinionated, unknown intellectuals, who had nothing, so far as he could see, to say to him.

Margaret Sargent belonged to this tiresome class. In memory of old times, he always talked to her a few minutes when he met her at parties, but her sarcasms bored him, and, unless he were tight, he would contrive to break away from her as quickly as possible. It irritated him to hear one day that she had applied for a job on *Destiny;* he was perfectly justified, he said to himself, in telling the publisher that she would not fit in. It would be intolerable to have her in the office. He owed her no debt; all that had been canceled long ago. And yet ... He sat musing at his desk. Why was it that she, only she, had the power to make him feel, feel honestly, unsentimentally, that his life was a failure, not a tragedy exactly, but a comedy with pathos? That single night and day when he had been almost in love with her had taught him everything. He had learned that he must keep down his spiritual expenses—or else go under. There was no doubt at all of the wisdom of his choice. He did not envy her; her hands were empty: she was unhappy, she was poor, she had achieved nothing, even by her own standards. Yet she exasperated him, as the spendthrift will always exasperate the miser who feels obliged to live like a pauper, lest his wealth be suspected and a robber plunder him. But there was more than that. What did he regret, he asked himself. If he had it to do over again, he would make the same decision. What he yearned for perhaps was the possibility of decision, the instant of choice, when a man stands at a crossroads and knows he is free. Still, even that had been illusory. He had never been free, but until he had tried to love the girl, he had not known he was bound. It was self-knowledge she had taught him; she had showed him the cage of his own nature. He had accommodated himself to it, but he could never forgive her. Through her he had lost his primeval innocence, and he would hate her forever as Adam hates Eve.

JAMES THURBER

What Are the Leftists Saying?

FOR A LONG TIME I have had the idea that it would be interesting to attempt to explain to an average worker what the leftist, or socially conscious, literary critics are trying to say. Since these critics are essentially concerned with the improvement of the worker's status, it seems fitting and proper that the worker should be educated in the meaning of their pronouncements. The critics themselves believe, of course, in the education of the worker, but they are divided into two schools about it: those who believe the worker should be taught beforehand why there must be a revolution, and those who believe that he should be taught afterward why there was one. This is but one of many two-school systems which divide the leftist intellectuals and keep them so busy in controversy that the worker is pretty much left out of things. It is my plan to escort a worker to a hypothetical, but typical, gathering of leftist literary critics and interpret for him, insofar as I can, what is being said there. The worker is likely to be so confused at first, and so neglected, that he will want to slip out and go to Minsky's; but it is important that he stay, and I hope that he has already taken a chair and removed his hat. I shall sit beside him and try to clarify what is going on.

Permission of the author. From *Let Your Mind Alone!*

Nothing, I must explain while we are waiting for the gentlemen to gather, is going to be easy. This is partly because it is a primary tenet of leftist criticism to avoid what is known as Oversimplification. This is a word our worker is going to encounter frequently at the gathering of critics and it is important that he understand what it means. Let me get at it by quoting a sentence from a recent review in *The Nation* by a socially conscious critic: "In so far as men assert and counter-assert, you can draw an assertion from the comparison of their assertions." As it stands, that is not oversimplified, because no one can point to any exact or absolute meaning it has. Now I will oversimplify it. A says, "Babe Ruth is dead" (assertion). B says, "Babe Ruth is alive" (counter-assertion). C says, "You guys seem to disagree" (assertion drawn from comparison of assertions). Here I have brought the critic's sentence down to a definite meaning by providing a concrete instance. Leftist criticism does not believe in that, contending that all thought is in a state of motion, and that in every thought there exists simultaneously "being," "non-being," and "becoming," and that in the end every thought disappears by being absorbed into its opposite. I am afraid that I am oversimplifying again.

Let us get back to our meeting. About sixteen leftist literary critics have now gathered in the room. Several are talking and the others are not so much listening as waiting for an opening. Let us cock an ear toward Mr. Hubert Camberwell. Mr. Camberwell is saying, "Sinclair Lewis has dramatized the process of disintegration, as well as his own dilemma, in the outlines of his novels, in the progress of his characters, and sometimes, and most painfully, in the lapses of taste and precision that periodically weaken the structure of his prose." This is a typical leftist critic's sentence. It has a facile, portentous swing, it damns a prominent author to hell, and it covers a tremendous amount of ground. It also has an air of authority, and because of this the other critics will attack it. Up speaks a Mr. Scholzweig: "But you cannot, with lapses of any kind, *dramatize* a process, you can only *annotate* it." This is a minor criticism, at best, but it is the only one Mr. Scholzweig can think of, because he agrees in general with what has been said about Sinclair Lewis (whose books he has never been able to read). At this point Donald Crowley announces that as yet nobody has *defined* anything; that is, nobody has defined "lapses," "dramatize," "process," or "annotate." While a small, excited man in shell-rim glasses is asking him how he would define the word "definition" in a world of flux, let us listen to Mr. Herman Bernheim. Mr. Bernheim is muttering something about Camberwell's "methodology" and his failure to "implement" his argument. Now, "methodology," as the leftist intellectuals use it, means any given wrong method of approach to a subject. "To implement" means (1) to have at the tip of one's tongue everything that has been written by any leftist since Marx, for the purpose of denying it, and (2) to possess and make use of historical references that begin like this: "Because of the more solidly articulated structure of French society, the deep-seated sentiments and prejudices of the northern French, and the greater geographical and political accessibility of France to the propaganda of the counter-Reformation," etc., etc.

The critics have by this time got pretty far away from Camberwell's analysis of Sinclair Lewis, but this is the customary procedure when leftists begin refuting one another's statements, and is one phase of what is known as "dialectic." Dialectic, in this instance, means the process of discriminating one's own truth from the other person's error. This leads to "factionalism," another word our worker must be familiar with. Factionalism is that process of disputation by means of which the main point at issue is lost sight of. Now, the main point at issue here—namely, the analysis of Sinclair Lewis—becomes even more blurred by the fact that a critic named Kyle Forsythe, who has just come into the room, gets the erroneous notion that everybody is discussing Upton Sinclair. He begins, although it is not at all relevant, to talk about "escapism." Escapism means the activities of anyone who is not a leftist critic or writer. The discussion, to our worker, will now appear to get so far out of hand that we must bring him a Scotch-and-soda if we are to hold his interest much longer. He will probably want to know whether one leftist intellectual ever agrees with another, and, under cover of the loud talking, I shall explain the one form of agreement which these critics have. I call it the "that he—but when" form of agreement. Let us say that one leftist critic writes in a liberal weekly as follows: "I like poetry, but I don't like Tennyson." Another leftist critic will write often in the same issue and immediately following the first one's article: "That he likes poetry, we must concede Mr. Blank, but when he says that Tennyson is a great poet, we can only conclude that he does not like poetry at all." This is, of course, greatly oversimplified.

Midnight eventually arrives at our party and everybody begins "unmasking" everybody else's "ideology." To explain what unmasking an ideology means, I must give an example. Suppose that I were to say to one of the critics at this party, "My country, 'tis of thee, sweet land of liberty." He would unmask my ideology—that is expose the background of my illusion—by pointing out that I am the son of wealthy bourgeois parents who employed an English butler. This is not true, but my ideology would be unmasked, anyway. It is interesting to note that it takes only one leftist critic to expose anybody's ideology, and that every leftist critic unmasks ideologies in his own special way. In this sense, Marxist criticism is very similar to psychoanalysis. Ideology-unmasking is a great deal like dream interpretation and leads to just as many mystic results.

A general midnight unmasking of ideologies at a gathering of leftist literary critics is pretty exciting, and I hope that a second Scotch-and-soda will persuade our worker to stay. If he does, he will find out that when your ideology is unmasked, you can't do anything with it, because it has no "social currency." In other words, anything that you say or do will have no more validity than Confederate money.

The party now breaks up, without ill feeling, because the critics have all had such a good time at the unmasking. A leftist critic gets as much fun out of disputation, denial, and disparagement as a spaniel puppy gets out of a steak bone. Each one will leave, confident that he has put each of the others in his place and that they realize it. This is known as the "united front." On our way out, however, I must explain to the worker the meaning of an extremely important term in Marxist criticism; namely, "Dialectical Materialism." Dialectical Materialism, then, is based on two fundamental laws of dialectics: the law of the permeation of opposites, or polar unity, and the law of the negation of the negation, or development through opposites. This second proposition is the basic law of all processes of thought. I will first state the law itself and then support it with examples . . . Hey, worker! Wait for baby!

RICHARD O. BOYER

Union President: Joseph Curran

WHEN, on the morning of January 29, 1936, the rubber workers of Akron, Ohio, called the first big sit-down strike in the United States, they started something which, for better or worse, changed the face of the nation. The fever spread to Flint, Michigan, where it hit the plants of General Motors; it broke out in Indiana, then in Chicago, then jumped all the way to the West Coast. By the time the epidemic died down, the C.I.O. was established firmly and had a total of four million members. While shop girls jitterbugged in department stores and college professors paraded with picket signs until their demands were met, the C.I.O. organized with enormous rapidity the rubber, glass, automobile, steel, mining, textile, clothing, oil, radio, lumber, packing, transport, shoe, fur, stevedoring, aluminum, communications, leather, and marine industries. In the ten years since the Akron sitdown, American organized labor has begun to figure in national politics on an effective scale, has had a great deal to do with keeping a President in office, and has grown in numbers more than it grew in the preceding fifty years—from three million members, in 1936, to fourteen million today, two-fifths of whom belong to the C.I.O. In the process, rough-and-ready young men who were unknown, uneducated workers in factories, mines, and mills have been swept along into positions of leadership. In the American tradition, they have quickly learned to make speeches, wear dinner jackets, receive the press, preside at banquets, dictate to secretaries, run newspapers, write columns, speak over the radio, be interviewed by *Fortune,* and perform for the newsreels. Within a decade, they have become a force in American industry, professional politicians have begun to keep an uneasy eye on them, and they have provided a new kind of American success story. The story of Joseph Curran, president of the National Maritime Union, is a perfect example.

Ten years ago, at the age of thirty, Curran was a sailor whose only home ashore was a bench in Battery Park. Today he is one of the country's most powerful men. In March, 1936, when he sullenly walked ashore in New York off the *California,* a Panama Pacific Line passenger ship, from which he had just been discharged for organizing a strike aboard her, he was not at all sure that he wouldn't be arrested for mutiny because of his activities. Because of what happened after that strike, however, he is now the president of the world's largest trade union of sailors, a vice-president of the C.I.O., and an official of the World Trade Union Federation. Instead of rising by getting to work on time, staying out of trouble, and being polite to the boss, he reversed the old formula for success and reached eminence by getting into all kinds of trouble, insulting the boss, and on many occasions refusing to go to work. His success sometimes mystifies even those who are closest to him. His size—six feet, two inches and two hundred and seventeen pounds—gives emphasis to a manner that is thoroughly truculent. One theory is that his success is based on other people's instinctive wish to placate him. Once, while he was still a sailor, he felt it necessary to chastise the chief mate of the *Santa Clara,* a Grace Line passenger ship on which he was a seaman; after that, the chief mate sent him his orders in writing, by bellboy. His fellow-seamen were equally cautious. "When Curran said the food was lousy, everyone said the food was lousy," one old shipmate recently recalled, "and if he said, 'Let's go to the movies,' everyone said, 'Let's go to the movies.' " It has also been suggested that Curran's faults are his principal assets. Whenever he shouts and curses and threatens, his constituents, some ninety thousand in number, say tolerantly, "He's just a roughneck sailor; he doesn't know any more than anyone else," and when it comes time again, they enthusiastically reëlect him to office. He has been president of the N.M.U. ever since it was organized. The members admire their president's wavy nose, rippled by fractures received in shipboard altercations on the Western Ocean, as oldtimers call the North Atlantic, but they are equally pleased when, resplendent in dinner jacket, he addresses a congress of shipowners, as he recently did at the Waldorf-Astoria. Sometimes, as Curran preens himself before a mirror while he is getting dressed for such as occasion, he is apt to be reminded of what happened right after he and his fellowstrikers were discharged from the *California*. A general seamen's strike was called on the East Coast, and the committee that directed it made him chairman. "They took up a collection and went out and bought me a business suit to make me look presentable," he says. He feels that stories which ascribe his success to violence are based on his appearance, or what he calls "my snoot."

Curran never got beyond the fifth grade, and at the time of the general strike he was utterly inexperienced in public affairs. Each day he had to deal with a dozen situations he had never encountered before, and he solved them all by bellowing. It was apparent to Curran even then that the labor movement was gaining ground swiftly. On the one hand, he was eager for the rewards of a strange, shore world, and on the other, he was suspicious of the landlubbers with whom he had to deal. He was especially wary of his secretary, Miss Dorothy Snyder, whom his colleagues hired for him after they had set up headquarters on Eleventh Avenue. She was bright and quick, and to Curran it seemed as if she willfully emphasized the slowness of his mind. When she hesitantly offered him advice on some minor matter, he would say, "What do *you* know?" Then he would follow the advice. In those days, he says, he could "throw a pretty good drunk," and when he went to parties he usually took along a bottle of Scotch. "This one's mine," he would say, and place it beside his chair. "He had a strong me-and-mine bias," one of his old friends says. "The more he'd drink, the further off he'd go on that tack." He had a hard time with the press, being unable to forgo ending difficult interviews by hollering, "Get the hell out!" "Now," he says complacently, "I'll even see a Hearst reporter." In the more complex world he had entered, he at first found it impossible to dictate a letter. Instead, he would simply swear at

Miss Snyder a while and then give up and tell her to write it herself. Miss Snyder, who left her job a few years ago to get married, still follows his progress proudly. "Now he can dictate as well as anyone," she recently said. "He used to write all his nouns with a capital letter and his spelling was awful. Now he can spell anything."

During the first days of the general strike, some newsreel people came to Curran and asked him to say a few words before the camera. They trapped him when he was wearing a black watch cap, blue dungarees, and a blue denim jumper. He was embarrassed and suspicious and miserable, and kept saying he was only a sailor and couldn't do it. Finally, a few remarks were printed in large letters on cardboard signs and placed above the camera, and Curran read them aloud. Today when he walks onto a platform, wearing a gray or blue double-breasted suit, with a stockade of pens and pencils in his breast pocket, he is poised and impressive. He has a lofty manner and a voice like the ripping of canvas; his words are polysyllabic and his sentences almost scan. After that first appearance before the camera, he began studying the dictionary, and he still reads it almost every day, his great, gray face, with its small, deep eyes and prowlike chin, set in a solemn scowl. A few weeks ago, when one of the other officials of the N.M.U. spoke of "chronological history," Curran was scornful. "Chronological history!" he said. "That's good. That's ver-ee good. Gee-zus-criz! Don't you know that's tautological?"

When Curran enters the large, imposing headquarters of the N.M.U., at 346 West Seventeenth Street, and walks into his own office, as handsome as anything in Hollywood, the strikes and the bloodshed that occurred when the N.M.U. was being organized, a mere nine years ago, probably seem very remote to him. He is even a little shamefaced when he remembers his first negotiations with the gentlemen—in general dignified, silver-haired old characters—who run the shipping companies. There was one named Blacktop, whom Curran always addressed as Blackbottom, and another whom he called Old Stoneface. He shakes his huge head when he recalls this conduct now, and clucks depreciatingly. "I was just a tough kid," he says. "In the early days of collective bargaining, I didn't want to hear any problems of the operators. In those days, it was just a flat argument, with the operators saying they had no money and with us saying they were damn liars. We do a large amount of industrial research now. We have to know an operator's business better than he does."

Curran often speaks of himself, with a dour, grudging modesty, as a product of the times. He says that his career would have been impossible if it hadn't been for the New Deal, the Wagner Labor Act, the C.I.O., and the state of the nation that brought them about. He likes to think, however, that he had a little to do with his success. His systematic study of Robert's "Rules of Order," he feels, has enabled him to conduct meetings with aplomb and authority. He owes his facility as an orator, he claims, to his system of picking out three people in an audience—"one on the right, one on the left, and one in the middle"—and addressing himself only to them. He believes that he has developed what might be termed a world viewpoint, which he attributes to the fact that the activities of the N.M.U. are worldwide. He points out that he has become an exceptionally well-read man. He recently remarked, in the course of a confused squabble he has been carrying on with the Communists in his union, that he has even read Marx, who he thinks is something of a screwbox. Curran himself has often been called a Communist, which he is not. When this happens, he says, "That's nothing to what they called Tommy." This is his way of referring to an earlier orator, Thomas Jefferson. All in all, Curran has covered a lot of ground in ten years.

Curran, an only child, was born on New York's lower East Side, in 1906, of Irish-American parents. He never knew his father, who died when he was an infant. He doesn't even know what his father's occupation was, but he thinks that he may have been a travelling salesman, because on Joe's birth certificate his father is designated as "a traveller." His mother, who died in 1934, was a professional cook. "She was a smart woman," Curran says. "She could read a book in four hours and tell you what was in it." However, he doesn't know much about her, either. "My mother was not given to talking," he says. "And she worked in rich families and had to board me out." Most of Curran's boyhood was spent in the home of a German baker in Westfield, New Jersey. That is the reason he can bake pies and cakes, and enjoys baking on his days off. In 1924, his mother married an Irish house painter named Christopher Tobin, whose latter years were made miserable by the Dies Committee, which took his fine Irish name and telescoped it into a name they said was Russian. It was claimed at one of the hearings held by the committee, which frequently attacked Curran and his union, that Curran's real name was Christobin and that he was a native of the Ukraine. While supposedly a resident of the Ukraine, he was, in fact, attending parochial school in Westfield. When he was fourteen, he felt out of place because he had grown so much bigger than the other children in his class and, though he was only in the fifth grade, insisted on quitting school and got a permit to go to work. He was lonesome as a child. "It was really rough," he says. "I want lots of kids. I don't want my kid, Joe Paul, to be an only child."

After leaving school, Curran found a job as an office boy in the New

York offices of the Gold Medal Flour Company, which were then in the Whitehall Building, overlooking the Battery and the harbor. It was the accident of this location, as much as anything else, that determined the course his life has taken. He spent much of his time watching the ships passing, and when he was sixteen, he decided to go to sea, and did. "Something told me I was home," he recalls. "The harder it got, the better I liked it. I never even got seasick. I was a fresh kid who thought he knew it all until the bos'n started kicking me around, and then I learned. Yeh. I got beat up, got no wages, lost weight from lack of food—but I was young and I liked it." He began to learn to splice ten-inch hawsers, rig up tackle, sling scaffolds, toss lines, overhaul gear, take soundings, lower lifeboats, batten down hatches, and stand watch at the wheel. He also learned to operate a steam capstan and a winch, take blocks apart and grease them, make cargo slings, lay paint on properly, lower booms, secure deck cargo, take a rolling hitch in a rope that would not slip, and swab and wash and chip and paint a ship. There is scarcely a recent book on the subject of tying knots that does not name him as an authority who gave the author advice. He learned how to keep himself clean by bathing in a bucket of salt water, and he learned how to do his laundry. "Before the union," he says, "if you saw a shower bath on a freighter, you would have thought you were crazy, and if you'd seen an electric toaster, you'd have fallen dead." He learned to adjust himself to living in a twenty-by-twenty fo'c'sle in whose three-tiered bunks twelve men slept. "Once, I had a top bunk under a dripping steampipe," he will remark, "and I learned how to curl up like a pretzel, so the scalding water wouldn't drip on me while I slept." He saw two sailors rip a shipmate to pieces with jagged pieces of wood. During a storm off Tasmania, he went down into the dark hold of a ship to disarm a Portuguese sailor who had gone insane and was wielding a fire axe. In the struggle, the sailor struck Curran in the back with the weapon. Possibly as a consequence, he still has a troublesome sacroiliac. "I don't know if it came from the axe or the lumpy straw mattresses we had to sleep on," he says now.

Curran has a collection of thousands of postcards he bought in ports around the world. Now and then he likes to go over them and reminisce. "It's always tough when a ship leaves port," he said on one such occasion recently. "You have to batten down the hatches, spread the tarpaulins, lower the booms into their cradles, and pile the guys, preventers, and stays on the hatch. The first night and day were always bad, especially on picket-fence ships—those that had eighteen to twenty-four booms, like the Luckenbach ships. When fellows came aboard, they'd say, 'Boy, look at that forest of sticks!' Usually everything was flying, which means hatches pen and booms up, gear lying all over the deck. Safety meant nothing in those days. You'd work all night and through the next day. Sometimes the ice on the tarpaulins would make you mighty miserable. A tarpaulin, well iced, will stand straight up and you can't bend it. Each hatch took as many as three or four, and they'd cut your hands to ribbons. On the Western Ocean, some of us used to laugh at the oldtimers who'd talk about iron men and wooden ships. 'Don't give a damn what you say, bud,' we'd tell 'em. 'Nothing's worse than this.' By God, after cutting their hands to shreds on frozen tarpaulins and stumbling over gear on an icy night, they wouldn't talk about iron men and wooden ships. If a guy did, he would be heaved right out of the fo'c'sle onto the deck and find his head in the scuppers. But if a ship was fair fast, soon she might be off Florida and all the wintry nights would be forgotten. But that Western Ocean! My God!"

Even worse than the Western Ocean were the periodic spells of unemployment. The International Seamen's Union, which was organized in 1892 and got up to a hundred and three thousand members just after the first World War, called a strike in 1921 and lost it disastrously. Its membership during the next decade averaged only four thousand. All through the twenties, the American merchant marine was suffering a depression. Fifty thousand men were competing for twenty thousand berths, and many of the men were willing to work without pay just to get food and lodgings. Wages, when a seaman could get them, were twenty-five dollars a month, there was no pay for overtime, a twelve-hour day was a short one, a single sheet (which was never changed during the course of a voyage) went with each bunk, a towel was practically unknown, and bedbugs and lice abounded. "In those days," Curran says, "when you quit a ship, it would take two or three months to get another. I had a very comfortable bench in the middle of Battery Park. I spent many starving days there. Used to use Australian bedsheets. That's what we call newspapers; you put them on top of you when you sleep on a bench. If you stuff 'em inside your coat, they'll keep you pretty warm. When I was lucky, I'd get a job washing dishes in a restaurant on Nassau Street. I'd start dishwashing at eleven A.M. You'd get one good meal when you went in and another when you went out, at four P.M. They paid one dollar. It kept me from being a bum, because I could wash my shirt there, too. With the dollar, you'd be able to keep indoors, and that was good on zero nights. You'd spend thirty-five cents for a flop at the Seamen's Church Institute on South Street. Then fifteen cents for cigarettes, and you'd have fifty cents left for breakfast and carfare. In those days, you didn't have a union hiring hall. You had to chase all over New York for a job. You'd get to a dock sometimes at two or three in the morning. Hundreds of other guys would be there. You'd wait until

noon, and then the shipping master would come out and say, 'Sorry. N
jobs.' "

After a few years, Curran began to lose his taste for his trade. He like
being at sea, but he didn't think so much of Battery Park. He made up h
mind to knuckle down and try to become an officer. Within the next tw
years, he succeeded, through study and hard work, in getting a berth a
bos'n, the sea equivalent of a foreman, on a ship. His men nicknamed hir
No Coffee Time Joe because he refused to let them knock off for fiftee
minutes for coffee during a watch. After a year, he got into a fight with th
first mate of the ship, lost his berth, and became a seaman again. Then h
decided that he would pick up some of the dogs he saw on his travels, r
tire from the sea, and go into business for himself as a kennelman. H
went so far as to buy two chows in China, a police dog in South Afric
and eleven spitzes in Odessa, but all of them either died or languished, s
he gave up his plans. He was still dreaming of escape and independenc
when, in 1928, a ship he was on touched Apia, a port in Western Samo
"I don't believe anyone will ever see anything more beautiful," he say
"The days and nights were soft and the water was a deep blue-green an
the sand was clean and very silver. There were all sorts of fruits—mangoe
coconuts, pineapples—and the fish! My God! The place was full of wi
boars. I decided to buy a two-masted schooner and live there all my lif
You could haul copra, and there were a couple of nickels to be made
fishing, too. And you could make a buck hauling scenery stiffs an
sponges." A scenery stiff, sometimes called a scenery bum, is a touri
"I got all the charts of the islands and brought them back to New Yo
with me," Curran continues. "I studied every reef and cove for years.
had my eye on a particular two-masted schooner. She was in New Be
ford, Massachusetts. She was a beauty—a little, bobtail schooner. She w
priced at six hundred dollars, and I started saving for her. I was going
have her rigged in such a way that I could sail her alone and hoist an
drop the sails from the wheel. I had it all planned so my jib, foresail, an
mainsail would have all hauling parts rove through blocks set in th
gunnel and run aft to cleats alongside the wheel, so I could drop the sai
at the wheel in case of a blow. I figured I could have her calked and stor
for three hundred, on top of the original six. But I could never make
Once I had four hundred dollars, but I was in Shanghai and she was
New Bedford."

In 1930, when the depression became acute, Curran, with thousan
of others, was on the beach much of the time. He was beginni
to lose faith in individual initiative, whether it concerned dogs an

ttle bobtailed schooners or being a seaman. The International Seamen's Union had for a long time been moribund, so a group of seamen got together and organized the Marine Workers Industrial Union, which Curran joined. When members of the union succeeded in getting berths, they would organize committees aboard ship. The chief duties of these committees were to attempt to persuade the management to improve the quality of the food and to deal with the captains as representatives of the crews on all matters except questions of navigation and discipline. Almost every American merchant ship has such a committee today, but the idea was then regarded as a blow against the moral order of the universe. For centuries, the tradition had been that a captain aboard his ship was a law unto himself. "For the crew to advise a captain on anything was like Arkansas Baptists trying to advise the Pope on a matter of faith," Curran says. It was only a few years since it had been officially held that American seamen were "deficient in that full and intelligent responsibility for their acts which is accredited to ordinary adults and as needing the protection of the law in the same sense which minors and wards do." This was the language of a Supreme Court decision in 1897, and it had not been reversed until 1915.

In 1934, as Curran studied his Australian bedsheets on his bench in Battery Park, he began to feel stirrings of hope. The N.R.A., which had just been set up by law, established the legal right of employees to bargain collectively and to join unions of their own choosing. "A kind of excitement was sweeping the country," Curran says. "You'd read of people forming unions in La Porte, Indiana, in La Crosse, Wisconsin, or some little whistle stop in Nebraska. Farmers were dumping milk in Iowa. Old Iron Pants Johnson was cracking down. The Blue Eagle was everywhere. I got caught up in the thing." Thousands of factory workers were joining a sort of union new to this country, one organized on an industry rather than a craft basis. The groundwork for the C.I.O. was being laid at labor conventions at which John L. Lewis and others attacked the American Federation of Labor's system of organizing on craft lines, declaring that it was outmoded and inefficient. Curran became indignant when, at an N.R.A. code hearing for the shipping industry, the International Seamen's Union, which belonged to the American Federation of Labor and then had only three thousand members, was chosen by the government as the East Coast seamen's union, instead of the independent Marine Workers Industrial Union, which had a membership of fourteen thousand. The I.S.U.'s officers immediately signed a contract with a number of shipowners stipulating that all seamen hired by them had to belong to the I.S.U. The Marine Workers Industrial Union disbanded, and its members joined the I.S.U. The I.S.U. was autocratically run and its members were constantly protesting, because, they said, they never knew what was in a contract affecting them until it was already signed. This dissatisfaction increased in the East when West Coast seamen were granted five dollars more a month than the East Coast men, as well as overtime pay and the right to have union instead of company hiring halls. When the I.S.U. officers, despite the protest, renewed the contract in January of 1936, Curran, along with thousands of others, was ready to act.

Curran heard the news of this contract when he was on the liner *California,* bound for New York on a return trip from San Francisco. When the ship, which was carrying four hundred cruise passengers, docked in San Pedro, the crew of three hundred and seventy-four, led by Curran, announced that they would not cast off the lines for the voyage to New York. The I.S.U. officials said the strike was unauthorized, and Daniel Roper, Secretary of Commerce, demanded that the strikers be arrested for mutiny. "On the third day of the strike," Curran says, "this mutiny talk began getting the crew restless, as such talk will. I didn't know anything about unionship then. I had a tiger by the tail and couldn't let it go. I didn't know how to compromise it. Everybody was keeping sober and we did any and all work except let go the lines. Davy Grange, the vice-president of the I.S.U., called up from New York and said, 'You have to sail the ship.' I told him, 'Go to hell. You sold us out.' Grange talked to Miss Perkins, the Secretary of Labor. Later we were told that Miss Perkins wanted to talk to me on the phone. The crew voted no. They thought it was a plot to get me off the ship and put me in irons. Finally, it was decided that we had to talk to Miss Perkins. The phone was six miles away from the ship. Twenty guys were appointed as my bodyguards, and all the crew was to pack their bags and leave the ship if we didn't get back in six hours. When I was brought to the phone, I was as nervous as a monkey. Miss Perkins said, 'You gotta bring the ship back. The Department of Commerce says it's mutiny.' I said, 'If we bring it back, it'll still be mutiny.' Then I said, 'What about the five dollars? What about the phony contract signed by the I.S.U.? If we come back, can we negotiate for ourselves?' She said, 'I'll use my good offices.' I said, 'What about the mutiny?' She said, 'I'll try to stop the charge.' I said, 'I'll have to talk to the crew.' But I figured this was the way out. I had that tiger by the tail and I was looking for a way to let it go. Here was a way to retire without losing face."

When the *California* arrived in New York, she was met by fifty patrolmen, twenty detectives, five agents from the Department of Justice, and a welcoming committee of marine workers and seamen who were parading outside the dock with signs saying "Ask for $5 More—Mutiny." The *Daily*

News carried a light-hearted story, headlined "Shades of H.M.S. *Bounty*," drawing an analogy to the eighteenth-century mutiny of British sailors against Captain Bligh. There were no arrests, but sixty-five of the crew, among them Curran, were discharged and logged two to six days' pay. This action resulted in a spontaneous general seamen's strike, as much against the leadership of the I.S.U. as against the shipping companies. Twenty thousand men participated in this strike, which lasted two and a half months and was a failure. At the end of that time, they decided to return to the ships and recruit more members for the rank-and-file movement. A Seamen's Defense Committee was organized, with Curran as its chairman. He remained ashore to direct its operations. Representatives of the committee met every incoming ship, despite the natural objections of the owners, on occasion getting by the dock guards by disguising themselves as Western Union messengers bearing flowers for arriving passengers. Once on a dock, they would "walk barges" to other ships at near-by piers. Rank-and-filers would also sail "schooner rig," which means stripped down to essentials—a few pairs of socks, a toothbrush, and a suitcase full of union literature. Aboard ship, the organizers threw every newspaper, magazine, and book in the crew's quarters overboard, on the theory that the crew would read the union material in sheer desperation, if for no other reason. The organizers sometimes began their work a bit belligerently. "All right, you guys," they would say. "We're members of the rank and file. Declare yourselves!" By September, 1936, forty thousand seamen had joined the movement. Then another strike was called.

The second strike, which enveloped all the Atlantic and Gulf ports, is usually referred to by N.M.U. men as "the big strike." It lasted three and a half months, and during it twenty-seven union men were killed and hundreds were injured. It occurred at the high tide of the C.I.O. drive, when neither labor nor management felt it could afford to doubt for an instant that it was right and when both sides were fighting fiercely. The seamen rented a hall at 164 Eleventh Avenue and set up headquarters there. Their day began at 6 A.M. with the dispatching of five thousand pickets to piers scattered from Staten Island, Hoboken, Jersey City, and Bayonne to the North River, the East River, and the Erie Basin. The men were relieved every four hours, and the picketing went on until nightfall. The hall was packed with a noisy swarm of seamen until late at night, and here and there, at tables in corners, committees on strategy, food, picketing, finances, publicity, legal aid, first aid, housing, and public speaking planned and argued and worked. A huge stewpot was always simmering on a gas range. Some seamen were sent to Washington Market to cadge food from the commission merchants, and others made the rounds of neighborhood grocers and bakers. If they were lucky, they would return with basket of cabbages, tomatoes, and carrots, bags of beans, stale bread, doughnuts coffee, and sometimes even meat. Others would be sent to Times Square and the waterfront saloons to "rattle the can" for contributions from the public. A member of the speakers' committee might call to one of the union's more eloquent speakers, John (Hot Cross) Bunn, "Hey, you with the phony Oxford accent! I want you to go up to Columbia and talk to some professors about support for the strike. And stay sober." Another group would be sent off on two rented launches to proselytize the crew of incoming ships by means of megaphones and signs. Sometimes, after the police had broken a picket line, the hall looked like a first-aid station just behind the front. If there were arrests, the legal-aid committee would round up lawyers and bail bondsmen. Longshoremen, who sided with the I.S.U., waded into the picket lines with baseball bats. The longshore men specialized in finding lone strikers and, in the waterfront term for beating a man up, "dumping" them. Curran had a group of bodyguards but, he says, he did not approve of the idea. "When something begins to happen, I don't want to be bothered by any bodyguards," he says. On one occasion, while picketing, he was hit over the head with a pool cue, and on another he received a glancing blow from an eight-pound iron rod and on still another a strikebreaking dope addict tried to strangle him with a clothesline.

The strategy committee, headed by Curran, was in almost permanent session during the strike. Some of its time went into discussing waterfront rumors that the companies were willing to settle. "The rumors were phonies to break morale," Curran now declares. Flying squadrons of seamen would be sent out every so often in borrowed Fords to check on the state of picket lines. Others would be directed to ferret out shipping crimps, or employment brokers, usually proprietors of seamen's boarding houses, who were supplying strikebreakers to the companies. "I found one on Staten Island," a seaman might say. "I cased the joint, and if we have men there at five in the morning, we can wreck it." Sometimes the hall was filled with an almost palpable tension, but generally, as the strike dragged on as food became scarcer and stomachs tighter and wives and children began to complain, the hall was a very gloomy place. The strikers took a great interest in the news of the other strikes that were going on all over the country; that seemed to give them a sort of comfort. "They're sitting down at Chevvy," a man would say, speaking of a General Motors plant in Flint as if it were only around the corner. "Even the goddam news papermen are striking," another would remark. Late every day, telegrams rom local committees elsewhere would begin coming in, telling of the rogress of the strike in other ports. (On December 24th, a wire reported hat seventy-five seamen had been injured in Houston when police broke picket line. Curran looked up from the telegram and said, "The Christmas Eve Massacre," which is what the event is still called by the N.M.U.) At about six in the evening, pickets would begin dropping in to warm hemselves and get something to eat, and the men who had been collecting money in Times Square and waterfront saloons would also return to the hall. The money would be counted in front of everyone, and would then be distributed among the men, at a quarter a head, as far s it would go. The quarter was to pay for a bed in one of the flophouses with which the housing committee had made arrangements. Those seamen who didn't get any money slept on the floor of the hall. "One night man came in and gave us five hundred dollars," Curran says. "That night we all slept in bed and there was plenty of meat in the stewpot." Another reat moment was the United States Supreme Court's decision in the case f the National Labor Relations Board v. the Jones & Laughlin Steel Corporation. It said, "Long ago we stated the reasons for labor organizations. We said that they were organized out of the necessities of the situation; hat a single employe was helpless in dealing with an employer . . . that union was essential to give laborers opportunity to deal on an equality with their employer. . . ." Curran had a large sign made of an excerpt rom the decision and tacked it up at headquarters.

The rank-and-file seamen won the strike. In May of 1937, forty thousand seamen, out of a total of fifty thousand, seceded from the I.S.U. and ormed the National Maritime Union, electing Curran its president. The National Labor Relations Board ordered the shipowners who had contracts with the I.S.U. to hold elections, so that the seamen could decide between the old I.S.U. and the new N.M.U. Of the sixty company elections round the country, the N.M.U. won fifty-six, by immense majorities, and the I.S.U. passed out of existence. Since then, seamen's minimum wages have risen from sixty-five dollars a month to a hundred and eighty-six-fifty. Today the union has a hundred and twenty-eight contracts, overing ninety thousand men on two thousand ships, and it has about two million dollars in its treasury. Curran believes that this is just the beginning. "Labor is on the move," he often says, and he even takes a wry and painful satisfaction in the fact that his constituents, through overruling him, recently gained by threat of strike a monthly raise of $41.50, he largest pay boost in maritime history. Before the unprecedented pay raise had been won, Curran had advised settling for an increase of $12.50. n turning down Curran's recommendation, rank-and-file members of

the union used such salty, sulphurous language that even Curran was a
little shocked. Shortly after he had been overruled, Curran, dressed in a
well-tailored suit and wearing a wristwatch, was doing what he calls
pacing the deck—walking up and down his handsome office, jingling the
coins in his pocket. A secretary was waiting for him to dictate a letter
answering the charge of a shipping executive that union members had
been disrespectful to a third mate. Curran's expression was grim as he
dictated a reply. The union, he said, would not countenance insubordination. Then, suddenly, his massive, ashen face relaxed into a smile.
"Gee-zus-criz!" he exclaimed, as if in surprise. "That's just the way I
was myself back in the old days!"

*When the Government went into art, the complaints were many and
bitter, until it became common knowledge that the revivals and original
productions of the Federal Theatre were the liveliest plays on Broadway—
and in a hundred cities and towns that had never before known a legitimate
theatre.* The Living Newspaper, *as Hallie Flanagan has told us in her sum-
ming-up of the achievement of the Federal Theatre, was berated by its
enemies as New Deal propaganda and by some of its friends for being ineffective as New Deal propaganda.* Triple-A Plowed Under *is a worthy
representative of the techniques and viewpoint of these plays. The state and
city guides of the Federal Writers Project never needed defenders; their
high quality is attested by the eagerness with which the book-buying public
has long awaited new editions of these eminently practical, handsome, and
well written books.* Pare Lorentz's The Plow That Broke the Plains *and*
The River *extended the limits of the film to include both soil conservation
and poetry; unfortunately, nothing less than the totality of the film can
recreate the effect that* The River *produced.*

NEW YORK PANORAMA

Metropolis and Her Children

THE RUMOR of a great city goes out beyond its borders, to all the latitudes of the known earth. The city becomes an emblem in remote minds; apart from the tangible export of goods and men, it exerts its cultural instrumentality in a thousand phases: as an image of glittering light, as the forcing ground which creates a new prose style or a new agro-biological theory, or as the germinal point for a fresh technique in metal sculpture, biometrics or the fixation of nitrogen. Its less ponderable influence may be a complex of inextricable ideas, economic exchanges, associations, artifacts: the flask of perfume which brings Fifth Avenue to a hacienda in the Argentine, the stencil marks on a packing case dumped on the wharf at Beira or Reykjavik, a flurry of dark-goggled globe-trotters from a cruise ship, a book of verse

> Under the stone I saw them flow
> express Times Square at five o'clock
> eyes set in darkness

read in a sheepherder's hut in New South Wales, or a Harlem band playing *Young Woman's Blues* from a phonograph as the safari breaks camp in Tanganyika under a tile-blue morning sky as intensely lighted as the panorama closed by mountains in the ceiling dome of the African section at the American Museum of Natural History.

The orbit of such a world city as New York also intersects the orbits of other world cities. New York, London, Tokyo, Rome exchange preferred stocks and bullion, ships' manifests and radio programs—in rivalry or well-calculated friendship. During the 1920's, for example, a jump spark crackled between New York and Paris. The art of Matisse, Derain, Picasso commanded the Fifty-Seventh Street market. The French developed a taste for *le jazz* and *le sport;* in an atmosphere of war debts and the Young Plan, the Americanization of Europe was mentioned. Paris, capital of the *Valutaschweine,* became the bourne of good and gay New Yorkers, the implicit heroine of a comedy by Philip Barry or a novel by Ernest Hemingway. The French replied, though not always in kind. Georges Duha-mel pronounced a jeremiad against the machine apocalypse in America and Paul Morand, an amateur of violence, explored the sensational di-versity of New York. These were symptomatic. The comments of Jules Romains went deeper and established fixed points for contrast with a later period.

All the rays of force alive in the modern world move inward upon the city, and the burning glass of its attraction concentrates them in the flame that is New York. Historically, it has been to an exceptional degree a city of accumulation: its methods promotion and commerce, its principle ag-grandizement. About a nucleus of Dutch and English—even French Huguenot—settlers it subsequently collected swarm after swarm of Irish, German, Italian, Jewish and Russian immigrants, a proportion of other nationalities, and Americans of many stocks from the seaboard and the interior. For the most part, those immigrants who remained in the city were compacted into districts especially suited to their exploitation, dis-tricts as verminous and sunless as the Cloaca Maxima. Here, in dwellings that reproduced the foetor of the slave ship in all but the promise of eventual liberty held out to the more intelligent or ruthless, they formed a crawling agglomeration. This was the frontier of New York and the grim apotheosis of the frontier in the United States, preserved almost un-touched into the third decade of the 20th century.

The shawled refugees from European want and oppression, most of whom crossed the ocean in immigrant ships under conditions of the ut-most squalor, were also transported by a succession of great New York trade vessels: the Black Ball and other Western Ocean packet lines, the world-ranging Donald McKay clippers, the first wood and iron steam-ships. These were conned through the Narrows by men off the superb Sandy Hook pilot schooners which had been worked out from the designs of Issac Webb in the 1830's, the hollow-entrance experiments of Griffiths in the 1840's, and the later masterly work of George Steers in such craft as the *Moses H. Grinnell* and the *America,* for which the *America's* Cup was named. Great numbers of immigrants and New Yorkers moved inland by way of the Hudson River sloops and steamboats, the Conestoga wagons, the Erie Canal barges and the railroads. Very early, therefore, the history of New York began to be a history of the successive phases in American transportation. As its lines of influence spread out into the interior, thickened and were fixed, it became more and more the commanding American city, the maker or merchant of dress silks and pannikins and spices, wines and beds and grub hoes. Long before the paramount age of sail ended, New York had taken on its alternate character as a great two-way transfer point and classification yard for men and goods and ideas moving between the other countries of the world and the great central plain of America. It has consolidated and enlarged this character with a multiplicity of functions which help to determine its position as the first city of the Western Hemisphere.

Approach to the City

For the American traveler coming home from Cape Town or St. Moritz or the Caribbean, and for those others who converge upon the city from Chicago and El Paso and Kildeer and Tonopah, New York has a nearer meaning. It is, in whatever sense, a substitute home town—a great apartment hotel, as Glenway Wescott wrote, in which everyone lives and no one is at home. In other eyes it may be a state fair grown to magnificence, a Main Street translated into the imperial splendor of Fifth Avenue. To such travelers the city is a coat of many colors—becoming to each, but not quite his own. It is both novelty and recognition that pleases him: the novelty of its actual and amazing encompassment, the recognition of great shafts and crowds and thoroughfares remembered from a hundred motion pictures, rotogravures and advertisements.

The man from another city will perhaps be least discommoded, his sense of the familiar both intensified and expanded. But to the men and women of the small towns, the sierras, the cornlands and grasslands, the seaboard coves and Gulf bayous—farmers, automobile mechanics, pack-rats, schoolteachers—New York cannot help but stand as a special order: the place which is not wilderness, the place of light and warmth and the envelopment of the human swarm, the place in which everyone is awake and laughing at three in the morning. These things are not altogether true, of course—but magic does not need to be true.

The traveler will know many things about New York and there will be guides to tell him many more, in the particular and the large; but he will see by looking, and find out by asking, and match the figure to the phenomenon. He may know that New York City is made up of five boroughs, four of which—Brooklyn, Queens, Richmond, the Bronx—compose like crinkled lily pads about the basking trout of Manhattan. He will not know, perhaps, that he and the other men and women who travel with him helped to make up a total of 68,999,376 visitors to the city in 1936, an off year. If he is an agronomist, he may find a certain perverse irony in the fact that the 198,330 acres of the five boroughs, without any tillage worth mentioning, supported an estimated population of 7,434,346 in 1937.

But it is less likely that the visitor who moves down one of those enormous radials that converge on New York from Seattle and Galveston and Los Angeles and Chicago will understand how Thomas Campanella's vision of a City of the Sun, published in 1623, has influenced the growth of such a modern metropolis as New York. Nor will he be aware, perhaps, that the verses of Walt Whitman and the paintings of "The Eight" and the landscape architecture of Olmsted the elder, quite as much as the Roeblings' Brooklyn Bridge and the Hoe press and the steel converters of Kelly and Bessemer, helped to create the social climate of the emerging city.

In the larger aspects of New York he may glimpse not only the results of the Randall Plan of 1811, but evidences of the influence of Geddes, Norton, Wright, McClellan, Bassett, Delano, Burnham, Keppel, James, the Olmsteds, Lewis, Whitten, Howard, Unwin, Wilgus, Mumford, Adams, McAneny, Stein, Perkins, Walsh, the indefatigable Moses, and a hundred others of the noble guild of city planners, up to and including the work of the Regional Plan of New York and Its Environs, the Port of New York Authority, the New York Department of Parks and the New York City Planning Commission. He will wish to know how the city changes, the extent and character of its physical property, and something about the nature and complexity of its functions. But he will understand that plant and function are never more than indicators of a series of cultural choices and directions. Finally, he will be made aware of these choices and directions at their source, in the character, convictions and behavior of New Yorkers themselves: the faces, vivid or distracted, washed in neon light the color of mercurochrome, faces of men and women who work and eat and make love in catacombs under the enormous pylons of their city.

The traveler approaches in bare winter or rainy autumn, in keen seaboard spring or the dog days. He drives a faded sedan with a child slung in a hammock cradle in the rear, or he takes the hot bouillon and crackers of the great airlines. He walks the glassed-in promenade deck of the *Normandie* or the open boat deck of the *Nieuw Amsterdam;* or he lounges in the doorway of the *Manhattan's* radio room. In the streamlined club cars of the Yankee Clipper, the Twentieth Century, the Royal Blue, the Broadway Limited, or in the day coaches of slower trains, he turns the pages of a national or trade journal published in New York—*Women's Wear, Collier's, Life, Variety, Printers' Ink*—and watches the conglomerate backyards of Albany-Bridgeport-Trenton slide past the window. Painted with slipstream whorls, his blunt-nosed bus trundles out of the lunch stop and bores Manhattan-ward again, the whipcord back of the driver twisted as he pulls out and around a great dark pantechnicon truck with small lamps at its clearance points.

The traveler is a fuel company executive returning from a trip through the West, a copy of *Saward's Coal Annual* wedged into the briefcase beside him; an elementary school principal from Lewiston, bound for special courses at Barnard College; a Cleveland printer out of a job, a men's wear buyer from Jacksonville, a Brooklyn clergyman on his return trip from Rome, a Pittsburgh engineer coming back from a South American cruise, a San Francisco divorcee loosed in Reno and remarried to a Hollywood fashion designer commuting to New York. These make up a composite American as alive and definite as Chaucer's pilgrims or Whitman's cameradoes of democracy.

But perhaps only the industrial engineer begins to comprehend the technical changes in transportation between Chaucer's time—or even Whitman's—and the 1930's. Unless the traveler drives his own car, he must resign himself to the helmsmen of the neotechnic age—locomotive engineers, ships' quartermasters, bus drivers, transport pilots—whose responsibilities have been reapportioned into a vast complex of schedules, maintenance men, radio directional and telephone signals, cartographers, traffic lights, instrument panels and routine instructions, all centered on New York.

The helmsmen themselves are aware of their place in this network. The locomotive engineer knows it, intent on the block signals aimed at and swallowed by the rush of his train, a full minute to be made up between Poughkeepsie and Grand Central Terminal. The bus driver gunning his coach in heavy traffic over US1 from New England, or the Albany Post Road, or the Sunrise Highway, or the loop over the Pulaski Skyway into the Jersey City mouth of the Holland Tunnel feels responsibility like a small knot between his shoulder blades: the need for quick and certain decisions, the judgment of space and time and the intent of drivers and a small boy heedless on a bicycle.

The pilot of Flight 16 eastbound, crossing the Alleghenies in cloud at 7,000 feet, knows it well. When his tally of instruments—altimeter, clock, air speed, bank and turn, artificial horizon—indicates that he has passed the outer marker, he reports by radio to the company dispatcher at Newark Metropolitan Airport, chief terminus for the New York district. Passengers rub at the bleared windows. But as he nears the inner marker at Martin's Creek, the mist begins to fade apart into soft translucent islands drenched with sun and the voice from the Newark radio control tower comes in with the tone of a man speaking clearly in the same room: "WREE to Western Trip 16, Pilot Johnson. Stuff breaking up fast. You are cleared at 3,000 feet to the range station. You're Number Two airplane."

In the chart-room of a transatlantic liner inbound from Cherbourg to New York, 200 miles off Fire Island in a pea-soup fog, the blasts of the automatic ship's siren at intervals of one minute vibrate amongst the polished metal or enameled instruments: the chronometers, telephone, radio compass, loudspeaker, mercury and aneroid barometers, gyro course-indicator and other devices of the new scientific navigation. The senior watch officer checks his chronometers against time signals from Nauen, Arlington and the Eiffel Tower. A seaman at the radio directional compass slowly swivels the frame of his antenna ring until the note of the Fire Island radio beacon—plangent as a tuning fork, but crisper—is loudest in his headphones. Making a cross-check, the junior watch officer sets down fathometer depth readings on a length of tracing paper in such a way that it can be laid over the chart for comparison with course and position marks.

Immobile in the dark wheelhouse, the helmsman concentrates on the lighted compass before him. No longer must he watch for the telltale flutter of the leech, or nurse his ship in weather seas. In the 330 years between Henry Hudson's *Half Moon,* steered into the future New York Harbor with a wheel-and-whipstaff rig that resembled a four-armed capstan with elongated bars, and the great express ships of the 1930's, already obsolescent in view of operating costs, irreducible vibration and other factors, the helmsman's responsibilities have been shorn away by engineers and technicians. The automatic steering device, or "Iron Mike," has even in part replaced him.

These new helmsmen of land and sea and air are the creatures of demanding time, their senses extended in the antennules of a hundred instruments. So they must necessarily regard the city a little as the gunnery officer does his target; but they too feel its magnetism. It comes to the traveler a great way off, like the intimation of any other dense human engagement. The expectant nerves contract, the mind is sensitized in advance. A familiar visitor, a New Yorker, waits for the sense of the city's resumed envelopment; but the bus passenger coming down over the Boston Post Road from New England watches traffic slow and thicken as the environs towns become larger, draw together, give off the effect of a brisker life. There is a moment in which he asks himself: "Are we in the city yet? Is this New York?" The visitor by rail, if he approaches from the south, may get hardly a glimpse of the towers before he tunnels under the river and coasts to a stop along the platform at Pennsylvania Station. Coming in from the north, he cannot help but be struck by the infinite pueblo of the Bronx.

But to the traveler by air, especially from the north or east, the city appears with the instancy of revelation: the slowly crinkling samite of its rivers and New York Harbor vaporous beyond, the Bronx splayed out and interwoven with the tight dark Hudson Valley foliage, Brooklyn and Queens and Staten Island dispersed in their enormous encampments about the narrow seaward-thrusting rock of Manhattan. Seen thus from above, the pattern of the island suggests a weirdly shaped printer's form. It is as if the lead rules had been picked out for avenues between the solid lines of type which are buildings. The skyscrapers—those characters too pointed to be equalized by the wooden mallet of the makeup man—prickle up along the lower rim of Central Park, through the midtown section, and most densely at the foot of the island.

These last are what the homebound traveler by water sees as his vessel comes through the Narrows into the Lower Bay, a journey and journey's end which has always somehow the quality of a public triumph. There stand the inconceivable spires of Manhattan—composed, repeating the upthrust torch of Liberty, at first almost without the sense of great weight, the distraction of archaic and heterogeneous detail. The forms of "gypsum crystals," a giant's cromlech, a mass of stalagmites, "the Cathedrals and Great White Thrones of the National Parks," an Arizona mesa, a "ship of living stone," a petrified forest, "an irregular tableland intersected by shadowy cañons," a mastodon herd, "a pin-cushion," the Henry Mountains in Utah, "a vertical aggregation," dividends in the sky: such metaphors reflect its diversity of association. As Melville's *Redburn* indicates, the term *skyscraper* itself—a noun full in the homely tradition of the American vernacular—was once synonymous with *moon-sail* and *cloud-raker* as the name for a ship's topmost kites.

Le Corbusier, celebrated French architect in the International style, refers to this massed upthrust as "the winning of a game: proclamation by skyscraper." And in the third book of Jules Romains' *Psyché*, Pierre Febvre thinks of it as "a rivalry of tumefactions constructed in haste on the rock of Manhattan, a typical fragment of American unreality." Taken together, both images—a sense of the grandiose subjective exemplified in architectural terms, and the perhaps consequent suggestion of imperfectly realized forms—help to clarify a profound intimation of the familiar experienced by many travelers, even those who have no acquaintance with the city. In one of the Regional Plan volumes, this intimation is dramatized, simply enough, by photographs on facing pages: one of lower Manhattan, the other of Mont-Saint-Michel, the ancient fortress rock of France, a cluster of towers about which the tides swirl like level avalanches.

The visual analogy is striking, but it does not end there. The image of the medieval castle-town has gone deep into the consciousness of western man. Preserved in masonry at Mont-Saint-Michel and Carcassonne, stylized in the perspectives of a hundred medieval and Renaissance painters, translated into fantasy in the fairy tales of Andersen and Perrault and the towers of Cloud Cuckoo Land, popularized in the colors of Dulac and Rackham and Parrish and the mass-production lampshade, it reappears in the apparition of lower Manhattan evoked by the new technology: the medieval image of power, the infantile or schizoid fantasy of withdrawal, the supreme image of escape to the inaccessible.

THE CONCEPT OF THE CITY

Historically, as Robert L. Duffus points out in *Mastering a Metropolis,* cities "have tended to grow up *around* something—a fortification, a temple, a market-place, a landing-place." In other words, the selection of site and arrangement have usually been determined by a choice of social function, a definite cultural emphasis. Sometimes it was relatively accidental. On the principle that travelers may be customers, a market town grew up at a crossroads. The walled towns of the Middle Ages, usually grouped about a castle for efficient defense, retained to some extent the lines of a military camp; but the exigencies of space within the walls made for a certain homogeneous and charming irregularity. The radial plans of the Renaissance, of which Karlsruhe is the most striking example, probably developed from the Greek and Roman cities clustered around a central temple or forum, although they retained some of the medieval irregularities.

Parallel with the unplanned growth of cities, there has always been a tradition of planned cities, conceived either as Utopias—by Plato in his *Republic,* More in his *Utopia,* Campanella in his *City of the Sun,* Bellamy in his *Looking Backward,* Samuel Butler in his *Erewhon,* to name only a few—or by architects and city planners for actual realization in stone and mortar. The geometrical design for Alexandria, and Wren's project for the rebuilding of London after the great fire were examples of this kind. Notable among them was the plan for Washington. Challenged by the unexpectedly possible, Jefferson studied the city patterns of Europe and with Washington and L'Enfant evolved the American capital city.

But it is significant that in general the tradition of abstract design, surviving through the Renaissance, through Karlsruhe and Palladio and Wren into the era of L'Enfant's Washington and Haussmann's renovation of Paris, is basically eclectic, corresponding almost exactly to the anachronistic revivals of the classic orders or the Gothic in architecture. But the criticism is not merely negative; it implies a basic disregard of the primacy of cultural function, of the possible and fruitful coördination between plant and function and environment in a new order of the city.

In any case, for good or ill, planned cities did not by any means represent the dominant mode in urban evolution. If there was one, it can only be called agglomeration; the gathering of flies around a stain of honey. More often than not, that honey was commerce, additionally sweetened by the perquisites of a capital city. Philip II, for example, deliberately built up the municipal strength of Paris as an offset to the challenge of the nobles, thus contributing to the new nationalism and the upswing of the merchant classes. Tudor London, clamorous with trades and spiky with the masts of ships, added central cells of industry to the commercial swarming of the city. After the great fires of the next century, Wren suggested that wherever possible industries should be relocated on the outer margins of the city—a recommendation seconded by Walter Curt Behrendt and the New York Regional Plan in the 1930's.

The advent of what Sir Patrick Geddes called the paleotechnic period, early in the 19th century, with its criteria of absolute utilitarianism, gradually created the inhuman ratholes of London and Glasgow and Birmingham and New York and Berlin—that "home city of the rent barracks." Dickens described a composite of industrial cities as Coketown. "It had a black canal in it, and a river that ran purple with ill-smelling dye;" and "the piston of the steam engine worked monotonously up and down, like the head of an elephant in a state of melancholy madness. It contained several large streets all very like one another, inhabited by people exactly like one another, who all went in and out at the same hours, with the same sound upon the same pavements to do the same work, and to whom every day was the same as yesterday and tomorrow, and every year the counterpart of the last and the next."

New York City, of all the great communities in the modern world, has been most acted upon by the agencies incident to the 19th century revolution in industry and techniques, most subject to the devastating consequences of 19th century *laissez faire* and the tensions of excessively rapid growth, most influenced by the multiplication and hypertrophy of functions, most compromised by a street plan which united some of the inconvenient features of the rigidly classical and the narrowly utilitarian, most unstable in the number and distribution of its population, most opportunistic in land uses, most anarchic in the character of its building, and most dynamic in the pulse and variety of its living ways.

In a history of some 330 years, of which hardly more than a century has been taken up with major growth, New York has somehow condensed and accommodated the stresses of 20 centuries in the evolution of Rome or

Paris. Such drastic foreshortening exacted a price and developed an opportunity. The price was paid and is being paid in the primary conception of the city as merely an accumulation: the largest size, the greatest number (even of units of quality), and the highest speed. It was paid in the ruthlessness—and the complementary meliorism that all this would somehow right itself—of what may be called the utilitarian imperative, which cut off waterside areas from public use, gobbled up available park sites, covered blocks with sunless tenements and no less sunless apartment houses, made night and day indistinguishable under the overhanging scarps of lower Manhattan, fostered duplication and speculation and high taxes in municipal government, and centered a terrific volume of traffic in a few sectors already overburdened by subway and elevated concentration, the lack of through highways and the density of building.

These became commonplaces, even rules of thumb. At a certain point, the practical effect was that a man could not go to the theater or visit a friend without a wholly disproportionate expenditure of time, energy, ingenuity and money. But in the deepest sense—the sense, that is, in which these processes were at once an expression and reflection of the New Yorker's cultural attitude toward his city—such factors tended to become psychological vested interests. The healthy dynamism of a developing metropolis was perpetuated as neurotic action for its own sake. The original necessity of enduring noise, dirt, conflict, confusion as symptoms of a transitional phase developed into a taste for the mindless intoxicant of sensation. Tall buildings convenient for intracommunication in such activities as finance became tall buildings for the sake of mere height and vainglory. In fine, the psychology of swift growth—its quick sense of the expedient, its prompt resource, its urgent energy, its prodigality in human waste, its impatience with deeper interrelationships and effects, byproducts or details—was carried over and intensified in a period which demanded consolidation, an assay of cultural attitudes and values, planning, a new concept of the city.

By 1938 the signs of this new attitude were already sharply manifest. Long before that, in 1931, Thomas Adams could write: "There is no city in the world that has a greater influence than New York. . . All over this continent it is imitated, even where it is said to be feared. Men say New York is a warning rather than an example, and then proceed to make it an example. Outside America, New York is America, and its skyscraper a symbol of the spirit of America. It is not only the largest city in the world, it is the greatest and most powerful city that is not a capital of a nation." There were jeremiads and panegyrics; this was a temperate statement of the fact.

All through the 1920's, New York had been not only the symbol of America but the daemonic symbol of the modern—the fortunate giant in his youth, the world city whose past weighed least heavily upon its future. Had not Paul Morand testified that the latest skyscraper was always the best? It was a city infallible in finance, torrential in pace, unlimited in resource, hard as infrangible diamonds, forever leaping upon the moment beyond. "You can get away with anything," said Ellen Thatcher in John Dos Passos' *Manhattan Transfer,* "if you do it quick enough." Speed—with its dividend, sensation—became the master formula in every human activity and technique: Wall Street, dancing, crime, the theater, construction, even death. "Don't get much time to sleep," said a Broadway soda clerk. "I have to sleep so fast I'm all tired out when I get up in the morning." This was rueful Eddington, the telescoping of time and space—a cliché of the period—in terms of the wear and tear on human metabolism. Photographers, draughtsmen, commentators all attempted to catch this loud moment or to translate it in terms of indefinite extension. An aseptic skyscraper city, an immense machine for living, was projected by such draughtsmen and writers as Hugh Ferriss, Sheldon Cheney, Raymond Hood and Norman Bel Geddes (of whom an anonymous satirist remarked in 1937 that he suffered from "an edifice complex").

In this period too New York had broken out full sail as the American capital of the arts and a world capital of major importance. This was in itself an extraordinary phenomenon. Other large, recently colonial cities —Melbourne, Rio de Janeiro, Toronto, even Mexico City—had shown no such versatile and autochthonous upsurge. It could be explained only in part by a reference to great concentration of wealth and commerce— as usual, a concentration in which artists had little share and against which, for the most part, they swung the shoulder of revolt. This cultural definition came out of the native genius of the city itself and was inseparably collateral with it. To a remarkable degree, the formulation and interpretation of that genius became the first task of the artist in New York.

Historians of another age may find the cultural rivalries of the Eastern seaboard cities in the middle of the 19th century as fruitful a source of social interpretation as their contests in trade. Philadelphia had receded, Charleston and Baltimore settled into their graceful mold. But Boston, as Van Wyck Brooks has superbly recreated it in *The Flowering of New England,* produced a culture articulated in all its parts. It is necessary to indicate more closely here the relative scale of that culture. Its perfect symbol, perhaps, was the figure of Hawthorne confronting the Marble Faun. Its faithfulness to a special Anglo-American tradition at once defined its limits and committed it to contest with the assimilative turbulence of its more democratic neighbor to the southward. Even in Emerson, perhaps, there was something of the merely benign clergyman; even in Thoreau, a little of the truant schoolboy decorating his metaphorical hut at Walden with the knickknacks of Athens and Rome. And even in Emily Dickinson's triumph of the microcosmic, it was possible to feel the sedate child who withdraws from the world to thread in quietude the quicksilver necklaces of the imagination. The neat coherence of parts, the good scholars competing for the prizes of the intelligence, the inflexibility of ethical referrents, the absence of that excess which is also the evidence of supreme vitality, the frugality and unanimity of pattern—all these were the sedate lamplight of a provincial culture, a culture comparable to that of Ghent in the late 14th century or 18th century Dublin and Stockholm.

But there were giants to the southward—men who had consorted with the buffalo and leviathan, who were privy to enormous griefs and ecstasies, who had faced the tremendous gales of the world in their most disintegrative onslaught. These men—Whitman and Melville—were of another breed, another stature; and they proclaimed themselves men of Manhattan. They came of the same Dutch-English stock, bred by that Empire State through which the commerce of the nation had begun to pour. *Moby Dick* appeared in 1851, *Leaves of Grass* in 1855. Both books were shunned or excoriated. Then and later, the culture of New York resembled the tumultuous cross-rips of Hell Gate. Museums, opera, the theater, libraries, lecture halls, schools, the superb education of street and waterfront: these were lavishly available, and Whitman in particular made good use of them. But the dominant tenor of the city was savage in its commercial excesses, ravenous in land use (though the salvaging of Central Park began a few years before the Civil War) and brutal in its disregard for health, amenities, the elementary kindness of life. The deeper significance of such personalities as Whitman and Melville is that they were archetypes of the city's character-to-be. Their decisive feeling for the supreme importance, the frequent nobility of the common man, their immersion by choice in his hopes and occupations—these were as foreign to the men of Boston, with their uneasy self-awareness in the role of scholar-gentlemen, as they would have been to that earlier New Yorker, the James Fenimore Cooper who wrote *The American Democrat*.

"He who touches the soil of Manhattan and the pavement of New York," said Lewis Mumford, "touches, whether he knows it or not, Walt Whitman." Certainly it was Whitman who conceived the city as an image of the democratic process—an historic reversal, it may be noted, of Thomas Jefferson's primary design. The city spoke out of Whitman's fiber: out of the broadest and most intimate lines of *A Broadway Pageant* and *Crossing Brooklyn Bridge,* out of

> Walt Whitman, a kosmos, of Manhattan the son,
> Turbulent, flashy, sensual, eating, drinking
>   and breeding,

or out of

> . . . submit to no models
>   but your own O city!

But in *Democratic Vistas* he faced all the implications of his image: splendor in the amplitude and onrush, "the sparkling sea-tides" and "masses of gay color" which were New York, but confession that to the cold eye appeared "pervading flippancy and vulgarity, low cunning, infidelity" and the rest, even to a degree beyond the average of mankind. But there were poets to be called up, poets to make "a literature underlying life;" to fertilize it, to create again and again the corrective vision of the city in an order more nobly human than itself. Whitman said it and said it plain:

> A great city is that which has the greatest men and women.

Did he not help to make good his own words?

But in its essence, Whitman's concept of New York as a symbol of the democratic maelstrom was a neo-romantic one. It rejoiced in the splendor of the fact, hewed close to it, made it Homeric. But was it not, even in that society of transitional latitude, precisely a begging of the question as to *what* means were to be applied to the creation of *what* forms for *what* ends—ends, that is, which might be translated concretely from the abstract *liberty, equality, fraternity, plenty?* Affirmation of greatness to nurture greatness, exultation in diversity for the use and promise of diversity, acceptance of barbarous poverty and wrong in the name of a more humane future, faith in the destiny of the free man intermingling freely with his fellows: these demanded a confident and practical vision of the city as a whole—a vision broader than Campanella's, as instrumental as the machine lathe—formulated and canalized in terms of New York's own native function and genius.

On the contrary, Whitman's noble disorder, with its hospitality to everything human, tended to emphasize precisely those impulses toward unoriented mass, energy, diversity which came to their anarchic ultimate at the end of the 1920's. It was Whitman's dynamic, with its dramatization of the common impulse, that prevailed in the evolving folkways of New York. Even in 1937, the city was most often presented in terms of speed, energy, quantity rather than as a correlative for human use and aspiration. Nor is it enough to point out, as Marie Swabey does in *Theory of the*

Democratic State, that the natural criteria of democracy are predominantly quantitative. The confusion inheres in the fact that big numbers have so often been used as if they were equivalent to definitions of quality— as if a tremendous number of housing units, even slum dwellings, some-how indicated a corresponding total of human happiness.

Side by side with the most devouring greed, it has almost always been possible to find a superb generosity of life in New York—even, in the late 1930's, signs of a nascent change of heart. If the vainglory of power be-gan to give way a little to the order of a genuine and mature society, there were men to be thanked for it—too many names for this place. These were the men who created and recreated values; who translated those values, under one form or another, into instruments of civic welfare; and who implemented the common aspiration. Together with that aspiration, the sum of their vision and accomplishments determined the living concept of New York: that basic unity, that prerequisite and final virtue of per-sons, which must be vital to the coherence of any human organization.

There were engineers—the Roeblings of Brooklyn Bridge, Clifford M. Holland of the Holland Tunnel, Nelson P. Lewis of the Board of Esti-mate and Apportionment, Singstad and Amman of the Port Authority— whose probity blossomed in highways and tunnels, or in the piers and cables of a bridge: such a bridge as Hart Crane had envisaged, a figure of the flight of time and the passage of mankind across the gulf. Stubborn bands and lone fighters—John Peter Zenger of the New York *Weekly Journal,* whose trial in 1735 vindicated free expression in the press; Nast and Parkhurst and the Lexow Committee; Seabury and the City Affairs Committee of the 1920's—these and a hundred others struck for the in-tegrity of a free commonwealth. Scientists and research technicians, who worked with sludge digestion tanks and chlorination and polyphase alter-nators, created a fresh environment available to the social imagination of an ampler culture. A John Dewey reground the tools of the mind; a Thor-stein Veblen challenged the directions of American civilization, especially those directions which New York had long controlled.

"A very little boy stood upon a heap of gravel for the honor of Rum Alley" in Stephen Crane's exact nightmare of the slums; John Dos Pas-sos' Ellen Thatcher murmured: "I think that this city is full of people wanting inconceivable things;" and Thomas Wolfe's Eugene Gant cried: "Proud, cruel, everchanging and ephemeral city, to whom we came once when our hearts were high . . ." These were novelists answerable to the truth of the living. There were men who created vivid museums, set up liberal schools, fought to establish capable hospitals. Even politicians who hoped for nothing but their own advantage sometimes inadvertently contributed to the civic total, as Tweed did in setting out the pleasant boulevard along Broadway north of Sixty-Fifth Street, later routed by the subway.

Painters and photographers—Albert Ryder and Thomas Eakins, the ancestors; Steiglitz and Paul Strand and Berenice Abbott; the genre work of Sloan, Glenn Coleman, Reginald Marsh, Lawson, Glackens, Kenneth Hayes Miller; John Marin's vision of the skyscrapers in a vibrating rondure of forms; Demuth's *My Egypt* and Billings' and Sheeler's stylization of industrial masses—these and others literally created the human face of the city for the endowment of its citizens. The work of Hardenbergh and R. H. Hunt, among the older men, and of McKim and Stanford White in the 1890's; Goodhue's churches and Snyder's neo-Gothic schools; the loft buildings of Ely Jacques Kahn; the skyscraper designs of Harvey Wiley Corbett and Raymond Hood; the model apartment groups laid out by Clarence Stein and Henry Wright, which helped to anticipate the Federal Government's plans for housing developments in the 1930's: these were among the factors that made New York architecture the most exciting and various, if not always the soundest, in the world. Too, Whitman had his poets—not often prophets, but men and women who struck a dark accusatory music from the city's agonism: Edna St. Vincent Millay, Hart Crane, Louise Bogan, Archibald MacLeish, Horace Gregory.

Forecast by such lively wine salesmen of the arts as James Huneker, a more thorough school of cultural commentators whose origins were mainly literary set out in the early 1920's to reexamine the pattern of New York as a prefiguration of the new America. Randolph Bourne's voice, and such books as Harold Stearns' *Civilization in the United States,* Waldo Frank's *Our America,* Paul Rosenfeld's *Port of New York,* Van Wyck Brooks' *America's Coming of Age* and William Carlos Williams' *In the American Grain* managed to make themselves heard above the noise of traffic. Lewis Mumford's broad and precise imagination, the warmth and vitality of his interpenetrating sense of the whole distinguished half a dozen volumes that culminated in the definitive *Technics and Civilization* and *The Culture of Cities.* There were, finally, the innumerable common heroes in the patient and immense body of the city: the workers in laboratories and hospitals who died of X-ray burns or a finger pricked at an autopsy; the riveter tumbled from his hawk's perch, falling voiceless and alone; orange-helmeted sandhogs coughing with silicosis or twisted with the bends; and the men who could work no more, the unremembered ones Stephen Crane found in the city's scratch houses in *An Experiment in Misery,* whose successors were still there when Joseph Mitchell published his sketch, *A Cold Night Downtown,* in 1938.

Together these engineers and artists and milk-wagon drivers forged a concept of the city, a unity for the city, out of the collective character and history of its inhabitants, just as the individuality of Paris was defined by Villon's reckless verses, the gardens of Marie Antoinette, Julian the Apostate's addresses to "my dear Lutetia," Victor Hugo, the engineer Eiffel, Marie Curie's dedication and Jules Romains' great antiphonal hymn. This unity, in fact, is at the root of the caricature visualized by outsiders as "a real New Yorker"—a certain large and shrewd liberality of thought and behavior, easy wit, compulsive energy, a liking for risk and the new, curiosity, restlessness.

There are those who consider that it is impossible to find any unity in the chaotic pattern of New York; or that, romantically enough, the emergence of unity would cancel its major charm. But the uneconomic and antisocial nature of many of the city's living ways demand a clear reorientation. The potential unity necessary to such reorientation already exists in the New Yorker's own concept of his city. In this shared consciousness —generated by a look, a grin, an anecdote as cabalistic to outsiders as the shop talk of mathematicians—the complex of the metropolis finds its organizing principle, deeper than civic pride and more basic than the domination of mass or power. To the degree that this principle, this wise geolatry, can be instrumented by the forms and processes appropriate to it, New York will emerge in greatness from the paradox of its confusions.

FEDERAL THEATRE PLAYS
Triple-A Plowed Under (Excerpts)

SCENE ELEVEN
(Triple-A Enacted)
CHARACTERS

VOICE OF LIVING NEWSPAPER

SECRETARY OF AGRICULTURE HENRY A. WALLACE

VOICE OF LIVING NEWSPAPER (*over* LOUDSPEAKER): Washington, May 12, 1933 —the AAA becomes the law of the land. It is hereby declared to be the policy of Congress . . .[1]

[1] *Vital Speeches,* October 21, 1935.

(*Spotlight on* SECRETARY WALLACE.)

SECRETARY WALLACE (*picking up sentence*): . . . to increase the purchasing power of farmers. It is, by that token, farm relief, but also, by the same token, National Relief, for it is a well-known fact that millions of urban unemployed will have a better chance of going to work when farm purchasing power rises enough to buy the products of city factories. Let's help the farmer. . . . It is trying to subdue the habitual anarchy of a major American industry, and to establish organized control in the interest of not only the farmer but everybody else. . . . The bill gives the Secretary of Agriculture the power to . . .[1]

(*Lights fade on* WALLACE. *The projection of a map of the United States, showing acreage reduction, comes up on the scrim.*)

VOICE OVER LOUDSPEAKER (*staccato*): . . . Reduce acreage. The visible supply of wheat diminished from two hundred and twelve million bushels in 1932 to one hundred and twenty-four million bushels in 1934.[2]

(*The projection changes to a number of little pigs in front of a number of large pigs, labeled "1933 production," the smaller pigs labeled "1934 production."*)

VOICE OVER LOUDSPEAKER (*continuing*): To curtail production. Hog production was cut from sixty million in 1933 to thirty-seven million in 1935.[2] *Projection changes to a slide depicting two loaves of bread. One is labeled "1933—10¢," the other "1934—11¢."*)[3]

VOICE OVER LOUDSPEAKER (*continuing*): To levy a tax on processing of basic farm commodities. Wheat advanced in price from 32 cents a bushel in 1933 to 74 cents a bushel in 1934.[2]

Blackout

SCENE TWELVE

(*Shirt Scene*)

CHARACTERS

VOICE OF LIVING NEWSPAPER

FARM BUREAU REPRESENTATIVE

FARMER

SHIRT SALESMAN

VOICE OF LIVING NEWSPAPER (*over* LOUDSPEAKER): Triple-A pays four million dollars daily.[4]

---

[1] Radio Speech—Farm and Home Hour——WJZ—March 18, 1933.
[2] *World Almanac,* 1936, pp. 352, 356, 365; *Ibid.,* 1934, p. 347.
[3] Ward Baking Company, New York, N. Y.
[4] *New York Times,* September 17, 1934.

(*Three spots directly overhead, stage right, center and stage left, light up as portals open.* FARMER *walks into spot right where he meets* FARM BUREAU REPRESENTATIVE.)

FARM BUREAU REPRESENTATIVE [1] : Check for reducing wheat acreage.

FARMER: Thanks, I need it. (FARM BUREAU REPRESENTATIVE *exits right,* FARMER *turns front in area of center spot.* SALESMAN *enters left, and* FARMER *and* SALESMAN *meet in area spot left. As* FARM BUREAU REPRESENTATIVE *and* FARMER *vacate spot right, that spot blacks; as* FARMER *vacates spot center, that spot blacks. The entire scene is played crisply, with no attempt at realism.*) Got a shirt?

SALESMAN: You bet.

FARMER: How much?

SALESMAN: One dollar.[2]

FARMER: It was seventy-five cents.

SALESMAN: Cotton's up—production's curtailed—there's a processing tax.

FARMER: What's it mean?

SALESMAN: You get check for planting no wheat—planter gets check for planting no cotton—planter pays more for bread of your wheat—you pay more for shirt of his cotton—that's where it comes from.

FARMER: Oh, well—when it was cheap I didn't have any money. I'll take it.

Blackout

SCENE THIRTEEN
(*Wheat Pit*)

CHARACTERS

VOICE OF LIVING NEWSPAPER
FOUR TELEPHONE MEN
SEVERAL RUNNERS
MAN AT BLACKBOARD
TWO GROUPS OF TRADERS—15 RIGHT, 15 LEFT

VOICE OF LIVING NEWSPAPER (*over* LOUDSPEAKER): Chicago, 1934.

(*The scene is a stylized representation of the Chicago Wheat Pit. Two ramps, their large ends set upstage, are joined by two four-foot platforms. Behind the platforms, elevated, is a blackboard; so that they can be seen over the small ends of the ramps, are open telephone booths. A large clock*

---

[1] Fictional character.
[2] Letter from William V. Lawson, Cotton and Textile Institute, 320 Broadway, New York, N. Y.

is next to the blackboard, right. Instead of numerals it depicts the months of the year. It has only one hand. This hand revolves slowly through the playing of the scene. Left of the blackboard is a large thermometer—to indicate increasing heat. The thermometer does not move in this scene.

There is a MAN *at each of the four telephones, and several* RUNNERS *between them and the men in the Pit. The Wheat Pit is filled with 30* TRADERS. *These* TRADERS *are divided into groups, left and right, one buying and one selling. At rise there is a din of voices. Immediately after rise a loud gong rings. The two* GROUPS OF TRADERS *speak in unison; those buying speak first, and those selling afterward. Their movements also are in unison—a movement which should be divided on a count of two beats to a measure or four beats to a measure, building tempo and volume of scene consistently until end.*

Right after gong is sounded, VOICE OVER LOUDSPEAKER *speaks.*)

VOICE: Triple-A enacted.

(*This same* VOICE *speaks throughout the scene, with a slightly increasing tempo. One* MAN *at blackboard continues his motions of writing through the scene.*)

TRADERS LEFT: Buying 500 May at 101.[1]

TRADERS RIGHT: Selling 500 May at a quarter.

TRADERS LEFT: Buying 500 May at 101.

TRADERS RIGHT: Selling at a quarter.

TRADERS LEFT: One.

VOICE OVER LOUDSPEAKER: Fair and warmer.[2]

TRADERS LEFT: Selling at one-eighth.

TRADERS RIGHT: A half.

LOUDSPEAKER (*crisply*): Fair and warmer.

Blackout

SCENE FOURTEEN [3]

(*Counter Restaurant*)

CHARACTERS

COUNTERMAN

CUSTOMER

(*As portals close on Wheat Pit, trucks move in right with counter.* COUNTERMAN *stands right of counter, appropriately dressed,* CUSTOMER

---

[1] *Journal of Commerce*, December 8 and 22, 1934.
[2] *New York Times*, August 12, 1934. Weather Bureau reports 1934 thus far driest and hottest on record.
[3] Creative.

left of counter. Light from overhead. Bowl and ladle on counter. CUS-
TOMER *very shabbily dressed, with hat over his eyes.)*

COUNTERMAN: Whadd'ya want?

CUSTOMER: A bowl o' oatmeal.

COUNTERMAN: Got three cents?

CUSTOMER: Got two cents.

COUNTERMAN: Not a chance. Got to have three cents.

CUSTOMER: It was two cents yesterday.

COUNTERMAN: Sorry, pal, prices went up today.

Blackout

SCENE FIFTEEN

(*Park Avenue Restaurant*)

CHARACTERS

MAN IN EVENING CLOTHES
WOMAN IN EVENING CLOTHES
WAITER

(Front light on Restaurant. Background suggests a modern room. A COUPLE *in evening clothes are seated at table.* WAITER *is taking the order. They are drinking cocktails.)*

MAN: . . . Imported Beluga caviar. Broiled royal squab, grilled mushrooms and a bottle of Chateau Yquem, '26. That's all for now. (*Exit* WAITER.)

WOMAN: Mmmmmmmmmmmmm . . . celebrating?

MAN: Right.

WOMAN: (*lifts glass*): What to?

MAN: Wheat.

WOMAN: Wheat?

MAN: Wheat.

WOMAN: All right. . . . Here's to wheat. (*They drink.*) Long may it wave.

MAN: And keep going up.

WOMAN: (*after a short pause*): Tell me, are you affected by these new proc-
cessing taxes?

MAN: Uh-huh.

WOMAN: You seem pretty cheerful about it.

MAN: Why shouldn't I, it's the consumer who pays. (*As she looks at him inquiringly, he picks up roll.*) When I buy this roll I pay the processing tax.

WOMAN: I thought you paid it on wheat and hogs and things like that.

MAN: Look, this roll, not so long ago, was wheat waving in the fields of Kansas. Somewhere between the harvesting of that wheat and this roll there was a processing tax.... (*He stops.*)

WOMAN: Go on.

MAN: That's all ... and it's the man who eats it who pays it.

WOMAN (*also after a slight pause*): I'm afraid it's just a bit complicated— for me.

MAN: Oh, well, wheat's up and I've been saving a lot of it to unload ... So what will it be, a new car or a sable coat?

WOMAN: Mmmmmmmmm!

MAN: O.K. Both.

Blackout

SCENE SIXTEEN
(*Drought*)

CHARACTERS

VOICE OF LIVING NEWSPAPER

A FARMER

FIRST VOICE

SECOND VOICE

VOICE OF LIVING NEWSPAPER (*over* LOUDSPEAKER): Summer, 1934: Drought sears the Midwest, West Southwest.[1] (*Light up on tableau of a* FARMER *examining the soil; a sun-baked plain, stretching away to a burning horizon. From the* LOUDSPEAKER *two voices are heard, one crisp, sharp, staccato—the other sinister and foreboding. The* VOICES *are accompanied by a rhythmic musical procession that grows in intensity, and leaps to a climax of shrill despair.*)

FIRST VOICE (*over* LOUDSPEAKER): May first, Midwest weather report.

SECOND VOICE (*over* LOUDSPEAKER): Fair and warmer.

FIRST VOICE: May second, Midwest weather report.

SECOND VOICE: Fair and warmer.

FIRST VOICE: May third, Midwest weather report.

SECOND VOICE: Fair and warmer.

FIRST VOICE: May fourth, Midwest weather report.

SECOND VOICE: Fair and warmer. Fair and warmer. Fair and warmer. Fair and warmer. (*The* FARMER *who is examining the soil straightens up and slowly lets a handful of dry dust sift through his fingers.*)

FARMER: Dust!

Close Travelers

---

[1] *New York Times*, August 12, 1934.

SCENE TWENTY-THREE
(*Supreme Court ... AAA killed*)

CHARACTERS

VOICE OF LIVING NEWSPAPER
VOICE OVER LOUDSPEAKER
SUPREME COURT JUSTICE ROBERTS—figure in silhouette
SUPREME COURT JUSTICE STONE—figure in silhouette
SEVEN OTHER SUPREME COURT JUSTICES—figures in silhouette
DANIEL O. HASTINGS, SENATOR FROM DELAWARE—in silhouette
ALFRED E. SMITH—in silhouette
EARL BROWDER—in silhouette
THOMAS JEFFERSON—in silhouette
FIRST MAN
SECOND MAN
THIRD MAN
A WOMAN
FOURTH MAN
FIFTH MAN

VOICE OF LIVING NEWSPAPER (*over* LOUDSPEAKER): January 6, 1936 . . . Supreme Court invalidates AAA in Hoosac Mills case.[1]

VOICE (*also over* LOUDSPEAKER): The majority opinion—Justice Roberts. (*As travelers open from rear, projection of Constitution is thrown on glass curtain. Discovered in shadow against projection are* JUSTICE STONE, THREE OTHER JUSTICES, *then* JUSTICE ROBERTS, *and the* FOUR REMAINING JUSTICES, *right.* ROBERTS *rises to one-foot platform directly in front of him.* FIVE JUSTICES *who concurred in his opinion, turn in profile as he begins to speak.*)

JUSTICE ROBERTS: . . . Beyond cavil the sole objective of the legislation is to restore the purchasing price of agricultural products to a parity with that prevailing in an earlier day; to take money from the processor and bestow it on the farmers. The Constitution is the supreme law of the land, ordained and established by the people. All legislation must conform to the principles it lays down. The power to confer or withhold unlimited benefits is the power to coerce or destroy. This is coercion by economic pressure. The judgment is affirmed.[2]

(*He steps down;* JUSTICE STONE *steps up.*)

VOICE OVER LOUDSPEAKER: The minority opinion—Justice Stone.

---

[1] *New York Times,* January 7, 1936.
[2] *Ibid.*

(*The* FIVE JUSTICES *concurring with* JUSTICE ROBERTS *turn to full front. The* TWO *concurring with* STONE *turn in silhouette.*)

JUSTICE STONE: Courts are concerned with the power to enact statutes, not with their wisdom. The only check upon their own exercise of power is our own sense of self-restraint. For the removal of unwise laws from the statute books, appeal lies not to the courts, but to the ballot, and to the processes of democratic government. So may the judicial power be abused. "The power to tax is the power to destroy," but we do not for that reason doubt its existence. Courts are not the only agents of government which must be assumed to have the capacity to govern.[1]

(*As* JUSTICE STONE *steps down,* SENATOR HASTINGS *enters, right, steps on higher platform at back, throwing his shadow into a much larger projection than that of the* JUSTICES.)

SENATOR HASTINGS: This re-establishes Constitutional government. It gives back to the State the power they intended to reserve when they adopted the Constitution. The chances are it will improve the condition of the country, as did the decision of the NRA.[2]

(HASTINGS *steps down and exits left.* ALFRED E. SMITH *enters right, steps on platform vacated by* HASTINGS.)

ALFRED E. SMITH: We don't want the Congress of the United States singly or severally to tell the Supreme Court what to do. We don't want any administration that takes a shot at the Constitution in the dark, and tries to put something over in contradiction of it, upon any theory that there is going to be a great public power in favor of it, and it is possible that the United States Supreme Court may be intimidated into a friendly opinion with respect to it. But I found, all during my public life, that Almighty God built this country, and he did not give us that kind of a Supreme Court.[3]

(SMITH *steps down, and exits left.* BROWDER *enters right; steps on platform vacated by* SMITH.)

EARL BROWDER: The reactionaries seek to turn both "Americanism" and the Constitution into instruments of reaction, but neither of these things belongs to them. Nowhere does the Constitution grant the Supreme Court power over Congress, but it does make Congress the potential master of the Supreme Court.[4] I repeat, the Constitution of the United States does not give the Supreme Court the right to declare laws passed by Congress unconstitutional.[5]

---

[1] *Ibid.*
[2] *New York Times,* January 7, 1936.
[3] *Ibid.,* January 26, 1936.
[4] *Daily Worker,* February 13, 1936.
[5] *Ibid.,* January 11, 1936.

(BROWDER *steps down and exits left.* THOMAS JEFFERSON *enters right, steps on platform vacated by* BROWDER.)

THOMAS JEFFERSON: There must be an arbiter somewhere. True, there must. But does that prove it is either the Congress or the Supreme Court? The ultimate arbiter is the people of the Union, assembled by their deputies in convention at the call of Congress or two-thirds of the States.[1]

(*Travelers slowly close, with* JEFFERSON *remaining standing on platform, center.*)

VOICE OVER LOUDSPEAKER: Farmers voted, by more than 6 to 1, for continuance of Triple-A.[2] (MEN *start crossing stage in front of travelers, from right to left.*)

FIRST MAN: The AAA is dead.... (*Exits left.*)

SECOND MAN: No more allotment checks ... (*Exits left.*)

THIRD MAN: What the hell're we agoin' to do this winter? (*Exits left.*)

A WOMAN: How're we goin' t' get coal? (*Exits left.*)

FOURTH MAN: They say the people wrote the Constitution ... (*Exits left.*)

FIFTH MAN: Them people have been dead a long time ... (*Also exits.*)

Blackout

SCENE TWENTY-FOUR
(*The Big "Steal"*)

CHARACTERS

VOICE OF LIVING NEWSPAPER
HENRY A. WALLACE, SECRETARY OF AGRICULTURE

VOICE OF LIVING NEWSPAPER (*over* LOUDSPEAKER): January 21st, Buffalo, New York, Court refunds processing tax on order of Supreme Court.[3] (*Pause*) Secretary Wallace. (*Lights on* WALLACE *speaking into microphone.*)

SECRETARY WALLACE: ... It doesn't make sense. In the Hoosac Mills case the Supreme Court disapproved the idea that the Government could take money from one group for the benefit of another. Yet in turning over to the processors this $200,000,000 which came from all the people, we are seeing the most flagrant example of expropriation for the benefit of one small group. You will get some idea of its size when you contrast these refunds with the profits of the processors in their most prosperous years.

[1] Jefferson's letter to Mr. Johnson, June 12, 1823—in *Congressional Digest*, December, 1935.
[2] *World Almanac*, 1936, p. 167.
[3] *New York Times*, January 21, 1936.

Cotton mills reported profits of $30,000,000 in 1920. Their processing tax refunds amount to $51,000,000 in cotton. Flour mills reported profits of about $20,000,000 on their wheat flour business in 1929. Their processing tax refunds amount to $67,000,000. Packers' profits on their hog business in 1929 were in the neighborhood of $20,000,000. Their tax refunds were $51,000,000.

This return of the processing tax under order of the Supreme Court is probably the greatest legalized steal in American history! [1]

Blackout

SCENE TWENTY-FIVE
(Soil Conservation)

CHARACTERS

VOICE OF LIVING NEWSPAPER
CHESTER A. DAVIS—ADMINISTRATOR OF AAA
FIRST REPORTER
SECOND REPORTER
MESSENGER
CLERKS, STENOGRAPHERS, ETC.

VOICE OF LIVING NEWSPAPER *(over* LOUDSPEAKER*)*: Washington, January 1936. Administrator Chester A. Davis.[2]

(Light upon CHESTER A. DAVIS; *this scene is played around his desk.)*

CHESTER A. DAVIS: . . . and we've got to find something to take the place of AAA . . . something that is constitutional, and that the various farm blocs will approve . . .

FIRST REPORTER *(slowly after a slight pause)*: Why don't you use the Soil Conservation Act passed last year? Sure, that's the one.

SECOND REPORTER: It's as broad as Barnum and Bailey's tent and it covers all the ground the AAA did.

CHESTER A. DAVIS *(scornfully)*: Impossible. That Act was just a temporary stop-gap dealing with the WPA or something. It has no bearing on this case.

FIRST REPORTER: I tell you it has. I was looking it over this morning and . . .

SECOND REPORTER *(excitedly)*: I was with him. It authorized conservation, acquisition of land, compensation for farmers who . . .

CHESTER A. DAVIS *(holding up his hand)*: Wait a minute.

---

[1] *New York Times,* January 29, 1936.
[2] Scene based on article in *Time* magazine, January 27, 1936.

(*He presses a button on his desk and speaks into the telephone*) Send in some copies of the Soil Conservation Act. (*There is an expectant silence as they regard each other. The* REPORTERS *are excited,* DAVIS *smiles skeptically.* A MESSENGER *enters and deposits some sheaves of paper on his desk.* DAVIS *takes one, and the* REPORTERS *make a dash for the others. As* DAVIS *reads, the* OTHERS *read along with him. When they break into speech, it is in tones of intense excitement.* CHESTER DAVIS *speaks up, reading*) The Soil Conservation Act passed on mmm (*mumbling*) . . . and authorized the creation of mm-mm-mm-mm-mm-mm-mm. *One:*—Conservation measures including methods of cultivation, the growing of vegetation and changes in the use of land . . . *Two:*—Co-operation of agreements with any agency or any person . . . *Three:*—Acquisition of lands or rights or interest therein . . .

SECOND REPORTER (*excitedly*) : *Four:*—United States Government contributions to those who conserve the soil, *in form of money, services, materials, or otherwise.*

FIRST REPORTER : *Five:*—The hiring of employees.

SECOND REPORTER (*more excited than he was before*) : *Six:*—The expenditure of money for *anything,* from the purchasing of law books right down to passenger-carrying vehicles. (*The words rushing out*) And most important of all . . .

Seven:—the transfer to this work authorized of such functions, moneys, personnel, and the property of other agencies in the Department of Agriculture as the Secretary may see fit!

CHESTER A. DAVIS (*who has become progressively more excited though inarticulate to this point—jumping up*) : My God, there's the farm program for 1936. (*Tremendous excitement, elation, his fingers begin to punch the various buttons on his desk, sending out a general alarm. Simultaneously,* SECRETARIES, ASSISTANTS, STENOGRAPHERS, CLERKS *rush in. He continues, shouting*) : Get my Planning Board together. Get my assistant, get me Wallace. Get me Wilson, get me Stedman, get me . . . (SECRETARIES, CLERKS, MESSENGERS *cross and crisscross from right to left as* DAVIS *gives orders.*)

Blackout

SCENE TWENTY-SIX
(*Finale*)

CHARACTERS

VOICE OF LIVING NEWSPAPER

DELEGATION OF FARMERS CARRYING PLACARDS, REPRESENTING:

South Dakota
Minnesota
North Dakota
Wisconsin
Nebraska
Iowa
Kansas
Idaho
Indiana

SECRETARY WALLACE ⎫
MAN IN EVENING CLOTHES ⎬ from Scene Fifteen
WOMAN IN EVENING CLOTHES ⎭

WOMAN STRIKE LEADER ⎫ from Scene Twenty
OTHER WOMAN ⎭

FARMER ⎫
DEALER ⎬ from Scene Three
MANUFACTURER ⎮
WORKER ⎭

A GROUP OF UNEMPLOYED WORKERS

A GROUP OF UNEMPLOYED FARMERS

VOICE OF LIVING NEWSPAPER: Huron, South Dakota, February 20th, 1936 . . .
Farmers meet in Convention to draft program.[1]
(*Portals part just sufficiently to admit line of* FARMERS *carrying banners of the States—South Dakota, Minnesota, North Dakota, Wisconsin, Nebraska, Iowa, Kansas, Idaho, and Indiana. Half of the* FARMERS *enter from the left, and go right in front of portals, the other half enter from right and go left in front of portals. As last* FARMER *enters, portals close and straight line evenly spaced is formed in front of portals.*)
VOICE (*over* LOUDSPEAKER): Now, while the Soil Conservation Act is being written, is the time to make Congress and the Administration feel the pressure of the organized good sense of the American farmers. We believe that the following main points represent what the farmers must

---

[1] *Farmers' National Weekly*, February 14, 1936.

have in order to live decently, and at the same time protect the interests of the other sections of the working population.[1]

FARMER FROM SOUTH DAKOTA: Past commitments for the benefit payments under the old AAA must be paid in full.

FARMER FROM MINNESOTA: Whatever legislation may be passed should include cash payments to working farmers *at least equal* to the benefit payments under the AAA.

FARMER FROM NORTH DAKOTA (*one step forward*): Additional cash relief if the benefit payments are inadequate for a farm family to maintain a decent American standard of living.

FARMER FROM WISCONSIN: A decent American standard of living means cost of production prices.

FARMER FROM NEBRASKA: Cost of production prices mean far higher prices than today, whereby the farmer can at least pay his bills, operating costs and living expenses.

FARMER FROM IOWA: Increased production is needed by the nation today, the United States Department of Agriculture reports.

VOICE (*over* LOUDSPEAKER): To feed one hundred and twenty-five million people according to the best standards, forty million acres would have to be added to production.

FARMER FROM KANSAS: Therefore we oppose the policy of reduction . . .

FARMER FROM IDAHO: . . . but we do not oppose soil conservation except when used as a means of giving the Secretary of Agriculture power to force farmers to reduce production of good land.

FARMER FROM INDIANA: There are adequate resources available to meet the financial obligation incurred in this program. We suggest diversion to farm relief of a large part of the immense war appropriations, and increasing taxation on the wealth and income of the great financial and industrial interests of this country. *With special emphasis on the giant corporations which handle food productions!*

FARMER FROM SOUTH DAKOTA: The farmer has been sold down the river. (*Curtains part revealing full stage set.* MAN *and* WOMAN *in evening clothes are on highest level upstage left.* SECRETARY WALLACE *is on intermediate level upstage.* WOMEN *from the Meat Strike scene are left center in front of* WALLACE, *and* MAN *and* WOMAN *in evening clothes and* UNEMPLOYED *are on ramp, right, while* FARMERS *are on ramp, left.* FARMERS *previously in line across footlights move toward ramp left, a few to proscenium, down right.* FARMER, UNEMPLOYED, *etc., when speak-*

---

[1] *Farmers' National Weekly*, February 7, 1936.

ing, step a little forward so that they may be marked apart from crowd. All on stage turn heads toward speaker to indicate source of voice. The reaction is particularly marked in case of LOUDSPEAKER, *with all heads turned toward voice and holding that position until* LOUDSPEAKER *is finished. Other definite and marked reactions in this scene are gesture on "up, up" of the* FARMERS, *and the "down, down" of the* WOMEN; *the movement of* FARMERS *and* UNEMPLOYED *as the* FARMER *steps forward between the two groups, and the gestures drawing them together on the line, "then our problem is the same," gestures toward and against* MAN *and* WOMAN *in evening clothes and* SECRETARY WALLACE *on lines such as "no charity," "jobs," "jobs," "We need help, not words." There should be a balanced reaction away from crowd in fear, disgust, etc., on the part of the* MAN *and* WOMAN *in evening clothes.*)

SECRETARY WALLACE: In 1935 the AAA paid benefits of five hundred and eighty million dollars.[1]

A FARMER:[2] Soil Conservation benefits must at least be equal to the benefits of the Triple-A.

MAN IN EVENING CLOTHES: We must carry on with soil conservation.

VOICE (*over* LOUDSPEAKER): A dollar one, a dollar two . . .

ANOTHER FARMER (*taking step forward*): Soil Conservation is the Triple-A in false whiskers.

STILL ANOTHER FARMER: Farm prices must stay up.

WOMAN (*strike leader*): Food prices must go down.

ALL FARMERS (*in chorus*): UP! UP!

ALL WOMEN: DOWN! DOWN!

FARMER[3] (*from Scene Three*): I can't buy that auto.

DEALER (*from Scene Three*): I can't take that shipment.

MANUFACTURER (*from Scene Three*): I can't use you any more. (*Jumps to intermediate level.*)

WORKER (*from Scene Three*): I can't eat. (*Jumps to intermediate level.*)

VOICE (*over* LOUDSPEAKER): There is now piled up in the banks a huge savings reserve, and it lays a basis for a new speculative boom—(*All look toward* LOUDSPEAKER.)

MAN IN EVENING CLOTHES:[4] Back to normalcy.

VOICE (*over* LOUDSPEAKER): . . . which may result in a far more disastrous collapse than any heretofore experienced.

---

[1] *New York Times*, March 4, 1936.
[2] Creative and digest of news.
[3] Digest of article "A.A.A. Philosophy" by Rexford G. Tugwell, *Fortune Magazine*, January 1934.
[4] Remainder of scene is creative.

MAN IN EVENING CLOTHES (*to woman with him*): The rugged individualism of our forefathers will solve our problem.

A FARMER: Our problems are of the soil.

AN UNEMPLOYED WORKER: Ours of the belly.

MAN IN EVENING CLOTHES: Of course we need the farmer.

VOICE (*over* LOUDSPEAKER): A dollar three, a dollar four. . . .

SECRETARY WALLACE: We have come to the time when we have to learn to live one with another. We have no more cheap land, no great foreign markets, no one to impose upon.

A FARMER: We need help, not words!

SECRETARY WALLACE: We, down in Washington, do not believe we have the final answer to the problem—but we believe that, no matter who is in power a year hence, the kind of thing exemplified in the Soil Conservation Act will be going forward.

ONE FARMER: We need help!

ALL FARMERS: We need help!

ONE UNEMPLOYED: We need food!

ALL UNEMPLOYED: We need food!

ALL FARMERS: We need food!

ONE WOMAN: We need a decent standard of living.

ALL WOMEN: We need a decent standard of living.

ALL UNEMPLOYED: So do we. We need a decent standard of living.

ALL FARMERS: So do we.

A FARMER: Then all our problems are the same!

ALL UNEMPLOYED: Then all our problems are the same.

WOMAN IN EVENING CLOTHES: All must be helped, John.

FARMER, UNEMPLOYED AND WOMEN: No charity!

AN UNEMPLOYED: Jobs!

ALL UNEMPLOYED: Jobs!

A FARMER: Help.

AN UNEMPLOYED: We need a State that permits no man to go hungry.

MAN IN EVENING CLOTHES: Rugged individualism.

A WOMAN: No profiteering.

ALL UNEMPLOYED: Jobs.

ONE FARMER: We can't harvest.

ALL FARMERS: We can't harvest.

ONE WOMAN: We can't buy.

ALL WOMEN: We can't buy.

ONE UNEMPLOYED: We can't eat!

ALL UNEMPLOYED: We can't eat!

VOICE (*over* LOUDSPEAKER. *News flashes of events that have occurred that day—especially with reference to a Farmer-Labor Party. Below are three flashes that were used).*[1]

Local Farmer-Labor Party conventions in Connecticut, Massachusetts, Pennsylvania and South Dakota declared for a national Farmer-Labor Party. Two country conventions at Minneapolis passed a resolution demanding that the State Farmer-Labor Party meeting in convention at Minneapolis March 17th take the lead in a national Farmer-Labor Party.

Washington: Before a cheering audience at the St. Nicholas Arena last night, Congressman Ernest Lundeen, of Minnesota, said: "Labor unions and farmer organizations will soon become irresistible political powers."

Great Falls, Montana: The semi-annual conference of the Farmers' Holiday Association held here today had as its major decision the endorsement of a resolution for the formation of a Farmer-Labor Party. This resolution was proposed by Reid Robinson of the Butte Miners' Union.

FARMER: We *need* you.

CHORUS OF FARMERS: We *need* you.

LEADER OF UNEMPLOYED: We need *you.*

CHORUS OF UNEMPLOYED: We need *you.* (FARMERS *and* UNEMPLOYED *jump close together, arms extended. Light on them is intensified. Lights on* WALLACE *and* WOMAN *and* MAN *in evening clothes fade. Tableau of* FARMERS, WOMEN *and* UNEMPLOYED *hold.*)

Curtain

---

[1] Daily spot newspaper quotes used, quotes changing wtih the news.

PARE LORENTZ

The River

✳

THE BODY OF THE NATION

BUT *the basin of the Mississippi is the* BODY OF THE NATION. All the other parts are but members, important in themselves, yet more important in their relations to this. Exclusive of the Lake basin and of 300,000 square miles in Texas and New Mexico, which in many aspects form a part of it, this basin contains about 1,250,000 square miles. In extent it is the second great valley of the world, being exceeded only by that of the Amazon. The valley of the frozen Obi approaches it in extent; that of the La Plata comes next in space, and probably in habitable capacity, having about eight-ninths of its area; then comes that of the Yenisei, with about seven-ninths; the Lena, Amoor, Hoang-ho, Yang-tse-kiang, and Nile, five-ninths; the Ganges, less than one-half; the Indus, less than one-third; the Euphrates, one-fifth; the Rhine, one-fifteenth. It exceeds in extent the whole of Europe, exclusive of Russia, Norway, and Sweden. *It would contain Austria four times, Germany or Spain five times, France six times, the British Islands or Italy ten times.* Conceptions formed from the river-basins of Western Europe are rudely shocked when we consider the extent of the valley of the Mississippi; nor are those formed from the sterile basins of the great rivers of Siberia, the lofty plateaus of Central Asia, or the mighty sweep of the swampy Amazon more adequate. Latitude, elevation, and rainfall all combine to render every part of the Mississippi Valley capable of supporting a dense population. *As a dwelling-place for civilized man it is by far the first upon our globe.*—MARK TWAIN's *Life on the Mississippi.*

FROM as far East as New York,
　Down from the turkey ridges of the Alleghenies
Down from Minnesota, twenty-five hundred miles,
　The Mississippi River runs to the Gulf.
Carrying every drop of water that flows down two-thirds the continent,
Carrying every brook and rill, rivulet and creek,
Carrying all the rivers that run down two-thirds the continent,
The Mississippi runs to the Gulf of Mexico.
Down the Yellowstone, the Milk, the White and Cheyenne;
The Cannonball, the Musselshell, the James and the Sioux;
Down the Judith, the Grand, the Osage, and the Platte,
The Skunk, the Salt, the Black, and Minnesota;
Down the Rock, the Illinois, and the Kankakee
The Allegheny, the Monongahela, Kanawha, and Muskingum;
Down the Miami, the Wabash, the Licking and the Green
The Cumberland, the Kentucky, and the Tennessee;
Down the Ouchita, the Wichita, the Red, and Yazoo—

Permission of the author.

Down the Missouri three thousand miles from the Rockies;

Down the Ohio a thousand miles from the Alleghenies;

Down the Arkansas fifteen hundred miles from the Great Divide;

Down the Red, a thousand miles from Texas;

Down the great Valley, twenty-five hundred miles from Minnesota,
   Carrying every rivulet and brook, creek and rill,

Carrying all the rivers that run down two-thirds the continent—

The Mississippi runs to the Gulf.

New Orleans to Baton Rouge,

Baton Rouge to Natchez,

Natchez to Vicksburg,

Vicksburg to Memphis,

Memphis to Cairo—

We built a dyke a thousand miles long.

Men and mules, mules and mud;

Mules and mud a thousand miles up the Mississippi.

A century before we bought the great Western River, the Spanish and
   French built dykes to keep the Mississippi out of New Orleans at
   flood stage.

In forty years we continued the levee the entire length of the great alluvial
   Delta,

That mud plain that extends from the Gulf of Mexico clear to the mouth
   of the Ohio.

The ancient valley built up for centuries by the old river spilling her
   floods across the bottom of the continent—

A mud delta of forty thousand square miles.

Men and mules, mules and mud—

New Orleans to Baton Rouge,

Natchez to Vicksburg,

Memphis to Cairo—

A thousand miles up the river.

And we made cotton king!

We rolled a million bales down the river for Liverpool and Leeds . . .

1860: we rolled four million bales down the river;

Rolled them off Alabama,

Rolled them off Mississippi,

Rolled them off Louisiana,

Rolled them down the river!

We fought a war.

We fought a war and kept the west bank of the river free of slavery forever.

But we left the old South impoverished and stricken.

Doubly stricken, because, beyond the tragedy of war, already the frenzied
cotton cultivation of a quarter of a century had taken toll of the land.
We mined the soil for cotton until it would yield no more, and then moved
west.
We fought a war, but there was a double tragedy—the tragedy of land
twice impoverished.
Black spruce and Norway pine,
Douglas fir and Red cedar,
Scarlet oak and Shagbark hickory,
Hemlock and aspen—
There was lumber in the North.
The war impoverished the old South, the railroads killed the steamboats,
But there was lumber in the North.
Heads up!
Lumber on the upper river.
Heads up!
Lumber enough to cover all Europe.
Down from Minnesota and Wisconsin,
Down to St. Paul;
Down to St. Louis and St. Joe—
Lumber for the new continent of the West.
Lumber for the new mills.
There was lumber in the North and coal in the hills.
Iron and coal down the Monongahela.
Iron and coal down the Allegheny.
Iron and coal down the Ohio.
Down to Pittsburgh,
Down to Wheeling,
Iron and coal for the steel mills, for the railroads driving
West and South, for the new cities of the Great Valley—
We built new machinery and cleared new land in the West.
Ten million bales down to the Gulf—
Cotton for the spools of England and France.
Fifteen million bales down to the Gulf—
Cotton for the spools of Italy and Germany.
We built a hundred cities and a thousand towns:
St. Paul and Minneapolis,
Davenport and Keokuk,
Moline and Quincy,
Cincinnati and St. Louis,
Omaha and Kansas City . . .

Across to the Rockies and down from Minnesota,
Twenty-five hundred miles to New Orleans,
We built a new continent.
Black spruce and Norway pine,
Douglas fir and Red cedar,
Scarlet oak and Shagbark hickory.
We built a hundred cities and a thousand towns—
But at what a cost!
We cut the top off the Alleghenies and sent it down the river.
We cut the top off Minnesota and sent it down the river.
We cut the top off Wisconsin and sent it down the river.
We left the mountains and the hills slashed and burned,
And moved on.
The water comes downhill, spring and fall;
Down from the cut-over mountains,
Down from the plowed-off slopes,
Down every brook and rill, rivulet and creek,
Carrying every drop of water that flows down two-thirds the continent
1903 and 1907,
1913 and 1922,
1927,
1936,
1937!
Down from Pennsylvania and Ohio,
Kentucky and West Virginia,
Missouri and Illinois,
Down from North Carolina and Tennessee—
Down the Judith, the Grand, the Osage, and the Platte,
The Rock, the Salt, the Black and Minnesota,
Down the Monongahela, the Allegheny, Kanawha and Muskingum,
The Miami, the Wabash, the Licking and the Green,
Down the White, the Wolfe, and the Cache,
Down the Kaw and Kaskaskia, the Red and Yazoo,
Down the Cumberland, Kentucky and the Tennessee—
Down to the Mississippi.
New Orleans to Baton Rouge—
Baton Rouge to Vicksburg—
Vicksburg to Memphis—
Memphis to Cairo—
A thousand miles down the levee the long vigil starts.
Thirty-eight feet at Baton Rouge

River rising.
Helena: river rising.
Memphis: river rising.
Cairo: river rising.
A thousand miles to go,
A thousand miles of levee to hold—
Coastguard patrol needed at Paducah!
Coastguard patrol needed at Paducah!

200 boats—wanted at Hickman!
200 boats wanted at Hickman!

Levee patrol: men to Blytheville!
Levee patrol: men to Blytheville!

2000 men wanted at Cairo!
2000 men wanted at Cairo!

A hundred thousand men to fight the old river.
We sent armies down the river to help the engineers fight a battle on a
    two-thousand mile front:
The Army and the Navy,
The Coast Guard and the Marine Corps,
The CCC and the WPA,
The Red Cross and the Health Service.
They fought night and day to hold the old river off the valley.
Food and water needed at Louisville: 500 dead, 5000 ill;
Food and water needed at Cincinnati;
Food and water and shelter and clothing needed for 750,000 flood victims;
Food and medicine needed at Lawrenceburg;
35,000 homeless in Evansville;
Food and medicine needed in Aurora;
Food and medicine and shelter and clothing for 750,000 down in the
    valley.
Last time we held the levees,
But the old river claimed her valley.
She backed into Tennessee and Arkansas
And Missouri and Illinois.
She left stock drowned, houses torn loose,
Farms ruined.

1903 and 1907.
1913 and 1922

1927.
1936.
1937!

We built a hundred cities and a thousand towns—
But at what a cost!
Spring and fall the water comes down, and for years the old river has taken
    a toll from the Valley more terrible than ever she does in flood times.
Year in, year out, the water comes down
From a thousand hillsides, washing the top off the Valley.
For fifty years we dug for cotton and moved West when the land gave out.
For fifty years we plowed for corn, and moved on when the land gave out.
Corn and wheat; wheat and cotton—we planted and plowed with no
    thought for the future—
And four hundred million tons of top soil,
Four hundred million tons of our most valuable natural resource have been
    washed into the Gulf of Mexico every year.

And poor land makes poor people.
Poor people make poor land.
For a quarter of a century we have been forcing more and more farmers
    into tenancy.
Today forty per cent of all the farmers in the great Valley are tenants.
Ten per cent are share croppers,
Down on their knees in the valley,
A share of the crop their only security.
No home, no land of their own,
Aimless, footloose, and impoverished,
Unable to eat even from the land because their cash crop is their only
    livelihood.
Credit at the store is their only reserve.
And a generation growing up with no new land in the West—
No new continent to build.
A generation whose people knew King's Mountain, and Shiloh;
A generation whose people knew Fremont and Custer;
But a generation facing a life of dirt and poverty,
Disease and drudgery;
Growing up without proper food, medical care, or schooling,
"Ill-clad, ill-housed, and ill-fed"—
And in the greatest river valley in the world.

There is no such thing as an ideal river in Nature, but the Mississippi is
*   out of joint.*
Dust blowing in the West—floods raging in the East—
We have seen these problems growing to horrible extremes.
When first we found the great valley it was forty per cent forested.
Today, for every hundred acres of forests we found, we have ten left.
Today five per cent of the entire valley is ruined forever for agricultural
*   use!*
Twenty-five per cent of the topsoil has been shoved by the old river into the
*   Gulf of Mexico.*
Today two out of five farmers in the valley are tenant farmers—ten per
*   cent of them share croppers, living in a state of squalor unknown to the*
*   poorest peasant in Europe*
And we are forcing thirty thousand more into tenancy and cropping every
*   year.*
Flood control of the Mississippi means control in the great Delta that must
*   carry all the water brought down from two-thirds the continent*
And control of the Delta means control of the little rivers, the great arms
*   running down from the uplands. And the old river can be controlled.*
We had the power to take the valley apart—we have the power to put it
*   together again.*

In 1933 we started, down on the Tennessee River, when our Congress
created the Tennessee Valley Authority, commissioned to develop navigation, flood control, agriculture, and industry in the valley: a valley that carries more rainfall than any other in the country; the valley through which
the Tennessee used to roar down to Paducah in flood times with more
water than any other tributary of the Ohio.

First came the dams.

Up on the Clinch, at the head of the river, we built Norris Dam, a great
barrier to hold water in flood times and to release water down the river
for navigation in low water season.

Next came Wheeler, first in a series of great barriers that will transform
the old Tennessee into a link of fresh water pools locked and dammed,
regulated and controlled, down six hundred fifty miles to Paducah.

But you cannot plan for water unless you plan for land: for the cut-
over mountains—the eroded hills—the gullied fields that pour their waters
unchecked down to the river.

The CCC, working with the forest service and agricultural experts, have
started to put the worn fields and hillsides back together; black walnut and
pine for the worn-out fields, and the gullied hillsides; black walnut and

pine for new forest preserves, roots for the cut-over and burned-over hill-sides; roots to hold the water in the ground.

Soil conservation men have worked out crop systems with the farmers of the Valley—crops to conserve and enrich the topsoil.

Today a million acres of land in the Tennessee Valley are being tilled scientifically.

But you cannot plan for water and land unless you plan for people. Down in the Valley, the Farm Security Administration has built a model agricultural community. Living in homes they themselves built, paying for them on long-term rates, the homesteaders will have a chance to share in the wealth of the Valley.

More important, the Farm Security Administration has lent thousands of dollars to farmers in the Valley, farmers who were caught by years of depression and in need of only a stake to be self-sufficient.

But where there is water there is power.

Where there's water for flood control and water for navigation, there's water for power—

Power for the farmers of the Valley.

Power for the villages and cities and factories of the Valley.

West Virginia, North Carolina, Tennessee, Mississippi, Georgia and Alabama.

Power to give a new Tennessee Valley to a new generation.

Power enough to make the river work!

EPILOGUE

We got the blacks to plant the cotton and they gouged the top off the
    valley.
We got the Swedes to cut the forests, and they sent them down the river.
Then we moved our saws and our plows and started all over again;
And we left a hollow-eyed generation to peck at the worn-out valley;
And left the Swedes to shiver in their naked North country.
1903, 1907, 1913, 1922, 1927, 1936, 1937—
For you can't wall out and dam two-thirds the water in the country.
We built dams but the dams filled in.
We built a thousand-mile dyke but it didn't hold;
So we built it higher.
We played with a continent for fifty years.

Flood control? Of the Mississippi?
Control from Denver to Helena;
From Itasca to Paducah;

From Pittsburgh to Cairo—
Control of the wheat, the corn and the cotton land;
Control enough to put back a thousand forests;
Control enough to put the river together again before it is too late . . .
    before it has picked up the heart of a continent and shoved it into the
    Gulf of Mexico.

The leading theme of the next group of selections is the crescendo of tensions in the years immediately preceding the war, when the war scare was beginning to create a small boom and to wipe out the effects of the second depression of 1937. Hollywood found its own characteristic modes of expressing the country's widespread concern with political action, and Dr. George Gallup devised a technique for measuring popular opinion that made him a formidable political influence. No book of these years can match in its evocation of local and universal horror The Invasion From Mars, *by the Princeton psychologist Hadley Cantril. For this methodical but inspired interpretation of the panic unleashed by the celebrated Orson Welles broadcast, a study based on investigations carried out by Dr. Gallup, is a singularly chilling glimpse into the human soul. Professor Cantril's terrified subjects, bedeviled by a world they never made, have their counterparts in the citizens of Jonathan Daniels's Fall River, where uncertainty and insecurity seek traditional scapegoats, and in Erskine Caldwell's pathetic Negro, who learns painfully that justice is reserved for his betters. Albert Maltz's happy man, who can escape from privation only by embracing death, is a blood brother of John Steinbeck's nameless, wandering Okies. To the young man of Irwin Shaw's story, who has accepted the as yet undeclared war as necessary, come the angels of Stephen Vincent Benét's nightmare, proclaiming the wrath to come. The dream of human happiness evoked by Shaw's hero must fade before the certainty that the Nazis are threatening to renew the reign of Chaos and Old Night.*

LEO C. ROSTEN

Politics Over Hollywood

DURING the world crisis in September 1939, four movie producers had tele-type machines installed in their offices to clatter out the minute-by-minute pulse beat of Europe; Hollywood parties rang with fevered talk and were gripped by dark apprehension; committees sprang up to aid Poland, France, Britain, China; and through every nerve of a community reputed to be somnambulistic there raced the throbbing pains of the world's agony. Those who knew Hollywood twenty years ago, or fifteen, or ten, would have been dumbfounded by the tension which electrified the men and women of the movie colony. "Hollywood," someone cried, "has put on political long pants."

Hollywood's rise to political consciousness is dramatic and revealing. Before 1934, roughly, the movie colony was dismissed as a never-never land of sunny skies, Sleeping Beauties, and ivory towers. The movie makers were elf-like creatures fondly believed (and expected) to behave like the fairy-tale princess who only knew she was blessed and thought of nothing but love. The harsher view found Hollywood politically indifferent, inno-cent and ignorant, populated by rich children who lolled in an arcadia of swimming pools and bonbons. The only "ism" in which Hollywood be-lieved, Dorothy Parker remarked, was plagiarism.

In one sense, the movie makers—directors and writers as well as actors—were not considered real people at all. To the public, they were characters out of folklore who lived under symbolic glass-bells. They were fair of face and full of grace, above want or care or concern. They were timeless, not contemporary. They had emotions, not ideas. They could love, but they could not think. Such mundane events as elections and tariffs, wars and blockades could not, presumably, touch their charmed and unreal exist-ence. It is not surprising that when Hollywood became articulate about war, unions, Fascism, boycotts, or the New Deal, a murmur of anguish rose in the land.

The public's consternation did not arise from what the demi-gods of the screen said, but from the fact that they talked at all. They were violating the pretty role to which they had been assigned in a million fantasies. They were breaking a spell. They were betraying public faith by stepping out of the romantic function they were supposed to serve and in which—precisely because it was exclusively romantic—they were adored. When a Joan Crawford denounced the invasion of Ethiopia, when a Fredric March pleaded for ambulances for Spain, it was like harsh voices destroying a cherished dream. It was easy and natural, at first, for the rudely awakened to cry "Communism!" Congressmen and editors, themselves subjects in the kingdom of the screen, expressed dismay at Hollywood's perfidy, and made headlines by smearing red herrings across the gossamer gowns of Beverly Hills. The loyal drudges of Earl Browder, on the other hand, saw visions of Lorelei on the barricades and foolishly allowed their hopes to soar into regions where common sense was exiled.

Ironically enough, it was the movie executives, who most feared any participation in politics by their glamorous employees, who gave Hollywood its first lesson in the school of hard political reality. The occasion was the bitter Merriam-Sinclair campaign for the governorship of California in 1934. This campaign represented Hollywood's first all-out plunge into the waters of politics. It is a case-study of Hollywood's political activism. Let us describe the history of the organizations and the salient political movements in the movie colony, and then analyze their meaning.

The candidates for the gubernatorial chair of California in 1934 were Frank E. Merriam, a dull Republican wheelhorse lacking in public appeal, and Upton Sinclair, *l'enfant terrible,* muckraker, radical, vegetarian, agnostic. Upton Sinclair had astonished everyone by a campaign which won him the Democratic nomination and threatened to storm the election heights as well. The movie executives were frightened; Sinclair was an outspoken critic and opponent of the motion picture industry, and his tax program threatened to hit Hollywood's studios harder than they had ever been hit before. It looked as though California, which had not had a Democratic governor in thirty-five years, might elect a reformer-Socialist who attacked big business, was dedicated to "production for use, not profit," and was the apostle of a messianic program built around the slogan, "End Poverty in California!"

The movement to beat Sinclair and EPIC took on the attributes of a crusade which bordered on panic. *Time* wrote that the campaign had become "a phobia, lacking humor, fairness, and even a sense of reality." When election betting reached even money on Sinclair's chances, the stocks of six leading California enterprises fell $60,000,000 in one day. The movie magnates joined the anti-Sinclair forces with desperate vigor. Louis B. Mayer of MGM, Republican State Committee vice-chairman, commanded the Hollywood sector; William Randolph Hearst hastened home from Bad Nauheim, Germany, to marshal his newspapers for the fight.

The movie leaders announced that they would be forced to take the entire motion picture industry out of California if Upton Sinclair were elected, and Joseph M. Schenck, a steadfact Democrat, declared in Miami: "If Florida is on the alert, it will benefit to the extent of $150,000,000 a year on the film industry if Sinclair is elected." (Oddly enough, the threat to leave California was followed by the construction of costly new sound stages—in California.) The legislature of Florida hurriedly welcomed the motion picture business by passing a law to exempt them from all taxes if they would migrate, and the incubus of a real-estate boom hovered once more over Florida.

The studio heads did more than issue sensational pronunciamentos. These alarums were, on the contrary, the least effective contribution Hollywood made to the Merriam cause. The producers raised a campaign fund of half a million dollars, partly by assessing their high-salaried employees one day's salary! The assessment was, of course, not so designated officially; it was a "request," but it was accompanied by delicacies of pressure and persuasion which left no room for doubt that refusals would be inexpedient. (The California papers did not publicize this singular tactic, but the *London News-Chronicle* managed to find news in the fact that it had been intimated to Katherine Hepburn that her studio might dismiss her if she came out in open support of Sinclair.) Many in Hollywood refused to be stampeded; Jean Harlow and James Cagney led an actors' rebellion against the "Merriam" tax, writers Gene Fowler, Jim Tully, Frank Scully, and Morrie Ryskind organized an Upton Sinclair committee; but most actors, directors, writers, and producers paid one day's salary into the Republican campaign chest.

Nor was this the big gun in Hollywood's attack on Sinclair. The producers' main barrage was a series of fabricated newsreels, of appalling crudity and immense effectiveness. Motion pictures were taken of a horde of disreputable vagrants in the act of crossing "the California border" and prepared to expropriate the God-fearing the moment Upton Sinclair was elected. The pictures were taken on the streets of Los Angeles with cameras from a major studio; the anarchists were actors on studio payrolls, dressed in false whiskers and dirty clothes, and wearing sinister expressions. These "newsreels" were distributed *gratis* to theatre owners, and were spread across the screens of leading theatres in every city in the state. The *Los Angeles Evening Herald & Express,* a Hearst paper, printed a large picture of a terrifying mob of young hoboes in front of a freight car, apparently arriving in Los Angeles to launch the Sinclair revolution. Unfortunately these harbingers of the Terror were recognizable as Frankie Darrow, Dorothy Wilson, and other reasonably familiar actors, and the picture itself was identified as a still from the film *Wild Boys of the Road.* Hollywood's "newsreels" deserved citation as *tours de force* of propaganda; *The New York Times* printed a two-column description of their content:

In one of the melodramas filmed and shown in Los Angeles, an interviewer approaches a demure old lady, sitting on her front porch and rocking away in her rocking chair.

"For whom are you voting, Mother?" asks the interviewer.

"I am voting for Governor Merriam," the old lady answers in a faltering voice.

"Why, Mother?"

"Because I want to save my little home. It is all I have left in this world."

In another newsreel there is shown a shaggy man with bristling Russian whiskers and a menacing look in his eye.

"For whom are you voting?" asks the interviewer.

"Vy, I am foting for Seenclair."

"Why are you voting for Mr. Sinclair?"

"Vell, his system worked vell in Russia, vy can't it work here?"

No comment on this prostitution of the screen can be more indicting than the editorial which appeared on the front page of the *Hollywood Reporter* eleven days before the Merriam-Sinclair election:

"When the picture business gets aroused, it becomes AROUSED, and boy, how they go to it. This campaign against Upton Sinclair has been and is DYNAMITE. It is the most effective piece of political humdingery that has ever been effected. . . . Never before in the history of the picture business has the screen been used in direct support of a candidate . . . never has there been a concerted action on the part of all theaters in a community to defeat a nominee . . . Maybe our business will be pampered a bit, instead of being pushed around as it has been ever since it became big business . . ."

It was the producers who gave the *coup de grâce* to Sinclair and elected Merriam. But in doing so they shocked the movie colony into a sudden awareness of movie politics and pressure. The Stop-Smash-Smear Sinclair campaign, and the producers' tax on studio personnel, coincided with the rise to power of the Screen Actors Guild and the fight of the Screen Writers Guild for recognition. The juxtaposition of events drove home a lesson in realism to Hollywood's talent groups.

Four years later, in May, 1938, when Governor Merriam was running for re-election against Culbert L. Olson, a group of movie celebrities met at the home of Miriam Hopkins and set up a "Studio Committee for Democratic Political Action." A letter signed by Melvyn Douglas was sent to Hollywood's actors, writers, directors, and technicians calling for members to join "a committee . . . working within the Democratic party, to support and extend the New Deal nationally and, primarily, to bring a new deal to California."

Many of Hollywood's writers, directors, and actors flocked into the organization, which took the title, Motion Picture Democratic Committee. The committee raised money for Olson, pamphleteered, held mass meetings, put on radio shows, sponsored a score of personal appearances and, in a classic gesture, asked Governor Merriam to contribute one day of *his* salary to the Olson campaign fund. Articulate, energetic, with a quick dramatic sense, the Motion Picture Democratic Committee played an important part in the campaign and helped score a signal victory in California politics, the election of a Democratic governor, Culbert L. Olson, for the first time in forty years. One producer summarized the movie colony's role in the 1938 election by remarking sadly, "I guess we started something in 1934."

Hollywood's earlier political gestures had been of the comic-opera genre. A Colonel Arthur Guy Empey had organized the Hollywood Hussars (in 1935), a band of knights prepared to gallop on their steeds to any emergency-flood or invasion, earthquake or revolution. Several movie stars were lured into this staunch regiment, notably Gary Cooper, but resigned when its proto-Fascist leanings became clearer.

Victor McLaglen organized a Light Horse Cavalry with a program as vague and penny-dreadful as the Hollywood Hussars. Both organizations aroused wide protests in the movie colony because of their vigilante overtones.

The political sympathies of Hollywood crystallized into less melodramatic patterns when, in 1936, several hundred movie celebrities attended a mass meeting and pledged themselves to a campaign against Fascism, Nazism, Communism, "and all other dangerous isms." Prominent in the crusade were David O. Selznick, Mrs. Fredric March, Herman Mankiewicz, Edwin Knopf, and others. The American Legion was strongly supported by film luminaries; the 1936 state convention was inaugurated on a sound stage which the Warner studio turned over to the Legion, and in 1939 the Legion created a Motion Picture Division of its Americanism Committee, with movie producer Walter Wanger as its chairman and a dozen Hollywood Legionnaires as members.

When Spain was torn by Civil War, and while the Japanese were raping China in the name of a "new order" for the East, a group of movie people organized the Motion Picture Artists Committee. Headed by Dashiell Hammett and allied with international organizations sponsored by Lloyd

George, the Duchess of Athol, and President Cardenas of Mexico, the Motion Picture Artists Committee threw itself into drives to aid China and Loyalist Spain. This Hollywood organization conducted an energetic campaign for the boycott of Japanese goods and an embargo on arms shipments to Nippon, urged the removal of the Spanish embargo so that the government at Madrid could buy arms and supplies, and shipped medical supplies, food, clothes, and toys to the wounded and the homeless in China and Spain. The championing of China won general approbation for the committee; its support of Loyalist Spain was another matter. This tragic conflict, so bitterly debated in the United States, was certain to make the Motion Picture Artists Committee the target of violent opposition and to invite the ubiquitous charge of "Communism."

It was the Hollywood Anti-Nazi League which brought the Communist issue to a clear and fateful head. The Anti-Nazi League, the most aggressive and controversial organization in Hollywood's history, was sponsored in 1936 by a group catholic enough to include such widely separated politicos as Rupert Hughes, Donald Ogden Stewart, Eddie Cantor, Dudley Nichols, Viola Brothers Shore, Gloria Stuart, and others. Republicans, New Dealers, movie producers, one hundred percenters, and liberals found a common ground for action in a movement designed to combat Nazi influence and Nazi propaganda. The Hollywood Anti-Nazi League was actively headed by Donald Ogden Stewart, Herbert Biberman, Alan Campbell, and Marion Spitzer; it claimed a membership of five thousand (probably an overstatement) at its peak, and in three years deposited almost $90,000 in its bank account. The League campaigned for a boycott of Nazi goods, published a weekly paper, put on a weekly radio program, and held mass meetings with speakers such as Congressman Jerry O'Connell, Thomas Mann, and Dr. John R. Lechner, Chairman of the American Legion's Americanism Committee. The organization scored two memorable *coups;* it exposed Leni Riefenstahl, Hitler's emissary who had come to Hollywood to peddle a Nazi film version of the Berlin Olympic Games, and it so successfully mobilized opposition to Vittorio Mussolini, who popped up in Hollywood fresh from his bombing expedition in Ethiopia ("Highly diverting . . . the bombs strike and the ground is thrown up in waves like the unfolding of a rose"), that the son of Il Duce was whisked out of the country by the infuriated Italian embassy.

The Hollywood Anti-Nazi League became a *cause célèbre* when the Dies Committee, the *Motion Picture Herald,* and the local press accused the organization of being used as a Communist "front" agency operated by a clique which followed the Communist party line with remarkable fidelity. No one charged the members of the league with Communist affiliation;

even Congressman Martin A. Dies declared that "the great majority of the members are not Communists." It was an inner circle that was indicted as either members of the Communist party, party stooges, or fellow-travelers of more than innocent cast. The leaders of the Hollywood Anti-Nazi League were challenged to clarify their position on Communism when anti-Communist resolutions were introduced from the floor. They reacted promptly; they fought down efforts to put the question to a democratic vote; they raised a hue and cry that the matter of Communism was irrelevant; and, using the classic *argumentum ad hominem,* they accused their critics of being everything from "wreckers" and "saboteurs" to "Fascist lackeys."

It is elementary logic to distinguish Hollywood from Communists-in-Hollywood, but when public opinion flared up against the methods and the purpose of Communist "front" organizations, the entire movie colony was smeared for the politics of a handful. Hollywood is a perennial springboard to the front pages; when Hollywood and "Communism" were linked, sensational publicity was sure to fall into the laps of the demagogues. It was not surprising that "Reds in Hollywood" became a theme song of the German-American Bund, the Silver Shirts, Father Coughlin, the Ku Klux Klan, and Fascist oracles of every hue. When Congressman Martin A. Dies made a careless attack on the film colony, suggesting that even Shirley Temple was being used by the Communist party, he gave the signal for the witch hunt.

All through 1939, especially whenever he asked Congress for funds, Mr. Dies declared that Communism was thriving in Hollywood; unfortunately for his case, he presented neither names nor evidence to support the charges. Mr. Dies sold two articles to *Liberty* in 1940, and the magazine printed a boxed notice over the articles which read: "For his statement of his case, [*Liberty*] has allowed him the fullest latitude within the laws of libel." The exposé proved to be tendentious and feeble. The farthest Mr. Dies would go was to assert that "forty-two or forty-three prominent members of the Hollywood film colony either were full-fledged members of the Communist party or active sympathizers and fellow travelers." No names were given. Mr. Dies admitted that movie producers "appeared to be very anxious to cooperate through their films in exposing and combating un-American activities"; but he suggested that "Communist influence was responsible for the subtle but very effective propaganda which appeared in such films as *Juarez, Blockade,* and *Fury.*"

All through the summer of 1940, too, Mr. Dies's accusations made the front pages of the land; all through the summer he promised that he would hold a hearing in Los Angeles which would expose Communism in both Hollywood and the films. Mr. Dies had stated that "a mass of verbal and documentary evidence" showed that less than fifty persons in Hollywood were Communist either formally or by sympathy—but the entire movie colony, the movie industry, and the movies were tarred with the red brush.

It is a vindication of Hollywood that the Dies committee failed to produce more facts to support the alarums anent movie Bolsheviks. This is not to say, of course, that there are no Communists in Hollywood. There are —just as there probably are in Orange, Texas. But to malign all of Hollywood because of the suspected politics of eighteen persons (according to Leech) or forty-three (the maximum Mr. Dies admitted suspecting) was an act of supererogation which deserved the quip "loaded Dies." The New York *Herald Tribune* editorialized: "The palpable injustice done . . . condemns the whole effort as a smear campaign."

The irony of the attack lies in the fact that Hollywood's leaders have for years been bitter and vociferous in their denunciation of Communists. Any other conception of the record and public declarations of the Messrs. Warner, Mayer, Schenck, Freeman, Zanuck, Schaefer, Wanger, *et al.,* betrays a dismal ignorance of the facts. The movie people's fear of Communism, like the fear of so many others in the land, had become a phobia which at one time tended to blind them to the Fascist threat. When Hollywood turned out full force, in rapid succession, for aid to Poland, Finland, the Netherlands, and Greece, the charge of wholesale Communism in the movie colony became patently inept. The final joker lies in the fact that Hollywood's leaders probably stand to the right of Mr. Dies and make even less distinction between a liberal and a Bolshevik. The representative from Texas has never denounced the New Deal with as much animus as some of the movie leaders have done in the presence of this writer.

It will be remembered that Mr. Dies asserted that "Communist influence" had injected "very effective propaganda" into *Juarez, Blockade,* and *Fury.* (Mr. Dies might have argued just as logically, as many Communists have done, that Hollywood is "Fascist" because of *Ninotchka, Comrade X, He Stayed for Breakfast, Public Deb Number 1,* and half a dozen more films which lampooned Communist theology.) Suppose we examine the content of these films, and then the political record of the studios and the men who produced them.

Juarez dramatized the fight of Benito Juarez against the ambivalent tyranny of Maximilian, whom Napoleon III had set up on the throne of Mexico. The picture eulogized Abraham Lincoln, and was almost overloaded with affirmations of democracy. The Communists attacked *Juarez* because of its sympathetic portrayal of Maximilian and Carlotta, and accused the writers of having falsified history. (The film deliberately ignored Juarez's anti-clericalism; Juarez had expelled the Papal Nuncio and other ecclesiastics who resisted his decrees.) Mr. Dies was apparently unfamiliar with those facts, or with the statement Lincoln made when he received Juarez's envoy: "You [enjoy] the respect and esteem of this government, and the good will of the people of the United States."

Blockade, the next movie on the list, was a melodrama about the Spanish Civil War which painfully avoided any reference to either the Loyalists or the Franco rebels. The meaning of the movie, in effect, was to appeal to "the conscience of the world"; it favored the shipment of food to Spain. If the cause of the legal government of Spain—with which the United States maintained sympathetic diplomatic relations to the end—was "Communist," then we should ask whether the majority of the American people who supported the Loyalist position were "Communists." (The adhesion of Generalissimo Franco to the Berlin-Toyko-Rome Axis soon convinced the doubtful that the democracies should have been on the side of the legal government.)

We come to the third movie indicted, *Fury. Fury* was a classic dramatization of mob violence. It contained no political characters, no political setting, and no political overtones. The assertion that this movie showed Bolshevik influence leaves this writer utterly nonplussed. The only group which could consistently denounce *Fury's* portrayal of lynching is the Ku Klux Klan.

Now let us examine the politics of the men who produced the three films. *Juarez* was produced by Warner Brothers, whose leaders, pictures, and politics have been cited by many scrolls and resolutions of the American Legion and the Daughters of the American Revolution. Mr. Dies had himself singled out the Warners, as being strongly anti-Communist. The Warner Brothers' patriotic shorts have for years been produced at a loss to the studio, and cast and filmed on a scale which has attested that the Warners have known they could not recover their costs. It was the Warner Brothers, furthermore, who gave free radio time each week for a year on their station (KFWB) to "America Marches On," one of the first anti-Nazi, anti-Communist programs in the country. Each dramatization featured an address by Dr. John R. Lechner of the American Legion, and the formal sign-off of the program was the statement, "Americans are opposed to Nazism, Communism, and Fascism."

Blockade was produced by Walter Wanger, who had organized and chairmanned a private group which refused to cooperate with the Hollywood Anti-Nazi League until it cleared itself of the charge of Communism. Mr. Wanger resigned from a New York organization because of its failure "to make clear its position with reference to Fascism AND Communism." In an open letter printed in the *Hollywood Citizen-News,* he had stated:

... I can see no excuse for intellectual straddling on this point. There can be no compromise between Fascism and Democracy. There can be no compromise between Communism and Democracy. There can, in short, be no compromise between Dictatorship and Democracy. The current controversy is between Dictatorship and Democracy, and I am on the side of Democracy.

Fury was made by MGM, whose chief, Louis B. Mayer, is a power in the Republican party, national Republican committeeman, and an old friend of Herbert Hoover, who played host to Mr. Mayer at the White House. The producer of *Fury,* Joseph L. Mankiewicz, was a moving spirit in the Aid-to-Finland drive and voted for Wendell Willkie in 1940.

These were the men accused of financing and producing "Communist" movies.

Anyone who attends the movies regularly must be impressed by the fact that Hollywood's output is to an overwhelming degree distinguished by utter political innocuousness. Hollywood shuns the political (and the realistic) because it must appeal to the widest of mass markets, and it dare not risk offending any substantial part of that market. Patriotic stories have always been at a premium in the motion picture industry. The Army and Navy pictures, a staple commodity from Hollywood's production lines, led pacifists to accuse Hollywood of militarism long before demagogues accused it of Communism.

The statement which Walter Wanger presented on a "Town Meeting of the Air" program puts the case for Hollywood trenchantly:

Hollywood made 350 pictures last year. Fewer than ten of these pictures departed from the usual Westerns, romances and boy-meets-girl story . . . I say the motion pictures can aid in national defense by giving us more, many more than ten out of 350 pictures which deal with democracy in the world crisis. . . . Where does Hollywood get its material? From popular books, plays, and magazine stories. Note the word "popular." Yet when we make a story which has already appeared in a national magazine, when we film a book which has already become a best seller, there are those who cry, "The motion pictures are beginning to propagandize." . . . The *Saturday Evening Post* . . . published a serial, *Escape.* Nobody accuses the *Saturday Evening Post* of war-mongering. But when Hollywood put this story on the screen . . . the cry went up, "Hollywood is going in for propaganda!"

The farce of "Communist Hollywood" was conceived in the days when political innocents assumed that any and all opposition to Fascism was Communist in origin or purpose. It will be to Hollywood's credit that its anti-Fascist activities predated the swing in American public opinion and diplomacy. It will be to Hollywood's credit that it fought the Silver Shirts, the German-American Bund, and the revived Ku Klux Klan at a time when few realized their ultimate menace.

"Causes" are always suspect, and humane acts can easily be attacked by the shallow and the ignorant as symptoms of dark, conspiratorial purpose. The movie people who donated funds to the migratory workers of California, to the wives and children of lettuce workers at Salinas, suffered the usual calumnies before the public came to believe the facts which cried for public action. Melvyn Douglas, Helen Gahagan, and half a dozen others who founded the Committee to Aid Migratory Workers were, of course, sticking their necks out; but they did send food, clothes, toys, and money to Americans whose welfare and liberty had been shockingly mistreated. James Cagney spoke for many picture people when he declared:

We were accused of contributing to radical causes. When you are told a person is sick or in need, you don't ask him his religion, nationality, or politics. . . . I am unequivocally opposed to subversive organizations of any kind. I am for this government and for American principles.

There was a time, not so long ago, when the charge "Communism!" was hurled against anyone—in Hollywood or in Boston—who held that Nazi Germany was a threat to America, that labor unions were legal organizations, that civil liberties should be protected with Jeffersonian courage, that the dispossessed in a free nation have a right to speak and live as free men and citizens. The nation now agrees with many of those who were labeled "un-American."

Despite its tennis courts and swimming pools, Hollywood was infected by the social insecurity of the times. Even the most sanguine apostles of escapism in the movie colony could not close their ears to the thunder of national change. Wherever men could read the papers or hear the radio, wherever they could sense the unrest which roared around the very foundations of their homes—there men cast worried glances at the political scene. It is naïve to assume that this was the work of malcontents or "agitators"; the political awakening of Hollywood was one small part of the political awakening of America.

In Hollywood, naturally, politics is more dramatic than in Shamokin. Hollywood politics is played by the most famous cast in the world. Hollywood politics is publicized by a brigade of publicists and newspapermen rivaled only in Washington. It was said earlier that dramatic acts appeal to dramatic personalities. Hollywood politics is dramatic, too. The movie makers react dramatically rather than politically. They react not simply as voters and citizens, but as virtuosos aware of the potency of their names and their influence. Show people do not test out their opinions, study political issues, or ponder the total implications of a political position. They rush into politics as into a benefit performance. They sign petitions with a flourish, make eloquent speeches and send out batches of long and defiant telegrams. Hollywood reacts to politics as it does to anything else—with fervid emotion and an infinite capacity for suffering. No chamber of commerce or civic league can produce either the breast-beating or the oratory of a Guild meeting or a Bel-Air living-room. "When Hollywood gets aroused, it gets AROUSED."

In the early stages of Hollywood's political awakening, it was *fashionable* to go left—with the right people. In the movie colony, said Frank Nugent, "affluence breeds ennui" and social consciousness is "a form of entertainment." Actors who had gone in for antiques, or actresses who had fancied the rumba, discovered the attraction of politics when political discussion began to dominate Hollywood's dinner tables. There was social pressure to familiarize one's self with the current world, and a new kind of deference was accorded those who performed as political experts. The radio talks of H. V. Kaltenborn and Raymond Gram Swing became almost as popular in Hollywood as the Jack Benny program. The level of political disputation in the movie colony was painfully immature, but the important point was that it was political.

In a world of war, unemployment, and social conflict, those who spend their time in spinning the pretty fables of the screen are troubled by a vague feeling of contempt for themselves, by a revulsion against the falsity of their purpose and the make-believe of their security. The movie people are obsessed by conscience; they are groping to participate in man's fight; they are driven by the urge to do "something significant."

The ivory towers of Hollywood have been undermined by the guilt and the frustration of those who inhabit them. The weekly amassing of immense salaries creates a disturbing sense of inequity in the souls of the movie colony's ex-salesmen, chorus girls, or lumberjacks. The Hollywoodian is haunted by the suspicion that his breath-taking fortune is not truly earned—*i.e.,* is not really deserved or morally justified. There are enough has-beens and might-have-beens floating around the movie colony to plague the children of fortune with the thought, "There, but for the grace of God, go I."

Political activity, Professor H. D. Lasswell has demonstrated, often serves as a form of individual therapy. Emotional insecurities are reduced when personalities set up heroes to love, villains to hate, devils to *blame*. The hostilities generated in the personality can be discharged with economy against symbolic objects. Hitler or Churchill, Roosevelt, the New Deal, the

Reactionaries, the Radicals—all these may become metaphorical Nemeses, and individuals preserve their inner equilibrium by discharging hate, fear, or tension to things outside the self. Let us not forget that identification with an heroic cause is eminently attractive to men in a culture like ours, which drives men into small and lonely universes.

To the personalities of Hollywood, lost and isolated in their own empty glory, profound gratification is to be found in organizations or causes which help them feel part of a significant movement, which help them feel at one with "the people." The gnawing doubts of egoism can be denied by the championing of altruistic creeds. Politics offers heroic roles, and what actor can resist an heroic part? Politics offered Hollywood the fresh and inspiring experience of martyrdom. Political activity sustains anxiety, and anxiety is a form of atonement for obscure remorse. Politics satisfies masochistic impulses. Politics is a legitimate way of getting into a bang-up fight, hurling great slogans and bitter anathemas, attacking old authority symbols, releasing inner rage against the figurative demons of the political world. Politics is a legitimate way of provoking that opposition in heated arguments which justifies and sanctions violent counter-aggression. Politics was made for the movie makers, once they discovered it.

But it was foolhardy to worry about genuine or dangerous revolutionists in Hollywood. The inhabitants of the movie colony are scarcely fit to accept the discipline and deprivations of a fanatical cause. The movie makers cannot remain consistent for long, personally or politically; they need quick and dramatic rewards. The stirring language and bravado gestures of protest movements are irresistible to the self-dramatizing, but actors become as bored with a political role as with a stage role if the rehearsals are prolonged and the big show is postponed.

The Hollywood Communist scare betrayed naïveté, a talent for head-lines, and an abysmal incomprehension of movie personalities on the part of those who pinned red labels on the movie colony.

The conflicts which dominated America reached into Hollywood as inexorably as anywhere in the land. The New Deal, public relief and public works, the persuasiveness of Franklin D. Roosevelt, the rise of unions and the crucial issue of collective bargaining—these won allegiance from glamour girls no less than from manicurists, from matinee idols as well as coal miners.

Hollywood was carried on the wave of the times—*despite* the omni-present lures of escapist living. Something happened in the movie business which surprised the executives: the actors and writers and directors were forced to the realization, after long and sad experiences, that in the last analysis they were employees. It seemed ludicrous, at first sight, to think of Clark Gable or Marlene Dietrich, Frank Capra or Gene Fowler as members of movie unions, paying union dues, pledged to a labor organization and ready to strike for it. It became less preposterous when one realized that even the movie makers who earn $1,000-$5,000 a week are *hired* men and women selling their services in a market which, despite its surface romance, is still a market. The Wagner act was a tocsin to Hollywood no less than to Pittsburgh. The movie makers, for all their generic individualism, moved toward the organization of their crafts because organization offered professional advantages and solved professional problems.

The years of unchallenged producer sovereignty, the tradition of draconic executives, the assumption that high salaries negated contractual status, the high-handed exercise of power by those who possessed it, provided fertile soil for the organization of Hollywood's employees. The concept of unionism and the meaning of organization seeped upward into the highest-paid levels of the film colony. The Screen Actors Guild, by threatening an industry-wide walkout, won higher basic rates for extras, greater security, and, above all, gave several thousand actors an outlet for their individual complaints and a channel for their common demands. The movie directors and writers, cameramen and publicists, organized themselves into occupational groups with common goals and protective purposes. Guilds—the choice of the word in preference to "unions" reveals the professional distaste for proletarian language—sprang up in Hollywood with bewildering speed, and the issues which gripped the nation as a whole were recapitulated in the industry of film making. Hollywood's guilds would not and could not have arisen had there not been a need for the functions they offered to fulfill.

Just before the Roosevelt-Landon campaign of 1936, a trade paper poll found Hollywood 6 to 1 for Roosevelt. Movie directors supported the President 8 to 1, actors 7 to 1, writers 5 to 1, laborers 8 to 1, agents 24 to 1—and executives, be it noted, 5 to 1. In the Roosevelt-Willkie campaign, Hollywood, like the rest of the country, was less emphatically Democrat and New Deal. The powerful Hollywood for Roosevelt Committee conducted a remarkable radio campaign in behalf of the President's third-term, and featured such movie celebrities as Pat O'Brien, Joan Bennett, Douglas Fairbanks, Jr., Alice Faye, Edward G. Robinson, Rosalind Russell, Henry Fonda, and many others. But a formidable battery of picture people supported Mr. Willkie: Louis B. Mayer, Bing Crosby, Walt Disney, Mary Pickford, Gary Cooper, Wallace Beery, Hedda Hopper, William Powell, Robert Montgomery, Harold Lloyd, Joan Blondell, Lionel Barrymore, Ann Sheridan, Adolphe Menjou, Morrie Ryskind, and a hundred more. The producers and executives were, on the whole, strongly pro-Willkie.

In the realm of international politics, Hollywood is more sensitive and more responsive than most communities in the land. There are several understandable reasons for the hypersensitivity. European politics cannot be ignored by an industry which, as a whole, derived from thirty-five to forty percent of its revenues from abroad (before the war broke out), nor by individual producers and studios that got as high as fifty percent of their income from outside the United States. Every time a nation was crushed under the juggernaut of Berlin or Rome, Hollywood felt the blow in its pocketbook. No other American product was strangled so quickly and automatically by the conquering regimes.

American movies, unlike American typewriters or washing machines, were *ipso facto* a threat to the Caesars. Goebbels hurled a systematic propaganda attack against Hollywood's films, and Hitler once honored Hollywood with special hatred in a radio harangue heard around the world. Wherever the Nazis and the Fascists moved, they cut the arteries of Hollywood's income. American movies became pawns in the gigantic game of power and conquest. Hollywood's product was outlawed in Germany, Italy, Soviet Russia, and in the nations which fell under the heel of conquest.

Foreign censorship taboos had for two decades familiarized Hollywood with the politics of entertainment (many American movies had been denied admittance to Spain, Poland, Turkey, Hungary, Brazil, Japan), and as the world plunged toward war, censorship became more severe and film quotas more oppressive. Hollywood's markets were crippled or obliterated by dictatorial action. Foreign propaganda films were taking over the markets closed to Hollywood by political fiat; and in those markets which remained more or less free—notably the South American countries—German and Italian films, made and used as deliberate instruments of foreign policy, were destroying the trade which Hollywood, in free competition, had enjoyed.

There was another and powerful reason for the movie colony's political sensitivity. Hollywood, we have said, is cosmopolitan. The movie people have friends, relatives, and memories which make Europe near and real. To Hollywood's British, French, German, or Hungarian colonies, the cold news of political events means mothers, fathers, sisters, friends. It is one thing to read about the cremation of Rotterdam; it is another to telephone your uncle in Holland and get no reply. It is one thing to hear of blood terror in Rumania; it is another to receive no answer to the frantic cables you send to the staff you met there last year. A substantial percentage of Hollywood had traveled and had known the life of a Vienna which was conquered, a Paris which was overrun, a London which was bombed. And even had the network of their personal lives been less wide, the malevolence of the new Caesars constituted a *personal* threat to the movie makers; after the Nazis smashed Warsaw they arrested the movie theatre owners who had ever shown films distasteful to the Third Reich, hanged them, and rolled them through the streets on portable gallows.

The fact that the movies are an international commodity drove politics home to Hollywood with a hard, unyielding impact. The paroxysms of power politics flung the impending chaos of the world into Hollywood's lap. The war on Hollywood antedated the firing of cannon. The political advertency of Hollywood preceded the political awakening of America.

RUSSELL MALONEY AND A. J. LIEBLING

Black Beans and White Beans:
Dr. George Gallup

THE FORTUNES of Dr. George Horace Gallup (Ph.D., State University of Iowa) are firmly bound up with the present Democratic administration. In the years between the end of the World War and the rise of the New Deal, there would have been no place in our economic system for an organization equipped, as Dr. Gallup says his American Institute of Public Opinion is equipped, to measure within three per cent of absolute mathematical accuracy the opinion of the electorate on current social and political questions. People just wouldn't have cared. These days, there is a sizable group which does care, passionately. The results of the Institute's surveys, familiarly known as "Gallup polls," appear three times a week (two surveys Sunday) in a hundred and six newspapers throughout the country, and are hopefully scanned by members of the once vested interests. The Democrats, with their Party firmly in office, presumably aren't interested in minute fluctuations of public opinion, but it is easy to understand a Republican's deriving considerable comfort from the discovery that national sentiment in favor of limiting the President's powers has grown seven per cent in a year, or that during the same period the conservative element within the Democratic Party has grown four per cent. Dr. Gallup, at least, is convinced that this is the case. "Most of my customers are conservative," he has said, "and most of my friends are liberals." His manner makes it plain that he is simply noting two facts: that the majority of newspaper publishers are conservative, and that the majority of his friends, the people he sees at lunch or on commuters' trains, are liberals. Dr. Gallup stands aloof from political partisanship. His aloofness probably would assay equal parts scientific detachment and business policy; obviously, it wouldn't do if he were known to support one or the other of the Parties.

Dr. Gallup once committed himself politically to the extent of saying that he thought the political division ought to be between liberal and conservative instead of between Democrat and Republican. "However," he added, "I'm not sure which side I'd be on." He does not give the impression of chafing under this enforced impartiality. His manner of speaking, though friendly and poised, is slightly diffident, as though he doubted the wisdom of advancing his personal opinion about anything. He is fond of quoting a maxim of Talleyrand's: "The only thing wiser than anybody is everybody." Dr. Gallup is merely the high priest of the oracle: the great Everybody speaks and he interprets.

Everybody is, for Dr. Gallup's purposes, three thousand people. This is best explained in terms of black beans and white beans, as Dr. Gallup has done in a pamphlet called "The New Science of Public Opinion Measurement." Dr. Gallup reproduces a table compiled by Professor Theodore Brown of Harvard, showing "probable error due to size of sample." Now, the reader who wishes to follow Professor Brown's (and Dr. Gallup's) reasoning will provide himself with a barrel containing black beans and white beans in equal proportions. If he will then perform, one thousand times, the operation of scooping up twenty-five hundred beans, determining the percentages of black and white beans, and mixing them back into the barrel, he will find that only three times out of the thousand have the percentages of black and white beans in his samples varied more than three per cent from the true proportion of beans in the barrel. All of which means that if you take one random sample of twenty-five hundred beans, there are nine hundred and ninety-seven chances in a thousand that you will come within a negligible three per cent of hitting the percentage of black and white beans in the whole barrel. Dr. Gallup, of course, works this formula backward. He dips up a sample of three thousand mixed beans (the five hundred extra are just an added precaution) and, with Professor Brown's assurance that his margin of error is probably not more than three per cent, announces that the percentages of black and white beans in his sample stand for the correct percentages of beans in the country, and that the beans think Roosevelt should keep us out of entanglements with foreign nations but should allow the sale of arms on a cash-and-carry basis.

To make sure that his three thousand beans are mixed fairly, Dr. Gallup makes his sample, as nearly as he can, a cross section of the nation at large, with a proper proportion of people in various classifications. In his own words: "The sample must contain the proper proportion of (1) voters from each state, (2) men and women, (3) farm voters and voters in towns of 2,500 population or less, 2,500 to 10,000, 10,000 to 100,000, 100,000 to 500,-000, and 500,000 and over, (4) voters of all age groups, (5) voters of above average, average, and below average incomes, as well as persons on relief, and (6) Democrats, Republicans, and members of other political parties." That is, if Dr. Gallup lined up (let us say) a thousand people of the same age, sex, income, Party allegiance, and locality, he and Professor Brown would be very much surprised if nine hundred and ninety-seven of them did not have the same opinion on whatever questions might be put to them. If this did not happen, if Brown and Gallup were confronted with the spectacle of a crowd of male, Democratic, forty-year-old, four-thousand-a-year natives of Sioux City divided into equal and opposing camps on some political question, they would stop believing in God.

Dr. Gallup's profound realization that, in spite of our puny pretensions to individualism, we are really quite a uniform little people is probably an accident of birth. He was born, brought up, and educated in the utterly normal Iowa. New Yorkers differ so much among themselves that the concept of the average American seems mythical. To Dr. Gallup, however, there is nothing odd in the idea that one man might represent, statistically, ten thousand or more of his own kind. He understands that the average man exists, and, furthermore, he likes and respects him. He has even, from long association, come to resemble one. Like most American men who were at college in the early twenties and haven't given much thought to clothes since, he wears a sort of uniform—loose, tweedy suits, white shirts with soft collars, heavy brogues, and shapeless hats. Though he is somewhat larger and more intelligent-looking than the average, his voice, coloring, and features would not make him stand out of a crowd, and his age—thirty-eight—undoubtedly represents some sort of median on a graph, something like the Peak Earning Years of a College-Trained Man. Once, prodded by an interviewer, Dr. Gallup sat down and answered all the questions his Institute had placed before the American public from 1935 to 1938. In almost every case he was in accord with the public verdict. His most heterodox beliefs were that women ought to be allowed to work even if their husbands held good jobs (public verdict, 82 per cent against) and that the President ought to be elected for a single six-year term (public verdict, 74 per cent against).

Gallup, whose parents named him George Horace arbitrarily and not after George Horace Lorimer, was born in Jefferson, a town of three thousand, in the flattest part of the state. His father was something of an eccentric; he once drove a covered wagon to Mexico for a pleasure jaunt. He was a staunch advocate of "dry farming," in which the land is ploughed very deeply to release underground moisture and which was frowned upon as a radical method at that time. Dr. Gallup says today that his father contributed to the formation of the Dust Bowl. He speaks of him with affection, but it is plain that he deplores his parent's deviation from the Iowa norm.

Financial disaster came to the Gallup family just after the World War. The elder Gallup, who was a big-scale land speculator, was holding ten thousand acres in Montana and Colorado. Land values fell suddenly, bringing down Mr. Gallup, and with him the Jefferson bank, which was in the venture with a $50,000 loan. Young Gallup, thrown on his own resources while he was a sophomore at the State University of Iowa, organized a towel service in the swimming-pool locker room. While he was a junior he became editor of the college paper, a weekly. Since there was no good daily in Iowa City, the college town, he turned the college paper into one, took general advertising, and made enough money to get himself through to graduation. This made such an impression on the university authorities that they asked him back as an instructor in journalism.

During his instructorship at the State University of Iowa, Gallup worked for a Ph.D. in journalism. His thesis described how he had developed and tested a method of measuring the reactions of newspaper readers to certain features by questioning a small, carefully selected number of them. This, of course, was the germ of the Gallup polls as we know them now. Next, Gallup went to Drake University, in Des Moines, as head of the Department of Journalism, and from there to Northwestern, in Evanston, Illinois. He continued to make his surveys of newspaper-reading publics, doing most of the work himself, in vacation time. In 1932 he was engaged, as vice-president in charge of copy research, by Young & Rubicam, a New York advertising agency which places much faith in the scientific approach. For the past eight years he has piled up statistics for Young & Rubicam, estimating the number of people who listen to the clients' radio programs or read their advertisements in the *Saturday Evening Post*. For this he uses the same tactics, and sometimes the same staff of assistants, he uses for gathering his Institute material. His cubicle at Young & Rubicam is No. 14 in a row of offices (there being, out of deference to some possible unscientific superstition, no office numbered "13").

By the autumn of 1935, Dr. Gallup had accumulated a bit of capital, and he set about organizing the American Institute of Public Opinion. In calling it an Institute, he was, of course, simply following a fashion among businessmen. "Institute" is the synonym for "organization" or "company" that came in about ten years ago, when "associates" began to pall. The American Institute of Public Opinion is, and always has been, a non-charitable, profit-making organization, although some naïve readers, misled by its name and its trademark, a picture of the Capitol dome, may have thought otherwise. Gallup's idea, which he has carried out in the four years since 1935, was to get the reaction of the American voter to questions of general interest about which there was any controversy and to syndicate his findings to newspapers. Sometimes his questions are no more inspired than the topic of a high-school debate ("Would you vote for a woman for President if she qualified in every other respect?"). Sociological questions, naturally, crop up now and then, and we have the voting American's opinions on birth control, sterilization, capital punishment, censorship, "mercy killing," aviation ("If someone paid your expenses, would you like to go to Europe and back by airplane?"), hitchhiking, Philippine independence, etc. But the Gallup poll, like any serious conversation in a club or barroom, always works round to That Fellow in the White House. Is he too friendly to organized labor or not friendly enough? (Forty-five per cent of the Gallup guinea pigs said too friendly.) Is relief being properly administered? Are we pursuing a proper course in international affairs? What about the Supreme Court? Justice Black? Inflation? The AAA? NRA? (Fifty-three per cent would like to see Roosevelt try it again.) The CCC? (Seventy-five per cent would like to see it militarized.) His test question, on the strength of which he got his first subscribers, was, in sporting parlance, a natural. He tested the reaction of the average man to New Deal spending: Did he think it was too much, too little, or just right? Everybody always thinks the government is spending too much. Many publishers were dourly pleased with this survey, which bore out their own notions, and decided to buy the Institute's service. The *Herald Tribune* signed up right away.

Obviously, the first real test of the Institute was to be the Presidential election of 1936. In addition to the Gallup poll, two other straw votes were being conducted that year—those of *Fortune* and of the *Literary Digest*. The *Digest* had conducted a dozen or so polls by the simple expedient of mailing out a couple of million ballot cards with return postage guaranteed. In other elections they had been, roughly speaking, accurate; that is, their percentages were sometimes wrong and their analysis of the electoral vote was not always reliable, but they had picked the winning candidate. For the past three elections, this has been a feat about as difficult as picking the winner of a Joe Louis fight. The *Digest* editors, however, had no qualms about the efficiency of their system. They sent out cards to a mailing list they compiled from the names of automobile owners and telephone subscribers, and sat back to wait for the result.

The *Fortune* poll was at this time directed by Paul Cherington, the first Professor of Marketing at the Harvard School of Business Administration and one of the pioneers in the field of scientific public-opinion polls. He set to work with a staff of interviewers, analyzed a well-selected cross section of the populace, and worked out a prediction of phenomenal accuracy. It predicted the popular vote with what proved to be, when the returns were in, an error of only 1.2 per cent. This, in prophetic circles, is par. To the editors of *Fortune,* who didn't believe that Roosevelt would be elected, it looked simply as if something had gone terribly wrong. After a series of fevered conferences, it was decided not to publish the results of the survey before the election. They were published after the election, but of course nobody cared by then. Meanwhile, the *Literary Digest* had picked Landon.

Gallup picked Roosevelt all right, but with an error of 6.5 per cent, a figure which would make him shudder today. He had not yet worked up the technique he now uses, which is based entirely on interviewing the public directly, but still relied to a certain extent on mail ballots. However, he had certainly predicted the election results better than anybody else, and since that time he has, in the fine old phrase, never looked back. Gallup was from the very start sanguine about his prospects, having been bred to a proper respect for the operations of mathematical formulæ. He promised his staff that as soon as he had thirty subscribers he would give a big party, with champagne. Later, just before he hit thirty, he raised the goal to fifty, then to sixty. When he passed sixty, he told his young men to go out and have some champagne, and to charge it to the Institute. Success had brought no desire for dissipation, and he stayed away from the celebration.

The American Institute of Public Opinion has two offices, one in New York, on East Forty-second Street, and one in Princeton. The editorial office, the New York one, which is handy to Dr. Gallup's Young & Rubicam office, is staffed by two young men, an office boy, and a stenographer. The young men are John Tibby, University of Pittsburgh '35, and William Lydgate, Yale '31. Here the findings of the Institute's researchers are worked up into news reports, and new questions are formulated for Dr. Gallup's final O.K. The office in Princeton takes care of mailing and receiving ballots, counting and tabulating votes, and paying interviewers. As a newspaper feature, the Institute is handled by an independent organization, the Publishers' Syndicate, in Chicago, which performs the usual duties of selling the service to newspapers and collecting payments. The reports of surveys are mailed to subscribing newspapers directly from Princeton. The Institute, which has thirty employees in Princeton, is the town's largest non-collegiate enterprise. The Gallup men blend into the university life and at a distance might be taken for young instructors. They go to all the Princeton football games, sitting on the visitors' side. They are unofficially helped out now and then by some of the professors in the social-science departments, who criticize the wording of their questions and suggest new and more impartial phrases. Dr. Gallup lives a few miles outside of Princeton. That's one reason he picked Princeton for a location; the other, of course, is that it provides a good, academic-sounding date line. Dr. Gallup's time is divided—as are the sources of his income, undoubtedly—about equally between Young & Rubicam and the Institute, which is entirely his own enterprise. He commutes to New York every weekday except Saturday, which he spends in the Princeton office. Perhaps one day in the middle of the week he takes an early train from New York and puts in an hour or so in the Princeton office before dinner. Almost every morning he looks in on Tibby and Lydgate in the New York office before going over to Young & Rubicam to take up the burdens of a vice-president.

The Institute is certainly in a healthy financial state, but the details are lacking. The "base rate" for subscribing newspapers is a dollar a week per thousand of circulation, but this is shaded for newspapers in big cities. It is one of the more expensive syndicated newspaper features. There are about a thousand people working part time as interviewers for the Institute. They are paid sixty-five cents an hour, and average somewhere between a dollar and a half and two dollars a week. Four surveys a week is the Institute's normal output, and about four thousand questionnaires are turned in weekly. Dr. Gallup figures their average cost, including postage and payment for interviewers, at forty cents. That's $1,600 a week for raw materials, and at least that much again must be added for salaries, office rent, etc.

The interviewers are picked out with the assistance of local institutions throughout the country—colleges, normal schools, and the like. They seem to be people who are above the necessity of working so hard for pin money and do the work partly for pleasure. Mr. Don F. Saunders, the young man in the Princeton office who directs the field-workers, says that among them are two college presidents. He will not identify them beyond denying that they are Conant and Butler. Each interviewer, when working, talks with about ten subjects a week, selected according to instructions from the Princeton office—one male, middle-class Republican, one wife of a man on relief, and whatnot. The selection of specific guinea pigs is entirely up to the interviewer, who is expected to use whatever public records are available, and his native wit. The names of those interviewed are never taken, on the theory that this does away with self-consciousness. The interviewers' instructions are not to let the subject read the questionnaire but to read out the questions, word for word, without amplification. If the subject seems confused, the interviewer reads the question again, slowly and carefully. If he still doesn't understand, the interviewer seeks out another person in the same classification. The interviewers are also warned, rather vaguely, that "a very effective system has been developed for detecting interviews which are not bona fide," but all this appears to mean, in actuality, is that a man from Princeton tries to look in on an interviewer occasionally and see how he's making out. Nobody is supposed to be interviewed more often than once a year.

Gallup and his colleagues are convinced that they never ask leading questions, but this seems to be debatable. For example: "In your opinion, which will do more to get us out of the depression—increased government spending for relief and public works or helping business by reducing taxes?" The phrase "helping business by reducing taxes" sounds like something that, in a lovely dream, an angel would say to J. P. Morgan. Seventy-nine per cent of Dr. Gallup's guinea pigs plumped for helping business by reducing taxes. Of course the vast majority of questions presented by the Institute propound no such sharply defined rights and wrongs. Also, Dr. Gallup conscientiously leaves in every ballot a place to check if the subject says he doesn't know or doesn't care. Curiously enough, the Institute staff finds that after seven years of the New Deal a great number of plain citizens are baffled by questions containing the words "economy" or "economic." This may or may not be an encouraging sign.

The Gallups—Dr. George Horace; Ophelia, his wife; and their two sons —live in a low, white, Early American farmhouse on three hundred acres of land. Anthropologists might find in his farming an analogy with the members of canoe-building Indian tribes who, when they move inland, pathetically continue to build useless canoes. His Princeton place has alfalfa fields and a silo, just like a Midwestern farm. The neighboring farmers raise dairy cattle; Dr. Gallup, although he couldn't possibly raise enough corn to feed them, raises beef cattle, as he learned to do in his birthplace.

Over and above living expenses, his farming costs him $3,000 a year. "A motorboat costs that much," he has said, "and I don't like motorboating." His private life, like that of any successful extrovert, offers nothing much to the biographer.

Dr. Gallup feels that his Institute is doing a real public service but that this is no reason he should not be paid for it. He is against government subsidy of sample-polling, because this might result in influence by the Party in power. He is utterly convinced that the voice of the people is right, and that three times a week is not too often to listen to it. Certain of his critics have said that his polls, even granting their accuracy, are a bad influence politically because foreknowledge of the outcome of an issue prevents healthful debate and minority activities. Dr. Gallup, in a recent lecture delivered at Princeton, answered that objection, and crushingly. He pointed to the continued existence of the Republican Party.

HADLEY CANTRIL

Being in a Troublesome World: The Historical Setting

THE CHARACTERISTIC THOUGHTS and judgments of any group of people are deeply rooted in the culture that surrounds them. The prevailing social conditions provide the context within which the individual must develop and make his adjustment. We naturally wonder if the social setting in the United States on October 30, 1938 was particularly conducive to the panicky behavior of people who happened to hear Orson Welles's broadcast of H. G. Wells's *The War of the Worlds*. Are the times more out of joint now than they were in the golden 'nineties or in 1925? Were there fewer people able to orient themselves properly in 1938 than there might have been in other historical periods had a comparable situation arisen? And if conditions were particularly disturbed, did they affect all people equally? These are essentially questions for the historian and sociologist of the future. But with our present perspective and our present evidence we can discern certain characteristics of the social background which contributed to the arousal of the panic.

Permission the author. From *The Invasion from Mars*. Princeton University Press.

INSTABILITY OF IMPORTANT SOCIAL NORMS

When a culture is highly stable and in a state of complete equilibrium, it means that the frames of reference of the individuals constituting the culture are in complete conformity with the norms of that culture. It means, furthermore, that the frames of reference of individuals are, for them, completely adequate pathways in an environment that is satisfying their needs. Such an ideal state of affairs has certainly never existed for long in any large cultural group. Unrest, change, frustration, dissatisfaction are the rule. For at least a segment of the population current norms are inadequate to meet personal physical and psychological needs. Individual frames of reference either do not conform to accepted norms, as is the case with the radical thinker, or do not adequately explain to the individual the dissatisfaction he is experiencing, as is the case with those who frankly confess they don't know what the remedy is, those who try one remedy after another, or those who land in the camp of a leader, such as Dr. Townsend, who has an oversimplified but understandable solution.

At the time of the Martian invasion many social norms, with their corresponding personal habits, were in a state of flux and change, many of the previously accepted social standards were either proving themselves inadequate to accommodate human needs or were in danger of being overthrown by outside ideologies. In either case many of the individuals who composed the culture were perplexed and confused.

Unsettled Conditions. Particularly since the depression of 1929, a number of people have begun to wonder whether or not they will ever regain any sense of economic security. The complexity of modern finance and government, the discrepancies shown in the economic and political proposals of the various "experts," the felt threats of Fascism, Communism, prolonged unemployment among millions of Americans—these together with a thousand and one other characteristics of modern living—create an environment which the average individual is completely unable to interpret. Not only do events occur that he is unable to understand, but almost all of these events seem to be completely beyond his own immediate control, even though his personal life may be drastically affected by them. He feels that he is living in a period of rapid social change, but just what direction the change should take and how it may be peacefully accomplished he does not know. For the most part, the potential consequences of forthcoming events are unpredictable.

This situation is not something known only to the public official, the big businessman, or the social scientist. The masses of people themselves know all this most poignantly. The material consequences of a disturbed eco-

nomic order are not difficult for anyone to recognize. And most important
for our purposes are the psychological consequences in terms of personal
anxieties, ambitions, and insecurities of this awareness that all is not right
with the world. A few random observations will illustrate what these unsettled conditions actually mean to people.

A recent poll of the American Institute of Public Opinion contained the
question, "If you lost your present job (or business) and could not find
other work, how long do you think you could hold out before you would
have to apply for relief?" [1] The answers to this question reflect the basic
insecurity of over half the population.[2]

Persons on relief already	17%
Could hold out one month or less	19
One to six months	16
Six months up to three years	13
Three years and over	35

The same ballot asked persons what social class they felt they belonged to
and of what income class they considered themselves to be members. The
answers to these two questions show that whereas only 6 per cent of the
population regards itself as belonging to the lower *social* class and 88 per
cent believe they are in the middle class, 31 per cent regard themselves as
members of the lower *economic* class. Hence for a quarter of the population
there is a discrepancy between their income and their social status.

Popular education, advertising, and mass media of communication have
deluged people with a knowledge of the potential abundancies of life.
They derive real needs for automobiles, central heating, indoor plumbing,
and dozens of other things which are now within their range of vision.
Even in our small sample of case studies, we found that when people were
asked to indicate from a list of eighteen possibilities, "Which of the following would you most like to have?" (such as a pretty home, travel, professional advancement), those persons with more than high school education checked twice as many things as less educated people. If education
should be further extended while economic conditions remained static,
one could safely predict that the discrepancy between the aspiration levels
and the achievement levels of the masses would become even greater.

---

[1] Release of April 2, 1939.

[2] See *Consumer Incomes in the United States,* a report of the National Resources Committee for a graphic account of income distribution in the United States during 1936. Also
the National Resources Committee report, *The Structure of the American Economy,* Part I:
Basic Characteristics, 1939. Although the report has been widely quoted, the real significance
of the low standards of living prevailing in the country are difficult to appreciate in any
personal context unless one can actually observe the consequences or feel their implications in
such books as *Grapes of Wrath, These Are Our Lives, Middletown in Transition.*

In the case of certain listeners to this broadcast, the general confusion in economic, political and social conditions does seem to have been a major cause of fantastic interpretation. And it was the people who were closest to the borderline of economic disaster who were most apt to take the program as news. We have already shown the high relationship between education and economic status and have seen that people of low education oriented themselves least adequately. But even when we equate people by their educational level and then compare their adjustment to the broadcast according to their economic circumstances, we find that poorer people tended to assume a false standard of judgment more frequently than others, irrespective of education (Table 14).

TABLE 14

PROPORTION OF PEOPLE IN DIFFERENT EDUCATIONAL AND ECONOMIC GROUPS WHO
INTERPRETED THE PROGRAM AS NEWS (CBS SURVEY)

Economic Status	Education		
	College (per cent)	High school (per cent)	Grammar school (per cent)
High	28	31	43
Average	25	34	45
Low	0	44	53

A few comments from the case studies will show how people felt, and why they were suggestible to news which perhaps seemed little less confused than the confused world they already knew.

"Everything is so upset in the world that *anything might happen.*"

"Things have happened so thick and fast since my grandfather's day that *we can't hope to know what might happen now.* I am all balled up."

"Ever since my husband lost his job a few years ago, *things seem to have gone from bad to worse.* I don't know when everything will be all right again."

"*Being we are in a troublesome world, anything is liable to happen.* We hear so much news every day—so many things we hear are unbelievable. Like all of a sudden 600 children burned to death in a school house, or a lot of people being thrown out of work. Everything seems to be a shock to me."

For many persons another bewildering characteristic of our present civilization is the mystery of science. For certain people without scientific training or without sufficient personal ability, initiative or opportunity to investigate the mechanisms surrounding them, the telephone, the airplane, poison gas, the radio, the camera are but specific manifestations of a baffling power. The principles by which such things operate are completely unknown. Such devices come from a world outside and lie within a universe of discourse completely foreign to the perplexed layman. Scientists in general are frequently referred to as "they." Many variations of this theme are found in the case studies. If science can create the things we have, why can't it create rocket ships and death rays?

"*I hear they are experimenting* with rocket ships and it seems possible that we will have them."

"So many odd things are happening in the world. *Science has progressed so far* that we don't know how far it might have gone on Mars. The way the world runs ahead anything is possible."

War Scare. This broadcast followed closely on the heels of a European war crisis. Not only did the crisis seem to be a very real one, but it was perhaps at the time a more widely known one than any in history—thanks to the medium of radio and the ingenuity and resourcefulness of the large broadcasting companies who had special reporters on the spot. During August, September and part of October 1938 millions of Americans were listening regularly to their radios, to the latest stories of a developing international crisis. Probably never before in the history of broadcasting had so many people in this country been glued to their sets. Stations at all hours were willing to interrupt prearranged programs for the latest news broadcast. Hence both the technique and the content of this broadcast tended to fit into the existing mental context which had resulted from world events of the previous weeks.

When our interviewers asked, "What major catastrophe could happen to the American people?" three-fourths of those in the frightened group as contrasted to half of those in the non-frightened group answered war or revolution. Evidence of the same feeling is seen in answer to the question, "What sort of a catastrophe did you think it was?" Here the largest single category of response, except that of a Martian invasion, was the belief that the catastrophe actually was an act of war or some foreign attack. Over a fourth of the people who were disturbed or frightened by the broadcast gave such answers. Further expression of the fear of war is revealed in the images that listeners had of the actual invaders. Although about half of the people who were frightened or disturbed had fantastic pictures of the invaders as Martians, giants, or creatures of semi-human form, almost one-fifth of them reported that they had visions of soldiers attacking with advanced military weapons. Persons in the frightened group were, then, apparently more concerned about war.

The European war scare left some persons bewildered and confused, with a very real, if vague dread of a new war. Others had definite ideas of the potential source of trouble, localizing it chiefly in Germany or Japan. The instability of the former peace-time norms and the fear that these would be upset in favor of new norms that were personally dangerous and unwanted was clearly reflected in the case studies.

"The war talk has us so upset. Conditions are so unsettled since Chamberlain went to see Hitler."

"I feel insecure because although we are not in the war, we are so near it. I feel that with new devices on airplanes, it is possible for foreign powers to invade us. I listened to every broadcast during the European crisis."

"I'm afraid of all those people in Europe, they could do anything."

"I felt the catastrophe was *an attack by the Germans,* because Hitler didn't appreciate Roosevelt's telegram."

"The announcer said a meteor had fallen from Mars and I was sure he thought that, but *in back of my head I had the idea that the meteor was just a camouflage.* It was really an airplane like a Zeppelin that looked like a meteor and *the Germans were attacking* us with gas bombs. The airplane was built to look like a meteor just to fool people."

"I felt *it might be the Japanese*—they are so crafty."

A few people interpreted the invasion as an extension of the war against the Jews.

"The Jews are being treated so terribly in some parts of the world, *I was sure something had come to destroy them* in this country."

"I worry terribly about the future of the Jews. Nothing else bothers me so much. I thought *this might be another attempt to harm them."*

The thrill of disaster. It is a well known fact that people who suffer deeply or whose lot in life is generally miserable frequently compensate for their situations by seeking some temporary change or escape from their troubles. Dull lives may be cheered with bright clothing or gaudy furniture, harassed breadwinners may become fixtures at the local beer hall, worried housewives may zealously participate in religious orgies, repressed youths may identify themselves for a few hours with the great lovers or gangsters of the silver screen. There are many socially accepted ways of escape from the responsibilities, worries, and frustrations of life—the movies, the pulp magazines, fraternal organizations, and a host of other devices thrive partially because their devotees want surcease from their woes.

In addition to these more obvious escapes, there are two other conditions that may resolve the problems such persons face. In the first place, some social upheaval may dissipate the circumstances that create the frustration. The early days after a revolution generally bring with them freedom and license. Sometimes the upheaval may be of such a nature that the individual will in the end be in a worse situation than he was before. But because of the intense worries or anxieties he has, he may consciously or unconsciously welcome the cataclysm. Take, for example, a bank clerk who has embezzled certain funds to help a needy family. His conscience may bother him and he may always have the dread that some day he will be caught. But one day the bank is blown up, all the records are destroyed and he himself is badly injured. It is not hard to imagine that such a man would greet such a catastrophe. A few persons represented in the case studies showed signs of welcoming the invasion and their consequent extermination because of the relief it would give them.

"*I was looking forward with some pleasure to the destruction of the entire human race* and the end of the world. *If we have Fascist domination* of the world, *there is no purpose in living anyway.*"

"My only thought involving myself as a person in connection with it was a delight that if it spread to Stelton *I would not have to pay the butcher's bill.*"

"I looked in the icebox and saw some chicken left from Sunday dinner that I was saving for Monday night dinner. I said to my nephew, '*We may as well eat this chicken*—we won't be here in the morning.'"

"The broadcast had us all worried but I knew *it would at least scare ten years' life out of my mother-in-law.*"

Another way in which people may get relief from their troubles is by submerging their own responsibilities and worries into a battle their whole society is having with some threatening force. We know, for example, that the suicide rate decreases in war time, presumably because potential suicides gain new securities and feel new responsibilities that are socially valued. Some of the frightened persons to the broadcast had a feeling of self-importance while they were listening or relaying vital information regarding the invasion to uninformed friends whom they thought they were helping. They were temporarily a member of the "in" group.

"I urged my husband to listen and said *it was an historical moment* possibly and he would be sorry afterwards to have missed it."

"*It was the thrill of a lifetime*—to hear something like that and think it's real."

"I had never heard anything like it before and I was excited even after I knew what it was about. *I felt like telling somebody all about it.*"

Others seemed to enjoy the broadcast despite their fear because the event was aligning them with other people in a conflict for rights, privileges, or ideals they had been carrying on alone or with a minority group. A Jewish woman reported, for example:

"I realized right away that *it was something that was affecting everybody, not only the Jews,* and I felt relieved. *As long as everybody was going to die,* it was better."

Although comparatively rare, these instances of an ambivalent attitude to the ensuing destruction do serve as a mirror of the times. Such persons would probably not have experienced any pleasure or relief from their worries had they lived in a more ideal social order where democracy was secure, where every person played a rôle, or where money, food, or houses were plentiful.

So far we have indicated that the broadcast would not have aroused an extensive panic if people had enjoyed greater educational advantages which they might have followed through with satisfying jobs, sufficiently rewarding to accommodate more of their needs. The times also seemed out of joint because of the threat of an impending war in which this country might become involved. These dislocations in the culture probably account in large measure for the emotional insecurity we have found so important and for the lack of critical ability discovered especially in the lower education and income brackets of the population.

Throughout the whole discussion so far we have stressed the personal and unique nature of the subjective context which the listener called upon to interpret the broadcast. In our analyses we have been forced to conceptualize these various contexts by using classificatory rubrics. But as the author of the *War of the Worlds* has pointed out, "the forceps of our minds are clumsy forceps and crush the truth a little in taking hold of it." [1] Before seeking any final generalizations with which to explain the nature of a panic, we shall turn therefore to case studies of a few individuals who were panic-stricken to see how the factors we have mentioned so far are in individual lives interwoven with individual listening experiences.

JONATHAN DANIELS

New Tenants

"THE JEWS," he said, "the damned Jews and the women!"

He was a bitter old man, a distinctly unpleasant old man, unshaven, unwashed. He was fat where maybe once he was strong, pasty and habitually inert on the bench in the little triangular park. But I think he put his pudgy

---

[1] H. G. Wells, *Experiment in Autobiography*. New York: Macmillan, 1934, p. 180. Permission the author. From *A Southerner Discovers New England*. The Macmillan Co.

finger not on justice but on the change which has taken place in Fall River. There were other men in the park, a good many of them younger and cleaner, filling the benches at an hour when work was going on. For work was going on, Fall River was climbing slowly up out of the depths of the despair which made it not only a place full of French and Portuguese unemployed and old Yankee families poor in a pinched comparison with the rich past, but also a city which had gone bankrupt when the pressure of the poor increased on a wealth which was no longer there.

The men in the little park looked well fed. They were warm in the sun. There seemed no lack of cigarettes among them. They had reading matter of a variety which extended (maybe not a great distance) from *The Daily Racing Form* to Father Coughlin's *Social Justice*. Yet about even the youngest of them there was a capon quality. The workers wanted in most of the new industries were women. In the roughly partitioned-off offices of little industries in huge old mills the new successful operators were not the immaculate, inheriting, young Yankees out of Harvard but the slim or paunchy Jews out of Krakow, Minsk, and the crowded streets of New York. The male and their old masters sat in parks or in old houses which still looked substantial from the street though there might be more heirlooms than income within. Recovery did not seem to lead back to the past.

That week, on the road which ran to the west from the Nantucket boat pier in New Bedford, I passed a sign which anounced that practically the entire village of Westport Factory, Massachusetts, would be sold at public auction: the mill, sixteen two-family dwellings, two cottages, and several parcels of land belonging to the company. They had built the first mill there in 1812. The village was a detail between New Bedford and Fall River, not as important, perhaps, as the pickets marching before the filling stations with their placards, "Tydol unfair to striking seamen." Socony, the Fall River pickets reported, was unfair, too.

There was a hideous, huge, green-towered church. A man in a shed was working very calmly with a big hammer on a tombstone. Children were pouring, like happy young bees from a hive, out of the parochial school. Only one little girl was deformed, frail and pitifully pigeon-toed and somehow pigeon-armed. The tenements to which they ran—the little lame girl moved like an old woman—looked clean and in good repair. There was little open evidence of horrid poverty. The big granite mills, rising like cliffs, with high delicate smokestacks, flanging slightly outward at the top, looked from a distance like the very picture of industrial solidity; but I had been riding New England long enough to know the signs of emptiness eager to be filled.

Everywhere they reminded me of my eighth-grade impression, from the days when eighth grades everywhere were fed from a Yankee spoon, of the poem of Dr. Oliver Wendell Holmes of Boston about the chambered nautilus which built vaster and nobler chambers until at last it was free— free as only the dead are. I never to my knowledge saw a nautilus but I am a friend from boyhood of its cousin the conch. And I have found hermit crabs and other creeping sea creatures in magnificent shells abandoned by their builders. In New England, as in the case of the nautilus, other life occupies the abandoned shells even if it does not fill them. That, I hope, is as good anthropology as zoology even if Dr. Holmes, professor of anatomy and physiology in the Harvard Medical School, did not write a poem about it. I doubt if anybody ever will. But there is a poem there: Maybe all of us live in the great halls the past built like little Jewish manufacturers struggling to meet chain-store prices, or like Portuguese girls at sewing machines making over and over the standardized dresses and needing the protection of minimum-wage laws. And some of us are just sitting hating Jews or an equivalent in a park. There's the plot for the poet: It's free.

In the park where the men sat, a former textile worker told me what he thought had happened to him and the others. He didn't take much stock in the talk about the South. He didn't think the Southern workers were as good as the Northern workers were, even if they did work cheaper. The new chain mills that had come in were doing all right. He'd seen what had happened in the mills that failed. They'd let the machinery get out of date. "Old clattery stuff," he said. In some of the mills they were using equipment that hadn't been changed since they were built. "They made plenty," he told me. "But they didn't pay it to us. They didn't buy new machines. What'd they expect?"

He nodded at the old man who had cursed the Jews.

"Of course, now, there's something to what he says. I can't get a job, but I got a daughter working for Schneierson's. Only thing is I don't see how you can blame the Jews. Nobody else around here ever was in business for love." He leaned across me toward the old man. "Name one who was," he dared.

The old man only made a noise which was a half a grunt and half a sniff. The textile worker laughed at his muttering, but I doubt whether he silenced it. I am afraid it will not soon be silenced anywhere.

I went beyond muttering to try to get facts. I have a deep prejudice, often placated by individuals, against chamber of commerce secretaries—formed, I suspect, when I was a young reporter. Young reporters being the apprentices of literature, even if they never become its practitioners, share with the masters a preference for murder over the poppycock patriotism of municipal promoters. It is a prejudice I have found generally justified in the search for truth and justice. Pudgy men personally, the worst of their tribe have sometimes conceived it as their duty to organize both the bruising and the bragging of the town, depending only upon whether the recipient of their attentions is the money investor or the labor organizer. Some of the same have treated me to some bad lying about poor causes. Now I have a hope based upon some evidence that such secretaries are decreasing, not because of any general advancing municipal morality in the United States but because of a creeping understanding among the municipal mighty that some brains are necessary if their towns are to survive the increasingly shrewd and ruthless war between the cities which goes on in these United States today.

I think Frank Dunham of Fall River may be one of those better and pleasanter men. At any rate he made me think he was glad to tell me the truth as well as point out to me the merits of his hard-hit town. I hope I'm not guilty of regional partiality, for though he was born in Bristol, Tennessee, his people were Yankee and he was only in the South a little more than long enough to be born. (Maybe there was an old Southern touch in the Fall River promise, "Progress—Prosperity—Peace." Peace in a crowded labor market where people had been hurt seemed a promise like the docility some stupid promoters once promised ignorant industrial itinerants in the South.)

A youngish-looking gray-haired man, Dunham spread across his desk in his long office the statistics of textile pay rolls falling, of empty industrial space, of dollars and people, of space filled, of new industries producing not only the coarse cotton goods of the past but a variety which ran from hats to shoelaces. He told me about the fire which had spread in 1927 from a watchman warming himself to blaze across the town. He remembered the expansive years when mill owners, preferring to pay local taxes rather than big Federal war taxes, had rather acquiesced in increasing assessments on their properties. They had been caught there when prosperity tumbled down. Then he suggested that we go across the street and see the members of the Board of Finance which had been put in like a set of receivers when the town had defaulted on its obligations in 1930.

I stopped him on the curb by the City Hall to look at a granite fountain which was not running any more. Only in the bottom bowl on one side there was a little pool of stagnant water with some trash in it. The granite letters still cried welcome:

Citizens and Strangers
Drink Freely of This

Cooling Stream,
It Will Promote
Temperance, Faith, Hope
And Charity.
The Records of 1882
Deposited Within Will
Rejoice Antiquarians

The fountain had been presented, the granite letters said in a nice distinction, to "citizens and mill operatives," by Henry D. Cogswell, D.D.S., of San Francisco, "who in 1833 as a factory boy marched to the music of the bell." Old Dr. Cogswell, it seemed probable from the date of his boyhood, may have made a killing filling teeth in California at a time when there was plenty of gold for that purpose and other purposes, too. It had been nice of him to remember Fall River, even if Fall River now seemed to have forgotten his fountain. I wondered how well it remembered him when he came back in 1882 to build what amounted to his monument. I think he deserved one even if he bought it for himself: He was the local boy who went off and made good; he was the boy who went to the West when the West was yawning open in promise to the young. For all I know, he was just a tooth puller; but the boy of 1833 was also the man of the past.

Dunham and I went in through an oak-paneled room which seemed in itself a symbol of an earlier time of fine carriage horses and plug hats, of a labor that ought to be grateful and even a management which was still confident that it was wise. In the smaller chambers beyond, elegant also in an outmoded fashion, were the two senior members of the Fall River Board of Finance. The Board, appointed by the Governor and composed at the outset of the solid, scrubbed, and cultured representatives of the Yankee economic aristocracy of Massachusetts, had in a real sense taken over the town in 1930 when the town defaulted on its obligations. But in the nine years its membership had changed. At one side of the ornate old-fashioned table sat little Edmund Coté, the French-Canadian chairman. His skin looked old, his hair was pasted in strands across the tight skin on his skull. His little eyes gleamed behind his modern rimless glasses. At his left was H. William Radovsky, a debonair, bald, middle-aged Jewish lawyer with an 1890 mustache long and a little bushy at the ends. He smoked a pipe like a Britisher or a Bostonian. Dunham introduced me. The other member, an Irish politician, was not in town. We talked about Fall River and finances. Dunham had already told me something about that story before we crossed to the City Hall. The really tough job had been done in the first years after the default in 1930. The Board members then had cut salaries and fired schoolteachers.

"They were called S.O.B.'s by half the town."

Nevertheless they had reduced the net debt of the city from ten to five million dollars. They had even reduced the tax rate in a town in which valuations on mill properties and machinery had come down from $100,-000,000 to $12,000,000. They had fed the poor even if, as some of the poor said, "all they give you in Fall River is rotten groceries." (The Board insisted that by the commissary system they saved money for the town and assured a balanced diet for the needy, eliminating the swapping of grocery orders for liquor and the purchase of hops and malt instead of meat and potatoes.) The Board as it aged and changed had less trouble than the original one. The Frenchman, the Jew, and the Irishman had moved away from the fiscal, moneylending guardianship of the National Shawmut and the First National Bank of Boston which had helped the original Board shape its financing. They had been able to get money cheaper elsewhere, Coté said.

"Dey didn't say anything to us," he said of the Boston banks, "but very likely dey didn't like it."

Radovsky made a slip in recounting the history of the Finance Board, and old man Coté corrected him. Afterwards he said, "Hymie ought to learn his lessons."

The old man moved from municipal finances to conditions in Fall River and New England. He talked in an argot which a long living in Fall River had not corrected. I remember his phrase "dose single woman" in his talk about relief. Forty per cent of the people on relief did not need it, he thought. He was sure there were no slums anywhere in New England like those in the South.

"Dose Negroes in de South don't live any better as in Haiti. I know. I went. Nothing like dat here. Nothing."

I did not argue. Indeed, there is nothing—or very little—in Massachusetts like the apparent poverty of the South. In New England, poverty, like everything else, has to be shut in for the fear of winter. It cannot be seen. But at Harvard, Paul Herman Buck, who won the Pulitzer Prize for *The Road to Reunion,* told me that when he took two fellow professors South in the summer they could not see Southern poverty for the flowers around the cabins. It is not easy not to be blind abroad. But there was poverty in Fall River deep and degraded and some also as proud and as pretending as that of some Southerners who long ago lost their money and their slaves.

When we went out Radovsky put on a jaunty brown hat and slipped into a smart green herringbone overcoat. He looked confident in his world, and so stylish in his dress as to make look almost nondescript an observant man of commerce whom I saw later. He was not fearful of Fall River's future, but he was thoughtful about the change from its past. We talked in his office, we talked looking at its people on its streets, we talked resting in a soda fountain where we had Coca Colas (somehow they are never quite as good in New England as they are in the South).

"We didn't have a damn thing here except cotton mills. We had a worse situation here than they did in Manchester. The whole thing happened at once there, and besides they had a good shoe industry which wasn't involved. But the liquidations began here in 1924. Every time we thought we'd hit bottom, somebody else would blow up."

He considered the causes of the disastrous procession. He named the familiar ones: low Southern wages, wage and hour restrictions, unions, taxes. But there was another reason.

"The old fellows who formed the mills worked up with them; they knew them from the bottom up; they knew the business and the labor. They sent their sons to Harvard and Yale and Dartmouth. Maybe they took law. They were interested in books and music. And yachting and things like that. Though they were the nicest fellows in the world, they did not understand the business as their fathers did. Then there was obsolete equipment, but that comes around to being a management fault."

"The last run of shad?"

"Yes, you can call it that."

"What's happened to them?"

He swung around on his stool at the soda fountain counter and regarded the town beyond the open door.

"Of course, I don't mean to suggest that all our old Yankee stock is run out. It hasn't by any means. Some of it is the best we've got. College hasn't made all of them soft—not by a long shot. But it's pathetic in some cases. Some of the old mill families are now like your old Southern families after the Civil War with big houses but no money. Some of them are having to make a hard struggle to keep up pretenses."

"Cake and wine on the sideboard even if there isn't bread in the pantry," I said.

"Something like that. The old mills that failed were almost altogether family-owned. I think only one moved South. The others failed where they sat. Right here in Fall River something like $75,00,000 was lost in their failure. You can guess what that meant to the people who lost it."

"What about the people who lost the jobs?"

There were relief figures to show some of that. There was the default-ing town in which the need for relief had pressed upon the disappearing wealth to show some of the community situation. Some thousands of people had simply disappeared. (Between 1930 and 1934, 240,000 New Englanders had moved from cities to farms, and a larger proportion had remained there than in the United States as a whole.) He thought—and the figures he showed me made me think so, too—that they had done a pretty good job in filling the 9,000,000 square feet of industrial space which was left idle. (That is almost half again as big a space as the Amoskeag vacancy in Manchester. That is a space big as two hundred football fields.) Some of the space had been filled fairly promptly by branches of chains of mills. But there was a lot of space left: It was filling with the familiar "diversified" industries, principally in the gar-ment business, attracted from New York City and other metropolitan areas by cheap factory space and the hope of abundant labor.

"Sweatshops?"

He looked, I thought, a little sad. "No. First the NRA and now the Massachusetts and the Federal minimum-wage laws prevent that. But Fall River has got about the lowest wage in Massachusetts."

He quoted out of memory the general terms of the state figures. Fall River was at the bottom, but in Massachusetts the state then limited hours in the ladies' garment industry to forty-eight and fixed the minimum wage at thirty-five cents an hour. The Federal law then limited the work-ing time to forty-four hours. Forty-four hours at thirty-five cents equaled $15.40. I knew that would not be considered a low wage in the South.

"The new industries want women workers?"

"That's a trouble," he said. "In the old days here the textile labor was about fifty-fifty, men and women. In the garment factories about 90 per cent of the employees are women. There's a great need for industries employing men."

I told him what the old man on the bench had said about the women and the Jews.

"The Jews seem to be the only people smart enough to take advantage of the chance."

"They work at their business?"

"All the time."

"And they haven't been to Harvard?"

He laughed. "No."

I offered him a cigarette and lit one myself.

"Sometimes I wonder," I said, "if these new Jews aren't more like the old Yankees than the sons of the old Yankees are."

He shook his head. "I don't know. They're the people that are making work in the mills. I don't know what we'd do without them."

"What are you doing with them?"

"What do you mean?"

"Does Fall River like them?"

He considered. "Not very much. I'm afraid that's growing. I think part of it is due to the overenthusiasm of the Jews for displays of racial-religious brotherly love. They're always getting the Protestant minister and the Catholic priest together with the rabbi in some joint service. That does more harm sometimes than good. You know Fall River is 85 per cent Catholic. All the Jewish stores closed when the Pope died. It didn't help."

"Suppose they hadn't closed?"

He laughed. "That might have hurt, too."

"So the old man wasn't just muttering for himself about the women and the Jews."

"I don't think there's any real feeling of resentment among the men over the fact that there are jobs for women and none for them. It's always been the custom here for several in a family to work and together make a good family income. It isn't anything new for the women to work. In the old mill days, as soon as the children were fourteen they were taken out of school and put in the mills. Last year we had the largest high-school class in the town's history despite the fact that the town's 15,000 smaller than it used to be."

He grinned over another puzzle. "But here's another thing. The more educated business-school girls in the garment factory offices make less than the less educated girls at the machines. Of course, there's a social difference between the girls in the offices and the girls in the plants, but some of the girls in the offices are beginning to think it isn't worth the difference in pay."

"A man's strength isn't so important any more—there are more jobs for the girls. Is the schooling important?"

"The children seem to think so."

"I wonder if they do?"

I knew that in the old days when Fall River was prosperous it was one of the most illiterate cities in the United States. Even in 1930 only Charleston in South Carolina among comparable cities had a larger ratio of people who were not able to read and write.

"I hope the children continue to have faith in the schools," I said, "but sometimes they seem to be in the schools only because they can't leave them for jobs. The Yankees went to Harvard and lost the mills, and the Jews didn't go to Harvard and are filling them again."

My Fall River acquaintance smiled slowly.

"You're not talking about Fall River now," he said, "and I'm not a philosopher."

We laughed. But I think I was talking about Fall River and a thousand other American towns as well. I know Fall River may need not only diversified industries but philosophers, also. It may need them most.

"I am and you are," I told him. "Or you'd better be."

And the rest of us, also. It was no simplicity of cause which emptied and silenced the vaster and vaster granite halls of Fall River's mills. There was no simplicity about the life which was creeping back into them. I drove by the little park where the old man had muttered his emotions. Some orators elsewhere were thinking and saying no more. The benches were still full of men. But not all the women were working in the factories. I passed a redheaded woman, pregnant and pushing a baby carriage. There were men working on a sea wall for the WPA near Tiverton, but, on the bridge there, nearly a hundred men were fishing in a pleasanter idleness than I had found in the park. Among the fishers was one middleaged woman who had just caught a very small fish. Beyond Portsmouth the road became emptier and sweeter: The dandelions were thick and golden in the grass. Behind stone fences a lovely big country house was almost surrounded by jonquils. There were cattle in the fields and a man plowing with a pair of horses. The earth came open in a deep furrow behind the blade of his plow.

ERSKINE CALDWELL

The People vs. Abe Lathan, Colored

UNCLE ABE was shucking corn in the crib when Luther Bolick came down from the big white house on the hill and told him to pack up his household goods and move off the farm. Uncle Abe had grown a little deaf and he did not hear what Luther said the first time.

Reprinted from *Jackpot* by Erskine Caldwell by permission of the publishers, Duell, Sloan & Pearce, Inc. Copyright 1940, by Erskine Caldwell.

"These old ears of mine is bothering me again, Mr. Luther," Uncle Abe said. "I just can't seem to hear as good as I used to."

Luther looked at the Negro and scowled. Uncle Abe had got up and was standing in the crib door where he could hear better.

"I said, I want you and your family to pack up your furniture and anything else that really belongs to you, and move off."

Uncle Abe reached out and clutched at the crib door for support.

"Move off?" Uncle Abe said.

He looked into his landlord's face unbelievingly.

"Mr. Luther, you don't mean that, does you?" Uncle Abe asked, his voice shaking. "You must be joking, ain't you, Mr. Luther?"

"You heard me right, even if you do pretend to be half deaf," Luther said angrily, turning around and walking several steps. "I want you off the place by the end of the week. I'll give you that much time if you don't try to make any trouble. And when you pack up your things, take care you don't pick up anything that belongs to me. Or I'll have the law on you."

Uncle Abe grew weak so quickly that he barely managed to keep from falling. He turned a little and slid down the side of the door and sat on the crib floor. Luther looked around to see what he was doing.

"I'm past sixty," Uncle Abe said slowly, "but me and my family works hard for you, Mr. Luther. We work as hard as anybody on your whole place. You know that's true, Mr. Luther. I've lived here, working for you, and your daddy before you, for all of forty years. I never mentioned to you about the shares, no matter how big the crop was that I raised for you. I've never asked much, just enough to eat and a few clothes, that's all. I raised up a houseful of children to help work, and none of them ever made any trouble for you, did they, Mr. Luther?"

Luther waved his arm impatiently, indicating that he wanted the Negro to stop arguing. He shook his head, showing that he did not want to listen to anything Uncle Abe had to say.

"That's all true enough," Luther said, "but I've got to get rid of half the tenants on my place. I can't afford to keep eight or ten old people like you here any longer. All of you will have to move off and go somewhere else."

"Ain't you going to farm this year, and raise cotton, Mr. Luther?" Uncle Abe asked. "I can still work as good and hard as anybody else. It may take me a little longer sometimes, but I get the work done. Ain't I shucking this corn to feed the mules as good as anybody else could do?"

"I haven't got time to stand here and argue with you," Luther said nervously. "My mind is made up, and that's all there is to it. Now, you go on home as soon as you finish feeding the mules and start packing the things that belong to you like I told you."

Luther turned away and started walking down the path towards the barn. When he got as far as the barnyard gate, he turned around and looked back. Uncle Abe had followed him.

"Where can me and my family move to, Mr. Luther?" Uncle Abe said. "The boys is big enough to take care of themselves. But me and my wife has grown old. You know how hard it is for an old colored man like me to go out and find a house and land to work on shares. It don't cost you much to keep us, and me and my boys raise as much cotton as anybody else. The last time I mentioned the shares has been a long way in the past, thirty years or more. I'm just content to work like I do and get some rations and a few clothes. You know that's true, Mr. Luther. I've lived in my little shanty over there for all of forty years, and it's the only home I've got. Mr. Luther, me and my wife is both old now, and I can't hire out to work by the day, because I don't have the strength any more. But I can still grow cotton as good as any other colored man in the country."

Luther opened the barnyard gate and walked through it. He shook his head as though he was not even going to listen any longer. He turned his back on Uncle Abe and walked away.

Uncle Abe did not know what to say or do after that. When he saw Luther walk away, he became shaky all over. He clutched at the gate for something to hold on to.

"I just can't move away, Mr. Luther," he said desperately. "I just can't do that. This is the only place I've got to live in the world. I just can't move off, Mr. Luther."

Luther walked out of sight around the corner of the barn. He did not hear Uncle Abe after that.

The next day, at a little after two o'clock in the afternoon, a truck drove up to the door of the three-room house where Uncle Abe, his wife, and their three grown sons lived. Uncle Abe and his wife were sitting by the fire trying to keep warm in the winter cold. They were the only ones at home then.

Uncle Abe heard the truck drive up and stop, but he sat where he was, thinking it was his oldest boy, Henry, who drove a truck sometimes for Luther Bolick.

After several minutes had passed, somebody knocked on the door, and his wife got up right away and went to see who it was.

There were two strange white men on the porch when she opened the door. They did not say anything at first, but looked inside the room to see who was there. Still not saying anything, they came inside and walked to the fireplace where Uncle Abe sat hunched over the hearth.

"Are you Abe Lathan?" one of the men, the older, asked.

"Yes, sir, I'm Abe Lathan," he answered, wondering who they were, because he had never seen them before. "Why do you want to know that?"

The man took a bright metal disk out of his pocket and held it in the palm of his hand before Uncle Abe's eyes.

"I'm serving a paper and a warrant on you," he said. "One is an eviction, and the other is for threatening to do bodily harm."

He unfolded the eviction notice and handed it to Uncle Abe. The Negro shook his head bewilderedly, looking first at the paper and finally up at the two strange white men.

"I'm a deputy," the older man said, "and I've come for two things—to evict you from this house and to put you under arrest."

"What does that mean—evict?" Uncle Abe asked.

The two men looked around the room for a moment. Uncle Abe's wife had come up behind his chair and put trembling hands on his shoulder.

"We are going to move your furniture out of this house and carry it off the property of Luther Bolick. Then, besides that, we're going to take you down to the county jail. Now, come on and hurry up, both of you."

Uncle Abe got up, and he and his wife stood on the hearth not knowing what to do.

The two men began gathering up the furniture and carrying it out of the house. They took the beds, tables, chairs, and everything else in the three rooms except the cook-stove, which belonged to Luther Bolick. When they got all the things outside, they began piling them into the truck.

Uncle Abe went outside in front of the house as quickly as he could.

"White folks, please don't do that," he begged. "Just wait a minute while I go find Mr. Luther. He'll set things straight. Mr. Luther is my landlord, and he won't let you take all my furniture away like this. Please, sir, just wait while I go find him."

The two men looked at each other.

"Luther Bolick is the one who signed these papers," the deputy said, shaking his head. "He was the one who got these court orders to carry off the furniture and put you in jail. It wouldn't do you a bit of good to try to find him now."

"Put me in jail?" Uncle Abe said. "What did he say to do that for?"

"For threatening bodily harm," the deputy said. "That's for threatening to kill him. Hitting him with a stick or shooting him with a pistol."

The men threw the rest of the household goods into the truck and told Uncle Abe and his wife to climb in the back. When they made no effort to get in, the deputy pushed them to the rear and prodded them until they climbed into the truck.

While the younger man drove the truck, the deputy stood beside them in the body so they could not escape. They drove out the lane, past the other tenant houses, and then down the long road that went over the hill through Luther Bolick's land to the public highway. They passed the big white house where he lived, but he was not within sight.

"I never threatened to harm Mr. Luther," Uncle Abe protested. "I never did a thing like that in my whole life. I never said a mean thing about him either. Mr. Luther is my boss, and I've worked for him ever since I was twenty years old. Yesterday he said he wanted me to move off his farm, and all I did was say that I thought he ought to let me stay. I won't have much longer to live, noway. I told him I didn't want to move off. That's all I said to Mr. Luther. I ain't never said I was going to try to kill him. Mr. Luther knows that as well as I do. You ask Mr. Luther if that ain't so."

They had left Luther Bolick's farm, and had turned down the highway towards the county seat, eleven miles away.

"For forty years I has lived here and worked for Mr. Luther," Uncle Abe said, "and I ain't never said a mean thing to his face or behind his back in all that time. He furnishes me with rations for me and my family, and a few clothes, and me and my family raise cotton for him, and I been doing that ever since I was twenty years old. I moved here and started working on shares for his daddy first, and then when he died, I kept right on like I have up to now. Mr. Luther knows I has worked hard and never answered him back, and only asked for rations and a few clothes all this time. You ask Mr. Luther."

The deputy listened to all that Uncle Abe said, but he did not say anything himself. He felt sorry for the old Negro and his wife, but there was nothing he could do about it. Luther Bolick had driven to the courthouse early that morning and secured the papers for eviction and arrest. It was his job to serve the papers and execute the court orders. But even if it was his job, he could not keep from feeling sorry for the Negroes. He didn't think that Luther Bolick ought to throw them off his farm just because they had grown old.

When they got within sight of town, the deputy told the driver to stop. He drew the truck up beside the highway when they reached the first row of houses. There were fifteen or eighteen Negro houses on both sides of the road.

After they had stopped, the two white men began unloading the furniture and stacking it beside the road. When it was all out of the truck, the deputy told Uncle Abe's wife to get out. Uncle Abe started to get out, too, but the deputy told him to stay where he was. They drove off again, leaving Uncle Abe's wife standing in a dazed state of mind beside the furniture.

"What you going to do with me now?" Uncle Abe asked, looking back at his wife and furniture in the distance.

"Take you to the county jail and lock you up," the deputy said.

"What's my wife going to do?" he asked.

"The people in one of those houses will probably take her in."

"How long is you going to keep me in jail locked up?"

"Until your case comes up for trial."

They drove through the dusty streets of the town, around the courthouse square, and stopped in front of a brick building with iron bars across the windows.

"Here's where we get out," the deputy said.

Uncle Abe was almost too weak to walk by that time, but he managed to move along the path to the door. Another white man opened the door and told him to walk straight down the hall until he was told to stop.

Just before noon Saturday, Uncle Abe's oldest son, Henry, stood in Ramsey Clark's office, hat in hand. The lawyer looked at the Negro and frowned. He chewed his pencil for a while, then swung around in his chair and looked out the window into the courthouse square. Presently he turned around and looked at Uncle Abe's son.

"I don't want the case," he said. "I don't want to touch it."

The boy stared at him helplessly. It was the third lawyer he had gone to see that morning, and all of them had refused to take his father's case.

"There's no money in it," Ramsey Clark said, still frowning. "I'd never get a dime out of you niggers if I took this case. And, besides, I don't want to represent any more niggers at court. Better lawyers than me have been ruined that way. I don't want to get the reputation of being a 'nigger lawyer.'"

Henry shifted the weight of his body from one foot to the other and bit his lips. He did not know what to say. He stood in the middle of the room trying to think of a way to get help for his father.

"My father never said he was going to kill Mr. Luther," Henry protested. "He's always been on friendly terms with Mr. Luther. None of us ever gave Mr. Luther trouble. Anybody will tell you that. All the other tenants on Mr. Luther's place will tell you my father has always stood up for Mr. Luther. He never said he was going to try to hurt Mr. Luther."

The lawyer waved for him to stop. He had heard all he wanted to listen to.

"I told you I wouldn't touch the case," he said angrily, snatching up some papers and slamming them down on his desk. "I don't want to go into court and waste my time arguing a case that won't make any difference one way or the other, anyway. It's a good thing for you niggers to get a turn on the 'gang every once in a while. It doesn't make any difference whether Abe Lathan threatened Mr. Bolick, or whether he didn't threaten him. Abe Lathan said he wasn't going to move off the farm, didn't he? Well, that's enough to convict him in court. When the case comes up for trial, that's all the judge will want to hear. He'll be sent to the 'gang quicker than a flea can hop. No lawyer is going to spend a lot of time preparing a case when he knows how it's going to end. If there was money in it, it might be different. But you niggers don't have a thin dime to pay me with. No, I don't want the case. I wouldn't touch it with a ten-foot pole."

Henry backed out of Ramsey Clark's office and went to the jail. He secured permission to see his father for five minutes.

Uncle Abe was sitting on his bunk in the cage looking through the bars when Henry entered. The jailer came and stood behind him at the cage door.

"Did you see a lawyer and tell him I never said nothing like that to Mr. Luther?" Uncle Abe asked the first thing.

Henry looked at his father, but it was difficult for him to answer. He shook his head, dropping his gaze until he could see only the floor.

"You done tried, didn't you, Henry?" Uncle Abe asked.

Henry nodded.

"But when you told the lawyers how I ain't never said a mean thing about Mr. Luther, or his daddy before him, in all my whole life, didn't they say they was going to help me get out of jail?"

Henry shook his head.

"What did the lawyers say, Henry? When you told them how respectful I've always been to Mr. Luther, and how I've always worked hard for him all my life, and never mentioned the shares, didn't they say they would help me then?"

Henry looked at his father, moving his head sideways in order to see him between the bars of the cage. He had to swallow hard several times before he could speak at all.

"I've already been to see three lawyers," he said finally. "All three of them said they couldn't do nothing about it, and to just go ahead and let it come up for trial. They said there wasn't nothing they could do, because the judge would give you a term on the 'gang, anyway."

He stopped for a moment, looking down at his father's feet through the bars.

"If you want me to, I'll go see if I can try to find some other lawyers to take the case. But it won't do much good. They just won't do anything."

Uncle Abe sat down on his bunk and looked at the floor. He could not understand why none of the lawyers would help him. Presently he looked up through the bars at his son. His eyes were fast filling with tears that he could not control.

"Why did the lawyers say the judge would give me a term on the 'gang, anyway, Henry?" he asked.

Henry gripped the bars, thinking about all the years he had seen his father and mother working in the cotton fields for Luther Bolick and being paid in rations, a few clothes, and a house to live in, and nothing more.

"Why did they say that for, Henry?" his father insisted.

"I reckon because we is just colored folks," Henry said at last. "I don't know why else they would say things like that."

The jailer moved up behind Henry, prodding him with his stick. Henry walked down the hall between the rows of cages towards the door that led to the street. He did not look back.

ALBERT MALTZ

The Happiest Man on Earth

JESSE FELT ready to weep. He had been sitting in the shanty waiting for Tom to appear, grateful for the chance to rest his injured foot, quietly, joyously anticipating the moment when Tom would say, "Why of course, Jesse, you can start whenever you're ready!"

For two weeks he had been pushing himself, from Kansas City, Missouri, to Tulsa, Oklahoma, through nights of rain and a week of scorching sun, without sleep or a decent meal, sustained by the vision of that one moment. And then Tom had come into the office. He had come in quickly, holding a sheaf of papers in his hand; he had glanced at Jesse only casually, it was true—but long enough. He had not known him. He had turned away. . . . And Tom Brackett was his brother-in-law.

Was it his clothes? Jesse knew he looked terrible. He had tried to spruce

Originally published in *Harpers Magazine,* June 1938. Reprinted here by arrangement with Maxim Lieber.

up at a drinking fountain in the park, but even that had gone badly; in his excitement he had cut himself shaving, an ugly gash down the side of his cheek. And nothing could get the red gumbo dust out of his suit even though he had slapped himself till both arms were worn out. . . . Or was it just that he *had* changed so much?

True, they hadn't seen each other for five years; but Tom looked five years older, that was all. He was still Tom. God! was *he* so different?

Brackett finished his telephone call. He leaned back in his swivel chair and glanced over at Jesse with small, clear blue eyes that were suspicious and unfriendly. He was a heavy, paunchy man of forty-five, auburn-haired, rather dour looking; his face was meaty, his features pronounced and forceful, his nose somewhat bulbous and reddish-hued at the tip. He looked like a solid, decent, capable business man who was commander of his local branch of the American Legion—which he was. He surveyed Jesse with cold indifference, manifestly unwilling to spend time on him. Even the way he chewed his toothpick seemed contemptuous to Jesse.

"Yes?" Brackett said suddenly. "What do you want?"

His voice was decent enough, Jesse admitted. He had expected it to be worse. He moved up to the wooden counter that partitioned the shanty. He thrust a hand nervously through his tangled hair.

"I guess you don't recognize me, Tom," he said falteringly, "I'm Jesse Fulton."

"Huh?" Brackett said. That was all.

"Yes, I am, and Ella sends you her love."

Brackett rose and walked over to the counter until they were face to face. He surveyed Fulton incredulously, trying to measure the resemblance to his brother-in-law as he remembered him. This man was tall, about thirty. That fitted! He had straight good features and a lank erect body. That was right too. But the face was too gaunt, the body too spiny under the baggy clothes for him to be sure. His brother-in-law had been a solid, strong young man with muscle and beef to him. It was like looking at a faded, badly taken photograph and trying to recognize the subject: the resemblance was there but the difference was tremendous. He searched the eyes. They at least seemed definitely familiar, gray, with a curiously shy but decent look in them. He had liked that about Fulton.

Jesse stood quiet. Inside he was seething. Brackett was like a man examining a piece of broken-down horse flesh; there was a look of pure pity in his eyes. It made Jesse furious. He knew he wasn't as far gone as all that.

"Yes, I believe you are," Brackett said finally, "but you sure have changed."

"By God, it's five years, ain't it?" Jesse said resentfully. "You only saw me a couple of times anyway." Then, to himself, with his lips locked together, in mingled vehemence and shame, What if I have changed? Don't everybody? I ain't no corpse.

"You was solid looking," Brackett continued softly, in the same tone of incredulous wonder. "You lost weight, I guess?"

Jesse kept silent. He needed Brackett too much to risk antagonizing him. But it was only by deliberate effort that he could keep from boiling over. The pause lengthened, became painful. Brackett flushed. "Jiminy Christmas, excuse me," he burst out in apology. He jerked the counter up. "Come in. Take a seat. Good God, boy"—he grasped Jesse's hand and shook it—"I *am* glad to see you; don't think anything else! You just looked so peaked."

"It's all right," Jesse murmured. He sat down, thrusting his hand through his curly, tangled hair.

"Why are you limping?"

"I stepped on a stone; it jagged a hole through my shoe." Jesse pulled his feet back under the chair. He was ashamed of his shoes. They had come from the Relief originally, and two weeks on the road had about finished them. All morning, with a kind of delicious, foolish solemnity, he had been vowing to himself that before anything else, before even a suit of clothes, he was going to buy himself a brand new strong pair of shoes.

Brackett kept his eyes off Jesse's feet. He knew what was bothering the boy and it filled his heart with pity. The whole thing was appalling. He had never seen anyone who looked more down and out. His sister had been writing to him every week, but she hadn't told him they were as badly off as this.

"Well now, listen," Brackett began, "tell me things. How's Ella?"

"Oh, she's pretty good," Jesse replied absently. He had a soft, pleasing, rather shy voice that went with his soft gray eyes. He was worrying over how to get started.

"And the kids?"

"Oh, they're fine. . . . Well, you know," Jesse added, becoming more attentive, "the young one has to wear a brace. He can't run around, you know. But he's smart. He draws pictures and he does things, you know."

"Yes," Brackett said. "That's good." He hesitated. There was a moment's silence. Jesse fidgeted in his chair. Now that the time had arrived, he felt awkward. Brackett leaned forward and put his hand on Jesse's knee. "Ella didn't tell me things were so bad for you, Jesse. I might have helped."

"Well, goodness," Jesse returned softly, "you been having your own troubles, ain't you?"

"Yes." Brackett leaned back. His ruddy face became mournful and darkly bitter. "You know I lost my hardware shop?"

"Well sure, of course," Jesse answered, surprised. "You wrote us. That's what I mean."

"I forgot," Brackett said. "I keep on being surprised over it myself. Not that it was worth much," he added bitterly. "It was running down hill for three years. I guess I just wanted it because it was mine." He laughed pointlessly, without mirth. "Well tell me about yourself," he asked. "What happened to the job you had?"

Jesse burst out abruptly, with agitation, "Let it wait, Tom, I got something on my mind."

"It ain't you and Ella?" Brackett interrupted anxiously.

"Why no!" Jesse sat back. "Why however did you come to think that? Why Ella and me—" he stopped, laughing. "Why, Tom, I'm just crazy about Ella. Why she's just wonderful. She's just my whole life, Tom."

"Excuse me. Forget it." Brackett chuckled uncomfortably, turned away. The naked intensity of the youth's burst of love had upset him. It made him wish savagely that he could do something for them. They were both too decent to have had it so hard. Ella was like this boy too, shy and a little soft.

"Tom, listen," Jesse said, "I come here on purpose." He thrust his hand through his hair. "I want you to help me."

"Damn it, boy," Brackett groaned. He had been expecting this. "I can't much. I only get thirty-five a week and I'm damn grateful for it."

"Sure, I know," Jesse emphasized excitedly. He was feeling once again the wild, delicious agitation that had possessed him in the early hours of the morning. "I know you can't help us with money! But we met a man who works for you! He was in our city! He said you could give me a job!"

"Who said?"

"Oh, why didn't you tell me?" Jesse burst out reproachfully. "Why as soon as I heard it I started out. For two weeks now I been pushing ahead like crazy."

Brackett groaned aloud. "You come walking from Kansas City in two weeks so I could give you a job?"

"Sure, Tom, of course. What else could I do?"

"God Almighty, there ain't no jobs, Jesse! It's a slack season. And you don't know this oil business. It's special. I got my Legion friends here but they couldn't do nothing now. Don't you think I'd ask for you as soon as there was a chance?"

Jesse felt stunned. The hope of the last two weeks seemed rolling up into a ball of agony in his stomach. Then, frantically, he cried, "But listen, this man said *you* could hire! He *told* me! He drives trucks for you! He said you *always* need men!"

"Oh! . . . You mean *my* department?" Brackett said in a low voice.

"*Yes,* Tom. That's it!"

"Oh, no, you don't want to work in my department," Brackett told him in the same low voice. "You don't know what it is."

"Yes, I do," Jesse insisted. "He told me all about it, Tom. You're a dispatcher, ain't you? You send the dynamite trucks out?"

"Who was the man, Jesse?"

"Everett, Everett, I think."

"Egbert? Man about my size?" Brackett asked slowly.

"Yes, Egbert. He wasn't a phony, was he?"

Brackett laughed. For the second time his laughter was curiously without mirth. "No, he wasn't a phony." Then, in a changed voice: "Jiminy, boy, you should have asked me before you trekked all the way down here."

"Oh, I didn't want to," Jesse explained with naïve cunning. "I knew you'd say 'no.' He told me it was risky work, Tom. But I don't care."

Brackett locked his fingers together. His solid, meaty face became very hard. "I'm going to say 'no' anyway, Jesse."

Jesse cried out. It had not occurred to him that Brackett would not agree. It had seemed as though reaching Tulsa were the only problem he had to face. "Oh, no," he begged, "you can't. Ain't there any jobs, Tom?"

"Sure, there's jobs. There's even Egbert's job if you want it."

"He's quit?"

"He's dead!"

"Oh!"

"On the job, Jesse. Last night if you want to know."

"Oh!" . . . Then, "I don't care!"

"Now you listen to me," Brackett said. "I'll tell you a few things that you should have asked before you started out. It ain't dynamite you drive. They don't use anything as safe as dynamite in drilling oil wells. They wish they could, but they can't. It's nitroglycerin! Soup!"

"But I know," Jesse told him reassuringly. "He advised me, Tom. You don't have to think I don't know."

"Shut up a minute," Brackett ordered angrily. "Listen! You just have to *look* at this soup, see? You just *cough* loud and it blows! You know how they transport it? In a can that's shaped like this, see, like a fan? That's to give room for compartments, because each compartment has to be lined with rubber. That's the only way you can even *think* of handling it."

"Listen, Tom—"

"Now wait a minute, Jesse. For God's sake just put your mind to this. I know you had your heart set on a job, but you've got to understand. This stuff goes only in special trucks! At night! They got to follow a special route! They can't go through any city! If they lay over, it's got to be in a special garage! Don't you see what that means? Don't that tell you how dangerous it is?"

"I'll drive careful," Jesse said. "I know how to handle a truck. I'll drive slow."

Brackett groaned. "Do you think Egbert didn't drive careful or know how to handle a truck?"

"Tom," Jesse said earnestly, "you can't scare me. I got my mind fixed on only one thing: Egbert said he was getting a dollar a mile. He was making five to six hundred dollars a month for half a month's work, he said. Can I get the same?"

"Sure, you can get the same," Brackett told him savagely. "A dollar a mile. It's easy. But why do you think the company has to pay so much? It's easy—until you run over a stone that your headlights didn't pick out, like Egbert did. Or get a blowout! Or get something in your eye, so the wheel twists and you jar the truck! Or any other God damn thing that nobody ever knows! We can't ask Egbert what happened to him. There's no truck to give any evidence. There's no corpse. There's nothing! Maybe tomorrow somebody'll find a piece of twisted steel way off in a cornfield. But we never find the driver. Not even a finger nail. All we know is that he don't come in on schedule. Then we wait for the police to call us. You know what happened last night? Something went wrong on a bridge. Maybe Egbert was nervous. Maybe he brushed the side with his fender. Only there's no bridge any more. No truck. No Egbert. Do you understand now? That's what you get for your God damn dollar a mile!"

There was a moment of silence. Jesse sat twisting his long thin hands. His mouth was sagging open, his face was agonized. Then he shut his eyes and spoke softly. "I don't care about that, Tom. You told me. Now you got to be good to me and give me the job."

Brackett slapped the palm of his hand down on his desk. "No!"

"Listen, Tom," Jesse said softly, "you just don't understand." He opened his eyes. They were filled with tears. They made Brackett turn away. "Just look at me, Tom. Don't that tell you enough? What did you think of me when you first saw me? You thought: 'Why don't that bum go away and stop panhandling?' Didn't you, Tom? Tom, I just can't live like this any more. I got to be able to walk down the street with my head up."

"You're crazy," Brackett muttered. "Every year there's one out of five drivers gets killed. That's the average. What's worth that?"

"Is my life worth anything now? We're just starving at home, Tom. They ain't put us back on relief yet."

"Then you should have told me," Brackett exclaimed harshly. "It's your own damn fault. A man has no right to have false pride when his family ain't eating. I'll borrow some money and we'll telegraph it to Ella. Then you go home and get back on relief."

"And then what?"

"And then wait, God damn it! You're no old man. You got no right to throw your life away. Sometime you'll get a job."

"No!" Jesse jumped up. "No. I believed that too. But I don't now," he cried passionately. "I ain't getting a job no more than you're getting your hardware store back. I lost my skill, Tom. Linotyping is skilled work. I'm rusty now. I've been six years on relief. The only work I've had is pick and shovel. When I got that job this spring I was supposed to be an A-1 man. But I wasn't. And they got new machines now. As soon as the slack started they let me out."

"So what?" Brackett said harshly. "Ain't there other jobs?"

"How do I know?" Jesse replied. "There ain't been one for six years. I'd even be afraid to take one now. It's been too hard waiting so many weeks to get back on relief."

"Well you got to have some courage," Brackett shouted. "You've got to keep up hope."

"I got all the courage you want," Jesse retorted vehemently, "but no, I ain't got no hope. The hope has dried up in me in six years' waiting. You're the only hope I got."

"You're crazy," Brackett muttered. "I won't do it. For God's sake think of Ella for a minute."

"Don't you *know* I'm thinking about her?" Jesse asked softly. He plucked at Brackett's sleeve. "That's what decided me, Tom." His voice became muted into a hushed, pained whisper. "The night Egbert was at our house I looked at Ella like I'd seen her for the first time. *She ain't pretty any more, Tom!*" Brackett jerked his head and moved away. Jesse followed him, taking a deep sobbing breath. "Don't that tell you, Tom? Ella was like a little doll or something, you remember. I couldn't walk down the street without somebody turning to look at her. She ain't twenty-nine yet, Tom, and she ain't pretty no more."

Brackett sat down with his shoulders hunched up wearily. He gripped his hands together and sat leaning forward, staring at the floor.

Jesse stood over him, his gaunt face flushed with emotion, almost unpleasant in its look of pleading and bitter humility. "I ain't done right for Ella, Tom. Ella deserved better. This is the only chance I see in my whole life to do something for her. I've just been a failure."

"Don't talk nonsense," Brackett commented, without rancor. "You ain't a failure. No more than me. There's millions of men in the identical situation. It's just the depression, or the recession, or the God damn New Deal, or . . . !" He swore and lapsed into silence.

"Oh, no," Jesse corrected him, in a knowing, sorrowful tone, "those things maybe excuse other men. But not me. It was up to me to do better. This is my own fault!"

"Oh, beans!" Brackett said. "It's more sun spots than it's you!"

Jesse's face turned an unhealthy mottled red. It looked swollen. "Well, I don't care," he cried wildly. "I don't care! You got to give me this! I got to lift my head up. I went through one stretch of hell but I can't go through another. You want me to keep looking at my little boy's legs and tell myself if I had a job he wouldn't be like that? Every time he walks he says to me, 'I got soft bones from the rickets and you give it to me because you didn't feed me right.' Jesus Christ, Tom, you think I'm going to sit there and watch him like that another six years?"

Brackett leaped to his feet. "So what if you do?" he shouted. "You say you're thinking about Ella. How's she going to like it when you get killed?"

"Maybe I won't," Jesse pleaded. "I've got to have some luck sometime."

"That's what they all think," Brackett replied scornfully. "When you take this job your luck is a question mark. The only thing certain is that sooner or later you get killed."

"Okay then," Jesse shouted back. "Then I do! But meanwhile I got something, don't I? I can buy a pair of shoes. Look at me! I can buy a suit that don't say 'Relief' by the way it fits. I can smoke cigarettes. I can buy some candy for the kids. I can eat some myself. Yes, by God, I want to eat some candy. I want a glass of beer once a day. I want Ella dressed up. I want her to eat meat three times a week, four times maybe. I want to take my family to the movies."

Brackett sat down. "Oh, shut up," he said wearily.

"No," Jesse told him softly, passionately, "you can't get rid of me. Listen, Tom," he pleaded, "I got it all figured out. On six hundred a month look how much I can save! If I last only three months, look how much it is—

a thousand dollars—more! And maybe I'll last longer. Maybe a couple years. I can fix Ella up for life!"

"You said it," Brackett interposed. "I suppose you think she'll enjoy living when you're on a job like that?"

"I got it all figured out," Jesse answered excitedly. "She don't know, see? I tell her I make only forty. You put the rest in a bank account for her, Tom."

"Oh, shut up," Brackett said. "You think you'll be happy? Every minute, waking and sleeping, you'll be wondering if to-morrow you'll be dead. And the worst days will be your days off, when you're not driving. They have to give you every other day free to get your nerve back. And you lay around the house eating your heart out. That's how happy you'll be."

Jesse laughed. "I'll be happy! Don't you worry, I'll be so happy, I'll be singing. Lord God, Tom, I'm going to feel *proud* of myself for the first time in seven years!"

"Oh, shut up, shut up," Brackett said.

The little shanty became silent. After a moment Jesse whispered: "You got to, Tom. You got to. You got to."

Again there was silence. Brackett raised both hands to his head, pressing the palms against his temples.

"Tom, Tom—" Jesse said.

Brackett sighed. "Oh God damn it," he said finally, "all right, I'll take you on, God help me." His voice was low, hoarse, infinitely weary. "If you're ready to drive to-night, you can drive to-night."

Jesse didn't answer. He couldn't. Brackett looked up. The tears were running down Jesse's face. He was swallowing and trying to speak, but only making an absurd, gasping noise.

"I'll send a wire to Ella," Brackett said in the same hoarse, weary voice. "I'll tell her you got a job, and you'll send her fare in a couple of days. You'll have some money then—that is, if you last the week out, you jackass!"

Jesse only nodded. His heart felt so close to bursting that he pressed both hands against it, as though to hold it locked within his breast.

"Come back here at six o'clock," Brackett said. "Here's some money. Eat a good meal."

"Thanks," Jesse whispered.

"Wait a minute," Brackett said. "Here's my address." He wrote it on a piece of paper. "Take any car going that way. Ask the conductor where to get off. Take a bath and get some sleep."

"Thanks," Jesse said. "Thanks, Tom."

"Oh, get out of here," Brackett said.

"Tom."

"What?"

"I just—" Jesse stopped. Brackett saw his face. The eyes were still glistening with tears, but the gaunt face was shining now, with a kind of fierce radiance.

Brackett turned away. "I'm busy," he said.

Jesse went out. The wet film blinded him but the whole world seemed to have turned golden. He limped slowly, with the blood pounding his temples and a wild, incommunicable joy in his heart. "I'm the happiest man in the world," he whispered to himself. "I'm the happiest man on the whole earth."

Brackett sat watching till finally Jesse turned the corner of the alley and disappeared. Then he hunched himself over, with his head in his hands. His heart was beating painfully, like something old and clogged. He listened to it as it beat. He sat in desperate tranquillity, gripping his head in his hands.

JOHN STEINBECK

The Grapes of Wrath

THE CARS OF THE migrant people crawled out of the side roads onto the great cross-country highway, and they took the migrant way to the West. In the daylight they scuttled like bugs to the westward; and as the dark caught them, they clustered like bugs near to shelter and to water. And because they were lonely and perplexed, because they had all come from a place of sadness and worry and defeat, and because they were all going to a new mysterious place, they huddled together; they talked together; they shared their lives, their food, and the things they hoped for in the new country. Thus it might be that one family camped near a spring, and another camped for the spring and for company, and a third because two families had pioneered the place and found it good. And when the sun went down, perhaps twenty families and twenty cars were there.

In the evening a strange thing happened: the twenty families became one family, the children were the children of all. The loss of home became one oss, and the golden time in the West was one dream. And it might be hat a sick child threw despair into the hearts of twenty families, of a hundred people; that a birth there in a tent kept a hundred people quiet and awestruck through the night and filled a hundred people with he birth-joy in the morning. A family which the night before had been ost and fearful might search its goods to find a present for a new baby. In he evening, sitting about the fires, the twenty were one. They grew to be units of the camps, units of the evenings and the nights. A guitar unwrapped from a blanket and tuned—and the songs, which were all of the people, were sung in the nights. Men sang the words, and women hummed he tunes.

Every night a world created, complete with furniture—friends made and enemies established; a world complete with braggarts and with cowards, with quiet men, with humble men, with kindly men. Every night relationships that make a world, established; and every morning the world orn down like a circus.

At first the families were timid in the building and tumbling worlds, but gradually the technique of building worlds became their technique. Then leaders emerged, then laws were made, then codes came into being. And as the worlds moved westward they were more complete and better urnished, for their builders were more experienced in building them.

The families learned what rights must be observed—the right of privacy n the tent; the right to keep the past black hidden in the heart; the right to talk and to listen; the right to refuse help or to accept, to offer help or to decline it; the right of son to court and daughter to be courted; the right of the hungry to be fed; the rights of the pregnant and the sick to transcend all other rights.

And the families learned, although no one told them, what rights are monstrous and must be destroyed: the right to intrude upon privacy, the right to be noisy while the camp slept, the right of seduction or rape, the right of adultery and theft and murder. These rights were crushed, because the little worlds could not exist for even a night with such rights alive.

And as the worlds moved westward, rules became laws, although no one told the families. It is unlawful to foul near the camp; it is unlawful in any way to foul the drinking water; it is unlawful to eat good rich food near one who is hungry, unless he is asked to share.

And with the laws, the punishments—and there were only two—a quick and murderous fight or ostracism; and ostracism was the worst. For if one broke the laws his name and face went with him, and he had no place in any world, no matter where created.

In the worlds, social conduct became fixed and rigid, so that a man must say "Good morning" when asked for it, so that a man might have a willing girl if he stayed with her, if he fathered her children and protected them. But a man might not have one girl one night and another the next, for this would endanger the worlds.

The families moved westward, and the technique of building the worlds improved so that the people could be safe in their worlds; and the form was so fixed that a family acting in the rules knew it was safe in the rules.

There grew up government in the worlds, with leaders, with elders. A man who was wise found that his wisdom was needed in every camp; a man who was a fool could not change his folly with his world. And a kind of insurance developed in these nights. A man with food fed a hungry man, and thus insured himself against hunger. And when a baby died a pile of silver coins grew at the door flap, for a baby must be well buried, since it has had nothing else of life. An old man may be left in a potter's field, but not a baby.

A certain physical pattern is needed for the building of a world—water, a river bank, a stream, a spring, or even a faucet unguarded. And there is needed enough flat land to pitch the tents, a little brush or wood to build the fires. If there is a garbage dump not too far off, all the better; for there can be found equipment—stove tops, a curved fender to shelter the fire, and cans to cook in and to eat from.

And the worlds were built in the evening. The people, moving in from the highways, made them with their tents and their hearts and their brains.

In the morning the tents came down, the canvas was folded, the tent poles tied along the running board, the beds put in place on the cars, the pots in their places. And as the families moved westward, the technique of building up a home in the evening and tearing it down with the morning light became fixed; so that the folded tent was packed in one place, the cooking pots counted in their box. And as the cars moved westward, each member of the family grew into his proper place, grew into his duties; so that each member, old and young, had his place in the car; so that in the weary, hot evenings, when the cars pulled into the camping places, each member had his duty and went to it without instruction: children to gather wood, to carry water; men to pitch the tents and bring down the beds; women to cook the supper and to watch while the family fed. And this was done without command. The families, which had been units of which the boundaries were a house at night, a farm by day, changed their boundaries. In the long hot light, they were silent in the cars moving slowly westward; but at night they integrated with any group they found.

Thus they changed their social life—changed as in the whole universe only man can change. They were not farm men any more, but migrant men. And the thought, the planning, the long staring silence that had gone out to the fields, went now to the roads, to the distance, to the West. That man whose mind had been bound with acres lived with narrow concrete miles. And his thought and his worry were not any more with rainfall, with wind and dust, with the thrust of the crops. Eyes watched the tires, ears listened to the clattering motors, and minds struggled with oil, with gasoline, with the thinning rubber between air and road. Then a broken gear was tragedy. Then water in the evening was the yearning, and food over the fire. Then health to go on was the need and strength to go on, and spirit to go on. The wills thrust westward ahead of them, and fears that had once apprehended drought or flood now lingered with anything that might stop the westward crawling.

The camps became fixed—each a short day's journey from the last.

And on the road the panic overcame some of the families, so that they drove night and day, stopped to sleep in the cars, and drove on to the West, flying from the road, flying from movement. And these lusted so greatly to be settled that they set their faces into the West and drove toward it, forcing the clashing engines over the roads.

But most of the families changed and grew quickly into the new life. And when the sun went down——

Time to look out for a place to stop.

And—there's some tents ahead.

The car pulled off the road and stopped, and because others were there first, certain courtesies were necessary. And the man, the leader of the family, leaned from the car.

Can we pull up here an' sleep?

Why, sure, be proud to have you. What State you from?

Come all the way from Arkansas.

They's Arkansas people down that fourth tent.

That so?

And the great question, How's the water?

Well, she don't taste so good, but they's plenty.

Well, thank ya.

No thanks to me.

But the courtesies had to be. The car lumbered over the ground to the end tent, and stopped. Then down from the car the weary people climbed, and stretched stiff bodies. Then the new tent sprang up; the children went for water and the older boys cut brush or wood. The fires started and supper was put on to boil or to fry. Early comers moved over, and States were exchanged, and friends and sometimes relatives discovered.

Oklahoma, huh? What county?

Cherokee.

Why, I got folks there. Know the Allens? They's Allens all over Cherokee. Know the Willises?

Why, sure.

And a new unit was formed. The dusk came, but before the dark was down the new family was of the camp. A word had been passed with every family. They were known people—good people.

I knowed the Allens all my life. Simon Allen, ol' Simon, had trouble with his first wife. She was part Cherokee. Purty as—as a black colt.

Sure, an' young Simon, he married a Rudolph, didn't he? That's what I thought. They went to live in Enid an' done well—real well.

Only Allen that ever done well. Got a garage.

When the water was carried and the wood cut, the children walked shyly, cautiously among the tents. And they made elaborate acquaintance-ship gestures. A boy stopped near another boy and studied a stone, picked it up, examined it closely, spat on it, and rubbed it clean and inspected it until he forced the other to demand, What you got there?

And casually, Nothin'. Jus' a rock.

Well, what you lookin' at it like that for?

Thought I seen gold in it.

How'd you know? Gold ain't gold, it's black in a rock.

Sure, ever'body knows that.

I bet it's fool's gold, an' you figgered it was gold.

That ain't so, 'cause Pa, he's foun' lots a gold an' he tol' me how to look. How'd you like to pick up a big ol' piece a gold?

Sa-a-ay! I'd git the bigges' old son-a-bitchin' piece a candy you ever seen.

I ain't let to swear, but I do, anyways.

Me too. Le's go to the spring.

And young girls found each other and boasted shyly of their popularity and their prospects. The women worked over the fire, hurrying to get food to the stomachs of the family—pork if there was money in plenty, pork and potatoes and onions. Dutch-oven biscuits or cornbread, and plenty of gravy to go over it. Side-meat or chops and a can of boiled tea, black and bitter. Fried dough in drippings if money was slim, dough fried crisp and brown and the drippings poured over it.

Those families which were very rich or very foolish with their money ate canned beans and canned peaches and packaged bread and bakery cake; but they ate secretly, in their tents, for it would not have been good to eat such fine things openly. Even so, children eating their fried dough smelled the warming beans and were unhappy about it.

When supper was over and the dishes dipped and wiped, the dark had come, and then the men squatted down to talk.

And they talked of the land behind them. I don't know what it's coming to, they said. The country's spoilt.

It'll come back though, on'y we won't be there.

Maybe, they thought, maybe we sinned some way we didn't know about.

Fella says to me, gov'ment fella, an' he says, she's gullied up on ya. Gov'ment fella. He says, if ya plowed 'cross the contour, she won't gully. Never did have no chance to try her. An' the new super' ain't plowin' 'cross the contour. Runnin' a furrow four miles long that ain't stoppin' or goin' aroun' Jesus Christ Hisself.

And they spoke softly of their homes: They was a little cool-house under the win'mill. Use' ta keep milk in there ta cream up, an' watermelons. Go in there midday when she was hottern' a heifer, an' she'd be jus' as cool, as cool as you'd want. Cut open a melon in there an' she'd hurt your mouth, she was so cool. Water drippin' down from the tank.

They spoke of their tragedies: Had a brother Charley, hair as yella as corn, an' him a growed man. Played the 'cordeen nice too. He was harrowin' one day an' he went up to clear his lines. Well, a rattlesnake buzzed an' them horses bolted an' the harrow went over Charley, an' the points dug into his guts an' his stomach, an' they pulled his face off an'—God Almighty!

They spoke of the future: Wonder what it's like out there?

Well, the pitchers sure do look nice. I seen one where it's hot an' fine, an' walnut trees an' berries; an' right behind, close as a mule's ass to his withers, they's a tall up mountain covered with snow. That was a pretty thing to see.

If we can get work it'll be fine. Won't have no cold in the winter. Kids won't freeze on the way to school. I'm gonna take care my kids don't miss no more school. I can read good, but it ain't no pleasure to me like with a fella that's used to it.

And perhaps a man brought out his guitar to the front of his tent. And he sat on a box to play, and everyone in the camp moved slowly in toward him, drawn in toward him. Many men can chord a guitar, but perhaps this man was a picker. There you have something—the deep chords beating, beating, while the melody runs on the strings like little footsteps. Heavy hard fingers marching on the frets. The man played and the people moved slowly in on him until the circle was closed and tight, and then he sang "Ten-Cent Cotton and Forty-Cent Meat." And the circle sang softly with

him. And he sang "Why Do You Cut Your Hair, Girls?" And the circle
sang. He wailed the song, "I'm Leaving Old Texas," that eerie song that
was sung before the Spaniards came, only the words were Indian then.

And now the group was welded to one thing, one unit, so that in the
dark the eyes of the people were inward, and their minds played in other
times, and their sadness was like rest, like sleep. He sang the "McAlester
Blues" and then, to make up for it to the older people, he sang "Jesus Calls
Me to His Side." The children drowsed with the music and went into the
tents to sleep, and the singing came into their dreams.

And after a while the man with the guitar stood up and yawned. Good
night, folks, he said.

And they murmured, Good night to you.

And each wished he could pick a guitar, because it is a gracious thing.
Then the people went to their beds, and the camp was quiet. And the
owls coasted overhead, and the coyotes gabbled in the distance, and into
the camp skunks walked, looking for bits of food—waddling, arrogant
skunks, afraid of nothing.

The night passed, and with the first streak of dawn the women came
out of the tents, built up the fires, and put the coffee to boil. And the men
came out and talked softly in the dawn.

When you cross the Colorado river, there's the desert, they say. Look out
for the desert. See you don't get hung up. Take plenty water, case you
get hung up.

I'm gonna take her at night.

Me too. She'll cut the living Jesus outa you.

The families ate quickly, and the dishes were dipped and wiped. The
tents came down. There was a rush to go. And when the sun arose, the
camping place was vacant, only a little litter left by the people. And the
camping place was ready for a new world in a new night.

But along the highway the cars of the migrant people crawled out like
bugs, and the narrow concrete miles stretched ahead.

STEPHEN VINCENT BENÉT
Nightmare with Angels

AN ANGEL came to me and stood by my bedside,
Remarking in a professorial-historical-economic and irritated voice,

"If the Romans had only invented a decent explosion-engine!
Not even the best, not even a Ford V-8
But, say, a Model T or even an early Napier,
They'd have built good enough roads for it (they knew how to build
roads)
From Cape Wrath to Cape St. Vincent, Susa, Babylon and Moscow,
And the motorized legions never would have fallen,
And peace, in the shape of a giant eagle, would brood over the entire
Western World!"
He changed his expression, looking now like a combination of Gilbert
Murray, Hilaire Belloc and a dozen other scientists, writers, and
prophets,
And continued, in angelic tones,
"If the Greeks had known how to coöperate, if there'd never been a Refor-
mation,
If Sparta had not been Sparta, and the Church had been the Church of
the saints,
The Argive peace like a free-blooming olive-tree, the peace of Christ (who
loved peace) like a great, beautiful vine enwrapping the spinning
earth!
Take it nearer home," he said.
"Take these Mayans and their star-clocks, their carvings and their great
cities.
Who sacked them out of their cities, drowned the cities with a green
jungle?
A plague? A change of climate? A queer migration?
Certainly they were skilful, certainly they created.
And, in Tenochtitlan, the dark obsidian knife and the smoking heart on
the stone but a fair city,
And the Incas had it worked out beautifully till Pizarro smashed them.
The collectivist state was there, and the ladies very agreeable.
They lacked steel, alphabet and gunpowder and they had to get married
when the government said so.
They also lacked unemployment and overproduction.
"For that matter," he said, "take the Cro-Magnons,
The fellows with the big skulls, the handsome folk, the excellent scribers
of mammoths,
Physical gods and yet with the sensitive brain (they drew the fine, running
reindeer).
What stopped them? What kept us all from being Apollos and Aphro-
dites

Only with a new taste to the nectar,
The laughing gods, not the cruel, the gods of song, not of war?
Supposing Aurelius, Confucius, Napoleon, Plato, Gautama, Alexander—
Just to take half a dozen—
Had ever realized and stabilized the full dream?
How long, O Lord God in the highest? How long, what now, perturbed
     spirit?"

He turned blue at the wingtips and disappeared as another angel ap-
     proached me.
This one was quietly but appropriately dressed in cellophane, synthetic
     rubber and stainless steel,
But his mask was the blind mask of Ares, snouted for gasmasks.
He was neither soldier, sailor, farmer, dictator nor munitions-manufac-
     turer.
Nor did he have much conversation, except to say,
"You will not be saved by General Motors or the pre-fabricated house.
You will not be saved by dialectic materialism or the Lambeth Conference.
You will not be saved by Vitamin D or the expanding universe.
In fact, you will not be saved."
Then he showed his hand:
In his hand was a woven, wire basket, full of seeds, small metallic and shin-
     ing like the seeds of portulaca;
Where he sowed them, the green vine withered, and the smoke and the
     armies sprang up.

IRWIN SHAW

Weep in Years to Come

THEY CAME out of the movie house and started slowly eastward in the
direction of Fifth Avenue. "Hitler!" a newsboy called. "Hitler!"

"That Fletcher," Dora said, "the one that played her father. Remember him?"

Permission of the author. From *Sailor Off The Bremen*. Originally published in *The New
Yorker*. Copyright, 1939, by Irwin Shaw.

"Uh huh," Paul said, holding her hand, as they walked slowly up the dark street.

"He's got stones in his kidney."

"That's the way he acts," Paul said. "Now I know how to describe the way that man acts—he acts like a man who has stones in his kidney."

Dora laughed. "I X-rayed him last winter. He's one of Dr. Thayer's best patients. He's always got something wrong with him. He's going to try to pass the stones out of his kidney this summer."

"Good luck, Fletcher, old man," Paul said.

"I used to massage his shoulder. He had neuritis. He makes fifteen hundred dollars a week."

"No wonder he has neuritis."

"He asked me to come to his house for dinner." Dora pulled her hand out of Paul's and slipped it up to his elbow and held on, hard. "He likes me."

"I bet he does."

"What about you?"

"What about me what?" Paul asked.

"Do you like me?"

They stopped at Rockefeller Plaza and leaned over the marble wall and looked down at the fountain and the statue and the people sitting out at the tables, drinking, and the waiters standing around, listening to the sound of the fountain.

"I can't stand you," Paul said. He kissed her hair.

"That's what I thought," Dora said. They both laughed.

They looked down at the Plaza, at the thin trees with the light-green leaves rustling in the wind that came down between the buildings. There were pansies, yellow and tight, along the borders of the small pools with the bronze sea statues, and hydrangeas, and little full trees, all shaking in the wind and the diffuse, clear light of the flood lamps above. Couples strolled slowly down from Fifth Avenue, talking amiably in low, calm, week-end voices, appreciating the Rockefeller frivolity and extravagance which had carved a place for hydrangeas and water and saplings and spring and sea-gods riding bronze dolphins out of these austere buildings, out of the bleak side of Business.

Paul and Dora walked up the promenade, looking in the windows. They stopped at a window filled with men's sports clothes—gabardine slacks and bright-colored shirts with short sleeves and brilliant handkerchiefs to tie around the throat.

"I have visions," Paul said, "of sitting in my garden, with two Great Danes, dressed like that, like a Hollywood actor in the country."

"Have you got a garden?" Dora asked.

"No."

"Those're nice pants," Dora said.

They went on to the next window. "On the other hand," Paul said, "there are days when I want to look like that. A derby hat and a stiff blue shirt with a pleated bosom and a little starched white collar and a five-dollar neat little necktie and a Burberry overcoat. Leave the office at five o'clock every day to go to a cocktail party."

"You go to a cocktail party almost every afternoon anyway," Dora said. "Without a derby hat."

"A different kind of cocktail party," Paul said. He started her across Fifth Avenue. "The kind attended by men with starched blue pleated bosoms. Some day."

"Oh, Lord," Dora said as they ran to escape a bus, "look at those dresses." They stood in front of Saks.

"Fifth Avenue," Paul said. "Street of dreams."

"It's nice to know things like that exist," Dora murmured, looking into the stage-lit window at the yellow dress and the sign that said "Tropical Nights in Manhattan" and the little carved-stone fish that for some reason was in the same window. "Even if you can't have them."

"Uptown?" Paul asked. "Or to my house?"

"I feel like walking." Dora looked up at Paul and grinned. "For the moment." She squeezed his arm. "Only for the moment. Uptown."

They started uptown.

"I love those models," Paul said. "Each and every one of them. They're superior, yet warm; inviting, yet polite. Their breasts are always tipped at the correct angle for the season."

"Sure," Dora said, "papier-mâché. It's easy with papier-mâché. Look. Aluminum suitcases. Travel by air."

"They look like my mother's kitchen pots."

"Wouldn't you like to own a few of them?"

"Yes." Paul peered at them. "Fly away. Buy luggage and depart. Leave for the ends of the earth."

"They got a little case just for books. A whole separate little traveling bookcase."

"That's just what I need," Paul said, "for my trips on the Fifth Avenue bus every morning."

They passed St. Patrick's, dark and huge, with the moon sailing over it.

"Do you think God walks up Fifth Avenue?" Paul asked.

"Sure," said Dora. "Why not?"

"We are princes of the earth," Paul said. "All over the world men slave to bring riches to these few blocks for us to look at and say 'Yes, very nice' or 'Take it away, it stinks.' I feel very important when I walk up Fifth Avenue."

They stopped at the window of the Hamburg-American Line. Little dolls in native costumes danced endlessly around a pole while other dolls in native costume looked on. All the dolls had wide smiles on their faces. "Harvest Festival in Buckeburg, Germany," a small sign said.

A private policeman turned the corner and stood and watched them. They moved to the next window.

" 'A suggestion to passengers to promote carefree travel,' " Paul read off a booklet. "Also, Hapag-Lloyd announces a twenty-per-cent reduction for all educators on sabbatical leave. They are 'Masters in the Art of Travel,' they say."

"I used to want to go to see Germany," Dora said. "I know a lot of Germans and they're nice."

"I'll be there soon," Paul said as they passed the private policeman.

"You're going to visit it?"

"Uh huh. At the expense of the government. In a well-tailored khaki uniform. I'm going to see glamorous Europe, seat of culture, at last. From a bombing plane. To our left we have the Stork Club, seat of culture for East Fifty-third Street. Look at the pretty girls. A lot of them have breasts at the correct angle, too. See how nature mimics art. New York is a wonderful city."

Dora didn't say anything. She hung onto him tightly as they went down the street. They turned at the corner and walked down Madison Avenue. After a while they stopped at a shop that had phonographs and radios in the window. "That's what I want." Paul pointed at a machine. "A Capehart. It plays two symphonies at a time. You just lie on your back and out come Brahms and Beethoven and Prokofieff. That's the way life should be. Lie on your back and be surrounded by great music, automatically."

Dora looked at the phonograph, all mahogany and doors and machinery. "Do you really think there's going to be a war?" she said.

"Sure. They're warming up the pitchers now. They're waiting to see if the other side has right-handed or left-handed batters before they nominate their starting pitchers."

They continued walking downtown.

"But it's in Europe," Dora said. "Do you think we'll get into it?"

"Sure. Read the papers." He glanced at the window they were passing. "Look at those nice tables. Informal luncheons on your terrace. Metal and glass for outdoor feeding. That would be nice, eating out on a terrace off those wonderful colored plates, rich food with green salads. With a view of mountains and a lake, and, inside, the phonograph."

"That sounds good," Dora said quietly.

"I could get an extra speaker," Paul said, "and wire it out to the terrace, so we could listen as we ate. I like Mozart with dinner." He laughed and drew her to a bookstore window.

"I always get sad," Dora said, "when I look in a bookshop window and see all the books I'm never going to have time to read."

Paul kissed her. "What did you think the first time you saw me?" he asked.

"What did *you* think?"

"I thought, 'I must get that girl!'"

Dora laughed, close to him.

"What did you think?" Paul asked.

"I thought"—she giggled—"I thought, 'I must get that man!'"

"Isn't New York marvelous?" Paul said. "Where did you say you come from?"

"Seattle," Dora said. "Seattle, Washington."

"Here we are on Madison Avenue, holding hands, shopping for the future . . ."

"Even if there was a war," Dora said after a while, "why would you have to get mixed up in it? Why would the United States have to get mixed up in it?"

"They got into the last one, didn't they?" Paul said. "They'll get into this one."

"They were gypped the last time," Dora said. "The guys who were killed were gypped."

"That's right," said Paul. "They were killed for six-per-cent interest on bonds, for oil wells, for spheres of influence. I wish I had a sphere of influence."

"Still," said Dora, "you'd enlist this time?"

"Yop. The first day. I'd walk right up to the recruiting office and say, 'Paul Triplett, twenty-six years old, hard as nails, good eyes, good teeth, good feet, give me a gun. Put me in a plane, so I can do a lot of damage.'"

They walked a whole block in silence.

"Don't you think you'd be gypped this time, too?" Dora said. "Don't you think they'd have you fighting for bonds and oil wells all over again?"

"Uh huh."

"And even so, you'd sign up?"

"The first day."

Dora pulled her hand away from him. "Do you *like* the idea of killing people?"

"I hate the idea," Paul said slowly. "I don't want to hurt anybody. I think the idea of war is ridiculous. I want to live in a world in which everybody sits on a terrace and eats off a metal-and-glass table off colored plates and the phonograph inside turns Mozart over automatically and the music is piped out to an extra loudspeaker on the terrace. Only Hitler isn't interested in that kind of world. He's interested in another kind of world. I couldn't stand to live in his kind of world, German or homemade."

"You wouldn't kill Hitler," Dora said. "You'd just kill young boys like yourself."

"That's right."

"Do you like that?"

"I'm really not interested in killing Hitler, either," Paul said. "I want to kill the idea he represents for so many people. In years to come I'll cry over the young boys I've killed and maybe if they kill me, they'll cry over me."

"They're probably just like you." They were walking fast now.

"Sure," Paul said. "I'm sure they'd love to go to bed with you tonight. I bet they'd love to walk along the fountains with the bronze statues in Rockefeller Plaza, holding hands with you on a spring Saturday evening and looking at the sports clothes in the windows. I bet a lot of them like Mozart, too, but still I'll kill them. Gladly."

"Gladly?"

"Yes, gladly." Paul wiped his eyes with his hands, suddenly tired. "Gladly today. I'll weep for them in years to come. Today they're guns aimed at me and the world I want. Their bodies protect an idea I have to kill to live. Hey!" He stretched out his hands and caught hers. "What's the sense talking about things like this tonight?"

"But it's all a big fraud," Dora cried. "You're being used and you know it."

"That's right," Paul said. "It's all a big fraud, the whole business. Even so, I got to fight. I'll be gypped, but by a little bit I'll do something for my side, for Mozart on a terrace at dinner. What the hell, it's not even heroism. I'll be dragged in, whatever I say."

"That's too bad," Dora said softly, walking by herself. "It's too bad."

"Sure," Paul said. "Some day maybe it'll be better. Maybe some day the world'll be run for people who like Mozart. Not today."

They stopped. They were in front of a little art store. There was a reproduction of the Renoir painting of a boating party on the river. There was the woman kissing the Pekinese, and the man in his underwear with a straw hat and his red beard, solid as earth, and the wit with his cocked derby hat whispering to the woman with her hands to her ears, and there was the great still life in the foreground, of wine and bottles and glasses and grapes and food.

"I saw it in Washington," Paul said. "They had it in Washington. You can't tell why it's a great picture from the print. There's an air of pink immortality hanging over it. They got it in New York now and I go look at it three times a week. It's settled, happy, solid. It's a picture of a summertime that vanished a long time ago." Paul kissed her hand. "It's getting late, darling, the hours're dwindling. Let's go home."

They got into a cab and went downtown to his apartment.

III

I should like to be able to offer the hope that the shadow over the world might swiftly pass. I cannot. The facts compel my stating, with candor, that darker periods may lie ahead. The disaster is not of our making; no act of ours engendered the forces which assault the foundations of civilization. Yet we find ourselves affected to the core; our currents of commerce are changing, our minds are filled with new problems, our position in world affairs has already been altered.

(*Message to Congress, September 21, 1939*)

The Summer of 1939 saw the birth of the Flushing Meadows World of Tomorrow and the Second World War. The hope that the United States could remain neutral led many people into the camp of isolationism, which found its most eloquent spokesman in Anne Morrow Lindbergh. The sense that an overwhelming evil had been let loose in the world led Mrs. Lindbergh to her confused interpretation of the course of future history. Reinhold Niebuhr, on the other hand, was moved by reading his morning mail to confound Utopian liberals by a summons to reality and a call to action. Archibald MacLeish's The Irresponsibles *launched the intellectuals on a guilty orgy of self-examination and self-castigation, while a citizen army was growing up that was before long to fight in all parts of the world.*

E. B. WHITE

The World of Tomorrow

I WASN'T really prepared for the World's Fair last week, and it certainly wasn't prepared for me. Between the two of us there was considerable of a mixup.

The truth is that my ethmoid sinuses broke down on the eve of Fair Day, and this meant I had to visit the Fair carrying a box of Kleenex concealed in a copy of the *Herald Tribune*. When you can't breathe through your nose, Tomorrow seems strangely like the day before yes-

Permission the author. From *One Man's Meat*. Originally published in *The New Yorker*. Copyright, 1939, by E. B. White. Harper & Brothers.

terday. The Fair, on its part, was having trouble too. It couldn't find its collar button. Our mutual discomfort established a rich bond of friendship between us, and I realize that the World's Fair and myself actually both need the same thing—a nice warm day.

The road to Tomorrow leads through the chimney pots of Queens. It is a long, familiar journey, through Mulsified Shampoo and Mobilgas, through Bliss Street, Kix, Astring-O-Sol, and the Majestic Auto Seat Covers. It winds through Textene, Blue Jay Corn Plasters; through Musterole and the delicate pink blossoms on the fruit trees in the everhopeful back yards of a populous borough, past Zemo, Alka-Seltzer, Baby Ruth, past Iodent and the Fidelity National Bank, by trusses, belts, and the clothes that fly bravely on the line under the trees with the new little green leaves in Queens' incomparable springtime. Suddenly you see the first intimation of the future, of man's dream—the white ball and spire—and there is the ramp and the banners flying from the pavilions and the brave hope of a glimpsed destination. Except for the Kleenex, I might have been approaching the lists at Camelot, for I felt that perhaps here would be the tournament all men wait for, the field of honor, the knights and the ladies under these bright banners, beyond these great walls. A closer inspection, however, on the other side of the turnstile, revealed that it was merely Heinz jousting with Beech-Nut—the same old contest on a somewhat larger field, with accommodations for more spectators, and rather better facilities all round.

The place is honeycombed with streets—broad, gusty streets, with tulips bending to the gale and in the air the sound of distant choirs. There are benches all along for the weary and the halt, but though science's failure to cope with the common cold had embittered my heart and slowed my step, the ball and spire still beckoned me on. It was not particularly surprising, somehow, when at last after so many months of anticipation and after so much of actual travail and suffering, when at last I arrived, paper handkerchiefs in hand, at the very threshold of Tomorrow, when I finally presented myself there at the base of the white phallus, face to face with the girl in the booth behind the little bars behind the glass window with the small round hole, expectant, ready, to see at last what none had ever seen, Tomorrow—it was not, somehow, particularly surprising to see the window close in my face and hear a bald contemporary voice say, "There will be a short wait of a few minutes, please."

That's the way it is with the future. Even after Grover Whalen has touched it with his peculiar magic, there is still a short wait.

The lady behind me was not surprised either, but she seemed apprehensive.

"Anything wrong in there?" she asked testily.

"No, Madam," said the guard. "Just some minor difficulty in the Perisphere."

The lady was not satisfied. "Is there anything in there to scare you?" she asked, looking at the Perisphere rolling motionless in the gray vapors that have hung for centuries above the Flushing Meadows.

"No, Madam," he replied. "The longest escalator in the world moves very slowly."

I clocked the wait. It was twenty minutes. Not bad, for a man who's waited all his life.

Much depends, when you ascend into the interior of the Perisphere, on the moment at which you happen to arrive at the top of the escalator and teeter off in a sidewise direction onto one of the two great moving rings that turn endlessly above the City of Man. If you arrive just as day has faded into night, and without any advance information about being shunted from an upward moving stairway onto a sidewise moving balcony, the experience is something that stays with you. I was lucky. The City of Man, when it first broke on my expectant sight, was as dark as a hall bedroom, and for a second or two I didn't catch on that I myself was in motion—except celestially. If I hadn't recognized Mr. Kaltenborn's electric voice, I would have felt lonelier than perhaps the situation warranted.

"As day fades into night," he said, with the majestic huskiness which science has given speech, "each man seeks home, for here are children, comfort, neighbors, recreation—the good life of the well-planned city."

Trembling in violet light beneath me, there it was—the towers, now to the adjusted eye dimly visible—"a brave new world [such a big voice you have, Grandpa!] built by united hands and hearts. Here brain and brawn, faith and courage, are linked in high endeavor as men march on toward unity and peace. Listen! From office, farm, and factory they come with joyous song."

I don't know how long it takes in there. Ten minutes, maybe. But when I emerged from the great ball, to begin the descent of the Helicline, it had come on to rain.

To be informative about the Fair is a task for someone with a steadier nose than mine. I saw all as in a dream, and I cherish the dream and have put it away in lavender. The great size of the place has been a temporary disadvantage these first few days, when the draftiness, the chill, the disorder, the murky bath of canned reverence in which many of the commercial exhibits are steeped have conspired to give the place the clammy quality of a seaside resort in mid-November. But this same great size, come the first warm, expansive days, will suddenly become the most valuable asset of the Fair. The refurbished ash heap, rising from its own smolder, is by far the biggest show that has ever been assembled on God's earth, and it is going to be a great place to go on a fine summer night, a great place to go on a sunny spring morning. After all, nobody can embrace Culture in a topcoat.

The architecture is amusing enough, the buildings are big enough, to give the visitor that temporary and exalted feeling of being in the presence of something pretty special, something full of aspiration, something which at times is even exciting. And the exhibition is cock-eyed enough to fall, as it naturally does, in line with all carnivals, circuses, and wonderlands. The buildings (there are two hundred of them) have color and a certain dash, here and there a certain beauty. They are of the type that shows up best in strong light. Like any Miami Beach cottage, they look incredibly lovely in sunlight, adorned with a necklace of vine shadow against a clear white skin, incredibly banal and gloom-infested on cloudy days, when every pimple of plaster shows up in all its ugly pretension. The designers of this twentieth-century bazaar have been resourceful and have kept the comfort of the people in mind. Experience has taught them much. The modern technique of sight-seeing is this: you sit in a chair (wired for sound) or stand on a platform (movable, glass-embowered) and while sitting, standing, you are brought mysteriously and reverently into easy view of what you want to see. There is no shoving in the exhibit hall of Tomorrow. There is no loitering and there is usually no smoking. Even in the girl show in the amusement area, the sailor is placed in a rather astringent attitude, behind glass, for the adoration of the female form. It is all rather serious-minded, this World of Tomorrow, and extremely impersonal. A ride on the Futurama of General Motors induces approximately the same emotional response as a trip through the Cathedral of St. John the Divine. The countryside unfolds before you in five-million-dollar micro-loveliness, conceived in motion and executed by Norman Bel Geddes. The voice is a voice of utmost respect, of complete religious faith in the eternal benefaction of faster travel. The highways unroll in ribbons of perfection through the fertile and rejuvenated America of 1960—a vision of the day to come, the unobstructed left turn, the vanished grade crossing, the town which beckons but does not impede, the millennium of passionless motion. When night falls in the General Motors exhibit and you lean back in the cushioned chair (yourself in motion and the world so still) and hear (from the depths of the chair) the soft electric assurance of a better life—the life which rests on wheels alone—there is a strong, sweet poison which infects the blood. I didn't want to wake up. I liked 1960 in purple light, going a hundred miles an hour around impossible turns ever onward toward the certified cities of the flawless future. It wasn't till I passed an apple orchard and saw the trees, each blooming under its own canopy of glass, that I perceived that even the General Motors dream, as dreams so often do, left some questions unanswered about the future. The apple tree of Tomorrow, abloom under its inviolate hood, makes you stop and wonder. How will the little boy climb it? Where will the little bird build its nest?

I made a few notes at the Fair, a few hints of what you may expect of Tomorrow, its appointments, its characteristics.

In Tomorrow, people and objects are lit not from above but from below. Trees are lit from below. Even the cow on the rotolactor appears to be lit from below—the buried flood lamp illuminates the distended udder.

In Tomorrow one voice does for all. But it is a little unsure of itself; it keeps testing itself; it says, "Hello! One, two, three, four. Hello! One, two, three, four."

Rugs do not slip in Tomorrow, and the bassinets of newborn infants are wired against kidnappers.

There is no talking back in Tomorrow. You are expected to take it or leave it alone. There are sailors there (which makes you feel less lonely) and the sound of music.

The living room of Tomorrow contains the following objects: a broad-loom carpet, artificial carnations, a television radio victrola incessantly producing an image of someone or something which is somewhere else, a glass bird, a chrome steel lamp, a terra-cotta zebra, some veneered book cabinets containing no visible books, another cabinet out of which a small newspaper slowly pours in a never-ending ribbon, and a small plush love seat in the shape of a new moon.

In Tomorrow, most sounds are not the sounds themselves but a memory of sounds, or an electrification. In the case of a cow, the moo will come to you not from the cow but from a small aperture above your head.

Tomorrow is a little on the expensive side. I checked this with my cab-driver in Manhattan to make sure. He was full of praise about the Fair, but said he hadn't seen it and might, in fact, never see it. "I hack out there, but I got it figured that for me and the wife to go all through and do it right—no cheap-skate stuff—it would break the hell out of a five-dollar bill. In my racket, I can't afford it."

Tomorrow does not smell. The World's Fair of 1939 has taken the body odor out of man, among other things. It is all rather impersonal, this dream. The country fair manages better, where you can hang over the rail at the ox-pulling and smell the ox. It's not only that the sailors can't get at the girls through the glass, but even so wholesome an exhibit as Swift's Premium Bacon produces twenty lovesick maidens in a glass pit hermetically sealed from the ultimate consumer.

The voice of Mr. Kaltenborn in the City of Man says, "They come with joyous song," but the truth is there is very little joyous song in the Fair grounds. There is a great deal of electrically transmitted joy, but very little spontaneous joy. Tomorrow's music, I noticed, came mostly from Yesterday's singer. In fact, if Mr. Whalen wants a suggestion from me as to how to improve his show (and I am reasonably confident he doesn't), it would be to snip a few wires, hire a couple of bands, and hand out ticklers. Gaiety is not the keynote in Tomorrow. I finally found it at the tag end of a chilly evening, far along in the Amusement Area, in a tent with some colored folks. There was laughing and shouting there, and a beautiful brown belly-dancer.

Another gay spot, to my surprise, was the American Telephone & Telegraph Exhibit. It took the old Telephone Company to put on the best show of all. To anyone who draws a lucky number, the company grants the privilege of making a long-distance call. This call can be to any point in the United States, and the bystanders have the exquisite privilege of listening in through earphones and of laughing unashamed. To understand the full wonder of this, you must reflect that there are millions of people who have never either made or received a long-distance call, and that when Eddie Pancha, a waiter in a restaurant in El Paso, Texas, hears the magic words "New York is calling . . . Go ahead, please," he is transfixed in holy dread and excitement. I listened for two hours and ten minutes to this show, and I'd be there this minute if I were capable of standing up. I had the good luck to be listening at the earphone when a little boy named David Wagstaff won the toss and put in a call to tell his father in Springfield, Mass., what a good time he was having at the World's Fair. David walked resolutely to the glass booth before the assembled kibitzers and in a tiny, timid voice gave the operator his call, his little new cloth hat set all nicely on his head. But his father wasn't there, and David was suddenly confronted with the necessity of telling his story to a man named Mr. Henry, who happened to answer the phone and who, on hearing little David Wagstaff's voice calling from New York, must surely have thought that David's mother had been run down in the B.-M. T. and that David was doing the manly thing.

"Yes, David," he said, tensely.

"Tell my father this," began David, slowly, carefully, determined to go through with the halcyon experience of winning a lucky call at the largest Fair the world had yet produced.

"Yes, David."

"We got on the train, and . . . and . . . had a nice trip, and at New Haven, when they were taking off the car and putting another car on, it was *awfully* funny because the car gave a great—big—BUMP!"

Then followed David's three-minute appreciation of the World of To-morrow and the Citadel of Light, phrased in the crumbling remnants of speech that little boys are left with when a lot of people are watching, and when their thoughts begin to run down, and when Perispheres begin to swim mistily in time. Mr. Henry—the invisible and infinitely surprised Mr. Henry—maintained a respectful and indulgent silence. I don't know what he was thinking, but I would swap the Helicline for a copy of his attempted transcription of David's message to his father.

My own memory of the Fair, like David's, has begun to dim. From so much culture, from so much concentrated beauty and progress, one can retain only a fragment. I remember the trees at night, shivering in their burlap undershirts, the eerie shadows clinging to the wrong side of their branches. I remember the fountains playing in the light, I remember the girl who sat so still, so clean, so tangible, producing with the tips of her fingers the synthetic speech—but the words were not the words she wanted to say, they were not the words that were in her mind. I remember the little old Stourbridge Lion, puffing in under its own steam to start the railroads bursting across America. But mostly the Fair has vanished, leaving only the voice of little David Wagstaff and the rambling ecstasy of his first big trip away from home; so many million dollars spent on the idea that our trains and our motorcars should go fast and smoothly, and the child remembering, not the smoothness, but the great—big—BUMP.

So (as the voice says) man dreams on. And the dream is still a contradiction and an enigma—the biologist peeping at bacteria through his microscope, the sailor peeping at the strip queen through binoculars, the eyes so watchful, and the hopes so high. Out in the honky-tonk section, in front of the Amazon show, where the ladies exposed one breast in deference to the fleet, kept one concealed in deference to Mr. Whalen, there was an automaton—a giant man in white tie and tails, with enormous rubber hands. At the start of each show, while the barker was drumming up trade, a couple of the girls would come outside and sit in the robot's lap. The effect was peculiarly lascivious—the extra-size man, exploring with his gigantic rubber hands the breasts of the little girls, the girls with

their own small hands (by comparison so small, by comparison so
terribly real) restrainingly on his, to check the unthinkable impact of his
mechanical passion. Here was the Fair, all fairs, in pantomime; and here
the strange mixed dream that made the Fair: the heroic man, bloodless
and perfect and enormous, created in his own image, and in his hand
(rubber, aseptic) the literal desire, the warm and living breast.

MURIEL RUKEYSER

For Fun

IT WAS LONG before the national performance,
preparing for heroes,
carnival-time, time of
political decorations and the tearing of treaties.
Long before the prophecies came true.
For cities also play their brilliant lives.
They have their nightmares. They have their nights of peace.
Senility, wisecracks, tomb, tomb.

Bunting, plaster of Paris whores, electrified unicorns.
Pyramids of mirrors and the winking sphinx,
flower mosaics on the floors of stores,
ballets of massacres. Cut-glass sewers,
red velvet hangings stained the walls of jails,
white lacquer chairs in the abortionists',
boxers, mummies for policemen, wigs
on the meat at the butchers', murderers
eating their last meal under the Arch of Peace.

The unemployed brought all the orange trees,
cypress trees, tubbed rubber-plants, and limes,
conifers, loblolly and the tamaracks,
incongruous flowers to a grove wherein

they sat, making oranges. For in that cold season
fruit was golden could not be guaranteed.

It was long before the riderless horse came streaming
hot to the square. I walked at noon and saw
that face run screaming through the crowd saying Help
but its mouth would not open and they could not hear.

It was long before the troops entered the city
that I looked up and saw the Floating Man.
Explain yourself I cried at the last. I am
the angel waste, your need which is your guilt,
answered, affliction and a fascist death.

It was long before the city was bombed I saw
fireworks, mirrors, gilt, consumed in flame,
we show this you said the flames, speak it speak it
but I was employed then making straw oranges.
Everything spoke: flames, city, glass, but I
had heavy mystery thrown against the heart.

It was long before the fall of the city.
Ten days before the appearance of the skull.
Five days until the skull showed clean,
and now the entry is prepared.
Carnival's ready.
Let's dance a little before we go home to hell.

REINHOLD NIEBUHR

An End to Illusions

THE MORNING NEWSPAPER brings reports of disaster everywhere. The morning mail acquaints me with the confusion created by these reports. My mail this morning, for example, contains four significant communications. The first is a letter from the Socialist Party informing me that my views on foreign affairs violate the party platform and asking me to give account of my nonconformity. The party position is that this war is a clash of rival imperialisms in which nothing significant is at stake. The second letter asks me to support an organization which will bring peace to the world by establishing "world education" and erecting a "world radio." It fails to explain how its world education is to seep into the totalitarian states and wean them from their mania. The third letter is from a trade union under Communist influence asking me to speak at a union "peace" meeting. The fourth is from a parson who wants me to join in an effort to set "moral force against Hitler's battalions," but it fails to explain just how this moral force is to be effective against tanks, flame-thrower, and bombing planes.

This mail increases the melancholy prompted by the morning's news. I answer the Socialist communication by a quick resignation from the party. I inform the trade union that my views would not be acceptable at its peace meeting. The proposal for a world radio is quickly consigned to a file which already contains eighty-two different recipes for world salvation. I start to answer the parson who wants to set "moral force" against Hitler, but overcome with a sense of futility and doubting my ability to penetrate the utopian fog in which the letter was conceived, I throw my reply into the wastebasket. Thus I save some time to meditate upon the perspective which informs this whole morning's mail and upon the vapid character of the culture which Hitler intends to destroy. This culture does not understand historical reality clearly enough to deserve to survive. It has a right to survival only because the alternative is too horrible to contemplate. All four letters are but expressions of the utopianism which has informed our Western world since the eighteenth century.

The Socialists have a dogma that this war is a clash of rival imperialisms. Of course they are right. So is a clash between myself and a gangster a conflict of rival egotisms. There is a perspective from which there is not much difference between my egotism and that of a gangster. But from another perspective there is an important difference. "There is not much difference between people," said a farmer to William James, "but what difference there is is very important." That is a truth which the Socialists in America have not yet learned. The Socialists are right, of course, in insisting that the civilization which we are called upon to defend is full of capitalistic and imperialistic injustice. But it is still a civilization. Utopianism creates confusion in politics by measuring all significant historial distinctions against purely ideal perspectives and blinding the eye to differences which may be matters of life and death in a specific instance

The Socialists rightly call attention to the treason of the capitalistic oligarchy which has brought the cause of democracy to so desperate a state

But we are defending something which transcends the interests of Mr. Chamberlain and the venality of M. Bonnet. Furthermore, the Socialists have forgotten how much they contributed to the capitulation of democracy to tyranny. It was a Socialist Prime Minister, Paul-Henri Spaak, who contrived the unrealistic neutrality policy of Belgium which was responsible for the German break-through at Sedan. The policy was unrealistic because it was based upon the quite untrue assumption that Belgium was imperilled equally by rival imperialistic powers. The peril was not equal at all, and history has avenged this lie in a terrible way. The Socialists of the Scandinavian countries were deeply involved in the parasitic pacifism of these small nations which scorned "power politics" and forgot that their security rested upon the British navy and the contingencies of a precarious balance of power. The Socialists of Britain willed to resist Hitler but did not will the means of resistance. As for Munich, I heard American Socialists give thanks that a madman with a gun was met by a man with an umbrella. If there had been two guns, rather than an umbrella and a gun, they said, the world would have been plunged into conflict. European Socialists have learned to repent of these errors under the pressure of tragic events, leaving only American Socialists to indulge the luxury of their utopianism.

The proposal for "world radio" and "world education" is merely a particularly fatuous form of the utopian rationalism and universalism which have informed the thought of liberal intellectuals in the whole Western world. These liberals have always imagined that it was a comparatively simple matter for the human mind to transcend the welter of interest and passion which is the very stuff of existence. They have not understood that man's very capacity for freedom creates the imperialist will to dominate, as well as the desire to subordinate life to universal standards. The five hundred American scientists who recently presented a memorial to the President favoring neutrality in the name of scientific impartiality seem not to have the slightest idea that scientific freedom is dependent upon the vicissitudes of political history. Their allusions reveal that modern culture completely misunderstands history precisely because it has learned a great deal about nature and falsely imagines that the harmonies and securities of nature are a safe asylum for man.

There seems to be absolutely no end to the illusions of which intellectuals are capable and no height of unrealistic dreaming to which they cannot rise. Aldous Huxley dreams in Hollywood of a method of making man harmless by subtracting or abstracting the self from selfhood and stumbles into a pseudo-Buddhistic mysticism as the way of salvation without understanding that this kind of mysticism annuls all history in the process of destroying the self.

When the intellectuals are not given to a vapid form of universalism they elaborate an impossible individualism. Bertrand Russell, who has now repented of his pacifism, wrote in an article recently reprinted in *The Nation* that any political view which made individuals the bearers of ideological forces was outmoded.[1] The fact is that Nazi collectivism with its primitive emphasis upon "blood and soil" is but a cruel and psychopathic emphasis upon organic and collective aspects of life which liberal individualism has outraged. As late as last February the *New Republic* promised to stand resolutely against any moral urge that might carry us into war because it knew so certainly that the "evils of a system" could not be cured by "killing the unfortunate individuals who for a moment embody the system." It failed to tell us that the individuals who for the moment embody a system might possibly fasten a system of slavery upon us which would not be for a moment. When Germany invaded Holland and Belgium and the situation of the western democracies became precarious, the *New Republic* forgot these individualistic scruples and solemnly warned that we could not afford to allow the British navy to be destroyed, though it did not tell us how we were to prevent it without imperilling the lives of unfortunate individual sailors and soldiers "who for the moment embody a system." The real fact is that we have no right to deal with the rough stuff of politics at all if we do not understand that politics always deals with collective action and that collective action invariably involves both guilty and guiltless among the individuals who for the moment embody a system.

The letter from the communistic trade union in my mail can stand as a symbol of the aberrations of those who frantically cling to Russia as their hope of salvation. The fear that a triumphant Germany will invade the Ukraine may bring Russia back on the side of the angels shortly, and then the rest of us will be told how wrong we were in judging Russia prematurely. Fortunately, we have no intellectuals of the standing of George Bernard Shaw and J. B. S. Haldane who, under the influence of the Russian obsession, talk such nonsense as these two men have permitted themselves.

The letter from the parson who wanted to set "moral force" against Hitler's battalions is a nice example of the sentimentalized form of Christianity which has engulfed our churches, particularly in America, and which has prompted them to dream of "spiritualizing life" by abstracting

---

[1] "What I Believe," in *The Nation*, March 3, 1940.

spirit from matter, history, and life. It is significant that this kind of "spiritual" religion identifies religious perfectionism with the morally dubious and politically dangerous dogmas of isolation. If we could only keep free of this European struggle we might still indulge our illusions about the character of human existence, which Christianity at its best illumines.

A survey of our culture gives us the uneasy feeling that Hitler was not quite wrong in his boast that he would destroy the world of the eighteenth century. In its more articulate forms our culture suffers from illusions which weaken its will and its right to survive. One can only be grateful for the common sense of common folk which has not been corrupted by these illusions and which in the hour of peril expresses itself in sound political instincts. But for this common sense we might capitulate to a system of government which declares war to be normal, because we do not believe in war. We might submit to a culture which glorifies force as the final arbiter, because we thought it a simple task to extricate reason from force. We might allow a primitive collectivism to enslave us, because we had false ideas of the relation of the individual to the collective forces of life. We might submit to tyranny and the negation of justice, because we had an uneasy conscience about the injustices which corrupt our system of justice.

Hitler threatens the whole world not merely because the democracies were plutocratic and betrayed by their capitalistic oligarchies. His victories thus far are partly due to the fact that the culture of the democracies was vapid. Its political instincts had become vitiated by an idealism which sought to extricate morals from politics to the degree of forgetting that all life remains a contest of power. If Hitler is defeated in the end it will be because the crisis has awakened in us the will to preserve a civilization in which justice and freedom are realities, and given us the knowledge that ambiguous methods are required for the ambiguities of history. Let those who are revolted by such ambiguities have the decency and consistency to retire to the monastery, where medieval perfectionists found their asylum.

ARCHIBALD MacLEISH

The Irresponsibles

HISTORY—if honest history continues to be written—will have one question to ask of our generation, people like ourselves. It will be asked of the books we have written, the carbon copies of our correspondence, the photographs of our faces, the minutes of our meetings in the famous rooms before the portraits of our spiritual begetters. The question will be this: Why did the scholars and the writers of our generation in this country, witnesses as they were to the destruction of writing and of scholarship in great areas of Europe and to the exile and the imprisonment and murder of men whose crime was scholarship and writing—witnesses also to the rise in their own country of the same destructive forces with the same impulses, the same motives, the same means—why did the scholars and the writers of our generation in America fail to oppose those forces while they could—while there was still time and still place to oppose them with the arms of scholarship and writing?

It is a question the historians will ask with interest—the gentle, detached, not altogether loving interest with which historians have always questioned the impotent spirits of the dead. Young men working in the paper rubbish of our lives, the old journals, the marginal notations, the printed works, will discover (or so they will think) that the scholars and the writers of our generation in this country had been warned of danger as men were rarely warned before. They will discover (or so they will think) that the common inherited culture of the West, by which alone our scholars and our writers lived, had been attacked in other countries with a stated and explicit purpose to destroy. They will discover that that purpose had been realized. They will discover that a similar purpose backed by similar forces, created by similar conditions, was forming here. And it will seem to them strange—ironical and strange—that the great mass of American scholars and American writers made no effort to defend either themselves or the world by which they lived.

They will make, of course, the necessary reservations. They will note that societies of scholars and associations of writers adopted resolutions declaring their devotion to civilization. They will note that certain young novelists and poets, the most generous and gallant of their time, unable to endure the outrage and injustice, gave up their lives as writers and enlisted in the hopeless armies to fight brutality with force. But of those who truly faced this danger not with their bodies but their minds, of those who fought the enemies of the intellect with the weapons of the intellect, devoting to that warfare all the strength, all the imagination, all the resources of courage and inventiveness, all the watchfulness by day and night, all the last reserves of hope and skill and pain which men must use whose lives and more than lives are put in danger—of those who fought this danger with the weapons by which this danger could be overcome, they will record the names of very few. And they will ask their question, Why did we, scholars and writers in America in this time, we who had been warned of our danger not only by explicit threats but by explicit action, why did we not fight this danger while the weapons we used best—the weapons of ideas and words—could still be used against it?

It is not a question for which we are altogether unprepared. We have been writing out our answer for many years now in action and inaction, in words and in silence—in learned articles in the scientific journals and in controversial articles in the general magazines, in blank faces after the passionate words, in bored eyes refusing to believe. The answer we have prepared, the answer we have written out for history to find, is the answer Leonardo is said to have given Michelangelo when Michelangelo blamed him for his indifference to the misfortunes of the Florentines. It is the answer of our kind at many other times and places. 'Indeed,' said Leonardo, 'indeed the study of beauty has occupied my whole heart.' The study of beauty, the study of history, the study of science, has occupied our whole hearts and the misfortunes of our generation are none of our concern. They are the practical and political concern of practical and political men, but the concern of the scholar, the concern of the artist, is with other, purer, more enduring things.

This is the answer we have written down for history to find. I doubt whether it will satisfy the ironic men who come to plague us on that waterfront where Tiresias was made to drink the blood and answer. I think indeed it will not satisfy them. For it has not satisfied ourselves. We say with great firmness and authority, speaking by our words and by our silence, that the misfortunes of our generation are economic and political misfortunes from which the scholar can safely hold himself apart. We say this with all the authority of the political scientists of the past to whom the misfortunes of the people were always political and economic and of no concern to the poet, the pure scholar, the artist intent upon his art.

We say it also with the authority of the political scientists of the present to whom all phenomena of whatever kind are, by hypothesis, economic and political. But though we say it we do not believe it. For we have observed these misfortunes. They have been acted out for us to see. And what we have seen is this: that the misfortunes of our time are not the misfortunes the philosophers, the theorists, the political scientists have described to us. They are not the practical concern of the practical man and therefore matters of indifference to the scholar. On the contrary, it is the practical man and the practical man alone—the man whose only care is for his belly and his roof—who can safely be indifferent to these troubles. The things he lives by are not menaced. And it is precisely the scholar, the poet —the man whose care is for the structures of the intellect, the houses of the mind—whose heart is caught. For it is the scholar's goods which are in danger.

It is perhaps because we have seen this and yet refuse to see it—because we know one thing and yet continue to declare another—that our minds are so confused and our counsels so bewildering. Nothing is more characteristic of the intellectuals of our generation than their failure to understand what it is that is happening to their world. And nothing explains that failure as precisely as their unwillingness to see what they have seen and to know what they do truly know. They have seen the crisis of their time—they have seen it spelled out, played out, fought out as few observers ever before in history saw the tragedy exposed. They know its ending. And yet they continue to pretend that they do not know. They continue to speak of the crisis of their time as though the war in Europe were that crisis—and the war, they say, is no concern of theirs. They continue to speak of the crisis as though the imperialistic maneuvers, the struggles for markets, the propaganda in the newspapers and the radio, were the crisis—and the maneuvers of imperialism, the propaganda of the press and the struggles for trade, they say, are no concern of theirs. And yet they know—they know very well because they have seen—that these things are not the crisis but merely its reflections in the mirrors of action. They know that behind the war, behind the diplomatic gestures, behind the black print on the page and the hysterical voices on the air there is something deeper and more dangerous—more dangerous to *them*. They know that it is a condition of men's minds which has produced these things—a condition which existed and exists, not only in Europe but in other parts of the world as well and not least in our own country. And they know that this condition of men's minds is not a practical, a political, phenomenon of no concern to the scholar and the man of thought, but something very different.

It is not, for example, a matter of purely practical and political interest that great numbers of men in various parts of the world wish passionately and even violently to give up the long labor of liberty and to surrender their wills and their bodies and even their minds to the will of a leader, so that they may achieve at least the dignity of order, at least the dignity of obedience. It is not a matter of purely practical and political significance that whole nations of men have gladly and willingly released themselves, not only from their rights as individuals, but from their responsibilities as individuals, so that they are no longer compelled to feel or to respect the individual humanity of others—or to feel or to respect the things that individual humanity has, over many centuries, created. It is not a matter of purely practical and political importance that governments which once, whatever they may have practiced, protested a respect for learning and the arts, should now permit themselves to show not only the power but worse, far worse, the *willingness,* the *purpose,* to enslave both learning and the arts. It is not a matter of purely practical and political importance that societies which once made part of the community of Western culture should now attempt by murder and outrage and exile to root out that culture and to replace it with private and parochial sciences and private and parochial arts so that frontiers are armed, for the first time in the history of the West, not only along the rivers and the mountains and the boundaries of nations, but across the common earth of culture, the free land that was never fenced before.

I think no honest man will say that these are matters of practical and political significance alone. I think any man who considers with coolness, and without the preconceptions of the dogmas, the character of the crisis of his time will admit, because he will have no choice but to admit, that this crisis is in essence a cultural crisis—a revolt of certain classes, certain conditions of men against the inherited culture of the West and against all common culture—a revolt by no means limited to those nations alone where it has been successful. Wars we have had before—many wars; murder also: inquisition of scholars: torture of askers: suppression and mutilation of truth. But in the past these things have been done, however hypocritically, in the name of truth, in the name of humanity—even in the name of God. The forms of culture were preserved—and in the preservation of a civilization as in the preservation of an art the forms are everything. What is new and unexampled in the times we live in is *the repudiation of the forms.* What is new is a cynical brutality which considers moral self-justification unnecessary and therefore—and this is perhaps its worst indecency—dispenses even with the filthy garment of the hypocrite. To use brutality and force, not in the name of Right nor in the name of God, but in the name of force alone, is to destroy the self-respect and therefore the dignity of the individual life without which the existence of art or learning is inconceivable. To lie, not in the name of truth, but in the name of lies, is to destroy the common basis of communication without which a common culture cannot exist and a work of learning or of art becomes unintelligible.

The truth is—the plain and simple truth of which we have so many painful evidences—that the disorder of our time, whatever else it may now be or may become, is in its essentials a revolt against the common culture of the West. For against what but the common culture did this disorder continue to struggle in Germany long after it had overthrown the former state? There was no domestic danger for it to fear. Against what but the Western respect for the dignity of the individual was aimed the long series of outrages against the Jews? The Jews were impotent when they were subjected to the worst abuses. Against what but the Western respect for the common, the nationless, creation of the artist was aimed the destruction of the work of men like Thomas Mann? Thomas Mann had already been repudiated by his people when they accepted the government of his enemies. Against what but the Western belief in the wholeness of Western civilization was aimed the assault upon a church which was no longer a danger to any ruler and the fabrication of a paganism which needed only the blond sopranos on the ends of wires to be Wagner at his worst?

Intellectuals in America and elsewhere—writers, scientists, the men of learning—have attempted to ignore these questions. They have pretended to themselves that the burning of books, the exiling of artists, the invention of mythologies were merely incidents—afterthoughts—decorations: that the true crisis was the crisis of food, the crisis of arms, the crisis created by political forces, by economic collapse—that they had, and needed have, no truck with it. They have been wrong. These things are not incidents. They are not afterthoughts. They are the essential nature of the revolution of our age. For without this attack upon the habits of the mind, the reliances of the spirit, that revolution could not, by any possibility, have succeeded.

The revolution of our age—the revolution which has finally emerged and declared itself in action—is not the great revolution of the masses of which generous men once dreamed: and which other and less generous men have now so meanly and so bloodily betrayed. The revolution of the masses was a revolution which proposed to set up one faith against another faith, one culture against another culture: a faith in man, a faith in the power of the patterns of men's lives, against a faith in institutions and in money; a culture of the people against a culture of the exploiters of the people. The revolution which has finally and successfully emerged in action has no such faith and no such culture.

It is a revolution of negatives, a revolution of the defeated, a revolution of the dispossessed, a revolution of despair. It is a revolution created out of misery by dread of yet more misery, a revolution created out of disorder by terror of disorder. It is a revolution of gangs, a revolution *against*. And the enemy it is against, the enemy it must destroy, is the enemy which, in all times and in all civilizations, has stood against the revolutions of the gangs—the rule of moral law, the rule of spiritual authority, the rule of intellectual truth. To establish the negative revolutions, the revolutions of which the only aim is power, the revolutions which have no means but force, it is necessary first to destroy the authority of the unseen sayings of the mind. It is necessary to destroy the things the mind has made. Caliban in the miserable and besotted swamp is the symbol of this revolution. As long as the unseen beauty in the air retains its voices and its seductive music and its stinging whips, the revolutions of the gangs are clumsy, blundering, grotesque, and foolish. They can bellow and threaten and boast and gesture with their arms, but in the end the invisible voices of the air, the invisible power of the ideal will master them. They have one hope of success and only one—the destruction of the whole system of ideas, the whole respect for truth, the whole authority of excellence which places law above force, beauty above cruelty, singleness above numbers.

It is the distinction of our time—perhaps unhappily its most memorable distinction—that it and it alone has provided the formula by which this overthrow could be achieved. Only in our time has the revolution of the gangs discovered a strategy and a leadership brutal enough, cynical enough, cunning enough to destroy the entire authority of the inherited culture and thereafter to seal the doors against the searching and the asking of the scholar's mind, the artist's mind, so that the revolution of force, the revolution of despair could flower and fulfill its possibilities. Only in our time has the revolution of the gangs shown itself openly and admittedly as the thing it is—a revolution of cruelty, cunning, and despair against the authority and the discipline of the mind.

It is to this disorder and not to some political and partisan dissension, not to some accidental economic breakdown—practical and political matters for the men of politics and practice—it is to this direct, explicit, and intentional attack upon the scholar's world and the scholar's life and the scholar's work that American scholarship has been indifferent. Or if not indifferent, then inactive, merely watchful—fearful, watchful, and inactive. And it is there that history will place its questions.

How could we sit back as spectators of a war against ourselves?

Did we suppose the newly discovered techniques of deception, of false-hood as a military force, of strategic fraud, were incapable of reaching us—incapable of crossing sea water? We had seen their methods drive their conquests through the countries of the world more rapidly than Alexander or Napoleon or Tamerlane or any other conqueror or killer.

Or was it something else we thought? Did we believe others would defend us? Did we think the issue was an issue of strategy, an issue of battles? Did we think the British and the French would win their war and so defend us? But we knew very well, because we had seen, that this war was not a war fought in the open on the military front, but a war fought in the back street and the dark stair—a war fought within the city, within the house, within the mind—a war of treason: a war of corruption: a war of lies. And against treason and corruption and lies, battle fleets and grand armies are impotent.

The questions answer themselves and yet provide no answer. For if we did not believe we were safe by sea water, or if we did not believe others would save us, then our failure to act in our own defense becomes a curious thing. What has prevented us from acting? Lack of courage? It is difficult to indict a generation for lack of courage. Lack of wisdom? There is wisdom enough in other matters.

I think, speaking only of what I have seen myself and heard—I think it is neither lack of courage nor lack of wisdom, but a different reason which has prevented our generation of intellectuals in this country from acting in their own defense. I think it is the organization of the intellectual life of our time. Specifically, I think it is the division and therefore the destruction of intellectual responsibility. The men of intellectual duty, those who should have been responsible for action, have divided themselves into two castes, two cults—the scholars and the writers. Neither accepts responsibility for the common culture or for its defense.

There was a time a century ago, two centuries ago, when men who practiced our professions would have accepted this responsibility without an instant's hesitation. A century ago the professions of the writer and the scholar were united in the single profession of the man of letters and the man of letters was responsible in everything that touched the mind. He was a man of wholeness of purpose, of singleness of intention—a single intellectual champion, admittedly responsible for the defense of the in-herited tradition, avowedly partisan of its practice. Where those who practice our several professions divide the learned world and the creative world between them in irresponsible and neutral states, the man of letters inhabited both learning and the world of letters like an empire.

He was a man of learning whose learning was employed, not for its own sake in a kind of academic narcissism, but for the sake of decent living in his time. He was a writer whose writing was used, not to mirror an abstract and unrelated present, but to illuminate that present by placing it in just relation to its past. He was therefore and necessarily a man who admitted a responsibility for the survival and vitality of the common and accumulated experience of the mind, for this experience was to him the air he breathed, the perspective of his thinking. Learning to him was no plump pigeon carcass to be picked at for his private pleasure and his private fame, but a profession practiced for the common good. Writing was not an ornament, a jewel, but a means to ends, a weapon, the most powerful of weapons, a weapon to be used. Whatever threatened learning or the ends of learning challenged the man of letters. Whatever struck at truth or closed off question or defiled an art or violated decency of thinking struck at him. And he struck back with every weapon masters of the word could find to strike with. Milton defending freedom of the mind in sentences which outlive every name of those who struck at freedom, Voltaire displaying naked to the grin of history the tyrants who were great until he made them small, Bartolomé de las Casas gentling cruel priests and brutal captains with the dreadful strokes of truth—Las Casas, Milton and Voltaire were men of letters—men who confessed an obligation to defend the disciplines of thought not in their own but in the general interest.

Had men like these been living in our time—had the intellectuals of our time been whole and loyal—it would, I think, have been impossible for the revolution of the gangs to have succeeded where success has been most dangerous—in the perversion of the judgments of the mind. Murder is not absolved of immorality by committing murder. Murder is absolved of immorality by bringing men to think that murder is not evil. This only the perversion of the mind can bring about. And the perversion of the mind is only possible when those who should be heard in its defense are silent.

They are silent in our time because there are no voices which accept responsibility for speaking. Even the unimaginable indecencies of propaganda—even the corruption of the word itself in Germany and Russia and in Spain and elsewhere—even the open triumph of the lie, produced no answer such as Voltaire in his generation would have given. And for this reason—that the man who could have been Voltaire, who could have been Las Casas, does not live: the man of intellectual *office,* the man of intellectual *calling,* the man who *professes* letters—professes an obligation as a servant of the mind to defend the mind's integrity against every physical power—professes an obligation to defend the labors of the mind and the structures it has created and the means by which it lives, not only privately and safely in his study, not only strictly and securely in the controversies of the learned press, but publicly and at the public risk and danger of his life. He does not exist because the man of letters no longer exists. And the man of letters no longer exists because he has been driven from our world and from our time by the division of his kingdom. The single responsibility, the wholeness of function of the man of letters, has been replaced by the divided function, the mutual antagonism, the isolated irresponsibility of two figures, each free of obligation, each separated from a portion of his duty—the scholar and the writer.

Why this substitution has come about—whether because the methods of scientific inquiry, carried over into the humanities, destroyed the loyalties and habits of the mind or for some other reason, I leave to wiser men to say. The point is that there has been a substitution. The country of the man of letters has been divided between his heirs. The country that was once the past and present—the past made useful to the reasons of the present, the present understood against the knowledge of the past—the country that was once the past and present brought together in the mind, is now divided into past on one side, present on the other.

Past is the scholar's country: present is the writer's. The writer sees the present on the faces of the world and leaves the past to rot in its own rubbish. The scholar digs his ivory cellar in the ruins of the past and lets the present sicken as it will. A few exceptions noted here and there—men like Thomas Mann—the gulf between these countries is complete. And the historical novels fashionable at the moment, the vulgarizations of science, the digests of philosophy only define its depth as a plank across a chasm makes the chasm deeper. That it should be necessary to throw such flimsy flights from one side to the other of the learned world shows how deeply and disastrously the split was made.

That scholarship suffers or that writing suffers by the change is not asserted. Scholarship may be more scientific: writing may be purer. Indeed there are many who believe, and I among them, that the time we live in has produced more first-rate writers than any but the very greatest ages, and there are scholars of a scholarship as hard, as honest, as devoted as any we have known. But excellence of scholarship and writing are not now in question. What matters now is the defense of culture—the defense truly, and in the most literal terms, of civilization as men have known it for the last two thousand years. And there the substitution for the man of letters of the scholar and the writer, however pure the scholarship, however excellent the writing, is a tragic and immeasurable loss. For neither the modern scholar nor the modern writer admits responsibilty for the defense.

They assert on the contrary, each in his particular way, an irresponsibility as complete as it is singular.

The irresponsibility of the scholar is the irresponsibility of the scientist upon whose laboratory insulation he has patterned all his work. The scholar has made himself as indifferent to values, as careless of significance, as bored with meanings as the chemist. He is a refugee from consequences, an exile from the responsibilities of moral choice. He has taught himself to say with the physicist—and with some others whom history remembers—'What is truth?' He has taught himself with the biologist to refrain from judgments of better or worse. His words of praise are the laboratory words—objectivity—detachment—dispassion. His pride is to be scientific, neuter, skeptical, detached—superior to final judgment or absolute belief. In his capacity as scholar the modern scholar does not occupy the present. In his capacity as scholar he loves the word—but only the word which entails no judgments, involves no decisions, accomplishes no actions. Where the man of letters of other centuries domesticated the past within the rustling of the present, making it stand among us like the meaning of a statue among trees, the modern scholar in his capacity as scholar leaves the present and returns across the past where all the men are marble. Where the man of letters of other centuries quarried his learning from the past to build the present the modern scholar quarries his learning from the past to dig the quarries.

It is not for nothing that the modern scholar invented the Ph.D. thesis as his principal contribution to literary form. The Ph.D. thesis is the perfect image of his world. It is work done for the sake of doing work— perfectly conscientious, perfectly laborious, perfectly irresponsible. The modern scholar at his best and worst is both these things—perfectly conscientious, laborious and competent: perfectly irresponsible for the saving of his world. He remembers how in the Civil Wars in England the scholars, devoted only to their proper tasks, founded the Royal Society. He remembers how through other wars and other dangers the scholars kept the lamp of learning lighted. He does not consider that the scholars then did other things as well as trim the lamp wicks. He does not consider either that the dangers change and can be greater. He has his work to do. He has his book to finish. He hopes the war will not destroy the manuscripts he works with. He is the pure, the perfect type of irresponsibility—the man who acts as though the fire could not burn him because he has no business with the fire. He knows because he cannot help but know, reading his papers, talking to his friends—he knows this fire has consumed the books, the spirit, everything he lives by, flesh itself—in other countries. He knows this but he will not know. It's not his business. Whose business is it then? He will not answer even that. He has his work to do. He has his book to finish . . .

The writer's irresponsibility is of a different kind. Where the modern scholar escapes from the adult judgments of the mind by taking the disinterested man of science as his model, the modern writer escapes by imitation of the artist. He practices his writing as a painter does his painting. He thinks as artist—which is to say he thinks without responsibility to anything but truth of feeling. He observes as artist—which is to say that he observes with honesty and truthfulness and without comment. His devotion, as with every honest painter, is devotion to the thing observed, the actual thing, the thing without its consequences or its antecedents, naked of judgment, stripped of causes and effects. The invisible world, the intellectual world, the world of the relation of ideas, the world of judgments, of values, the world in which truth is good and lies are evil—this world has no existence to the honest artist or to the honest writer who takes the artist for his model. His duty is to strip all this away—to strip away the moral preference, the intellectual association.

He sees the world as a god sees it—without morality, without care, without judgment. People look like this. People act like that. He shows them looking, acting. It is not his business why they look so, why they act so. It is enough that he should 'make them happen.' This is the whole test, the whole criterion, of the work of the writer-artist—to show things as they 'really happen': to write with such skill, such penetration of the physical presence of the world, that the action seen, the action described, will 'really happen' on his page. If he concerns himself with motive at all he concerns himself with the 'real' motive, meaning the discreditable motive which the actor conceals from himself. His most searching purpose is to find, not the truth of human action, but the low-down, the discreditable explanation which excuses him from care. The suggestion that there are things in the world—ideas, conceptions, ways of thinking—which the writer-artist should defend from attack: the suggestion above all that he was under obligation to defend the inherited culture, would strike him as ridiculous.

Artists do not save the world. They practice art. They practice it as Goya practiced it among the cannon in Madrid. And if this war is not Napoleon in Spain but something even worse than that? They practice art. Or they put the art aside and take a rifle and go out and fight. But not *as artists*. The artist does not fight. The artist's obligations are obligations to his art. His responsibility—his one responsibility—is to his art. He has no other. Not even when his art itself, his chance to practice it, his need to live where it is practiced, may be in danger. The writer-artist will write a bloody story about the expense of blood. He will present the face of agony as it has rarely been presented. But not even then will he take the weapon of his words and carry it to the barricades of intellectual warfare, to the storming of belief, the fortifying of conviction where alone this fighting can be won.

There are examples in history of civilizations made impotent by excess of culture. No one, I think, will say of us that we lost our intellectual liberties on this account. But it may well be said, and said with equally ironic emphasis, that the men of thought, the men of learning in this country were deceived and rendered impotent by the best they knew. To the scholar impartiality, objectivity, detachment were ideal qualities he taught himself laboriously and painfully to acquire. To the writer objectivity and detachment were his writer's pride. Both subjected themselves to inconceivable restraints, endless disciplines to reach these ends. And both succeeded. Both writers and scholars freed themselves of the subjective passions, the emotional preconceptions which color conviction and judgment. Both writers and scholars freed themselves of the personal responsibility associated with personal choice. They emerged free, pure and single into the antiseptic air of objectivity. And by that sublimation of the mind they prepared the mind's disaster.

If it is a consolation to the philosophers of earlier civilizations to know that they lost the things they loved because of the purity of their devotion, then perhaps this consolation will be ours as well. I doubt if we will profit by it or receive much praise.

1940.

PAUL ENGLE

America, 1941

WESTERN MUSE, who by the curved prow over
The salty water wandered from the edge
Of hungering Europe to this country where
All through long June bees ride the ruddy clover,

Wild dogwood dangles from the Catskill ledge
And goldenrod is more a flower than the rose,
More native autumn-colored—let the live air
Be in my lungs no song drier than drouth
Or corn leaves brittle when the cold wind blows,
Tongue's touch worn from the words. Give me away,
The power of plain talk in a plain man's mouth,
To tell the marvelous horror of our day.

I cannot ask my tongue to cheat the eye,
Naming alone the mounting meadowlark
When the blue bird-way gleams where the bombers fly.
I will not range in any measured rime
Only the child's night cry, dreading the dark,
The wind's voice varied with the altering suns,
When the true sound and temper of our time
Is the gigantic arrogance of guns.

Muse of muskies lashing the Minnesota
Lake, of Alabama pine growing
Green from the red earth, the Dismal Swamp
Gray with old water, golden Dakota
Wheat tall with the early autumn sowing,
Utah range brown as a sunburned face—
How can I praise you without hollow pomp
When on our same round world, balanced in space
As on a trained seal's nose a turning ball,
All blacked-out Europe, crouched for the bomb's thud,
Colors its eyes only with the tall
Smoke of its burning home, its crawling blood?

Muse of American summer when days start
Full of vacation laughter, free of the clock
To loaf in hills where the honey locust hums—
How, in a heartless age, can I find heart
To praise the brilliant morning and not mock
The dread of continents when daylight comes
Laying the land bare to the bomber's chart?

Muse of our time, let my talk be act.
It's too late now to make the frightened head
An air-raid shelter walled by the skull's tough bone
To will away the brute, exploding fact.

Mind, believe what my candid eyes have shown.
Truth, be in my mouth as daily bread.

Muse of American men, help me find
Words that will tell the wonder of this place,
Continent bounded by the gray gull's flight,
Where liberty now nourishes the mind
As blood makes bone alive and gives eyes sight—
And find those lands where the already blind
Tear freedom from a man as eyes from his face,
Taking away hope and the loved light.

While in these days over our harvest field
A long wind twitches the lion-tawny wheat,
Let each word leave my mouth like autumn yield,
Grain ripened in the sun and good to eat.
I want the natural wisdom of a child
To tell the pity of Europe's people now,
Common men and women, proud of the piled
Manure in their yard, the calf dropped by their cow;
All those in cities hoping for a raise,
A new house out where the kids had room to play,
Those desperate for a job in the feared days,
Young girls doing their hair the latest way.

Now while on their face continual sorrows
Fall and are not turned back by any hand,
Give me the aviator's metal eye
To hunt bright hope beyond the rainy sky,
To find beyond river and hill tomorrow's
Flying weather and a field to land.

E. J. KAHN, JR.

My Day

ONE OF THE QUESTIONS frequently asked of a selectee by civilians he encounters on the rare excursions he makes into their sheltered world is "Well, what do you *do* all day, anyway?" Well, we do lots of things. The component parts of my routine at Camp Croft were varied slightly from day to day, but on the whole I found it hard to tell one day from another. On my typical day I was aroused, along with thirty or so roommates, at five-thirty in the morning by a fellow who had spent the night in charge of company headquarters and who bounded briskly into the barracks, snapped on the lights with a flourish, shouted, "Let's go," and vanished again into the darkness outside before I had time to say thanks. A bugle was also blown, but we didn't always hear it. We had only ten minutes in which to prepare for reveille, so most of the boys, having dislodged themselves from their beds, hurriedly started putting their clothes on, at the same time encouraging reluctant risers near them, by a stiff nudge or two, to follow their example. At five-forty a staff sergeant's whistle blew and we lined up in front of our barracks for roll call. When we had been found all present or accounted for, we scrambled back indoors. We were then completely at leisure, until breakfast at six-fifteen, to wash, make our beds, sweep under them, arrange our shoes neatly under the beds, tie the laces on the shoes we had arranged, and dust the whole display. We performed some of these chores to the musical accompaniment of Stan Shaw's all-night phonograph-record program on one of the boys' radios, a broadcast some of us used to listen to in New York as we went to bed.

At the sound of another whistle we walked to our company mess hall, a long, low building a hundred yards away, and as we filed in we paused at the door to receive our daily ration of milk, a half-pint bottle. About two hundred and fifty men ate there, seated ten at a table. Our food had already been set out by soldiers who were on duty as waiters for the day, and we began eating when a cook blew a whistle. Before each of us was a thick china cup, a china plate, a knife, a fork, a spoon, and, at some

---

Originally published in *The New Yorker*. Reprinted from *The Army Life* by permission of Simon and Schuster, Inc. Copyright, 1942, by E. J. Kahn, Jr.

breakfasts, a cereal bowl. We were continually informed by our mess
sergeant, a man evidently unimpressed by such conversationally worth-
while meals as those which once took place at the Mermaid Tavern, that it
was pointless and in fact improper to mix talking with eating and that our
table repartee should be limited to "Pass the butter, please" and "Reach for
it yourself." After breakfast some of us lined up in front of the barracks
and then roamed across the company area, stripping it of such undesirable
matter as cigarette butts, matchsticks, and bits of paper. The rest of us
returned to our barracks to finish sweeping and to wipe off any ledges or
shelves we suspected an inquisitive officer might finger.

By seven-fifteen, we were ready to go to work. Most of our days were
divided into hourly periods. We worked for fifty minutes and then had a
theoretically ten-minute break, which was rarely longer than ten minutes
and was frequently shorter, depending on how many things we were required to do during it. Each break began and ended with a whistle blast,
and in between we often ran in and out of the barracks to gather up equipment as orders were shouted to us. We sometimes changed our accessories
as often as a débutante. One morning, for instance, we were told to fall
out in khaki hats. After doing so, we were told to go back inside and
get our denim hats. We neatly stowed our khaki hats away and fell out
in denims, only to learn that at Croft they are worn exclusively by prisoners. It developed that what we should have done was to wear our khakis
and carry the denims, which were to be turned in at the supply room,
where they would presumably await our admittance to the guardhouse.

On a typical day our work started off with a brisk dose of calisthenics,
which we performed not to musical rhythms but to our own raucous count.
Each exercise we did, we were told, would develop some especially useful
muscle, and the officers who served as physical-education instructors, while
warning us not to bend those knees as we strove earnestly to touch our
toes, were apt to urge us on by announcing that every uncomfortable position we got ourselves into was for our own good. You don't have to be
in the Army long to learn, from some superior or other, that everything
you do, or that is done to you, is for your own good.

During the ten-minute break allotted to us after calisthenics we returned to the barracks and picked up the resplendent accessories of our
regular drill uniforms, which consisted, all told, of blue denim fatigue
blouses and trousers; canvas cartridge belts, with canteen, bayonet, and
first-aid kit attached; rifles; leggings; and wide-brimmed khaki field hats
that will no doubt eventually inspire some little Daché creation that all
the smart girls will be wearing. From eight-fifteen until nine o'clock we
were occupied with close-order drill, without which we would never be

able to give a decent account of ourselves in a Fifth Avenue victory parade. Close-order drill consists of marching in formation. You move at attention, maintaining, when under way, a steady speed of one hundred and twenty steps to the minute, holding your rifle on your shoulder at a precise angle, and looking straight ahead at the neck of the fellow in front of you, a monotonous and singularly unappealing view.

Close-order drill was followed by fifty minutes of what is called extended-order drill, which we were learning for use in areas more combative than Fifth Avenue. During this period we moved around a field in squads of a dozen or so men in long, loose lines, and at frequent intervals were compelled to fall flat on the ground, no matter how unreceptive the ground might appear to be. More often than not, we would be running when we got the order to drop. The Army has an approved way of performing every movement, and we were given explicit instructions about falling. You hit the ground first with your rifle butt, which is clasped firmly in the right hand. Your knees hit next, and, a fraction of a second later, your whole left side. Immediately you roll over into a prone position, bring your rifle butt up to your right shoulder, and there you are, ready to shoot. Very simple.

We were finished with extended-order drill at ten o'clock, by which time we were tired enough to call it a number of days. We would accordingly be astonished to learn that our schedule then demanded a five-mile hike. On hikes we marched at route step—keeping in step not required and talking permitted—with our rifles slung by their straps over our shoulders and our packs, like overweight jockeys, riding high on our backs. We got back to the barracks just in time to collect our mail before lunch, which was served at noon. We received mail twice daily, and once on Sunday. Two letters and a medium-sized package of cookies were regarded as fair compensation for a hike. Probably the saddest fellow in the camp the day we returned from our first long march was the one who stopped lamenting a blister long enough to open a promising-looking envelope forwarded to him from his home, only to discover that it contained a letter from his draft board. It wanted to know where he was.

We would usually be finished with lunch, known in the Army as dinner, by twelve-twenty, and we had the next forty minutes to ourselves, unless, of course, somebody with more authority wanted them. At one o'clock our afternoon began. We were likely to spend the first two hours of it at a movie theater, where we divided our time impartially between cat naps and films about the training of an infantryman. The majority of Army pictures are produced by the Signal Corps, and the actors are almost all Army men, who accomplish with dexterity and poise various movements our officers hope we will some day be able to duplicate. The only member of any of the casts known to me as a nonprofessional is a silver-haired Hollywood actor of whose identity I am uncertain. As a wise old medical officer, a sort of antiseptic Frank Craven, he plays the narrator's role in an animated treatise on sex hygiene I witnessed twice within my first three weeks of service. When he turned up a while later in a regular Hollywood picture about a reformed jewel thief, his first appearance on the screen drew more cheers from the soldier audience than a sweater girl would have.

After our siesta at the movies we went back to our company drill ground for bayonet practice. We stood in two facing rows and, at appropriate intervals, growled ferociously at our supposed opponents and made threatening gestures at them. Bayoneting is as precise a sport as fencing, with a set of conventions no less strict. We were taught a series of ten movements designed to wear down the resistance of, if not actually cut to small pieces, the most formidable enemy, and we were taught to execute them in a definite order beginning with something called the long thrust and going on from there to a series of violent slashes, smashes, and jabs. The only thing that worried us about bayonets was that our opponents might have a set of movements of their own that would interfere with the proper completion of ours, or that they might refuse to co-operate by simply not remaining erect long enough for us to go all the way through our lessons.

Our working day ended at four-thirty in the afternoon. However, there were still plenty of things to keep us from feeling idle. If, for instance, we had carried our beds and bedding outside in the morning, we naturally had to carry these inside and reassemble them. At five-twenty-five we went to Retreat, presenting arms in formation while the camp colors were lowered. While waiting for this ceremony to occur, we took showers and shaved, if we had time; otherwise, we cleaned up after supper. The Army expects every soldier to shave once a day.

Supper came immediately after Retreat, and after supper we were free. Frequently, however, we had a few incidental extra-hour duties to perform, such as cleaning our rifles, turning in our laundry, receiving our laundry, signing the payroll, getting paid, receiving or turning in equipment, or writing letters home. Some men, of course, would go to the movies or hang around at the canteen. At nine o'clock the lights in the barracks went out and everybody with a half-finished letter would rush down to the latrine, where the lights remained on all night and seats of any kind were in great demand. By eleven every man was required to be in his bed. It seemed like a long day, but, as one sergeant explained to a new private who happened to remark that at home he had enjoyed the luxury of a fifty-hour week, "In the Army, fellow, your day begins at midnight." And when, the private hopefully inquired, did it end? "Midnight," the sergeant said.

MARK VAN DOREN

Total War

❋

FOR THE GRAY TEMPLES, for the slippered feet
That bounded such a life as, bent to grace,
Looks brittle now, looks breakable, the word
Nevertheless is shatter; the shocked face

Must fly on other errands, the pale shins
Must brown, must bruise themselves, and all that trunk
Be fragments; the cohesive thought be shrapnel
Peppering cold skies. The sands are sunk

That pedestaled our figure, that as one
Mock granite sounded echo to our soul;
Whose end is now this grit, these million grains
That star a blackened heaven, where no whole

Ever again may shape. Yet, gentlemen,
Be shivered. What was habit now is myth.
Is mumbling. Let it go. A huger form
Waits round the world: man still, and monolith.

With the Japanese attack on Pearl Harbor came a break in the tension; the task ahead was so clear as to obscure most other problems. John O'Hara's old Harvard man and some of his fellows crowded the buildings along Constitution and Pennsylvania Avenues. "The loyal opposition" was the new term used to describe an unfamiliar phenomenon in our polit-

From *The Seven Sleepers* by Mark Van Doren by permission of the publishers, Henry Holt and Company, Inc. Copyright, 1944, by Mark Van Doren.

ical life. Wendell Willkie, defeated candidate for President in 1940, emerged as a serious-minded, winning personality with a profound conviction that the inhabitants of one world could be brought to see the wisdom of sharing that world rather than destroying it. The education of Mr. Willkie at the time seemed a propitious omen; but he died too soon and his lesson is in danger of being discarded or forgotten. The bright hope of the United Nations, before it hardened into reality at Lake Success and Turtle Bay, appears in all its pristine splendor in both Mr. Willkie's book and Norman Corwin's play.

JOHN O'HARA

Graven Image

THE CAR TURNED in at the brief, crescent-shaped drive and waited until the two cabs ahead had pulled away. The car pulled up, the doorman opened the rear door, a little man got out. The little man nodded pleasantly enough to the doorman and said "Wait" to the chauffeur. "Will the Under Secretary be here long?" asked the doorman.

"Why?" said the little man.

"Because if you were going to be here, sir, only a short while, I'd let your man leave the car here, at the head of the rank."

"Leave it there *anyway,*" said the Under Secretary.

"Very good, sir," said the doorman. He saluted and frowned only a little as he watched the Under Secretary enter the hotel. "Well," the doorman said to himself, "it was a long time coming. It took him longer than most, but sooner or later all of them—" He opened the door of the next car, addressed a colonel and a major by their titles, and never did anything about the Under Secretary's car, which pulled ahead and parked in the drive.

The Under Secretary was spoken to many times in his progress to the main dining room. One man said, "What's your hurry, Joe?" to which the Under Secretary smiled and nodded. He was called Mr. Secretary most

Reprinted from *Pipe Night* by John O'Hara by permission of the publishers, Duel, Sloan & Pearce, Inc. The story originally appeared in *The New Yorker.* Copyright, 1943, by John O'Hara.

often, in some cases easily, by the old Washington hands, but more frequently with that embarrassment which Americans feel in using titles. As he passed through the lobby, the Under Secretary himself addressed by their White House nicknames two gentlemen whom he had to acknowledge to be closer to The Boss. And, bustling all the while, he made his way to the dining room, which was already packed. At the entrance he stopped short and frowned. The man he was to meet, Charles Browning, was chatting, in French, very amiably with the maître d'hôtel. Browning and the Under Secretary had been at Harvard at the same time.

The Under Secretary went up to him. "Sorry if I'm a little late," he said, and held out his hand, at the same time looking at his pocket watch. "Not so very, though. How are you, Charles? Fred, you got my message?"

"Yes, sir," said the maître d'hôtel. "I put you at a nice table all the way back to the right." He meanwhile had wigwagged a captain, who stood by to lead the Under Secretary and his guest to Table 12. "Nice to have seen you again, Mr. Browning. Hope you come see us again while you are in Washington. Always a pleasure, sir."

"Always a pleasure, Fred," said Browning. He turned to the Under Secretary. "Well, shall we?"

"Yeah, let's sit down," said the Under Secretary.

The captain led the way, followed by the Under Secretary, walking slightly sideways. Browning, making one step to two of the Under Secretary's, brought up the rear. When they were seated, the Under Secretary took the menu out of the captain's hands. "Let's order right away so I don't have to look up and talk to those two son of a bitches. I guess you know which two I mean." Browning looked from right to left, as anyone does on just sitting down in a restaurant. He nodded and said, "Yes, I think I know. You mean the senators."

"That's right," said the Under Secretary. "I'm not gonna have a cocktail, but you can. . . . I'll have the lobster. Peas. Shoestring potatoes. . . . You want a cocktail?"

"I don't think so. I'll take whatever you're having."

"O.K., waiter?" said the Under Secretary.

"Yes, sir," said the captain, and went away.

"Well, Charles, I was pretty surprised to hear from you."

"Yes," Browning said, "I should imagine so, and by the way, I want to thank you for answering my letter so promptly. I know how rushed you fellows must be, and I thought, as I said in my letter, at your convenience."

"Mm. Well, frankly, there wasn't any use in putting you off. I mean till next week or two weeks from now or anything like that. I could just as easily see you today as a month from now. Maybe easier. I don't know where I'll be likely to be a month from now. In more ways than one. I may be taking the Clipper to London, and then of course I may be out on my can! Coming to New York and asking *you* for a job. I take it that's what you wanted to see me about."

"Yes, and with hat in hand."

"Oh, no. I can't see you waiting with hat in hand, not for anybody. Not even for The Boss."

Browning laughed.

"What are you laughing at?" asked the Under Secretary.

"Well, you know how I feel about him, so I'd say least of all The Boss."

"Well, you've got plenty of company in this goddam town. But why'd you come to me, then? Why didn't you go to one of your Union League or Junior League or whatever-the-hell-it-is pals? There, that big jerk over there with the blue suit and the striped tie, for instance?"

Browning looked over at the big jerk with the blue suit and striped tie, and at that moment their eyes met and the two men nodded.

"You *know* him?" said the Under Secretary.

"Sure, I know him, but that doesn't say I *approve* of him."

"Well, at least that's something. And I notice he knows you."

"I've been to his house. I think he's been to our house when my father was alive, and naturally I've seen him around New York all my life."

"Naturally. Naturally. Then why didn't you go to *him?*"

"That's easy. I wouldn't like to ask him for anything. I don't approve of the man, at least as a politician, so I couldn't go to him and ask him a favor."

"But, on the other hand, you're not one of our team, but yet you'd ask me a favor. I don't get it."

"Oh, yes you do, Joe. You didn't get where you are by not being able to understand a simple thing like that."

Reluctantly—and quite obviously it was reluctantly—the Under Secretary grinned. "All right. I was baiting you."

"I know you were, but I expected it. I have it coming to me. I've always been against you fellows. I wasn't even for you in 1932, and that's a hell of an admission, but it's the truth. But that's water under the bridge—or isn't it?" The waiter interrupted with the food, and they did not speak until he had gone away.

"You were asking me if it isn't water under the bridge. Why should it be?"

"The obvious reason," said Browning.

" 'My country, 'tis of thee'?"

"Exactly. Isn't that enough?"

"It isn't for your Racquet Club pal over there."

"You keep track of things like that?"

"Certainly," said the Under Secretary. "I know every goddam club in this country, beginning back about twenty-three years ago. I had ample time to study them all then, you recall, objectively, from the outside. By the way, I notice you wear a wristwatch. What happens to the little animal?"

Browning put his hand in his pocket and brought out a small bunch of keys. He held the chain so that the Under Secretary could see, suspended from it, a small golden pig. "I still carry it," he said.

"They tell me a lot of you fellows put them back in your pockets about five years ago, when one of the illustrious brethren closed his downtown office and moved up to Ossining."

"Oh, probably," Browning said, "but quite a few fellows, I believe, that hadn't been wearing them took to wearing them again out of simple loyalty. Listen, Joe, are we talking like grown men? Are you sore at the Pork? Do you think you'd have enjoyed being a member of it? If being sore at it was even partly responsible for getting you where you are, then I think you ought to be a little grateful to it. You'd show the bastards. O.K. You showed them. Us. If you hadn't been so sore at the Porcellian so-and-so's, you might have turned into just another lawyer."

"My wife gives me that sometimes."

"There, do you see?" Browning said. "Now then, how about the job?"

The Under Secretary smiled. "There's no getting away from it, you guys have got something. O.K., what are you interested in? Of course, I make no promises, and I don't even know if what you're interested in is something I can help you with."

"That's a chance I'll take. That's why I came to Washington, on just that chance, but it's my guess you can help me." Browning went on to tell the Under Secretary about the job he wanted. He told him why he thought he was qualified for it, and the Under Secretary nodded. Browning told him everything he knew about the job, and the Under Secretary continued to nod silently. By the end of Browning's recital the Under Secretary had become thoughtful. He told Browning that he thought there might be some little trouble with a certain character but that that character could be handled, because the real say-so, the green light, was controlled by a man who was a friend of the Under Secretary's, and the Under Secretary could almost say at this moment that the matter could be arranged.

At this, Browning grinned. "By God, Joe, we've got to have a drink on this. This is the best news since—" He summoned the waiter. The Under Secretary yielded and ordered a cordial. Browning ordered a Scotch. The drinks were brought. Browning said, "About the job. I'm not going to say another word but just keep my fingers crossed. But as to you, Joe, you're the best. I drink to you." The two men drank, the Under Secretary sipping at his, Browning taking half of his. Browning looked at the drink in his hand. "You know, I was a little afraid. That other stuff, the club stuff."

"Yes," said the Under Secretary.

"I don't know why fellows like you—you never would have made it in a thousand years, but"—then, without looking up, he knew everything had collapsed—"but I've said exactly the wrong thing, haven't I?"

"That's right, Browning," said the Under Secretary. "You've said exactly the wrong thing. I've got to be going." He stood up and turned and went out, all dignity.

MARQUIS W. CHILDS

The Education of Wendell Willkie

❧

IN THE whispering gallery that is Washington there was one preoccupation in the spring of 1940 that almost overshadowed the war in Europe. It was an election year and whether France fell or whether England fell Americans would observe their inalienable right to choose a president. The question was the third term. Only one man could answer that and those around the President said they honestly believed he did not know himself.

That an election should cut athwart the world crisis was one of the ironies of the inflexible American system. But there it was and it had to be got through with. The poisonous whisperers said that the administration intended to suspend the elections and perpetuate itself in power. That was part of the miasmal breath which all through this period seemed to have its origin in the Axis swamp.

The wonder was that when the turmoil of the '40 election had ended so little damage had been done. It was a proof, if any proof had been needed, of the vigorous functioning of the American political system even in a time of grave peril and uncertainty.

I had decided early, perhaps a year before the Democratic convention, that Roosevelt would run for re-election. The reasons, it seemed to me,

Permission the author. From *I Write from Washington* by Marquis W. Childs. Copyright, 1942, by Marquis W. Childs. Harper & Brothers.

were obvious. Ruling out personal desires and the exhilarating thought of the stature in history of the first third-term president, you could imagine what was in the minds of F.D.R. and those closest to him. They believed, as any reasonable man must have believed at that point, that collaboration with Great Britain was essential; not in the old isolationist, save-the-empire sense at all; but with the realization that we were faced with the most formidable foe in our entire history and that anything we could do to hold off that foe we must do. If the Republicans were to win, then isolationists, and isolationists in the narrowest sense of the word, would take over all the key positions in Congress.

No matter what the Republican President might believe with respect to the world crisis, he would have to cope with Hamilton Fish, for example, as chairman of the House Committee on Foreign Affairs; or should Fish decide to take instead the more powerful position of rules committee chairman, he would then have George Holden Tinkham on foreign affairs. In short, he would have two strikes on him before he got up to bat. You could call that a rationalization, but it happened to be the cold, hard fact. The Ham Fishes and the Tinkhams were aching to get into power. Incidentally it was at this time that Fish's office became a sort of congressional headquarters for the Nazi agent, George Sylvester Viereck.

Of course, there were also practical reasons why Roosevelt should run again. Politicians want to win elections. They are in politics to win. And there was apparently no other man in sight who could win. The third term was a risk, looking at it from the practical point of view of the bosses and politicos in the party, but it was not so great a risk as running one of the New Deal satellites.

It is just here, it seems to me, that the debate over the third term begins. If Roosevelt had not so completely dominated his own administration . . . If he had developed a man to succeed him . . . If he had been willing to step back . . . If . . . If . . . If . . . That is the way the argument will run, I believe.

There was no doubt that Roosevelt overshadowed the party just as he overshadows his time. But there were also men who might have been pushed forward if the President had been of a mind to push them. One of them was Robert H. Jackson, who had seemed to me five years before to have a high political potential. I had watched him present the government's tax case against Andrew Mellon, as difficult and involved a legal action as could well be imagined, involving the vast structure of the Mellon empire and how it was put together and then taken apart.

Jackson, at that time counsel for the Bureau of Internal Revenue, was to rise rapidly. Along with a keen mind, he had a warm, pleasant personality; a disarming frankness and honesty. There had been reports in 1938 that Roosevelt wanted Jackson to run for governor of New York. This was to be part of the buildup. Then, so the New Dealers said, Jim Farley stepped in the way. Farley had his own ambitions. He was loyal to Roosevelt, dog loyal, but that same loyalty did not extend to the men whom the President had gathered around him. They were not the kind of men whom Farley understood or trusted. They were intellectuals, idea men, before they were politicians.

After a brief period as assistant attorney general in charge of antitrust prosecutions, during which time he brought Thurman Arnold into the government, Jackson became solicitor general. The solicitor general represents the government in the Supreme Court. He is the government's law specialist, in contrast with the attorney general who is primarily an administrative officer at the head of the big business that is the Department of Justice. In this office Jackson shone with such a luster that lawyers' lawyers could not remember his equal. Even the crusty conservatives on the Supreme Court respected his technical skill, the breadth of his law, even while they sniffed contemptuously at the New Deal arguments he presented.

In 1939, Jackson was appointed attorney general. The political gossip had it that this was a move to make him more conspicuous and therefore more eligible for the nomination in '40. While that may have been the intent, the effect was directly the opposite. The outstanding qualities that Jackson had were somehow lost in the vast administrative tangle of the D. J. with its twenty-four thousand lawyers, wardens, turnkeys, clerks, secretaries. True, he inherited the confusion left behind by his predecessor in office, Frank Murphy. But in any event he never got around to making the remedial changes he had talked about for so long. And he was unhappy in his complicated new job. He could be ticked off as a possible candidate.

Harry Hopkins had sent up a boomlet, going so far as to establish a residence in his home state of Iowa, returning to Grinnell, the old home town, to be photographed in homely simplicity. The President, so Harry's friends said, had tapped him. Then there was Paul V. McNutt, he of the handsome visage and real, not make-believe, political past. You had to look hard to find any politics in the background of Jackson, Hopkins, or Henry Wallace, but McNutt had Indiana in his vest pocket. Unofficially McNutt launched his campaign when he flew back from the Philippines, where he was governor general, to give the Gargantuan cocktail party which he has never quite lived down. Thousands of guests, hogsheads of Martinis, tables groaning with those unhealthy little comestibles that are the sign of the mass cocktail party in Washington.

Jim Farley was the only candidate who without any stalling or fooling around told the world he wanted to run for President. He stuck to that all through the grim, grisly convention in Chicago. He was a candidate with a manager, a headquarters, two of everything. And only now and then did his smile crack a little at the edges. It was for "Big Jim" a heartbreaking ordeal. His was the simple logic of the professional politician. For all of his political life he had given Roosevelt complete and unswerving loyalty and now his friend owed him the same kind of loyalty. Instead his friend had decided to violate the rules and run for a third term. There were men around Farley who did him a distinct disservice by abetting his resentment and flattering his ambition.

Each morning in a room at the Stevens full of crystal chandeliers Farley received the press. Giving off wisecracks, as jaunty as ever, he knew nevertheless that while he still held the office of Democratic national chairman the real power was just across narrow Balboa Street in the Blackstone Hotel, where in a small bedroom opening off from a big living room done in sickly green and imperial purple Hopkins had a direct wire from the White House. Against overwhelming odds, Hopkins was trying to give a solemn, respectable look to a spectacle that could at best be counted a grim, inevitable choice in the face of a threatened world collapse.

The national schizophrenia was painfully evident in that convention. The New Dealers wanted to wind the whole thing up in two days or less and show the country that the Democratic party realized it was no time for bands and hoopla. But Farley was determined to go through with five days of conventioning and, if he could not have the nomination, at least he could dictate, as Democratic national chairman, the way the gathering should be run. And Mayor Kelly who was host had promised the hotels five days of business as part of the bargain that brought the Democrats to his city.

So for the better part of an uncomfortable week the motions were gone through with. The man who got all the dead cats and overripe tomatoes was Hopkins. I happened to be in his room when a delegation of indignant interventionists led by Herbert Agar came to call. They had heard that there was to be a compromise on the foreign affairs plank, an evasion of the issue of aid to Britain, and they railed at the slight, gray man who was the intermediary between the power a thousand miles away and the convention. Hopkins said little.

There was little that he could say. Once again it had been assumed that, in the face of a national election, the party would take on the neutral coloration that would make it possible for marchers of every shade of opinion to fall in.

Down the street at the Congress Hotel was a Wheeler-for-President headquarters. Three or four rooms were hung with photographs and posters. Pretty girls passed out Wheeler buttons. But the senator himself took all this with a certain cynicism. Publicly he insisted his name would go before the convention. When the time came for nominations, however, Montana was silent. Wheeler had stepped aside, unwilling for the sake of the record to go through with the form as Farley did.

Apparently he felt that the weak compromise plank on foreign affairs had been triumph enough. That plank contained empty rhetoric about not sending Americans boys to fight in foreign wars on foreign soil. Put in to appease Wheeler, Walsh, and the other isolationists in the party, this same obeisance to isolationist emotions was to recur throughout the campaign that followed.

On the night that Roosevelt was nominated a "demonstration" of sizable proportions was put on. In the hot, smoky atmosphere of the stadium, it had all the fine spontaneity of a parade ground formation. Mayor Kelly's director of sewers was discovered to have led the cheering from a master microphone concealed somewhere in the subterranean depths of the great hall. Banners emblazoned with huge photographs of Roosevelt were joggled up and down as sweaty demonstrators milled about in the viscous air.

It was not a pretty spectacle but undoubtedly it coincided with the desires of the great majority of delegates. Political commentators who wrote otherwise were merely indulging in wishful thinking. A large number of the delegates represented powerful state and city machines. These professionals were fairly certain of winning with Roosevelt. The President's choice of Wallace as a running mate did not please the pros. The boys from the Bronx had heard that he was an omphalos gazer who consulted the ghost of a Sioux Indian chief on difficult matters. But second place was merely a detail. They may have accepted the inevitable without enthusiasm, but the laborers in the Democratic vineyard went back home feeling fairly confident and relatively happy.

Chicago had been in painful contrast to the Republican get together at Philadelphia. A meteor had flashed across the political heavens in Philadelphia and the blaze of light had sent a quickening excitement across the country. Jealous Democrats said it had been rigged up, with Wall Street paying for the fireworks and directing their display. But no amount of carping could conceal the fact that an exciting new personality had jumped with both feet onto the national stage.

Willkie's reputation had been expanding for two or three years. The build-up had been carefully engineered, no doubt of that. When the moment arrived, however, the man himself burst through the trappings with the full force of his strong will. And if the convention was stage-managed to end in a close heat with victory for Willkie, as the Democrats were to whisper, Willkie himself gave no evidence of having heard about it.

During that week in Philadelphia he was sustained by coffee, cigarettes, and the tension that mounted as the hour of balloting drew near. I had not known Willkie before Philadelphia. Duke Shoop of the Kansas City *Star* took me over to his headquarters in the Benjamin Franklin Hotel and we pushed our way through the eager hangers-on to find in the inner sanctum a big, square-jawed man with rumpled hair who looked as though he had not slept for thirty-six hours—as he had not.

"I don't know," he said in the warm, husky voice that was so appealing when you heard it at first hand, "how this thing is going to turn out. I think I've got a good chance but I don't want to say any more than that at this time."

An incident occurred while we were with him that was prophetic of the struggles Willkie was to have with the determined amateurs who surrounded him. Over the protests of one of these amateurs several news photographers came into the room to make some special shots of Willkie, an arrangement that had been previously agreed to. The debate became shrill and acrimonious as we tried to talk on the other side of the room with the defender of the great man plainly losing his temper, something you must never do with news photographers as Willkie himself well knew. After two or three minutes he stepped over to end the dispute. "Now look, Joe," he said to his friend, "you're very tired. I want you to go down to your room and sleep for twelve hours. There's one thing we can't afford and that's to have anybody lose his temper." Sheepishly the valiant amateur retired and the news photographers went to work.

In spite of the efforts of his eager champions, or it may have been because of them, Willkie won the horse race at Philadelphia. Certainly that was one of his assets. He was as fresh as paint with no color of professionalism. Americans who spoke disparagingly of "politics" and "politicians" could now vote for a man who was as innocent as a babe of any political background.

In the thrill of Philadelphia you could almost forget momentarily the horrors across the Atlantic. The station wagon set had come down from New York for the big show. The town was gay with the right hats. There were good parties all over the place.

A convention of politicians is also a convention of newspaper men. The talk never ends, good talk, full of loud, ribald laughter. We saw each other at closer range than in Washington. Each convention time, I came to have a new respect for the judgment of Raymond P. Brandt of the *Post-Dispatch* Washington bureau for whom and with whom I worked. His is a judgment formed on twenty years of Washington and it is merciless and sure. Then there is that veteran of veterans, Henry Hyde of the Baltimore *Evening Sun,* who for nearly fifty years has been chasing political fires with the same miraculous enthusiasm. With him always is round, owlish-eyed H. L. Mencken, who collects conventions with the zeal of an anti-quarian. Someone always has a new story, a new rumor, a tender new canard. There are feverish and futile expeditions to smoke-filled rooms where great things are allegedly afoot. Sleep is forsworn. And when there is nothing else to do, the convention itself offers a mild entertainment.

Willkie appeared in person at the last session at Philadelphia. It was a good show. He had a dynamic youthful quality, a simple directness, that broke through the hackneyed pattern of the political convention. A high moment, indeed, it was perhaps *the* high moment of the entire Willkie campaign. The Democratic performance that followed in Chicago seemed by contrast even more stale and empty than it was.

The relentless surge of events across the Atlantic inevitably pushed politics aside. President Roosevelt called on Congress to pass the draft act. Even though it was an election year, this could not wait. Nor was there any inclination, except on the part of the die-hard minority, to make the draft a political issue. Willkie approved its passage as did most other responsible Republican leaders.

There were reasons other than political for opposing the draft act. A military critic of the rank of Hanson Baldwin of the New York *Times* pointed to the need for a highly trained mechanized force rather than for a mass army. He pointed out that the building of cantonments throughout the country would take men and materials that might be better used in immediately equipping a smaller force. It was a cogent argument, the force of which was not entirely obvious until the draftees were installed in the raw new camps with little or nothing to do and little or nothing to do it with.

The draft act was adopted on September 16, 1940. While it had been debated for a considerable time, not then or for many months later were its implications faced. We took this step by indirection. The word defense came to be the key word in our vocabulary. At the same time that the slow machinery of the draft was being put in motion and the training centers were being planned, the campaign orators had begun to talk about "foreign wars" and the American boys who must never be allowed to jeopardize their lives on foreign soil. We wanted to go on believing that virtuous, isolated America could have no part in the vile world's quarrel.

In a political year there were not alone military considerations in the steps the administration took to prepare for "defense." Part of the propaganda was that Roosevelt and the New Dealers wanted to take the country into a war of their own making. It would be a New Deal war and under the false threat of that war Roosevelt would perpetuate the New Deal in office for another four years; a powerful propaganda line, the weight of which was to be felt long after the election.

When little Harry Woodring was summoned to the White House and told that he must resign, his adversary, Assistant Secretary of War Louis Johnson, assumed he would succeed to the office. The President had told him that he would get it, if and when Woodring stepped down. But the President had other plans.

He had asked Henry L. Stimson to be secretary of war. Stimson at seventy-three was an eminently respectable Republican who had been the head and front of the group in America that opposed Axis aggression. His moral imperative was as clear and as certain as that of Cordell Hull. It had in fact been enunciated in 1931 when Stimson, as secretary of state, sought to persuade the British to stand up against the Japanese who were then on the first lap of their avowed world conquest. Stimson had taken a strong stand on the Japanese invasion of Manchukuo and it was a galling and humiliating experience to have the British let him down. Sir John Simon in the Foreign Office in London was making the same old moves on the same old chess board of power politics. Ever since that failure and humiliation Stimson had followed with growing anger and indignation the Axis successes. He was to come into the Roosevelt cabinet out of a sense of patriotic duty, aware perhaps of the political implications of his appointment but convinced too that in such a crisis political considerations were decidedly secondary.

To the vacant post of Secretary of the Navy the President named another eminently respectable Republican, Colonel Frank L. Knox, who had been the G.O.P. candidate for Vice-President four years before. There were reports that several other Republicans had first been offered this post. But Knox, if he knew this, harbored no minor resentments. He too was happy to accept. It would give him not only an opportunity to exercise his strenuous patriotism, modeled after that of his patron saint, Theodore Roosevelt, but it would also bring him into the larger sphere for which he had long felt himself suited. At sixty-six the good colonel was full of a jaunty optimism that soon took within its broad compass the Navy and all its symbols and accouterments. It was a job to his liking and he made the most of it. In a short time he had far more grizzled and sea going a mien than even the veteran admirals.

With that cunning sense of timing which he has displayed throughout his political career, the President announced Knox's appointment on the second day of the Republican convention in Philadelphia when tempers and temperatures were running high. The news was received in Philadelphia with loud and angry cries. Knox was guilty of treachery and he was roundly denounced by all the right-thinking in convention assembled. While this was going on, the doughty colonel far from the strife and sweat of Philadelphia was playing golf in New Hampshire. He enjoyed the joke almost as much as the President.

No matter what the Republicans might say about the inclusion of these decoys in the Cabinet, the fact was that they gave to the Roosevelt administration a different coloration. As Secretary of War, Stimson took some of the curse off the draft act. It was an unprecedented thing to do in peace time—to conscript the youth of the nation. With Stimson and Knox in office this seemed more nearly the act of a national, rather than a partisan, administration. This impression was of course carefully fostered as the election drew nearer.

In the summer, before the fury of the campaign had begun, the President took one of those bold steps which now and then he executes with such masterly skill. While there had been printed rumors in advance, the exchange of fifty destroyers for bases in the Atlantic burst with dramatic suddenness on the public. It was a transaction that satisfied almost every public desire. While England was given material aid in her struggle against desperate odds, this could not be accounted the principal motive for the transaction, since in exchange we were granted the right to construct a chain of bases on English soil from Newfoundland south to British Guiana. Even the die-hard Chicago *Tribune* could approve the destroyer deal, going so far as to claim credit for its origin. It strengthened our sense of defensive security at the same time that it eased our conscience in the light of the terrible news that came from blitzed Britain. Seldom has the President's creative imagination found a more happy outlet.

Against this background the campaign of 1940 began. Willkie had gone to Elwood, Indiana, and there his acceptance speech had been something of a diminution from the high pinnacle of enthusiasm of Philadelphia. The qualities that he was to display throughout the campaign were already obvious. He had a supreme self-confidence in his own powers. It was a self-confidence that transcended all advice, but especially he was suspicious of professional politicians. His was to be a new kind of campaign. The American people were tired of politics, tired of the old political speeches.

This went for small things as well as big. While he was still at Elwood, a friend from Washington had tried to persuade the candidate to take some lessons in voice placement. It would save his energy in the ordeal that was to come, the friend argued, and make it possible to speak oftener and with greater ease. Willkie would have none of this. It was sissy stuff, he said. The American people were tired of a smooth voice and a Groton-Harvard accent.

That was just before the start of the long swing to the West coast. In Chicago Willkie's voice grew rasping. Roaring like the bull of Bashan all through downstate Illinois the next day, his voice grew hoarser and hoarser. At Rock Island it was only a pathetic croak and panic seized his advisers as they feared that his throat had been so strained that he might be unable to speak for days to come. Without Willkie's knowledge telegrams were hastily dispatched to famous throat physicians in various parts of the country. The first to reach the ailing candidate was a noted specialist from Chicago. Considerable persuasion was required before Willkie would even see the man. He didn't need a doctor, he croaked. When the famous physician was finally admitted he was treated by the patient with scant courtesy. Departing indignantly, he muttered that what that man needed was not a doctor but a policeman.

From Hollywood another specialist had been summoned. Doctor Harold Gray Barnard of Beverly Hills, accustomed to treating the throats of radio and motion-picture stars, was better equipped to handle the temperamental Willkie. The energetic Doctor Barnard became a fixture on the train, fussing over Willkie like a mother hen charged with responsibility for a bold and astonishing duck. After he became reconciled to the idea of a doctor, a symbol of weakness and softness, as Willkie had first interpreted it, the candidate even welcomed the attentions of the throat specialist.

Willkie is an incorrigible talker. He would campaign all day, often speaking from street corner to street corner like an aldermanic candidate, yet at eleven-thirty or midnight he would go on talking so long as he had an audience of one in his private car. Little Doctor Barnard would stand unhappily at the edge of a knot of people while Willkie's hoarse voice rasped on. "My God, I can't make him stop," he would moan pitifully. "He goes right on night and day."

Willkie is a man of tremendous force of will. In a small way, this was demonstrated when, after a brief rest in Kansas City, he overcame what had been almost a paralysis of the muscles of his throat and went on to make on schedule one of the most important speeches of his campaign. He is also a man of tremendous partisanship. With Willkie there are no shadings of gray. You are either for him or against him and he simply cannot understand it, if, granted you are a fairly normal human being, you are not with him.

This is of course the mark of the amateur in politics. The professional takes his opposition with far more philosophy and understanding. Very early Willkie had begun to alienate the professional Republicans. They simply did not speak the same language. Joe Martin, Republican leader in the House and soundly grounded in the politics of his native New England, would come away from a conference with Willkie troubled and unhappy, divided in his loyalty between this new and startling apparition and the familiar politics of the past. Among Martin's flock in the House an antipathy toward Willkie grew up which was almost greater than their hatred of Roosevelt. In the Republican cloakroom they cursed that so-and-so whom they had been duped into accepting at Philadelphia. Such reactionary isolationists as Dewey Short, aptly described as the Ham Fish of the Ozarks, could hardly be restrained by Martin from expressing openly their resentment and bitterness.

Thus between the amateurs and zealots who guided the Willkie campaign and the professionals a widening gulf was created. On the train was a good-natured, tame professional, Representative Charlie Halleck of Indiana, but he was largely window dressing. Smiling Charlie sat in on the conferences with the publishers and the high-powered publicists who were constantly advising Willkie, but he readily confessed that his voice in the councils was a small one. That, incidentally, is one minor conclusion which seems fairly obvious on the basis of Willkie's experience. Publishers make poor political advisers. They were always hopping on and off the campaign train, ready to pour out torrents of advice. They were working as hard as they could for Willkie and he was naturally inclined to take their advice.

His intense partisanship was to lead him into paths that might well have proved destructive. There was the dickering that led up to John L. Lewis's support on which Willkie himself pinned so much hope. Out of his relationship with Lewis in the course of his venture in Mexican oil, William Rhodes Davis had developed a friendship with the massive leader of the miners. Now Davis came forward and let it be known that he would put up the money to pay for a nation-wide radio hookup in which Lewis would declare for Willkie.

Although no definite assurances had come from the labor leader, Davis seemed supremely confident that he could deliver his friend. Delilah was confident that her Samson, who in the days when he organized the CIO had been a very great Samson indeed, would appear at the barber shop at the proper time. In New York was a very off-the-record meeting at which the terms of the deal were discussed. This followed earlier negotiations carried on by a go-between concerning Willkie's labor speech in Pittsburgh. Davis, whose Nazi connections had by that time been widely advertised, agreed to pay for the broadcast, which would cost about fifty-five thousand dollars. The Hatch clean politics act was in force and to get around it the oil adventurer and his associates set up a kind of political black bourse, exchanging checks at a furious rate to insure that no one individual would be listed as giving more than five thousand dollars. Shrewd Republican lawyers scanned all these transactions, scrutinizing the checks with almost microscopic care to make sure that there was no technical violation of the law. Finally the money was siphoned through the Democrats-for-Willkie Club which was publicly listed as the sponsor of the Lewis broadcast.

The net effect of that broadcast appears to have been almost nil. Willkie's middle-class following was disturbed that the mahatma of labor should proclaim in such a Jovian voice his support of their man. But this was not sufficient to drive them out of the Willkie camp. On the other hand it is highly doubtful if any considerable number of labor votes were gained for the Republicans by Lewis's lurid performance. A small group personally loyal and others financially dependent on the big boy may have followed his lead but the number was small.

Willkie told me after it was all over that he had never heard of Davis before Sam Pryor, Republican National Committeeman for Connecticut, told him of the oil man's willingness to pay for the Lewis broadcast. It had simply appeared to him as a fortunate windfall. If it had been known to the Democrats at the time they might well have exploited the episode to Willkie's ruin. My feeling was that a candidate whose managers were about to accept so substantial a gift under such circumstances should have known more about the giver.

By that time Willkie was so passionately bent on winning that he did not want to ask any questions. In the same way, in the passionate heat of the moment he was led into saying things that later he would regret. Departing from his prepared manuscript again and again or ignoring it altogether, he would say to his audiences in the closing weeks—"You mothers, you fathers"—that Roosevelt if re-elected would have the boys on the transports on the way to a foreign war within three months. In the year that followed Willkie was to go a long way beyond this fiery partisanship. His education was to progress rapidly in the throes of a crisis which would brush aside all but the blindest or the meanest partisanship.

What struck me all through the campaign was that only a very little bit in the way of a positive, constructive program might have won for the Republicans. There were reports that Willkie was about to espouse the cause of the small business man; that he would take a strong stand for breaking up the big monopolies. This, so the report went, would have brought into his camp that volatile trust buster Thurman Arnold. I believe that such a move might have gone a long way toward turning the trick. People all over the country seemed to be waiting for something positive, something to hope for in the future.

Yet Willkie remained supremely confident that he could win by the very force of his personality. I remember a half a dozen of us had a session with him in his private car somewhere in Iowa on the way back from the West coast. Bob Sherrod of *Time* asked him, with respect to his pro-British foreign policy, what he would do once he were in the White House with such recalcitrants as Ham Fish and the incredible Tinkham. Willkie brushed this aside impatiently, saying that once he was elected, with the power of the presidency behind him, such details could easily be taken care of. And I am sure he believed that. We from Washington looked skeptical.

That campaign swing was a rare experience. In the first place there was a grand crowd on the train. Dick Wilson of the Des Moines *Register-Tribune*, Bill Lawrence, then with the United Press, Jim Wright of the Buffalo *Evening News*, Tom Stokes for Scripps-Howard, Doris Fleeson of the New York *Daily News*, Shoop of the Kansas City *Star*—you could not ask for a better crowd. Four or five of us would meet in Jim Wright's drawing room for dinner about nine or nine-thirty to review the events of the day with a running commentary that was scarcely flattering to the principals. Talk in the dining car, or in someone's compartment, lasted until four or five in the morning as we rolled across the vastness of America. I remember Henry Suydam of the Newark *Evening News* in a lyrical description of one of Ambassador Bullitt's fancier dinner parties in Moscow. It was at this same predawn session that a solemn editor from New York warned us that if Roosevelt were re-elected all land would be nationalized three months after his inauguration. Moreover, he believed it.

The drama of Willkie in action against the broad sweep of the American land was irresistible. Washington is at best an artificial city, divorced from the deeper realities of American life. It is like Hollywood in that all the inhabitants live on a single industry and that industry depends on the caprice of the public throughout the country. Washington is a state of mind and most newspaper men as well as most politicians welcome the chance to escape it occasionally. We were, of course, traveling at the end of a meteor at the speed of light, but nevertheless the strength of the land and the people was borne in on us. "Only the strong can be free," Willkie said again and again, "and only the productive can be strong." You could not help but feel the productive strength of America, real or latent, and the man on the back platform with the raucous voice and the free gestures seemed to symbolize that strength.

Willkie seemed to be speaking in a moment of pause between two worlds, a moment of deliberate hesitation between one world and another. He said at the end of his Western tour that he saw the light of a spiritual hunger in the thousands of faces turned up to him and this was no mere political figure of speech. The people were puzzled and uncertain. They listened earnestly, hopeful, to what this big man from the East had to say.

When I got back to Washington, I tried to put something of this in a piece for the paper, something of the beauty and strength and loneliness of the great country I had seen again; in the mood of autumn, the mood of pause before change; the warm September sun that never once failed to shine on the crowds. Willkie weather, said the Republicans.

In the stockyards of Chicago men sat on fence rails along the sorting pens, men in leather jackets. They gave no sign of what they thought of the speaker who roared at them. They listened but without any expression whatsoever. Here was Carl Sandburg's hog butcher to the world, the air full of an acrid stench, a faint haze of smoke. Men in bloody aprons standing on the sidewalk to see the procession go by, grinning good-naturedly, turning back into the great cavernous plants. Downstate Illinois was a blaze of sunlight, the last full glow of summer shining on the comfortable-looking towns, Joliet, Galesburg, Peoria. Missouri was like that, too, and Kansas, comfortable and contented looking in this pause.

At Tulsa there had been drama, the kind of drama Willkie rises to: a huge outdoor stadium, a full moon, a vast crowd, and Willkie grown eloquent, carried along on the tide of his own free-flowing oratory. Amarillo was the morning heat of Texas and little boys jeering. In the small hill towns of New Mexico the people had a lost and lonely look. They had come from miles around for this rare event, a presidential candidate in search of their scattered votes. It was hard to believe that this quick-talking stranger from the East could know what they needed and wanted. Washington, and New York, too, were very far away. Albuquerque was drama again: "Viva Villkie!" splitting the air, the largest political meeting in the history of the state, the chairman said with pride; the floodlights, the crowd yipping and whooping with good-natured abandon.

In the early morning the gray sky was low over the Albuquerque airport and everyone, even, amazingly enough, Willkie, was in a subdued mood. The airport is a plateau above the brown, smoothed-off mountains, above the town. The three planes were ready, the take-off perfectly timed, at ten-minute intervals, one, two, three. Phoenix was a brief pause in flight. A rush from the airport in a long file of cars. Willkie under the fierce Arizona sun was sweating like a truck horse. Around the speaker's platform built before the big bank of bleachers they had massed the products of the region—bales of cotton, mounds of grapefruit and oranges, sides of beef, jars of honey. Professionals on the train grumbled because Willkie was wasting his time in a state with only three electoral votes. But such an argument would not make a dent on Willkie. This was America and he wanted to campaign in every corner of it.

March Field came with a rush through bumpy air, down into the heat, gray and brown hangars and burnished silver planes in ranks along the edge of the smooth carpet we landed on. You can never remember what Southern California is like, the waxy green of the orange groves, the endless highways lined with filling stations and cheeseburger stands, women in slacks, old women, young women, children in sun suits. The people in California seem somehow almost as luxuriant as the vegetation, filled to bursting with a kind of energy and enthusiasm that the vistor cannot cope with. We paraded for miles through the environs of Los Angeles, a nerve-racking assignment with near crashes at every main intersection.

At Fresno in the San Joaquin Valley, John Steinbeck's valley, the air was dry and full of a powder of dust, the sky blue and immense. Willkie spoke in a park in the center of town. People who had followed the parade, mostly children let out of school, spilled into the green, shaded area and clustered around the bandstand. Here and there men were lying on the grass, itinerant workers in ragged overalls, lying in a state of such indifference or exhaustion that they gave no sign they knew the crowd was there or the voice was speaking, lying with closed eyes while the scurrying youngsters dodged around them.

It was as though they had been barred from the normal, prosperous American world that Willkie addressed. They had accepted, it seemed, a kind of exile. And was that true, less dramatically, elsewhere? Was it only the decently dressed, middle class that came out to the train or the auditorium? Is there a class in America in economic and political exile? These were some of the questions that came to mind seeing the lifeless men there on the dusty grass.

San Francisco is another California. Arriving at night, the hills terraced with light and the pungent smell of low tide in the air, you have a sense of exhilaration that no other town in the country can give. At the end of every street is a breath-taking vista, the bay, the bridges, an expanse of sky at the top of one of San Francisco's hills. This was real drama, inherent drama, and the San Franciscans seemed to walk with conscious pride, knowing the quality of their city and not too excited about a presidential candidate campaigning on their street corners. In the late afternoon sun, the hills that roll back from the Golden Gate were tawny colored, the red of the bridge a warm terra cotta. And the wind blows strong off seven thousand miles of ocean.

Seen from a car window, sleepily, Lake Crescent in Oregon was incredibly blue with the dark pine slopes going up from it. Although the railway passes so close, it has an untouched look. Over Portland there was a smoke haze from the fires that came at the end of a dry summer and the great mountains, Rainier and Hood, were obscured in the blue haze. The Northwest has grown accustomed to visits of Presidents and presidential candidates. Tacoma was indifferent, the workers in a millyard stony cold. At Seattle the crowd was warmer, cheering wildly in a packed stadium. Crowds and crowd reaction, it is evident, mean little. So much depends on whether the crowd is hand-picked, what time of day it is, what day of the week. A candidate touring a city on Saturday afternoon, for example, will draw twice the crowd he would get on Monday morning.

The way back East by the northern route had seemed endless. There is so much empty space. Small things are remembered. Standing on the station platform at Missoula, Montana, I watched a girl come toward me, her eyes looking straight into mine with a look that had something of candor, something of contempt. "You can go on wearing that if you want to," she said, her eyes on the official Willkie badge on my lapel, "but it isn't going to do you any good." She hadn't even paused, saying this in a measured, deliberate voice full of youthful confidence, and pride, too, perhaps.

North Dakota was one long horizon, the waving grass stretching from sky to sky. By a curious inverse ratio like one of those laws in high school physics, more politicians climb on the candidate's train in sparsely settled country than in populous regions. There are few jobs that pay as much as the jobs in politics. Along the railroad right of way the ring-necked pheasants flew up into the light as the train rushed by. The progenitors of these pheasants were brought from Mongolia to settle down in perfect ease in the Dakotas.

No one could miss the richness of Iowa. The fall-plowed earth was black and soft under a gentle haze. Iowa is a much-maligned state, not flat, not dull, but rolling and lovely. The sun sets in Iowa with a long, lingering beauty, seen across fields in which the corn shocks march row on irregular row. Willkie spoke at noon in Iowa Falls, a peaceful town with a green square. Mrs. Sabra Calkins, aged ninety-four, who has seen most Presidents since Buchanan, had been brought out to hear him.

After Chicago it was a wild dash against time. The long special train thundered down through the Mohawk Valley in the late afternoon, faster than the Century, faster than the Broadway. Then the change to a plane, with minutes counting. The lights of Schenectady below. They are waiting, a national network, millions of listeners. And Willkie made it, to the rising and falling scream of the motorcycle sirens, made it with two and a half minutes to spare.

When it was over, I tried to write something of what I felt about that swing around America. Newspapers are pretty formalized and the tendency always is to keep what you write within the formal pattern. Breaking over with impressions that were highly personal, I was apprehensive. But a wire of warm congratulation from my managing editor, Ben Reese, was my reward. He said he thought it was the best piece of writing in the *Post-Dispatch* in a long time and that was praise from Sir Hubert. Dour Fitzpatrick, whose Scottish skepticism goes into so many of his brilliant cartoons, wrote that I seemed to be taking a last lingering look at the corpse and I could see what he meant. I felt that the country was on the verge of a profound change. I think the people sensed it, too, that fall. Much in the America we had known was to go. A greater, richer, stronger America might come out out of the ordeal ahead of us. Or we might forfeit our birthright, the wonderful heritage of spirit, of earth, of people. But nothing would be quite the same again. The high wind of change was in the air.

The election was a hurdle to be got over. And when it was over, a thankful sigh went up from Washington and from the country. Not in a day, however, would the bitter words spoken in that contest be forgotten. The dark cloud of rhetoric would linger on, blurring and confusing the issues. President Roosevelt took his campaign statements more seriously than his interventionist backers believed he would. It was one reason why the Axis could strike in its own time.

In the interval between election and inauguration I went on a lecture tour that extended across western Canada to Victoria. My wife and I soon discovered that Canadians were assuming that the pattern would be the same as in 1916 and 1917. They seemed to feel that we would be actively in the war by April or May of 1941 at the latest. In turn I tried to be as realistic as possible. I said everywhere I spoke that I felt there would be no change of status before June 30 at the earliest. I pointed out that Wheeler of Montana had been elected by a larger majority than he had ever received before, several times larger than that given the President in Montana; that Walsh of Massachusetts and other isolationists who had been re-elected would come back doubly determined "to keep us out of war."

The President and his frail friend and adviser, Harry Hopkins, had gone away together for a cruise. On deck, under the warm sun of the Caribbean, they evolved the lease-lend concept. By sustaining Britain with planes, guns, and tanks, meanwhile guarding our own shores, we should not have to fight abroad. This theme the President sounded again and again in the weeks that followed. The British were fighting our battle and it was up to us to furnish them with the sinews of war. It was a clever line, a disarming line, but those who accepted it literally were scarcely prepared for the grim realities to come.

Willkie went to England. It was the most brilliant stroke he had made since Philadelphia, and without knowing anything about what led up to the decision, I guessed that he had broken away from the advisers who had pulled and hauled at him all through the campaign and had stepped out on his own. His journey captured the imagination of people on both sides of the Atlantic. And it was the perfect answer to the ugly whispering campaign that implied he had pro-Nazi sympathies. In the factories and in the pubs Willkie met the defenders of Britain, a meeting which neither will soon forget.

Straight off the return clipper, he came to Washington for such a carefully staged drama as the capital delights in. The marble and crystal caucus room in the Senate Office building was crowded as it had never been crowded before. Even veteran senators who waited until near the hour set for Willkie's appearance found it difficult or impossible to break through the crowd at every entrance. Wizened little Carter Glass of Virginia was literally pulled through by guards to whom he had appealed.

For Willkie it was the perfect entrance and he made the most of it. He seemed to radiate assurance and determination as a lane was made for him into the packed hearing chamber. And he read his prepared statement in a warm, confident voice. Britain could not have had a better advocate. There was only one embarrassment. That came when Bennett Clark and one or two other isolationists on the foreign affairs committee questioned Willkie about statements he had made during the campaign: that Roosevelt's re-election, for example, would mean sending American boys into foreign wars. For a moment the witness appeared discomfited. He ran his big hands through his rumpled hair.

"Why, senator," he said, "that was just a bit of campaign rhetoric and you know it as well as I do."

For a moment he looked a little shamefaced, like a small boy who has been made to confess to teacher. But this could not daunt his exuberant assurance for long. If nothing else, a strong sense of righteousness would have sustained him. He had learned a great deal in a short space of time.

A few nights later some of us who had been on the campaign train with him gave him a dinner. In the reunion was something of the excitement and the humor of that barn-storming tour. On such an occasion Willkie is at his best. His talk is frank and uninhibited, salted with his convictions and prejudices freely and bluntly expressed. He loves it, talking with men in a room through a long, convivial evening. His trip to England had made him more serious, more convinced of America's duty and responsibility.

"It's all right to talk about collaboration with Great Britain now," said Jay Hayden of the Detroit *News,* shrewdly drawing him out. "But don't you think that when this war is over the Republican party is going back to isolation? They always have and they always will."

Without a moment's hesitation Willkie came back with an answer for that one.

"Look," he said, his index finger raised in the familiar admonitory gesture, "if we go back, it will be so far back that neither you nor I nor anyone in this room can be a party to it. It will be way back. We can never let that happen."

Yes, he had learned. He had learned that the conservative party under a two-party system cannot afford the luxury of reaction. It must offer a positive policy as an alternative to the policies of the party in power. That was the lesson which the parties on the right in Germany never learned—and the result was Hitler. Thenceforward Willkie was to wrestle manfully with the Republican party, seeking to convert the more bigoted and stubborn elements in the great lump of the G.O.P. to enlightenment. Whether he will succeed is still a question. And on the answer depends not a little the future of Americans everywhere.

WENDELL L. WILLKIE

One World

IT WAS only a short time ago—less than a quarter of a century—that the allied nations gained an outstanding victory over the forces of conquest and aggression then led by imperial Germany.

Reprinted from *One World* by permission of Simon and Schuster, Inc. Copyright, 1943, by Wendell L. Willkie.

But the peace that should have followed that war failed primarily because no joint objectives upon which it could be based had been arrived at in the minds of the people, and therefore no world peace was possible. The League of Nations was created full-blown; and men and women, having developed no joint purpose, except to defeat a common enemy, fell into capricious arguments about its structural form. Likewise, it failed because it was primarily an Anglo-French-American solution, retaining the old colonial imperialisms under new and fancy terms. It took inadequate account of the pressing needs of the Far East, nor did it sufficiently seek solution of the economic problems of the world. Its attempts to solve the world's problems were primarily political. But political internationalism without economic internationalism is a house built upon sand. For no nation can reach its fullest development alone.

Our own history furnishes, I believe, another clue to our failure. One of our most obvious weaknesses, in the light of what is going on today, is the lack of any continuity in our foreign policy. Neither major party can claim to have pursued a stable or consistent program of international co-operation even during the relatively brief period of the last forty-five years. Each has had its season of world outlook—sometimes an imperialistic one—and each its season of strict isolationism, the Congressional leadership of the party out of power usually, according to accepted American political practice, opposing the program of the party in power, whatever it might be.

For years many in both parties have recognized that if peace, economic prosperity, and liberty itself were to continue in this world, the nations of the world must find a method of economic stabilization and co-operative effort.

These aspirations at the end of the First World War, under the presidency of Woodrow Wilson, produced a program of international co-operation intended to safeguard all nations against military aggression, to protect racial minorities, and to give the oncoming generation some confidence that it could go about its affairs without a return of the disrupting and blighting scourge of war. Whatever we may think about the details of that program, it was definite, affirmative action for world peace. We cannot state positively just how effective it might have proved had the United States extended to it support, influence, and active participation.

But we do know that we tried the opposite course and found it altogether futile. We entered into an era of strictest detachment from world affairs. Many of our public leaders, Democratic and Republican, went about the country proclaiming that we had been tricked into the last war, that our ideals had been betrayed, that never again should we allow ourselves to become entangled in world politics which would inevitably bring about another armed outbreak. We were blessed with natural barriers, they maintained, and need not concern ourselves with the complicated and unsavory affairs of an old world beyond our borders.

We shut ourselves away from world trade by excessive tariff barriers. We washed our hands of the continent of Europe and displayed no interest in its fate while Germany rearmed. We torpedoed the London Economic Conference when the European democracies, with France lagging in the rear, were just beginning to recover from the economic depression that had sapped their vitality, and when the instability of foreign exchange remained the principal obstacle to full revival. And in so doing, we sacrificed a magnificent opportunity for leadership in strengthening and rehabilitating the democratic nations, in fortifying them against assault by the forces of aggression which at that very moment were beginning to gather.

The responsibility for this does not attach solely to any political party. For neither major party stood consistently and conclusively before the American public as either the party of world outlook or the party of isolation. If we were to say that Republican leadership destroyed the League of Nations in 1920, we must add that it was Democratic leadership that broke up the London Economic Conference in 1933.

I was a believer in the League. Without, at this time, however, arguing either for or against the provisions of the League plans, I should like to point out the steps leading to its defeat here in the United States. For that fight furnishes a perfect example of the type of leadership we must avoid in this country if we are ever going to fulfill our responsibilities as a nation that believes in a free world, a just world, a world at peace.

President Wilson negotiated the peace proposals at Versailles, including the covenant of the League, without consultation with or the participation of the Republican leadership in the Senate. He monopolized the issue for the Democratic party and thereby strategically caused many Republicans—even international-minded Republicans—to take the opposite position. Upon his return the treaty and the covenant were submitted to the United States Senate for ratification. And there arose one of the most dramatic episodes in American history. I cannot here trace the details of that fight which resulted in rejection on the part of the United States of world leadership. It is important for us today, however, to remember the broad outlines of the picture.

First, as to the Senate group, the so-called "battalion of death," the "irreconcilables," or the "bitter-enders." Here was a group that had no party complexion. In its leadership the name of the Democratic orator,

James A. Reed, occupies as conspicuous a position as that of the Republican, Borah. At the other extreme was the uncompromising war President, Woodrow Wilson, who insisted on the treaty with every *i* dotted and every *t* crossed. Between them were the reservationists, of various complexions and opinions, and of both Republican and Democratic affiliation.

We do not know today, and perhaps we never shall know, whether the man who was then Republican leader of the Senate, Henry Cabot Lodge, whose name we now associate with the defeat of the League, truly wanted the League adopted with safeguarding reservations or whether he employed the reservations to kill the League. Even his close friends and members of his family have reported contrary opinions on the subject.

But we do know that when this question passed from the Senate to the two great political conventions of 1920, neither of them stood altogether for, or altogether against, the treaty as it had been brought home by the President. The Democratic Convention in its platform did not oppose reservations. The Republican platform adopted a compromise plank which was broad enough to accommodate the firm supporters of the League in the Republican ranks. The anti-League delegates found safe footing there too.

Both platforms were ambiguous; the parties had no consistent historical position about the co-operation of the United States with other nations. The confusion was doubled by the attitude of the Republican candidate, Warren Harding, an amiable, pleasant man of no firm convictions. There was no doubt that Cox's position on the Democratic ticket was a fairly definite support of the Wilson treaty, though his party platform left open the possibility of reservations and many of the Democratic leaders were strongly in opposition. But no one was certain whether Harding was merely pulling his punches against the League or whether he intended to support it upon election, in a modified form. All that was clear was that he felt he had to make some opposition to the League since it had been made a political issue by the Democrats. In private conversation, he gave each man the answer he wanted. It was not until after the election returns were in that Harding spoke frankly of the League as "now deceased."

The election, ironically, had turned primarily on different questions. The great cause of America's co-operation with the world was put to the test of an election dominated by local issues through the fault of both parties. The Democratic party and its leaders unwisely sought to monopolize the international position and the Republican party equally unwisely allowed itself to be pushed strategically in the opposite direction. The time is approaching when we must once more determine whether America will assume its proper position in world affairs, and we must not let that determination be again decided by mere party strategy.

I am satisfied that the American people never deliberately and intentionally turned their backs on a program for international co-operation. Possibly they would have preferred changes in the precise Versailles covenant, but not complete aloofness from the efforts of other nations. They were betrayed by leaders without convictions who were thinking in terms of group vote catching and partisan advantage.

If our withdrawal from world affairs after the last war was a contributing factor to the present war and to the economic instability of the past twenty years—and it seems plain that it was—a withdrawal from the problems and responsibilities of the world after this war would be sheer disaster. Even our relative geographical isolation no longer exists.

At the end of the last war, not a single plane had flown across the Atlantic. Today that ocean is a mere ribbon, with airplanes making regular scheduled flights. The Pacific is only a slightly wider ribbon in the ocean of the air, and Europe and Asia are at our very doorstep.

America must choose one of three courses after this war: narrow nationalism, which inevitably means the ultimate loss of our own liberty; international imperialism, which means the sacrifice of some other nation's liberty; or the creation of a world in which there shall be an equality of opportunity for every race and every nation. I am convinced the American people will choose, by overwhelming majority, the last of these courses. To make this choice effective, we must win not only the war, but also the peace, and we must start winning it now.

To win this peace three things seem to me necessary—first, we must plan now for peace on a world basis; second, the world must be free, politically and economically, for nations and for men, that peace may exist in it; third, America must play an active, constructive part in freeing it and keeping its peace.

When I say that peace must be planned on a world basis, I mean quite literally that it must embrace the earth. Continents and oceans are plainly only parts of a whole, seen, as I have seen them, from the air. England and America are parts; Russia and China, Egypt, Syria and Turkey, Iraq and Iran are also parts. And it is inescapable that there can be no peace for any part of the world unless the foundations of peace are made secure throughout all parts of the world.

This cannot be accomplished by mere declarations of our leaders, as in an Atlantic Charter. Its accomplishment depends primarily upon acceptance by the peoples of the world. For if the failure to reach international understanding after the last war taught us anything it taught us this:

even if war leaders apparently agree upon generalized principles and slogans while the war is being fought, when they come to the peace table they make their own interpretations of their previous declarations. So unless today, while the war is being fought, the people of the United States and of Great Britain, of Russia and of China, and of all the other United Nations, fundamentally agree on their purposes, fine and idealistic expressions of hope such as those of the Atlantic Charter will live merely to mock us as have Mr. Wilson's Fourteen Points. The Four Freedoms will not be accomplished by the declarations of those momentarily in power. They will become real only if the people of the world forge them into actuality.

When I say that in order to have peace this world must be free, I am only reporting that a great process has started which no man—certainly not Hitler—can stop. Men and women all over the world are on the march, physically, intellectually, and spiritually. After centuries of ignorant and dull compliance, hundreds of millions of people in eastern Europe and Asia have opened the books. Old fears no longer frighten them. They are no longer willing to be Eastern slaves for Western profits. They are beginning to know that men's welfare throughout the world is interdependent. They are resolved, as we must be, that there is no more place for imperialism within their own society than in the society of nations. The big house on the hill surrounded by mud huts has lost its awesome charm.

Our Western world and our presumed supremacy are now on trial. Our boasting and our big talk leave Asia cold. Men and women in Russia and China and in the Middle East are conscious now of their own potential strength. They are coming to know that many of the decisions about the future of the world lie in their hands. And they intend that these decisions shall leave the peoples of each nation free from foreign domination, free for economic, social, and spiritual growth.

Economic freedom is as important as political freedom. Not only must people have access to what other peoples produce, but their own products must in turn have some chance of reaching men all over the world. There will be no peace, there will be no real development, there will be no economic stability, unless we find the method by which we can begin to break down the unnecessary trade barriers hampering the flow of goods. Obviously the sudden and uncompromising abolition of tariffs after the war could only result in disaster. But obviously, also, one of the freedoms we are fighting for is freedom to trade. I know there are many men, particularly in America, where our standard of living exceeds the standard of living in the rest of the world, who are genuinely alarmed at such a prospect, who believe that any such process will only lessen our own standard of living. The reverse of this is true.

Many reasons may be assigned for the amazing economic development of the United States. The abundance of our national resources, the freedom of our political institutions, and the character of our population have all undoubtedly contributed. But in my judgment the greatest factor has been the fact that by the happenstance of good fortune there was created here in America the largest area in the world in which there were no barriers to the exchange of goods and ideas.

And I should like to point out to those who are fearful one inescapable fact. In view of the astronomical figures our national debt will assume by the end of this war, and in a world reduced in size by industrial and transportation developments, even our present standard of living in America cannot be maintained unless the exchange of goods flows more freely over the whole world. It is also inescapably true that to raise the standard of living of any man anywhere in the world is to raise the standard of living by some slight degree of every man everywhere in the world.

Finally, when I say that this world demands the full participation of a self-confident America, I am only passing on an invitation which the peoples of the East have given us. They would like the United States and the other United Nations to be partners with them in this grand adventure. They want us to join them in creating a new society of independent nations, free alike of the economic injustices of the West and the political malpractices of the East. But as partners in that great new combination they want us neither hesitant, incompetent, nor afraid. They want partners who will not hesitate to speak out for the correction of injustice anywhere in the world.

Our allies in the East know that we intend to pour out our resources in this war. But they expect us now—not after the war—to use the enormous power of our giving to promote liberty and justice. Other peoples, not yet fighting, are waiting no less eagerly for us to accept the most challenging opportunity of all history—the chance to help create a new society in which men and women the world around can live and grow invigorated by independence and freedom.

NORMAN CORWIN

Program to Be Opened in a Hundred Years

First produced January 13, 1943

ANNOUNCER (*slowly, quietly, importantly*). Ladies and gentlemen, what follows now is not to be heard today. This is a program for a date as yet unfixed; roughly, one hundred years hence.

Heavy transmission tone for three seconds.

Music: A twenty-first century motif, underscoring newness and strangeness. It resolves before:

NARRATOR (*impressively—this is a world-wide hookup—with a distinctness that is thoughtful rather than elocutionary*).

Greetings, citizens of the world, on this the hundredth anniversay of the great victory over Fascism.

We are earthcasting from the world city of Unison, U.S.A., western capital for the United Nations.

Greetings; and ready.

Ready.

SPEAKER (*quietly—a gentleman; all you want your great-grandson to be*).

Good zenith to you, in all zones, in all islands, in all continents.

One hundred years ago as this hour struck on the clocks of Greenwich, the fathers of our fathers won for us the century just now closed. They won it by the weight and the persuasion of steel and flame, and by the blood of their bodies, and by a violence never seen before that time; nor, thanks to them, since that time.

None is here today of the magnificent unknown, of the majestic masses of men and women who undertook that war. None can see for himself what uses we have made of the gifts they gave us. The young men who took Berlin and Tokyo are since returned to the earth, the anger gone out of them, the blood of the enemy rusted on their bayonets. The workers arise no more to the factory whistle; their hands are long ago unhinged. None who suffered the unutterable agonies is able to be with us.

The homeless are gone home.

Speech is little. Speech is a gust of wind on the face of deep waters. There are no words in our joined tongues fit to celebrate the memory of the common people of the decade 1940, now all dead. Therefore let us celebrate their name with spatial silence—silence, pole to pole, and around the girdle of the globe.

Let no man speak.

An interval of silence.

SPEAKER. Let China be the first to speak as she was first to fight in that war which was already ten years old by the Sunday of Pearl Harbor.

Fellow citizen of China!

CHINESE (*not a trace of accent; such nonsense was long ago forgotten*).

I crossed the Pacific Ocean from China to come here today in five hours. At the time of the siege of Tokyo it took as many days to cross, the voyage being sometimes even perilous.

The distances between continent and continent are shorter, but what should this mean if the distance between man and man were not likewise shorter? What should it avail that our new telescopes explore the valleys of the planet Mars if we were just as far as ever from the shores of brotherhood?

But happily we have made progress in several directions. It was not easy. Not even with the end of Fascism did our forefathers quit distinguishing between the yellow and the white races, the white and black. That was slower coming, but when it did come, world democracy came closer by a giant bound.

SPEAKER. Now from the Russias, from the Soviet Republics, first to stop the Germans.

Fellow citizen of Russia!

RUSSIAN. I came by the Wallace Intercontinental Highway, over the Bering Bridge between Siberia and Alaska, by road from Jeffersongrad on the Volga to Timoshenkoville on the Missouri. Once, before our countries were allied in war, there was no trade, no traffic, not even diplomatic courtesy between us. The only thing we shared was mutual distrust. Then came the barbarian with his week-end treacheries—one of a June Sunday, one of a December. Our first bond was the battle; afterward, we sat together in the peace, and worked together in the settlement. Now there is a highway linking us, there is honor and respect between us; industry is in our lands and agriculture in the desert and the tundra; the commonwealth of common people grows with each new season.

Like the Americans, we Russians are a people bred to peace, but gifted in the ways of war. Mild when unprovoked, but tough when need be—such is the secret of the happy state.

These hundred years have buried Fascism. Much has been done. The cure for cancer of the flesh was found hardly ten years ago, but cancer of the soul was cured the day it was decided every man has equal title to an equal share of opportunity; to useful work; to the governing of his own society; and to bread and peace.

SPEAKER. And now a friend descended of the people of our German enemy.

GERMAN. The sins of our Fascist fathers belong to them, and lie buried with them in their deep disgrace. We, the children of these tragic fathers, rejoice with you, the children of their conquerors, in what was their defeat and our victory.

SPEAKER. We celebrate today because there are no border guards at any point along the earth, and passports have disappeared from all the customs. And we are proud of this, and look with satisfaction on our accomplishment. But this is not recent. This is no twenty-first century invention. It is but a new use of an old American idea, remodeled and expanded for the modern world.

Almost three hundred years ago in the city named Philadelphia—Philadelphia being then as now the Greek word for Brotherly Love—a band of un-united states, facing a common enemy, united. They did not know it then, but they had made a working model of the future world. I speak now for that nation. In our few centuries we have had many enemies—enemies who spoke our language and who didn't speak our language. We, who were of the mingled people of all lands, fought in the mingled wars. We fought those who are this day at our side; co-holders of the earth; co-partners in its enterprise; co-keepers of the peace.

America is a fair land, but each land is fair where a city could be named for the same thing Philadelphia was named for—and be worthy of the name. All lands are fair where a man can enjoy the fruits of his labor, and speak freely, and know neither fear nor want. These are the matters for which the poor endured and the young gave up their years and the defenseless died among the ruins of their homes, and the great peoples poured out their blood. These are the matters. These are the works to be commemorated.

Let us continue to remember, and, remembering, continue.

*   *   *

From Mr. Corwin's notes to the play

This is a slight exercise on an idea which seems to me worth expanding. It is admittedly unfinished, but little can be done to round it out until the political evolution of the war affords a sounder basis for speculation.

The absence of a Briton from this program is of course conspicuous, but I would be glad to yield the floor to any prophet who, as of January, 1943, could (or at this writing nine months later, can) foresee the shape of The British Empire to come. The righting of wrongs in India and Palestine, the democratizing of colonial policy, the status of England herself with relation to Europe and America, are problems upon whose solution I chose not to inflict guesses. I have notions about what ought to be done, but in this piece I was proposing a hope and not a blueprint. . .

Missing from the actual broadcast were the allusion to the Wallace Highway (Vice-President Henry Wallace on November 8, 1942, proposed such an intercontinental artery) and the exchange of courtesies between two great allies in the naming of towns after each other's heroes. The sentence was deleted because of apprehensions (not my own) that it might be mistaken to imply the socializing of America or the Americanizing of Russia. Rather than invite accidental or deliberate misconstruction on somebody else's airtime, I allowed the cut. Nevertheless, I still believe the angle is valid, and I recommend it to whomever it concerns. . .

We became, under the stress of war, the most-informed and possibly the best-informed nation in the world. News, political commentary, and strategic analysis were spewed at us from every side, and our new national heroes, like John Marquand's war correspondent and John Bainbridge's commentators, were the men who manufactured the millions of words we daily consumed. It seems surprising, in retrospect, that journalists, readers, and listeners succeeded in retaining their sanity. Selden Menefee, examining America through the speculum of the public-opinion polls, found the nation united and determined; but Margaret Mead, looking ahead, was concerned to know whether the acknowledged toughness and resilience of the American character could be pressed into the service of more enduring ideals than those of military victory.

OGDEN NASH

Everybody Tells Me Everything

I FIND it very difficult to enthuse
Over the current news.
The daily paper is so harrowing that it is costly even at the modest price
of two cents;
It lands on your doorstep with a thud and you can't bear to look at it but
neither can you forbear, because it lies there with all the gruesome fascination of something that fell or jumped from the thirtieth floor and lit
on a picket fence.
And you think that perhaps a leisurely perusal of some unsensational
literary magazine will ease the stress,
And there you find an article presenting a foolproof plan for the defense
of some small nation which unfortunately happened to get swallowed
up by a nation not so small just as the article presenting the foolproof
plan for its defense slid off the press.
And you furtively eye your radio which crouches in the corner like a
hyena ready to spring,
And you know that what you want is Baby Snooks or Dr. I. Q. and you
know that what you will get is Elmer Davis or a European roundup or
Raymond Gram Swing.
Wherever you turn, whatever escapist stratagem you use,
All you get is news,
And just when you think that at least the outlook is so black that it can
grow no blacker, it worsens,
And that is why I do not like to get the news, because there has never
been an era when so many things were going so right for so many of
the wrong persons.

JOHN BAINBRIDGE

Business Behind the Lines: Major George Fielding Eliot

❊

SINCE MUNICH, Major George Fielding Eliot, the popular military expert who is sometimes advertised as America's outstanding authority on the war, has been heavily engaged on all the main journalistic fronts. Skillfully deploying himself, he has successfully assaulted most of the publishing strongholds in the New York area. Besides turning out a daily article of military comment, which appears in the *Herald Tribune* locally and in thirty-four other papers from coast to coast, he has stormed the book publishers with two vigorous volumes. He has engineered a turning movement toward the magazine field and directed a withering barrage along the entire front, running from the *New Republic* to the *Independent Woman*. With this hard campaign behind him, he has swept on to overrun the lecture platforms and the radio studios, delivering scores of lectures and analyzing the war from one to five times a week for the Columbia Broadcasting System. Such widespread use of his forces has led some observers to suggest that Major Eliot may be overextending his lines of communication. If the Major intends to top the literary output of the military wizards of the past, he still has, of course, some little distance to go. Caesar put out ten volumes of commentaries; Napoleon's correspondence and written works fill more than two dozen volumes; Karl von Clausewitz, the illustrious German military writer, who was perhaps the greatest theorist of them all, produced ten tomes, not counting two volumes of letters he dashed off to his wife; and Frederick the Great, when not too busy fighting the Seven Years' War and playing on his flute, knocked out twenty-four volumes of prose and six of verse. Still, all signs point to a record for Major Eliot. This war is young and the Major has just begun to write.

Major Eliot lives and sometimes works in a pleasant six-room apartment on upper Madison Avenue. The other members of the household are his wife, his secretary, and a colored maid named Janet. Only Janet wears

a uniform. The Major's attractive wife, whom he addresses as Toots, usually ambles around the house in cerise silk lounging pajamas. His secretary, a pretty young lady with red hair, ordinarily wears a more conventional ensemble. Most of the time Major Eliot dresses in the casual board-
ing-house style affected by Major Hoople. Mapping strategy at his desk
in the late afternoon, he is apt to be wearing a day's growth of whiskers,
a damp white shirt unbuttoned at the neck, rumpled black trousers, gray
silk socks unsupported by garters, and a pair of battered bedroom slippers. It is hard to imagine him in uniform. He is six feet tall and weighs
some two hundred and thirty pounds. He has stooped shoulders, a formidable nose, graceful hands, and sagging jowls. Although the Major is only
forty-eight and in good health, he normally looks as weary as if he had
just returned from duty on the Russian front. Actually, he has seen no
active service for about a quarter of a century, and there is slight prospect
of his putting down his pen for the sword. He has been in readiness
for the government to call upon him, but so far nothing has happened.
He accepts the situation philosophically. "On the whole," he says, "I think
I am doing something more useful." He is not the only one who thinks so.
For his service on the journalistic firing line, Major Eliot earns an income
said to be in the neighborhood of $40,000 a year, or about five times the
salary of General George C. Marshall, Chief of Staff of the United States
Army.

Major Eliot's income is, if anything, low for a man who is conceded
by his competitors to be the founder and leader of a new American industry. This is called the military-expert industry. Since Joshua reported
what happened at Jericho, men have written about war. There have been
recorders of wars past, prophesiers of wars to come, reporters who saw
wars happen, and historians who told how and why they happened.
But never before has a group of self-acknowledged experts, operating
thousands of miles from the battle fronts, set themselves up in the business of selling omniscient, day-by-day dope about a war to the general
public. It is a by-product of total war. The military-expert business is run
by a bunch of men who, in the years between the 1918 armistice and
Munich, comprised a kind of underprivileged national group. Born kibitzers, with what amounts to a tic of talking about war, the military
experts, then still amateurs, were about as popular as the fans at the ball-
park who insist on explaining, to anyone who will listen, the philosophy
of the bunt. The apathy with which the experts were regarded was not
the result of a public distaste for experts as a class. Americans love experts.
During the agitated twenties, Dr. Coué was acclaimed for his eleven-

word panacea, Freud was honored for discovering sex, and Wall Street diviners, like Evangeline Adams and Herbert Hoover, were sanctified for predicting, up to within a few hours of the crash, that our economic system would reach a plateau of permanent prosperity. Dr. Townsend was enshrined during the hard times of the thirties for promising fifty dollars on every maid's day out, Major Angus was feted for his exuberant economic notions, and Howard Scott was briefly glorified for thinking up Technocracy. However, through all these dark years of peace the military experts were as frustrated as Sir Basil Zaharoff. Lacking a major war, they had no raw material to work with and nothing to put on the market. A few of them wrote books in which they reprocessed some of the old wars, but the public was not much interested. Sitting on a high stool and wearing a green eyeshade, Major Eliot worked his way through many of these lean years as a Kansas City accountant. In 1929, another incipient military expert, who was later to turn up on the newspaper *PM* with the nom de plume of The General, was attending grammar school, wearing short pants.

Sitting in a classroom or on a bookkeeper's bench, a boy or man who was interested in war as a hobby needed considerable imagination to see himself hailed within a decade as a professional military wizard. The potential experts had plenty of imagination. They were boys and men of vision and of faith. They read about war, talked about war, and made up war games to be played on their living-room floors. Instinctively, they always figured that they had something to sell, but it took a total war to create a market. Major Eliot and his colleagues suddenly found that, with such a war imminent, theretofore bored people would not only tolerantly listen to talk about their hobby but would pay for the privilege. The military experts had arrived. They were ready to cash in. Faced with a war too vast for any one individual to understand, censorship limiting the news and propaganda coloring it, this period has become the worst of times for bewildered citizens and the best of times for military experts. They produce the answers, perhaps a little vague or inconclusive, but always comfortingly authoritative in tone, nicely packaged, ready-made, and quotable, and they can be relied upon to deliver their product regularly, like milk. The military-expert business is booming, and only peace can stop it.

Mainly because he got in on the ground floor and now sells his goods to more customers than any of his competitors, Major Eliot is the acknowledged grand old man of the military-expert industry. The business is largely in the hands of a group conveniently known in the field as the Big Five. In addition to the Major, there are Fletcher Pratt, military consultant to *Time* and author of a column of military comment which is syndicated to fifty newspapers here and abroad by the Overseas News Service and until recently appeared in the New York *Post;* Hanson W. Baldwin of the *Times;* Lowell Limpus of the *News;* and The General of *PM.* The eminence of these five can be judged by the fact that their combined output is distributed in this country and abroad to an audience of approximately one hundred million customers. Considering the market, the expert industry would seem to qualify as big business, but in other respects it bears more resemblance to a cottage industry. Like weavers before the Industrial Revolution, the experts are able to turn out their product in their homes, they employ simple tools, and they are loosely organized along the lines of the thirteenth-century craft guilds. Like the medieval guildsmen, who got together to protect their trade monopoly and one another, the experts have banded together, in an informal way, for their joint protection. An expert would apparently as soon blaspheme his mother as utter a single uncomplimentary syllable about a brother expert's product or craftsmanship. When Major Eliot, at dinner parties, speaks of Hanson Baldwin, for example, he refers to the *Times* expert as "the best military man in town, whom I love like a brother." Baldwin says nice things about the Major, whom he calls George. Fletcher Pratt has nothing but good to say of Eliot, whom he calls George, *and* of Baldwin, whom he calls Hans. Hans and George both agree that Pratt, known familiarly as Fletch, is also top rank, the customary term of approbation used by professional swivel-chair strategists. Limpus and The General are also unable to disguise their admiration for their colleagues.

It would be difficult to comprehend Major Eliot's preëminence among the guildsmen without glancing briefly at his benevolent competitors. Sartorially, his toughest competitor is Fletcher Pratt. A perky, bespectacled little man of forty-five with a bulging forehead and a wispy mustache, Pratt specializes in naval warfare and picturesque apparel. He favors droopy tweeds, noisy plaid shirts, and orange foulard neckties, and in cold weather he shrouds himself in an exotic fur coat that trails the floor. The coat, a rare possession, is made of genuine Australian wombat and cost $3,500. Sweeping around in his wombat, in an accurate impersonation of the late Paul McCullough, Pratt sets a dazzling sartorial pace for his fellow-experts. Pratt spent his childhood on an Indian reservation near Buffalo, where his father was employed as an overseer. He was born too late to see any Indian fighting, and during the First World War he was employed by the War Library Association, which collected books for men at the front. After the war he spent several years on the staffs of assorted small literary monthlies which failed, and then he began to write fiction. He became a military expert about ten years ago, shortly after selling a haunting story to a pulp magazine about an invasion of Madagascar by giant octopuses, which ate up half the inhabitants.

Pratt has developed into such a stern military critic that he looks down his nose at Julius Caesar. The greatest Roman of them all, Pratt points out in one of his books, "never became a great general," his strategy was "hackneyed and obvious," and his tactics were "infantile." With the same severity, Pratt analyzes the strategy and tactics of the present war from a bizarre apartment in the Chelsea section, where he lives with his wife, a cat, and a half-dozen caged monkeys—four noisy marmosets and two Humboldt's woollies. He composes at a desk near the monkeys' cages, and his writing is lively. His style, he said once in an interview, derives from the Icelandic sagas, Carlyle, Macaulay, and Winchell. He finds this unique blend handy in his work at *Time*, to which he gives advice on military matters and goes over manuscripts looking for technical errors. Unlike Major Eliot, who can always see a ray of sunshine in even the most thunderous Allied reverses, Pratt is almost invariably harshly pessimistic. Analyzing the recent battle of the Coral Sea, for example, he rushed into print with the shivering, syndicated observation that it looked "like a defeat, a bad one." His conclusion was based largely on the fact that our fleet was going in what seemed to him to be the wrong direction. By the next day Pratt, but not the fleet, had made a U turn. "This," he wrote, referring to the battle he had lost the day before, "is a victory." The day after that he disappeared from the columns of the *Post* and has not been heard from locally since. In contrast to Pratt's mercurial behavior, Major Eliot's reaction to the Coral Sea engagement was serene; from the beginning he appraised it as a victory, though "only the first round," in a cool, shrewd analysis implying that we could expect to see more fighting in the Pacific before the war was over.

Notwithstanding Major Eliot's glowing recommendation, Hanson Baldwin, the Major's fraternal competitor on the *Times*, works under a double handicap in the expert business. He is an Annapolis graduate and an experienced reporter. The only one of the Big Five to have graduated from either the United States Military or Naval Academy, Baldwin spent three years on active duty as ensign and a lieutenant (j.g.) after completing his course at Annapolis in 1924. He began his newspaper career on the Baltimore *Sun*, switching to the *Times* as a general reporter a couple of years later. Since 1937, he has had the title of military and naval correspondent. Now thirty-nine, tall, and lean, Baldwin looks as earnest as a clergyman and writes in a vein as grave and irreproachable as a funeral oration. In contrast to the negligée Eliot, he never gets down to work until he is dressed, shaved, brushed, pressed, and looking very sharp.

Perhaps Major Eliot's breeziest competition is furnished by Limpus, of the *Daily News* and the only guildsman whose military career has been directly influenced by General MacArthur. It happens that MacArthur was superintendent of West Point in 1922, when Limpus was expelled for flunking an examination. Born in Alpine, Indiana, forty-four years ago, the *News* expert's martial exploits have had a consistently abortive cast. He was a soldier in France during the World War, thus sharing with Major Eliot the distinction of being one of the two big-time military experts who have actually been in a war, and, though he failed to see any fighting, he attained the rank of regimental sergeant major. Even in the Reserves, which he joined in 1923, he did not exactly flourish. Shortly after being promoted to a captaincy, he flunked his physical examination and was transferred to the inactive list. Except when he dabbles in military affairs, Limpus seems to avoid his peculiar hex. He has been employed by the *News* as a reporter and feature writer since 1924 without any noticeable trouble. As a political writer before the current war, he had produced several books about civic figures as well as a history of the local Fire Department. These accomplishments, together with his oddly sensational military background, qualified him, in the opinion of the *News* management, as a military expert. Limpus differs from Major Eliot in being an exponent of the gee-whizz school of military analysis. He thinks of the war as a gigantic chess game, reports it as if it were a sporting event, and roots like a cheerleader for our fellows to win. In conversation he refers to big generals by their first names and carries around their autographed pictures.

The only competitor who outranks Major Eliot is the anonymous character known to *PM* readers as The General. There has been a rather high turnover in *PM* generals, but the one who is spoken of among the staff as *The* General is a downy-faced youth of twenty-six named Leonard Engel, who was the first to hold the command and only recently resigned. *PM*'s General (ret.) has been described as no bigger than the whiskey in a weak highball, but actually he stands something over five feet and weighs close to a hundred and thirty pounds. Unlike Limpus, one of whose grandfathers commanded a Northern volunteer company in the Civil War, or Pratt, both of whose grandfathers served in the Union Army, or Eliot, whose wife's father was a Confederate trooper, Engel boasts that he has nothing military whatever in his background. Engel, tense, dark, and loaded with exposés, became a military expert rather late in life, having first toyed with the ideas of careers as a geneticist, a chemist, or an anthropologist, and then taken a job as an aeronautical writer on *Time*. He left this job a few days before

PM began publication, when, he says, Marshall Field called him up and asked if he wanted to be a general. The newspaper, Engel learned, had engaged an elderly, retired major general of artillery to write its war column but had discovered that the old gentleman's copy sounded like something on the French and Indian War. Engel was commissioned to ghost for the retired officer, but was soon operating almost entirely on his own, turning out sensational scoops, such as the column which appeared a couple of days before the Nazis invaded Russia clearly proving such a move unthinkable. Wearying of the rigors of *PM* military life, Engel resigned his commission last fall. His post was filled by I. F. Stone, a member of *PM*'s Washington bureau, who soon got tired of playing general and requested a demotion. The war column is currently being prepared by a former press agent and reporter named Charles A. Michie. The old major general has watched the younger men come and go, sticking to his post and giving each new general his fatherly guidance. Although retired from active duty, Engel is still a practicing expert. He was called in recently by *Fortune* as a consultant on an article concerning the Russian Army, and he is rushing work on a comprehensive book about war for Random House. "They look forward to it as the most important book of the decade," Engel told one of his friends the other day. He was called up recently by his draft board. Because he has something known as congenital ocular nystagmus, the ex-General was rejected by the Army.

With men who know the experts best, it's the Major two to one. By most independent readers, Major Eliot is regarded as the stronger, the deeper, the naturally finer type of expert. No one else can deliver a military dictum with the Major's overwhelming force. This is because he is a master of military double-talk, a jargon peculiar to military experts and perhaps the biggest trick of their trade. The hallmark of a genuine expert is a specialized vocabulary, heavily weighted with military words and phrases that were once almost the exclusive property of chiefs of staff. As a result of their education by the experts, even laymen can now spruce up their conversation with such words as "deploy," "terrain," "matériel," "task force," "theatre of operations," and "pincers movement." Using this colorful language, the Major could make a collision between two rowboats on the lake in Central Park sound like the Battle of Jutland. "On the south face of the Smolensk salient," a typically informative dispatch reads, "the Russians appear to be counter-attacking in considerable strength. There is as yet no certainty that the Germans have crossed the Dnieper in force anywhere along the line from Smolensk to Orsha, Mogilev and Rogachev. . . . This shoulder of the salient appears to be holding fast; and it is always possible that if the Russians can make good the line of the

Dnieper on the front indicated, and can collect strong counter-attacking forces, they may be able to debouch from this river with telling effect against the flank and rear of the German troops in the vicinity of Vitebsk." Sometimes it is easier to decode. For instance:

We ought to give thought, not only to our concentration of offensive power against our objective in the main theater, but the security of our base, our lines of communication, our strategic flanks, and our interests in other parts of the world.

In the foregoing warning Major Eliot is clearly rendering into professional double-talk the Boy Scout motto, "Be Prepared."

Major Eliot's military comments may be impressive enough in print, but they are unforgettable on the air. To hear the Major talk for thirty seconds is to be convinced of his uncontestable vocal superiority over his competitors. He has a voice as sedative as a bored bullfrog's. In a hypnotic baritone he reports momentous events with the verve of a clerk broadcasting daily quotations on the Chicago livestock market. The Major always, whether orally or in print, makes it crystal-clear that opportunities are golden, experience is bitter, flies are in the ointment, and, regardless of how famine may gnaw at the vitals, nobody can have his cake and eat it too without winding up in a grave dilemma. His command of the well-established idiom is excelled only by his ability to sweep aside whatever is extraneous and penetrate to the very heart of any subject. On the Selective Service measure, when it was being debated in Congress, the Major sagely remarked:

The purpose of any draft bill is to make available sufficient man power for the defense of the nation.

On the repeal of the arms embargo in 1939:

We have taken a step which may be of material assistance to one set of belligerents and of proportionate material injury to the other.

On the submarine menace last winter:

The increasing rate of sinkings of merchant vessels in American coastal waters is a cause for the gravest concern.

On last spring's campaign in the Crimea:

The Russians have made initial gains, but whether they will be able to expand these into decisive accomplishments will depend largely on the forces available to each side which can be brought to bear in this theater.

On the second front:

There are risks to be taken if the war is to be won. Among those risks, we might well weigh the chances of an invasion of Norway—it would certainly bring us great and immediate advantages if it could be successfully accomplished.

Although Major Eliot usually prefers his prose ungarnished, like the meat and potatoes which comprise his favorite dish, he occasionally permits himself a sprinkling of literary parsley. Scolding the Russians during the Finnish war for putting up loudspeakers and harassing the enemy with propaganda, the Major let his words take wing:

Grim old Suvarov must be turning in his grave, and the shade of Nikolai Nikolaievitch blushing with shame. Not by such means did Russian armies storm the redoubts of Plevna or scale the icy slopes of the fortress of Erzerum.

A reader of Major Eliot's column is occasionally inclined to get the feeling that, though the Major is less terse than he might be, his words of embellishment are as soothing as a light massage. For example, the Major discusses a possible German attempt to invade England:

Initially, this will be a contest of air power plus sea power. Germany's conquests on the continent have been due to her admirable coördination of air and land power. In order to produce the same combination in England, it is necessary for Germany to get her land power to the island, across the water. Her sea power is very small, comparatively. It is on her air power that she must depend for the preparatory work, and for the major part of the escort duty. Her air power must break down British resistance at the point of landing or landings, and protect against British sea power the German land power while it is on the way across the intervening water, during which time it is helpless to protect itself.

Major Eliot's day, which begins around nine, when he rises, slips into his bathrobe and bedroom slippers, and shuffles off to breakfast, is roughly as exciting as that of any typical small manufacturer engaged in turning out war goods. Like most other entrepreneurs favorably affected by the war, the Major has recently expanded his plant. Until several weeks ago, he always prepared his product in a back room of his apartment, assisted only by his secretary. Now he is installed in spacious quarters on the fourteenth floor of the Herald Tribune Building on West Forty-first Street, and employs a staff of four. The office walls are lined with several hundred books, pamphlets, and magazines, the floor is carpeted in a rich blue which matches the heavy drapes, maps abound (including a pin-studded map of the world covering nearly an entire wall of the Major's private office), the furniture is highly polished, and everything, except the Major, looks very slick. He smokes cigarettes constantly, letting them burn down to a dangerously short stub and allowing the ash to drop off and flutter down over his clothes. In addition to his secretary, the office staff consists of a switchboard operator, a filing clerk, and an executive assistant. The latter, a former dancer and actress who assists in gathering material and planning articles, is an expert, in her own right, on ocean shipping.

Except on the occasions when Major Eliot spends the day working at home, he arrives at his office around eleven. After handling his mail, which ordinarily includes a couple of letters from inventors trying to enlist his interest in designs for unsinkable battleships or plans for setting afire the surface of the Rio Grande to forestall an invasion via Mexico, he turns to the military news of the day. His usually reliable sources include radio broadcasts, newspapers and popular magazines, Army and Navy service journals, press releases from a number of government departments, and a variety of dope sheets, like the Kiplinger and the Whitehall letters. The Major dictates everything, from his newspaper column to his books. He is reluctant to say just how long he spends preparing a daily column, but he has a reputation of being a very speedy worker. Whereas other radio commentators may spend five or six hours writing a script, Major Eliot has such a thorough grasp of his subject that he can work up his remarks in something like thirty minutes. As a rule, the Major spends six days a month in Washington. Apparently because of his position as a war industry leader, he never talks much, even when prodded, about his excursions to the capital, where he is often seen at off-the-record press conferences open to certain accredited journalists. He says he picks up much of his background information on these secret missions talking with the men on duty in the public-relations office of the War Department, but such a statement is probably the result of over-modesty.

Being the dean of military experts is a responsibility that weighs heavily on the Major. Like the other men in the industry, he believes it is his mission to contribute to molding what he calls "an informed and vigilant public opinion." Large-scale educational efforts of this kind are bound to take a long time and suffer a few reverses. Some Army men, perhaps because of professional jealousy, are inclined to make fun of the entire military-expert industry. They are fond of repeating a fanciful story about how Major Eliot once prepared an impressive article in which he explained that certain rapid Russian troop movements during the Finnish war had been made possible by a railroad which, it turned out later, didn't exist. Humorists in the War Department named the mythical line in honor of its intrepid builder. It has become accepted military procedure to explain perplexing troop movements with the brief comment: "Moved via Major Eliot Railway."

With the exception of Major Bowes, probably no major in the country has been more roundly honored than Major George Fielding Eliot, the military expert. Although he has never, like his colleague on the air, received from his admirers a two-pound clear Havana cigar, a cast-iron razor, or the skin of a wildcat, Major Eliot has been showered with the approval of some five million men, women, and children who follow his daily column in the *Herald Tribune* and thirty-four other newspapers. While his curiously penetrating voice has never moved the Sioux to confer upon him, as they did upon Major Bowes, the name Chellmig-whasket, or Chief of the Air, Major Eliot's millions of radio fans have adopted him as their favorite military expert. Though his lecture tours have been less extensive than the tours of the Major Bowes units, his following among members of women's clubs and businessmen's associations is impressive. He has also made personal appearances at the Military Academy at West Point and, being an amphibious man, at the Naval War College in Newport. His appearance at West Point did not necessarily constitute an endorsement of his product by the War Department, since other folk who have been booked at the Academy include such military figures as Miss Elissa Landi and Mr. Alexander Woollcott. For a former accountant, Major Eliot has nevertheless come a long way. His career is not only an inspiration to all restless C.P.A.'s but also a model for any resourceful young man who wants to train himself for a position in America's new and booming military-expert industry.

Becoming the dean of military experts was not easy for Eliot. He was an only child; his mother died when he was three and his father, a Brooklyn insurance broker specializing in marine policies, didn't raise his boy to be a soldier. In 1902, when George was eight, his father, who had married again, went to Australia on a business trip. Although he intended to stay only a few months, he took along his wife and George and, once there, discovered such attractive business possibilities that he decided to remain. The family settled in St. Kilda, a suburb of Melbourne, and there George attended grammar school. His father was determined that George should grow up to be a businessman, and tutored him relentlessly in arithmetic. This gave George a distaste for figures but came in handy later on when he went into bookkeeping work. After George had been in a Melbourne grammar school for four years, his father noticed that the boy was beginning to talk with an Australian accent. Evidently preferring a Jersey accent, the elder Eliot shipped George back to the States to attend Montclair Academy. When, two years later, the young man returned to Australia, he enrolled at the University of Melbourne, where, despite his father's objections, he became a member of the University of Melbourne Rifles, a cadet corps, something like the R.O.T.C. in this country. The Major-to-be took well to military life and during his senior year held the post of regimental commander, the top rank for a college cadet.

Flirting with the notion of a military career after college, George was constantly opposed by his father, who, in those days before military-experting had become a paying propostion, urged the lad to be sensible and get into a remunerative line, such as insurance or accounting. To give his son a proper start, the elder Eliot found him a job as a clerk in the auditor's office of the Victorian Government Railways. As soon as war was declared in 1914, however, George quit working for the railroad and, without telling his father, joined up. Because of his cadet training, he was inducted into the Australian Imperial Force as a second lieutenant. He was made a first lieutenant after a few weeks, promoted to the rank of temporary captain about a year later, and during the last three months of the war held the grade of acting major. He was mustered out in 1918, after having seen action in the Dardanelles campaign and on the Western Front. He was twice wounded, once when the palm of his left hand was pierced by a bayonet and once when he was struck on the head by the butt of a German rifle. Both wounds left small scars.

When the armistice was signed, Eliot, taking advantage of a regulation allowing an extended leave to soldiers who had served for four years, was on a troopship bound for Australia. His father had died while he was away and his stepmother died soon after his return. Undecided about a career, he worked for the railroad again for a short while and then, after settling his father's estate, moved to Canada. He arrived in Vancouver in the fall of 1919. Practically everyone he met in Canada told him conditions in the States were very bad, so he knocked around the Dominion for a couple of years, working most of the time as an ambulant bookkeeper. One day in a bar he met a travelling salesman from Kansas City, who said that things in K.C. were looking up, so he made for K.C., where he got a job working for an accounting firm. His first assignment was to audit the books of the shirt factory in the Missouri State Penitentiary, and after that he took on a number of more prosaic jobs. Although he considered himself qualified to be a bookkeeper, he knew little about accounting practice. "I kept my mouth shut and watched what the others did," Eliot says, "and I came out all right." By boning up on his trade at night in textbooks, he managed to keep himself steadily employed. He wasn't happy in his work but he stuck at it for the next six years.

During this dreary period in Kansas City, Eliot, who had as yet no intimation of his eventual calling, nevertheless laid the groundwork for the strategy by which he was to pull himself out of an accounting foxhole and become, as subsequently advertised in *Look,* an "outstanding American military authority." Joining the Officers' Reserve Corps as a lieutenant, he was quickly promoted to a captaincy in Intelligence. The Captain, however, aspired to be the very model of a modern major, so he began to attend evening lecture courses given by Regular Army officers and do a fair amount of military homework in the hope of getting a promotion. A dispirited accountant by day and an enthusiastic soldier by night, Eliot made a distinguished record at night school. He also worked hard on correspondence courses provided by the War Department. Taking such subjects as first aid, military hygiene, and map reading, Major Eliot completed the necessary number of courses with passing grades. To supplement his studies, he spent a couple of weeks at an Army camp each summer.

After three years of this stringent regimen, Captain Eliot was ready to be commissioned a major. In order to do this he had to pass an oral examination given by the late Colonel E. L. Butts, noted as the originator of Butts' Manual, which is a system of physical exercises performed with a rifle. In a room in the Kansas City post office, Colonel Butts listened while Captain Eliot figured out and expounded the solution of an intricate hypothetical military problem. The examination took about three hours. Shortly afterward Major George Fielding Eliot came into being. Although the Major resigned from the Reserves in 1930, he has never yielded to the temptation to drop his title. Some peevish Army folk complain that this is overdoing the matter of loyalty to the service.

Major Eliot's literary career, like his commission, had its genesis in Kansas City. Walking home from his accounting chores one day in 1926, he picked up a copy of a new pulp magazine called *War Stories*. He was at once struck with the idea that he, too, could write war stories. He knocked out a short story titled "On the Outpost Line," based on a friend's experience in the World War, and sent it along. It was accepted and he received a check for $100 and a request for more of the same. The Major was glad to oblige and presently was contributing to many other magazines, such as *Battle Birds, Thrilling Adventure,* and the *Lone Eagle.* The moment his income from writing warranted the move, he dropped his accounting. Like other successful writers of the period, the Major soon migrated to New York and Greenwich Village. He wasn't happy there. He was vexed by his carefree neighbors, who dropped in occasionally and interrupted his creative work. "They thought you were a writer and had no respect for your time," he says, still annoyed when he thinks about it. He moved from Fourth Street to Twelfth Street to Commerce Street to Darien, Connecticut. There, at last, he was unmolested. He later moved to upper Madison

Avenue, where he now lives and has the advantage of operating on interior lines, such as the Fifth Avenue Coach and the Madison Avenue Bus.

In his pulp writing, Major Eliot appears to have been more heavily influenced by Edgar Rice Burroughs than by Karl von Clausewitz, the great German military writer. His short stories, written fast and loose, were considered first-rate by both the editors and the readers of pulps. Their heroes, such as Sergeant Jack Martin, "late of Massachusetts, despite his Australian uniform," who loped across the Desert of Sinai on the trail of a ruthless spy, were frequently Americans who had migrated to Australia in their youth. A story called "Tribes of Terror" is representative of the Major's military writing of this period. The editor's blurb, printed beneath the title, reads, "The Job Was Too Much for an Army—but Bill Brand Dared It Alone! Smashing Adventure in Abyssinia!," and the story begins:

> Bill Brand leaned across his polished desk until his grim, bronzed face was within a foot of the florid countenance of Colonel Ponsonby-Thorpe, C.M.G., D.S.O., Commandant of the Somaliland Camel Corps.
>
> "You know what I think?" he snarled. "I think you're a lot of lousy four-flushers! You're leaving a better man'n any of you'll ever be, to be murdered by a pack of stinking fuzzie-wuzzies—because he's got a contract that you'll fall heir to if he croaks. That's what I think," he added, straightening up and running a hard eye round the semi-circle of officers grouped behind the chief.

Colonel Ponsonby-Thorpe, C.M.G., D.S.O., as the story unfolds, refuses to lend Bill Brand a camel, so Brand walks across the desert, meeting with many thrilling adventures, such as being captured by desert tribesmen, hurled into a pit filled with death-dealing cobras, digging his way out of a dungeon, and escaping from an erupting volcano. After running this impressive obstacle race, Bill Brand is complimented by a friendly native, who observes, *"Franghi,* it is in my mind that you are a man of parts."

Aside from turning out sagas about men of parts at a couple of cents a word, Major Eliot's only professional military writing during this stage of his career consisted of three or four contributions to the unofficial Army and Navy service journals. For *The Infantry Journal,* he prepared an article about the French Foreign Legion. His point was that the Legion wasn't as bad as the movies depicted it. Although these articles paid very little, the Major was indirectly rewarded by the fact that he met his future wife through one of them. Disagreeing with the review in the *U. S. Naval Institute Proceedings* of a book about the Dardanelles campaign, the Major wrote a short rebuttal in the same periodical. The author of the book, commanding officer of a battleship based at Norfolk, was so pleased that he invited the Major to drop down for a visit. The Major accepted, and aboard the S.S. Robert E. Lee going to Norfolk, he met a former schoolteacher, Miss Sara Elaine Hodges. Four months later they were married in a simple ceremony quite without military pomp and circumstance.

After a honeymoon in Florida, where the Major whipped out a serial story for *Liberty*, which had as its background a war between Japan and the United States, he and his bride returned to New York. To judge from his writings at that time, he was no less concerned about the international military scene than he is now. In April, 1936, several weeks before the outbreak of the Spanish Civil War, Major Eliot was merely looking in the wrong direction, his attention then being focussed on Russia. His name appeared that month over a story in *Thrilling Adventure*, which was headed by the blurb, "Pete Kendall, American Engineer, Meets Breath-Taking Perils as He Comes to Grips with the Masked Commissar!" A year later there is evidence of a temporary change in the Major's interest. He took up G-men. Although he knew little about crime and punishment beyond whatever he had picked up from the ledgers of the shirt factory in the Missouri State Penitentiary, Major Eliot had acquired a few source books on criminology and was turning out book-length pulp stories under the pseudonym of C. K. M. Scanlon. A month before the incident at the Marco Polo Bridge, which marked the beginning of the Sino-Japanese War, C. K. M. Scanlon wrote a short story which carried the blurb, "The Federal Bureau of Investigation Matches Guns and Wits Against a Nationwide Criminal Combine of Hijackers Who Defy the Law! Follow Dan Fowler on an Exciting Trail of Big-Time Crime!"

The fortunes of war and of military experting are such that it took a couple of peaceful editors to get Major Eliot on the trail of a big-time career. With a friend named Colonel R. Ernest Dupuy, who had been his collaborator on some pulp stories, the Major approached a book publisher in 1937 with an idea for a military novel. "To hell with the novel," the editor said. "Write me a factual book about what the next war's going to be like." Six months later the joint predictions of the prophets were published in a book titled "If War Comes." Although many of their prognostications turned out to be on the dreamy side, the Major is unabashed. "We're only mortals," he says modestly. The book had a small sale. "Nobody wanted to read about war then," the Major reflects today.

One man who wanted to read about war so much that he had studied Eliot's and Dupuy's book was the editor of the *New Republic*, Bruce Bliven, who was preparing a supplement on American Defense for his journal. He invited Eliot—Dupuy was living in Washington and thus less accessible—to contribute an article on the technical aspects of the problem. These aspects were blocked out one day in February, 1938, when Bliven and Eliot went to lunch at the New Weston Hotel and sat around the dining room until five o'clock, deciding what kind of army, navy, and air forces this country ought to have. During the next few months Major Eliot turned out about a dozen *New Republic* pieces. He impressed the editor not only with his copy but with his writing speed. When Bliven called the Major one Wednesday morning to inquire about an article promised for the following day, the Major was reassuring. "I've just got to write a short novel before I get to your piece," he said. "I'll be through with that by midnight, and then I'll get to you." The Major delivered the goods.

Eliot soon had offers from other editors who had seen his *New Republic* articles. Completely emancipated from the pulps by the middle of 1938, he was turning out articles for magazines like *Current History, The American Mercury,* and *Harper's.* Instead of detailing the whiz-bang exploits of Special Agent Dan Fowler, Pete Kendall, and Sergeant Jack Martin, the Major became concerned with the adventures of Neville Chamberlain, Edouard Daladier, and Adolf Hitler. Meanwhile, he had written "The Ramparts We Watch," a book which developed the comforting thesis that the defense of America could be accomplished without either a tremendous expansion of our armed forces or industrial mobilization. The book sold 10,600 copies. "Then," the Major recalls today, "the dam broke." Spilling into his commodious lap came offers for more books, articles, and lecture engagements. After knocking out a book on air power, he hurried off to Europe in the summer of 1939 to get material for still another book. He intended in this, he says, "to cover the European military situation from soup to nuts."

Major Eliot made a dash through England, France, Poland, the Balkans, and the Middle East, talking with military and naval men. Before leaving England, he made a transatlantic broadcast for the Columbia Broadcasting System, and an agent representing him in New York started negotiations with Columbia to put him on as a regular commentator. Late in August, as Eliot was having lunch with a British admiral in Cairo, he received a cable from C.B.S. advising him that he would be taken on as its military analyst. Seeing that history was moving too fast for him, he decided to drop his book and rushed back to England. On the second of September, the day after the Germans began their blitz against Poland, the Major stepped to a microphone in London and confidently predicted:

It is my opinion that the Army of Poland is going to give a first-rate account of itself in the struggle which has been thrust upon it. . . . The Polish Army will not be easily destroyed nor quickly overwhelmed. . . . The Germans will not have an easy time of it moving large numbers of troops very far inside the Polish frontiers.

A prophet not without honor in his own country, Major Eliot returned home to receive a stirring welcome from his lecture and literary agents and to be deluged with offers. "I felt," the Major now says, "that I had arrived."

Since that momentous day Major Eliot has developed into this country's leading military expert. As a rule, in his experting, he tries to avoid prophecy. "It doesn't do much good," he says flatly. Although he frequently declares that it is impossible to be a military genius without taking risks, he prefers a more conservative system for himself. His method, while not like betting on every horse in a race, is something like betting across the board on five out of seven entries. In order to avoid any semblance of rashness, he gracefully takes one step backward for every step forward. He seldom trips. Considering the need for Allied reinforcements during the Norwegian campaign, the Major wrote:

Before this arrival of German reinforcements takes place, the British may begin to arrive. Or they may not.

Speaking of the Germans' use of field artillery in Russia:

There is, however, nothing to support the further supposition that artillery has been used offensively against Russian tanks; it may or may not have been.

Analyzing the Turkish-Bulgarian nonaggression pact, he said:

This may be just such another double-cross, engineered, if not participated in, by Hitler and Stalin, or it may not.

The Major, in addition to doing wonders with the "or it may not" theme, can play countless variations on the theme of "I will let you know later." For example:

It seems likely that a change of some sort in the Mediterranean naval picture is about to take place, but as usual it is difficult to ascertain very far in advance what its nature is going to be.

Or:

As to Moscow, we should be able to form a more accurate judgment very soon.

Despite these and other precautionary devices, the Eliot system sometimes breaks down. When the Admiral Graf Spee, after being attacked by three British cruisers, arrived in Montevideo, Major Eliot promptly explained what might happen. The Spee, he said, might make a break for the open sea, alone. ("Her losses of personnel are not crippling.") On the other hand, she might make a break, but with assistance. ("It is not beyond the realm of possibility" that two other German pocket battleships are rushing to rescue the trapped ship.) "Of course," the Major added, "the Spee may not go out at all." Still, she might come out—fighting. ("On balance, one may guess that she will come out. . . . The German high command may think it best to sacrifice the Spee in the hope that she will do so much damage before she goes down as to justify their order.") All this covered a commendable variety of possibilities, though, as it turned out, not the right one.

Naturally, neither Major Eliot nor anyone else can be expected to deliver infallible military judgments. As the Major himself often profoundly says, "Nothing is certain about war except its uncertainty." It may, therefore, be instructive to measure a few of the Major's expert judgments against those of an ordinary, inexpert citizen. Such a person was discovered recently by the Inquiring Fotographer of the *Daily News,* who asked a number of men he met on the street whether the war predictions they had made as armchair generals had come true. One man, a barber from the Bronx, replied sadly:

I was wrong. I didn't think the Germans were so strong and the Russians fooled me, too. I thought we could hold the Philippines and I was sure that Singapore would hold. I'm so wrong that I won't predict the future any more.

Like the barber from the Bronx, Major Eliot, whose trade requires him on occasion to make predictions, didn't think the Germans were so strong, either. Writing in *This Week,* the *Herald Tribune's* Sunday supplement, in June, 1938, he observed:

What is plain from an examination of these various facts and figures is that Germany is by no means ready for war and that the combined power of the Franco-British alliance is comfortably superior to that of the Rome-Berlin Axis. . . .

In *The American Mercury* about three months before the war began:

Today one may confidently state that the German Army could not fight the French, single-handed, with any hope of genuine success.

Developing this view the same month in *Current History,* the Major noted:

As a matter of cold fact, the Germans are far less ready for war than they were in 1914, they lack the resources for a struggle of any duration, their Italian ally is the weakest and most vulnerable in Europe, their economic and financial situation is uncertain (to say the least) and their armed forces are suffering the pains of rebirth begun only four years ago.

Speaking in St. Louis three months after the war had started, Major Eliot was saying:

This is one time when we're strong enough to stay out of war. It's nonsense to worry about our getting in.

Six days before the Germans marched into the Soviet Union in June, 1941, the Major's column appeared in the *Herald Tribune* under the heading "Major Eliot Doubts Nazis Will Wage War on Russia Now." Subsequently, like almost everyone else in the world except a few unreasonable Russians, Major Eliot found it difficult to believe that the Russians would put up much of a fight. A week after the invasion he noted that "the balance in favor of an early German success seems such that the Western opponents of Hitler's Reich would be blind and stupid indeed not to take the fullest advantage of the priceless opportunity presented to them by the present German involvement in Russia." Two weeks passed and the Major was still wary:

We may hope that Russian resistance will last on into the winter, but we have no assurance that it will.

Four more weeks of Russian resistance and the Major was still up in the air:

While it seems quite possible now that there may be a stabilization of the front and a winter campaign in Russia, it is by no means certain.

In August, far from the end of a limb, he said:

The Russian situation may be assessed as one of serious gravity, without going so far as to say that a military or industrial collapse is imminent.

In November, after noting some Russian successes:

. . . the Germans have not yet given up; they are still seeking a decision; they may make further gains; they may even take Moscow.

So it has gone. The Major is pleased with his record on Russia. "I think I was righter than most," he says, and he doubtless was. The odds of military guesswork being what they are—as unfair to experts as they are to statesmen and field marshals—Major Eliot's score may well be a little better than par for the business. He was right, for example, on October 22, 1939, when he wrote that Yugoslavia probably could not withstand a German attack for long, and when, on April 30th of this year, he said that a crisis was near in Madagascar, and when, on May 3rd, four days before the engagement in the Coral Sea, he wrote that a naval battle was impending in the South Pacific.

In believing that the Philippines and Singapore would hold, the barber from the Bronx made the common mistake of underestimating the Japanese, and so did several million other Americans, including the Major. Among many statements pooh-poohing Japanese power, perhaps the clearest was contained in a lecture Eliot delivered at Town Hall less than a month before Pearl Harbor:

Japan is in no case to fight a war with a group of major opponents. Her army is sadly out of date, having not one fully armored division, and being short of tanks, armored cars, anti-tank and anti-aircraft artillery, modern engineering equipment and modern communication devices. . . . As for Japanese air power, it is almost non-existent. . . . The American, British and Dutch naval and air forces are fully capable of isolating Japan from the world and bringing to bear the pressure of full blockade—a pressure which Japan could not long endure, but which she lacks the strength to break by force.

When the attack on Pearl Harbor came, the Major said in a broadcast that "this attack is of a suicidal nature, from which few of the ships, aircraft and personnel participating have any hope of returning." As for Hong Kong, Major Eliot was under the impression that it was "well equipped and munitioned and tactically very strong" and that "it would take a long time—months, perhaps—to reduce it by any means possessed by the Japanese."

Throughout most of the Malayan campaign, Major Eliot kept his followers bucked up. Even when things began to go badly for the British, the Major still had good news; once he broadcasted over C.B.S.:

To those who tend to become discouraged because of continual reports of British withdrawals and Japanese advances in Malaya, the present scene on the island of Luzon offers a heartening antidote, where the troops of General Douglas MacArthur are demonstrating that Japanese attacks can be stopped, that even infiltration tactics cannot penetrate at will into well-organized defensive positions properly disposed in depth. This is of considerable importance, for there is every reason to suppose that the British have organized just such a defensive position covering the tip of the Malay Peninsula and far enough from Singapore to keep Japanese artillery out of range of the dockyard, the harbor and the city itself.

Even when Singapore fell, Major Eliot, who will never be accused of defeatism, pointed out that, after all, we still had Sumatra and Java, and when they were all but completely lost, he closed a thoughtful column with the hope that "even now, at the eleventh hour and the fifty-ninth minute, something may yet be accomplished by boldness and determination."

Occasionally during the Malayan campaign, the Major became a shade less optimistic. For example, in late January, when outnumbered British troops were falling back with great haste under enormous Japanese pressure, the Major's column appeared under the heading "Major Eliot Sees Counter-Attack as Only Way to Save Singapore." This strategical advice, in the opinion of some non-military observers, compared favorably with the medical advice prescribed by W. C. Fields to the patient suffering from insomnia: "Be sure to get plenty of sleep."

A while ago Major Eliot pointed out to an interviewer that before he came along there was in this country no recognized writer on military affairs. "I wanted to fill that niche in American letters," he said. It is perhaps too early to say whether he has succeeded. It may be well to await further developments. Although it is difficult to ascertain very far in advance what the verdict of history will be, it may possibly place the Major in the hall of fame next to such other military experts as Caesar, Napoleon, and Clausewitz. Or it may not.

JOHN P. MARQUAND

Really Simple Fellows, Just Like You or Me

꘎

READERS of *I Call the Turn* may recall perusing, perhaps with dubious pleasure, the human and warm thumbnail biography of Walter Newcombe that appeared on the rear of what is known in the publishing trade as the "dust jacket." This was prefaced by an informal snapshot of Walter taken when Walter was spending a week end at Happy Rocks, his publisher's country home. Thus it gave a mistaken idea of the luxury of Walter's surroundings, for only a few cynics realized that Walter was not comfortably at home. Walter was standing in front of the great fieldstone fireplace surrounded by shelves, ceiling high, of books which had been purchased from an English gentleman's library. This gave the impression that Walter was versed in the classics, which was not true, because Walter had stopped with Dickens' *Dombey and Son,* had let the Russians go with a hundred pages of *Crime and Punishment,* had read *Julius Caesar* and *The Mill on the Floss* in school English, and had done limited work on *The House of the Seven Gables* while at Dartmouth. In this photograph the camera had caught Walter swaying slightly, like the Tower of Pisa, a defect which was only partially corrected by the retouch artist of the Publicity Department. Walter was dressed informally in a gabardine coat, white flannels and tennis shoes. His eyes, without his glasses, looked innocent and startled, but his lips were compressed in a thin, determined line. The thumb of his right hand was thrust into the side pocket of his jacket and his other four fingers hung limply downward.

When you saw the photograph, the opening sentence of the biography—"Walter Newcombe, no relation to Thackeray's Colonel Newcombe, if you please"—seemed on the whole superfluous. It might be better if publishers did not assign bright boys and girls from Yale and Vassar to write about their authors with glowing human interest.

In those all too rare moments [the sketch concluded] when Walter Newcombe is not on the plane to Lisbon, perchance on his way to see his old friend General Wavell in Cairo or may it be to hobnob for a while with some other world figure, say the Generalissimo or Madam Chiang Kai-shek in their bungalow at Chungking—he lives a quietly harassed life trying to finish another of his commentaries on this changing world. (The sooner the better, say his readers!) As this is written, Mr. and Mrs. Newcombe and their daughter Edwina are safely tucked away in the gardener's cottage of his publisher's country estate, where Mr. Newcombe complains that his portable typewriter is continually getting mixed up with two dachshund puppies and his daughter's roller skates. Someday, Mr. Newcombe says, he is going to write a book about Edwina.

Most of this was an imaginary half-truth, for Walter was never fond of dogs, and he did all his writing in an office in New York; but there was one bit of that "blurb" which was illuminating—a single sentence which must have come from something which Walter had said himself.

Newcombe's career as a journalist, which saw its inception in Boston, really began when he joined those distinguished ranks of young men—and young women too—who first spread their creative wings in New York's old Newspaper Row, who hobnobbed with Heywood Broun and F. P. A. of the old *Tribune,* with Cobb of the *World,* and with Don Marquis of the *Sun* . . .

It is doubtful whether Walter ever hobnobbed, except in the vaguest sense, with any of these individuals, but this was only a detail. All that was interesting was that Walter had thrust behind him those awkward days and all that kindly environment of the old telegraph desk. He always said that he only began to find himself when he walked into the City Room one morning and got himself a job on what he ever afterwards loyally called "the Paper"—or "the Old Sheet," in New York.

Walter appeared there in one of those critical journalistic periods when many New York dailies could not adjust to the changing styles and tastes of the Twenties. The Paper was like a little country in the throes of a social revolution. There were the same frantic changes of policy and format. In desperation the owner of the Paper had moved to town, completely abandoning his previous pursuits, and appeared at his office every day. There was a continual transfusion of new blood. Correspondents were snapped back from Europe and put on the slot, or were set to running the Morgue or taking wrappers off exchanges. New cartoonists came and went with new managing editors, city editors, promotion experts, dramatic editors, and feature writers for the new women's page. They all appeared like Kerenski as possible saviors of the Paper, but they were gone like a summer shower. Later, when people who worked there tried to remember Walter, it was very difficult, but then at this time you never knew who your boss would be the next morning, or whether you might be looking for a new job yourself in the afternoon. Besides, Walter had only been there for a little while before he was sent to the London Office.

In the past twenty years, the United States has been most fickle in its selection of types for hero-worship. It is difficult to realize, in the light of the present, that Bankers and Business Executives once were heroes, in the Twenties. Jeffrey Wilson could remember when the circulation of periodicals such as the *American Magazine* was built largely on the heroic backlog of Big Business. Pages were filled with photographs of bankers at play, and with inspiring interviews with men like the late Messrs. Schwab and Vanderlip, telling the youth of America how they, too, could succeed. This, of course, was before Bankers and Executives were swept away into the Limbo of disrepute when the dam of the depression broke, and before some wag at the Senate hearing placed that midget on the knee of Mr. Morgan.

After the Bankers came a new type of hero. He was the Man in White; he was that quiet, nerveless soldier fighting his lonely battle on the murky frontier of Science, strangling microbes, manufacturing artificial hearts, so that America might live. This era brought us *The Microbe Hunters* and *The Hunger Fighters* and young Dr. Kildare and hospital nurses and horse-and-buggy doctors and *Arrowsmith* and doctors' Odysseys; but by the middle of the Thirties the Doctor too began to lose his dramatic punch. That was when the Foreign Correspondent at last came into his own.

We discovered that the Foreign Correspondent was not a disreputable, disillusioned journalistic wastrel. The Foreign Correspondent, it all at once appeared, was not a stoop-shouldered man, bending over a typewriter or bickering with the cable office or living amid the smell of cabbage in some dingy apartment on the Boulevard Saint-Germain. The Correspondent, we suddenly realized, was a debonair man of the world, a streamlined troubadour who hobnobbed, as they said on Walter's jacket, with nearly everyone. The doors of the Chancelleries were open to him. Brüning, Hitler, Mussolini, Dollfuss, Simon, Churchill, King George and Léon Blum, Trotsky, Lenin, Stalin, the Shah of Persia, the Duke of Windsor, Gandhi, the Old Marshal, the Young Marshal, Sun Yat-sen, Kemal Ataturk, Konoye, Beneš, Tojo, and Prince Chichibu—all these gentlemen were familiar and rather amusingly uncomplex figures to Your Foreign Correspondent. There seemed to be no barrier of language, no shyness, no secret repressions when Your Correspondent tapped upon their doors. They might be in their palaces or in a political dungeon or devoting their attention to an attack of gallstones or international anarchy, but they still had lots and lots of time to see Your Correspondent; and they were genial, ordinary fellows, too, not stand-offish or stuck up, but very much like you or me. It seemed that they enjoyed ping-pong, or cattle raising, or a good laugh, or some quaint American gadget like an automatic cigarette lighter, or the latest volume of Edgar Wallace, just like you or me. It seemed that they all had all sorts of personal habits, just like you or me. They picked their teeth and they put their bridgework in a glass of water every night. They smoked cigarettes or drank warm milk. They loved dogs and rolypoly children. They were tousle-headed, florid-faced, tranquil, clear-eyed, filmy-eyed, lethargic, dynamos of nervous energy, and they put you at ease at once, just like you or me.

They were always in a disarming mood when they saw Your Correspondent, just a little tired, just a little wistful as they gazed back upon their achievements—when they saw Your Correspondent. Taken off their guard that way—something in Your Correspondent's personality must have done it, although really he was an ordinary fellow, too, just like you or me—they were trapped into being amazingly revealing. It is true that they were tactful and only too aware of the weight of state secrets, so that often they told Your Correspondent confidences off the record which may be revealed fifty or sixty years from now, confidences a bit too heady for you or me at present. Yet even so, subconsciously they gave still more. They gave by a lift of the eyebrow, by a nervous tic of the larynx, by an involuntary fidgeting in their padded chairs, by a far-off look out of the window at the chimney pots of London, at the majesty of the Dolomites, at the minarets of Istanbul, at the miniature quaintness of the Nippon countryside—but Your Correspondent understood those hidden meanings. There was an invariable communion of souls between Your Correspondent and his subject which resulted in a mutual perfection of comprehension and a wholesome and mutual respect each for the other—Your Correspondent went away from there feeling that he had made another friend. Although he could never tell you or me quite all about it (because not the greatest writer in the world could wholly express the essence of that communion), still Your Correspondent brought away something that he would always remember—the sad lilt of a voice, the brave self-confidence of a laugh, the silence of that austere little room in the palace, or perchance the snap of a coal in the grate while outside yellow fog billowed through the streets of London. Your Correspondent saw it all. He felt, as he never had before, the gathering of great imponderable forces in the making, the tramp of peoples inexorably on the march, the gathering of the clouds signifying what?

It didn't matter what. Your Correspondent saw it; he sensed it; he vibrated with it. It turned out that Correspondents were not the humdrum lads whom we used to know. The *apéritifs* of Europe's capitals, the rice wine of Japan, had done a lot to change them in the middle 1930's. The world knew it when suddenly they broke away from their newspaper columns and began to give a jaded, worried nation the benefit of their personal confessions. There were *Personal History* and *The Way of a Transgressor* and *I Write as I Please;* but there is no need to call the roll of those volumes—*Inside Europe*—*Assignment in Utopia*—*Inside Asia*—those men had seen everything.

When *World Assignment* by Walter Newcombe was published it is said that his publisher, Sinclair Merriwell, was somewhat dubious. In fact, Mr. Merriwell admitted as much himself with rueful humor that made the tables rock with sympathetic laughter at one of those Book and Author Luncheons at the Hotel Astor. He actually thought—publishers, you know, never do know a good thing, even when it is right under their noses—that Mr. Newcombe's manuscript, which he had brought timidly to the office himself, believe it or not, all done up in a cardboard hot-water bottle carton, was just another of those books. But the Book-of-the-Month Club had taught him better and so also had the public, the most intelligent public in the world. Mr. Merriwell wanted right here and now to apologize to the public, and to tell them that they knew more about books than he did. They had given *World Assignment* the accolade. They had seen its inner quality, that literary essence which raised it above mere adventure, mere personal chronology, mere journalistic analysis.

Yet, what was that quality? Once, in a confidential mood and very much off the record, Walter's publisher had said that he was everlastingly damned if he could say.

"Don't quote me," he said, "but I took it to balance the list. There was too much whimsy-whamsy and we needed something heavy, but who ever heard of Newcombe? But that's the beauty of publishing. I had never heard of him, and now he's a great friend of mine—one of my best friends, and we have him tied up for his next two books as long as they aren't fiction."

It was easy enough to say that the works of Walter Newcombe possessed a plus quality of literary essence, as his publisher put it in that speech at the Astor, but it was more difficult to define what that essence was. When the Stanhope Agency added Walter to its literary stable, George Stanhope expressed it differently.

"Walter Newcombe," Stanhope said, "certainly has a whole lot on the ball."

Yet, when pressed to be more specific, George Stanhope could not tell what it was that Walter had on the ball. *World Assignment* was on the whole quiet and unoriginal compared with the efforts of his competitors. To Walter, Paris was not "a jewel encircled by the loving but avaricious arms of the silver Seine." What impressed him more than the width of the boulevards was the stone buildings. "They have a spaciousness," Walter wrote, "which somehow always reminds me of the steps of the New York Public Library." He did not react like Napoleon when he beheld the pyramids. He was mainly amazed that you could walk right up the sides. Rome, Walter observed, had been disfigured by Mussolini, much more than by King Victor Emmanuel, because Mussolini had uncovered a great many more pagan ruins than were necessary. Teheran, in Persia, Walter found, was a conglomeration of French-looking villas, hardly worth a visitor's time. What had interested him most was the sight of some crabs by a drain in one of the Shah's palace gardens—crabs, although Teheran was exactly so-many miles away from the Caspian Sea. Somehow Peking was not what he had thought it would be in the least. All the buildings were the same height except the Pekin and the Wagon-Lits Hotels. And China did not smell as badly as he had expected it to. In Tokyo he had trouble with the sunken bathtubs made of mosaic blocks in Mr. Frank Lloyd Wright's earthquake-proof hotel. Walter confided to his readers that he had scraped himself severely in one an hour previous to his being received by Prince Chichibu.

His reactions to the great figures in his world gallery of portraits were equally unexciting. If it had not been for the background of the Quirinal Palace, Mussolini would have reminded him of a friend of his who had been in the engineering company which had built the George Washington Bridge. When Herr Hitler lost his self-consciousness, as he did after the first few moments of their meeting, Walter observed that he was "quite a lot of fun." (This remark was deleted from the annotated and revised war edition of *World Assignment*.) If Stalin's hair had been a little shorter and he had been minus a mustache, Walter would have thought that he was entering the room of his old High School principal.

Jeffrey thought it was hardly fair to take these extreme samples from *World Assignment* and set them all together, as they gave an exaggerated impression of stupidity and gaucheness. The truth was that there was a dullness in Walter's work which lent it the authenticity of Daniel Defoe.

An innocence about his paragraphs and periods, a completely gullible acceptance of everything he saw, were exasperating until they became almost subtle. Walter saw everything, and he put down everything. This may have been the "plus quality" of Walter's work. Every reader of *World Assignment* felt that he knew exactly what Walter meant, and yet each reader closed the book with a different impression. If you did not like Mr. Léon Blum, you were sure that Walter did not. If you did like Léon Blum, you could grasp the conviction of Walter's enthusiasm.

In his later works his world stood a little more breathless, waiting for the turn of fate, its drama moving forward with the inexorable sweep of Greek tragedy. He began to write of shepherd's pipes ushering in the spring above the anemone-incrusted hills of Greece, their brave notes rising above the rumble of approaching forces. Yet even through these picturesque periods, Walter still remained simple. And that perhaps was the whole answer to Walter Newcombe—the guileless simplicity that had made him say, "But she's a statue, Mr. Jenks." He was still walking down the path of life saying that she was only a statue, in a great many different ways.

MARGARET MEAD

If We Are to Go On

❇

WE HAVE a certain kind of character, the American character, which has developed in the New World and taken a shape all its own; a character that is geared to success and to movement, invigorated by obstacles and difficulties, but plunged into guilt and despair by catastrophic failure or a wholesale alteration in the upward and onward pace; a character in which aggressiveness is uncertain and undefined, to which readiness to fight anyone who starts a fight and unreadiness to engage in violence have both been held up as virtues; a character which measures its successes and failures only against near contemporaries and engages in various quantitative devices for reducing every contemporary to its own stature; a character which sees success as the reward of virtue and failure as the stigma for not being good enough; a character which is uninterested in the past, except when ancestry can be used to make points against other people in the success game; a character oriented towards an unknown future, ambivalent towards other cultures, which are regarded with a sense of inferiority as more coherent than our own and with a sense of superiority because newcomers in America display the strongest mark of other cultural membership in the form of foreignness. What is the possible role for such a character structure—after winning the war—in working towards building the world anew?

We may ask first whether such a character has a future; whether it was not specially suited to pioneer conditions when success could be regarded as the reward for industry and abstinence; and whether the chief reason why puritanism flowered in America while withering in England was not just this favorable condition. It takes very special circumstances to back up a belief in the close connection between virtue and success. Most other cultures have had to construct their ethical systems on a less exacting model. The peoples have suffered for the sins of their kings; one evil deed has corrupted the land. Theories of reincarnation have permitted the notion that the luck fluctuates from one incarnation to another, or the whole problem of success was shelved altogether and each man took the fortune which a blindfold fate meted out to him. Christianity traditionally dealt with the problem in terms of heaven and hell, and those whose lot in no sense matched their effort or their deserts might flourish or suffer on earth; but all these inequalities were righted in heaven. The belief in the after-life was a particularly flexible method of reconciling a man who was exhorted to goodness, to a life without earthly rewards. But the essence of puritanism, although it retained all the color and terror of hell fire, was a belief that there was a relationship here on earth between good behavior and good deserts. God prospered the good man and withdrew from the evil man, and success could be taken as an immediate outward and visible sign that one had so lived as to find favor in the sight of God. Very few peoples have ever trafficked long with such an unmanageable moral code, but the peculiar conditions of American life promoted this attitude rather than diminished it. In Europe if one were born one of ten sons, and one's neighbor was an only son, and the inheritance consisted of farms of the same size, nine of the ten, if it were entailed—all of the ten, if it were not— were desperately unlucky. But in America, the nine could go somewhere else and often prosper more than the brother who remained at home. The favors conferred by birth were obscured by the opportunity to wrest favors by hard work and enterprise.

The American version of luck, best exemplified in the press stories of Hollywood success which have been analyzed by Rosten,[1] point up our

---

[1] In *Hollywood: The Movie Colony.*

essential puritanism by insisting that when sudden, undreamed-of, un-heard-of success and fame befalls some unknown movie star, she should have no birthright claim to it. She was not, the careful press stories explain, even pretty—they had to alter the molding of her nose. She is not the right height—when she plays with the star she prefers she has to stand on a box. Her success, her luck, is an artifact pure and simple, synthetic from start to finish. It might have happened to anybody. It might have happened to you and me. This is an excellent example of what the anthropologist means by the regularity of culture: that an apparent contradiction, like these tales of great and absolutely undeserved good fortune, when it is analyzed more closely nevertheless fits in with other ideas in the culture which it appears to contradict. The American logic is: Be intelligently good and you will be successful. As for those who cannot in any sense be shown to have been specially good, who have not worked or saved or slaved or supported their widowed mothers while they burnt the midnight oil and finished night school—when they succeed, we represent their great good fortune as due to a capricious turn of a wheel rather than tolerate the notion that those who benefited so greatly had some single initial advantage. The assumption that men were created equal, with an equal ability to make an effort and win an earthly reward, although denied every day by experience, is maintained every day by our folklore and our daydreams.

Running through this emphasis that work brings its own rewards and that failure is squarely the fault of him who fails is another thread for which the sanction is not guilt but shame. Shame is felt perhaps most strongly over the failures of other people, especially one's parents, who have not been successful, have not worked hard enough to have an inside bathroom or an automobile or to send one to a private school, to live on the right street, or go to the right church. As class is an expression of economic success, then it follows that to belong as a child or adolescent in a class below others is a statement that one's parents have failed, that they did not make good. This is bad enough when they have not risen, unbearable if they have started to fall even lower. Deeper than our disapproval of any breaking of the ten commandments lies our conviction that low economic estate is something dreadful and that a failure to keep moving upward is an unforgivable sin. If one analyzes the novels of American life and the case histories of adolescents which have been collected by American sociologists, this terrible shame of children over their parents' failure—a failure which the parents themselves may well handle in terms of guilt rather than shame—comes out very strongly. Success and conformity—outward conformity made possible by economic success—these are the marks that,

one is a good American. So the boy or girl who is held back by the idiosyncrasies of rich parents from conformity to the standards of the adolescent group may suffer almost as much as if he were held back by poverty. Whatever the cause, the lack of conformity attests to the difference and so to the inferiority of his parents, those parents whose status in the world defines his—until he has made his own.

The only non-European people of whom we have any record who have ever tried to build a society on such a close relationship between sin and worldly success are the Manus, where endemic malaria makes it possible for illness to be regarded as punishment for sin and the recovery from malaria—which almost always follows in a day or so—as the reward for atonement. But the Manus do not include in their decalogue that one should honor his father and his mother. As soon as they begin to fail, to drop out of the race for success, their children can turn upon them and heap abuse upon their heads, thus saving themselves from involvement in their moral failures. But for Americans to whom honoring parents has been insisted upon just to the degree that immigration which sets a premium on Americanization and a premium upon rise in economic level has rendered it almost impossible to carry it out—this easy way out is not there. "Blood is thicker than water," and we are not permitted to disown our poor relations—who carry the taint of failure in all their doings—but must continue to recognize them. The simple directness with which an English family disowns those on whom breeding has not taken, who have not learned to behave according to the family standard, is not for us. Our obscure desire to escape from our origins, which is present in all but those few families whose status is a function of their ability to trace genealogies where no one else can, carries with it its own sanctions. To deny one's origins is wrong and, by extension, to fail to face the failure—the ultimate moral turpitude of one's kin—is also wrong. And for handling these shames over the sins of others we have no formula except bitterness and misery. After all, you can repent of your own sinfulness and work harder or you can accept your own sinfulness and go to the devil with a certain grim pride in your own temerity; but you cannot gracefully accept other people's sins for which you can take no responsibility and yet in whose consequences you share. Thus class membership, for all but the upper upper, becomes a possible source of shame to Americans; it is the outward and visible sign of how far our particular parents did not get. While pride is possible in terms of the distance that they came, the distance has to be almost the whole mythological gamut from log cabin to the White House before it can be really satisfying. One's own position is continually compromised by the things that one's ancestors did not do, such as not coming to Boston earlier, not making better deals with the Indians, not going West in '49, not buying the right land. In a hundred ways present conditions show that other people's ancestors were, not more fortunate, for that one could bear with a good grace, but more enterprising than ours.

This is our character; this our need for success. That need has been terribly frustrated since 1929. A whole generation of fathers have faced their growing children with bowed heads because they had somehow failed; a whole generation of children have grown up under the shadow of that failure, believing in many cases that someone—the Federal Government, or somebody—should do something about it, anxious for a panacea which would assuage the guilty unhapipness of their parents or anxious for some scapegoat on which to vent their resentment. Fortunately, the desire for the panacea has been stronger than the desire for a scapegoat. While the men at well-covered dining tables, to which the only repercussions of disaster came dimly in discussions of the sale of a yacht or a country estate, have found a scapegoat necessary to absorb their sense of defeat, those parents whose apparent failure to find jobs has meant no bread for their children have, touchingly enough, felt far less hostility. They have for the most part continued to believe in the American dream that those who are good shall be happy, that all who are willing to work can work and buy a little home of their own. But neither among the angry men who rage about That Man in the White House nor among the Okies wandering over the country has there developed, as yet, any final questioning of the assumption upon which Americans have lived for generations—that the world is a wide, wide place with room for all who come to it with willing hands, good hearts, and hard heads.

When we talk about saving America from the fate that menaces her now, we can mean many different things. We can mean that we wish to protect our foreign markets and so protect the present economic system. Men may be quite willing to send other men to die for this great cause; but they will not go themselves. Dying for foreign markets has always been someone else's, and a helpless someone's, job. Or we may mean saving our soil from foreign conquest, from the actual print of tank treads on our soil. This Americans will to some extent die for, but not with the same fervor that an Englishman or a Norwegian will. For after all, the soil of the United States is not laced tightly with the bones of a thousand of our ancestors nor built securely and firmly into our whole picture of life. The soil of America as it enters our picture of the world is empty and open, uncut forests and unplowed plains. It does not matter that such forests and plains don't exist any more, they are part of our picture, just as secure hedgerows are part of the English picture. Invasion by foreigners—aren't we, in fact, always being invaded by foreigners, not always armed with guns—but still, you know, every Italian carries a stiletto, and certainly the Californians' treatment of the Okies did not differ greatly from an attitude towards an invading army. Always invaded, always outraged, with the best families' names always disappearing from the news columns and the names of new people, names you can't spell, cropping up. Our feeling about invasion, although it is there, cannot inspire a holy crusade. We will fight and fight hard if invaded, but we will find nothing to boast of or sustain us afterwards, as we tell over the tale—and pride in our own good behavior is essential to our picture of ourselves.

We talk about saving the American way of life—and this stands for a number of vague things such as refrigerators and automobiles and marrying whom you like and working for whom you like and not having to be regimented and wrapped up in yards of governmental red tape. Or it may mean something more; it may mean saving that dynamic principle which associates success and goodness. Our character structure is based upon having a job to do which can be done, just as the Manus savage's goodness was based upon associating his failure to work with a disease from which he got well. If we cannot again work and move in a world where there is some relationship between our success and our effort and willingness to work, this American character is doomed to disappear with the physical frontier which fostered it. This insistence upon a relationship between what we do and what we get is one of our most distinguishing characteristics. On it is based our acceptance of men for what they have become rather than for what they were born. On it is based our faith that simple people, people like ourselves, are worthy of a hearing in the halls of the great. On it is based our special brand of democracy. Americans who are once convinced that it's all a matter of pull, of who you know, that working hard doesn't get you anywhere nowadays, that it's all a racket anyhow —which is the cynical obverse of believing that effort and success are linked—are not a desirable breed. No one who was interested in building the world anew would conceive of asking such people to help. Once we lose our moral keystone to an orderly world, the whole structure comes crashing down about our heads, leaving us with a type of American who has neither vision nor humility, who lacks the will and the purpose which have helped us shape a great country from an untouched wilderness, who lacks even the constructive fire which might come from bitterness and a genuine hatred of those who have brought him to such a pass. That there are already many such Americans it is impossible to deny, just as it is impossible to ignore those scattered areas in American life in which all ideals have been sacrificed to a limbo of cynical grabbing—politics being the most notable example; business ethics often being another. In whole areas of life, Americans have ceased to see any element of moral responsibility, and they have nothing else, no valuation of style or breeding or of sheer virtuosity to put in the place of moral purpose. Traditionally we have disallowed these European valuations and insisted on our own; if we discard or discredit our own, we have nothing.

It is this cynicism which could well form the basis of an American fascism, a fascism bowing down before any character strong enough and amoral enough to get away with it, to get his. This note is found running through the admiration for Hitler which runs like a muddy sewer underneath so much outwardly patriotic conversation. There are very few Americans who can identify with Hitler in his cold destructiveness, but they can identify with his success in getting away with it, in the way in which he has made monkeys of his opponents. The belief that all life is a racket and the strongest racketeer gets the biggest pile of loot is the bastard brother of the belief that life is real and life is earnest. Its presence in this country, in the tone of our music, in the flavor of our jokes, in the wisecracks which are on every lip, cannot be dismissed lightly. It stands as a terrible warning of what may come from any concerted attack upon our success creed as sentimental, unreal, and outdated. Those who see a worship of success as the worship of seven devils, should ponder deeply the story of the worse devils who entered the room so swept and garnished. A puritan who goes to the devil, who sells his soul and knows it and is ready to burn in hell and keep his word, has a certain grim and terrible dignity. But a puritan who has lost his puritanism has nothing left but a cynicism that clatters like invisible handcuffs tying his hands forever from any deep commitment or great purpose.

Yet this American character which has done great things, which built cities faster than cities had ever been built before, which created a civilization in which men were more nearly equal than they had ever been before, which created a civilization which could dream of freeing the whole world—does depend upon valuing success. Shall we say that the day of these crude equations between personal morality and enterprise and a million dollars or at least a Ford car is over, and over for good; that when the American dream, which was nourished on a historical accident and lies sick upon a despoiled continent, is played out, we now have nowhere to go, except back to our origins, accepting some political system made in Europe? Shall we accept this verdict, bow our heads and let the winds of the old world mow us down? Or will Americans fight to continue to be themselves and for the right to define themselves as the champions of the good life?

If we are to keep it, we must do two things: we must redefine success without, however, breaking the thread which ties success to effort; and we must find a place which, like the great plains of the New World, gives us a wide stage on which to act out our parts. In the past when there were no new lands and no new gold mines, there were new inventions. The automobile brought us a tide of prosperity as surely as did the building of the railroads. For a little while men believed, some men still believe, that we have within us on this continent the power through making new inventions to open up more and more frontiers, new stages for industriousness and enterprise. But the closing in of the world, until all the peoples of the earth must rise or fall together, has changed that frontier and given us, instead of new inventions—to be built on American soil and sold to ourselves and perhaps the world—the chance to become devoted entrepreneurs of a whole world that must be built new, according to a new plan. Those who read Henry Luce's *American Century* with approval think that was what he was trying to say. Those who reject his phrasing reject it because they think that he is preaching a new imperialism in which Americans, tall and well fed and mechanically trained, will go about the world building dams and factories, lending money and sending armies to collect the interest or protect our investments. They think that he is replacing the old imperialism, which rested upon a sense of responsibility or divine right, by a new imperialism which will rest upon nothing but the lust for wealth, power, and conquest. That intelligent people can read *The American Century* two ways—that some read it and see the mark of what someone has euphemistically called "the clean fascists," while others can read it and fail to find this mark—represents the dilemma in which we stand today. Many who feel the strength and vigor of America still stirring are forced to phrase their faith in the ruthless terms of American big business, while many who have faith in a world where other values rule look with no faith at the ideals of Americans around them. The second group think they know the goal but can find no one to work towards it; they feel that the others trust Americans so exuberantly and crudely that the goal seems inevitably compromised.

Can we not take this sense of moral purpose—so intolerable when it sets itself above the world, but so indomitable when it sets itself to a hard job—and shape from it a tool with which the building of a new world can be done? Granting that Americans have a genius for seeing themselves on the side of the good and right, can we not use that genius and the energy which comes from a gleaming and almost intolerable self-approval when things are going well? Can we not tackle the job of post-war planning as we once tackled the wilderness, given energy by a belief that we are right, and given canniness and a willingness to work on new inventions by the belief that we must succeed in order to prove that we are right? Get the distaff ready and God will send the flax . . . if it is a good enough distaff.

For our willingness to work on inventions, our belief that problems are to be solved by purposeful thought and experimentation, is another aspect of this type of character structure. In most of the civilizations of which we have record, man had an alibi for not using his mind; the world was as God had made it and willed it to be; balances were righted in heaven; Fate or Chance or the order of the universe were responsible; and man's job was to fit in rather than to seek to change that which was there, to cultivate various virtues like dignity or resignation rather than to seek to reshape the world. Only in those societies which shifted success from heaven to earth, and so put the whole impact of religion back of efficiency, could we have a type of character in which it became a virtue to do the kind of thinking which lies back of invention, a virtue to set problems and solve them. For the puritan did not believe that man was saved either by faith or good works, but that he was saved by *intelligent* works. Much of the energy which has made man the constructive inventor of the last two centuries was generated by fear of the guilt he would feel if failure should prove to him and his neighbors that he had somehow done wrong. There are those who are so disgruntled with most of our inventions and with the violence to other human values which is implicit in this American cult of success that they would gladly scrap the whole show, return to a fixed status society, in which one's happiness came from being rather than from doing and food was guaranteed because of what one was born, a human being of a given age and sex.

But before we fling aside this peculiar drive towards efficiency and success which has been developed by the middle-class, success habit of mind, it is worth while asking whether this is not just the mechanism that we need to build a new world. The very impetus under which our reformers work, the moral passion with which they denounce social iniquity, are all fathered by this puritan tradition. As it has provided energy to conquer time and space and bind the whole world together as a physical unit—never to be split apart again—may it not also provide the energy to make the inventions which will bind the world together as a social unit? Is not this character structure, this driving will to prove that one is good by being successful, a tool made ready to forge a new world?

If we can once harness American shrewdness, that mixture of mysticism and a knowledge of machinery which has been so falsely dubbed "practicality," to the problem of making social inventions, we will be going a long way towards starting on a new road. The American who is asked to devise a way of handling synthetic rubber does not talk about human nature, man's right to natural rubber, the religious incompatibility of synthetic rubber and an ethical ideal, the racial dynamism of rubber, or the meaning of rubber for freeing the proletariat. He thinks first and foremost about his problem. Rubber has such and such qualities. He wishes to make a substance which has such and such qualities. From what materials, with what machines, using what processes will he work?

Our social thinking has been hampered by our lack of recognition that social organization is also a matter of invention. The use of fire is not inherent in humanity, although human beings functioning on this earth would have been very limited had the use of fire not been discovered. Language is not inherent in humanity, but the discovery and elaboration of languages has enormously enhanced our dignity and scope as human beings. War is not inherent in humanity. Warfare was an invention which accompanied the development of group solidarity, itself also an invention in living together. Just as we would not expect people to eat their food raw or stop talking merely because someone told them that fire and language were wrong or "unnatural," we cannot expect that warfare, which is the most adequate invention to date for protecting one's own group against the purposeful depredations of other groups, will be given up because it is branded as ethically unacceptable. It will not be given up until we invent something better. The old *lex talionis,* the eye for an eye and tooth for a tooth, was not given up until courts of law and justice were invented. Barter was not abandoned merely because someone sat on a local molehill and described it as clumsy and inefficient. It was abandoned when money, which was more efficient, was invented.

There are those who will object that warfare is inefficient, that it involves an expenditure of human life in a way which no one can condone and everyone must condemn. But that is just from our own point of view. The efficiency of any invention must be judged in terms of the goals for which one is working. Dive bombing is inefficient if you care more about the lives of your airmen than about the destruction of enemy battleships; it is terrifically efficient if you do not. As long as nations care more for the preservation of their political entity and autonomy than about anything else, then warfare is efficient. We have now reached a point where a great body of people have ceased to believe that nationalism is a goal or value by which one can judge the efficiency of social techniques. We want a world without war more than we want to be merely a strong nation. That is a simple, clear issue. Our enemies want a world with strong nations, built and perpetuated by wars. For them life is a continuous war, punctuated by armistices. For us, life has come to be seen as a peaceful, orderly existence, punctuated by wars. What is efficient for them is not efficient for us. But, in a very terrible sense, our enemies still have the choice of weapons, for the very simple reason that the weapons, the tools we need to build a peaceful world, have not yet been invented. It is not merely that they, warring states, attacked us and so forced us to fight. It is also that in the intervals when they were sharpening up their weapons and refurbishing their arms, we had no alternative to offer that was good enough. The world is so constructed today that if one army marches against another, the other army must obey the rules of war, must fight or surrender. Not until we develop a comparable strategy of peace, a plan of social organization which is so all-embracing that all who encounter it have no choice except to begin to play by that set of rules, will we have made the necessary inventions which will supersede war.

We have made such inventions inside our national states. If one man hit another five hundred years ago, the other man had no choice except to hit back or be dishonored. He was trapped in the rules of personal, hand-to-hand fighting whether he fought or not. Today, he need neither fight nor be dishonored; he can merely hand the drunk or disorderly or insane person over to the nearest policeman. He is as firmly embraced by rules of orderly procedure as his ancestor was embraced by rules of disorderly procedure. It is not so much that people today think brawls on the street are wrong, and shrink with a fine ethical fury from indulging in them, and call up conscientious scruples and sanctions against violence. A man may be a believer in violence or a Quaker; but on Fifth Avenue at ten o'clock in the morning, if he encounters violence he will call a policeman. A new invention has superseded an old. But it will, of course, only supersede the old as long as the ideals of the society are congruent with it. It is significant how civil law, which was compatible with steadily widening areas of social order, disappears as the glorification of warfare comes back under fascism. When I insist that the only way to get rid of an accepted social invention which we no longer wish to use is to make a new invention, I can give no guarantee that that new invention will of itself, unsupported by the whole direction of the culture, win out. But equally certain is it that without the inventions with which to implement order, we cannot hope to have any order in a world which contains such a full panoply of inventions for implementing disorder.

There is no necessary connection between warfare and human nature. Human nature is potentially aggressive and destructive and potentially orderly and constructive. Possibly some individuals are born with a slight preference for one type of behavior over the other, but this has never been demonstrated. But whether the bulk of a community will delight in violence, murder and rapine, or in a quiet pursuit of agriculture, of trade or knowledge, is wholly dependent upon the cultural tradition within which each generation of children is reared. Warfare is simply a sanctioned form of social behavior into which the most diverse character structures will fit if they are convinced that the use of this form is congruent with the aims which they hold most dear. Nor have we any absolute proof that those who believe in war fight better than those who believe in peace. Those who believe in war as a way of life carry with them certain liabilities which those who believe in order do not. The man whose male honor depends upon war can be wholly wrecked by defeat. The man who takes up his rifle to defend his home, convinced that he has no other choice but repudiating the trappings of militarism, has no such vulnerability. He is not proving he is a man by fighting. He has already proved that by living in an orderly world for which he is now willing to fight, and die, if necessary. Upon the faith that such a citizen soldier, who has no personal impulse to power or destructiveness and whose investment in battle is simply all that he believes worth fighting for, is stronger than the professional soldier of a warrior state, depends our greatest hope of victory. Our enemy is fighting for the right to keep on fighting indefinitely; we are fighting for the right to stop and build a stable world. The method we are using is his method. He has chosen the weapons; he has chosen his seconds; he has chosen the place and the hour. Unless we can pit against him an abiding determination to make an invention which will outlaw his, he is stronger than we. Unless we can say, yes, we are playing your game now and we intend to beat you at it, but afterwards, we will invent a better game and never again are we going to be caught playing yours, we have no hope. Proposals in Congress for a great standing army after the war are confessions of defeat, confessions that we cannot make the necessary inventions, that we are going to accept the enemy's definition of the world. Every proposal for a permanent army—which is called an army and phrased in the old jargon of war—is a step which weakens us as a people. We will not fight for the love of fighting; we will not fight because we are afraid not to fight lest we be dubbed cowards; we will not fight for mere survival. And when I say this I am not making ethical remarks or commencement speeches. I am not preaching pacifism; I am merely describing, scientifically, a condition which exists and which the captains and the kings must take into account.

Erich Fromm suggested in his *Escape from Freedom* that no people, once having tasted freedom and turning back towards slavery, could escape a terrible penalty in maladjustment and neurosis. It is probable that the same statement can be made about people who have tasted and loved order based on peace. They can be annihilated by those who love war; but they themselves cannot be made to love it. If our generals and our admirals will hold before their troops the chance of remaking the world, they will fight with every energy that is in them. To the extent that our generals and admirals want victory, want to go down in history as the winners of a world conflict, they must do this. If they are trapped instead in defense of a profession which they think of as immortal instead of belonging to one great phase of history, they will defend the permanent necessity of war.

Yet, to attack our professional soldiers because they practice their art well is again a suicidal act. To disarm when you have no technique for keeping your adversary disarmed is a form of silly wishful dreaming *within the framework of war,* characteristic of so much pacifist thinking. Most pacifists take their clues from war itself and think that by sinking battleships or insulting generals we need have no more of it. Not until we tackle this problem as calmly as we would tackle a problem of inventing a new synthetic to replace an old, not until we see it as calling, not for heroics or sermons, but for inventive thinking, will we get anywhere at all.

If the American people are told that they are fighting to get peace they feel trapped in contradictory nonsense, for, of course, it is nonsense. You don't get peace by war; you only get armistices. To pause between wars makes good sense to a warlike people. That is why it is the Nazis and their sympathizers among the United Nations keep talking about a negotiated peace. The point of a negotiated peace is so that everybody can stop, have a breathing spell, and fight more efficiently in the future. War to the finish is never the slogan of people who like war. Like the head-hunters of New Guinea, war-mongering leaders realize that if you kill all the people whom you habitually head-hunt, there will later be no one for your young men to prove their manhood on. Head-hunters' victims, like game, must be preserved. Unless we say frankly that we are fighting in order to get the chance to set the world in the kind of order that we want, a kind that the military nations do not want, and fighting for that chance alone, Americans will smile cynically at our oratory. But if we are to say this, we must mean it. We must see the job ahead as a job, not a matter of capital ships and power politics, but a challenging, practical job, a problem in organization which can be solved just as Americans have solved the problems of mass production. And we must see it as our duty—if we are to call ourselves good—to fight for the right to do this next big job uninterrupted. When the Indians and other European nations interfered with the job which we had decided to do on this continent, we pushed them aside without scruples. It lies within the American character to see a job as so important, and so pre-eminently our own, that, to the extent that we work hard enough, think intelligently enough, and pay enough attention, we have the right to tell other people to keep off the grass or only come on it if they mean to work at the same job as hard as we. To say we are fighting this war so as to have a chance to make the next, the needed, inventions, makes sense in American terms; and we can only win the war if we fight it in terms that do make sense—to Americans.

SELDEN MENEFEE

The Polls Tell the Story

THE OPINIONS of the people who did the working and the fighting in World War I are shrouded in mystery. "Public opinion" was merely a phrase, representing whatever the politicians and journalists wanted it to represent. This war is different. Since the American Institute of Public Opinion began operation in 1935, it has become possible to gauge roughly nationwide opinion on nearly every important issue.

The tools of opinion measurement are still far from perfect, of course. Theoretically a "sample" of 3,000 people, or even fewer, is large enough to give an accurate picture of the nation's attitudes if the sample is carefully chosen. To qualify, it must be a faithful miniature of the total population in regional location, size of towns, proportion of farmers, age, sex, race, and especially occupational and economic status. Actually, biased interviewers or incompetent interviewing in only a few areas may throw the results off; and if no election is in the offing to provide a check on the measurement of opinion, the "uncontrolled variables" may never be found out.

There are other pitfalls, too, including (1) prejudice in the selection of questions to be asked; (2) biased wording of the questions; (the "Have you stopped beating your wife?" type of question, which the polls try to avoid, but which occasionally slips in); (3) the reluctance of some people to express their frank opinions on controversial issues, especially when the person interviewing them comes from a different economic class; (4) lack of time for a well-considered reply where the issues at stake are complex; and (5) misinterpretation of results by the polling agency, consciously or unconsciously—as by failure to take the "don't know" answers into ac-

Reprinted from *Assignment: USA*. Copyright, 1943, by Selden Menefee, Reynal & Hitchcock, Inc. N. Y.

count where they bulk large, or by giving undue weight to opinions on questions concerning which the public is ill-informed.

But allowing for these possible shortcomings, and taking the exact wording of every question into account, the public opinion poll can be extremely valuable as an index to what the people are thinking. We know that the polls are reasonably accurate—usually within four percentage points on election results. Dr. Gallup overestimated the Republican vote by about 6 percent in the 1936 presidential election, but by 1940 he had reduced his error to half that figure. The *Fortune* poll missed the 1940 election results by only two-tenths of one percent. Compared with the unscientific *Literary Digest* poll, these predictions are something to crow about. And where a check has been made by two or more polling agencies on the same question, or on similar ones, the results have usually turned out to be almost identical.

Let's take a look at the state of American opinion toward the war and the home front in the year 1943. The figures used below are taken from Gallup, *Fortune*, National Opinion Research Center and Office of Public Opinion Research polls, some of which have not hitherto been published. They are supplemented by a few observations of my own.

THE WAR AND THE ENEMY

The American people do not question the necessity of fighting this war through to the bitter end. Less than one in ten favors seeking an immediate peace through some sort of compromise. Nevertheless only two-thirds of the people claim to have a clear idea of what we are fighting for. And most of these think in negative terms—of beating the Nazis and Japan, rather than of establishing a just and permanently peaceful world order. This is an improvement over the early months of the war, when only half of us had a fair notion of what it was all about; but it still casts a grave reflection on (1) lack of specific war aims, and (2) our government's inadequate information policy. In the summer of 1942, less than two-tenths of the people were able to name the Four Freedoms correctly.

Four-fifths of the people feel that they are doing something to help win the war. But a great many also feel that all of us should buy more war bonds, sacrifice more through stricter rationing and participate more in the Red Cross and other war organizations. Less than half of us think that "the people of this country are taking the war seriously enough." Two-thirds of us believe that business executives and workers are doing all they can to help win the war, and over half feel that government officials are doing likewise. But only a third think that labor leaders are pulling their share in the contest.

As for the war itself, in the summer of 1943 most people agreed that Hitler would be beaten in the last half of 1944, but that Japan would hold out for another year. The invasion of North Africa had brought a drop in the estimated over-all length of the war, from almost three to less than two years.

Mainly because of the belief that it will take longer to defeat Japan than Germany, most people think that the Japanese are the greater military threat to this country—over half, as opposed to a third who believe Germany is the principal menace. Racial feeling is high against Japan. In one poll, the Japanese were characterized by various interviewees, among other less printable things, as "barbaric, evil, brutal, dirty, treacherous, sneaky, fanatical, savage, inhuman, bestial, un-Christian and thoroughly untrustworthy." Only a few more than half of us feel that the Japanese government is our major enemy, not the people of Japan. But in the case of Germany, nearly three-fourths of us hold that the Nazi government, rather than the German people, is the real foe.

Two-thirds of us believe that we will be able to get along better with Germany than with Japan after the war is over. If the people of Germany and Japan were starving after the war, most Americans would be willing to give or sell them food. But one-third of us would oppose sending any food to Japan, while only one-sixth would take such a stand toward Germany.

Only 39 percent of us would allow Japan to join our post-war union of nations, and 44 percent would admit Germany; three-fourths favor joint action with Britain and China.

Anti-Japanese feeling runs highest on the Pacific Coast, of course, but it is strong in every region. When the execution of American flyers by the Japanese was announced, war bond sales took a sharp jump throughout the country. There is strong agitation against the evacuated Japanese in such States as Colorado, Wyoming and Arkansas. In Jackson, Michigan, I found that the town had been almost torn asunder by a proposal of the YWCA to allow a Japanese-American girl to attend Jackson Junior College. The local press fought the plan, which was finally killed by the board of education.

What We Think of Our Allies

We have a realistic attitude toward Russia. More than four-fifths of us firmly believe that we should try to work with Russia as an equal partner both in fighting the war and in working out the peace. This in spite of the fact that many of us expect trouble around the peace conference table. Half of us think the Soviets "will make demands that we can't agree to."

About forty percent think that Russia will try to bring about Communist governments in other European countries, and nearly thirty percent couldn't make up their minds on this question. But only about a fourth of the people think that Russia is likely to make a separate peace with Hitler as soon as she finds it to her advantage. After years of mutual suspicion and fear, attitudes toward Russia are growing constantly more friendly, even in the Northeast where Catholic elements are strong.

I found Bridgeport citizens enthusiastically cooperating in writing individual letters of friendship to the citizens of Gorky, in the Soviet Union, in a campaign sponsored by Russian War Relief. In Northampton a committee headed by a Congregational minister was conducting a city-wide drive for clothes for the Russian people. (In Toledo, Ohio, and other places, the Parent-Teachers' organizations have conducted similar drives through the schools.) In Greenfield, Mass., I asked a local editor what the Republican people of Franklin County thought about Russia. "They're very favorably disposed," he answered. "We have some White Russians in this town, and they've been interpreting their country to the people hereabouts. Even the Poles here are inclined to favor Russia, in spite of their government-in-exile." These reactions could be duplicated in nearly any city in the land.

Nonetheless feeling toward Russia remains colored by fear of communism—a fear long reinforced by conservative propaganda. When the people were asked, "On the whole, which country do you like best today—Britain or Russia?" over half said Britain, one-sixth said Russia, and close to one-third couldn't make up their minds.

Despite strong anti-British feeling in such centers of isolationism as Boston, a vast majority of our people heartily approve of the British war effort. This friendly attitude, though qualified somewhat by sympathy for the Indian Nationalist movement, has grown as the British war machine has gathered strength. Our strongest, most unanimous admiration, however, is reserved for China. After the first dismal half-year of our war in the Pacfic, we have come to realize fully the valor of our Chinese allies in holding out alone against Japan for six long years.

WANTED: A DECENT POST-WAR WORLD

This war differs from the last in one very important respect. This time our eyes are on the post-war world. We are determined to prevent future wars, and two-thirds of us believe that there is a fairly good chance of doing so. We are also worried about the economic slump which may follow this war. At the turn of the year Dr. Gallup asked this question: "Aside from winning the war, what do you think is the most important problem facing this country today?" Here are the main answers:

Solve economic situation, prevent inflation and another depression	16%
The food shortage, here and abroad; need for more food production	12%
To make a lasting peace, to end future wars	11%
Farm labor shortage; manpower problem	10%
Postwar conditons; reconstruction of the world	8%
A job for everyone after the war; prevention of unemployment	7%

Four out of the six most common answers, be it noted, were concerned with post-war conditions at home and abroad. This realistic attitude is one reason for the relative lack of emotionalism, the soberness with which we are fighting this war.

In 1937 only 23 percent of the people in this country favored joining the League of Nations. By the fall of 1942, the proportion had risen to 70 percent. The strength of public opinion on our post-war policy is shown by the finding early in 1943 that 76 percent thought we should "take an active part in world affairs" rather than "stay out of world affairs as much as we can." This was a new high in internationalism; the minority (isolationist) view dropped from about 26 percent of all persons questioned in October 1942 to 14 percent in January 1943. The *Fortune* Survey revealed in June 1943 that sentiment for playing a larger part in world affairs than before the war had risen from 58 percent just before Pearl Harbor to 77 percent, and that the group who held the opposite view had dropped from 18 to 12 percent.

Seventy-four percent of all persons questioned by the Gallup poll in April felt that the countries fighting the Axis should set up an international police force after the war is over to try to keep peace throughout the world. Only one person in seven opposed the idea. The strong sentiment for this proposal, which had grown from 46 percent in August 1939, stands in glaring contrast to the refusal of the U.S. Senate to commit itself on the same issue when it was polled by the Associated Press in April 1943.

The sentiment for a world organization to prevent future wars is almost universal, regardless of political affiliation. In November 1942, when the State of Massachusetts conducted a referendum on the question of calling "at the earliest possible moment a convention of representatives of all free peoples to frame a Federal Constitution under which they may unite in a Democratic World Government," three people out of every four voted "yes," regardless of whether they supported isolationist Henry Cabot Lodge or pro-Administration candidate Joseph Casey for the Senate in the same election. In another local referendum held at the same time in Boulder, Colorado, 79 percent of the people voted for joining a union of nations after this war. It will be hard for the politicians of either party to ignore such clear expressions of public opinion.

The Ball-Burton-Hatch-Hill proposal for a United Nations government to police the world provoked widespread discussion throughout the country. This was the first definite post-war world plan offered in high official circles, and the way the people grasped at it was an indication of their psychological need for more definite and positive war aims.

On the steps of a Kentucky hotel I heard an Administration Democrat deliver himself of a diatribe against Roosevelt for not giving his full support to the Ball resolution. "He ought to hang his head in shame," he said. "Here he's been advocating collective security and quarantining the aggressors all these years, and when some Republican Senators offer him their support what does he do? Plays party politics, instead of accepting it like a gift from heaven. He's courting trouble. If he doesn't change his ways the same thing will happen to him that happened to Wilson."

A little later, Representative Fulbright of Arkansas introduced in Congress his resolution stating "that the Congress hereby express itself as favoring the creation of appropriate international machinery with power adequate to establish and maintain a just and lasting peace among the nations of the world, and as favoring participation by the United States therein."

This proposal, much vaguer than the "B2H2" plan, was approved by 78 percent of the population, opposed by only 9 percent. What the public was saying, in effect, was: "We think the general principle of participating in world affairs is preferable to a general policy of isolationism such as we followed after the last war. Just how this new policy is going to be worked out and be put into effect, we do not know; but we favor trying to arrive at some basis for full American participation in enforcing the peace that will follow this war."

And if it comes to delegating the power to make the peace, twice as many of us would prefer to entrust the President (58 percent) as Congress (28 percent) with this great responsibility.

WANTED: A JUST PEACE

A small opinion poll in Valparaiso, Indiana, using return postcards, obtained an 83 percent favorable reply to the question, "Should the government take steps now, during the war, with our Allies to set up a world organization to preserve the peace?" The important thing, however, was the relatively high degree of interest shown. On this question 27 percent of the people queried—a new high record for the Valparaiso poll—took the trouble to mail back their ballots, compared with less than 10 percent on questions concerning voting age and other domestic issues.

The National Opinion Research Center found that 74 percent of us were generally favorable to the notion of joining a "union of nations" after this war. Three out of every five believed that "the Allies should start talking and preparing *now* for the kind of peace we want after the war." In order to "try out a union of nations as a possible way of preventing wars," a clear majority of us are willing: (1) "to stay on a rationing system in this country for about 5 years to help feed the starving people of other countries"; (2) "to pay more taxes for a few years while the new union is being organized, even if people in the other countries can't afford to pay as much"; and (3) "for part of the American Army to remain overseas for several years after the war to help establish order."

The things most of us are not willing to do include (1) considering most of the Lend-Lease materials as aid to the Allies and not expecting any payment for them; (2) giving up our Army, Navy and Airforce, if all other nations do the same; (3) forgetting about reparations payments; and (4) "allowing foreign goods to come into this country and compete with the things we grow or make here—even if the prices are lower." The inconsistencies of these views show the need for further education if popular enthusiasm for post-war planning is not to be sidetracked by misunderstanding of what is needed for a permanent peace.

Fortune found, however, not only that three-quarters of us favor sending money and materials to help other nations get back on their feet after the war, but that about three-fifths think that by doing so we will increase trade, making this country more prosperous than ever. Only one in five thought that such a program would lower living standards in this country. Here is a sign that our desire to collaborate in the post-war world has a stable basis in self-interest. If those who write the peace build their program on this basis, the danger of relapsing into post-war isolationism should be minimized.

We have no widespread desire to annex territory after this war. Six-sevenths of us think we should have more military bases outside the country than we had before the war; but aside from this, less than a third want to acquire other types of territory.

Nor do we have much of the vindictiveness that we displayed against Germany during and after World War I. Here are the percentages choosing various proposals as to what should be done with Germany after she surrenders:

Set up a United Nations council for ten years or so, and eventually make her adopt a democratic government and see that she sticks to it 37%

Bring to trial and execute all found to be leading Nazi officials 31%

Make Germany use all her available men, money and materials to rebuild the damage done in other countries 27%

Set up an international government in Germany for 100 years .. 21%

Do nothing to Germany but see to it that she stays within her own boundaries 13%

Carve Germany up and divide her among some of the United Nations 11%

Kill a Nazi for every person killed by the Germans in occupied countries 4%

The fact that only 4 percent of the people want to take revenge on the rank and file of Nazis, and only 11 percent want to carve Germany up, shows that we are inclined toward a reasonable rather than a vindictive peace. We can't agree on all the details of the peace, but we do know that the kind of peace we made after World War I is not good enough this time.

WANTED: JOBS AND SOCIAL SECURITY

There is less apparent interest in domestic than in international post-war problems, judging from the polls. But I found in talking to people that fears of inflation, post-war depression and unemployment were common and that government planning is relied on to prevent a collapse of our home economy after the war. These fears will be intensified as victory draws closer.

Our people are incurable optimists, however, particularly in good times. Four-fifths of those now employed believe their jobs will continue after the war is over. Of those who don't think so, only one in three expects to have enough money saved up to tide his family over; but only one in twenty anticipates much difficulty in finding a new job. *Fortune* found that 46 percent believe "young men after this war are going to have a better chance to get ahead than young men had before this war," while 17 percent think the opposite will be true.

Once the war is over, the public believes, a year or more will be required before war plants can be changed over to making peace-time goods and the armed forces drawn back into civilian life. There will be lots of unemployment, or at least some unemployment, in this period. Two-thirds of our labor leaders think that unemployment will be "extensive," while two-thirds of our business executives feel that unemployment will be only "moderate," according to a survey made by the Office of Public Opinion Research. Enforced savings now, through Social Security, would be the best way of taking care of this problem, rather than relying on Government-made jobs, relief or charity. If there is widespread unemployment after the war, seven people out of ten believe the government should provide assistance to the unemployed until they find jobs again.

The people feel strongly that it is the Government's responsibility to see that our service men get jobs after the war. Three out of four Americans told interviewers of the National Opinion Research Center that "If there aren't enough jobs after the war for all the men in the armed forces, it should be up to the government to guarantee jobs for them." Of these, about half favored a public works program which would not compete with private business to bridge the gap, and another quarter were for government subsidies to business. Less than a tenth thought that the Government should "take over and run some private businesses" if unemployment got out of hand.

During the transition period, wage and price controls will continue to be essential to keep our economy running, according to an NORC poll. Food rationing will have to be continued for a time, but gasoline rationing can safely be abandoned, most people think. High taxes are taken for granted after the war by 95 percent of us.

There will always be some Americans in need of the basic necessities of life, according to the representative American. To help care for them we should continue to have old-age and unemployment insurance, under the present Social Security law, and extend it to include all workers in all occupations. Furthermore, a similar plan should be worked out to take care of working people when they are sick. Close to nine-tenths of the people expressed these views. The Gallup poll found in April that only a third of the people had heard of the National Resources Planning Board's proposal for "cradle-to-grave" social security, but of those who had, 70 percent were in favor of it. In August, a third of the people wanted to see "many changes and reforms" after the war, while 58 percent wanted to have the country remain "pretty much the way it was." But some of the latter group probably thought of the New Deal period when they wanted to go back to pre-war days.

OPINION ON THE ADMINISTRATION

The people by and large approve the job the President is doing, although not without qualifications. The percentage expressing approval dropped from about 80 percent to less than 70 percent during the Congressional election campaign, rose sharply after the North African invasion, and stood at 75 percent early this year. A clear majority of voters in every social stratum except business executives favored Roosevelt for President in 1944 if the war is still on—but not if it is over. A *Fortune* Survey taken in the spring showed that 70 percent thought that the President had been doing a good job of running the war, but only 56 percent similarly approved his wartime record on the home front. In July 1943 the Gallup poll estimated that 73 percent approved the way Roosevelt was handling our foreign policy, but the vote was only 49 percent in favor of the President's handling of home front problems, with 42 percent opposed and the remainder undecided. Apparently the coal strikes and Congressional attacks on the Administration had had at least a slight effect.

Criticisms of the Administration fall into three main categories, according to Gallup: inefficient and sloppy administration; too much politics in home front affairs; and poor handling of the labor situation.

My own impressions check closely with this. I heard very frequently that "bureaucracy is getting out of hand; the Government has too many employees, and there is too much duplication of functions." The Administration is also accused of vacillating on questions which affect the lives of almost everyone. Resentment is especially high because of the delay in settling such problems as the control of manpower, the size of the Army and the drafting of fathers.

According to the Gallup poll, four-fifths of the people approve of the Selective Service system, a slight majority favors drafting manpower for our war industries where necessary, and three-fourths of all war workers and others alike are willing to work a minimum 48-hour week. In the light of these figures, it is easy to understand the widespread criticism of Washington's failure to adopt long ago an all-out war policy on manpower, and to let the average American know just where he stands in the picture.

Five-sixths of the people accept rationing as necessary. But only 45 percent thought that a good job had been done in rationing food stuffs, while 37 percent said "a fair job" and 13 percent "a poor job." The dissenters didn't like some of the methods by which rationing had been placed in effect. Most people favor the surprise technique, as in the case of shoe rationing. Announcements ahead of time that coffee and canned goods were to be rationed seemed to most people a major blunder, since nothing was done to prevent hoarding by an unscrupulous minority. Minor nuisances such as the "tire inspection racket" and the ill-considered temporary ban on sliced bread seemed to be most irritating of all.

Political bickering in Washington came in for a good share of homespun cussing. Congressional sniping at the President was resented by his supporters, and conservatives were outraged by Roosevelt's alleged ambitions for a fourth term. All factions joined in deploring personal feuds among Washington executives. The Jeffers-Patterson dispute, the argument between Secretary Knox and the Truman Committee over ship losses, the Wallace-Jones fight and the Hull-Welles affair left a bad taste in the mouths of most people to whom I talked.

In March 1943, Dr. Gallup asked the people whether they would like to write a letter to a Government official about some aspect of the war program. Almost half said "yes," and mentioned most prominently these problems, in the following order of importance: rationing, food production, the draft, post-war plans for the international scene and post-war plans for social security at home. Personal, immediate problems came first, as might have been expected.

ON TAXES AND INCOME

The slowness of Congress in passing some form of pay-as-you-go tax legislation was hard for most citizens to stomach. A Virginia woman said, "Why don't they get together instead of squabbling all the time? The people are for it. But Congress is holding it up just like it did the $50 pay for soldiers."

The Gallup poll showed that two-thirds of the people were for changing to a current basis as long ago as November 1942, and by March 1943 the proportion had risen to three-fourths of all employed taxpayers. The 1942 income tax rate was accepted as fair by five out of every six employed taxpayers, but they wanted it deducted from their paychecks. The eventual change to this new policy was a tribute to the effectiveness of the public opinion poll as a means of democratic pressure on Congress. But Congress did not go as far as it could in closing the inflationary gap between income and consumer production; for most people were ready to take an additional deduction of 15 percent from their paychecks for war bonds.

Three out of four people definitely favor a limit on the amount of profit a business can make during wartime, the National Opinion Research Center found. And almost as many favor some limit on wages. More than half thought that the incomes of such people as industrialists and movie stars should be limited to $25,000 after their taxes had been deducted. When Congress overruled the President's executive order limiting incomes to this figure, there was bitter criticism in labor circles. According to one union leader, "That's class legislation of the rankest sort. They put a ceiling on our wages, and at the same time take it off of the big shots' salaries. Why?"

A Seattle shipyard worker put it more forcefully: "I don't mind paying my taxes. What I do mind is seeing them rich so-and-sos get away with murder. I saw in the paper where they knocked down that $25,000 limit.

That's the way it is. A guy like me tries something and where does it get him? In jail, most likely. But them rich guys get away with it every time."

ON LABOR AND BUSINESS

Two-thirds of the people are critical of the Administration's labor policy, to which they attribute jurisdictional disputes and wildcat stoppages in war industry. Four-fifths of the general public and of union members alike think that unions should be required to register a financial statement with the Government each year. A general ban on strikes in war plants was favored by four-fifths of the general public and two-thirds of the war workers themselves, according to a Gallup poll in May. Three-fourths of the general public and two-thirds of the union members registered their approval of making it a crime to advocate a strike in a government-operated war plant. After the first coal strike, over a third of the people said they were less in favor of labor unions than they were a year earlier. Few of them had much use for John L. Lewis—only 9 percent were favorable, while 87 percent were disapproving.

Businessmen and workers alike think that business men would be better off under a Republican regime than under a Democratic one. And a plurality of business men and workers alike feels that the workers will be better off if the Democrats win the 1944 election than if the Republicans win.

Small business men feel discriminated against under the present system of letting war contracts. "The little fellow hasn't got a chance today," one Bridgeport contractor complained to me. "He depends on quality of work, and he can't outbid the big companies on war jobs. If he does get a contract, he hasn't got the pull that's needed to get priorities on the material he's got to have. I found it cheaper to go out of business."

A Government survey early in 1943 showed that only one small businessman out of every eight was using his equipment at capacity. Nearly a third claimed they could more than double their production without new machinery or equipment—if they could get the labor and materials they needed. They felt that the Government favored big business, that Government red tape had stopped them, and that they weren't given sufficient time to prepare bids for war jobs. "Contracts ought to be let by negotiation, to give the little plants a look-in," one machine shop operator told me.

The polls show that an alarming amount of latent anti-Semitism exists in this country. Early in 1943 the question was asked, "Do you think that Jewish people in the United States have too much influence in the business world, not enough influence, or about the amount of influence that they should have?" Half of the people said too much, a third said about the right amount, and only 2 percent said not enough. Another poll showed that three people out of five believed "the Jews have too much power in the United States." The danger in this situation is pointed up by another poll result: a third of the people think that "there is likely to be a widespread campaign in this country against the Jews."

On Our War Information Policy

At the end of 1942, only 69 percent of the people felt that the Government was giving them as much information as it should about the war. A few months later, a *Fortune* poll showed that 43 percent thought the government had done a good job in giving out news about the war, 36 percent rated our news policy as fair, and 11 percent thought it was a poor job. There is a strong feeling that our military bigwigs hold up unfavorable news much longer than is justified as a precaution against aiding the enemy. Resentment was especially rife over the suppression of shipping losses in the winter of 1942-1943. "My God," one indignant Indiana shopkeeper exclaimed, "What do they think we are? Babies? Let us know the worst. We'll fight that much harder. Their excuse is that they don't want to help the enemy. Well, the way I figure is the enemy knows about how many ships he's sunk. And he adds a few for good measure when he brags about them. Looks like we could at least be honest with ourselves." I heard widespread discussion, all of it adverse, when the story of Japanese losses in a naval battle in the South Pacific was released a day earlier than estimates of our own losses.

The most violent criticism of our information policy, however, came when the complete story of the 1942 raid on Tokyo was released more than a year after the fact. Silence for a few weeks or even months was admittedly sound strategy if it helped American airmen to escape from the Japanese-occupied areas of China. But the censorship continued long after it had any utility, in the opinion of most people who follow the war news closely.

On the whole the picture is encouraging. The American people are ready for whatever sacrifices are necessary to win this war. They are critical of anything that stands in the way. They may not be well informed on every issue, or always consistent in all their opinions. But they are basically in agreement on all major democratic aims of the war and for the peace to come. This is in a very real sense a people's war, and our citizens are determined that it shall be followed by a people's peace, both at home and abroad.

Such perpetual problems as race prejudice could hardly have been ex-
pected to disappear merely because the country was united in war against a
common enemy; hatred went underground and emerged in various forms,
as described by Robert McLaughlin and St. Clair McKelway, sometimes at
a Southern way station, sometimes at the Plaza. The neuroses of civilized
existence flowered under the pressures of war; Robert M. Coates's people
attempt to escape the psychological strains under which they labor by re-
treating into dialogues with imaginary partners, thus convincing the taxi
driver that everyone has gone mad. But, at last, even a skeptic like A. J.
Liebling (and why were the skeptics and pessimists so consistently the most
intelligent and the most correct of us all?) could feel that we had turned the
corner and might somehow, after all, be saved.

ROBERT McLAUGHLIN

A Short Wait Between Trains

THEY CAME into Forrest Junction at eleven-thirty in the morning. Seen from
the window of their coach, it wasn't much of a town. First there were the
long rows of freight cars on sidings with green-painted locomotives of the
Southern Railway nosing strings of them back and forth. Then they went
past the sheds of cotton ginners abutting on the tracks. There were small
frame houses with weed-choked lawns enclosed by broken picket fences,
a block of frame stores with dingy windows and dark interiors, a small
brick-and-concrete bank, and beyond that the angled roof and thin smokestacks of a textile mill.

The station was bigger than you would expect; it was of dirty brick
and had a rolling, bungalow-type roof adorned with cupolas and a sort
of desperate scroll-work. The grime of thousands of trains and fifty years
gave it a patina suggesting such great age that it seemed to antedate the
town.

Corporal Randolph, a big, sad Negro, said, "Here we is."

Private Brown, his pink-palmed hand closed over a comic book, looked
out the window. "How long we here?" he asked.

Originally published in *The New Yorker*. Reprinted from *A Short Wait Between Trains*
by Robert McLaughlin, by permission of Alfred A. Knopf, Inc. Copyright, 1944, 1945, by
Robert McLaughlin.

"Until one o'clock," said Randolph, getting up. "Our train west is at one o'clock."

The two other privates—Butterfield and Jerdon—were taking down their barracks bags from the rack. Other passengers bunched in the aisles— two young colored girls in slacks; a fat, bespectacled mother and her brood, with the big-eyed child in her arms staring fixedly at the soldiers; tall, spare, colored farmers in blue overalls.

As they waited for the line to move, Jerdon said, "Who dat?"

Grinning, Brown answered, "Who dat say 'Who dat?'"

Jerdon replied in a nervous quaver, "Who dat say 'Who dat?' when I say 'Who dat?'"

They both began to laugh and some of the passengers looked at them with half-smiles and uncertain eyes.

Butterfield said, "Even the kid thinks you're nuts."

The child in the fat woman's arms looked at him sharply as he spoke, then her eyes went back to Jerdon and Brown.

"You think I'm nuts, baby?" asked Jerdon. "Is it like the man say?"

The line of passengers began to move.

"That baby don't think I'm nuts," said Jerdon. "That baby is sure a smart baby."

Their coach was up by the engine, and they descended to the platform into a cloud of released steam, with the sharp pant of the engine seemingly at their shoulder.

A motor-driven baggage truck, operated by a colored man wearing an engineer's cap, plowed through them. The three privates, with their bags slung over their shoulders, stood watching the corporal. He was checking through the papers in a large manila envelope marked "War Department, Official Business." It contained their railway tickets and their orders to report to a camp in Arizona.

"Man," said Brown, "you better not lose anything. We don't want to stay in this place."

"This don't look like any town to me, either," said Jerdon.

Butterfield, slim, somewhat lighter in complexion, and a year or two older than the others, looked around him. "Hey," he said, "look what's up there."

The others turned. Down the platform they could see two white soldiers armed with carbines and what appeared to be a group of other white soldiers in fatigues. A crowd was forming around them.

"They're prisoners of war," said Butterfield. "You want to see some Germans, Brown? You say you're going to kill a lot of them; you want to see what they look like?"

Brown said, "That what they are?"

"Sure," said Butterfield. "See what they've got on their backs? 'P.W.' That means 'prisoner of war.'"

The four soldiers moved forward. They stood on the fringe of the crowd, which was mostly white, looking at the Nazi prisoners with wide-eyed curiosity. There were twenty Germans standing in a compact group, acting rather exaggeratedly unconscious of the staring crowd. A small mound of barracks bags was in the centre of the group, and the eyes of the prisoners looked above and through the crowd in quick glances at the station, the train, the seedy town beyond. They were very reserved, very quiet, and their silence put a silence on the crowd.

One of the guards spoke to a prisoner in German and the prisoner gave an order to his fellows. They formed up in a rough double column and moved off.

Little boys in the crowd ran off after them and the knot of watchers broke up.

When the four soldiers were alone again, Brown said, "They don't look like much. They don't look no different."

"What did you think they'd look like?" Butterfield asked.

"I don't know," said Brown.

"Man, you just don't know nothing," said Jerdon. "You're just plain ignorant."

"Well, what did *you* think they'd look like?" Butterfield asked Jerdon.

Jerdon shifted his feet and didn't look at Butterfield or answer him directly. "That Brown, he just don't know nothing," he repeated. He and Brown began to laugh; they were always dissolving in laughter at obscure jokes of their own.

A trainman got up on the steps of one of the coaches, moved his arm in a wide arc, the pant of the locomotive changed to a short puffing, and the train jerked forward.

The colored baggageman came trundling back in his empty truck and Corporal Randolph said to him, "They any place we can leave these bags?"

The baggageman halted. "You taking the one o'clock?"

"That's right."

"Dump them on the truck. I'll keep them for you."

Randolph said, "Any place we can eat around here?"

"No, they ain't."

"Where we have to go?"

"They ain't no place," the baggageman said, looking at them as though curious to see how they'd take it.

"Man," said Jerdon, "we're hungry. We got to eat."

"Maybe you get a handout someplace," said the baggageman, "but they sure no place for colored around here."

Butterfield said sourly, "We'll just go to the U.S.O."

"Oh, man, that's rich," Brown said, and he and Jerdon laughed.

"They got a U.S.O. in this here town?" Jerdon asked the baggageman.

"Not for you they ain't," said the baggageman.

"Man, ain't that the truth," replied Jerdon.

Randolph said stubbornly, "We got to get something to eat."

The baggageman said, "You want to walk to Rivertown you get something. That the only place, though."

"Where's Rivertown?" Butterfield asked.

"Take the main road down past the mill. It's about three, four miles."

"Hell, man," said Jerdon, "I'm hungry now. I don't have to walk no four miles to get hungry."

"You stay hungry then," said the baggageman, and went off.

"Well, ain't this just dandy?" said Brown.

The men all looked at Corporal Randolph, who transferred the manila envelope from one hand to the other, his heavy face wearing an expression of indecision.

Butterfield said, "There's a lunchroom in the station. You go tell them they've got to feed us."

Randolph said angrily, "You heard the man. You heard him say there's no place to eat."

"You're in charge of us," Butterfield said. "You've got to find us a place to eat."

"I can't find nothing that ain't there."

"You're just afraid to go talk to them," said Butterfield. "That's all that's the matter with you."

Brown said, "Corporal, you just let Mr. Butterfield handle this. He'll make them give us something to eat." He and Jerdon began to laugh.

"O.K.," said Butterfield. "I'll do it."

Brown and Jerdon looked at Randolph.

"My God," said Butterfield, "you even afraid to come with me while I ask them?"

"You're awful loud-talking—" Randolph began, angrily but defensively.

"You coming with me or not?" Butterfield asked.

"We're coming with you," Randolph said.

The four soldiers went into the colored section of the station and walked through it and into the passage that led to the main entrance. The lunchroom was right next to the white waiting room. The four men moved up to the door, bunching a little as though they were soldiers under fire for the first time.

Butterfield opened the screen door of the lunchroom and they followed him in. There were five or six tables and a lunch counter and, although it was around twelve, only a few diners. A cashier's desk and cigarette counter was by the door, and seated behind it was a gray-haired woman, stout and firm-chinned and wearing glasses.

Butterfield went up to her, rested his hands on the edge of the counter, and then hastily removed them.

She looked up.

Butterfield said quickly, "Is there any place we could get something to eat, Ma'am?"

She looked at him steadily, then her eyes shifted to the others, who were looking elaborately and with desperation at their shoes.

"This all of you?" asked the woman.

"Yes, Ma'am, there's just us four."

"All right," she said. "Go out to the kitchen. They'll feed you."

"Thank you, Ma'am."

Butterfield, trailed by the others, started back toward the kitchen.

"Just a minute," said the woman. "Go out and around to the back."

They turned, bumping each other a little, and went back out the door.

Brown said, when they were outside, "Mr. Butterfield, he sure do it."

"That's right," said Jerdon. "You want to look out, Corporal. That Butterfield, he'll be getting your stripes."

Butterfield and Randolph didn't answer, didn't look at each other.

In the kitchen they found a thin, aged colored man in a while apron and a young, thick-bodied colored girl, who was washing dishes.

"What you want?" asked the cook.

"Something to eat."

"Man, we're hungry," Jerdon told him. "We ain't put nothing inside us since before sun-up. Ain't that right, Brown?"

"Since before sun-up *yesterday,*" said Brown.

"The lady say you come back here?" asked the cook.

"That right."

The cook took their orders and, as he worked, asked them what camp they were from, where they were going, how long they'd been in the Army. He told them about his two sons, who were in the Engineers at Fort Belvoir.

"Labor troops," said Butterfield. "A bunch of ditch diggers and road menders."

The cook stared at him. "What the matter with you, man?"

Butterfield didn't answer. He lit a cigarette and walked to the serving window, looking out at the woman at the cashier's desk.

Brown and Jerdon went over to the girl washing dishes, and Corporal Randolph, his manila envelope under his arm, listened mournfully to the cook.

Suddenly Butterfield threw away his half-smoked cigarette and called to the others, "Come here and look at this."

"What?" said Randolph.

"You come here and see this."

They all came over, the cook, the girl, the three other soldiers.

Sitting down at the tables in the lunchroom were the twenty German prisoners. One of their guards was at the door with his carbine slung over his shoulder, the other was talking to the cashier. The other diners were staring at the Nazis in fascination. The prisoners sat relaxed and easy at the tables, lighting cigarettes, drinking water, taking rolls from the baskets on their tables, and munching them unbuttered, their eyes incurious, their attitudes casual.

"God damn! Look at that," said Butterfield. "We don't amount to as much here as the men we're supposed to fight. Look at them, sitting there like kings, and we can't get a scrap to eat in this place without bending our knee and sneaking out to the kitchen like dogs or something."

The cook said severely, "Where you from, boy?"

"He from Trenton, New Jersey," said Brown.

Butterfield stared around at them and saw that only Randolph and the cook even knew what he was talking about and that they were both looking at him with troubled disapproval. Brown and Jerdon and the girl just didn't care. He turned and crossed the kitchen and went out the back door.

The cook said to Randolph, "I'll wrap some sandwiches for him and you give them to him on the train." He shook his head. "All the white folks around here is talking about all the nigger killing they going to do after the war. That boy, he sure to be one of them."

Randolph cracked his big knuckles unhappily. "We all sure to be one of them," he said. "The Lord better have mercy on us all."

ST. CLAIR McKELWAY

The Touchin' Case of Mr. and Mrs. Massa

A Boogie-Woogie Ballad

✖

OH, LET'S FIX us a julep and kick us a houn'
(Sing "Yassah! Yassah! Yassah!")
And let's dig a place in de col', col' groun'
For Mr. and Mrs. Massa!

[Boogie-woogie]

Oh, this Mr. and Mrs. Massa have always lived in old Virginia and old
North Carolina and old South Carolina and old Alabama and old Kentucky and old So Forth and old So On and nobody has ever understood
the colored people the way they do because down in old So Forth and old
So On is where the white folks understand the colored folks like no other
white folks on earth understand colored folks. Yassah, Massa! Yassah!

[Boogie-woogie]

Oh, before the war and for some time afterward Mr. and Mrs. Massa understood the colored folks so well that they had a washerwoman they paid $1.50
a week and a cook they paid $1.75 a week and a butler they paid $2.25 a
week and it was mighty lucky for these colored folks that the washerwoman was the cook's mother and the butler was the cook's husband because this enabled the three of them to live cozily in the fifth one-room
shack from the left on the other side of the railroad tracks and thus pay
$0.85 less a week for rent than the total of their combined salaries.

[Boogie-woogie]

Oh, and over and over the total of their combined salaries Mrs. Massa
every other week gave the cook a ham bone outright and Mr. Massa every
other month gave the butler a whole quarter of a dollar extra right out of a
clear sky. It was manna, Mammy! Manna!

[Boogie-woogie]

Oh, but after the war had been going along for a while the butler, whose
name was Charles F. Parker, came to Mr. Massa and told him he was going

to quit because he had been offered a job as a counterman in the cafeteria of a defense plant at a salary of $15 a week plus three meals a day and Mr. Massa understood the colored folks so well he told Charles F. Parker that up to then he (Mr. Massa) had been able through influence to persuade the local draft board not to draft him (Charles F. Parker) but that if he (Charles F. Parker) quit his job as butler he (Mr. Massa) would have to persuade the draft board to go ahead and draft him (Charles F. Parker). Swing low, sweet Lincoln!

[*Boogie-woogie*]

Oh, but then Charles F. Parker told Mr. Massa that as he (Charles F. Parker) understood the situation after conversations with the draft board he (Charles F. Parker) had already been classed as 4-F owing to a number of physical disabilities, including chronic hoecake poisoning, and that therefore he thought he would take the job at the defense-plant cafeteria but with all due respect to Mr. Massa, etc. and etc. Hit that hoecake, boys! Hit it!

[*Boogie-woogie*]

Oh, so Mr. and Mrs. Massa saw the straws in the wind, saw which way the wind was blowing, and also recognized the trend of the time, so they took another tack, changed face, turned over new leaves, and each gave Charles F. Parker fifteen cents as a bonus and wished him success in his new job and raised the washerwoman (Esther G. Henderson) from $1.50 a week to $1.75 a week and raised the cook (Mrs. Charles F. Parker) from $1.75 a week to $1.85 a week with the understanding that Mrs. Esther G. Henderson would help out Mrs. Charles F. Parker in the kitchen and that Mrs. Charles F. Parker would wait on the table. Pass the hominy grits, boys! Pass it!

[*Boogie-woogie*]

Oh, but at the end of the first week under the new arrangement Mrs. Charles F. Parker came to Mrs. Massa and said she was going to quit because she had been offered a job as cook at the defense-plant cafeteria at a salary of $22.50 per week plus three meals a day and Mrs. Massa jus' had to cry. Weep some mo', my lady, oh, weep some mo'!

[*Boogie-woogie*]

Oh, and then the washerwoman (Esther G. Henderson) came to Mrs. Massa and said she was going to quit because she was eighty-two years old and her back ached and her daughter and son-in-law were going to support her for nothing, and Mrs. Massa jus' had to cry some mo'!

[*Boogie-woogie*]

Oh, and then one day a week after that Mr. and Mrs. Massa were walking back home after a dinner at the Old Southern Greek Chop-house and they saw Charles F. Parker and Mrs. Charles F. Parker and Esther G. Henderson coming out of the colored section of a movie house after having seen a Technicolored feature featuring Jack Benny and Mr. and Mrs. Massa noticed that Charles F. Parker had on a new suit and looked happy and that Mrs. Charles F. Parker had on a new dress and looked happy and that Esther G. Henderson had on a new shawl and looked happy and moreover was still laughing at the jokes Jack Benny had made inside the movie house and Mr. and Mrs. Massa saw the three of them go into a three-room stucco bungalow where Esther G. Henderson had a room all to herself and Mr. and Mrs. Charles F. Parker had a room all to themselves and then Mr. and Mrs. Massa looked at each other understandingly and tears came into the eyes of Mrs. Massa and Mr. Massa put his hand on her shoulder and said to her softly, "Nevah you mind, there'll be a reckonin' one of these days!"

[*Boogie-woogie*]

Oh, and so Mr. and Mrs. Massa finally closed up the house in old So Forth and old So On and came to New York and leased a suite at the Savoy-Plaza and the Savoy-Netherlands and the Savoy-So Forth and the Savoy-So On and any time you want to listen day or night as well as any time you don't want to listen day or night they will tell you for hours without stopping how they understand the colored people like no other white folks on earth understand colored folks and how the war and high wages are jus' ruinin' everything down in old So Forth and old So On and how never you mind there's goin' to be a reckonin' one of these days. Reckon twice and hit it again, boys! Hit it!

[*Boogie-woogie*]

Oh, and the bones of Mr. and Mrs. Massa are not growing cold and their heads are not bending low and no angel voices are calling to them and if nobody will carry them back to old So Forth and old So On, oh, then . . .

[*Boogie-woogie*]

Let's fix us a julep and kick us a houn'
(Sing "Yassah! Yassah! Yassah!")
And let's dig a place in de col', col' groun'
For Mr. and Mrs. Massa!

ROBERT M. COATES

Meanwhile

IT WAS a time when I was having a series of very bad dreams. I had all the typical ones. I'd be walking on a crowded street and the crowd would be full of familiar faces, old friends, even, but though I tried to greet them, to make them notice me, they all ignored me, walking past me with eyes stonily averted and chill, inexpressive profiles. . . . (Conversely, sometimes I'd go into a restaurant that I knew, or some such establishment—the dream that I remember best of this sort was about a bank—and I'd find everything subtly different, all the personnel changed and the new ones all strangers to me, and the atmosphere hostile and ominous. In the bank dream, I still remember the faces of the tellers, stony-eyed and forbidding behind their wicketed windows, and how I went from window to window, searching for a face that was familiar to me. . . .) I'd be walking down the Rue de Rivoli in Paris, and coming to the corner of the Rue Castiglione. . . .

I'd be doing some familiar, accustomed thing, and suddenly everything about it would turn strange. In one dream that I had, for instance, I had stopped late at night to buy a morning paper, surely something I did every night of my existence in those times. And the newsstand I stopped at was one I knew well, too. It was over on Twenty-third Street, and it had a roof and a box-like enclosure where the proprietor could sit in comfort, and the old man who ran it had been at some pains to fix up his tiny habitation. There was a kerosene lantern hanging from the ceiling inside, and a sliding glass panel between his seat and the shelf where the papers were piled outside, and in my waking life I had grown used, when I stopped there, to seeing the familiar old face peering out and the old hand reaching claw-like to pick up the pennies where I had dropped them. In my dream, though, the old man wasn't there.

There was no one in the newsstand, and no light in the kerosene lantern. There was only the box-like enclosure, standing dark at the edge of the curb, and around it the frosty gray sidewalk and beyond that the dimmed-out, empty street; and I was at a loss to know what to do, for I only

had a five-dollar bill and I wanted a paper. Then I noticed that the shelf
outside was littered with money.

It was as if the old man had been away for weeks or as if he had left
his life's savings; there was a fortune there, but though puzzled and perhaps a little envious, I put aside temptation; I made change for myself
scrupulously, more or less as the old man might have done. I took four
ones, a half dollar, a quarter, two dimes, and a *News* and a *Tribune;* I was
walking off down the street with the newspapers under my arm and the
money still in my hand when I heard startled cries and then more cries,
deeper, angrier, then the sound of running feet, the piercing shrilling of a
police whistle, all the shouting turmoil of a pursuit, overtaking me.

I ran. I was guilty, though I knew not of what, and I ran; and even as
I ran, twisting this way and that through the dark unfamiliar alleys that
presented themselves in my path, I was conscious of a guilt that was not my
guilt, of a blame that was not my blame. . . .

(I would be in a haunted house, but a house that was haunted not by
any definable thing, even anything so near to a thing as a ghost, but
by merely a sense of evil. There would be evil everywhere: in the dust
that puffed up from between the cracks of the floor as I walked on it; in the
air; in the reflection of a mirror on the wall—reflecting me; in the light that
lay over the landscape outside the window. . . . But no evil that I could
touch, that I could feel, that I could see.) I would wake up sweating, to
hear the fierce hooting shrilling of the fire engines, hurtling somewhere
through the streets outside, and as they drew nearer (if they drew nearer)
the angry hammering clangor of the bells.

"Why not give them a chance?" said the man. "Take those kids, seventeen, eighteen years old—if they want to go, why not let them? I think
they ought to lower the draft age, both ends, instead of raising it. The
kids, they're young, and they don't think much; they'd make the best soldier material. And you've got to remember too that for lots of them
they'd be eating better, getting better clothes, better treatment every way
than they'd ever had before in their lives; why, they tell me that in some
of those hill-billy companies half the men never even had shoes on before
they got in the Army!

"But with us older men, it's a hell of a lot different. We've got responsibilities."

Money dreams, worry dreams, everything but sex dreams; there was no
time for sex at that period. Before the war, I had long, involved, rather
literary dreams: a dream in which I had set out to find, in a region that was
partly Paris and partly the section just east of Madison Square, a café called

"The Wandering Jew," it seemed I had to find it or else suffer some loss or punishment; a dream in which I had found myself walking, pall-bearer fashion, beside a freight car in a long line of slowly moving freight cars, and at the side of every other car in the train a bum or a hobo was walking, also like a pallbearer, and we walked on, and it was solemn and peaceful and pleasant—until suddenly the train took a curve that I hadn't expected (was it something to do with the locomotive of history?) and I found myself walking alone, down a long stretch of empty track. And the loneliness and the terror. . .

But my dreams now were different. In one that constantly recurred, I would be walking down the Rue de Rivoli in Paris, the light bright on the street outside, the sun caracoling among the arches, and as I came to the corner of the Rue Castiglione—but then something would always happen to bar my way. Sometimes it would be the crowd, grown suddenly ugly and ominous, swarming watchful and sharp-eyed around me, while I flapped my arms and tried vainly to get away. Sometimes it would be the street, tilting up unclimbably. Sometimes it would be, simply, darkness. . . .

"Well, this Darlan business," the man said. "It's quite true he may be anti-British and he's probably anti-American too. But if we're going to play ball with Vichy, and it looks as if we've got to, then we've got to play ball with Darlan too. It's a simple matter of political expediency. After all, we've got to let the French pick the men they want."

"Well, this Tito-Mikhailovitch business—you hear a lot of talk about how the Yugoslavs want Tito, as if that proved anything! We're at war, and we've got to pick the man and the men that are going to be useful to us. Times like this, we can't afford to knuckle under to anybody, and if the Yugoslavs don't like Mikhailovitch, well, that's just their hard luck."

"Well, the Finns. I know all that stuff about the Germans using Finland for bases, and the losses on the Murmansk run and so on, just as well as you do. But you know, somehow I just can't blame them, the Finns, I mean. Hate dies hard, and they took an awful beating from the Russians. And as far as that goes, what the hell are we sending all that stuff to the Reds for, anyway?"

"Take it easy," the man said. "You'll see. We can talk a lot here, but it's the boys in the State Department that really know what's going on."

It is easy to see I was worried, in that period. It was odd, too, how often I kept running across slightly mad people, slightly crazy people, in the streets and in other public places.

Formerly, it had been only rarely that I had seen them—those old ladies with incongruous hats and haunted eyes, sitting mumbling their food at isolated tables at the Automat and glaring at the other diners; the old men with raggedy hair and wild gestures who'd go lurching through the noonday crowds on Sixth Avenue as if drunk, but not drunk with drinking; the women, black-clad and wraith-thin, who would suddenly burst into shouts of obscenity as the crowd halted at a street crossing—now, it seemed, I saw them everywhere. No longer were all of them elderly, either. At the little cigar store and luncheonette on West Twenty-eighth Street where I sometimes bought my afternoon paper, the woman who ran the place met me at the door one day with a white, scared face. "I don't know what to do," she whispered, and she gave a jerk of her head toward a girl sitting at the soda fountain. "She came in here and said she was broke, and would I please give her a cup of coffee. And all so gentle and innocent, too. And now look at her."

I glanced past her at the girl. She was only about twenty, I'd guess, and she was decently dressed, with a sharp little pointed face peering fox-like over a bedraggled fur neckpiece, and she was sitting hunched over her cup of coffee, staring at her reflection in the mirror and mumbling.

"I'll give 'em as good as they send," she was saying. "Don't you worry about that. I'll send 'em. They'll go way up the river when I get after 'em, way up that deep river, and then down, down, down. I'll down 'em," she said, "Down the hatch," and she was lifting the cup to drink when she caught sight of me and whirled on the stool. "Get the hell out of here!" she shouted, and she drew the cup back as if to throw it at me. I got out, though the woman who ran the place gazed at me despairingly. But, good Lord, it was her problem, wasn't it, not mine?

"Don't you worry," the man said. "A good deal of that criticism you hear is just irresponsible meddling. You've got to remember, the State Department . . ."

"Maybe Darlan *was* a mistake," the man said. "But in a way it wasn't our problem. It was strictly a question for the military, and you've got to remember, at the time . . ."

"Oh, Spain, Spain. That's all water under the bridge. I wish people would quit talking about Spain," the man said. "We all make mistakes, and anyway I'm still not convinced things aren't better as they are, with Franco, than they would have been if the Communists had got control . . ."

"I'm not worried about South America," the man said.

I can tell you, there were times when I got a little slug-nutty myself. "ALLIES PLAN TRIBUNAL TO ASSESS WAR GUILT," I remember the headlines saying one day, and I found myself wondering for a moment what tribunal would be called, and when, to assess my responsibilities. I had so many things on my conscience.

There was my guilt at having permitted the war to come about at all— because there was no avoiding or evading the fact that I was responsible, just as much as anyone else—and before that, the greater guilt of allowing the world to degenerate to a point where wars could still happen. And beyond that, the long train of other errors, both major and minor, that I might have prevented. . . . I can tell you, it was a very worried little man who might have been seen, of an evening, walking up Lexington Avenue in a brown overcoat and a gray felt hat, his cigar cocked at a jaunty angle (if he had had a cigar), and his keen eyes quick to observe the vagaries of the humankind around him.

(And the plump little woman I met there, quietly dressed, walking up past the Hotel Amsterdam as I walked down; without warning, she pointed at no one in particular and her face twisted up in rage. "I know all your tricks, you Brooklyns," she shouted in a voice as deep and resonant as a man's. "All your damn' stinkin' tricks, I know 'em. You won't get me!" Then she dropped her hand and walked on again, to all appearances as quiet and reserved as a Sunday-school teacher. A man just ahead of me, who had been more or less in range of her pointing finger, looked startled for an instant. Then he glanced round at me and grinned. . . . Well, maybe having all those nuts around wasn't such a bad thing after all. Occasionally, they gave you a laugh.)

"Well, the Nazis, the Fascists," the man said. "I know. But I can't help thinking, maybe that's just the kind of treatment those Europeans need. And you've got to remember, a strong government. . . ."

Or like that taxi driver I got talking to that night, in the bar on Third Avenue. He was standing at the street end of the bar, dawdling over a glass of beer, and there was nobody else much in the place and so pretty soon we got talking. "By God, sir," he said. He was one of those old-time, red fellows, who looked as if he'd once been a private chauffeur before he turned hackie. "It's a funny thing. Or maybe, not being in my line of business, you mightn't have noticed it. But it seems to me nowadays that nearly everybody you run into, before you know it they start talking to themselves.

"Where I notice it most is in the cab. I get a fare, maybe up on Madison, but it don't matter where, it can happen all over; and I'll know it's a man alone I've got in the back behind me, because, God sakes, didn't I see him when he got in? But you know, when you get into traffic sometimes you can forget, and there's many's the time, when I've gone a few blocks, I have to look back to make sure, because from all the jabbering that's going on, there might be two or three fellahs sitting there.

"I'll look back, and be damned if the fellah won't be sitting all alone there, and yet him jabbering away, maybe arguing just like he was arguing with somebody or maybe giving him a dressing-down. You know, anyway, talking. I had one man tonight just before I come in here, picked him up on Central Park West and took him down to Grand Central, and by God, sir, you'd think he was trying a case in the law courts, the way he went at it.

"'Now, now, take it easy,' he'd say, like he was trying to soothe somebody down. 'I know how you feel,' he'd say, and then his voice would go mumbling down till I couldn't hear what he was saying. And then all of a sudden he'd start up again. 'Well, O.K., then, by God!' he'd say, loud enough to make you jump. 'If that's how you feel about it, O.K.,' and off he'd go again; it made your flesh creep, sort of.

"Finally, when we hit a red light, down around Columbus Circle, I turned right around in my seat and looked at him. I didn't say a word, because I didn't want to, but you know, I really looked at him—but do you think that stopped him? Not him. He kept on talking away, off and on, all the way till I dropped him at Grand Central. . . . What is it, anyway?" said the taxi driver. "Is it the war, or something? I can't figure it out."

A. J. LIEBLING

Toward a Happy Ending

PEARL HARBOR had left slight trace on the public mind, it seemed to a man coming off a boat in mid-January of 1942, but it had closed the second phase of the war. The first had ended with the disaster of the Pétain armistice. The second had been a negative success because our side had avoided collapse. The third, however unpromisingly it might start, however long it might last, was bound to end in the defeat of the avowedly fascist powers, because the combination of peoples they had attacked was too big, too strong, and too game for them. Hitler's chance to own the world had depended on a successful bluff. If, with the aid of the French industrialists and their counterparts in Great Britain and the United States, he could have secured a dominance of the West without war, isolating Russia, he might have brought it off. He still had had a chance as long as he could keep Russia and the United States neutral. But with all the holders of high cards in the game he was in the position of a poker player who has tried to steal a pot with no pair. He could keep on raising until he ran out of chips in order to delay the showdown; that would be an insane card player's reaction. His situation made me, personally, extremely and perhaps unreasonably happy. Millions of men meriting better than I have lived and died in humiliating periods of history. Free men and free thinking always get a return match with the forces of sadism and anti-reason sometimes. But I had wanted to see a win, I had wanted my era to be one of those that read well in the books. Some people like to live in a good neighborhood; I like to live in a good age. I am a sucker for a happy ending—the villain kicked in the teeth, the stepchildren released from the dark basement, the hero in bed with the heroine. Maybe the curtain will go up on the same first act tomorrow night, but I won't be in the audience.

By 1942 I had my personal hurts as well. I had Suzette's letter, which had taken nearly a year to reach me, telling of her father's death, cold, undernourished and humiliated, in the Montmartre flat where we had so often broken bread. Jean, the son, had won a Croix de Guerre and had been demobilized, Suzette had written—I could imagine him dodging about France to avoid conscription for German factory labor. Sauvageon, living in the *zone interdite* between occupied and unoccupied France, had managed to get a letter out to me too, through Switzerland. He had written of the mass emigration of the Alsatians and Lorrainers who had chosen to retain their French nationality.

The third round would be the good one, I thought, and I didn't stay long at home waiting for it to begin. I made the return trip to England by another Norwegian ship, this time a fast one that traveled without escort. The chief excitement of this trip was a long series of after-dinner checker games between me and the chief engineer, Johansen, who referred to himself as "some of the oldest engineers afloat." I once beat him with a quadruple jump, in a game for three bottles of beer.

London had changed more than New York since our entry into the war. It was full of Americans now, and one more attracted about as much attention as an extra clam at a shore dinner. I felt like an until recently only child whose mother has just given birth to quintuplets. And I was more of a stranger to the American news sources with whom I now had to deal, the Army and Navy Public Relations offices, than correspondents who had been in London for only three months, because the organizations had been set up since the time I had left.

I had a high idea of what the American Army in the European theater of operations would eventually be, and my first clues to it did not disappoint me. There were few ground combat troops in Great Britain as yet and many less Air Corps people than I had expected to find, but the preparations of the Services of Supply indicated how great the fighting force would soon be. The S.O.S. was building, for example, a depot in the South of England for the repair of American Army motor vehicles, and from its size one could get a fair idea of how many vehicles would be in operation and how big an army they would serve. It was like estimating an elephant's size from the print of one foot. The dimensions of the A.E.F. would certainly be elephantine, which pleased me because it indicated that the Government had not been impressed by the Sunday-supplement strategists who talked about an exclusively air war.

I knew that the quality of American troops would be good, once they had paid their entry fee with a couple of bobbles, because Americans are the best competitors on earth. A basketball game between two high-school teams at home will call forth enough hardness of soul and flexibility of ethic to win a minor war; the will to win in Americans is so strong it is painful, and it is unfettered by any of the polite flummery that goes with cricket. This ruthlessness always in stock is one of our great national resources. It is better than the synthetic fascist kind, because the American kid wears it naturally, like his skin, and not self-consciously, like a Brown Shirt. Through long habit he has gained control over it, so that he turns it on for games, politics, and business and usually turns it off in intimacy. He doesn't have to be angry to compete well.

While I had been away from London, Manetta, the manager of the Savoy Grille, had taken over the restaurant in my old hotel in Half Moon Street, and it was now one of the busiest and noisiest pubs in London, with a British version of a swing band, no tables available on less than three days' notice, American colonels crowding the members of refugee governments away from the ringside, and Jack, the cockney bartender who during my first visit had drooped disconsolately in front of a fine assortment of whiskies, now overworked and understocked, like the wine waiter. The hotel portion of the establishment looked much as it always had, although because of the Americans it was harder to get a room. Some of the old county women, having booked weeks in advance, would arrive there and in time descend from their rooms, leading either a spaniel or a small grandniece wearing a blue hair ribbon. They would march stiffly toward the once tranquil dining room, hear the first blast of the swing band, enter the gabble of the cocktail lounge where the new clientele waited for tables, and then turn and hobble desperately away, dragging dog or child after them.

. London had the atmosphere of a town where people are gathering for a gold rush or an opera festival; everybody felt that something good was going to begin soon. Psychologically we had already passed to the attack. The correspondents, while they waited to be let in on the time and place, wrote stories about the growing American forces in Britain. After three years of going out to French, British, and Polish troops for stories, I enjoyed the novelty of being with Americans, although the uniform I now had to wear when I went out to troops made me feel that I was play-acting. I had passed through British railway stations so often and so unremarked in mufti that the salutes of British noncoms now took me by surprise and I was generally well past the saluter before I realized I had left him with a poor view of American military courtesy. It would have been hopeless to explain each time that a correspondent didn't rate a salute—I was bald enough and old enough to be a field officer and was wearing an officer's uniform.

The Air Corps, which was just beginning to take over a few British fields, reminded me of a football squad beginning its training for the season. It would win a lot of games if it was not rushed into heavy competition too soon. My favorite unit in the first weeks was a Flying Fortress bombardment group that resembled a football squad physically too. There is an official maximum size for fighter and medium bombardment pilots, but the really big boys in the Air Corps get into the big ships, where there is relatively a lot of head room. The commander of one squadron of the group had been All-Southern at Mississippi State; one of his pilots had played tackle for Alabama in the Rose Bowl, and another had understudied an All-American halfback at Duke; Tommy Lohr, a rugged little lightweight back from Brown, was another pilot in the group, and altogether they would have made a good squad for any coach in a normal season. But this time they had other business.

The original public-relations crew in London, being for the most part newspapermen who had recently acquired uniforms and lived in deadly fear of irritating real soldiers, were not of much help in getting out to see troops. According to them the C.O. of any unit a correspondent wanted to see was sure to be busy, and anyway there were no living accommodations for newspapermen at the flying field. I arranged all that with my Fortress fellows by always occupying the bed of a man who had gone on forty-eight-hour leave to London. While the man was in London he would sleep in my room at the hotel. When the regular occupant of the bed at the field returned there was always somebody else going up to town and I would move into his bed while he took mine in London. I never really interviewed anybody, just lived around the place and learned by osmosis, until I sometimes thought of myself as a redundant member of the group, a goldbricker nobody had yet caught up with. We were living in hutments and sleeping on cots; there were toilets that flushed and showers; between meals and after dinner we would sit in the lounge of the officers' club, where there were deep chairs and a bar. In retrospect, after we all got to Africa, it seemed a most luxurious period.

The Fortresses made their first flights over France while I was living with this group. The accuracy of their bombing, even in their first raids, astonished officers of British Bomber Command and the Ministry of Economic Warfare, who had selected the targets. The British thought at first that these were selected crews of veterans and that the accuracy couldn't be retained in large-scale operations. But I knew that they were boys who had had at most a year and a half in the Air Corps, and that there were thousands more like them at home. The factories would furnish the planes, the American system of public education would furnish the crews; it couldn't be anything but a win. And the ground forces, I felt confident, would be up to the air people in efficiency. The factories and the schools would work for them, too. And the good American food that the boys had eaten had given them the bone and lungs and recuperative power that no Nazi state system of physical education could superimpose on rickety frames.

The boys themselves, I thought, were the best proof they had something to fight for. Four officers fly in each Fortress, and every one of them at that time had to be a college man. You could look around the lounge in the evening and see 250 officers, all giving a common impression of fitness and good humor. There wasn't a raddled, vicious face in the lot. They had come from state universities and technical schools and little denominational colleges all through the country, where tuition fees were nominal or nonexistent. This brazen public defiance of the profit system had resulted in the creation of our greatest national asset. They hadn't had to spend their elementary-school days getting up competitive examinations which would admit them to secondary school, or their secondary-school days preparing competitive examinations for college. They had had time to play. Some of them were sons of rich men, a few were sons of mechanics, and most were in between, but there was no trace of class accent to distinguish one from another. There were regional accents, of course. And the standard of training in all those schools that to me had for years been just names in columns of football scores must have been pretty good, because the kids could all do their stuff as well as the few members of the group who had been to Ivy colleges.

I hadn't been with so many Americans so young in twenty years, and I thought they had an edge on my own college generation, although maybe I was less than fair in retrospect because I had been an insecure, intolerant undergraduate myself. All the boys had to do, I thought, was to look around at each other and they would understand that democracy was worth defending. The noncoms they flew with, six sergeants to a Fortress, were just as different from products of other regimes as the officers. They were all high-school men, even though in civil life they had clerked in grocery stores or driven laundry trucks. They had no idea that they were bound down in any social class, and they thought for themselves about everything they saw and did. They were good stuff.

The officers of the different ships wore no insignia to show which Fortress they belonged to, but it was easy to pick out crewmates in the lounge of the club. They were the men who usually occupied adjacent chairs, engaged in long sessions of insulting one another, and lent one another money in crap games. One of my favorites, a boy named Jones from Memphis, used to sit next to the phonograph, changing the records. The songs they liked were full of sobs: "I'll Be Around When He Is Gone," or "Someone's Rocking My Dream Boat," or "This Is the Story of a Starry Night." A psychiatrist has since told me that he considers such fare extremely depressing for men about to go out on bombing missions, but there were no suicides. I never hear those songs now without seeing the faces of the kids in the lounge, and sometimes I forget which of them are dead.

There was one Fortress pilot whom his colleagues called the Baron, who once told me that his only ambition for after the war was to sit in the grandstand at the Yankee Stadium every afternoon and watch the ball game. He was known as the Baron because once when he had been doing some drinking in the club he had said, "When we get to Germany I will be a baron if I feel like it because my family has a castle on the Rhine and I can walk in and claim it any time." His father had been an officer in the German Army in the war previous to this one, but that did not prevent the Baron from being the kind of suburban boy who shoots a good game of pool, plays semipro baseball on Sunday while he is still in college and officially an amateur, and is perennially worried about a pending charge of driving while under the influence of alcohol. When the home-town papers began to arrive at the station after the first few Fortress raids the fellows from small cities had a lot of fun reading each other their clippings. One town had had a Joe Snodgrass Day in honor of a navigator from there who had been in a raid, and it had raised a fund of $62 to buy candy and chewing gum for him, but not cigarettes because some of the subscribers objected to smoking. The Baron said to me, "In the town I come from the people think I am a bum, and I guess they would be surprised I am here at all." He had played varsity baseball at three colleges, none of them tough academically, and you could deduce that he had not been exactly a studying type from the fact that he had been thrown out of two of them. He was a good pilot, and he flew in a careless, easy-looking way. "Flying is the hardest thing in the world to learn," he once said to me, "and the easiest thing to do after you've learned it." He had met a co-ed at the third college where he had played ball, and married her. He was always showing new acquaintances a picture of his wife, tall and dark, and she was very pretty. The Baron had a hard time emotionally in England. He didn't like anything he had heard about Hitler, but it used to make him angry when Englishmen referred to Germans as Huns. "My old man is all right," he used to say.

Quite a while afterward I met a bomber crew from that group in Africa, and they told me they thought the Baron had been killed over Lorient. "At least, when we last saw that ship it was blazing and only five hundred feet off the ground, and nobody had bailed out," the bombardier said. "It wasn't the Baron's regular crew. There was something the matter with a supercharger in his own ship that morning, and the pilot of the ship he was lost in had a heavy cold and the co-pilot was green, so the Baron volunteered to fly them. That was a raid when we had to come down lower than usual to get through cloud over the target. We don't know whether flak or fighters got the Baron's ship, but just as it made the turn after bombing, smoke and flames began pouring out of it and it began losing altitude. They could have bailed out all right, but they were heading into a group of German fighters, so they kept the guns going and they blew two 109's to bits on the way down. They were too goddam busy to jump."

I used to sometimes try to get fliers talking about what they wanted after the war, but most of them had ambitions rather like the Baron's. One fellow wanted to stay on his honeymoon until all his bonus money ran out, another wanted to play golf all day and poker all night every night and drink whisky constantly, and a lot of them wanted to stay in the Air Corps or get jobs in commercial aviation. They didn't have very much to say about the future of the world, if they thought about it. They weren't vindictive, either. They liked to hear me talk about my Polish friends. "I guess those boys are really bloodthirsty," they would say with objective astonishment. "It's better for us not to get mad," one of them said to me. "The type of precision bombing we do you've got enough to do without being angry."

President Roosevelt, one of the most remarkable personalities of modern times, is seen here in several guises: first, through two of his aides, Harry Hopkins and former Vice-President Henry A. Wallace, each in his own way a projection of the President's mind. Mr. Wallace is, of course, considered by many to be the only true successor of Mr. Roosevelt as leader of the New Deal, and surely represents, with Mr. Hopkins, one extreme of the thought of Mr. Roosevelt, who notoriously assumed a variety of viewpoints before making up his mind.

William Allen White reviews the whole history of the Roosevelt administration from the standpoint of an enlightened, independent conservative, who had complained in 1926: "We have just got to grind along and develop a leader and it is a long, slow task calling for all our patience. How long. Oh Lord, how long! What a joy it would be to get out and raise the flaming banner of righteousness." Later, he was to comment dourly: "Well, six years brought the man! And when he came, I some way did not 'get out and raise the flaming banner of righteousness.'" Mr. Lerner's review of the President as a war leader is less dispassionate than Mr. White's survey, but gives a vivid impression of the President's Protean quality. And the celebrated Teamsters Speech, rather than some weightier address, has been chosen as showing Mr. Roosevelt in full exercise of his powers as a showman and politician.

The extraordinary spectacle of Washington in wartime is recreated in Jonathan Daniels's "Thursday Afternoon"—that Thursday afternoon of which everyone can remember the smallest detail: how and where he heard the news and what he and everyone else thought and said.

GEOFFREY T. HELLMAN

House Guest: Harry Hopkins

HARRY L. HOPKINS, special adviser and assistant to the President, chairman of the Munitions Assignments Board, and one of the seven members of the War Mobilization Committee, is fifty-two, Iowa-born, sympathetic toward the poor and tolerant of the rich, and a bettor on horses, cards, and the time of day; the survivor of two serious abdominal operations and the recipient of a weekly liver-extract inoculation; a trustee of the First Methodist Church of Grinnell, Iowa; the refuser of a number of honorary college degrees; talkative, candid, informal, and garterless; the possessor of a sallow, heavily lined, irregular face animated by intent, suspicious eyes; the public disburser of several billion dollars annually and the private accumulator of no capital whatever; an ex-Secretary of Commerce whose tenure of office was largely spent sick in bed; introverted, sociable, emotional, pleasure-loving, and hard-working; whimsical, blunt, a tease, a devotee of the telephone, impatient of detail, and a man who has enjoyed the benefits of psychoanalysis; next to Roosevelt, the country's first really influential appreciator of the importance of American friendship with Soviet Russia; an early champion of a powerful American air force; a lover and competent purveyor of wit and anecdote; an amateur of fungus who has a clear idea of the difference between mushrooms and toadstools; sardonic, thoughtful, intuitive, resourceful, and political-minded; a master of the knack of making other people feel important, a man who is better in an emergency than in a non-emergency, a worshipper of Franklin Roosevelt and Winston Churchill; contemptuous of protocol, especially when it involves the State Department; a reformed social worker who is now indifferent to all issues except the prosecution of the war; and, since the death of Louis Howe, the President's closest intimate.

Hopkins' detractors, many of them Roosevelt-haters to whom he is a convenient symbol, think he looks rather fishy, that his charm is gooey, and that he is a sort of left-wing Rasputin. His admirers, who were once mostly social workers but today are mostly liberal businessmen on the W. Averell Harriman-Robert A. Lovett order, are satisfied with his appearance, which they find ramshackle but boyishly attractive, and they admire him for, among other things, the effective part he has played in a war policy that is becoming increasingly fruitful and his complete loyalty to the President. Hopkins, who looks like an animated piece of Shredded Wheat, has never been sardonic with or about Mr. Roosevelt, but in the days before the war he did occasionally tease his boss. Several years ago, when he was Works Progress Administrator, he attended a meeting in the White House at which an expert on unemployment problems suggested that part of the WPA be converted into a national educational system. "You know, Harry, that's a great idea," the President said. Hopkins, who likes to sit well down on his spine and stare at fellow-conversationalists over the top of his spectacles, allowed his backbone to slide down a notch or two farther and gazed coldly at the President. "Harry, listen," said Mr. Roosevelt, waving his yellow cigarette-holder commandingly, "that would be a wonderful idea." "Well that's fine Mr. President," said Hopkins, who sometimes talks without commas, like an old-fashioned telegram. "We've been doing that for three years."

Hopkins and his third wife, the former Mrs. Louise Macy, a good-looking girl with a determined chin who used to be the Paris editor of *Harper's Bazaar,* live in two rooms—one large, one small—in the White House, facing the south lawn. The small room is Mrs. Hopkins' bedroom. The large room, which Hopkins uses as a combined bed-and-living room, served as a Presidential office until the time of Theodore Roosevelt, during whose administration the office wing of the White House was built and who was the first president to have his office outside the mansion. A plaque over the fireplace of this room reads, "In this room Abraham Lincoln signed the Emancipation Proclamation." It contains a big, archaic, four-poster bed with a green canopy, as well as a sofa, a desk, a large map of the world, several comfortable chairs, and one moderately comfortable chair with a metal tag on its back which is inscribed, "Secretary of Commerce, December 24, 1938—September 18, 1940." It is customary for Presidents to present outgoing Cabinet members with their Cabinet chairs and to replace the chairs at their own expense, so Hopkins tells friends that it cost Mr. Roosevelt seventy-four dollars to fire him. The room does not contain a closet, and Hopkins keeps his suits in a wardrobe which stands, not too accessibly, behind his desk. In the wardrobe, too, is a gray felt Scott & Co. $7\frac{1}{8}$-size hat, initialled "W.S.C.," which Churchill pressed upon him one chilly summer day in 1941 when he arrived hatless at Chequers, the Prime Minister's country place outside London.

The Hopkinses, who were married in July last year, live in the White House at the insistence and pleasure of the President, whose bedroom is on the same floor, and they have done little to give their home an air of permanency. Mrs. Hopkins has brought down from New York her colored maid, a girl who has already reconciled herself to the White House rule that no laundry may be carried uncovered through the halls, but the wife of the Presidential adviser has left a good deal of her modern furniture in storage in Manhattan and she has not bothered to do any interior decorating. Practically the only possessions the Hopkinses have in their suite are his books, a Capehart radio-phonograph, and a few dozen wedding presents—glassware, silver, cocktail shakers, and so on—which stand on top of the bookcases in the big room. (The Hopkinses get setups for drinks by calling the White House pantry.) The décor of Lincoln's old office is not precisely in the *Harper's Bazaar* tradition, but Mrs. Hopkins has come to have a certain affection for it. "It has a queer atmosphere of its own," she says. The Hopkinses have ducked putting their address in the current Washington *Social Register* by appending the entry "See Dilatory Domiciles" after their names and then carefully forgetting to have themselves listed in the Dilatory Domiciles addition to the volume. The 1942-43 *Who's Who* does not mention Hopkins' office, which is in a recently built wing of the White House, and it lists as his home a house in Georgetown which he left on May 10, 1940, when he came to dinner at the White House and was asked by his host to stay on. He borrowed a pair of pajamas, sublet his house for the remainder of his lease, and never returned to it.

The Hopkinses breakfast in their rooms, and five mornings a week Mrs. Hopkins leaves the house at eight-thirty to work as a captain of nurses' aides in a Washington hospital. She gets back around four. She and her husband dine with the President, or Mrs. Roosevelt, or both, about five nights a week. Grace Tully, the President's personal secretary, is often present, too. Dinner is at seven-fifteen sharp, and unless guests have been invited it is informal and served either in Mr. Roosevelt's study or in the upstairs hall adjoining this study. Black-tie affairs, with guests, are held in a downstairs dining room. After dinner there is frequently a movie, either an advance showing of a Hollywood feature or an Army or Navy picture, after which Roosevelt and Hopkins may work in the President's study while Mrs. Hopkins curls up with a good book. About once a week the Hopkinses dine with friends—the Lovetts, the Robert E. Sherwoods, or the James V. Forrestals, for instance—or go out to a sea-food restaurant. Hopkins is partial to cold boiled lobster, and he does not permit the state of his health, which is on the mend but far from good, to interfere with how much he eats or with the tempo of his eating, which is lively. Unlike his wife, he does not care for intellectual guessing games; after dining with friends, he prefers bridge, poker, or gin rummy. His social behavior is unconventional. Once, turning up for dinner at the house of an old crony, he pulled out an electric razor and shaved himself before the entrance-hall mirror.

As chairman of the Munitions Assignments Board, Hopkins presides over a group of British and American generals and admirals. In accordance with the basic strategic plans made by the Combined Chiefs of Staff, this board, which meets every Wednesday, apportions munitions and other military supplies produced in the United States to the Allied forces. The board decides, for instance, how many bombers of a certain type shall be sent in a given time to China, to Russia, and so on. It works through three subcommittees—one on ground-force matters, one on air matters, one on naval matters. When the subcommittees agree, the board generally approves their decisions; when they disagree, it acts as a court of appeals and decides between them. The Combined Chiefs of Staff have the power of vetoing the Munitions Assignments Board's rulings, but Hopkins and the other board members usually consult General Marshall and the other chiefs of staff before making their decisions, so this power is seldom invoked.

Hopkins has been an articulate propagandist for all-out aid to Russia ever since the summer of 1941, when, as supervisor of the lend-lease program, he visited Moscow during the period of heavy German air raids on that city and had three long talks with Stalin. W. Averell Harriman went to Russia some weeks later and Stalin told him that he liked Hopkins' candor. A few days after the Moscow conferences, Hopkins accompanied Churchill on a battleship from England to the Atlantic Charter meeting with Roosevelt, which Hopkins arranged. "I had the Russian story for the President," he has said since. "The congressmen who passed the lend-lease bill certainly never thought of Russia, since she was not at war with Germany at the time, but then *no* specific country was mentioned in the bill. The political implications of extending lend-lease to Russia have never bothered me." On his return from the meeting, Roosevelt explained to the Army and Navy chiefs the importance of immediate aid to Russia.

Hopkins still thinks that the Russian front is the most important one. His influence in the Munitions Assignments Board has consistently reflected this belief. He is also chairman of the President's Soviet Protocol Committee, which was established early this year to assure adequate treatment of Soviet requests for the sinews of war. "I've carried that banner around town. Marshall is fine about it," he recently told a friend. Hopkins spends about a third of his working time in board activities, conferring with its members and sub-committee members seven or eight times a week, in addition to attending the Wednesday meeting. The other members of the board, who appreciate the fact that Hopkins is more often than not a spokesman for the President, listen to his suggestions with respect. "He's a civilian chairman with a three-hundred-and-sixty-degree point of view," one of them said a few weeks ago. "He approaches problems without any preconceived opinion. He will argue all around a question, and sometimes you will mistake an argument of his for a conclusion, but actually he's just boxing the compass to make up his mind." In group discussions, Hopkins, one of whose favorite expressions is "We must have a meeting of minds," employs a technique of at first needling practically everyone on hand, including the men with whom he secretly agrees, on the theory that this tends to clear the air and paves the way for the most logical decision. He then abandons his secrecy and often delivers an opinion coinciding with that of someone whom he has just severely badgered. In his old WPA days, in the late nineteen-thirties, this odd procedure gave his fellow-conferees many an anxious moment. Once, in the course of one of the first meetings of WPA officials, Hopkins brought up the question of whether women should be paid the same wages as men. With the exception of Aubrey Williams, then assistant Works Progress Administrator, everyone agreed that they should not. Williams said he thought they should. "Oh you do?" said Hopkins. "What makes you think you could get away with it?" Williams said he didn't care whether he could get away with it or not. "Do you know who disagrees with you?" said Hopkins. "The Secretary of Labor, a woman." "Pay 'em the same," said Williams doggedly. Hopkins went on to plague his assistant at some length, and Williams became rather glum. "Well fellows thank you very much," Hopkins finally said. "Aubrey's right about this and that's what we'll do." At the end of the meeting, he departed with Williams. "What's the matter with those other fellows?" he asked Williams.

"Harry punished me quite considerably," Williams has since observed reminiscently. "He's a phenomenal character, always searching for integrity in methods and always thinking of the effect of everything on the President."

All of Hopkins' activities are colored, and most of them are made possible, by the circumstance that he lives in the White House and has the President's ear as no other man has. He is the chief liaison between Roosevelt and all the Allied governments, and between Roosevelt and the other men, both civilian and military, who run the United States. Roosevelt and Hopkins think alike on an astonishing number of points; they share a concern for the average man and a preference for the society of the rich, the gay, the talented, and the wellborn; they are alike in that this concern has now very definitely taken second place in their minds to their wish to win the war as quickly as possible; they share intuitiveness, a mixture of idealism and political shrewdness, and a relish for fairly ribald anecdote and the exercise of irony, a weapon that has a sharper edge in Hopkins' hands than in the President's. Hopkins has been described as a physical extension of the President; he has a dressing-gown run of Roosevelt's floor in the White House and his host invites him at any time of the day or night to supply conversational digests of important reports on the war and to relay information and messages from the men with whom he must keep in touch, from General Marshall to Donald Nelson. The President has confidence in Hopkins' opinions, in his summarizing of the opinions of others, and in his discretion. "He knows I keep my mouth shut," Hopkins says. Hopkins doesn't mind keeping his mouth shut, but he sometimes is depressed by the thought that some of the history of this period will probably never be known to the public, and in private conversation he has remarked upon the importance of some of Roosevelt's remarks and casual mots, without, however, saying explicitly what they were.

On a typical day, Hopkins will be in constant direct or telephonic contact with Roosevelt, Hull, Marshall, Nelson, James F. Byrnes, Robert Sherwood, General H. H. Arnold, Stimson, Knox, J. Edgar Hoover, and Lord Halifax. Among the matters which he has taken up with the President, after consulting with the authorities involved, are how big the armed forces should be, the percentage of Negroes they should include, how big a part participation in combat should have in military promotions, and problems of handling rationing, strikes, and censorship. If, as has happened, General Marshall is in a hurry to get the President's signature on an order and Mr. Roosevelt is in a particularly busy meeting, Hopkins is the man, and the only man, who can walk into the meeting and push the paper under the President's nose. "I make myself available to people who've got something to say about the war," Hopkins once said. "It takes a lot of time—some of it wasted. I do a lot of errands, but they're good errands."

The precise nature of many of Hopkins' activities and the precise extent of his influence on the President are matters which Hopkins has done little to clear up. "I deal a lot with foreign governments like Russia, China, England, and Canada on things concerned with warfare," he says to people who ask him what he does. "The President can't see all these people or read all these things, so there are many things that I do that relate to these things. I try to lighten the President's terrific burden." At the time Hopkins was appointed Secretary of Commerce, he was asked by a Senate investigating committee what his reaction would be if the President laid down a policy in which he did not concur. He replied, "I'm a member of a team. I may try to influence a policy, but once the policy is set I'm in there fighting for it five minutes later."

Mr. Roosevelt's unique accessibility to his house guest has naturally excited a certain amount of envy, and Hopkins, who has no use for roundabout methods, has made no great effort to dissipate it. Depending on his mood, he is either indifferent to or touchy about hostile newspaper publicity. "I've reached a point in life where nothing can hurt me," he sometimes says. Occasionally, though, he tells friends that the newspapers are crucifying him. He and his wife have denied the rumor, spread by the Washington *Times-Herald* and the Chicago *Tribune,* that Lord Beaverbrook gave Mrs. Hopkins a $500,000 emerald necklace, presumably because of Hopkins' lend-lease favors to England. "Cissie Patterson is on my neck," Hopkins once said sadly, discussing this canard. He is bitterer about the insinuations certain anti-Roosevelt papers have made that he does not always pay his own way. "By God, I took a tour at the Naval Hospital and it was out of my own pocket," he said lately, discussing an illness which had been described by a part of the nation's press as a drain on the taxpayers' money. "These bastards say I didn't pay for it, but I paid my own way there." Sometimes, however, Hopkins treats with a lighter touch reports that he receives unusual concessions of one sort and another. One of these credited him with a complimentary suite at the Statler Hotel in Washington. On a Saturday night shortly afterward, Hopkins, along with the Sherwoods and the Sam Rosenmans, was enjoying a few drinks in the Statler barroom. Midnight, Washington's deadline for public drinking on Saturdays, approached while the party was still convivial. "Well, we'll go to one of my seventy rooms here and finish," said Hopkins, with a rueful smile.

Hopkins gets ten thousand dollars a year as special adviser to the President, and he picks up extra spending money by writing occasional articles —about rationing, Russia, and so on—for the *American Magazine.* Stephen Early, the White House press secretary, and John Hertz, the banker and owner of Count Fleet, sometimes give him tips, which he takes, on horse races, and he thinks he makes a little money out of this hobby. He used to go to the races quite a bit, but he hasn't gone once since the United States entered the war. "The war is a damn personal thing to me and while the war is on I take my relaxation privately, not publicly," he says. John Hertz is an old friend of his, and Hopkins regrets never having seen Count Fleet run.

Hopkins was a social worker, mostly in New York, for nearly twenty-five years before he went to Washington as Works Progress Administrator, and he is comparatively temperate in his reaction to friends and associates who reprove him for temporarily neglecting the sort of social-betterment ideas that used to possess him. Mrs. Roosevelt, whose regard for Hopkins is thought by many students of the New Deal to antedate her husband's affection for him, is among those who mourn the passing, or at least the eclipse, of Hopkins the social worker. "Mrs. Roosevelt thinks I've confined myself too much to the war and that I don't watch the social program any more," Hopkins told a friend the other day. "There may be something to it. I don't know. I just confess that my interests have for the time being moved exclusively to winning the war."

One man to whom the disappearance of Hopkins the social worker was an agreeable surprise is Winston Churchill. Hopkins, who has taken four trips to England on Roosevelt's behalf, made the first early in 1941, while England was standing up to the Axis single-handed. France had fallen, the German-Soviet pact was still in effect, the prospect of our participation in the war was doubtful, and Churchill was eager to court his visitor, and through him the President and the American people. He arranged a dinner at the country home of Ronald Tree, secretary to the British Ministry of Information, at which Hopkins was to be guest of honor and which he himself and two or three Cabinet ministers would attend. In the library, after dinner, the Prime Minister passed around some first-class cigars and embarked on his theme for the evening, one which he had selected after devoting considerable thought to the expressed objectives of the New Deal and to the humanitarian doings of his American listener. England was really fighting for the Forgotten Man, he said in substance, and then launched into a social-service talk of impressive scope, which tied the war up with any number of freedoms. He wound up after about half an hour. Nobody spoke for a moment after he had finished; everyone else was waiting uneasily for the reaction of President Roosevelt's representative, who had slumped farther and farther down on his spine. "Well, Mr. Prime Minister," Hopkins finally said, "neither the President nor myself gives a damn about what you've been saying. All we're interested in in Washington is how we can beat that son of a bitch in Berlin."

Churchill smiled the smile of a relieved grandson of the seventh Duke of Marlborough and pulled out a fresh cigar. The rest of the evening was devoted to thoroughly down-to-earth conversation. Hopkins, whose father ran a harness shop in Iowa, has visited Churchill three times since, and he has seen a great deal of him on the Prime Minister's three stays in the White House, where Churchill had the bedroom directly across the hall from the Hopkins apartment. Except for the President, Hopkins admires the Prime Minister more than anyone else in the world.

Harry Hopkins, special assistant and adviser to the President, chairman of the Munitions Assignments Board, and for more than three years a guest in the White House, was born in Sioux City, Iowa, in 1890. His father, the late David A. Hopkins, was a harness dealer who moved to Nebraska from Sioux City in 1892 and nine years later, when Harry was eleven, settled in Grinnell, Iowa, where he gradually switched over from selling harnesses to running the town's only newspaper-and-magazine store. He also kept candy on hand and continued to handle the leather goods left over from his harness shop. A tall, portly man, he tended counter in his shirtsleeves and sold cigarettes without a license. Grinnell was, and is, a rather innocent town, with a strong Methodist flavor, and the senior Hopkins, a salty, erratic, irreligious, outspoken, quarrelsome character with so compelling a passion for bowling that he eventually left town to take over the bowling-alley concession in a hotel in Spokane, Washington, was known as Dad Hopkins and was generally regarded as the town's most picturesque ornament. Harry's mother, who was born in Ontario, was a zealous churchgoer, a onetime president of the Methodist Home Missionary Society of Iowa, conventional, reliable, and the opposite of her husband in nearly every particular. She brought up her five children (a sixth died in childhood) to attend church frequently, to ignore their comparative poverty, to eschew liquor, and to work hard. In his early teens Harry beat carpets, scrubbed floors, and milked cows; summers he earned money by working on nearby farms. He also spent a good deal of time swapping funny stories with his father, a man who believed in letting carpets alone. Hopkins is a thoughtful man who likes to ponder his personality and antecedents. "What makes a fellow tick?" he once inquired of an acquaintance, and, without pausing for a reply, went on to analyze which traits he had inherited from which parent. The analysis got nowhere. Old Grinnell friends have figured out that he owes his ability to take a position and stand by it to his mother, and his geniality and wit to his father. Hopkins has one sister, Mrs. Frank L. Aimé, a social worker who lives in Riverdale. One of his brothers died a few years ago; the two others are a Tacoma, Washington, physician and a Portland, Oregon, businessman.

Hopkins went to Grinnell College, a coëducational institution, where he was a successful campus politician and athlete. During the summer vacation after his freshman year, his mother took him to New York for a few days. Hopkins was pleasurably stimulated by the metropolis, and after returning home he kept thinking about the excitements of the East. In 1912, the year he was graduated from college, he was delighted when one of his professors, who was connected with Christodora House, a Manhattan settlement house, had him appointed head of a summer camp for boys which this organization ran near Bound Brook, New Jersey. He has since explained that he became a social worker in order to get to New York. He stopped off at Chicago en route; the Republican Presidential convention was being held there, and he got into it (by posing as Elihu Root's secretary) just in time to hear Theodore Roosevelt, who was bolting to the Progressive Party, make a speech saying that thieves were running the Republican Party. He went on to Baltimore, where he heard William Jennings Bryan denounce Tammany. He then proceeded to Bound Brook, where he surveyed his duties and surroundings with astonishment. "I'd never seen a Jewish boy before in my life," he once said. "Also, you'd go on hikes and picnics, plan baseball games, and struggle to discipline the boys," he went on. "I'd never disciplined anyone and they made a sucker out of me." In his early youth, Hopkins was too busy playing basketball and squiring girls to acquaint himself with the doctrine of flux as reflected in the works of Horatio Alger and Heraclitus, so his own more recent activities have been a source of surprise to himself. His intimates have come to include such sophisticates as the Herbert Bayard Swopes, Bernard Baruch, Quentin Reynolds, the John Hay Whitneys, and the W. Averell Harrimans, and "There's always a civilized way to do things" has become one of his favorite expressions, but he still finds it difficult to realize that he sleeps in the room in which Lincoln signed the Emancipation Proclamation, that he has both lunched and dined with the King of England in a single day, that his relationship with Mr. Roosevelt is almost that of an alter ego, and that he is, by virtue of this relationship, the second most influential man in the country and one of the dozen or so most influential men in the world.

Hopkins is a man of considerable humility and simplicity, and his wonder at his career is no less today than it was long before his doings had achieved any great degree of importance. In the fall following his New Jersey summer's amazement, he was again amazed when he became a case worker at Christodora House. He lived at the settlement, on Avenue B, and started mixing with a class of people he had never encountered in Grinnell, where actual privation was rare. "I really got exposed to New York," he told a friend once. "I climbed tenement stairs, listened to the talk of Morris Hillquit and William English Walling, went to Cooper Union meetings, and really got exposed to the whole business of how the working class lived and to their poverty and joviality. Many's the bottle fight I saw in those days. Real gangsters would walk into the settlement dances—Lefty Louie and others—just to bedevil us, and you'd try to throw them out. You know. Really tough. That's when I found out there was such a thing as a gangster. I got a dose of it, and not by books."

After a couple of years of watching bottle fights and ushering gangsters off the dance floor, Hopkins, who had meanwhile married a fellow-Christodora worker, Miss Ethel Gross, and set up housekeeping in a rented house in Yonkers, became a district supervisor in the Family Welfare Department of the Association for Improving the Condition of the Poor. He supplemented the study of this organization's case workers' reports by visits to the families involved, and he became even more surprised at the poverty and joviality he encountered. In 1915 he left the Association to become executive secretary of the New York City Board of Child Welfare, which had been established partly as the result of an economic survey of widows and their children which Hopkins himself had helped to make for the Association. This survey took him all over Manhattan, drawing out charwomen in tenement houses, and once again he found a minimum of gloom. Hopkins is an easygoing, wisecracking, sympathetic, conversational individual with a liking for nearly everyone who isn't a stuffed shirt, and a good many old-time social workers around town suspect that during his Association days a number of ordinarily truculent paupers became jovial through pure contagion. He later acquired a knack of cheering up the rich as well as the poor, and today he prides himself on his ability to get along with all kinds of people. "Now, you take this business of Louie," he said a few months after his marriage last summer to his third wife, the former Mrs. Louise Macy, a Pasadena girl who was once the Paris editor of *Harper's Bazaar* and is accustomed to moving in rather urbane circles. "Three-fourths of her friends I think are fine." Mrs. Hopkins appreciates the successful effort her husband has made to get along with people like Mrs. Carmel Snow, the editor of *Harper's Bazaar,* a magazine which does not reflect the problems of charwomen and touches only lightly on the problems of Presidents, and she in turn has adjusted herself to Hopkins' friends, who run more to prime ministers, Cabinet members, ambassadors, co-ordinators, and four-star generals.

Hopkins' career as a social worker was advanced rather than interrupted by the first World War, during which, after being rejected because of poor eyesight when he tried to enlist in the Army, he served as manager of the Southern Division of the Red Cross in New Orleans, dealing largely with the economic problems of servicemen's families. After the war he returned to the Association for Improving the Condition of the Poor as assistant director. In 1924 he became director of the New York Tuberculosis Association, and under him it soon transcended its name. It amalgamated under its control a number of other public-health organizations, among them the New York Heart Association and various charity dental and social-hygiene associations, changed its name to the New York Tuberculosis and Health Association, and began to operate on a really large scale, selling more Christmas seals than ever before. By this time, Hopkins, although far from reconciled to the condition of the poor, was no longer surprised by it, but he soon began to be astonished by the problems of the sick and his commanding position amid these problems. His wonder at the influential niche which he occupied was shared by others, notably the medical men with whom he came in constant contact. Hopkins is a person of quick perception and retentive memory, one who learns more from conversation than from books, and he didn't bother to bone up on medical matters to any appreciable extent. Sitting on boards largely populated by doctors, he occasionally displayed a grasp of science which they considered loose or was guilty of medical gaffes that would make even an interne shudder. Accompanied by celebrated physicians on money-raising expeditions, he would sometimes intimate to men of means, in an offhand but enthusiastic way, that if such-and-such a sum were forthcoming for research, a cure for heart disease would be discovered within five years. His medical colleagues would enter pained demurrers. Many of them still feel that Hopkins would undoubtedly be the last man on a submarine to be invited to perform an emergency appendectomy, but they appreciate his talent for raising money and for efficient organizational expansion. According to Dr. Alfred Cohn, a member of the board of directors of the Tuberculosis Association and a heart specialist on the staff of the Rockefeller Institute, Hopkins ran the Association with uncommon skill. "He is a man of good will with a sense of responsibility," Dr. Cohn has said. "He created an atmosphere in which other men of good will could work. He thought of himself simply as a catalyzer."

Hopkins began to develop serious emotional problems in his latter Association days; in 1930 he had himself psychoanalyzed, and the stenographers in his office followed his progress, to which he never alluded explicitly, with interest. "Don't take marriage too seriously," Hopkins, fresh from a treatment, would advise them. "Give your husband plenty of rope." Hopkins and his first wife were divorced that same year, and a few months later he married Barbara Duncan, a girl employed by the Tuberculosis Association. The first Mrs. Hopkins, who has not remarried, is now an employee of the Red Cross in Rhode Island; she and Hopkins had three sons, David, Robert, and Stephen, who are in the Navy, the Army, and the Marines respectively.

The next big sociological surprise in Hopkins' life was the late Jesse Isidor Straus, who, as chairman of the New York State Temporary Emergency Relief Administration, in 1931 arranged for Hopkins to become a statewide catalyzer by appointing him the executive director of that organization. Mr. Straus, who was president of Macy's and later served as ambassador to France, was neither poor nor particularly jovial; he liked the people around him to know exactly what they were talking about, he constituted Hopkins' first intimate contact with an urbanely autocratic man of affairs, and for some weeks he baffled Hopkins. "I thought: by God, this is a new kind of man I've met in my life," Hopkins later remarked. "If you can't get along with him it's your own fault. Soon we got on famously." The two men got along so well that a year later, when Straus retired from the chairmanship of the TERA, he recommended Hopkins to Governor Roosevelt as his successor. Roosevelt accepted the suggestion. Earlier, Straus had invited Hopkins to come to work at Macy's as a sort of idea man. Hopkins, whose salary as a social worker was hovering around $10,000, was in the habit of talking about going into business in order to make money, but he never really meant it, and he declined Straus's offer.

Hopkins' Washington career dates from 1933, when Roosevelt made him head of the Federal Emergency Relief Administration. By 1934, four million families were on relief and the FERA was distributing around $150,000,000 a month to them. Hopkins, who upon arriving in Washington had said to a friend, "Well, I'm not going to last six months here, so I'll do as I please," developed a magisterial impatience with persons who referred to federal aid as coddling or vote-fishing. "I have a real quarrel with people who say such things while seated at a comfortable dinner table drinking cocktails," he remarked. In 1935, when he became Works Progress Administrator, he said, in a radio speech dealing, among other things, with chambers of commerce, "They sit in pompous conclaves now and then and bring forth such ideas as giving the needy unemployed a ham sandwich and letting it go at that. I believe the days of letting people live in misery, of being rock-bottom destitute, of children being hungry, or of moralizing about rugged individualism in the light of modern facts—I believe those days are over in America." During his three years as head of the WPA, Hopkins got $10,000 a year and supervised the distribution of over ten billion dollars for public works. For several years he had favored work relief rather than the dole as a solution of the national unemployment problem, and he plunged happily into the initiation and direction of projects involving everything from road building to post-office murals.

Louis Howe, Roosevelt's confidential secretary, died in 1936, and not long after this Hopkins became the preferred intimate and, after the fall of James A. Farley from favor, the chief political adviser of the President. He began to acquire enemies on a coast-to-coast scale, and in the fall of 1938

Arthur Krock, the major Washington correspondent of the New York *Times* and spokesman for a good many people who suspected that Hopkins' stewardship of federal-aid funds was not altogether divorced from political considerations, credited Hopkins, in his column, with the remark "We will spend and spend, tax and tax, elect and elect." In a letter to the *Times* Hopkins denied having said this, and he also denied it in the course of a Senate investigation which preceded the ratification of his appointment as Secretary of Commerce, late in 1938. According to Krock, whose source was an article by Frank Kent in the Baltimore *Sun,* Hopkins made the statement at a race track in the presence of at least two prominent New Yorkers. Krock was not willing to give the names of these men to the Senate committee. H. L. Mencken, a less reticent man, has included the remark, under "Electioneering," in his "New Dictionary of Quotations":

"We will spend and spend, and tax and tax, and elect and elect."
Ascribed to Harry L. Hopkins: To Max Gordon at the Empire racetrack, Yonkers, N. Y., Aug., 1938.

Mr. Mencken has followed this up, under "Electricity," with:

"I'll put a girdle round the earth
In forty minutes."
Shakespeare: A Midsummer Night's Dream, II, c. 1596.

Hopkins is flattered by the juxtaposition, but he still doesn't think he ought to be in the book.

Hopkins is a man of indifferent health, and the fortitude with which he has survived periods of intense suffering has probably been a factor in the growth of the President's affection for him. Hopkin's first siege of physical ailment began in his WPA days. He has a weak stomach, and on airplane trips of inspection around the country he often made speeches and played poker with local dignitaries while in a condition so shaky that it would have discouraged most men from addressing even their best friends or from playing solitaire. His second wife died in the fall of 1937, after a long illness, and a couple of months later Hopkins went to the Mayo Brothers' Clinic for an ulcer operation. He has been in and out of the Mayo Clinic and other hospitals a half-dozen times since, and in 1939 he rented a farm near Grinnell with the announced intention of ending his days there, perhaps rather soon. He was being mentioned as a possible Presidential candidate, and some cynical political observers interpreted the Iowa farm, which Hopkins never actually lived on, as a strategic as well as a therapeutic measure. Hopkins thrives on emergencies, and in May, 1940, on the day Germany invaded Belgium and Holland, he rose from the sickbed he had occupied for several months and dined at the White House, where, by invitation and practically by command, he has lived ever since. Two months afterward he was well enough to take charge of the third-term "draft" at the Chicago convention. Later in the year he accompanied Roosevelt on the cruise to the Bahamas on which the idea of lend-lease was worked up, and in January, 1941, he made the first of four trips to England as Roosevelt's personal envoy to Winston Churchill.

Hopkins, who is not a hypochondriac, likes to discuss his health and to tell people that it used to be nearly impossible for him to digest anything, that half of his insides have been removed, and that he was finally cured by a series of treatments so mysterious and so widely scattered that the doctors never knew what actually cured him. "They gave me stuff they'd never given before," he says with some pride. "I took plasma transfusions and all sorts of drug injections through my arms, my ankles, and the backs of my hands. I had some kind of malnutrition. It resembled everything they'd ever heard of, from beri-beri to sprue. They don't know what cured me, they tried so many things." Occasionally, declining professional aid, Hopkins has acted as his own doctor. Several years ago, while week-ending near New York, he called a friend in Washington and told him he was dying. The friend got in touch with the President's household at Hyde Park and arrangements were made to speed medical aid to Hopkins' bedside. The friend's telephone rang again in a few minutes and Hopkins said, "I'm about eight miles out of New York. Can you get someone to bring me a *Racing Form?*" In the summer of 1939, when the King and Queen of England were here, Hopkins, then Secretary of Commerce, attended a garden party in their honor at the British Embassy. Half an hour after he had arrived, he sneaked off behind some bushes, where an inquisitive elderly lady, spotting him through the foliage, found him sitting on the ground with his shoes off. "I'm here because my feet hurt," Hopkins explained. Elderly ladies generally like Hopkins; he got on well with the President's mother, the late Mrs. James Roosevelt, and he was one of the few political visitors to Hyde Park to whom the senior Mrs. Roosevelt's frequent query, "Who are all these queer people, Franklin?," did not apply.

The war has acted as a tonic to Hopkins, but it has also made him less carefree. He has an explosive, penetrating laugh, but it has been heard rather infrequently since December 7, 1941. That day he was lunching alone with the President in the White House study when Secretary of the Navy Knox telephoned the news. His last marriage has also brightened up his life. He met his bride in March, 1942, when, in response to a letter from Mrs. Lawrence Lowman, a former *Harper's Bazaar* editor, asking whether he could help a friend of hers, Louise Macy, get a job in Washington, he asked Mrs. Macy to meet him at the St. Regis one morning. After half an hour's talk, he said he would see what he could do. He went to England shortly afterward, and on his return, in April, invited Mrs. Macy to dinner in New York. He offered her a job in the OPA, but she was in the middle of a nurse's-aide course by this time and shook her head. Hopkins has always been susceptible to good-looking, gay, companionable women, of which Mrs. Macy is one, and he resolved to see her again. During the next two months he saw her eight or nine times; she spent one weekend at the White House and two at Hyde Park, at Mrs. Roosevelt's invitation.

On June 22nd Hopkins took Mrs. Macy to a Russian War Relief rally at Madison Square Garden, where, sharing the speakers' platform with Ambassador Litvinov, he paid tribute to the fighting spirit of Russia, which he had visited the year before. After the rally, Hopkins took Mrs. Macy to El Morocco, where they talked until it was time for him to catch the 12:50 train to Washington. "I had never dreamed of getting married again," Hopkins now says. "I got to my room the next morning and thought: you're in love with her, you talked like a sixteen-year-old last night. Churchill was here and I asked him to dine with the nicest girl he'd ever seen. I telephoned Louie to come down. I wanted to get it settled before dinner." Hopkins proposed to Mrs. Macy, who did not shake her head this time, in the Harrimans' suite at the Mayflower, where she had gone to change for dinner. "Marie Harriman came in just as I was going to kiss her," Hopkins later complained to a friend. Churchill and the engaged couple drove to the British Embassy for dinner, and the Prime Minister was the first person to be told of their plans. Later in the evening, Hopkins walked into the President's study, advised his boss to hang on to his chair, and said that he was going to be married. Mr. Roosevelt laughed and said he bet he knew who the girl was. When his guess was confirmed, he said, "That's wonderful!," and insisted that the Hopkinses should live at the White House. "It was all done in good company," Hopkins says, recalling the evening's events. Hopkins went to England two weeks later, and on his return, in late July, he and his fiancée were married in the President's study.

By his second marriage, Hopkins has an eleven-year-old daughter, Diana, a bright and fanciful child whom Mrs. Roosevelt invited to live at the White House not long after the death of her mother, in 1937, when Hopkins was in the Mayo Clinic. Diana later returned to her father, who had rented a house in Georgetown, but she went back to the White House with him in 1940, and Mrs. Roosevelt has continued to take a motherly interest in her. Diana's friends include Winston Churchill, but he is not often here, and the President's wife used to worry whether the little girl's rather solitary life at the White House was a good thing for her. She once communicated her apprehension rather forcibly to Hopkins, a loving but busy father. "That's totally unimportant. The only important thing is the war," said Hopkins, who likes to use this dodge when anything of a purely civilian nature confronts him. "Harry, it's *not*," said Mrs. Roosevelt. Mrs. Roosevelt has worried a good deal less about Diana since Hopkins' third marriage. Diana has a room on the floor above the Hopkins apartment, and Mrs. Hopkins, who is her husband's junior by fifteen years, is an affectionate and thoughtful stepmother, whom Diana finds highly sympathetic. She has given Hopkins domestic companionship without interfering with his friendship with the President, and Hopkins, who does not expect to stay on at the White House when Roosevelt leaves, looks forward someday to setting up a home with her and Diana in New York. He is not sure what he will do when that day comes—he would rather like to edit a magazine on public affairs—but he is reasonably sure that he will live in New York. "I've liked New York since the first day I saw it," he said a few evenings ago, relaxing with friends at a non-White House dinner. "It's a wonderful place to live. You mind your own business, see the people you want, go to the theatre at the last moment, hear some music. I love it. None of this commuting life. I want no part of that. I want to live right in Manhattan. I think Sundays in New York are the tops. I like *every*thing about that town, from its smells to the cops, from its parks to—" Hopkins waved his hands vaguely, at a loss for further encomiums.

Although the President's special adviser and chairman of the Munitions Assignments Board awaits, with the gusto of an O. Henry, the day when he can exchange conversations about bombers, rationing, and military strategy for the simple and complicated pleasures of truly urban life, he has not forgotten the sharp and far from festive impression which Manhattan made on him when he came to it, fresh from Iowa, thirty years ago. "I thought the economic system which bred such poverty was terrible and I think so now," he recently told a friend. "The poor are not poor because they're bad or lazy. Anyway, I don't see why, because a man is lazy, his wife and children shouldn't eat. A man drinks, he is a drunkard. Well, what are you going to do with his wife and children? I believe people are poor in the main because we don't know how to distribute the wealth properly. I've got away from the notions I once had about a socialist state. I think it can be done under a capitalist economy. WPA showed that. Twenty-five million got their income under that. I think that after this war, if you run up a debt of two hundred billion dollars, the country can stand it. It's resilient. Now we spend around seven billion a month on the war. We certainly can spend a few billion a year after the war. We must get the right relationship between government and private enterprise. The government is in this thing and in it for good."

HENRY A. WALLACE

Broadcast to the Little Businessmen of the Nation

WHEN WE THINK of America we think of a fortunate country where a little man can get ahead through his own efforts. That is what Thomas Jefferson was talking about when he used the words "Life, Liberty, and the Pursuit of Happiness." Jefferson laid great emphasis upon agriculture and feared the day when people would leave farms and crowd together in great cities. We know now that special precautions must be taken if the growth of cities is not to produce the dire results Jefferson feared. The little man whose strength is the vitality of the nation must be preserved. When this war has been won we want every man in America who has ambition and a willingness to work hard to have the opportunity to prove in a market free from unfair restraints that he has something to add to the productivity and happiness of this nation.

Everyone has been able to contribute something during this war. On the Pacific Coast last month I visited several airplane plants where nearly half of the workers were women, and where many of the men workers would not have been allowed to work three years ago because of physical handicaps. Nevertheless these women and the so-called rejects are turning out bombers in one-half the man hours that so-called superior labor used three years ago. Truly "the stone which the builders rejected has become the chief corner-stone." I am mentioning this great accomplishment because I am firmly convinced that small business depends for its prosperity very largely on full employment and an expanding economy. Unless business, labor and government plan together for full use of man power, resources, and skills, small businessmen will be ruined by the tens of thousands.

Reprinted from *Democracy Reborn* by Henry A. Wallace, Reynal & Hitchcock, Inc., N. Y.

The people of the United States are united in their determination to win this war. American industry, American business, and American agriculture can look forward to a bright future if the markets of peace are expanded to take the place of the markets of war. We cannot have free enterprise unless the world is at peace.

We must maintain the peace. The Teheran Conference has laid the ground work. All peace loving nations will be given an opportunity to co-operate in rebuilding the shattered world and perfecting a permanent organization for peace.

I believe in free enterprise. Free enterprise means free and open opportunities for all capitalists, workers, industrialists and traders—to produce the goods and services which are the only true basis of national wealth and well-being. Free enterprise means that each and every industry is open to new capital and new firms—that all firms have free access to raw materials, to labor, to technologies—that producers have free access to the markets in which they sell—that all individuals, in accordance with their several abilities and irrespective of color, race, and creed, have equal opportunities to work at their chosen jobs.

Free enterprise is not privileged enterprise. Monopolists define free enterprise falsely as freedom from government interference for monopolies. Free enterprise really means freedom for everyone and not ruthless domination by a few. Free enterprise does not mean freedom for cartels to plot against the national interest. Free enterprise does not mean freedom for monopolies to exploit consumers while denying jobs to workers.

Farmers more than any other class of our people love to produce to the limit. Therefore, they are gravely concerned when big industrialists reduce the foreign market for farm products by asking the Congress to raise tariffs on industrial products while they reduce the domestic market for farm products by plowing workers out on the streets. The farmer wants, and has always wanted, an abundance of farm and industrial products. But it is suicide for him to stand for abundance all by himself. He tried that after the last war and especially in 1930, 1931 and 1932. At that time industry cut its production in half and reduced prices very little. The farmer did the reverse. He cut his prices in two but reduced his production very little. All the farmer got out of trying to run an abundance show all by himself was bankruptcy. But he still believes in abundance and he wants full markets, provided by a reasonable tariff policy and full employment at good wages. Full employment, full production, good wages and reasonable prices are the vital essentials of prosperity for the farmer, the worker and the small businessman.

The phenomenal success of American industry in producing for war has demonstrated convincingly that we can produce a national income of from 150 to 200 billion dollars in the early postwar years, and that that income can be progressively enlarged if we preserve a free and dynamic economy. Full use of our resources in all-out production for peace can create a level of well being for the common man such as has heretofore been available only to a privileged minority. The common man knows this. He will never again accept an economic organization which falls short of this goal.

In our great wartime production effort the strategy has been determined by the needs of the armed forces and only the execution of the tactics has been left to the separate business units. Nevertheless, I am confident that equally amazing goals can be achieved in peacetime by free, private enterprise, if our business and labor leaders have sufficient faith in free enterprise to give their unqualified support to the full use of all our resources, to the measures necessary to enable free enterprise to serve the public interest.

Business can discharge its public responsibilities and preserve itself only by maintaining conditions of *genuine* free enterprise. The price of survival and progress is the whole-hearted acceptance of healthy competition—competition in price as well as in quality and service. Let us understand fully the implications of free enterprise, the duties which it imposes and the opportunities which it opens:

It is a fundamental of free enterprise that no individual or group shall control the market, with power to exclude new investment, new enterprises, new methods, or workers. So far as small businesses are concerned, the mere absence of local capital markets is a restraint on their ability to grow and expand. The present high concentration of investment banking in New York City is in itself incompatible with free enterprise, for only the large national corporations have access on reasonable terms to that capital market.

Restrictive agreements limiting capacity, curtailing output, fixing prices, assigning markets—all of these manifestations of the cartel at home or abroad must be forever abolished.

The basic technologies of modern industry must be restored to, and remain a part of the public domain. This is not an attack on the patent system; it is a necessary measure to make the patent system conform to its constitutional purpose—to promote the progress of science and the useful arts. It must become impossible to use patents to monopolize entire industries. The solution is simple—all patents should be subject to open licensing at a reasonable fee—one which affords a reasonable return to the inventor and promotes the wider and wider use of the patent. And no license should be permitted to stipulate how much the licensee shall produce, what he shall charge, or where he shall sell.

The government's tax policies have an important influence on business activity. In a peace-time economy, the tax program should have a double objective—to bring in the necessary revenue and to encourage the production of the largest possible national income. Taxes which impair the ability of consumers to purchase the products of agriculture and industry, or which discourage the investment of venture capital in new undertakings, must be avoided in our drive for all-out production. The tax program can and should be framed with attention to the larger objectives of the economy—full use of all our resources.

A public works program of all units of government should be planned far in advance, carried to the point of preparing blueprints and contracts, and then all postponable projects should be held in abeyance until the construction activity is needed to balance a prospective decline in business activity. Likewise, the government should seize the opportunity afforded by periods of business prosperity to accelerate its program of debt retirement, and thereby improve its credit position and help control the credit inflation which might otherwise lead to an early recession. Government fiscal policies can go far to reduce, and to compensate for, fluctuations in business activity.

Above all it is necessary for our leaders in industry, agriculture, and trade to understand the responsibilities of both business and government in assuring continuing full employment of all resources. Business policies must be framed with this long-run objective in view. Forward looking businessmen will welcome the co-operation of government in maintaining full employment, without sabotaging the national economy by treating such government activities as attacks upon free enterprise.

In recent speeches I have dealt with the necessity for developing balanced regional economics in the South and the West, as part of a full-production national economy. The per capita income in the South and West must be raised to the point where adequate markets will exist for the output of farm and factory. All obstacles to such regional developments should be removed.

In the building of our postwar national economy, particular attention must be given to the opportunities for small business enterprises. Small business provides an outlet for new ideas and products, a training ground for new leaders, and an effective competitive check on big business, which might otherwise confuse mere size with efficiency. The greatest contribution which government can make to the progress of small business is the creation and preservation of genuine free enterprise. Given access to the necessary technologies and to the capital markets, small enterprise in industry and trade will flourish. And such small business, by reason of its inherent resilience and flexibility, can become the mainstay of our regional economics, the balance wheel of the national economy.

Competition must remain the indispensable foundation of free enterprise. When competition exists, enterprise is free and the necessity for governmental regulation of industry is at a minimum. Where competition is suppressed or restricted, technological progress is blocked, efficiency diminishes, markets contract and the national income shrinks. The government must either aid in preserving healthy competitive conditions, or assume increasing responsibility for the management of industry.

We have an unparalleled opportunity to return to a free enterprise economy. The necessities of war have exposed domestic restraints and broken foreign cartel restraints. Improvements in technology have created new inter-industry competition which threatens the power of entrenched monopolies. New light metals and alloys will compel the aluminum and copper industries, and even the steel industry, to develop cheaper methods of production and seek new markets for their products. Some technical advances will enable small plants to operate economically in industries heretofore dominated by one or two firms.

The greatest opportunity lies in the war plants built with government funds. In the manner of their postwar use lies the acid test of whether we are sincere in our determination to reestablish genuine free enterprise. We must not regard such plants as liabilities to be disposed of hastily; we must not allow the disposition of these plants to add to the concentration of control in industries which are already monopolistic. The plants must be kept in full production to create the enlarged national income required to support a new American standard of living. As a final sale of these war plants would probably result in their being acquired sooner or later by a few large concerns, I have suggested that title should remain in a federal agency, and that these plants should be leased to independent producers who will create new competition and new production.

Whether or not we have free enterprise and the full use of all productive resources depends on our understanding that our way of life is at stake, and on the determination of all of us to test every private and public policy by whether it contributes to the full use of all our resources or whether it tends toward the destruction of full production.

We shall win the military victory. We must have a peaceful world thereafter. We must preserve America as a land of economic opportunity for all of our people. This must be the Century of the Common Man.

[*March 17, 1944.*]

W. L. WHITE

The Last Two Decades

I HAD HOPED to tell the story of the last two decades of my father's life not in my own words but largely in his, making it a mosaic of the letters and editorials he wrote on the fast-changing scene, hoping that the contrast would not be too great between my selection and his narrative.

I find that this last hope is impossible. For in his account of the previous five decades he tempers what he then wrote and thought with that mellowness which only comes with the years, at some times because they had taught him tolerance, at others because time had drained off the emotion of the hour and he could look back with kindly detachment.

Often the value in what he said lay not in its permanence but in his saying aloud, in earthly phrases and with the terrifying frankness of a child, what many thought but few dared whisper.

So, for instance, with his epitaph of Frank Munsey, the newspaper proprietor whose consolidations had thrown thousands of reporters, editorial writers, and printers out of work. In the Gazette (December 23, 1925) he wrote:

"Frank Munsey, the great publisher, is dead. Frank Munsey contributed to the journalism of his day the great talent of a meat packer, the morals of a money changer and the manners of an undertaker. He and his kind have about succeeded in transforming a once noble profession into an eight per-cent security. May he rest in trust!"

So, also with his more mellow four-line epitaph on Woodrow Wilson:

> "God gave him a great vision.
> "The Devil gave him an imperious heart.
> "The proud heart is still.
> "The vision lives."

Early in the twenties, at about the time his own narrative leaves off, he fired the Gazette's first editorial gun against the inevitable rise of postwar prejudice:

"An organizer of the Ku Klux Klan was in Emporia the other day and the men whom he invited to join his band at ten dollars per join, turned him down.

. . . To make a case against a birthplace, a religion, or a race, is wicked, un-American and cowardly. The Ku Klux Klan is based upon such deep foolishness that it is bound to be a menace to good government in any community. . . . American institutions—our courts, our legislators, our executive officers—are strong enough to keep the peace and promote justice and good will in the community. If they are not, then the thing to do is to change these institutions and do it quickly, but always legally. For a self-constituted body of moral idiots who would substitute the findings of the Ku Klux Klan for the processes of law, to try to better conditions, would be a most un-American outrage which every good citizen should resent. . . . It is to the everlasting credit of Emporia that the organizer found no suckers with $10 each to squander here."

However, this prediction was wrong, and the following week he had to admit:

"The Ku Klux Klan is said to be reorganizing in Emporia. It is an organization of cowards. Not a man in it has the courage of his convictions. It is an organization of traitors to American institutions. Not a man in it has faith enough in American courts, laws and officials, to trust them to maintain law and order. . . . It is a menace to peace and decent neighborly living and if we find out who is the Imperial Wizard in Emporia, we shall guy the life out of him. He is a joke, you may be sure. But a poor joke at that."

The tide, however, was too strong at this point to be checked. By 1924, Emporia had a Ku Klux mayor, and in the primary elections for governor, Klan-endorsed candidates had won both the Republican and the Democratic nominations.

So, on September 20, my father announced that he was entering the race as an independent for governor, because:

"I want to offer Kansans afraid of the Klan and ashamed of that disgrace, a candidate who shares their fear and shame.

"The issue in Kansas this year is the Ku Klux Klan above everything else. It is found in nearly every county. It represents a small minority of the citizenship and it is organized for purposes of terror, directed at honest law-abiding citizens; Negroes, Jews and Catholics. These groups in Kansas comprise more than one-fourth of our population. They menace no one. Yet, because of their skin, their race, or their creed, the Ku Klux Klan is subjecting them to economic boycott, to social ostracism, to every form of harassment, annoyance and every terror that a bigoted minority can use.

"Kansas, with her intelligence and pure American blood, of all states should be free of this taint. I was born in Kansas and lived my life in Kansas. I am proud of my state. And the thought that Kansas should have a government beholden to this hooded gang of masked fanatics, ignorant and tyrannical in their ruthless oppression, is what calls me out of the pleasant ways of my life into this disgraceful but necessary task. I cannot sit idly by and see Kansas become a byword among the states. . . . I call to my support all fair-minded citizens of every party, of every creed, to stop the oppression of this minority of our people. It is a national menace, this Klan. It knows no party. It knows no country. It knows only bigotry, malice and terror. Our national government is founded upon reason, and the Golden Rule. This Klan is preaching and practising terror and force. Its only prototype is the Soviet of Russia."

As the campaign progressed, my father warmed up his vocabulary to pay his respects to the Republican candidate:

"The gag rule first came into the Republican Party last May. A flock of dragons, Kleagles, Cyclops and Furies came up to Wichita from Oklahoma and called a meeting with some Kansas Terrors, Genii and Whangdoodles. . . . A few weeks later, the Cyclops, Kleagles, Wizards, and Willopses-wallopuses began parading in the Kansas cow pastures, passing the word down to the shirt-tail rangers they were to go into the Kansas primaries and nominate Ben Paulen."

Although Paulen was presently elected, my father received about the same number of votes as the Democratic candidate; and he felt that the hundred and fifty thousand-odd votes which he had piled up had demonstrated to politicians that the Klan endorsement was, in fact, a handicap as there was in Kansas a larger anti-Klan vote than there were Klansmen. At all events, the Klan presently disappeared from Kansas politics; and on May 5, 1926, my father fired in the Gazette his parting shot:

"Doctor Hiram Evans, the Imperial Wizard of the Kluxers, is bringing his consecrated shirt tail to Kansas this spring, and from gloomy klaverns will make five Kansas speeches. We welcome him. Enter the wizard—sound the bull roarers, and the hewgags. Beat the tom-toms.

"He will see what was once a thriving and profitable hate factory and bigotorium now laughed into a busted community; where the cock-eyed he-dragon wails for its first-born, and the nightshirts of a once salubrious pageantry sag in the spring breezes and bag at the wabbly knees.

"The Kluxers in Kansas are as dejected and sad as a last year's bird's nest, afflicted with general debility, dizziness on going upstairs, and general aversion to female society."

But there is deeper wisdom in that analysis of the Ku Klux Klan which he presently wrote for the magazine World Tomorrow, and which has a sobering similarity to the postwar years of World War II. He felt that:

"We who think we have grown-up minds have our own mental distempers. We are going through our own years of bitter disillusion. The great guns of the Western Front smashed so much more than the little French towns and the flesh and blood of the soldiers.

"They [the people] counted on the faith of the world, the ideals of the world, the high hopes of the world. Amid the ruins, they are all broken and sad. We should not be angry if the child minds about us show a strange perversity and a wicked bigotry which is bound to pass as humanity readjusts itself after the breakdown of civilization."

But even with the passing of the Klan my father was not happy in the Roaring Twenties. As early as 1926, he saw the times of the Big Bull Market with sad clarity:

"What a sordid decade is passing! It will be known in American history fifty years hence as the time of terrible reaction. . . . It will not be the story of a weak man like Harding nor a silent and unemotional man like Coolidge. They are mere outer manifestations of the inner spiritual traits of the people. The spirit of our democracy has turned away from the things of the spirit, got its share of the patrimony ruthlessly and gone out and lived riotously and ended by feeding among the swine.

"Corruption is rampant in high places. Special privilege is unleashed and shameless. The fourth-rater is coming into prestige and power in business, in politics, in religion. . . . Perhaps the whole thing is epitomized by the rise and fall of Harding. The story should not be written now. It would hurt too many hearts. But when it is written, it will be a bitter and awful thing.

"If Roosevelt had lived [my father, of course, refers to Theodore] it might have been different. But who knows? Times are made more or less by leadership, but there is the other half of the equation, which is that times develop leaders. It would have been an uphill and terrible struggle, possibly a fruitless and tragic struggle, ending in sad defeat for the old Colonel had he lived in these times. Perhaps if he had lived, he would not have permitted public sentiment to sag as it has sagged. One doesn't know. Nothing is as futile as the ifs of history.

"We have not come to the turn of the lane. The manifestations in Iowa, in the Dakotas and in Wisconsin are sporadic,—little isolated dust storms on the desert, whirling fitfully, meaning little except as evidence of a gathering storm which is not yet even upon the horizon.

"The nation has not yet been shocked out of its materialism. Of course, Coolidge is a tremendous shock absorber. His emotionless attitude is an anesthetic to a possible national conviction of sin. . . . We have just got to grind along and develop a leader and it is a long, slow task calling for all our patience. How long, Oh Lord, how long!

"What a joy it would be to get out and raise the flaming banner of righteousness! Instead of which we sit in our offices and do unimportant things and go home at night and think humdrum thoughts.

"What a generation!" [1]

It is on the whole not surprising that this malcontent, who so clearly rejected the validity and the permanence of that Best of All Possible Worlds, should have been blacklisted in 1928 by the D.A.R. along with a list of liberals and pacifists which included Dean Roscoe Pound of the Harvard Law School, President Mary E. Woolley of Mount Holyoke College, Felix Frankfurter, then a professor in the Harvard Law School, Clarence Darrow, Rabbi Stephen S. Wise, Norman Hapgood, and David Starr Jordan.

---

[1] When this editorial, more than a decade later, was published in an anthology, my father added the following footnote: "Well, six years brought the man! And when he came, I some way did not 'get out and raise the flaming banner of righteousness.' "

This temporarily roused my father out of his discontent to produce the following gentle pastoral idyll on the subject of the good ladies of the D.A.R. whose leaders were:

"developing a taste for those idle, apoplectic old gentlemen in red flannels who escape the boredom of their rich wives by sitting in club windows in Washington and bemoaning the decadence of a growing world. The nice old girls of the present D.A.R. administration have been hypnotized by the brass buttons of the retired Army officers and lured into this red-baiting mania by the tea-gladiators of Washington."

When Mrs. Brosseau, then the D.A.R.'s president, retorted with spirit, he charged that she had:

"put the entire D.A.R. membership list on the sucker list of the superpatriots [because her black list had singled out] organizations affecting colored people, Jews and Catholics . . . the peculiar enemies of the Ku Klux Klan. The D.A.R. has yanked the Klan out of the cow pasture and set it down in the breakfast room of respectability, removing its hood and putting on a transformation. Mrs. Brosseau is a lovely lady with many beautiful qualities of heart and mind, but, in her enthusiasm, she has allowed several lengths of Ku Klux nightie to show under her red, white and blue."

The year 1928 also saw the nomination of Herbert Hoover (my father had been one of his early western supporters) and his campaign with Governor Smith in which the most noisy issue was Prohibition, combined, in the South, with a seldom-voiced anti-Catholicism. My father was, of course, a deeply convinced Prohibitionist. There were bigots in this movement, but I wonder if any subsequent generation can understand that there were also many most earnest, if mistaken idealists who poured into the movement the enthusiasm of a deep hope that Prohibition could abolish alcoholism, and that it would be a tremendous step forward in human happiness. No Marxist ever poured higher hopes and more selfless energy into his panacea than did the Prohibitionist of the last generation. Furthermore, my father, who had so often and so brilliantly interpreted to the nation the hopes and fears, aspirations and prejudices of the Middle West and of country towns, shared their deep and instinctive distrust of the big-city political machine which was epitomized by Tammany.

All through the economic storm which broke six months after President Hoover's inauguration, my father's basic faith in his old friend remained unchanged. But even as early as 1930 he began to doubt not Hoover's program, but his ability to hold popular confidence. He felt that Hoover, who

"has some sort of shrinking horror of connecting his office with causes, should be told by his advisors that in extraordinary times of turmoil and panic, the Presidential office must take leadership in the country.

"He must . . . appeal to the people. He must dramatize his cause or the cause loses, and with the cause his fortune falls.

"Go to the people, Mr. President. They are dependable. Lincoln, Roosevelt and Wilson found the people a tower of strength and of refuge. Whoever is wise and honest and brave, they will follow to victory. But their leader must take them into his councils. They will repay candor with confidence."

And this same note is sounded in his political epitaph on Herbert Hoover written just after the Roosevelt landslide in 1932. He felt that Herbert Hoover had:

"suppressed the drama which another man, with a politician's instinct for hero-izing himself in any crisis, might have turned to his own advantage. If he had any illusions, and certainly the President had few, . . . one was a blind faith that some way democracy in the end would be able to see with its own eyes the truth. He believed that the people could see it clearly and logically without drama, without a hero in whose struggles they could see a story, and so feel their way to the truth. But, alas, the President was wrong in attributing a logical habit of mind to men in the mass. They must emotionalize their thinking. They need a story. They learn their truth in parables.

"He will be known as the greatest innocent bystander in history. But history will also write him down an earnest, honest, intelligent man, full of courage and patriotism, undaunted to the last.

"Here is tragedy . . . a brave man fighting valiantly, futilely to the end."

My father's first reaction to the New Deal was bewilderment. A month after the inauguration of President Roosevelt, he was writing:

"Strange things are moving across this American world of ours. The country seemed to want dramatic action. Roosevelt is supplying the want.

"It isn't in the books. The Constitution is straining and cracking. But, after all, the Constitution was made for the people, and not the people for the Con-stitution. We are toying gayly with billions as we once played cautiously with millions. We are legerdemaining a huge national debt which is to be paid Heaven knows when or where or how. It is bewildering—this new deal—the new world. How much is false, how much is true, how much is an illusion of grandeur, a vast make-believe, only time will tell.

"In the meantime, the wizard in the White House works his weird spell upon a changing world."

But by 1934 he found compensation because,

"for thirty years, now, the Editor of the Gazette has been hammering away for a larger participation of the average man in the wealth of this nation—less for superintendence, interest and profits,—more for wages. We have clamored for higher income taxes, for devastating inheritance taxes, for workmen's com-pensation, unemployment insurance, old-age pensions, for all the measures which Colonel Theodore Roosevelt used to call 'social and industrial justice.' President Roosevelt's new first assistant secretary of the treasury is described as believing in the following social reforms:

Higher income and inheritance taxes.
Federal grants for the unemployed.
A more equitable distribution of wealth.
Unemployment and old-age pensions.
Minimum wages.
National economic planning.
Public works and mortgage relief.

"Franklin Roosevelt has packed his whole government in Washington full of men like that. Congress has given him broad powers. He surrounds himself with leaders like Eccles, Tugwell, Ickes, Wallace, Frances Perkins and Morgenthau who believe in all these reforms. It is plain as a barn door that we are getting our revolution through the administrative arm of the government, without legislation.

"Well, in these sad days of depression, the Gazette gets a great laugh out of this. In fact, you may catch us grinning at any hour of the day or night to think of what has happened in this land of the free. We hope the conservative Democrats who were lambasting Hoover a year and a half ago are enjoying what they got.

"These are great days—if not happy ones."

In the summer of 1933, as a reporter for the North American Newspaper Alliance, my father attended the London Economic Conference, witnessed the short-lived struggle for power between Raymond Moley and Cordell Hull, and at the end of the conference, with my mother, took a short trip to the Soviet Union avoiding Germany where Hitler had just come to power. In Moscow they spent most of their time with the veteran reporters —Maurice Hindus, Walter Duranty, Eugene Lyons, Louis Fischer and William Henry Chamberlin, who even then had varying points of view. Russia in 1933 was undergoing not a depression but a famine in the south as a result of the collectivization of the land and the liquidation of the Kulaks. The American reporters in Moscow knew that an estimated three million people were dying in the Ukraine, although no reporters had visited this region nor could news of the famine be cabled abroad.

Back in Emporia, my father was making up his mind about Roosevelt. He was greatly pleased when the President came out foursquare for the Child Labor Amendment, pointing out in the Gazette:

"It is that sort of thing that makes the people love him. He may make mistakes—loads of them, but the folks know he is brave and honest, and that he is never going to be caught . . . hesitating in a crisis. Roosevelt has his weaknesses, but his strength is so fine and fair that the people will forgive him when they find he is wrong; and he can start all over again with new confidence."

As the New Deal's economic program came into view he felt:

"Evidently the President is aiming at something of the same target at which both the fascists and the communists are shooting; that is to say, the socialization of capital, the regimentation of industry and agriculture, and, finally, a more equitable distribution of wealth, a guarantee of a minimum standard of living for all who have worked honestly. . . . Obviously, he is not greedy for power. No one can deny that he is seeking the larger good of the American people. It is evident that he is no dictator. He has none of the faults and few of the virtues of a tyrant. Instead . . . a yearning for peace, for justice and for self-respect, for the people of this country and for the world."

He also felt:

"In all this tremendous change from the old democracy of individual laissez faire to the new democracy of socialized capital, no question of honesty, no scandal . . . has come to the American people."

And yet:

"Far be it from the Gazette to carp. We are supporting the administration and the whole alphabet thereunto appertaining. But are the American people ready for the revolutionary change, the fundamental break with our American past that is necessary if this revolution takes hold permanently? Today, it is a palace revolution which has captured Washington. How far and how deeply in the hearts of the American people has it gone? These questions are not asked by an impertinent enemy but by a sincere friend whose fond and fervent hope is that the day he long has sought is really here."

Yet occasionally, my father had honest doubts as to whether this long sought day was really desirable:

"Roosevelt's greatest problem can be stated thus: Can government chain its dollars, harness them to the common good, and still retain free men and free institutions? It has never been done before. Political liberties always go down when economic liberty is circumscribed. But this is a new world. Our democracy for a hundred years has been a new order, but it is more deeply rooted here than in Europe. Probably America can do this strange thing—establish a new revolution of free men with their dollars in shackles."

It was a question which later was to trouble the economist Hayek, who gave a different answer. In these years, my father's occasional criticisms of the Roosevelt program were always friendly. In sounding the knell of the NRA, he pointed out that its mistake was

"taking all business at one fell swoop, which recalls the epitaph on Bill Nye's famous dog, Epaminondas, who in his insatiable thirst for gobbling everything, gobbled off a plasterer's mixing board a bellyful of plaster of paris, which hardened; when he died, Bill Nye took the dog from around his monument and wrote these soulful words: 'Here lies Epaminondas, interior view. He bit off more than he could chew.'"

Meanwhile, Alfred Landon was looming over the flat prairie horizon as a probable Republican Presidential candidate. He had been elected governor of Kansas in 1932 and again in 1934 in the face of Democratic landslides somewhat because of his abilities and largely because in both campaigns the independent candidacy of John R. Brinkley (a goat gland doctor who had been barred by the State Medical Board from practicing in Kansas) had subtracted many thousands of votes from what otherwise would have been a Democratic majority, with the result that Landon emerged in 1935 as the only Republican governor in the land to survive two Democratic landslides.

Landon was the son of an old Kansas Bull Mooser who had been my father's friend since the golden days of 1912. He was supported by what remained of the Roosevelt Progressives in Kansas. The reader has seen that my father's old Kansas political friends meant much in his life, and so can understand that in this situation he had little choice, whatever he may have felt and written previously about Roosevelt. For Landon was as yet unknown outside the state. Over the nation, my father was probably the best known Kansan, and his opposition at this stage would have been fatal. Furthermore, my father, who was personally fond of Landon, wanted tremendously to believe that Landon was a true Bull Moose Progressive; and there was a considerable body of evidence to justify this hope.

Yet his praise of Landon, while generous, could hardly be criticized as hysterical. Late in 1935, he editorialized on the Landon boom, pointing out that Landon's Kansas friends

"will not claim him to be a superman. They will not point to him as a miracle worker.

"But he will go forward and not back. That we know. . . . We make no bond for anything else. Take him or leave him."

Early in 1936 when the private cars of prominent Republicans on pilgrimage were already a familiar sight in the Topeka switchyard, my father wrote his first serious editorial estimate of Landon, pointing out that he:

"is now going into that rarefied atmosphere where the great currents of American politics run swift, capricious and mercilessly cold. . . . Political geography has taken him where he is; a successful Republican governor of a midwestern state who, as La Follette's Monthly declares, is not too progressive to offend the conservatives, and not too conservative to lose the support of the liberals.

"But political geography does not make a man President. He must measure up to certain spiritual requirements. He must have moral courage, or, if not that, the backing of great material forces—money for instance. He must have intellectual strength—or, lacking that, a great charm which to the moron mind substitutes for intellectual endowment. He must have insight—instinctive and canny. Or to make up that lack, he needs a crafty political acumen and a manipulating ability that amounts to genius. . . . Every man has latent forces. . . . In the next three months, only one man can make Governor Landon President, and that man is Alfred Mossman Landon. He, himself, must make each great and final decision.

"But if he does not have these extraordinary qualities—if some hell-born breed of events thrusts him luckily into power without the strength to do the job, God help his country in a time like this.

"In the meantime, all of Kansas is proud to see him take the upward journey, proud and happy that their friend and fellow Kansan is on his way. And as he goes, he has their blessing.

"But in the high bleak thin air—he walks alone."

However, my father followed him to the Republican convention at Cleveland, at which he was a Landon delegate and also a member of the platform committee. His principal contribution to the campaign was a small book "What It's All About," in which he gave outsiders a picture of Governor Landon. However, he hit at the President in a ringing Republican editorial when Roosevelt invaded Kansas to speak at Wichita two weeks before the campaign's close. Pointing out that

"our old American smiler declared that Kansas would not have pulled through the last few years of drouth and depression if it had not been for 'federal aid in many fields of endeavor,' "

he charged that the President's logic was

"slick as goose grease and false as hell. . . . Who in the world thinks 'it is wrong to give federal assistance'? We Republicans are just as much for . . . it as the slick old thimble-rigger who passed so felicitously through Kansas yesterday. . . . Where the Republican plan differs from the Democratic practice is in our promise that this federal aid shall be administered by the states, counties, and cities . . . following local knowledge and wisdom. [Otherwise you] build up a great political machine centered in Washington and pay for it with waste and extravagance. . . . It's sensible if you are a Democrat but mad as a hoot owl if you are a taxpayer."

It was on this Kansas trip that the President, when his train paused in Emporia, told the crowd that, anyway, he was appreciative of "Bill White's support for three and a half years out of every four."

The next two years of my father's life were fairly well occupied with the preparation of his book "A Puritan in Babylon," published in 1938, which was actually a political and economic study of the 1920's done in the form of a biography of Calvin Coolidge. It was, from the standpoint of scholarship and research, perhaps his most important book to date.

Meanwhile, war was approaching, a subject on which he had few illusions. Certainly not many are to be found in his editorial of November 11, 1933. Here he pointed out:

"Fifteen years ago came the Armistice and we all thought it was to be a new world. It is! But a lot worse than it was before.

"Ten million men were killed and many more maimed, fifty billion dollars' worth of property destroyed, the world saddled with debts.

"And for what? Would it have been any worse if Germany had won? Ask yourself honestly. No one knows.

"Is this old world as safe for democracy as it was before all these lives were lost?

"There is no democracy east of the Rhine. Tyrants have risen where constitutional monarchs ruled twenty years ago. . . . The boys who died just went out and died. To their own souls' glory, of course—but what else? . . . Yet the next war will see the same hurrah and the same bowwow of the big dogs to get the little dogs to go out and follow the blood scent and get their entrails tangled in the barbed wire.

"And for what?

"Look at Russia, ruled by the proletarian tyrant!

"Behold Germany, governed by paranoiac sadists!

"Italy has lost her liberty to fill her stomach and enthrone the rich!

"Poland, the Balkans, and Central Europe—a super powder magazine— waiting for the match to blow civilization back to the dark ages!

"What a glorious war! All wars are like that. The next one will be worse.

"War is the devil's joke on humanity. So let's celebrate Armistice Day by laughing our heads off.

"Then let us work and pray for peace when man can break the Devil's chains and nations realize their nobler dreams!"

This was probably the prevailing American viewpoint in the late twenties and middle thirties. It was to change with events, as was his own. When, after signing a pact, Russia and Germany closed in on Poland, he became chairman of that committee which presently secured the repeal of the American embargo on arms, thus enabling the British and French to buy munitions in this country. Of all this I know little at first hand since I had already left for Europe as a war correspondent; but the committee was substantially the nucleus for the more powerful group which, as America, stunned by fear, watched the fall of France, was later to rise under his chairmanship as the Committee to Defend America by Aiding the Allies.

While the first German tanks were fumbling through the Ardennes Gap, he was writing:

"As one democracy after another crumbles under the mechanized columns of the dictators, it becomes evident that the future of Western civilization is being decided on the battlefield of Europe. . . . Terrible as it may seem, the people of our country cannot avoid the consequences of Hitler's victory and of those who are or may be allied with him. . . . It would be folly to hold this nation chained to a neutrality policy determined in the light of last year's facts. . . . America must spend every ounce of energy to keep the war away from the Western hemisphere by preparing to defend herself and aiding with our supplies and wealth the nations now fighting to stem the tide of aggression. . . . It is for us to show the people of England, of France, of Belgium and Scandinavia that the richest country on earth is not too blind or too timid to help those who are fighting tyranny abroad.

"If they fail, we shall not have time to prepare to face their conquerors alone."

It is superficially a most curious fact that the "William Allen White Committee," then so bitterly denounced by Bundists and Communists as a group of irresponsible interventionist war-mongers, should be headed by a man who believed with a great earnestness that this country should not enter the war, nor, in aiding the Allies, take any step which would give the Axis casus belli.

Actually, a minority of the committee, which toward the end may have become a majority, believed (I happened to share its view) that the sooner American soldiers were sent overseas, the better chance we should stand of preventing an otherwise inevitable and permanent Axis conquest of Europe.

This was never my father's view. If his name was of value to that committee because it savored, not of the war-fevered eastern seaboard, but rather of the traditionally isolationist Midwest, they had also to accept the handicap that his own convictions represented the average opinion of America more accurately than any Gallup Poll, and this average opinion was presently to reach a state aptly characterized by Mark Sullivan as "a case of split personality—mass schizophrenia" in the conflicting beliefs that Hitler's defeat was a matter of life and death for America, but that under no circumstances should we declare war.

Probably his principal service to the committee was in connection with the campaign of 1940 when, on several occasions, he served as a liaison between Willkie and the President in a largely successful attempt to prevent the Roosevelt foreign policy from becoming the principal issue of the campaign. But early in 1941 he resigned as active head of the committee after a somewhat heated and complicated dispute as to whether or not it should favor American naval convoys for our Lend-Lease aid to the British. His position, presently expressed in a letter to one of the committee's members, was:

"When the President is for them, I'm going to support them, of course. But I do not believe that our organization should keep nagging him and needling him while he is hesitating. I do not believe that he and Secretary Hull have changed their minds since they both spoke to me about convoys, and both protested against their use. Perhaps they should change their minds; I don't know. But I don't think our organization is doing any service to the President in building up public sentiment that will force his hand."

In May, he was writing to his old friend, Oswald Garrison Villard:

"I hoped I would never see another war. I shall never encourage the coming of another war. But if it comes, this summer or next summer . . . I see nothing to do but to fight it with all our might and all our hearts. And that's not a pleasant prospect for a man who realizes the utter futility of wars in the past and who can only hope rather vainly that, out of this war, men may learn wisdom in the end.

"But how can they learn wisdom through hate and rancor and suspicion and all the hell's mint of counterfeit coins of wisdom that will be spread across the world in the currency of our spiritual commerce? . . . I should like to postpone it for another year by any device that will keep England afloat while we prepare. In that year, much might happen. . . . Possibly the Nazis will not be able to go through another winter. That may be wishful thinking. . . . I'm hoping rather than thinking."

Even on the eve of Pearl Harbor, he was writing:

"I am one of those in the 75 per cent of Americans who, for a year, have been ringing up in the Gallup Poll as favoring the President's foreign policy. I am also of the 95 per cent who have been ringing up in the Gallup Poll for this same period as wishing to avoid war."

Meanwhile, Russia had come into the war. Possibly because, when he headed the committee, the American Communists had so viciously attacked him, one can detect a note of cautious restraint in his salute to this new ally. Writing for the Gazette two days after Hitler's attack, he pointed out that between Stalin and Hitler,

"the two dictators who are clashing along the long boundary line between the Slavic and the Nordic civilizations in Europe, it is small choice. . . . Both are conspicuous international liars. . . . Both have betrayed and murdered their best friends. Both are tyrants, ruthless of human life, utterly impervious to the claims of dignity for the human spirit. So both hate democracy with craven hate."

Although he felt that Stalin's "lust for power was fairly well confined in the boundaries of his country," and that he was "at the moment fighting America's most dangerous enemy," his conclusion was that America, England, Scandinavia, Holland, Belgium, and France, "indeed all honest men who love freedom all over this globe," could now take a deep breath and "wish that it shall be a battle to the death"—a grim view which he modified two days later, when the Russians seemed to have halted the German attack:

"What a miracle it would be if those slab-sided, gawky, bewhiskered Bolsheviks stand-up-and-fall-down steppers on their own feet—should hold the Nazi champions long enough to let the people in Germany know that their omnipotent Führer was just a dub of common clay. Then, indeed there would be a celebration; a shindy as the old-fashioned posters used to say, 'platform dancing in the grove and fireworks in the evening!' "

Yet some mistrust still persisted, for still later he was writing to an old Kansas friend of isolationist tendencies that the world would never be safe until Hitler was licked—

"and, if you ask me, this world won't be safe even then . . . unless Joe Stalin is shoved back in his corner."

My father was still preoccupied with his estimate of Roosevelt and, in a letter to another correspondent, found the President

"a great puzzle. I am fond of him. He has done everything I ever asked, but I have asked for precious few things. In the summer of 1940, because I was chairman of the Committee to Defend America by Aiding the Allies, he talked in utmost confidence with me and let me talk in turn confidentially to Wendell Willkie, which I did and I hope with some effect. At least we kept the foreign issue out of the campaign as far as possible.

"I knew the President nearly twenty years ago and have liked him. I suppose he knows my weaknesses, and I am sure he knows that I know his, and we have put up with each other. Each of us probably feels in his heart that in certain matters he tolerates fools gladly. On that basis we have erected what might pass for a friendship. But I miss what I found in Theodore Roosevelt—a certain ruggedness, the ability to quarrel bitterly with a man and then take him to his heart and forget the quarrel. . . .

"Yet he has done so many fine things. He has started us down so many roads that long had been blocked by an arrogant plutocracy that I cannot ask perfection and I am glad he came."

Now and then in these closing years, he glanced shrewdly into the future, as in his letter to Alfred M. Landon in mid-July of 1942. Landon had sent him a proposed speech, to which my father replied, objecting:

"You emphasized the difficulties rather than the needs for some kind of world organization to save the peace. I have no plan. I don't string along with Clarence Streit. I follow Hoover closer than any other one man as he set forth the case in his book. But it is wiser to prepare the popular mind to accept as inevitable some kind of organization rather than to raise the obstacles . . .

"When I look into the future, even two or three years, I am shocked, indeed horrified, at the inevitable spectacle that rises before me no matter who wins the war. The duties of a decent victor will be burdens and not tokens of triumph."

Some flavor of the placid routine of these closing years is given in a letter to Edna Ferber written in July of 1942:

"I am working on my autobiography. Every morning at half past seven the stenographer comes out to the house. I lie on the porch in the hammock and dictate fifteen hundred words or so, and by half past eight or nine go down to the Gazette office, take care of my letters, then come home and sleep, do my editorials in the afternoon for the next day's paper, and knock off at half past five and call it a day.

"I get up as much copy as anyone around the shop and, of course, have my finger in a lot of local pies. Just now I'm helping to nominate a governor and am busier than a man falling out of a balloon without a parachute. But it would be pretty terrible not to be a part of things.

"Of course, the war has got me down, and I know it is a long war, terrible next year and maybe worse the year after. But by 1945 I think we can see day-light if we can just keep out of inflation. That is the hell fire and damnation that looms ahead of us, and I am scared stiff."

My father's fatal sickness began in the fall of 1943, but in the earlier part of the year the time he could spare for active politics was devoted to an attempt (it was unsuccessful) to organize the Kansas Republican delega-tion for Wendell Willkie in the 1944 convention and election. He had pre-viously written Justice William A. Smith of the Kansas Supreme Court:

"I'm 100 per cent sold for life on Wendell Willkie and if I am the only man in Kansas who is following him . . . I am going to do it. I have made my living by being a pretty good judge of men, and never since Teddy Roosevelt have I known a man on whom I have pinned my faith as I pinned it on Wendell Willkie. I think one of the most courageous things any man ever said in public life was Willkie's 'campaign oratory' statement. It was not discreet, but it was deeply honest. Only three times in public life have I seen such honesty. The pretension that a candidate's utterances are omniscient when everyone knows he is talking damned nonsense is one of the large reasons why the American people lose faith in democracy."

So in May of 1943, he was writing to Thomas W. Lamont that:

"Of course, I am for Willkie, I still have faith that he will be able to breast the tide and buck the isolationist reaction against him. . . . This is a hunch and a guess. I have no facts to support it and have been wrong before; I may be wrong this time."

During the same spring, he paid his respects to another Republican candidate in a Gazette editorial in which he said:

"The same forces in the Republican party that gathered about Taft in 1912 and that nominated Harding in a 'smoke-filled room' in 1920, . . . seem deter-mined to force the nomination of Governor Bricker of Ohio as Republican Presi-dential nominee. And who is Governor Bricker? Alice Roosevelt is said to have defined him in five words: 'Bricker is an honest Harding.'

"That leaves little more to be said. He is a man who is trying to capitalize the tremendous discontent among Republicans and among Democrats who hate the New Deal. . . . He hopes to get by without saying anything, without getting on either side of the momentous questions of the hour—domestic and foreign.

"A man who can stand in American politics, aspiring for a high office, with-out the intelligence, the courage, or the honesty to make some declaration upon the most important issue that has ever faced this old earth, certainly is not the kind of man for the Republicans of this country to rally around. . . . Surely the Republican party, which came to power more than eighty years ago under Abraham Lincoln by saving the country from disunion and by freeing 4,000,000 slaves, the Republican party which guided the country while a continent was settled, . . . cannot be so craven that it would conspire to steal into victory with no issue but Bricker and a bellyache."

This tribute he presently sent to Willkie with the comment that it had "raised hell clear across the continent," as a result of which he had received

"a stack of letters as thick as a hired girl's leg. I just had to take a sock at that bird, and I hope this will find you the same."

In addition, that spring, he sent Willkie several letters of strategic advice, arguing that he should

"avoid the President when you possibly can. Don't wisecrack at him, but when you have something to say, don't pull your punches or slap his wrist. Sock him with all you've got, but with a dignity that becomes a patriot and a great cause."

In general, however, he urged him to:

"Attack the fundamental domestic policy of the New Deal and not the President. Handle him with tongs. Explain why deficiency spending will bring us to the brink of ruin. Tell the people that the extension of governmental powers into planned economy in time of peace is the denial of liberty inevitably. For the very theory of planning requires that man shall become a wooden figure without will, without individuality, that he shall be, in short, that powerless human sheep, the economic man, a social and political eunuch.

"The people are ready to hear this. They are yearning for new leadership. We are entering an interregnum. Either Hitler and the storm troopers, the boys in the pool hall under the leadership of Ham Fish, Martin Dies, Gerald Nye and Colonel McCormick will come out and take leadership and bash the heads of liberals everywhere, or you will take leadership, and the time is short."

To another Republican leader who asked his opinion on a new Republican platform, he wrote:

"We should . . . denounce all government coddling, either to capital in the form of protective tariff, or to labor in the form of special privileges. And we should not be mealy-mouthed about either. The strength of the Republican party is the middle class—the small businessman, the independent operator in any line of mercantile or industrial business. He is the man who should be considered in writing our platform. I'm getting pretty sick of the pussyfooters who try to catch the WPA and the National Association of Manufacturers with the same kind of talk. Personally, I want neither of them."

He was also looking ahead toward the end of the war, which he had predicted for 1945, and in another letter says:

"After unconditional surrender . . . we are in for a ten-year struggle in which we must put our American energies, our American production, and the full strength of American credit—not into a grand do-good adventure, not into making the world beautiful and utopian, but into a cold-blooded, hardboiled attempt to put world civilization back on its feet. The capitalist system must not break down. Unless capitalism is willing to organize, to sacrifice, to envision its own self-interests in the renewal and revival of civilization, war will be a failure. . . . And a weary, disheartened world will turn to some totalitarian tyranny and we shall regiment mankind in inevitable economic slavery."

Something of the same note is in his letter to Mr. and Mrs. Raymond Robbins in which he says:

"As we approach the peace, . . . we are standing in slippery places. I get more and more frightened at the limitations of our political institution and the tremendous, unbelievable size of the political job before us, and the economic commitment we must make in the next two or three years if the peace shall become really a victory and not a prelude to a debacle.

"And the fourth term bothers me. . . . Every year that Roosevelt is in the White House he deteriorates physically and also . . . in leadership due to the natural distrust of the country for a man who has such faith in himself and so little in God that he believes he is indispensable. People know, deeply and instinctively, that when a man becomes indispensable to a democracy it is no longer a democracy; and that weakens the President for the greatest task that has ever faced any man on this planet.

"It may take another false peace and another war to develop the stern qualities in the people that will make them worthy of the great leader who is necessary to do the work ahead of us. I suppose we should not be silly and expect it to be done overnight . . . but be grateful if it could be done in a century."

His criticisms of the President, while frequent, were never bitter. On his return from the Teheran Conference, my father, in an editorial, pointed out:

"He saw more of an amazing world than Marco Polo. He saw in North Africa alone as much conquered land as Alexander saw when he wept for new worlds to conquer. He performed a feat so strange even in modern war, so amazing and unbelievable, that if it had been prophesied fifty years ago men would have stoned the prophets for impiety.

"Biting nails—good, hard, bitter Republican nails—we are compelled to admit that Franklin Roosevelt is the most unaccountable . . . President that this United States has ever seen. He has added a vast impudent courage to a vivid but constructive imagination, and he has displayed his capacity for statesmanship in the large and simple billboard language that the common people can understand; moreover, that the people admire, even when it is their deadly poison. We have got to hand it to him.

"Well, darn your smiling old picture, here it is! Here, reluctantly, amid seething and snorting, it is. We, who hate your gaudy guts, salute you."

Still later, he was writing to Henry J. Allen:

"The President is a baffling case. For ten years he has been staging himself as the champion of the underdog. But I doubt if he really understands the underdog well enough to love him intelligently in spite of his faults. And from now on out, if I was the underdog, I should bury my bones against the day of hunger.

"He is too many for me. Like you, I think he inordinately wants a Fourth Term, but I don't know why. You think he wants power. I think he wants to sit in, to win hand after hand, and maybe take quite a pot with him as he passes through the portals of history. Theodore always had one eye on history; . . . he played a bold hand, did what he thought was right, and defied the world, the flesh, and the devil, which is something that F. D. R. just can't do. He can defy Wall Street when Wall Street is groggy, and anyway Wall Street doesn't have many votes. But he has never offended any minority that has supported him when that minority was wrong and when any intelligent man must have known it was wrong.

"And yet, if he can die before 1944, he will leave a great name in history. Lincoln was beloved of the gods, who took him just before he started to fight the Republican radicalism led by Thaddeus Stevens on reconstruction. If Lincoln had gone into that fight, God knows how he would have come out at the inevitable defeat."

And in late August of his final year he was writing to Harold B. Johnson:

"It is the tragic weakness of the Roosevelt administration that after twelve years he has so entirely denuded the Democratic party, that it has not one available leader who can carry on the work which he has started. As you know, I have never been greatly excited about Roosevelt as a dictator. He laughs too easily. He is too soft-hearted in many ways. . . . But he has functioned much like a dictator in chopping off the political heads of possible rivals—not with a snickersnee, not with a machine gun, but with soft soap, kicking them upstairs or choking them to death on taffy."

So often, in those final months and weeks, as old age was closing relentlessly down on him, my father was trying to peer into the future. "We must," he wrote in a cautioning letter to Roger Straus, a devoted Dewey supporter,

"pick a man of size this time. . . . For the peace will bring problems as urgent and as important as the problem of war."

Yet always he could bring his gentle irony to bear on himself, even on his own eager interest in the future. For he concludes:

"This started out to be a note of gratitude and here it is, an old man, babbling about those years when he will be merely a ripple under the daisies."

MAX LERNER

The Enigma of FDR

I

THERE is a tendency among liberals to blame the State Department for our present foreign policy. But while their instinct is probably sound in seeing the State Department as the shaping force, the final responsibility must rest on the President, and I am certain that he would wish it thus.

But to say that is to state the self-evident. What remains is the big enigma about FDR: how someone with his greatness of spirit and his record of liberalism could identify himself with so illiberal and blind a policy as we seem to be pursuing in North Africa, France, Spain, and seem to be preparing toward the rest of Europe.

I have no pipeline to FDR's mind. But one thing is clear at the very start. He is an equilibrium President, at his best when he has to play contending forces off against each other. All his conditionings in public life have been to ride chaos, with a perilous but sure balance. That is why he is the greatest leader in a crisis that the modern world has seen; and all the greater because, while dictators require intelligence and will, democratic leaders require those qualities plus a delicate and dizzying finesse.

I think FDR enjoys the whole game of political finesse as he enjoys few things else. I think everyone will agree now that he did a magnificent job in bringing American strength into the war without breaking our fragile national unity. And a good job also in making American weight felt in the war even before we had entered it formally.

What then has happened to him? I think he is still trying to play the game of finesse when what is required instead is social clarity and forthrightness. He seems to see the problem of France, for example, as an equilibrium problem—one of balancing De Gaulle against Peyrouton and Noguès, the Fighting French against the collaborationists.

You will see that I do not think our present policy consists of any grand design on FDR's part, but is attributable rather to a lack of design, and to an ingrained and natural way of doing things. He is deeply preoccupied with the military aspect of the war, and his natural tendency not to stir up trouble is reinforced in North Africa and Spain by military considerations. Moreover, he leans heavily on such advisers as Leahy and Berle. Add to that his knowledge that a militant American policy of supporting the forces of economic democracy and the underground in Europe might again stir the sleeping dogs of political catholicism in America. Add to that his liking for power politics and his unwillingness to give the Russians an unnecessary card in the postwar game by helping to create Popular Front governments on the Continent.

I have tried to set down these elements of tactic and belief as sympathetically as I have known how, despite my disagreement with what they add up to. I think the President is well intentioned, but—on foreign policy—thus far I think he is wrong.

For the fact is that we live in an era of vast and far-reaching social change. The impulses throughout the world have for some time been the impulses toward combining three elements into one world; an expanding economy, democratic freedom, and world peace. In the struggle to achieve these, the war has been only an initial skirmish. We may win the skirmish and still lose the campaign. And the campaign can be won only if those three impulses are encouraged and fulfilled all over the world.

President Roosevelt has, within America, fought bravely for all three. And even his foreign policy has over a decade been more progressive than that of any President since Wilson. His great shaping ideas in this field have made history: the Good Neighbor idea in Latin-American affairs; the idea of "quarantining" Nazi aggression; the idea of America as the arsenal of the democracies; the idea of Lend-Lease; the idea of the Four Freedoms; the idea of the United Nations.

Where his foreign policy failed signally was in Spain during the fascist civil war, at Munich when we accepted the betrayal of Czechoslovakia, and now in North Africa. In the trial balance, the credits far outweigh the debits.

But you cannot approach the making of a postwar world with a ledgerbook. You must approach it, as Harold Laski said the other day in his open letter to the President, with a broad and bold determination that this is a liberating war, a war to end exploitation. I believe that the President has it in him to be a great peace leader on a world scale as well as a great war captain. But to do that he will have to break with the policies of his current advisers on foreign affairs, and see the world and the future not through State Department blinkers, but through the eyes of the great democrat that he is himself.

2

I wrote yesterday of the enigma of President Roosevelt's foreign policy. But it would be unfair to assess his entire record as war President by that. There is no comparable enigma in his conduct of the war itself.

Here I have no hesitation in saying that FDR has proved the greatest war President we have had, and this the best-run war in American history. Consider the record. As an industrial power we were heap big injun, but as a military power we were second-rate. We got into a war whose major entries had either been in it long before us, or else had been preparing for years. We had to build an army and air force almost overnight.

Then take the record of the home front proper. Here the picture reduces itself to three main elements—production, stabilization, freedom.

Production was fearfully slow in getting started. Blunders were made originally in the estimates of raw-material requirement. It took us a while to discover that curtailment of civilian production is not the same as conversion to war production. It took us a while to replace the system of priorities by a system of allocation. But the production lines did eventually get rolling.

In the fight to stabilize prices and wages and rents, it has seemed at times as if the President were carrying the burden almost alone. He had to deal with a hostile Congress and an apathetic press and highly organized lobbies. If he seems now to have the situation pretty well in hand, it is his own victory, and for it he deserves some kind of medal or other.

That goes for freedom as well. There were thousands of little dogmatists on the Left and the Right, each marooned on his own island of righteousness who prophesied that if America entered the war it would mean the end of our civil liberties. Well, we are in the war and we still have our liberties . . . so completely in fact that every petty Roosevelt-hater in the country is given columns of space to cry to high heaven against the man who runs a total war without destroying his freedom.

The President has been much criticized as an administrator, often by people who can only parrot the familiar charges that he does not know how to delegate power nor how to fire anyone. Actually the President is a shrewd administrator, who doesn't operate according to the textbooks, but gets results. Most of the "muddles" about which the papers cry muddle about for a while and finally get solved. FDR's technique is to let things simmer, to patch and mend, until there are calls for action from every quarter—and then to strike suddenly and give the country the action it pleads for, summary and comprehensive.

I do not say that his home front policy has had no faults and weaknesses. But I think most people follow blindly the lead of the press and cry about the wrong ones.

The President's basic weakness lies in his appeasement of powerful groups within the country which have, on the whole, not been for an all-out war. He has appeased the business groups, he has appeased the Tory wing of his own party. As with other men, his weakness is a phase of his strength. His strength lies in his adaptability, his mastery of the art of compromise. His weakness lies in carrying that art too far.

His basic appeasement, of course, was to turn the war economy over to the dollar-a-year men to run their own way. One could argue that, given our structure of business power, he could scarcely have done otherwise. One could argue that since we are the only great power in the war where the conservatives form the opposition in press, Congress and industry, the President had no choice if he was to lead a unified nation into war.

Having said this, the historian of the future will have to say also that the size of the big corporate unit and the structure of corporate power were strengthened during the war, rather than weakened; that Congress has had some success in its campaign of attrition against our social gains of the past decade; and that inquisitions by the Dies Committee and the Civil Service Commission made the life of a liberal within the Administration an almost intolerable one.

What does it all add up to, when you add and subtract and strike a trial balance? It adds up to a seasoned and mature democratic leader, guiding the frail bark of a crisis state through rapids and shallows with incredibly skillful powers of maneuver; a leader who is best at the things that his heart is really in, but whose hand has not lost its cunning at whatever he turns it to; a leader who believes in making haste slowly; a leader who is probably more of a political tactician than a social thinker, and who sometimes does not reckon with the final social cost of concessions and appeasements; but finally a leader who has measured up to the war emergency with a stature unexampled in democratic history.

I have tried to set all this down not as an advocate nor as a partisan, but as an historian. In the end only a people that is trained to take the long view is worthy of having great leaders.

3

The President, at yesterday's press conference, had another of those bantering exchanges with reporters on the question of whether he would run again. This has now become one of the rituals without which a Roosevelt press conference would be unrecognizable. As with most rituals, the meaning has dropped out while the form remains. No reporter any longer expects that his fourth-term questions will be answered except by banter, yet he thinks up new ways of asking them. Nor does the President any longer expect that his answers will be taken with anything but disbelief, yet he continues to find new ways of shrugging off the questions. And everything is good-natured.

If the President treats this as a genial but unimportant ritual, it is mainly to postpone campaign discussion as long as possible and keep the attention of Americans on what is important. That is, I think, the key to his outlook. He is sometimes wrong and often right in his specific judgments. But whether wrong or right, the thing he cares most about is perspective. He can show a rhinoceros-hide toughness and good humor in meeting criticism on any particular issue. But accuse him of putting the wrong things first, or of muddling up things like the war, or relations with Russia, which are in the foreground of his preoccupations, and you may get one of his infrequent flare-ups. For it is perspective that is his test of statesmanship. He is not touchy about personal attacks, as other men are, and he has suffered his share of them. But he has a feeling for history and the world framework, and an awareness of his place in one and America's role in the other.

It is evident from every one of FDR's speeches and statements since D-Day that he feels we have rounded another of the nightmare corners in our journey through the world's darkness. Few will ever know how heavily that nightmare weighed on the President. He knew how high the invasion stakes were, and how tragic a wrong decision could be. It is pretty well known that it was he who pushed the decision through at the Teheran Conference, and he who—when last-moment doubts were raised before the invasion date—insisted that there should be no further postponements.

Is it any wonder then that the President has seemed a new man, in health and mood? More than anything else, this had been his sickness: the brooding sense of possible sequels to the single biggest decision he has ever had to make during his whole tenure of the Presidency.

However often I have been the President's critic, I am newly impressed with the essential rightness of his big perspectives. During the depression, he saw that recovery was impossible except through reform of the economic structure and he fought for the reforms militantly. When the war shadows hung over the world, he tried—despite his mistakes about Spain and about Munich—to prepare American opinion for our inevitable entrance into the war, and to make us meanwhile a belligerent neutral. After Pearl Harbor he cared only about three things: to build an effective war economy, to rivet down a firm working accord with our allies, and to make the American people see that the war in the East and the war in Europe were part of the same struggle. Under his leadership we have built and equipped the greatest armed forces in our history, and launched their most successful strategic campaigns.

As we look back at the troubled twelve years of his tenure, the specific issues that harassed and enraged us fade out and the large outlines remain, clearer now than they could ever have been when they were being shaped. That is the President's strength with the people. He aims always at the big things that affect their lives and living standards and destinies, however high the price he may have to pay in concessions to the reactionaries, however long the wait. And the people sense this in him, and respond to it.

That is one of the things the people around the President should see more clearly. The campaign against him will once more this year, as in past years, be piddling and dirty. The instinct of the President's supporters will again be to defend him against every little mudclod hurled at him. They will be wrong. They will try to make the President out as a man who has never made a mistake. Again they will be wrong: he has made plenty, which is natural for any human being. If they are wise they will work in the President's own spirit, and spend their energies laying bare the large outlines of what the American people have been able to accomplish under his leadership. For the fact is that whatever chance Dewey or anyone else may have is in itself due to the fact that under the President America has kept itself safe and free and its world whole. In that lies FDR's greatness.

Only you wouldn't suspect it, reading the papers and the *Congressional Record*. You would think that of all the people in the world who deserve some credit for the successful invasion, the one man who should get none at all is the Commander-in-Chief of our armed forces, and the leading figure in United Nations decisions.

—April 14, 15, June 15, 1944.

FRANKLIN D. ROOSEVELT

Speech before the International Brotherhood of Teamsters, AFL, September 23, 1944

✻

WELL, here we are together again—after four years—and what years they have been!

I am actually four years older—which seems to annoy some people. In fact, millions of us are more than eleven years older than when we started in to clear up the mess that was dumped in our laps in 1933.

We all know certain people will make it a practice to depreciate the accomplishments of labor—who even attack labor as unpatriotic.

They keep this up usually for three years and six months. But then, for some strange reason, they change their tune—every four years—just before election day.

When votes are at stake they suddenly discover that they really love labor, and are eager to protect it from its old friends.

I got quite a laugh, for example—and I am sure that you did—when I read this plank in the Republican platform adopted at their national convention in Chicago last July:

"The Republican party accepts the purposes of the National Labor Relations Act, the Wage and Hour Act, the Social Security Act, and all other Federal statutes designed to promote and protect the welfare of American working men and women, and we promise a fair and just administration of these laws."

Many of the Republican leaders and Congressmen and candidates, who shouted enthusiastic approval of that plank in that convention hall, would not even recognize these progressive laws if they met them in broad daylight.

Indeed, they have personally spent years of effort and energy—and much money—in fighting every one of those laws in the Congress, in the press and in the courts, ever since this Administration began to advocate them and enact them into legislation.

That is a fair example of their insincerity and their inconsistency.

The whole purpose of Republican oratory these days seems to be to switch labels. The object is to persuade the American people that the Democratic party was responsible for the 1929 crash and depression, and the Republican party was responsible for all social progress under the New Deal.

Imitation may be the sincerest form of flattery—but I am afraid that in this case it is the most obvious common or garden variety of fraud.

There are enlightened, liberal elements in the Republican party, and they have fought hard and honorably to bring the party up to date and to get it in step with the forward march of American progress. But these liberal elements were not able to drive the old guard Republicans from their entrenched positions.

Can the old guard pass itself off as the New Deal? I think not.

We have all seen many marvelous stunts in the circus, but no performing elephant could turn a handspring without falling flat on his back.

I need not recount to you the centuries of history which have been crowded into these four years since I saw you last.

There were some—in the Congress and out—who raised their voices against our preparations for defense—before and after 1939—as hysterical war mongering, who cried out against our help to the Allies as provocative and dangerous.

We remember the voices.

They would like to have us forget them now. But in 1940 and 1941 they were loud voices. Happily they were a minority and—fortunately for ourselves, and for the world—they could not stop America.

There are some politicians who kept their heads buried deep in the sand while the storms of Europe and Asia were headed our way, who said that the Lend-Lease Bill "would bring an end to free Government in the United States," and who said "only hysteria entertains the idea that Germany, Italy or Japan contemplates war upon us."

These very men are now asking the American people to entrust to them the conduct of our foreign policy and our military policy.

What the Republican leaders are now saying in effect is this:

"Oh, just forget what we used to say, we have changed our minds now—we have been reading the public opinion polls about these things, and we now know what the American people want. Don't leave the task of making the peace to those old men who first urged it, and who have already laid the foundations for it, and who have had to fight all of us, inch by inch, during the last five years to do it—just turn it all over to us. We'll do it so skillfully—that we won't lose a single isolationist vote or a single isolationist campaign contribution."

There is one thing I am too old for—I cannot talk out of both sides of my mouth at the same time.

This Government welcomes all sincere supporters of the cause of effective world collaboration in the making of a lasting peace. Millions of Republicans all over the nation are with us—and have been with us—in our unshakable determination to build the solid structure of peace. And they, too, will resent this campaign talk by those who first woke up to the facts of international life a few short months ago—when they began to study the polls of public opinion.

Those who today have the military responsibility for waging this war in all parts of the globe are not helped by the statements of men who, without responsibility and without knowledge of the facts, lecture the chiefs of staff of the United States as to the best means of dividing our armed forces and our military resources between the Atlantic and Pacific, between the Army and the Navy, and among the commanding generals of the different theatres of war.

When I addressed you four years ago, I said:

"I know that America will never be disappointed in its expectation that labor will always continue to do its share of the job we now face, and do it patriotically and effectively and unselfishly."

Today we know that America has not been disappointed. In his order of the day, when the Allied armies first landed in Normandy, General Eisenhower said:

"Our home fronts have given us overwhelming superiority in weapons and munitions of war."

I know that there are those labor baiters among the opposition who, instead of calling attention to the achievements of labor in this war, prefer the occasional strikes which have occurred—strikes which have been condemned by every responsible national labor leader—every national leader except one. And that one labor leader, incidentally, is certainly not among my supporters.

Labor baiters forget that, at our peak, American labor and management have turned out airplanes at the rate of 109,000 per year; tanks, 57,000 per year; combat vessels, 573 per year; landing vessels, 31,000 per year; cargo ships 19,000,000 tons per year, and small arms ammunition, 23 billion rounds per year.

But a strike is news, and generally appears in shrieking headlines—and, of course, they say labor is always to blame.

The fact is that, since Pearl Harbor, only one-tenth of one per cent of man-hours have been lost by strikes. But even those candidates who burst out in election-year affection for social legislation and for labor in general still think you ought to be good boys and stay out of politics.

And, above all, they hate to see any working man or woman contribute a dollar bill to any wicked political party.

Of course, it is all right for large financiers and industrialists and monopolists to contribute tens of thousands of dollars—but their solicitude for
that dollar which the men and women in the ranks of labor contribute is
always very touching.

They are, of course, perfectly willing to let you vote—unless you happen
to be a soldier or sailor overseas, or a merchant seaman carrying the munitions of war. In that case they have made it pretty hard for you to vote—for
there are some political candidates who think they may have a chance if
only the total vote is small enough.

And while I am on the subject of voting let me urge every American
citizen—man and woman—to use your sacred privilege of voting, no matter
which candidate you expect to support. Our millions of soldiers and
sailors and merchant seamen have been handicapped or prevented from
voting by those politicians and candidates who think they stand to lose by
such votes. You here at home have the freedom of the ballot. Irrespective of
party, you should register and vote this November. That is a matter of
good citizenship.

Words come easily, but they do not change the record. You are old
enough to remember what things were like for labor in 1932.

You remember the closed banks and the breadlines and the starvation
wages; the foreclosures of homes and farms, and the bankruptcies of business; the "Hoovervilles," and the young men and women of the nation
facing a hopeless, jobless future; the closed factories and mines and mills;
the ruined and abandoned farms; the stalled railroads and the empty docks;
the blank despair of a whole nation—and the utter impotence of our Federal Government.

You remember the long, hard road, with its gains and its setbacks, which
we have traveled together since those days.

Now there are some politicians, of course, who do not remember that
far back, and some who remember but find it convenient to forget. But
the record is not to be washed away that easily.

The opposition has already imported into this campaign the propaganda
technique invented by the dictators abroad. The technique was all set out
in Hitler's book—and it was copied by the aggressors of Italy and Japan.

According to that technique, you should never use a small falsehood; always a big one, for its very fantastic nature will make it more credible—if
only you keep repeating it over and over again.

For example, although I rubbed my eyes when I read it, we have been
told that it was not a Republican depression, but a Democratic depression
from which this nation has been saved—that this Administration is responsible for all the suffering and misery that the history books and the

American people always thought had been brought about during the twelve ill-fated years when the Republican party was in power.

Now, there is an old and somewhat lugubrious adage which says:

"Never speak of rope in the house of one who has been hanged."

In the same way, if I were a Republican leader speaking to a mixed audience, the last word in the whole dictionary that I think I would use is that word "depression."

For another example, I learned—much to my amazement—that the policy of this Administration was to keep men in the Army when the war was over, because there might be no jobs for them in civil life.

Why, the very day that this fantastic charge was first made a formal plan for the method of speedy discharge from the Army had already been announced by the War Department—a plan based upon the wishes of the soldiers themselves.

This callous and brazen falsehood about demobilization was an effort to stimulate fear among American mothers, wives and sweethearts. And, incidentally, it was hardly calculated to bolster the morale of our soldiers and sailors and airmen fighting our battles all over the world.

Perhaps the most ridiculous of these campaign falsifications is the one that this Administration failed to prepare for the war which was coming. I doubt whether even Goebbels would have tried that one. For even he would never have dared hope that the voters of America had already forgotten that many of the Republican leaders in the Congress and outside the Congress tried to thwart and block nearly every attempt which this Administration made to warn our people and to arm this nation. Some of them called our 50,000-airplane program fantastic.

Many of those very same leaders who fought every defense measure we proposed are still in control of the Republican party, were in control of its national convention in Chicago, and would be in control of the machinery of the Congress and of the Republican party in the event of a Republican victory this fall.

These Republican leaders have not been content with attacks upon me, or my wife, or my sons—they now include my little dog, Fala. Unlike the members of my family, he resents this. Being a scottie, as soon as he learned that the Republican fiction writers had concocted a story that I had left him behind on an Aleutian island and had sent a destroyer back to find him— at a cost to the taxpayers of two or three or twenty million dollars—his Scotch soul was furious. He has not been the same dog since.

I am accustomed to hearing malicious falsehoods about myself—such as that old, worm-eaten chestnut that I have represented myself as indispensable. But I think I have a right to object to libelous statements about my dog.

But we all recognize the old technique. The people of this country know the past too well to be deceived into forgetting. Too much is at stake to forget. There are tasks ahead of us which we must now complete with the same will and skill and intelligence and devotion which have already led us so far on the road to victory.

There is the task of finishing victoriously this most terrible of all wars as speedily as possible and with the least cost in lives.

There is the task of setting up international machinery to assure that the peace, once established, will not again be broken.

And there is the task which we face here at home—the task of reconverting our economy from the purposes of war to the purposes of peace.

These peace-building tasks were faced once before, nearly a generation ago. They were botched by a Republican Administration. That must not happen this time. We will not let it happen this time.

Fortunately, we do not begin from scratch. Much has been done. Much more is under way. The fruits of victory this time will not be apples to be sold on street corners.

Many months ago, this Administration set up the necessary machinery for an orderly peacetime demobilization. The Congress has now passed legislation continuing the agencies needed for demobilization—with additional powers to carry out their functions.

I know that the American people—business and labor and agriculture—have the same will to do for peace what they have done for war. And I know that they can sustain a national income which will assure full production and full employment under our democratic system of private enterprise, with Government encouragement and aid whenever and wherever it is necessary.

The keynote of all that we propose to do in reconversion can be found in the one word—"jobs."

We shall lease or dispose of our Government-owned plants and facilities and our surplus war property and land on the basis of how they can best be operated by private enterprise to give jobs to the greatest number.

We shall follow a wage policy which will sustain the purchasing power of labor—for that means more production and more jobs.

The present policies on wages and prices were conceived to serve the needs of the great masses of the people. They stopped inflation. They kept prices on a stable level. Through the demobilization period, policies will be carried out with the same objective in mind—to serve the needs of the great masses of the people.

This is not the time in which men can be forgotten as they were in the Republican catastrophe which we inherited. The returning soldiers, the workers by their machines, the farmers in the field, the miners, the men and women in offices and shops, do not intend to be forgotten.

They know they are not surplus. Because they know that they are America.

We must set targets and objectives for the future which will seem impossible to those who live in and are weighted down by the dead past.

We are even now organizing the logistics of the peace just as Marshall, King, Arnold, MacArthur, Eisenhower and Nimitz are organizing the logistics of this war.

The victory of the American people and their allies in this war will be far more than a victory against fascism and reaction and the dead hand of despotism and of the past.

The victory of the American people and their allies in this war will be a victory for democracy. It will constitute such an affirmation of the strength and power and vitality of government by the people as history has never before witnessed.

With that affirmation of the vitality of democratic government behind us, that demonstration of its resilience and its capacity for decision and for action—with that knowledge of our own strength and power—we move forward with God's help to the greatest epoch of free achievement by free men the world has ever known or imagined possible.

JONATHAN DANIELS

Thursday Afternoon

SOMEWHERE between the human swarm and the constitutional abstraction, there is, I am convinced, a Government of the United States. I have been hired to watch it. I have been hired to work for it. It is not easily seen. It seems reasonable, nevertheless, to believe that it is there. Its capital is not merely between Maryland and Virginia, but also somewhere between American awe and American derision, between the statistics and the bewilderment, between the political scientists and the political people. It rises like a monument and a mirage on the shores of the Potomac. Every citizen either feels its hand on his shoulder or has his hand out for its favor—often both. But even Presidents keep looking over their shoulders at the country. That hot wind in Washington is the country blowing on the back of Washington's neck.

I have blown. And I have also felt it singeing the bottom of my hair. I have met people who have seen the government. I have even met clerks who were confident they were it. I have sat within the paneled elegance provided for scholarship in the gleaming white Supreme Court Building and listened while a learned Justice, speaking a vernacular which he did not take from the Constitution, expressed the considered view that some of his colleagues had only the vaguest notion as to what the government is. I suspect that the Government of the United States is both the forest and the trees, and that we are the forest. And I begin to believe that nobody, including the dullest scholars of theoretical unrealities, the doctrinaires and the disenchanted, can write about it except as an autobiographical enterprise. We have just finished dealing in our greatest war with some notions about the citizen and the State. We do not confuse them. But I am America. So is everybody else between the big Lakes and the warm Gulf. America—God bless us or help us—is what we are.

The republic of the atomic age is still the government of a very human people, and the problems of people coming together for government may still be more significant than disintegrating the atom. Uranium is very mild stuff beside Americans. We are still at least as dependent upon politicians as upon physicists. We almost forget that the atomic bomb was a political product. And I know that there was at least one moment when the whole process of its development was threatened because some business men who had not become adept bureaucrats issued orders in WPB which they had not cleared with other bureaucrats in the same agency. Guarding scarcities and unaware of atomic plans, in 1942, they sent firm orders down to Tennessee prohibiting the construction of new power plants needed to produce electricity required by the physicists in the process of smashing the atom.

I did not start out to find the Government of the United States. Nothing, indeed, could have been further from my mind. I went out to look at the country itself, late in 1940, when the defense boom was pouring a golden stream across the land. I got to Tennessee before the physicists did. And the thing that impressed me was the people. I talked to them in new-turned mud around the rising camps and the big growing dams, by the rivers and the trailers and the juke boxes, in crowded bars and overwhelmed city halls.

Down in the country under the nation's planners, some of whom were in new army and navy uniforms, the people themselves were like the pioneers putting the power of America together again—pioneers at a gold rush. They took the wages, grinning about them. They would have worked for less, but if any army wanted to count every countryman a carpenter, they would not argue. They lived in the woods. They slept in the back seats of their cars, and cooked out of cans. And, among them, the big, rich confusion from Washington was an easy American joke. I think I was the man who first brought back the joke from the crowded country towns to the effect that the defense boom had brought them cooperators, coordinators and cohabitators and they did not know which did the most harm. Also, the story about the Louisiana Negro who looked at his wages, made sure that there had been no mistake, and whooped his not unpatriotic feeling:

"Thank God for Hitler!"

I guess that looking and writing about government as it hit the country ("at the local level," Washington called it) is the way I got into government and began to look at it from the inside. The inside was not quite new to me. I grew up in Washington as a Cabinet member's boy. The statesmen and the politicians, the admirals and the newspapermen, used to come for meals with the family. I remember best that most of them told good jokes. Also, I particularly remember William Jennings Bryan's eating; it was a spectacle for the admiration of a small boy whose own hungers seemed always certainly infantile afterward. I was shocked when a small Republican schoolmate suggested, as we passed the White House on the way home from Keith's Vaudeville, that even Woodrow Wilson had to go to the bathroom. It was logical, but somehow appalling.

I was smuggled into the House Chamber when Wilson asked the Congress for war in 1917. I remember war coming then, not in terms of the challenging ring of Wilson's voice, but of the beat of the hoofs of the horses, Nip and Tuck, pulling the carriage in which Father and I drove home through the dark Washington streets from the excited Capitol. My heart seemed to beat with the sound of their hoofs. Government and America seemed suddenly altogether grander than the politicians who came to our house. My own father, tired and serious in the carriage, seemed grand, too. I have not changed that idea since. Indeed, I have had reason to extend it to other men in a growing faith in the possibility of patriots in places of power—and that such patriots are to be found among Democrats and Republicans, liberals and conservatives alike.

That infantile view of the inside of government was a long time ago. When I went to Washington, in 1942, I had watched government from the outside for twenty years, in the basement of the City Hall in Louisville, in the Legislature at Raleigh, in the press gallery in Washington. I had been writing in Munich when Hitler was just beginning; but, to destroy my reputation as a political interpreter at the outset, he had seemed to me just a little less interesting than Huey P. Long. Then I came back and looked at businessmen a while instead of politicians, as an editor of *Fortune*. Even then the similarities were more striking than the differences. I began traveling around America seeing the American bust and then the American boom. Each seemed a phase of the tossing and turning of Americans in the American dream.

I went into government, I think, by way of a huge hall in Atlantic City. There, though Democrat and New Dealer, as critical outsider I spoke of governmental confusion. Charles P. Taft, the President's son and a good Ohio Republican but an early and able wartime bureaucrat, spoke in its defense. I can report now that it was much more fun on the outside raising hell than it was on the inside trying to make sense. Pearl Harbor blew me into Washington as a sort of professional man from the country in a capital which was more than ever concerned about the country. Charlie Taft grinned a little when I came in, but gently. Also, he told me a story about government, which he had inherited from President Taft, about an army colonel in Texas who had a thousand men who had never seen a horse and a thousand horses who had never seen a man—and all he had to do was to make a cavalry regiment. It is a story that will stand even in the atomic age.

Without the expression of undue pride, I think I can say that I participated in bureaucracy in its most difficult form in the Office of Civilian Defense. I know that other civilian veterans of the war in Washington will debate that. I still respect the idea that, through OCD, Federal, State and local governments might cooperate together from hamlet to continent in crisis. Those who designed OCD for home defense did not underestimate the patriotic energies of American volunteers. But I can testify that they minimized the violence still implicit in mobilized American individualism. I know that in the chaos which grew when no bombs fell, I was lucky to get out of OCD.

In a Washington which can be darker than most cities under its shade trees, I worked only seven months in that belabored war agency. I escaped to a room in the basement of the State Department doing a hush-hush job which, being secret, was also secure. The rats which came out of the holes with the heat pipes did not disturb me. Down the quiet hall was a room in which, I remembered, a nice old gentleman in an alpaca coat (I suppose he must have been a bureaucrat, too) had shown me when I was young the bullet the surgeons had taken from Lincoln's skull.

The room in the basement would have been a quiet place in which to spend part of a war. The quietness did not last. I became Administrative Assistant and later Press Secretary to President Roosevelt. Those jobs were not designed for serenity. But, if there was any place from which to see the government, I had it. Congress had specifically exempted my job from the Hatch Act, which prohibits the participation of government employees in politics. So, I suppose I was politician by Act of Congress. But fortunately or unfortunately, I think I was created long before a spectator by Act of God.

I not only saw the White House. I also saw government, in the agencies and departments, branches and bureaus under and around it, in a Washington in which Cabinet officers are not less human than taxi drivers. That government is a business not merely of conferences and Congress, but of cocktail parties and hotel rooms, of bishops and John L. Lewis, of little lost girls from Minnesota typing steadily all day long in huge typing pools, of bureaucrats in The Lobby and The Press as well as in the Veterans' Administration. Its powers include not merely the President and Supreme Court Justices, career ambassadors out of Groton and a Texas school for the deaf, but also such figures as old man Bernard M. Baruch sitting on a park bench playing a role originally written by Anatole France, and Tommy Corcoran playing his accordion as well as his government for his clients.

It was crowded from the slums around the Capitol to the mansions over Rock Creek. There were all sorts of people in the crowding. I doubt that any sample of America was missing. I remember the millionaires in their new navy uniforms in the big houses on Kalorama Road and down below them the old converted mansions turned into boarding houses bulging with country girls. People moved in and out of Washington like a procession.

Items of it stick in my mind: an insistent patriot with hands that tapered like those of an Assyrian rug peddler with the same combination of sensitiveness and indecency in his fingers; a pretty stepmother walking very primly through Lafayette Square with a solemn, sallow child; a young novelist awkward as a new officer; an official's discarded favorite talking like a jilted girl; Harry Hopkins looking like Death on its way to a frolic; the unwashed, unfed people disgorged from the early Pullmans to the shortage of taxicabs; Senators with their vests unbuttoned in the evening; Congressmen dancing at the Shoreham, the dipsomaniac wife of a tough official, the Assistant Secretary of State who picked his nose and rolled the result into neat little balls; Henry Wallace grinning; Harry Truman blushing and looking at the floor; Mrs. Gifford Pinchot's red hair, the perfumed pre-war smell of the women in the Mayflower, the Saturday bridge games in Eric Johnston's suite, Georgetown gardens in May, the pretty young wife of the elderly Cabinet officer; and gay Catholic Presidential Secretary Bill Hassett singing:

> Would you leave gaiety
> All to the laity,
> Father O'Flynn?

Perhaps they do not sound like the items of government. They are as much its items, nevertheless, as an income tax blank or a questionnaire. Perhaps I remember the lively items best. Some of us could be happier if the psychologists were right and there were no memory of pain. But it was not all gay. Washington is the capital not only of pride but of complaint, too. It can also be the capital of hurt feelings and hard work. It abounds in phonies. But at least as many of them are visitors from out of town as residents of its marble corridors. There are simple people there worth any man's conversation. And some are sad. There are Negro messengers, Irish politicians, Jewish lawyers, demagogues who sometimes look like statesmen, and statesmen who often act like demagogues. It is a town of people clinging in political insistence to small-town residences while they are dependent for life on room service at the Mayflower. There are pathetic rich lobbyists who had a notion, when they were young, that they wanted to be statesmen, and statesmen secretly envious when the lobbyists reach for the check. And Washington certainly has a great American corps of devoted public servants more interested in their jobs than concerned about their pay. Frustration is often normal. Ambition is standard. Envy can be malignant in a town in which everybody can know everybody else's pay.

Washington has many of the characteristics of a company town. Also, as is not generally the case in company towns, those who do business with the company, who sell to it and who hope to profit from it, live there, too, or have their representatives living there. More newspapermen than there are members of Congress are always looking at the company's books. It is a teeming place of people rubbing up against each other and energetically exercising their personalities. There is a basic similarity to Hollywood in the exhibitionism of the successful and the sycophancy of the hopeful. But most of the national indiscriminate belaboring of the bureaucrats hits the wrong people.

"I am a bureaucrat," I said when I was in Washington.

But I remember my associate, William McReynolds, laughing his low

Kansas laugh which thirty-nine years in the government service had not made less Kansan.

"You're boasting," he said.

I think he is right. One of the worst troubles with bureaucracy in the expanded American Government has been the acute shortage of really first-class bureaucrats. A good many business men who came to Washington as officials began to understand that after they had tangled themselves in their own lines once or twice. Some just stayed tangled and mad about it. And some bureaucrats who stay longest remain dull as long as they stay. Unfortunately, if bureaucrats are effective, there are always places at better pay for them in the huge bureaucracy of business which grows, largely from their ranks, in the office buildings around the government ones.

I was not a bureaucrat. Bill McReynolds was right about that. I hope I am still a reporter. I had had, with other newspapermen, to listen to enough politicians and officials say that they used to be newspapermen themselves. Franklin Roosevelt never quite got over having been an editor of the *Harvard Crimson*. And Harold Ickes, now in his seventies, was still a reporter in the Chicago of the days before the story came through that somebody had shot McKinley.

"I used to be a government official myself," I can say with the proper note of patronizing reminiscence of the escaped.

But I am still a reporter. And I hope a reporter who can look not only at the stuffing in Senatorial shirts but also, beyond the preserved Constitution in the case in the Library of Congress, to the swarming government of Americans around it. I am also anxious not to write any inside story. Others will do that. What I am concerned about is the wide-open story of a government which has grown big beside us and with us and is still as bewildering as we often are ourselves. I am not a political scientist (indeed, I doubt that there is any such science). But I looked. I enjoyed the chance to see. Seen at its worst, the Government of America is worth seeing. What I report is only one man's view of a government which deserves all men's eyes.

As big as it is, that government is not easy to see all in one place at one time. But I think I saw it clearest and best for myself and for the inrushing pattern of the American future the night that Harry Truman, as the clock under the portrait of Woodrow Wilson in the Cabinet Room passed 7:09, suddenly ceased to be "Harry" and became "Mr. President." Then within the time it takes for the clicking of cameras, he was the almost superstitiously honored man-symbol of America who can still, after our pattern of reverence, be described in the native argument in the American language as one angry truck driver would describe another.

Just fifteen minutes before sunset that evening they had found him in the pleasant hide-out office of bald-headed Sam Rayburn, Speaker of the House, on one of the maze of hardly used corridors in the Capitol. The Vice-President, dry after presiding over hours of Senatorial debate on a water treaty, had come to join the Speaker and other convivial officials and friends in late afternoon relaxation. "Harry" smiled through his thick lenses as he came in eager for the Speaker's bourbon. He got the telephone call instead.

It was nearly dark when he drove into the White House grounds. And behind him, swiftly in the deepening twilight of a hot April, the Government of the United States began racing through the guarded gate. Then the people came to mass themselves against the great iron fence: A mass, that grew through the evening, of patient and pathetic people, curious citizens and spectators before history. Ed Stettinius, beautiful, rich young man, ran across Executive Avenue from the State Department where before him Cordell Hull had talked to Jap diplomats in the language which in Cordell Hull's Tennessee youth had been reserved for United States Revenue officers. All the Cabinet came, except Postmaster General Frank Walker, who had been caught by the news in Lynchburg, Virginia. Sam Rayburn, his bald head gleaming above his grim face, led Democratic Congressional leaders through the newspapermen who swarmed around the big mahogany table in the lobby of the Executive Offices. Minority Leader Joe Martin, a Republican partisan as implacable as any of the Democrats, hurried across Lafayette Square from his apartment in the hotel built where that other Massachusetts man, pessimistic old Henry Adams, had watched democracy with an erudite fastidiousness. Senators arrived. The Chief Justice of the United States came, and Bob Hannegan, the moon-faced Irishman who had risen from the precincts of St. Louis to national chairmanship of the party in power. Harry Truman walked slowly along the covered back gallery by the rose garden from the White House residence to its offices to meet them. In the long Cabinet Room he looked like a little man as he sat waiting in a huge leather chair. Mrs. Truman was late in arriving.

The government waited, for the government had come in the personages described by the Constitution, in its human pieces and checks and balances and powers—as human as the men in Philadelphia who had designed their functions. They were the men of Lincoln's central imperative preposition—the "by" people of democracy.

Chief Justice Stone wore no robe of judicial sanctity. He was an aging, kind-eyed man in a blue serge suit—the sort of suit professors get chalk on and which scholars wear bright at the elbows and the seat. Somehow, Tru-

roared him out to his Connecticut Avenue apartment where he ate a roast beef sandwich in a neighbor's flat. Behind him the big reception clerk spoke an old day's-end speech above the noises of the lobby:

"The President has left his office."

He spoke transition.

It was not easy then to see what transition was. There had been no such transition in America in great crisis since Lincoln died and Andrew Johnson took the oath in the parlors of Kirkwood's Hotel. In an April, too, Johnson swore to defend the Constitution in a future which was to be filled with the furies of the American struggle through anger and aspiration, corruption and partisanship toward the American destiny. Nobody could count the similarities and differences between the futures beyond 1865 and 1945. Times, not men, had changed: Johnson was a tailor until he was thirty-four; Truman was a haberdasher when he was thirty-eight. Haberdasher and tailor together could perhaps have counted the change in costume and appearance. There was not a beard in the Cabinet Room when Truman took his oath. But the same tempestuous, teeming, determined America was around it.

It was the same oath. Chief Justice Stone repeated it in the lobby to the swarm of newspapermen.

He smiled: "It is a good one if you live up to it."

And it is a good Constitution. It is no mere document. It is certainly not the mere body of the determinations of men in the past. It is the strange informal and inflexible, solemn and irreverent, ruthless and sentimental system by which we live as a people together. We know that our politicians are the damnedest set of men on earth—and that together they make the greatest government in the world. Much of it the Founding Fathers would not recognize. Some citizens and foreign visitors do not like it—and may get a false notion that many of us don't like it either. We ourselves cuss it, cherish it, cheat it, and argue about it. We shall probably do so eternally and certainly as long as we do we shall be what men have always meant when—hesitating, in observation, between dismay and admiration—they have called us Americans.

The people standing quiet in the street before the White House that April night understood that. The President was dead, and they stood in sorrow; the President drove past them into the night, and they saluted him in loyalty. They waited in grief, without fear. There was nothing strange about the future; they had faced it before. It would be America; they are it.

man waiting was still "Harry," whose room on the seventeenth floor at the Stevens in Chicago the summer before had been so full of sweaty well wishers. He wore his solemnity and his affability together. All around the room, the Congress of the United States was a collection of people, shocked puzzled, a little wary, and as precise as well-trained children in the pro prieties of the hour. The Executive Branch stood about the room or sat in the big chairs as the men most hurt and most uncertain in change. There was an uneasy feeling of an era ending and of careers interrupted. There was an eager feeling present, too, concealed but tangible. The clock under Woodrow Wilson was speaking of the future.

Here was change. No American feared any tumult such as might else-where attend such change. But in it men wore masks as solemn as the Constitution itself. The heartbroken were self-contained. So were those whose hearts quickened. The masks were worn—but the masks were off, too. There was time for the proprieties but not for prolonged pretenses. Men moved in unconscious nakedness which showed in the tone of voice they used in speaking to the little man who was to be Bigness so soon. A certain sleekness slipped into the words addressed to him by attendants and some statesmen. There was real grief, there was also patriotism, shrewdness, understanding of power and a wonder about its directions. There was order and dignity. Here, also, was the whole human struggle of a nation. Here were States' Rights, the division of powers, the hope and push of the Right and the Left. Here were the insistent contending Amer-ican regions, the conflict of minority rights and majority rule, little am-bitions and big questions, privilege and politics. Around the little man in the chair were the same forces that have been shaping America around the written document from the beginning.

Mrs. Truman came in, sad and a little frightened. The Government of the United States arrayed itself in an arc of faces across the end of the room. Before it the Chief Justice repeated the great oath. In his flat Missouri voice the President responded from a little sheet of paper. America spoke its greatest man-pledge under the glare of lights and the clicking of cameras. There were more newspapermen and photographers than officials there. They sprawled over the Cabinet table. They quarreled almost automat-ically among themselves. And the President took the oath a second time, not for greater certainty but for more pictures.

He was not Harry Truman any longer; he never would be again. The prison of the Presidency dropped around him. The Secret Service scurried beside him as he moved. The personages shook his hand and fell away. The President of the United States walked down the hall to the big lobby past the wide mahogany table. His car had turned into a procession which